The Law of Compulsory Purchase

The Law of Compulsory Purchase

Second edition

General Editor
Guy R G Roots QC, MA (Oxon)

Senior Editor
Michael Humphries QC, LLB (Hons)

Editors
Robert Fookes MA (Oxon), Barrister
James Pereira MA (Cantab), LLM (London), Barrister

Bloomsbury Professional

Bloomsbury Professional Limited, Maxwelton House, 41–43 Boltro Road, Haywards Heath, West Sussex, RH16 1BJ

Bloomsbury Professional, an imprint of Bloomsbury Publishing Plc

A CIP Catalogue record for this book is available from the British Library.

ISBN 978 1 84766 746 5

Typeset by Phoenix, Chatham, Kent
Printed and bound in Great Britain by Martins the Printers, Berwick upon Tweed

Foreword to the first edition

The law of compulsory purchase and compensation is to be found in a multiplicity of statutes and statutory instruments and in many hundreds of cases decided by the superior courts and by the Lands Tribunal. Nearly all of this material is now available online. The practitioner who has to advise upon this branch of law and the advocate who has to present a case in which it arises are confronted by two problems. The first is the great range and diversity of the sources, which carries with it the danger that something material to the particular case may be missed, and the second is the apparent complexity of the law itself. On the one hand, therefore, a textbook on the law of compulsory purchase and compensation needs not only to refer to the statutory provisions and the cases but to do so in a way that enables those that are relevant to the matters in issue to be readily identified. And, on the other hand, the law must be expounded in a way that both simplifies what can be simplified and explains with clarity the difficult areas.

This work was first published in 2000 in the form of a two volume loose leaf version that included all the statutory and certain other material that is now available online. This new bound version retains essentially the same exposition of the law that appeared in the loose leaf format, and it is now in a form that is more convenient for the present-day user and more appropriate for the standard textbook that it has become. It is to be warmly welcomed.

Today the emphasis is on deciding cases justly and expeditiously and in ways that are proportionate to what is at stake and to the financial position of the parties. By making the law accessible and comprehensible in the way that it does, this book will continue to assist all of us engaged in this process.

George Bartlett QC
President of the Lands Tribunal
March 2008

Preface

For at least two hundred years, compulsory acquisition of land has been critical to economic and social development in the United Kingdom. The need to acquire land compulsorily will continue into the future. However, the law relating to compulsory purchase and compensation, being spread across several statutes of varying antiquity and many judicial decisions, can appear daunting.

The aim of this work is to provide a comprehensive guide to the law and practice in this field, while making it as accessible as possible. This work is intended for use by practitioners in the field of compulsory purchase and compensation, particularly lawyers, surveyors and valuers, acting for both landowners and acquiring authorities, but the structure, style and indexing are intended to make it accessible to occasional users and students.

This work was first published in 2000 in two volume looseleaf format with statutory and other relevant sources (which will continue to be available and updated). For those who prefer the convenience of a single volume, the publishers published essentially the same text in single volume bound format without the source materials. The first edition was published in 2008. This second edition comprehensively updates the text. The statutory and other material can be found nowadays on line, albeit not presented in the same convenient updated and referenced format as will be found in the looseleaf version of this work. For those who prefer the two volume looseleaf, it will continue to be available and service updates will continue to be provided to subscribers.

Guy Roots QC
Michael Humphries QC
Robert Fookes
James Pereira

May 2011

Contents

Table of Statutes

D

E

Table of Statutory Instruments

Table of Cases

B

C

D

G

H

J

K

L

R

S

Y

Z

Division A

Introduction

Contents

References in bold are to paragraph numbers.

Chapter 1

Introduction

Contents

A Introduction

[1]

For at least two hundred years, compulsory acquisition of land has been essential for economic and social development in the United Kingdom. Our canals, railways, roads, electricity generation and transmission, water supply, sewage disposal, schools and hospitals are but the most obvious examples of the types of development which would not have been capable of achievement if it had not been possible to acquire all the land required without the consent of the owners. The need to acquire land compulsorily will continue into the future and may well prove to be an important factor in achieving more sustainable development by the assembly of sites for urban regeneration in order to reduce the need for development on greenfield sites[1].

1 See, eg, *Towards an Urban Renaissance: Final Report of the Urban Task Force chaired by Lord Rogers of Riverside* (June 1998) DETR and ODPM Circular 06/04, Part 1, para 1.

[2]

Parliament has created a system which enables certain bodies to acquire land without the owner's consent in circumstances where they have been authorised by Parliament to do so, subject to strict adherence to procedures laid down by Parliament and subject to the payment of compensation assessed in accordance with rules provided by Parliament. Thus, the law relating to compulsory purchase and compensation is primarily derived from Acts of Parliament, but these are supplemented by numerous judicial decisions through which important principles have evolved. Much of the statute law can be traced back to the middle of the nineteenth century and, in some cases, the courts have been forced to interpret it in a manner which has little perceptible relation to the actual words used, representing a judicial effort to keep the primitive wording of the statutes in some sort of accord with the realities of an industrial age[1].

1 See, eg, the speech of Lord Wilberforce in *Argyle Motors (Birkenhead) Ltd v Birkenhead Corpn* [1975] AC 99, HL, at 129B.

[3]
This chapter explains the scope and purpose of **Division A** of this work. This Division introduces the subject of compulsory acquisition and compensation as follows:

(1) **Chapter 2** contains an outline of the history and evolution of the present system of compulsory acquisition in England and Wales and the prospects for changes to the system.
(2) **Chapter 3** explains the nature of compulsory acquisition and the justification of public interest.
(3) **Chapter 4** outlines the human rights dimension.
(4) **Chapter 5** explains the special rules which apply where land, which has been acquired by compulsion, is disposed of.

B The aim and structure of this work

[4]
Being spread across several statutes of varying ages and so many judicial decisions, this branch of the law can appear daunting. The aim of this work is to provide a comprehensive guide to the law and practice relating to compulsory purchase and compensation, while making it as accessible as possible, not by oversimplification, but by setting it out in a well-defined structure and by stating the main propositions in the text as clearly as possible, fully supported by notes which provide detailed references to cases and other material and elaboration where appropriate. This work is intended for use by practitioners in the field of compulsory purchase and compensation, particularly lawyers, surveyors and valuers, acting for both landowners and acquiring authorities, but the structure, style and indexing are intended to make it accessible to occasional users and students.

[5]
The 'system' of compulsory purchase comprises four distinct elements: *powers, authorisation procedures, implementation mechanisms* and *compensation*. While these are obviously linked, it is convenient to consider them separately. The *power* to acquire land compulsorily has to be provided by statute and is always ancillary to the primary functions of the body in question. When a body wishes to exercise such a power, it must then follow the procedures for obtaining *authorisation* to make the acquisition. After being duly authorised, it must follow the mechanisms for achieving the *implementation* of the acquisition. A right to *compensation* flows from the exercise of the power.

[6]
Thus, the four Divisions of this work that follow the introductory matters explained in **Division A**, reflect the nature of the system of compulsory purchase described above as follows:

(1) **Division B** explains the *powers* to acquire land by agreement and compulsorily. It also explains the circumstances in which a landowner can require a body to acquire his land as though the body had made a compulsory purchase order.

(2) **Division C** explains the *procedures for securing authorisation* to acquire land compulsorily.
(3) **Division D** explains the *mechanisms for implementing* a compulsory purchase so that the acquiring authority obtains possession of the land.
(4) **Division E** explains the right to and assessment of *compensation* for compulsory purchase.

[7]–[150]
The two Divisions which then follow explain the rights to compensation which arise in a variety of circumstances where no land has been taken from the claimant. Thus:

(1) **Division F** explains, first, the right to compensation where no land has been taken but the value of the claimant's land has, nonetheless, been depreciated by works authorised by statute (referred to as 'injurious affection') and, second, the right to compensation for depreciation in the value of property caused by the use of public works.
(2) **Division G** explains the rights to compensation where decisions are taken which restrict the manner in which land can be used or developed and where bodies have powers to enter onto land, without acquiring it, to do such works as lay pipes and cables.
(3) Finally, **Division H** explains the process for determining questions of disputed compensation and the procedures in the Upper Tribunal (Lands Chamber), formerly known as the Lands Tribunal.

Chapter 2

Evolution of the system

Contents

A Introduction

[151]

Our rule of law has, since Magna Carta[1], protected the ownership of land. Expropriation has only been possible when duly authorised by law. Since the need to acquire land without the owners' consent has existed for very many years, a body of law has evolved which enables this to occur, while striking a balance between the safeguards for the individual and the need to acquire land in the public interest.

1 '... no freeman shall be ... disseised of his freehold or liberties ... but ... by the law of the land' (Magna Carta, Chapter 29).

[152]

This Chapter briefly explains the historical background to the present system and the prospects for change.

[153]

Early examples of a form of compulsory acquisition are the inclosures authorised in the eighteenth and nineteenth centuries by Acts of Parliament. Inclosures followed a procedure which included the hearing of objections and the determination of claims for compensation by commissioners. In the late eighteenth and nineteenth centuries, infrastructure schemes like canals, railways and harbours were constructed under the authority of Acts of Parliament. In addition to authorising the execution of the works, ancillary powers were granted to acquire the necessary land. Such Acts were self-contained in the sense that they included specific provisions governing the procedures to be followed and providing for compensation to be paid. Parliamentary Bills followed a procedure which enabled objectors to be heard before the powers were granted by the passing of the Act.

B Evolution of the procedures

[154]
By the middle of the nineteenth century, Acts authorising the execution of works for the purpose of undertakings which required land to be acquired compulsorily had become sufficiently frequent that it was decided to standardise compulsory purchase procedure and compensation. This was achieved by the Lands Clauses Consolidation Act 1845 (LCCA 1845). The LCCA 1845 did not itself provide the power to acquire land compulsorily – that depended upon a specific Act passed for that purpose, which came to be referred to as the 'special Act'[1] – but, from the passing of the LCCA 1845, all Acts which authorised the compulsory purchase of land incorporated, but without repeating, provisions of the LCCA 1845[2]. While the provisions of the LCCA 1845 were generally not new, the process of drawing them together and applying them uniformly to all compulsory purchases represents the birth of our present system of compulsory purchase. Parallel legislation, the Railways Clauses Consolidation Act 1845, made similar provision specifically for railway schemes and included procedures, known as the mining code, which could be applied in respect of land containing or adjacent to minerals.

1 LCCA 1845, s 2 and the Compulsory Purchase Act 1965 (CPA 1965), s 1(2).
2 LCCA 1845, s 1.

[155]
In the late nineteenth and early twentieth centuries, when the functions of local authorities were greatly extended into such fields as housing, highways, public health, water supply and sewage disposal, it was recognised that compulsory acquisition would be needed frequently and it would have been cumbersome for each authority to promote an Act of Parliament every time it wanted to build some houses, or a road or a sewage works. A new procedure was introduced, involving an application to a minister for a 'provisional order'. Notice would be given and, in the event of objections, these would be heard by commissioners at a public inquiry. After the commissioners had reported, the minister could confirm the order which then had to be the subject of confirmation by Act of Parliament.

[156]
The provisional order procedure was itself cumbersome and was gradually replaced by the system now in place for the majority of circumstances in which bodies have compulsory purchase powers. Many bodies are now given general powers to make compulsory purchase orders for purposes ancillary to their primary functions, although the mere existence of such powers does not authorise the purchase of a specific parcel of land. To acquire a particular parcel of land, it is necessary for a body to make a 'compulsory purchase order', specifying precisely the land to be acquired and to secure the minister's confirmation of the order. Since the minister is answerable to Parliament, a degree of Parliamentary control is retained over the expropriation of private property. The general use of compulsory purchase orders was introduced by the Local Government Act 1933; the

procedure for making and confirming compulsory purchase orders was consolidated in the Acquisition of Land (Authorisation Procedure) Act 1946 and is now contained in the Acquisition of Land Act 1981.

[157]
The procedure for implementing a compulsory purchase originated in the LCCA 1845, and similar provisions are now contained in the CPA 1965 which are described in **Division D**. Under these Acts, the acquiring authority has to commence the process by serving a 'notice to treat'. If it requires possession before compensation is agreed or settled, it can take it following service a notice of entry. Once compensation is agreed or determined, completion of the purchase follows normal conveyancing procedures. Acquiring authorities now have available an alternative mechanism known as the general vesting declaration. The Compulsory Purchase (Vesting Declarations) Act 1981 provides a procedure for transferring title to the acquiring authority without conventional conveyancing; compensation is negotiated or determined and paid later.

[158]
Where a promoter does not possess a general power to make a compulsory purchase order, it continues to be necessary for him to obtain an Act of Parliament to be authorised to acquire land compulsorily, unless his scheme is of a type to which the Act 1992 or the Planning Act 2008 applies. The Transport and Works Act 1992 introduced a procedure (explained in **Division C**) for authorising railway and other transport proposals enabling the Secretary of State to make an order having a similar effect to a private Act. Instead of objections being heard by parliamentary committee, they are heard at a public inquiry. Such an order can grant compulsory purchase powers as ancillary to authorising the promoter's scheme. The Planning Act 2008 introduced a new system for scrutinising and authorising major infrastructure projects. Sections 122–134 are concerned with compulsory purchase of land for such projects. These provisions and the associated secondary legislation are explained in **Division C**.

C Evolution of the principles of compensation

[159]
The evolution of the principles of compensation is described in more detail in **Division E**; the following is a brief outline. The LCCA 1845 also contained provisions relating to compensation. Under that Act[1], two kinds of compensation were available to an owner whose land was acquired: the value of his land taken and the loss of value caused to his other land by reason of it being severed or otherwise injuriously affected. The LCCA 1845 did not prescribe the basis for assessing these elements of compensation and principles were developed through judicial decisions which provide the foundation of the present code. The value of the land came to be interpreted as the value to the owner, taking account of the fact that the purchase was compulsory. Over time, it became the practice to reflect the compulsory nature of the acquisition by adding 10% to the market value of the property acquired. The value

to the owner also included all other losses caused to the claimant personally by reason of being dispossessed; this developed into a distinct element of compensation, now called disturbance, but, to this day, this rests on judicial decision, rather than express statutory right.

1 LCCA 1845, s 63.

[160]–[170]

Those principles were modified by the Acquisition of Land (Assessment of Compensation) Act 1919 (ALACA 1919) primarily to eliminate the 10% addition to market value. The ALACA 1919 introduced the rules, which are now to be found in the Land Compensation Act 1961, s 5, which govern the valuation of the land taken. The element of the total figure of compensation which is attributable to the value of the land taken is now to be assessed as open market value without any account being taken of the fact that the purchase is compulsory. The other two elements of compensation (severance and injurious affection, and disturbance) remain, albeit developed by judicial decisions. The Land Compensation Act 1973 introduced important improvements to the compensation code. Further amendments were made by the Planning and Compensation Act 1991 and the Planning and Compulsory Purchase Act 2004.

[171]

The Lands Tribunal was created in 1950[1] as a specialist forum to deal with compensation and other land- and valuation-related issues. The Tribunals, Courts and Enforcement Act 2007 introduced a re-organisation of tribunals including the Lands Tribunal. The jurisdiction of the Lands Tribunal to determine compensation in consequence of compulsory purchase or other actions authorised by statutes has been transferred to the Upper Tribunal (Lands Chamber) as explained in **Division H**.

1 Lands Tribunal Act 1949.

D Prospects of future change

[172]

A variety of criticisms of the present system of compulsory purchase have been made in recent years, particularly on the ground that it is said to be slow and bureaucratic. Concerns have been expressed that it needs to be modernised and streamlined in order to meet the need to assemble inner city sites for urban regeneration. For example, the Environment, Transport and Regional Affairs Committee has said that it was:

> ' … very concerned about problems of land assembly and the failure to bring brownfield land into use for housing. The traditional way of dealing with these problems is the compulsory purchase order which has been little used in recent years. It is slow. A streamlined compulsory purchase order would be helpful and is urgently required …'[1]

Another example is the Urban Task Force Report, which said:

'... there is a wide spread reluctance among many other local authorities to exercise their powers of compulsory purchase. Other than the problem of lack of resources, the four main reasons for this reluctance are the inherent bureaucracy of the process, uncertainty over powers, a loss of skills and the inadequacy of the compensation provisions.'[2]

Criticisms have also been made of the rules for assessing compensation and the mechanism for determining questions of disputed compensation. Examples are the Report of the City University Business School[3] and the Report of the Urban Task Force[4].

1 Environment Transport and Regional Affairs Committee *Tenth Report: Housing* (22 July 1998), para 252.
2 *Towards an Urban Renaissance: Final Report of the Urban Task Force Chaired by Lord Rogers of Riverside* (June 1998) DETR, p 228.
3 *The Operation of Compulsory Purchase Orders: A Report by the City University Business School for DETR* (May 1997) Stationery Office.
4 *Towards an Urban Renaissance: Urban Task Force Report*, p 231.

[173]

In order to examine the validity of these criticisms, the Department of the Environment, Transport and the Regions (DETR) embarked, in 1998, upon a review of compulsory purchase law and procedure, with the assistance of a group of practitioners and representatives of local authority and property interests[1]. An interim report[2] was published in January 1999 and the Final Report was published in July 2000[3]. It was acknowledged[4] that the basic framework of our existing system is sound, but there may be elements of the law which need refinement, and there is a case for consolidation of the statutes and codification of some of the principles established by judicial decision. The matter was referred to the Law Commission, which published two reports for consultation[5] and subsequently two final reports[6]. Certain limited changes were enacted in the Planning and Compulsory Purchase Act 2004[7]. In December 2005, ODPM announced that it had decided not to progress the Law Commission's proposals, although a few relatively minor issues may be addressed when legislative opportunities arise[8].

1 Compulsory Purchase Policy Review Advisory Group (CPPRAG).
2 *Fundamental Review of the Laws and Procedures Relating to Compulsory Purchase and Compensation: Interim Report* (January 1999) DETR.
3 *Fundamental Review of the Laws and Procedures Relating to Compulsory Purchase and Compensation: Final Report* (July 2000) DETR.
4 Keynote Address by Nick Raynsford MP, Parliamentary Under-Secretary of State for the Environment, Transport and the Regions at the National Symposium, '*Compulsory Purchase: An Appropriate Power for the 21st Century?*', proceedings published by DETR in August 1999.
5 *Towards a Compulsory Purchase Code (1) Compensation*, Law Commission Consultation Paper No 165, and *Towards a Compulsory Purchase Code (2) Procedure*, Law Commission Paper No 169.
6 *Towards a Compulsory Purchase Code (1) Compensation*, Law Commission Paper LC 286 and *Towards a Compulsory Purchase Code (2) Procedure*, Law Commission Paper LC 291. See also the comments of the House of Lords in *Waters v Welsh Development Agency* [2004] 1 WLR 1304.
7 Part 8 which deals with compulsory purchase was brought into force on 31 October 2004: PCPA 2004 (Commencement No 3) Order, SI 2004/2593.
8 *Government Response to Law Commission Report: Towards a Compulsory Purchase Code*: Office of the Deputy Prime Minister (December 2005), presented to the House of Commons in a written statement on 15 December 2005. The Court of Appeal has twice criticised the Government for failing to adopt the Law Commission's recommendations: *Greenweb v London Borough of Wandsworth* [2008] EWCA Civ 910 and *Transport for London v Spirerose Ltd* [2008] EWCA Civ

1230 at [69]–[79]. On 10 March 2011, the Government rejected an attempt to add clauses to the Localism Bill in order to reform the Land Compensation Act 1961, ss 14–20 (planning assumptions), but the minister did undertake to give such reform further consideration: Statement of Minister of State, Department for Communities and Local Government, Official Report of Public Bill Committee, Localism Bill, pp 939–946.

[174]–[350]

In order to respond to the point made by the Urban Task Force (in the passage cited above) that there had been a loss of skills in local authorities and others having compulsory purchase powers, which had contributed both to the reluctance to use compulsory purchase powers and to slowness, inefficiency and bureaucracy, when they were used, CPPRAG recommended that a comprehensive manual and best practice guide be prepared. This recommendation was accepted[1] and the manual entitled 'Compulsory Purchase Procedure Manual' was first published in November 2001[2]. Further guidance on the use of compulsory purchase powers is now contained in ODPM Circular 06/2004.

1 *Fundamental Review of the Laws and Procedures Relating to Compulsory Purchase and Compensation: Interim Report* (January 1999) DETR, para 8.7.12. A draft was issued for consultation, but the final version has not yet been published (October 2000).

2 *Compulsory Purchase Procedure Manual*. This is updated periodically and is available by subscription from TSO Parliamentary and Legal Bookshop.

Chapter 3

The nature of compulsory purchase

Contents

A Introduction

[351]
Compulsory purchase is a euphemism for expropriation in exchange for a payment which is assessed in accordance with principles which seek to provide the financial equivalent to the loss imposed upon the landowner without reflecting the gain to the expropriator. Compulsory acquisition is authorised as an exception to the general protection afforded to property and is justified on the grounds that the public interest outweighs the landowner's interest. Thus the *public interest* is fundamental to compulsory purchase in the law of England and Wales[1]. Public interest is also fundamental to the power to acquire land compulsorily without infringement of human rights, as is explained in **Chapter 4** of this Division. Since land can only be acquired compulsorily where it is justified in the public interest, there are restrictions upon the use to which land so acquired may be put (explained later in this Chapter) and there are special rules which govern the disposal of land compulsorily acquired (explained in **Chapter 5** of this Division).

1 Although the making and confirmation of compulsory purchase orders are administrative acts involving the exercise of discretion, there is scope for judicial review of the decision to confirm a compulsory purchase order, as is explained in **Division C**. The principles applicable are the familiar '*Wednesbury/Ashbridge*' principles: see *R v Secretary of State for Transport, ex p de Rothschild* [1989] 1 All ER 933, CA.

B Justification for the use of compulsory powers

[352]
The basis upon which compulsory purchase is justified is necessity in the public interest, as explained by Lord Denning MR in the following passage from his judgment in *Prest v Secretary of State for Wales*[1]:

> 'It is clear that no minister or public authority can acquire any land compulsorily except the power to do so be given by Parliament: and Parliament only grants it, or should only grant it, when it is necessary in the public interest. In any case, therefore, where the scales are evenly balanced – for or against compulsory acquisition – the decision – by whomsoever it is made – should come down against compulsory acquisition. I regard it as a principle of our constitutional law that no citizen is to be deprived of his land by any public authority against his will, unless it is expressly authorised by Parliament and the public interest decisively so demands[2]. If there is any reasonable doubt on the matter, the balance must be resolved in favour of the citizen.'

1 (1982) 81 LGR 193, CA. This passage and the passage from the judgment of Watkins LJ cited below were cited with approval by Lord Hope in *R (on the application of Sainsbury's Supermarkets Ltd) v Wolverhampton City Council* [2010] UKSC 20, [2010] 4 All ER 931 at [10].
2 See *A-G v De Keyser's Royal Hotel Ltd* [1920] AC 508, HL.

[353]
In the same judgment, Lord Denning endorsed Forbes J's expression of the principle in *Brown v Secretary of State for the Environment*[1]:

> 'It seems to me that there is a very long and respectable tradition for the view that an authority that seeks to dispossess a citizen of his land must do so by showing that it is necessary, in order to exercise the powers for the purposes of the Act under which the compulsory purchase order is made, that the acquiring authority should have authorisation to acquire the land in question.'

Forbes J went on to deal with necessity in the context of the acquiring authority itself already having possession of other suitable land, saying:

> '… then it seems to me that no reasonable Secretary of State faced with that fact could come to the conclusion that it was necessary for the authority to acquire other land compulsorily for precisely the same purpose.'

1 (1978) 40 P&CR 285 at 291.

[354]
Also in *Prest v Secretary State for Wales*[1], Watkins LJ said[2]:

> 'The taking of a person's land against his will is a serious invasion of his proprietary rights. The use of statutory authority for the destruction of those rights requires to be most carefully scrutinised. The courts must be vigilant to see to it that that authority is not abused. It must not be used unless it is clear that the Secretary of State has allowed those rights to be violated by a decision based upon the right legal principles, adequate evidence and proper consideration of the factor which sways his mind into confirmation of the order sought.'

In *R v Secretary of State for Transport, ex p de Rothschild*[3], Slade LJ referred to the judgments in the cases of *Prest* and *Brown* and, while holding that they did not create special rules as to the burden of proof, commented[4] that they gave:

> 'a warning that, in cases where a compulsory purchase order is under challenge, the draconian nature of the order will itself render it more vulnerable to successful challenge …'

1 See para **[351]** fn 1.
2 At 211. For an explanation of the comments made by Watkins LJ concerning the onus of proof, see *R v Secretary of State for Transport, ex p Rothschild* [1989] 1 All ER 933, CA per Slade LJ at 937h–938f. See also the discussion of the cases referred to above by Laws J in *Chesterfield Properties plc v Secretary of State for the Environment and Stockton-on-Tees Borough Council* (1997) 76 P&CR 117 and by Harrison J in *London Borough of Bexley v Secretary of State for the Environment, Transport and the Regions* [2001] EWHC Admin 323, [2001] 18 EGCS 172.
3 [1989] 1 All ER 933, CA.
4 [1989] 1 All ER 933 at 938e–f.

C What is acquired by compulsory purchase

[355]
A compulsory purchase of land usually involves the acquisition by the acquiring authority of the freehold, together with any estates and interests in the land which have been carved out of the freehold[1], although some statutes authorise the acquiring authority to acquire a right only where that is sufficient for the authority's purposes. The meaning of land, the estates and interests which may be acquired, and the circumstances in which rights over land may be acquired are all matters which are explained in detail in **Division B**. Compulsory purchase is to be distinguished from requisitioning, which involves only the taking of possession, without the acquisition of an estate or interest; requisitioning normally only occurs in connection with defence and wartime activities.

1 The acquiring authority is not bound to acquire all the existing interests in the land it requires if it can achieve its objectives without doing so. For example, it may acquire the freehold interest and then allow leases to expire by the effluxion of time if it does not require possession of the land until after the leases have expired: see further **Division D [309]**.

D The purchase price: compensation

[356]
This process of acquisition is referred to as a purchase, despite the unwillingness of the 'seller', because his title to the land in question is acquired for a monetary payment referred to as compensation, the main element of which is the open market value of the land assessed as though he was a willing seller. The basis upon which the compensation is assessed is fully described in **Division E**. The fundamental principle underlying the compensation code was expressed by Lord Justice Scott in a well-known passage from the case of *Horn v Sunderland Corpn*[1], as follows:

> '[Compensation] is the right to be put, so far as money can do it, in the same position as if his land had not been taken from him. In other words, he gains a money payment not less than the loss imposed on him in the public interest, but, on the other hand, no greater.'

1 [1941] 2 KB 26 at 42.

E Bodies authorised to acquire land compulsorily

[357]
Historically, the Crown could acquire land under the royal prerogative; even if this power still exists, its use would be confined to wartime emergencies

and is of academic interest only[1]. For all practical purposes, since compulsory acquisition of land occurs only where it is authorised by statute, the relevant statute will specify the body by whom the power may be exercised. In addition to government departments, many local authorities and other public bodies have general powers to acquire land compulsorily, subject to confirmation in relation to a particular case, but such powers are not confined to bodies of a public nature. Many of the railway and other infrastructure schemes for which Parliament granted authorisation in the nineteenth century were promoted by commercial companies seeking to profit from their activities. Today, especially since the privatisation of the nationalised industries, there are also many commercial companies which have compulsory purchase powers. This does not alter the requirement that, in any particular case, a compulsory purchase is not to be authorised and confirmed, unless it is shown to be in the public interest. The term 'acquiring authority' tends to be used to refer to any body exercising compulsory purchase powers, even if the body is not strictly an authority.

1 For consideration of the royal prerogative and its relationship with statutory powers, see *Burmah Oil Co Ltd v Lord Advocate* [1965] AC 75, in which Lord Radcliffe said at 115:

> 'The Crown has never claimed or sought to exercise in time of peace a right to take land except by agreement or under statutory power.'

F Restrictions on the use of land compulsorily acquired

[358]–[500]

Land which has been compulsorily acquired may only be used for the purposes for which the acquiring authority was authorised to acquire it[1]; this includes any ancillary or incidental purpose[2]. For example, land acquired for coastal protection purposes cannot be used to create a promenade[3], and land acquired for housing purposes cannot be used to construct a road serving a function independent from housing[4]. The purpose for which land was being used when it was acquired may be continued temporarily, pending the commencement of the purpose which justified the acquisition[5]. A body which has acquired land by the exercise of compulsory purchase powers may not, by contract, agree not to use it in a way which would be inconsistent with the purpose for which the land was acquired[6]. It may, however, enter into restrictive covenants, so long as these are consistent with the purpose for which the land was acquired[7].

1 *A-G v Manchester Corpn* [1906] 1 Ch 643.

2 *A-G v Great Eastern Rly Co* (1880) 5 App Cas 473, HL at 478.

3 *Webb v Minister for Housing and Local Government* [1965] 2 All ER 193, CA.

4 *Meravale Builders Ltd v Secretary of State for the Environment* (1978) 36 P&CR 87, QBD. See also *Hanks v Minister of Housing and Local Government* [1963] 1 QB 999; *R v Inner London Education Authority, ex p Westminster City Council* [1986] 1 All ER 19; *Procter and Gamble Ltd v Secretary of State for the Environment* [1992] 1 EGLR 265, CA.

5 *A-G v Teddington UDC* [1898] 1 Ch 66, Chancery Division; *A-G v Hanwell UDC* [1900] 2 Ch 377, CA.

6 *Ayr Harbour Trustees v Oswald* (1883) 8 App Cas 623, HL. See also *Stourcliffe Estates Co Ltd v Bournemouth Corpn* [1910] 2 Ch 12, CA; *R v Hammersmith and Fulham LBC, ex p Beddowes* [1987] QB 1050.

7 *Stourcliffe Estates Co Ltd v Bournemouth Corpn* [1910] 2 Ch 12, CA.

Chapter 4

The human rights dimension

Contents

A Introduction

[501]
While a detailed exposition of human rights law and principles is outside the scope of this work, the subject is undoubtedly of relevance to the law relating to compulsory purchase and compensation. Consequently, this Chapter provides an outline of the provisions of the European Convention on Human Rights (ECHR) and the Human Rights Act 1998 (HRA 1998) which are of principal relevance to compulsory purchase.

B European Convention on Human Rights

[502]
The United Kingdom is a signatory to the ECHR[1], which came into force as an international treaty in 1953. The Convention comprises a statement of rights, which signatory states guarantee, and incorporates machinery and procedures for their enforcement through the European Commission of Human Rights and the European Court of Human Rights in Strasbourg. A number of cases have reached the European Court which have a bearing on compulsory purchase law.

1 The full title is the 'Convention for the Protection of Human Rights and Fundamental Freedoms', Rome, 4 November 1950 (Cmd 8969).

[503]
The provisions of the ECHR which are likely to be of most relevance to compulsory purchase law are as follows.

Article 2:

> 'Everyone's right to life shall be protected by law …'

Article 6:

> 'In the determination of his civil rights and obligations … , everyone is entitled to a fair and public hearing within a reasonable time by an independent and impartial tribunal established by law …'

Article 8:

> 'Everyone has the right to respect for his private and family life, his home and his correspondence. There shall be no interference by a public authority with the exercise of this right except such as is in accordance with the law and is necessary in a democratic society in the interests of national security, public safety or the economic well-being of the country, for the prevention of disorder or crime, for the protection of health or morals, or for the protection of the rights and freedom of others.'

Article 1 of the First Protocol:

> 'Every natural or legal person is entitled to the peaceful enjoyment of his possessions. No one shall be deprived of his possessions except in the public interest and subject to the conditions provided for by law and the general principles of international law. The preceding provisions shall not, however, in any way impair the right of the state to enforce such laws as it deems necessary to control the use of property in accordance with the general interest …'

C Human Rights Act 1998

[504]
The HRA 1998 came fully into force on 2 October 2000, incorporating the provisions of the ECHR into domestic law. The provisions which are of principal relevance to compulsory purchase may be summarised as follows. Primary and subordinate legislation must be interpreted so far as possible in a manner which is compatible with the ECHR[1]. Where UK legislation is found to be incompatible with the ECHR, the UK courts may make a declaration of incompatibility[2]. The UK courts must take account of relevant decisions of the ECHR and other institutions[3]. 'Public authorities' must not act in a way which is incompatible with the ECHR[4]. The term 'public authority' is defined as including courts, tribunals and any person certain of whose functions are of a public nature[5]. A person who claims that a public authority has acted in a manner incompatible with the ECHR may bring proceedings against the authority in the UK courts, may rely on the ECHR in any legal proceedings[6] and may obtain such relief as is appropriate, including an award of damages[7]. To be entitled to relief, a person must be a 'victim' of an act which the ECHR makes unlawful[8].

1 HRA 1998, s 3.
2 HRA 1998, s 4.
3 HRA 1998, s 2.
4 HRA 1998, s 6.
5 HRA 1998, s 6(3).
6 HRA 1998, s 7.
7 HRA 1998, s 8.

8 HRA 1998, s 7(1). The concept of the victim has some similarity with the concept of sufficient interest to bring judicial review proceedings, but may be somewhat narrower in scope. The person must have been directly affected or there must be a risk of direct effect.

D Relevance to compulsory purchase

[505]

Although the ECHR guarantees the right to peaceful enjoyment of property, it is clear from Article 1 of the First Protocol that compulsory acquisition of land does not involve an infringement of the ECHR so long as it is done in the public interest[1] and is subject to the law laid down by statute[2]. Similar considerations apply to Article 8. States are given a 'margin of appreciation' in deciding for themselves what constitutes sufficient public interest to justify a compulsory acquisition[3].

1 Public interest is fundamental to the law of compulsory purchase in England and Wales, see **Division A, Chapter 3**.

2 The first part of Article 1 states: 'Every natural or legal person is entitled to the peaceful enjoyment of his possessions. No one shall be deprived of his possessions except in the public interest and subject to the conditions provided for by law and by the general principles of international law …' For an explanation of Article 1, see *Lithgow v United Kingdom* (1986) 8 EHRR 329, para 106.

3 See the comments of Ouseley J about the margin of appreciation in *Trailer and Marina (Leven) Ltd v Secretary of State for the Environment, Food and Rural Affairs* [2004] EWHC 153, at para 63.

[506]

The system of compulsory purchase in England and Wales enables a landowner who objects to a compulsory purchase to be heard at a public inquiry before the order is confirmed. There is a right to challenge a decision to confirm an order on legal grounds, as described in **Division C**. It is considered that these procedures comply with art 6, which provides a right to a fair trial in relation to civil rights and obligations at least in relation to compulsory purchase orders made by bodies other than ministers[1].

1 In *Bryan v UK* (1995) 21 EHRR 342, the European Court of Human Rights held that the procedure under the Town and Country Planning Act 1990, in relation to appeals against enforcement notices, complied with art 6. The same may not apply to compulsory purchase by ministers; see for example *County Properties Ltd v Scottish Ministers* 2000 SLT 965 in which it was held that there had been a breach of art 6 where a listed building application was called in by the Scottish Minister and Scottish Heritage, an Executive Agency, was an objector to the application. In *R (on the application of Holdings & Barnes) plc v Secretary of State for the Environment, Transport and the Regions* [2001] 1 EGLR 33, the Divisional Court held that confirmation by the Secretary of State of a compulsory purchase order to implement a Highways Agency road scheme was lawful but not compatible with the Human Rights Act 1998. An appeal was made direct to the House of Lords who reversed the judgment of the Divisional Court [2001] UKHL 23, [2003] 2 AC 295.

[506.1]

The High Court has considered the concept of 'proportionality' in relation to compulsory purchase in a number of cases. In *Baker v First Secretary of State*[1] a local authority sought to compulsorily purchase, under the Housing Act 1985, a residential property in extreme disrepair. The landowner argued that she would carry out the necessary repairs. The council rejected this as she was elderly, out of work and had no funds to finance the repairs. The compulsory purchase order was confirmed. The landowner then challenged the decision on the grounds that it involved a breach of Article 8 of the Convention and Article 1 of the First Protocol. The High Court rejected the challenge but drew attention to two aspects of proportionality being 'proportionality of means' and 'proportionality of ends'. Nicholas Blake QC (sitting as a deputy High Court judge) said:

> 'That consideration [ie what is the best of a number of possible solutions] has to be reflected in the decision making process. Proportionality is not simply whether at the end result the balance is fair, but whether, in getting there, it has been decided that the most appropriate course of conduct is also the least interfering with human rights, having regard to the public benefit to be achieved and the different means of achieving it.'

1 [2003] EWHC 2511 (Admin). See also the judgment of Sir Thomas Bingham MR in *R v Ministry of Defence, ex p Smith* [1996] 1 All ER 257; the judgment of Sullivan J in *Tesco Stores Ltd v Secretary of State for the Environment, Transport and the Regions and Wycombe District Council* (2000) 80 P&CR 427 at 429; and the judgment of Harrison J in *London Borough of Bexley v Secretary of State for the Environment, Transport and the Regions* [2001] EWHC Admin 323, [2001] 18 EGCS 172.

[506.2]

In a number of subsequent decisions, the courts have considered whether proportionality in the context of compulsory purchase requires it to be considered whether acquisition compulsorily is the least intrusive means of achieving the public benefit sought, or whether the test of proportionality is satisfied provided that the order strikes a fair balance between the public benefit sought and the interference with the rights in question. The latter test (fair balance) is less stringent than the former (least intrusive means). The weight of authority at present supports the proposition that the fair balance test is the correct test for proportionality in the context of confirmation of a compulsory purchase order[1]. It has been held that, in challenges to the proportionality of a decision, it is for the court to determine on an objective basis whether the decision was proportionate[2]. It has also been held that the general requirement that there be a compelling case in the public interest to justify confirmation of a compulsory purchase order will usually ensure that the requirements of the ECHR are met[3].

1 *Belfields Ltd v Secretary of State for Communities and Local Government* [2007] EWHC 3040 (Admin), [2007] All ER (D) 367 (Dec) at [20]; *Lisa Smith v Secretary of State for Trade and Industry* [2007] EWHC 1013 (Admin), [2007] All ER (D) 59 (May) at [43]; *Pascoe v First Secretary of State* [2006] EWHC 2356 (Admin), [2006] 4 All ER 1240 at [83]; *Bexley London Borough Council v Secretary of State for the Environment, Transport and the Regions* [2001] EWHC Admin 323, [2001] 18 EGCS 172 at [34]–[35]; see also the approach taken in *Sole v Secretary of State for Trade and Industry* [2007] EWHC 1527 (Admin), (2007) 151 Sol Jo LB 746. See also **Division C Chapter 6**, where these cases are referred to in the context of challenges to the validity of CPOs.

2 *Lisa Smith v Secretary of State for Trade and Industry* [2007] EWHC 1013 (Admin), [2007] All ER (D) 59 (May) at [58], following *R (SB) v Governors of Denbigh High School* [2006] UKHL 15, [2007] 1 AC 100 at [30], where it was said that the court was required to adopt an approach that went beyond that traditionally adopted in judicial review, and employed a heightened intensity of review that enabled the court itself to judge, on an objective basis, whether the measure is proportionate or not. By contrast, see *R (Powell) v Secretary of State for Communities and Local Government* [2007] EWHC 2051 (Admin), [2007] All ER (D) 137 at [12], where Sullivan J held that the court could only intervene if the balance struck was irrational.

3 See *Bexley London Borough Council v Secretary of State for the Environment, Transport and the Regions* [2001] EWHC Admin 323 at [46]; *Tesco Stores Ltd v Secretary of State for Transport and the Regions* (2000) P&CR 427 at 429.

[507]
With regard to compensation for compulsory purchase, although this is not expressly mentioned in the ECHR, the reference in Article 1 of the First Protocol to 'the conditions provided for by law and the general principles of international law' is taken to mean that compensation must be paid. States are given a margin of appreciation as to the basis upon which compensation is assessed and legitimate objectives of public interest may justify reimbursement at less than the financial equivalent to what the claimant has lost[1]. As is explained elsewhere, the fundamental principle which underlies the assessment of compensation for compulsory purchase in England and Wales is that the claimant has the right to be put, so far as money can do it, in the same position as if the land had not been taken from him[2]; compensation assessed on this basis will not infringe the ECHR.

1 For example, *James v UK* (1986) 8 EHRR 123, and *Lithgow v UK* (1986) 8 EHRR 329. In *Lithgow*, the European Court said (at para 121): 'The Court further accepts the Commission's conclusion as to the standard of compensation: the taking of property without payment of an amount reasonably related to its value would normally constitute a disproportionate interference which could not be justified under Article 1. Article 1 does not, however, guarantee a right to full compensation in all circumstances, since legitimate objectives of 'public interest', such as pursued in measures of economic reform or measures designed to achieve greater social justice, may call for less than reimbursement of the full market value.'
2 See **Division A, Chapter 3** and, for a detailed exposition of compensation law, **Division E**.

[508]
While it appears, therefore, that the principle of compulsory acquisition and the system which now exists for authorising and implementing a compulsory acquisition is in conformity with the ECHR, the conduct of a particular acquisition may nevertheless be the subject of proceedings in the domestic courts, in which the ECHR is cited[1]. In view of the wide definition of the term 'public authority'[2], it may be concluded that all bodies upon which compulsory acquisition powers are conferred would be treated as falling within this category and, consequently, would be potential defendants to proceedings under the HRA 1998. Similarly, all bodies with power to confirm CPOs may be regarded as 'public authorities'. With regard to compensation, in general terms, there appears to be no conflict between the principles which exist already and the ECHR, although individual cases may, nevertheless, provide scope for human rights issues to be raised.

1 See **Division C, Chapter 6**.
2 See para **[504]**.

[509]
In the context of the ECHR, a distinction has emerged between, on the one hand, compensation for compulsory acquisition and, on the other hand, compensation for the imposition of restrictions upon the use and development of land. Article 1 of the First Protocol confirms the ability of a state to impose restrictions upon the use and development of land. In England and Wales, where central or local government has the power to impose such

restrictions, a statutory right to compensation is in many cases provided. Such rights to compensation are described in **Division G** of this work. However, so far as the ECHR is concerned, Ouseley J has commented[1] as follows:

> 'It is better to say that … there is no presumption in favour of compensation in a control of use case, and that its availability is one of the factors relevant to whether a fair balance has been struck between the public interest and an individual's rights. The payment of compensation would generally support a finding of non-violation but many instances existed where a fair balance had been struck notwithstanding the absence of such provision.'

In the same case, the Court of Appeal commented[2]:

> 'The right analysis seems to us to be that provided the state could properly take the view that the benefit to the community outweighs the detriment to the individual, a fair balance will be struck, without any requirement to compensate the individual. Should this not be the case, compensation in some appropriate form may serve to redress the balance, so that no breach of Art. 1, Protocol 1 occurs.'

1 *Trailer and Marina (Leven) Ltd v Secretary of State for the Environment, Food and Rural Affairs* [2004] EWHC 153 at [80], upheld *R (on the application of Trailer and Marina (Leven) Ltd v Secretary of State for the Environment, Food and Rural Affairs and English Nature* [2005] 1 P&CR 495, CA.

2 [2005] 1 P&CR 495, CA at [58].

[510]–[650]

Finally, reference should be made to Article 2, the right to life, which may have some relevance to compulsory purchase. Projects which threaten public safety or public health may give rise to proceedings which rely on this article.

Chapter 5

Disposal of land acquired by compulsion

Contents

A Introduction

[651]
Where land has been acquired by the exercise of compulsory powers (or under the shadow of compulsory powers), the acquiring authority may wish to dispose of it either because it wishes to arrange for another person or body to fulfil the purposes of the acquisition or because the land has become surplus to requirements. In the former case, it is not unusual for local authorities and other agencies to acquire land in order to assemble a site suitable for development but with the intention that the land, once assembled, will be transferred to others who will carry out the development. There is no reason in principle why the acquiring authority should not dispose of the land in such circumstances so long as the terms of disposal (such as a commitment to carry out development) are consistent with the purposes for which the land was acquired. It may be necessary to ensure that the terms of disposal comply with any obligation imposed upon the acquiring authority to secure the best consideration (which is a topic outside the scope of this work). The terms of any such arrangements may be relevant to the question whether a compulsory purchase order should be confirmed or whether a confirmed compulsory purchase order is susceptible to challenge in the High Court. The procedure for confirming a compulsory purchase order and for High Court challenges are explained in **Division C**. This chapter is primarily concerned with the disposal of land which has become surplus to requirements.

[651.1]
Where land acquired by the exercise of compulsory powers has become surplus to requirements, the acquiring authority may wish, or be required, to dispose of that land. Powers exist under Pt X of the Local Government, Planning and Land Act 1980 (LGPLA 1980)[1] for the Secretary of State to compile and maintain a register of land held by public bodies, which, in the opinion of the Secretary of State, is not being used or sufficiently used for the performance of the body's functions or the carrying on of their functions[2], and to direct such public bodies to dispose of the same[3].

1 As amended by the Local Government Act 1988, s 31, Sch 5.
2 LGPLA 1980, s 93.
3 LGPLA 1980, s 98.

B The 'Crichel Down Rules'

[652]

The 'Crichel Down Rules'[1] set out the non-statutory arrangements under which surplus government land, which was acquired by or under a threat of compulsion, should be offered back to former owners, their successors or sitting tenants, as the case may be. The general principles underlying the rules are commended to local authorities and other statutory bodies, as well as private sector bodies to whom public land holdings have been transferred (for example, on privatisation), although it is recognised that their approach to the disposal of surplus land must depend on their particular functions and circumstances. The basic principal behind the 'Crichel Down Rules' is that, where a government department wishes to dispose of land to which the rules apply, former owners will, as a general rule, be given first opportunity to repurchase the land previously in their ownership, at current market value, provided that it has not been materially changed in character since acquisition[2]. Where only part of the land had been materially changed in character, then the general obligation will be to offer back only that part which has not been materially changed.

1 Published originally in the 1950s, the 'Crichel Down Rules' are now contained in Part 2 of the Memorandum to ODPM Circular 06/2004. The previous (1992) version of the rules was reported at [1993] JPL 325.
2 In *Blanchfield v A-G of Trinidad and Tobago* [2002] UKPC 1, [2002] 4 LRC 689, the Privy Council confirmed that the Crichel Down Rules apply where a public body are to dispose of land, and not merely where it ceases to be used for the purpose for which it was acquired. In such a context, the obligation does not arise unless the authority wishes to retain the land or transfer it to another public body for public purposes.

[653]

Paragraph 15 of the 'Crichel Down Rules' sets out exceptions to the general obligation to offer back the land to a former owner[1]. One exception is where the disposal is in respect of a site for development or redevelopment, which comprises two or more previous land holdings and there is a risk that a fragmented sale of the site would realise substantially less than the best price that can be reasonably obtained for the site as a whole[2]. A potential exception to this exception, however, exists where a consortium of former owners has indicated a wish to purchase the land collectively[3].

1 For a decision under the exception in what is now paragraph 15(2) see *R v Secretary of State for the Environment, Transport and the Regions, ex p Wheeler* (2000) 82 P&CR 1. For a decision under the exception in what is now para 15(6) see *R v Secretary of State for Defence, ex p Wilkins* [2000] 3 EGLR 11.
2 Paragraph 15(6) of the 'Crichel Down Rules' (ODPM Circular 06/2004 Memorandum Part 2).
3 Paragraph 15(6) of the 'Crichel Down Rules' (ODPM Circular 06/2004 Memorandum Part 2) and *R v Trent Regional Health Authority and Secretary of State for Health, ex p Westerman Ltd and Erewash BC* (1995) 72 P&CR 448.

[653.1]

Paragraphs 20–25 of the 'Crichel Down Rules' set out the appropriate procedures to be followed by Government departments where it is decided that property to be disposed of is, by virtue of the rules, to be offered back to its former owners.

C The best consideration that can be reasonably obtained

[654]

Section 123 of the Local Government Act 1972 (LGA 1972) provides that a 'principal council'[1] may dispose of land held by them in any manner they wish, but that, except with the consent of the Secretary of State, a council shall not dispose of land under this section, otherwise than by way of short tenancy, for a consideration less than the best that can be reasonably obtained. In *R v Darlington BC, ex p Indescon Ltd*[2], Kennedy J held that:

> ' … a court is only likely to find a breach or an intended breach by a council of the provisions of s 123(2) of the Local Government Act 1972 if the council has (*a*) failed to take proper advice or (*b*) failed to follow proper advice for reasons which cannot be justified or (*c*), although following proper advice, followed advice which was so plainly erroneous that in accepting it the council must have known, or at least ought to have known, that it was acting unreasonably.'

In exercising its powers under s 123, a local authority will be required to have regard to all the circumstances of the transaction[3].

1 LGA 1972, s 270 defines a 'principal council' as a meaning 'council elected for a principal area' and a 'principal area' as meaning 'a non-metropolitan county, a district or a London borough, but, in relation to Wales, means a county or county borough'.
2 [1990] 1 EGLR 278.
3 *R v Lancashire CC, ex p Telegraph Service Stations Ltd* (1988) 153 LG Rev 510.

[655]

Where an authority has been directed to dispose of land under the LGPLA 1980, s 98 the LGA 1972, s 123 does not require the authority to delay a sale until a time when better price might be obtained and the s 98 direction contains an implied consent to sell at less than the best consideration reasonably obtaininable[1].

1 *R v Secretary of State for the Environment, ex p Manchester City Council* (1987) 54 P&CR 212.

[656]

DCLG Circular 6/03 gives guidance for authorities on the disposal of land for less than the best consideration that can reasonably be obtained. Where it is not possible to make a reasonably reliable estimate of the open market value of the land because of the absence of comparable transactions and the lack of experience in the relevant market, an authority which is disposing of land may be entitled to offer the land for sale in the open market, rather than first offering the land to the previous owners[1].

1 In *Tomkins v Commission for the New Towns, ex p Tomkins* (1988) 58 P&CR 57, the Commission for the New Towns was held to be entitled to offer land for sale on the open market, rather than offering the land first to the previous owner, where the land had development value, which, in the particular circumstance, made it difficult to accurately assess its open market value.

D Adverse rights over the land disposed of

[657]
Easements and restrictive covenants do not prevail against an acquiring authority where land compulsorily acquired is used for the statutory purposes of that authority[1]. Unless specifically extinguished by the compulsory purchase, however, such interests may revive against a subsequent purchaser[2].

1 *Kirby v School Board for Harrogate* [1896] 1 Ch 437. See also **B[828]** and **D[1605]**.
2 *Marten v Flight Refuelling Ltd* [1962] Ch 115, [1961] 2 All ER 696; *Bird v Eggleton* (1885) 29 Ch D 1012.

[658]
By virtue of the Town and Country Planning Act 1990 (TCPA 1990), s 237, where land has been acquired or appropriated by a local authority for planning purposes, then the local authority or a successor in title will be authorised to carry out building operations on the land, notwithstanding interference with adverse rights over the land, such as easements and restrictive covenants. In order for land to be validly appropriated for planning purposes, it is necessary to show that it is required for activities or purposes for which the land could have been acquired compulsorily under the TCPA 1990, s 226[1]. Even so, adverse rights are not extinguished by s 237.

1 *London Borough of Sutton v Bolton* (1993) 68 P&CR 166.

[658.1]
In *Thames Water Utilities Ltd v Oxford City Council*[1], the High Court held that the power to override easements and other rights granted by the TCPA 1990, s 237, where planning permission has been granted for development, would allow building works to go ahead in breach of a restrictive covenant, but would not then allow the use of the building in breach of the covenant. This decision, which turned upon the precise wording of the immunity granted by s 237, had significant implications for those carrying out development pursuant to a planning permission, but with a proposed use in breach of a restrictive covenant. This decision potentially affected other similar statutory provisions in the Local Government, Planning and Land Act 1980, Sch 28, para 6; the New Towns Act 1981, s 19; the Housing Act 1988, Sch 10, para 5, the Leasehold Reform, Housing and Urban Development Act 1993, Sch 20, para 5 and the Regional Development Agencies Act 1998, Sch 6, para 2. The Planning Act 2008, s 194 and Sch 10 has enacted amendments to all these statutes the intended effect of which is to remove the effect of the decision in *Thames Water Utilities Ltd v Oxford City Council*.

1 [1999] 1 EGLR 167. It is submitted that there must be some doubt as to the correctness of this decision. See also **Division D [1605]–[1606]**.

E Rights of pre-emption

[659]–[800]
A specific right of pre-emption has sometimes been given in enactments granting compulsory purchase powers[1]. Whether a former owner or

successor in title of land compulsorily acquired, can take advantage of any such right of pre-emption will be a matter of detailed interpretation of the enactment granting the right[2].

1 *Blanchfield v A–G of Trinidad and Tobago and Chaguaramas Development Authority* [2003] UKPC1, [2002] 4 LRC 689.
2 See, eg, *Freedman v British Railways Board and National Carriers Ltd* (1992) 69 P&CR 13.

Division B

Powers of compulsory purchase

Contents

References in bold are to paragraph numbers.

Chapter 3 Purchase of land by agreement

Chapter 4 Purchase and blight notices

Chapter 1

Compulsory purchase powers

Contents

A Introduction

[1]
Compulsory purchase is the acquisition of land, or an interest in land, without the agreement of the owner. Statutory powers are required to authorise the compulsory transfer of title and lawful entry onto the land. Without statutory authority, title would not pass without the agreement of the owner, the taking of the land would amount to trespass and its use could be a nuisance. Compulsory purchase needs to be distinguished from requisition, which is the taking of possession of the land without the agreement of the owner, but where no title passes[1].

1 Enactments giving power of requisition usually make this clear in their titles. See, for example, the Requisitioned Land and War Works Act 1945.

[2]
The statutory powers which enable an acquiring authority to purchase land by compulsion are contained in what may be called the 'compulsory purchase code'. The compulsory purchase code, however, does not just provide an acquiring authority with the primary power to purchase land by compulsion, but also sets out the procedures by which the compulsory purchase of particular land is authorised, the way in which compulsory purchase is implemented, and the rules by which compensation is assessed.

[3]
It can be seen, therefore, that the compulsory purchase code in England and Wales comprises four principal elements, being:

(*a*) the primary power granted to an acquiring authority to purchase land by compulsion;
(*b*) the procedures governing the authorisation of a compulsory purchase;

(*c*) the implementation of compulsory purchase; and
(*d*) the assessment of the compensation to be paid.

The remainder of this section examines the first of these elements of the compulsory purchase code. The other three elements are explained in other Divisions of this work.

B Powers granted to an acquiring authority to purchase land by compulsion

[4]
Government departments, local authorities and other public bodies having statutory functions[1] may need to acquire land or interests in land in order to carry out their functions and, for that purpose, they will require express statutory power if they wish to purchase land by compulsion, save possibly where the Crown retains certain residual powers under the royal prerogative in time of war. Indeed local authorities and other statutory bodies will also require express statutory power to purchase land by agreement[2]. At one time, compulsory purchase powers were commonly contained in local or private Acts which related to the area or undertaking of a particular public body, but they are now usually granted by public general Acts.

1 Such as the Environment Agency, the Civil Aviation Authority and the Post Office.
2 For a discussion of acquisition by agreement see **Division B, Chapter 3**.

[5]
Until the privatisation of the former nationalised industries, it was unusual for private individuals or companies to be able to rely on powers of compulsory purchase contained in public general Acts, a rare example being the Pipelines Act 1962. Where such bodies wished to acquire land by compulsion, it was usual for the necessary powers to be sought by private Act and, indeed, that remains the approach today where appropriate compulsory purchase powers are not otherwise available[1]. Since the mid-1980s, however, a great number of public utility companies operating in regulated industries, such as the various statutory undertakers[2], have been given statutory functions which may require them to acquire land, although in most other respects they will operate as normal companies. Such companies do not need statutory powers to acquire land by agreement[3], but do require such powers to acquire land by compulsion. This trend has now been accelerated by the Planning Act 2008 which enables an applicant for a development consent for a major infrastructure project to seek the inclusion of compulsory purchase powers as 'ancillary matters'.

1 See, for example, the Gulf Oil Refining Act 1965, which authorised the Gulf Oil Company to build an oil refinery in Milford Haven.
2 Acquisition of Land Act 1981 (ALA 1981), s 8(1) defines the term 'statutory undertakers' for the purposes of that Act.
3 Although such an object must be contained in the company's articles and memorandum of association.

[6]
In all such cases, however, a company acquiring under statutory powers must remain within the powers granted or fall foul of the doctrine of ultra

vires. So, for example, where a local authority, in the exercise of its powers as a housing authority, seeks to acquire land both for housing and quite unrelated highway purposes, the courts will strike down such a compulsory purchase order as being ultra vires and therefore invalid[1]. Section 23 of the ALA 1981 provides that 'any person aggrieved' by a compulsory purchase order who desires to question its 'validity' on the grounds that its authorisation is not empowered by the ALA 1981, may make an application to the High Court. Section 24 of the ALA 1981 provides that, on such an application, the court may quash the order or any provision contained therein. The opportunity to challenge the validity of compulsory purchase orders is dealt with in **Division C, Chapter 6**.

1 *Meravale Builders Ltd v Secretary of State for the Environment* (1978) 36 P&CR 87.

[7]
Compulsory purchase powers may therefore be granted to an acquiring authority by:

(*a*) royal prerogative;
(*b*) local or private Act; or
(*c*) public general Act.

1 Royal prerogative

[8]
Ministers and government departments requiring land are given statutory powers to acquire land by compulsion in much the same way as are local authorities and other public bodies. In time of war or other national emergency, the Crown does probably retain some residual power under the royal prerogative to acquire land by compulsion without recourse to statutory authority. Where appropriate statutory powers do exist, however, then the Crown will not be able to proceed under the royal prerogative, but should exercise its statutory powers of compulsory purchase in the normal way[1].

1 *A-G v De Keyser's Royal Hotel Ltd* [1920] AC 508.

[9]
Where the Crown takes land under the royal prerogative in time of war, the House of Lords has decided in *Burmah Oil Co (Burma Trading) Ltd v Lord Advocate*[1] that compensation should be payable to expropriated owners. Although the principle survives, the effect of this particular decision was, however, retrospectively overturned by the War Damage Act 1965. Certainly, any residual powers that the Crown does still retain under the royal prerogative are, in practice, of little significance in the modern law of compulsory purchase.

1 [1965] AC 75.

2 Local or private Acts

[10]–[20]
At one time, any public or private body wishing to obtain compulsory purchase powers had to do so by securing a local or private Act of

Parliament. Such a body was required to promote a local or private Bill that specified the land to be acquired and the purpose for which it was being acquired. Persons affected were notified and entitled to petition against the Bill. Until the enactment of the Land Clauses Consolidation Act 1845 (LCCA 1845), now largely superseded by the Compulsory Purchase Act 1965 (CPA 1965), a local or private Act granting compulsory purchase powers had also to provide for the procedure to be followed in the acquisition and for the compensation to be paid. After the passing of the LCCA 1845, however, certain provisions were automatically incorporated into an authorising enactment.

[21]

A local or private Act may also incorporate the provisions of the Railways Clauses Consolidation Act 1845 giving power to exclude minerals from the purchase of land[1] and restricting the working of minerals[2]. These powers are now available under the ALA 1981, s 3 and Sch 2, where that Act applies. Without such powers, the minerals underlying any land acquired would be included in the purchase.

1 Railways Clauses Consolidation Act 1845, s 77.
2 Railways Clauses Consolidation Act 1845, ss 78–85.

[22]

Although less common now, local or private Acts are still sometimes sought for particular projects where the promoter does not have the necessary statutory powers; examples are the Channel Tunnel Act 1987 and the Crossrail Act 2008.

[23]

The procedure for promoting a private Bill is set out in standing orders of each House of Parliament. Before a private Bill can be introduced and read for the first time, the objects of the Bill must be advertised and plans and other documents displayed in the locality in which the undertaking is proposed. Those whose interests are directly affected by the Bill, such as owners, lessees and occupiers, must be separately notified by the promoters of the Bill. A promoter must deposit a petition for the Bill and the Bill itself in Parliament by 27 November each year. A private Bill may be introduced in the Commons or the Lords and such Bills are divided roughly equally between the two Houses. The first reading of the Bill simply comprises its title being read out by one of the clerks. Opponents of a private Bill will have *locus standi* to petition against it, where their property or interests are directly and specially affected, and owners, lessees and occupiers of land proposed to be compulsorily purchased under the Bill will have sufficient *locus standi* for that purpose. In the Commons, the *locus standi* of a petitioner will be determined by the Court of Referees following deposit of the Bill, whilst, in the Lords, such issues are determined by the select committee at the committee stage. The second reading of a private Bill gives an opportunity for debate and determines whether the Bill is unobjectionable in terms of national policy, on the assumption that the facts stated in its preamble are correct. Next follows the committee stage which for a private Bill will be consideration by a small committee of four members in the Commons and five in the Lords. The promoters and opponents of a private Bill have the opportunity to be represented by counsel before the committee and to call evidence. Departmental representatives or ministers may give evidence before the committee, but are not subject to cross-examination, although questions may be put through the committee chairman. If contested, the promoters must first prove the preamble to the Bill, which states the facts giving rise to it and its objects. If the committee finds the preamble of the Bill proved, it will then go on to consider the individual clauses. If the preamble is not proved, then the Bill fails. Opponents of a Bill may argue against the preamble and put down amendments to the individual clauses. After a private Bill has passed through its committee stage, it is reported, as amended, to the whole House. For a private Bill, this is usually a formality. Immediately the report stage is completed, a Bill is read for the third time. On its third reading, a Bill will only be debated if six or more members give notice and only minor verbal amendments may be made. The Bill is then sent to the other House. Once a private Bill has passed through both Houses, it will receive royal assent and become a private Act.

[24]
The cumbersome nature of the private Bill procedure ultimately led to the passing of the Transport and Works Act 1992 (TWA 1992), which provided a simplified authorisation procedure for the promoters of works relating to certain rail, tram, trolley, guided bus and inland waterways schemes.

3 Public general Acts

[25]
Public general Acts generally grant statutory power to acquire land for a specific purpose, but do not identify the particular land to be acquired or the particular project for which it is to be acquired. Such statutory powers of compulsory purchase are now numerous and the principal powers are listed in the schedule to this chapter.

[26]
In the past, some public general Acts conferred compulsory purchase powers which did not require further authorisation once the land to be acquired has been identified by the acquiring authority. Such Acts, however, were always unusual and it is extremely unlikely now that they would be encountered in normal practice[1]. It is current practice for a public general Act, which gives power to take land for a specific purpose without actually identifying the land itself, to specify a procedure which authorises the particular purchase, once the land to be acquired has in fact been identified.

1 See, eg, the Admiralty (Signal Stations) Act 1815, ss 1, 4 (no longer in force).

C Some practical points in considering compulsory purchase powers

[27]

In order to purchase land by compulsion an acquiring authority must exercise some statutory power and is thus subject to the principle of ultra vires; in other words, it must act within its powers. It is necessary, therefore, to examine exactly what powers are available to an acquiring authority and whether they are sufficient for that authority's purpose. These issues may be examined under the following headings:

(1) The acquiring authority.
(2) The purpose for which the land is to be acquired.
(3) The land and interests in land required by the acquiring authority.
(4) Adverse third party rights.
(5) The powers available.
(6) Pre-condition to exercise of compulsory purchase power.
(7) Identification of the procedure for acquiring a particular piece of land.
(8) Minerals
(9) Powers to enter land without compulsory purchase

Section D of this chapter lists many of the principal powers of compulsory purchase which are currently available to acquiring authorities, and groups these under broad subject heading[1].

1 The statutes granting these powers are numerous and the majority are not printed in this work.

The acquiring authority

[28]

The term 'acquiring authority' is defined in the ALA 1981, s 7 as including, in relation to a compulsory purchase, the Minister, local authority or other person who may be authorised to purchase land compulsorily[1]. The term 'local authority' is defined in the same section to include billing and precepting authorities under the Local Government Finance Act 1992 (ie principally district councils and county councils), as well as various other bodies.

1 See the ALA 1981, s 7(1).

[29]

It should be noted that local authorities may be able to acquire land in more that one capacity, for example, as highway authority, housing authority, or coast protection authority. In each case, however, it is important to ensure that the local authority is acting in the appropriate capacity in exercising any particular power of compulsory purchase.

The purpose for which the land is to be acquired

[30]–[40]

A power of compulsory purchase will always specify the 'purpose' for which it may be exercised, even if that purpose is expressed in fairly general terms.

Thus the Road Traffic Regulation Act 1984, s 40 authorises a local authority to compulsorily purchase land for the purposes of, inter alia, s 32 (providing parking spaces), a fairly specific purpose. By contrast, the Town and Country Planning Act 1990 (TCPA 1990), s 226 provides, inter alia, for a local authority to compulsorily purchase land in its area if it thinks that the acquisition will facilitate the carrying out of development, redevelopment or improvement of the land; a rather wider purpose.

[41]
In general a power with a wide purpose should not be used in place of a more specific power where one exists. So, for example, para 2 of App A to ODPM Circular 06/2004 provides that: '... the First Secretary of State ... may refuse to confirm an order if it seems to him that this general power [in s 226 of the Town and Country Planning Act 1990] was being used in a way intended to frustrate or overturn the intention of Parliament by attempting to acquire land for a purpose which has been explicitly excluded from a specific power.'

[42]
Section 121 of the Local Government Act 1972 states that a principal council may compulsorily acquire land 'for any purpose for which they are authorised by this or any other public general Act to acquire land', in other words, for which they are authorised to acquire land by agreement. Thus although stating no purpose itself, it does rely on that purpose being identified in some other Act.

[43]
It is important, therefore, that the acquiring authority is clear as to its purpose in acquiring the land, and clear also that that purpose falls within the ambit of the authorising power being exercised. This is often important in the drafting of the order itself. Section 226(1) of the TCPA 1990, for example, identifies two purposes, one of which was mentioned above, those being:

(*a*) the authority thinks that the acquisition will facilitate the carrying out of development, redevelopment or improvement on or in relation to the land; or
(*b*) the land is required for a purpose which it is necessary to achieve in the interests of the proper planning of an area in which the land is situated.

ODPM Circular 06/2004 (App A, para 4) provides the following guidance for those intending to use the powers under s 226:

> 'The Secretary of State takes the view that an order made under subsection (1) of section 226 should be expressed in terms *either* of paragraph (a) *or* paragraph (b) of that subsection.'

It goes on to make clear that the appropriate letter (*a*) or (*b*) should be quoted and the wording of the order, and that paragraph reproduced.

[44]
Acquiring authorities should be particularly wary of the perils of changing the purpose for which land has been acquired. The Court of Appeal has held

quite clearly that a compulsory purchase order cannot be confirmed for another purpose than, or for a purpose additional to, that for which it was made[1]. Furthermore, although the confirming authority may confirm a compulsory purchase order with or without modifications[2], this power to modify a compulsory purchase order may only be used sparingly and as para 51 of ODPM Circular 06/2004 says: 'Some minor slips can be corrected, but not significant matters such as the substitution of a different, or insertion of an additional, purpose.'

1 See *Procter and Gamble Ltd v Secretary of State for the Environment* (1991) 63 P&CR 317.
2 ALA 1981, s 13. Notwithstanding the advice in the circular that the power to modify should be used sparingly, in practice, it is quite common for the confirming authority to modify a compulsory purchase order to remove plots from the order when requested to do so by the acquiring authority (for example, where the acquiring authority has reached agreement with a landowner).

The land and interests in land required by the acquiring authority

[45]
Clearly, an acquiring authority must decide what land and/or interests in land it requires to achieve its purpose. If it includes too much land, it may not be able to justify the acquisition or part of the acquisition; too little land and it may not be able to achieve its objective. In most cases such issues are unlikely to give rise to problems, but that is by no means always the case. Perhaps more difficult, is whether an authority needs to acquire the freehold or leasehold title, or whether some lesser right (eg an easement) in the land would be sufficient. Clearly, if challenged on this point at a compulsory purchase order inquiry, an authority would need to be able to justify its proposed acquisition of the greater interest in land.

[46]
The meaning of 'land' for the purposes of compulsory purchase is examined in **Division B, Chapter 2**.

Adverse third party rights

[47]
An acquiring authority intending to acquire land for some statutory purpose will need to be aware of adverse third party rights affecting the land, and whether it, or its successors, will be bound by any such rights. This issue is examined in **Division D, Chapter 2**.

The powers available

[48]
As mentioned above, as a generality, an authority should seek to use a more specific compulsory purchase power, rather than a general power, provided that the specific power is sufficient for the particular purpose.

[49]
It may be that all the necessary powers to compulsorily purchase both the land and any interests in land are contained in the principal Authorising Act, but this is not always so. Some Authorising Acts do not, for example, grant to local authorities the power to compulsorily purchase new interests in land. Indeed, this was the main issue in *Sovmots Investments v Secretary of State for the Environment*[1] which finally went to the House of Lords in 1977, although the problem itself was largely resolved by the Local Government (Miscellaneous Provisions) Act 1976, s 13. Section 13 provided that where a local authority may be authorised by compulsorily purchase order to acquire 'land' for any purpose, it also had power to purchase 'such new rights over the land as are specified in the order'. Thus a power to compulsorily purchase new rights in land will now be available to a local authority even though not included in the principal Authorising Act.

1 [1979] AC 144.

[50]–[60]
It is obviously important to ensure, however, that all necessary powers have been identified and are sufficient for the intended purpose.

Pre-condition to exercise of compulsory purchase power

[61]
There may be a legal/factual pre-condition to the exercise of a compulsory purchase power and it is important therefore that an acquiring authority is satisfied that any such pre-condition is discharged before commencing compulsory purchase order proceedings.

[62]
By way of example, if it appears to the Secretary of State that reasonable steps are not being taken for properly preserving a listed building, the Planning (Listed Buildings and Conservation Areas) Act 1990, s 47 gives him power inter alia to authorise a local authority to compulsorily acquire that building. Section 48, however, provides that the compulsory purchase of a building under s 47 shall not be started unless at least two months previously the authority or the Secretary of State has served a 'repairs notice'. The proper service of such a notice more than two months before is, therefore, a necessary factual pre-condition to the commencement of compulsory purchase proceedings.

[63]
Clearly it will be important for an acquiring authority to be aware of, and observe, any such pre-condition and failure to do so could result in judicial challenge to the decision to make the compulsory purchase order or to the order itself if confirmed.

Identification of the procedure for acquiring a particular piece of land

[64]
As mentioned earlier, the authorising Act will identify the procedure to be followed in acquiring a particular piece of land, and in most cases, but not always, this is by incorporation of the compulsory purchase order procedure in the ALA 1981. Where other procedures for progressing a compulsory purchase order are prescribed these will usually be set out in the appendices to the authorising Act.

Temporary possession of land

[65]
An acquiring authority may wish to take temporary possession of land, often in connection with the construction of some wider development project. Occasionally, the authorising Act may specifically grant power to an acquiring authority to take temporary possession on land for such purposes[1]. More usually, however, the authorising Act will not grant a specific right to take temporary possession of land. In these circumstances, acquiring authorities may be able to acquire such temporary rights by agreement. Failing agreement, however, an acquiring authority may be forced to acquire the freehold in the relevant land. In these circumstances many acquiring authorities will give the landowner a written undertaking to return the surplus land at the end of the temporary period. It may be possible to take this temporary possession into account when assessing compensation (eg, although the freehold was taken, it was only taken for (say) six months and then the land was returned). Where it would not be appropriate to hand back the temporarily taken land, or where the landowner does not want it, the acquiring authority may wish to dispose of it in the open market. Although the 'Crichel Down rules' do not strictly apply in these circumstances, an acquiring authority may wish to have regard to the principles contained within them.

1 See, eg, s 23 of the London Docklands Railway (Lewisham) Act 1993, and also ss 32 and 43 of the Railway Clauses Consolidation Act 1845.

Minerals

[66]
An acquiring authority, when preparing a compulsory purchase order, should consider carefully whether it needs to acquire any minerals that may be in the land to be taken.

Powers to enter land without compulsory purchase

[67]–[350]
It is worth bearing in mind that certain statutory bodies have powers to enter onto, and, in some cases, carry out surveys or even works without actually

acquiring any interest in the land. For example, the Environment Agency has powers under the WRA 1991, s 160 to lay pipes or under ss 161–162 to control pollution. In most case, the exercise of such rights triggers a right to compensation which is ex.plained in **Division G** of this work.

D Schedule: Compulsory purchase of land – principal powers

[351]–[400]
The schedule below summarises the principal powers authorising the compulsory purchase of land or interest in land contained in public general Acts. The schedule is arranged thematically under the following broad headings:

(*a*) Local authorities – general
(*b*) Airports and aviation
(*c*) Education
(*d*) Energy
(*e*) Environmental protection
(*f*) Fire and rescue services
(*g*) Highways and traffic
(*h*) Housing
(*i*) Infrastructure
(*j*) Land drainage
(*k*) Military and defence
(*l*) Miscellaneous
(*m*) National Health Service
(*n*) Pipelines
(*o*) Police
(*p*) Ports, harbours and shipping
(*q*) Regional, urban and rural development
(*r*) Telecommunications
(*s*) Town and country planning
(*t*) Transport
(*u*) Wales – general
(*v*) Water, sewage and rivers

Authorising Act	*Body with compulsory purchase powers*	*Section*	*Purpose*	*Comments*
Local authorities – general				
Local Government Act 1972	A principal council (s 270)	s 121	Any purpose for which authorised to acquire land	
	A district council (on behalf of parish or community council)	s 125	For any of the functions of a parish or community council where that council has been unable to purchase land by agreement under s 124 of the Act	
Local Government (Miscellaneous Provisions) Act 1976	A local authority (s 44)	s 13	Acquisition of 'new rights' in or over land for any purpose for which authorised to acquire land	
Agriculture, forestry and food				
Forestry Act 1967	The Minister of Agriculture, Fisheries and Food	s 40	Land suitable for afforestation or for any purpose connected with forestry (s 39)	The procedure for making a compulsory purchase order under this Act is set out in Sch 5, Pt I, and the CPA 1965 is incorporated subject to modifications in Sch 5, Pt III

Food Act 1984	A local authority	s 110	For purposes of the Act	The power of compulsory purchase under s 110 does not apply to the power to acquire an existing market undertaking under s 50 of the Act
Airports and aviation				
Civil Aviation Act 1982	The Civil Aviation Authority	s 42	For the performance of its functions	
		s 44	Power to obtain rights over land to secure safe and efficient use for civil aviation purposes etc	
	An air traffic licence holder	s 42A	For any purpose connected with the carrying out of activities authorised by the licence	
	The Secretary of State	s 49	For purpose of providing or improving any highway which is to be provided or improved in pursuance of an order under s 48(1)	
Airports Act 1986	A Relevant Airport Operator	s 59(1)	Acquisition of land for any purpose connected with the performance of the operator's functions	

Authorising Act	*Body with compulsory purchase powers*	*Section*	*Purpose*	*Comments*
Airports Act 1986 – *contd*		s 59(3), (4)	Applies Civil Aviation Act 1982, s 44 to any relevant airport operator	
Education				
Education Act 1996	A local education authority	s 530	For purposes of any school or institution which is, or is to be, maintained by local education authority, or otherwise required for its purposes under Act	
Energy				
Atomic Energy Authority Act 1954	The United Kingdom Atomic Energy Authority	s 5	For the performance of its functions	
Opencast Coal Act 1958	The Coal Authority	s 4	Facilitating the working of coal by opencast operations	'Compulsory rights orders' granted under s 4 give temporary rights of occupation and use of land
Gas Act 1965	A public gas transporter (Gas Act 1995, Sch 4, para 7(1))	s 12	For purpose of acquiring right to store gas in underground gas storage	
	A public gas transporter (Gas Act 1995, Sch 4, para 7(1))	s 13	Compulsory purchase of land or rights in connection with wells, boreholes and shafts	

Gas Act 1986	A public gas transporter (Gas Act 1995, Sch 3)	s 9(3) and Sch 3 (as amended by the Gas Act 1995, Sch 3)	General duty of public gas transporter set out in s 9(1)	
Electricity Act 1989	A licence holder	s 10 and Sch 3	For any purpose connected with carrying on its licensed activities	
Coal Industry Act 1994	The Coal Authority	s 4C	For the purpose of preventing or mitigating the effect of a discharge of water from a coal mine	
Environmental protection				
Water Resources Act 1991	The Environment Agency	s 154	Required by the Agency for the purposes of, or in connection with, the carrying out of its functions	
		s 156	Acquisition of land for fisheries purposes	
		s 168(4)	Acquisition of land pursuant to a 'compulsory works order' (s 168(1))	
		s 182	Acquisition of mineral rights	In relation to minerals etc, Sch 23 has effect instead of the ALA 1981, Sch 2

Authorising Act	*Body with compulsory purchase powers*	*Section*	*Purpose*	*Comments*
Fire and rescue services				
Fire and Rescue Services Act 2004	A combined fire and rescue authority	s 3(3)(*f*)	For purposes of its functions	
Highways and traffic				
Highways Act 1980	A highway authority, being the Secretary of State or a local highway authority	ss 239–240	Acquisition of land in connection with construction, improvement etc of highways	s 238(1) provides that acquisition may be by compulsion or by agreement
		s 241	Acquisition of land between improvement line and boundary of street	s 238 provides that acquisition may be by compulsion or by agreement
		s 242	Acquisition of land for execution of works in connection with certain bridges	s 238 provides that acquisition may be by compulsion or by agreement
		s 243	Acquisition of land for cattle grids etc	s 238 provides that acquisition may be by compulsion or by agreement
		s 244	Acquisition of land for road ferries	s 238 provides that acquisition may be by compulsion or by agreement

		s 245	Acquisition of land for buildings etc needed for discharge of functions of highway authority	s 238 provides that acquisition may be by compulsion or by agreement
		s 246(1)	Acquisition of land for mitigating adverse effects of constructing or improving highway	s 238 provides that acquisition may be by compulsion or by agreement
		s 250(1)	Acquisition of rights over land by creating new rights as well as acquiring existing rights	
		s 250(2)	Acquisition of 'exchange land', where acquiring common, open space or allotment	
Road Traffic Regulation Act 1984	A local authority	s 40	For purposes of providing parking spaces	
Housing				
Housing Act 1985	A local housing authority	s 17(3)	For provision of housing accommodation under Pt II of the Act	

Authorising Act	*Body with compulsory purchase powers*	*Section*	*Purpose*	*Comments*
Housing Act 1985 – *contd*		s 243	Within a 'housing action area', for purposes of securing or assisting in securing the improvement of the housing accommodation in the area as a whole, the well-being of persons residing in the area, and the proper and effective management and use of that accommodation (s 239(2))	
		s 300(3)	Purchase of houses liable to be demolished or closed pursuant to order under ss 264–265	
	A county council	s 29	Provision of accommodation for employees of county councils	By s 29(2), a county council may acquire land 'in the same way' as local housing authority under this part of Act (ie s 17)
Housing Associations Act 1985	A county council	s 34(1)	Acquisition of land for erection of housing by housing association, where the district council are unwilling to acquire the land	County council may exercise powers of district council under Pt II of the Housing Act 1985

	The housing corporation in England, or the Secretary of State in Wales (Government of Wales Act 1998, Sch 16, para 24(2))	s 88(1)	For purposes of selling or leasing the land to a registered social landlord or unregistered self-build society, or itself providing dwellings or hostels
Housing Act 1988	A housing action trust	s 77	For purpose of achieving its objectives and performing its function
Local Government and Housing Act 1989	A local housing authority (s 100(1) and Housing Act 1985, ss 1 and 2)	s 93(2)	Within a 'renewal area', for purposes of improvement or repair of premises, the proper and effective management and use of housing accommodation, and the well-being of persons residing in the area (s 93(3))
Housing and Regeneration Act 2008	The Housing and Communities Agency	s 9 and Sch 2	For the purposes of its objects, including the improvement of the supply and quality of housing in England (s 2)
Infrastructure			
Planning Act 2008	An applicant for a Development Consent Order	s 120 and Sch 5, para 1	For the purposes of enabling the proposed development as set out in s 122

Authorising Act	*Body with compulsory purchase powers*	*Section*	*Purpose*	*Comments*
Land drainage				
Land Drainage Act 1991	An internal drainage board	s 62(1)	Any purpose in connection with performance of functions	
	A district council, London borough or the Common Council of the City of London	s 62(2)	For purposes of ss 14–17 and 66 of the Act	
Military and defence				
Defence Act 1842	The Secretary of State for Defence	ss 16 and 19	Lands, buildings, or other hereditaments wanted for the service of the ordinance department, or for the defence of the realm	The ALA 1981 does not apply
Military Lands Act 1892	The Secretary of State for Defence	s 1(1)	For the military or naval purposes of Her Majesty's armed forces	s 2 incorporates the Lands Clauses Acts and applies the provisional order procedure
	A territorial, auxiliary and volunteer reserve association (TAVRA) (Territorial Army)	s 1(2)	For the military purposes of Her Majesty's armed forces	s 2 incorporates the Lands Clauses Acts and applies the provisional order procedure

	A county council	s 1(3)	On behalf of TAVRA for the military purposes of Her Majesty's armed forces	ALA 1981 procedures apply by virtue of ALA 1981, s 1(2)
Land Powers (Defence) Act 1958	The Secretary of State for Trade and Industry	s 13	Land for construction of oil installations for defence of the realm	Procedure set out in Sch 2
Miscellaneous				
Small Holdings and Allotments Act 1908	A borough council, district council or parish council	s 25	For providing allotments	See s 39 for procedure. The ALA 1981 is applied by ALA 1981, s 1(2)
Coast Protection Act 1949	A coast protection authority	s 14	Acquisition of land required for carrying out of coast protection work, or for protection of which it is proposed to carry out such work (s 4)	
Prison Act 1952	The Secretary of State	s 36	Acquisition of land required for the alteration, enlargement or rebuilding of a prison, or establishment of a new prison, or for any other purpose connected with the management of a prison	
Slaughterhouses Act 1974	A local authority (s 34)	s 30	For purposes of Pt I of the Act (other than those of s 14)	

Authorising Act	*Body with compulsory purchase powers*	*Section*	*Purpose*	*Comments*
Refuse Disposal Amenity Act 1978	A county council or district council	s 7	Acquisition of land for any of purposes of Act	
Animal Health Act 1981	A local authority (s 50)	s 55	Acquisition of land for provision of wharves for landing etc of imported or other animals, and for use for burial of carcasses etc and for any other purpose of the Act	
Industrial Development Act 1982	The Secretary of State	s 14	Acquisition of land to provide or facilitate provision of premises in any 'development area' or 'intermediate area' as defined by s 18	
Food Act 1984	A local authority	s 110	Acquisition of land for the purposes of the Act	
Postal Services Act 2000	Universal service provider	s 95 and Sch 5	Acquisition of land for any purpose in connection with provisions of universal postal service	
Courts Act 2003	The Secretary of State	s 3	For purposes of public services	To be had together with s 288 of the Town and Country Planning Act 1990

National Health Service and social services				
National Health Service Act 2006	The Secretary of State	s 211	For the purposes of the Act	
	A Primary Care Trust	s 18 and Sch 3 para 22	For the purposes of its functions	
	A National Health Service trust	s 25 and Sch 4 para 27	For purposes of its functions	
National Health Service (Wales) Act 2006	The Welsh Ministers	s 159	For the purposes of the Act	
	A Local Health Board	s 11 and Sch 2 para 20	For the purposes of its functions	
	A National Health Service trust	s 18 and Sch 3 para 27	For the purpose of its functions	
Pipelines				
Pipe-lines Act 1962	A person proposing to place a pipeline across land	s 11	Land for pipeline construction	For procedure and compensation see Schs 2 and 3 and CPA 1965, s 37
		s 12	Rights over land for pipeline construction	For compensation see s 14

Authorising Act	*Body with compulsory purchase powers*	*Section*	*Purpose*	*Comments*
Police				
Metropolitan Police Act 1886	The Police Receiver	ss 2 and 4(11)	Construction of police buildings	See Road Traffic Regulation Act 1984, s 97(5), in relation to traffic wardens
Local Government Act 1972	A police authority	s 121	Any purpose for which authorised to acquire land	A police authority under the Police Act 1964, s 3, is deemed to be a 'principal council' for the purposes of s 121: see Local Government Act 1972, 146A(1)(*b*)
Ports, harbours and shipping				
Harbours Act 1964	A harbour authority (s 57(1))	s 14 and Sch 2	A harbour revision order may confer on harbour authority power to acquire land by compulsion for purpose of its being used as the site of works, or for some other purpose of the harbour (Sch 2, para 7)	
Docks and Harbours Act 1966	A harbour authority (s 50(1) and the Harbours Act 1964, s 57(1))	s 36	References to a harbour in s 14 of and Sch 2 to the Harbours Act 1964, shall include references to an 'inland clearance depot' (s 36(4))	

Transport Act 1981	Associated British Ports	s 8 and Sch 3, para 19	For purposes of its business
Regional, urban and rural development			
Regional Development Agencies Act 1998	A regional development agency (s 41)	s 20	For the purposes of a regional development agency as set out in s 4 of the Act, or for purposes 'incidental' thereto (s 20(1))
Housing and Regeneration Act 2008	The Housing and Communities Agency	s 9 and Sch 2	For the purposes of its objects, including the regeneration or development of land or infrastructure in England (s 2)
Telecommunications			
Communications Act 2003	A code operator	s 118 and Sch 4	Required by the operator – (a) for, or in connection with, the establishment or running of the operator's network; or (b) as to which it can reasonably be foreseen that it will be so required.

Authorising Act	*Body with compulsory purchase powers*	*Section*	*Purpose*	*Comments*
Town and country planning				
National Parks and Access to Countryside Act 1949	A local planning authority for a National Park	s 12(4)	Provision of accommodation, meals, refreshments, camping spaces and parking places	
		s 13(8)	Improvement of waterways for purposes of open-air recreation	
	Natural England, Scottish Natural Heritage or the Countryside Council for Wales	ss 17, 18 and 103	Establishment and maintenance of nature reserves	
	A local planning authority	ss 76 and 103	Public access to land for open-air recreation	
	The Secretary of State	s 77	Public access to land for open-air recreation	
	A local planning authority	ss 89(5) and 103	Planting of trees	
	A local authority	ss 89(5) and 103	Treatment of derelict land	

Caravan Sites and Control of Development Act 1960	A local authority	s 24(5)	To provide sites where caravans may be brought
Countryside Act 1968	The Countryside Council for Wales	s 4(3)(*a*)	To make and carry out, or promote the carrying out, of any experimental scheme designed to facilitate the enjoyment of the countryside etc
	A local authority	s 7(4)	To provide a country park
		s 9(5)	Acquisition of land near common land required in the interests of persons resorting to the common land for open air recreation
		s 10(4)	To provide camping sites for holiday and recreation purposes
	Natural England or the Countryside Council for Wales	s 15A	Where expedient for purpose of conserving flora, fauna, or geological or physiographical features of special interest
Ancient Monuments and Archaeological Areas Act 1979	The Secretary of State	s 10	Acquisition of ancient monument for purposes of its preservation
		s 16	Acquisition of easements and other similar rights over land in vicinity of monument

Authorising Act	*Body with compulsory purchase powers*	*Section*	*Purpose*	*Comments*
Local Government, Planning and Land Act 1980	An urban development corporation	s 142	Land in urban development area; land adjacent to such an area if required for purposes connected with discharge of functions; for provision of services in connection with discharge of functions	
	A local highway authority	s 143	Construction or improvement of road needed in connection with urban development area	
New Towns Act 1981	A New Town development corporation	s 10	Land within area of New Town; land adjacent to such an area if required for purposes connected with discharge of functions; for provision of services for the purposes of the New Town	The procedure for making a compulsory purchase order under this Act is set out in Sch 4, Pt I
	A local highway authority	s 11(1)	Construction or improvement of road needed in connection with New Town	The procedure for making a compulsory purchase order under this Act is set out in Sch 4, Pt I and II

	The Secretary of State	s 11(2)	Construction or improvement of road needed in connection with New Town	The procedure for making a compulsory purchase order under this Act is set out in Sch 4, Pt III
Wildlife and Countryside Act 1981	Natural England	s 28N	For the acquisition of sites of special scientific interest	Applies s 103 of the National Parks and Access to Countryside Act 1949
Town and Country Planning Act 1990	A local authority (s 226(8)) or a joint planning board (s 244)	s 226	Acquisition of land (a) if the authority thinks that the acquisition will facilitate the carrying out of development, redevelopment or improvement, or (b) which is required in order to achieve proper planning of area	
	The Secretary of State	s 228	Land necessary for the public service	This includes land for courts etc appropriate for discharging duty in relation to courts (see Courts Act 2003, s 3)
	The Secretary of State	s 165	Acquisition of land where a blight notice has been served in respect of land, the land falls within paras 7–9 of Sch 13, and the relevant development corporation for the New Town or the relevant urban development corporation, has not been established	

Authorising Act	*Body with compulsory purchase powers*	*Section*	*Purpose*	*Comments*
Town and Country Planning – *contd*		s 228	Acquisition of land necessary for the 'public service' (s 228(5)); or for the public service and to meet proper planning of area or to secure best of most economic development or use of land	
Planning (Listed Buildings and Conservation Areas) Act 1990	A county council, county borough, district council, London borough council, English Heritage, joint planning board or Broads Authority (the appropriate authority s 47(7))	s 47(1)(*a*)	If reasonable steps are not being taken to preserve a listed building	
	The Secretary of State	s 47(1)(*b*)	If reasonable steps are not being taken to preserve a listed building	
Environment Act 1995	A National Park authority	s 65(7) and Sch 8	Various	Sch 8 gives a National Park authority various powers in relation, inter alia, to land

		s 70 and Sch 9	Various	Sch 9 gives a National Park authority various powers in relation, inter alia, to land
Transport				
Transport Act 1962	The British Railways Board or the British Waterways Board	s 15	For the purposes of their business	
Transport and Works Act 1992	A person authorised by a works order	s 1 and Sch 1, para 3	For construction or operation of a railway, tramway, trolley vehicle system, or guided transport system	ALA 1981 does not apply
Wales – general				
Welsh Development Agency Act 1975	The Welsh Development Agency	s 1(7)(*h*) and s 21A	For purposes of WDA specified in s 1(3)	s 21A and Sch 4 (both as inserted by Government of Wales Act 1998, Sch 13) define the power conferred by s 1(7)(*h*)
		s 16(3)(*b*)	For purpose of reclaiming land which is derelict, neglected or unsightly etc (s 16(1))	s 21A and Sch 4 (both as inserted by Government of Wales Act 1998, Sch 13) define the power conferred by s 16(3)(*b*)
Water, sewerage and rivers				
Water Industry Act 1991	A water undertaker or sewerage undertaker (s 219(1)	s 155	Required by undertaker for purposes of, or in connection with, the carrying out of its functions	

Authorising Act	*Body with compulsory purchase powers*	*Section*	*Purpose*	*Comments*
		s 188 and Sch 14	Acquisition of mineral rights	In relation to minerals etc Sch 14 has effect instead of the ALA 1981, Sch 2
Transport and Works Act 1992	A person authorised by a works order	s 3 and Sch 1, para 3	Construction of an inland waterway, or the carrying out of works which interfere with rights of navigation	ALA 1981 does not apply

Chapter 2

The subject matter of compulsory purchase

Contents

[401]
In contemplating a compulsory purchase of land, an acquiring authority will need to understand the nature of the estates and interests in that land which it will need to acquire or extinguish in order to carry out its purposes. There may also be interests in the land which the authority may safely ignore. Furthermore, an understanding of these estates and interests will be vital in the assessment of compensation. For the owner of an estate or interest in land, these matters are no less important. The purpose of this section is to give a general understanding of the subject matter of compulsory purchase.

A The meaning of 'land'

[402]
The term 'land' is not defined in either the Acquisition of Land Act 1981 (ALA 1981) or the Compulsory Purchase Act 1965 (CPA 1965) other than to make clear, in ss 7(1) and 1(3) respectively, that it includes anything falling within any definition of that expression in the enactment under which the purchase is authorised. Some such authorising enactments do expressly define 'land', whilst others do not.

[403]
An example of a definition of 'land' in an authorising Act is given in of the Town and Country Planning Act 1990 (TCPA 1990), s 336(1), which defines the term as 'any corporeal hereditament, including a building, and, in relation to the acquisition of land under Pt IX, includes any interest in or right over land'.

[404]
In the absence of a definition in the authorising Act, the Interpretation Act 1978, Sch 1 defines 'land' as including 'buildings and other structures, land covered with water, and any estate, interest, easement, servitude or right in or over land'[1].

1 In relation to the physical extent of 'land', see *Bocardo SA v Star Energy Weald Basin Ltd* [2010] UKSC 35, [2010] 3 All ER 975.

[405]
The Land Compensation Act 1961 (LCA 1961) is not an authorising Act, but, in s 39(1), defines 'land' as 'any corporeal hereditament, including a building as defined by this section, and includes any interest or right in or over land and any right to water' and defines 'building' as including 'any structure or erection and any part of a building as so defined, but does not include plant or machinery comprised in a building'. This definition is, however, for the purpose of the LCA 1961, namely the assessment of compensation, and does not purport to define what may be acquired.

B Estates and interests in land which may be acquired

[406]
The estates and interests in land which may be acquired are considered under the following headings:

(1) Legal freehold.
(2) Legal leasehold.
(3) Legal interests in and rights over land.
(4) Equitable interests in and rights over land.

1 Legal freehold

[407]
Section 1(1) of the Law of Property Act 1925 (LPA 1925) provides that:

> 'The only estates in land which are capable of subsisting or of being conveyed or created at law are:
> (*a*) An estate in fee simple absolute in possession;
> (*b*) A term of years absolute.'

These two legal estates correspond to the more widely used expressions 'freehold' and 'leasehold'. In general terms, a freehold estate is one whose duration is uncertain, whereas a leasehold estate is for a period whose duration is fixed or capable of being fixed.

[408]
An acquiring authority exercising compulsory purchase powers over land will usually wish to acquire the largest legal estate in land, being the legal fee simple absolute in possession. The term 'fee simple' denotes an inheritable estate in land that is capable of being inherited by any heir so long as there are heirs to inherit. The word 'absolute' means that the fee simple is without any restriction which would prevent it from enduring for as long as there are heirs to inherit. The term 'in possession' means that a present right to immediate enjoyment is given. This is not, however, the same as 'physical possession' and the LPA 1925, s 205(1)(xix) makes it clear that it 'includes receipt of rents and profits or the right to receive the same, if any…'.

[409]
Where an authority only wishes to acquire an estate or interest in the land less than the legal fee simple absolute in possession, it must have express statutory power to do so[1]. In practice, an acquiring authority will often find that lesser estates and/or interests have been carved out of the legal freehold and, in these circumstances, it is important that the acquiring authority knows which estates and/or interests it must acquire, which it may extinguish, which it may ignore and when it will have to pay compensation. These lesser estates and interests, both legal and equitable, are identified and discussed in the next few paragraphs of this chapter.

1 *Sovmots Investments Ltd v Secretary of State for the Environment* [1979] AC 144, HL.

[410]–[420]
In principle, where lesser estates and interests have been carved out of the legal fee simple absolute in possession, this should not have any effect on the total compensation to be paid by an acquiring authority. Such lesser estates and interests having a value to be compensated will reduce the value of the legal freehold and should not be an additional financial burden on the acquiring authority. In reality, however, it will sometimes be the case that the value of the various legal parts is greater or lesser than the whole.

[421]
In the LPA 1925, s 205(1)(ix) 'land' is defined as including:

> '... land of any tenure, and mines and minerals, whether or not held apart from the surface, buildings or parts of buildings (whether the division is horizontal, vertical or made in any other way) and other corporeal hereditaments; also... a rent and other incorporeal hereditaments, and an easement, right, privilege, or benefit in, over, or derived from land; ... '

Thus the earth itself, minerals, buildings and 'corporeal hereditaments' (that is, physical objects attached to the land so as to become part of it) are part of the land and will be conveyed under a compulsory purchase. Objects attached to the land are known as 'fixtures'. Where crops have become severed from the land, they may be sold separately, whether it be to the acquiring authority or another party. Indeed, even where crops (such as timber) have not been severed from the land, they may still be valued separately from the remainder of the land.

[422]
Chattels not affixed to the land (which are known as 'fittings') and intangible interests, such as goodwill, do not form part of the land, but may still be the subject matter of a claim for disturbance.

2 Legal leasehold

[423]
The second legal estate in land identified by the LPA 1925, s 1(1) is the 'term of years absolute', more commonly known as 'leasehold'. This legal estate in land is inferior to the legal freehold as it must be for a limited duration. A

'term of years absolute' must be for a fixed term of years, although, by s 205(1)(xxvii) of the Act, it can include a period for less than a year and would therefore encompass a weekly or monthly tenancy. Thus, in *Lace v Chantler*[1], a lease 'for the duration of the war' was held not to be a legal lease, as it was not for a period which was fixed or capable of being fixed.

1 [1944] KB 368.

[424]
Compulsory purchase powers grant to an acquiring authority the right to compel a leaseholder to assign his interest in the land. Where the acquiring authority also holds the freehold or other reversionary interest, then, unless there is reason to keep the interests separate, the lease will merge with the reversionary interest. An acquiring authority may not, however, create and take a leasehold interest in land without express statutory authority.

[425]
Although 'a term of years absolute' may include a term of a year or less, or from year to year, the law of compulsory purchase and compensation treats a person who has no greater interest than as a tenant for a year, or from year to year, differently from persons with a greater leasehold interest.

[426]
Section 5(1) of the CPA 1965 requires an authority exercising compulsory purchase powers to serve a 'notice to treat' on 'all the persons interested in, or having power to sell and convey or release, the land', which would appear to include a person with no greater interest than as a tenant for a year or from year to year. Normally, however, an acquiring authority will not serve a notice to treat on such a tenant, but will simply allow the remaining term to expire or acquire the reversionary interest and serve notice to quit, in either of which cases, the tenancy will not have been terminated by the compulsory purchase, and so, no compensation will be payable[1]. The same principle will apply if the owner of the reversionary interest himself gives notice to quit[2]. Alternatively, an acquiring authority may serve a notice to treat on some other interest in the land to be acquired, followed by notice of entry under the CPA 1965, s 11 in which case, if a tenant for a year or from year to year is required to give up possession before the expiration of his term, compensation will be payable under the CPA 1965, s 20. The leading authority of *Newham London Borough v Benjamin*[3] decided that, even where a notice to treat had been served on a person with no greater interest than as a tenant for a year or from year to year, that only meant that compensation should be assessed in the manner directed by the Act; in other words, in accordance with the CPA 1965, s 20.

1 *Syers v Metropolitan Board of Works* (1877) 36 LT 277.
2 *Ex p Nadin* (1848) 17 LJ Ch 421; *Ex p Merrett* (1860) 2 LT 471.
3 [1968] 1 All ER 1195. See also **Division D** paras **[1321]–[1325]**.

[427]
Security of tenure under the Agricultural Holdings Act 1986 (agricultural tenancies), Landlord and Tenant Act 1954 (business tenancies), or the Rent

Act 1977 or Housing Act 1988 (residential tenancies) does not prevail against compulsory purchase.

[428]
Leasehold interests are considered further in **Division D, Chapter 5**.

3 Legal interests in and rights over land

[429]
The fundamental difference between an estate in land and an interest in land is that an estate gives the right to possession of the land, whereas an interest merely gives rights over someone else's land.

[430]–[440]
Section 1(2) of the LPA 1925 provides that:

> 'The only interests or charges in or over land which are capable of subsisting or of being conveyed or created at law are:
> (*a*) An easement, right, or privilege in or over land for an interest equivalent to an estate in fee simple absolute in possession or a term of years absolute;
> (*b*) A rentcharge in possession issuing out of or charged on land being either perpetual or for a term of years absolute;
> (*c*) A charge by way of legal mortgage;
> (*d*) … and any other similar charge on land which is not created by an instrument;
> (*e*) Rights of entry exerciseable over or in respect of a legal term of years absolute, or annexed, for any purpose, to a legal rentcharge.'

[441]
The term 'easement, right or privilege' in or over land will include such easements as rights of way, rights to light, rights to support and rights to water, together with rights, such as *profits a prendre*. Such 'easements, rights, or privileges' may exist as legal interests in land only if, in duration, they are 'equivalent to an estate in fee simple absolute in possession or a term of years absolute'; in other words, to be legal, such interests must be perpetual or for a fixed term. Restrictive covenants do not fall within s 1(2) above and can, therefore, exist only as equitable interests in land.

[442]
Sections 14–17 of the CPA 1965 deal with the acquisition of land subject to mortgage. Section 14 gives an acquiring authority the right to purchase or redeem the interest of a mortgagee in land subject to compulsory purchase by paying off the principal and interest due on the mortgage, together with certain costs or charges. Section 14 applies whether or not the acquiring authority has previously purchased the mortgagor's interest in the land, known as the equity of redemption. Where the mortgage debt on any land is likely to exceed the value of the land itself, an acquiring authority are unlikely to want to purchase or redeem the mortgage, but should, instead, serve a notice to treat on both the mortgagor and the mortgagee. In these

circumstances, compensation will be settled or determined by the Upper Tribunal under the CPA 1965, s 15.

[443]
A rentcharge is a right entitling the beneficiary to receive a periodic sum of money from the owner of land charged with that payment and should not be confused with the right to receive rent under the terms of a lease. Section 18 of the CPA 1965 provides that the compensation to be paid by an acquiring authority for the release of a rentcharge over land subject to compulsory purchase shall be settled by agreement or, failing agreement, be determined by the Upper Tribunal. If on payment of the agreed or determined compensation, the person entitled to a rentcharge does not release it or fails to make good title, the acquiring authority may pay the compensation into court and execute a deed poll under the CPA 1965, s 9(3) thereby extinguishing the rentcharge.

4 Equitable interests in and rights over land

[444]
If an estate or interest in land is not contained in the LPA 1925, s 1(1) or s 1(2) it can only take effect as an equitable estate or interest.

[445]
Equitable interests in land may arise in a number of circumstances, including:

(1) The interests of a beneficiary under a trust. The creation of successive interests in land by way of strict settlement under the Settled Land Act 1925 or trust for sale under the LPA 1925 and, more recently, 'trusts of land' under the Trusts of Land and Appointment of Trustees Act 1996, will give rise to such beneficial interests. The equitable interest of a beneficiary under such a trust will not usually bind an acquiring authority purchasing the land, but will, instead, be 'overreached', that is, transferred to the purchase moneys.
(2) Interests arising under contracts to create legal estates and interests. Contracts to create legal estates or interests in land cannot be enforced as a matter of law; the legal remedy being damages for breach of contract. Equity, however, will order specific performance of such a contract and the application of the equitable maxim that 'Equity regards as done that which ought to be done' means that equity will regard such a contract as an equitable interest in land. Estate contracts are registerable as Class C land charges under the Land Charges Act 1972[1].
(3) Legal interests not created in the prescribed manner. A legal estate or interest in land can only be created or transferred by deed made pursuant to the LPA 1925, s 52 or, since 31 July 1990, the Law of Property (Miscellaneous Provisions) Act 1989, s 1. An interest not created in the prescribed manner may, however, take effect as an equitable interest. Thus, a right of way across land created in writing, but not by deed, would only take effect as an equitable easement.

(4) Interests arising under restrictive covenants. Restrictive covenants are enforceable in law as between the original contracting parties, but not against subsequent purchasers of the land, due to the legal concept of 'privity of contract'. In certain circumstances, however, equity will allow a restrictive covenant to run with the land. Restrictive covenants are registerable as Class D land charges under the Land Charges Act 1972 (LCA 1972).

1 Entry as a land charge in the land charges register in Plymouth should not be confused with registration of title under the Land Registration Act 1925, which is entirely separate and relates to conveyancing.

[446]
Where a landowner gives another person a bare licence to use or occupy land, this will not create any interest in the land and no compensation will be payable by an acquiring authority[1]. In recent years, however, the courts have begun to apply equitable remedies to protect certain contractual licences by the use of constructive trusts and the concept of estoppel. There is authority, for example, that, in certain circumstances, equity will protect a licensee of land with an irrevocable licence by imposing a constructive trust, which will bind an acquiring authority and require the equitable interest created to be compensated[2]. Furthermore, the LCA 1972, s 37 permits a 'disturbance payment' to be paid to any person 'displaced from any land' in consequence of the acquisition of the land by an authority possessing compulsory purchase powers. To be entitled to claim such a payment, the person displaced must be in 'lawful possession' of the land[3], which would include a licensee[5], and have no interest the acquisition or extinguishment of which would entitle him to compensation.

1 *Frank Warr & Co Ltd v LCC* [1904] 1 KB 713.
2 *DHN Food Distributors Ltd v Tower Hamlets London Borough Council* [1976] 3 All ER 462.
3 Land Compensation Act 1973 (LCA 1973), s 37(2)(*a*).
4 *Wrexham Maelor Borough Council v MacDougall* [1993] RVR 141.

C Acquiring, interfering with and creating interests in and rights over land

1 Acquiring the benefit of existing interests in and rights over land

[447]
Subject to the definition of 'land' in the authorising enactment, a power of compulsory purchase will give the right to acquire the land and all the interests vested in the land. Thus, if the land to be acquired has the benefit of a legal interest in or right over other land, such as an easement or *profit a prendre*, the acquiring authority will take the land with the benefit of that interest or right as would any other purchaser.

[448]
In respect of registered land, the Land Registration Act 1925, s 2(1) provides that only legal estates are capable of substantive registration and that all other interests must take effect as 'overriding' or 'minor' interests. This is

slightly misleading, however, as the Land Registration Act 1925, s 3(xi) defines 'legal estates' as meaning 'estates, interest and charges' which exist at law under the LPA 1925. Thus, the benefit of a legal interest identified in the LPA 1925, s 1(2) should appear on the register of title.

[449]
Section 62(1) of the LPA 1925 provides that:

> 'A conveyance of land shall be deemed to include and shall by virtue of this Act operate to convey, with the land, all buildings, erections, fixtures, ... liberties, privileges, easements, rights, and advantages whatsoever, appertaining to the land, or any part thereof, or, at the time of conveyance, ... enjoyed with the land or any part thereof.'

Thus, a conveyance made pursuant to a compulsory purchase of land will include words, imported by s 62, which have the effect of making an express grant to the acquiring authority of any easements or other rights benefiting the land. Unless special provision is made in the authorising Act, however, there is no general power to purchase just an existing easement or right in land, without taking the land as a whole[1].

1 *Sovmots Investment Ltd v Secretary of State for the Environment* [1979] AC 144.

2 Interfering with the burden of existing interests in and rights over land

[450]–[460]
Unless there is express statutory power to do so, a compulsory purchase of land does not acquire adverse interests in, or rights over, the land to be acquired, which benefit land not being acquired, and a notice to treat need not be served in respect of such interests[1].

1 *Clark v School Board for London* (1874) 9 Ch App 120.

[461]
Some compulsory powers do expressly provide for the extinguishment of adverse interests in or rights over the land, or at least provide limited immunity from such rights for subsequent owners of the land[1], usually subject to the payment of compensation. In *Thames Water Utilities Ltd v Oxford City Council*[2] the High Court held that the power to override easements and other rights granted by the TCPA 1990, s 237 where development has been granted in accordance with planning permission, would allow building works to go ahead in breach of a restrictive covenant, but would not then allow the use of the building in breach of the covenant. The effect of this decision has now been reversed by a new s 237(1A) (inserted by the Planning Act 2008). However, the general caution remains that not all compulsory purchase powers provide for the extinguishment of adverse rights over or interests in land.

1 See, for example, the Housing Act 1985, s 295, the TCPA 1990, s 237 and the Channel Tunnel Rail Link Act 1996, s 7.
2 [1999] 1 EGLR 167. It is submitted that there must be some doubt as to the correctness of this decision. See also **Division D [1605]–[1606]**.

[462]
In respect of registered land, the Land Registration Act 1925, s 20(1)(*b*) provides that the disposition of a freehold estate shall take effect, 'subject … unless the contrary is expressed on the register, to the overriding interests, if any, affecting the estate transferred or created' and s 23(1) provides a similar provision in respect of a registered leasehold interest. The rights which can take effect as overriding interests are listed in the Land Registration Act 1925, s 70(1)(*a*)–(*m*) and include legal easements and *profits a prendre* (s 70(1)(*a*)) and local land charges (s 70(1)(i)). Although not within s 70(1), the case of *Celsteel Ltd v Alton House Holdings Ltd*[1] has established that equitable easements are also 'overriding' interests which will bind a purchaser of land. Section 2(1) of the Land Registration Act 1925 provides that those interests which are not substantively registerable (that is legal interests under the LPA 1925, s 1(2)) or 'overriding', 'shall take effect in equity as minor interests'. 'Minor' interests will include rights under restrictive covenants and estates contracts, such as options to purchase land. A 'minor' interest is unenforceable against a subsequent purchaser of the registered title, unless noted on the register[2]. Thus, in respect of registered land, 'overriding' interests and 'minor' interests noted on the register will continue to bind the land, unless specifically acquired or extinguished.

1 [1985] 1 WLR 204.
2 Land Registration Act 1925, s 59(6).

[463]
Similarly, in respect of unregistered land, legal interests in the land under the LPA 1925, s 1(2) interests registered as land charges under the Land Charges Act 1972 and other equitable interests which are not registerable as land charges and of which the acquiring authority has notice, will continue to bind the land unless specifically acquired or extinguished.

[464]
It is important to note, however, that, even though such adverse interests or rights may continue to bind land compulsorily acquired, they will not be exercisable against an acquiring authority using the land for purposes authorised by statute[1], although, if the land is later sold, those adverse interests or rights may become exercisable against subsequent owners[2].

1 *Kirkby v School Board for Harrogate* [1896] 1 Ch 437; *Long Eaton Recreation Grounds Co v Midland Rly Co* [1902] 2 KB 574; *Brown v Heathland Mental Health National Health Service Trust* [1996] 1 All ER 133.
2 *Marten v Flight Refuelling Ltd* [1961] 2 All ER 696; *Bird v Eggleton* (1885) 29 Ch D 1012; *Clarke v School Board for London* (1874) 9 Ch App 120.

[465]
Where the activities of an acquiring authority interfere with adverse interests in, or rights over, the land, the person with the benefit of such an interest or right may be able to claim compensation for injurious affection under the CPA 1965, s 10. In such circumstance, it is usual for the authority interfering with the interests or rights to negotiate for the extinguishment, or partial extinguishment, of those interests or rights, upon the payment of compensation.

3 Creating and taking new interests in and rights over land

[466]

In *Sovmots Investments Ltd v Secretary of State for the Environment*[1], the House of Lords held that a local authority's powers of compulsory purchase were limited to those expressly conferred by statute and could not be extended by necessary implication to include powers not so conferred[2]. Thus, a power to compulsory acquire 'land' does not entitle an authority to create and take new easements or rights over land, unless the Act authorising the purchase specifically provides for the same[3]. The effect of this decision was, however, reversed for local authorities with the passing of the Local Government (Miscellaneous Provisions) Act 1976, s 13. Section 13 provided that, where a local authority is authorised by compulsory purchase order to compulsorily purchase land, it is also authorised to purchase such 'new rights' over land as are specified in the order and, for these purposes, 'new rights' means rights which are not in existence when the order specifying them is made.

1 [1979] AC 144. See also *Pinchin v London and Blackwall Rly Co* (1854) 5 De GM & G 851; *Hill v Midland Rly Co* (1882) 21 Ch D 143.

2 This contrasts with the position where there has been an acquisition of land by agreement which may, in certain circumstances, lead to the implied grant of all those easements which are necessary to the reasonable enjoyment of the property: see *Wheeldon v Burrows* [1921] 1 Ch 200 at 225; *Pwllbach Colliery Co Ltd v Woodman* [1915] AC 634 at 646. These cases are discussed by Lord Edmund-Davies in *Sovmots Investment Ltd v Secretary of State for the Environment* [1977] 2 All ER 385 at 397.

3 See also *Pinchin v London and Blackwall Rly Co* (1854) 5 De GM & G 851; *Hill v Midland Rly Co* (1882) 21 ChD 143.

[467]

A number of Acts authorise the creation and taking of new rights over land without the land itself being purchased[1], although, in many cases, these are not true easements as there will be no dominant tenement[2]. Statutory rights over land of this sort are often called 'wayleaves' and are used extensively by statutory undertakers for the laying of water mains, sewers, gas pipelines and electricity pylons and cables.

1 See, for example, the Highways Act 1980, s 250, the Electricity Act 1989, Sch 3, the Water Industry Act 1991, ss 158 and 159, the Water Resources Act 1991, s 154, the Gas Act 1986, Sch 3 and the Pipelines Act 1962, s 12. DETR Circular 1/81, paras 78–81 gives guidance on the use of powers under s 250 of the Highways Act 1980.

2 The four rules of recognition for an easement are set out in *Re Ellenborough Park* [1956] Ch 131.

[468]

Section 28 of and Sch 3 to the ALA 1981 deal with the acquisition of new rights over special kinds of land, being the land of a statutory undertaker, a local authority, National Trust land, and/or commons, open spaces etc. Section 28 identifies a number of provisions[1] that authorise the compulsory purchase of new rights over land and applies to such acquisitions the particular procedures in Sch 3 to the Act. Previously, the procedural provisions of the Acquisition of Land (Authorisation Procedure) Act 1946 applied to these authorising enactments.

1 The provisions identified in the ALA 1981, s 28 are the Local Government (Miscellaneous Provisions) Act 1976, s 13(1), the Development of Rural Wales Act 1976, s 6(5), the Local

Government, Planning and Land Act 1980, s 142(4), the Highways Act 1980, s 250, the Telecommunications Act 1984, s 34(3), the Gas Act 1986, Sch 3, para 1 and the Electricity Act 1989, Sch 3, para 1.

D Other aspects of land

1 Acquiring strata of land only

[469]
Without express statutory power or the agreement of the landowner, an acquiring authority cannot acquire only a stratum of land, but must acquire the freehold of the entire land[1]. Specific powers to acquire a stratum only of land are granted where necessary, and the London Transport Act 1969, for example, is one of a number of Acts authorising the London Transport Executive to acquire strata of land for the purposes of the London Underground.

1 See Forbes J in the first instance decision in *Sovmots Investments Ltd v Secretary of State for the Environment* [1976] 1 All ER 178 at 188 (this case went to the Court of Appeal and the House of Lords, but not on this point). In *English Property Corpn plc v Royal Borough of Kingston-upon-Thames* (1998) 77 P&CR 1,CA, it was accepted (being agreed between the parties) that a stratum of land cannot be acquired except with the agreement of the landowner. In relation to the physical extent of 'land', see *Bocardo SA v Star Energy Weald Basin Ltd* [2010] UKSC 35, [2010] 3 All ER 975.

2 Minerals

[470]–[480]
Unless otherwise excluded, the acquisition of 'land' will include the acquisition of any mines and minerals forming part of the land. Mines and minerals may, however, be expressly excluded from a compulsory purchase by applying the 'mining code'. The 'mining code' is now contained in the ALA 1981, s 3, Sch 2 which re-enacts the Railways Clauses Consolidation Act 1845, ss 77–85. The 'mining code' enables an acquiring authority to exclude mines and minerals from a compulsory purchase of land and, subject to the provisions of the code, allows the original owner to work them.

3 Severed land

[481]–[800]
Where the boundary of an acquiring authority's proposals severs a unit of land ownership so that part falls within the area of land to be compulsorily acquired and part outside it, the owner of the land will have to decide whether to sell only part of the land, and claim compensation for depreciation of the retained part, or, alternatively, whether to seek to require the authority to purchase the whole. The statutory provisions governing land severance are contained with the CPA 1965, s 8, the Compulsory Purchase (Vesting Declarations) Act 1981, Sch 1 and the LCA 1973, ss 53–57. These provisions are discussed in **Division D, Chapter 2**.

Chapter 3

Purchase of land by agreement

Contents

A Introduction

[801]

An acquiring authority may negotiate and contract to purchase land by agreement in one of three broad circumstances. First, an authority may have the opportunity to purchase land in the open market and not need to resort to the use of, or the threatened use of, its compulsory purchase powers. Secondly, an authority may enter negotiations to purchase land by agreement, but decide to obtain compulsory purchase powers by way of insurance, in case negotiations break down. Thirdly, an authority may start compulsory purchase proceedings, but find that an owner is willing to sell his interest in the land. In each of these circumstances, however, the doctrine of 'ultra vires' means that a statutory body will still need statutory powers to acquire land by agreement, even if the vendor is willing to sell and compulsory purchase powers are not actually necessary. Most statutory provisions which confer compulsory purchase powers now also confer the power to acquire land by agreement. A few statutes only allow an acquiring authority to acquire land by agreement and contain no powers of compulsion[1].

1 See, for example, the Open Spaces Act 1906, s 9; the Agriculture Act 1970, s 48 and the Land Compensation Act 1973 (LCA 1973), ss 22(2), 26(1), (2).

[801.1]

An authority with compulsory purchase powers may enter into negotiations with a landowner prior to, or indeed following, the submission of a compulsory purchase order for confirmation. ODPM Circular 06/2004 gives the following encouragement at para 24 to prospective acquiring authorities:

'Before embarking on compulsory purchase and throughout the preparation and procedural stages, acquiring authorities should seek to acquire land by negotiation wherever practicable. The compulsory purchase of land is intended as a last resort in the event that attempts to acquire by agreement fail. Acquiring authorities should nevertheless consider at what point the land they are seeking to acquire will be needed and, as a contingency measure, should plan a compulsory purchase timetable at the same time as conducting negotiations. Given the amount of time which needs to be allowed to complete the compulsory purchase process, it may often be sensible for the acquiring authority to initiate the formal procedures in parallel with such negotiations.'

[801.2]
In carrying out negotiations to acquire land by agreement, it is important that parties are careful, where appropriate, to ensure that negotiations are clearly conducted 'subject to contract'. This issue arose in the Court of Appeal decision in *Secretary of State for Transport v Christos*[1], where a claimant argued that a 'subject to contract' agreement to settle a claim at a certain price meant that:

(*a*) there was a binding contract at that price; and/or
(*b*) the acquiring authority was estopped from arguing for a lower value in the Lands Tribunal.

The Court of Appeal ultimately rejected these arguments holding that:

'It is true that, following the notice to treat given by the acquiring authority and the counter-notice given by Mr and Mrs Christos, it was not open to either party to withdraw from the compulsory acquisition of the property. It was, however, open for either party to withdraw on the amount to be paid, as the offer to settle for £500,000 "subject to contract" signified that was not intended to be legally binding until the exchange of formal contracts.'

It is important, however, that parties which do not intend to be bound by a 'subject to contract' agreement make this clear in negotiation and, in particular, mark correspondence accordingly.

1 [2003] EWCA Civ 1073, [2004] 1 P&CR 228.

B Statutory power to acquire land by agreement

[802]
A specific power to acquire land by agreement is now contained within most statutory provisions granting powers of compulsory purchase[1]. In many of the older Acts granting local authorities power to purchase land by agreement, there was a requirement for the approval of the minister[2]. This requirement was, however, removed for all such Acts by the Town and Country Planning Act 1959, s 22.

1 See, eg, the Town and Country Planning Act 1990 (TCPA 1990), s 227, which provides that the council of any county, district or London borough may acquire by agreement any land which they require for any purpose for which a local authority may be authorised to acquire land under s 226. The latter section grants to certain local authorities power to acquire compulso-

rily any land in their area for development, redevelopment or improvement, or for other planning purposes.

2 See, for example, the National Parks and Access to Countryside Act 1949, s 103(3).

[803]

In most cases, an acquiring authority will rely on a specific power to acquire by agreement, but, for local authorities the Local Government Act 1972 (LGA 1972), s 120 provides a 'principal council'[1] with a useful general power to acquire land by agreement, whether situated inside or outside its area, for the purposes of 'any of their functions under this or any other enactment' or for 'the benefit, improvement or development' of their area. This power is sometimes used where the authority intends to use land for more than one purpose. Section 120 also enables a principal council to acquire land by agreement, where the land is not immediately required for the purpose for which it is acquired, and provides that, until it is required for that purpose, it may be used for the purpose of any of the council's functions. Clearly, the purposes for which the land is to be acquired by agreement under this section must themselves be within the powers of the council (ie not ultra vires)[2].

1 The LGA 1972, s 270, defines a 'principal council' as a meaning 'council elected for a principal area' and a 'principal area' as meaning 'a non metropolitan county, a district or a London borough but, in relation to Wales, means a county or county borough'. LGA 1972, s 128(3) disapplies the Town and Country Planning Act 1959, s 22 to 'principal councils'.

2 See *Costello v Dacorum District Council* (1981) 79 LGR 133; on appeal (1982) 81 LGR 1 and also *R v Somerset County Council, ex p Fewings* [1995] 1 All ER 513.

[804]

Section 3 of the Compulsory Purchase Act 1965 (CPA 1965) provides (as amended) that:

> 'It shall be lawful for the acquiring authority to agree with the owners of any of the land subject to compulsory purchase, and with all parties having an estate or interest in any of the land, or who are by Schedule 1 to this Act or any other enactment enabled to sell or convey or release any of that land, for the absolute purchase, for a consideration in money or money's worth, of any of that land, and of all estates and interests in the land.'

Section 1(3) of the CPA 1965 makes it clear that 'subject to compulsory purchase' means that such a purchase is authorised by a compulsory purchase order. The words 'or money's worth' were added to s 3, with effect from 25 September 1991, and would, for example, allow a land swap[1]. Schedule 1 to the Act gives owners under certain legal disabilities, power to sell to the acquiring authority and makes provision for the measure of compensation in such circumstances. Similar provisions are contained within the Land Clauses Consolidation Act 1845 (LCCA 1845), ss 6–15. Although the provisions of the LCCA 1845 were intended to be incorporated automatically into all acquisitions of land by a statutory body[2], some later Acts expressly incorporated the provisions. Section 38 of and Sch 6 to the CPA 1965 amend those later Acts so as to translate references to the Land Clauses Acts into references to the corresponding provisions of Pt I of the CPA 1965.

1 Amendment made by the Local Government, Planning and Land Act 1980, s 70, Sch 15, para 3.
2 LCCA 1845, s 1.

[805]
An agreement to purchase land is not affected by the three-year time limit imposed on the compulsory purchase of land by the CPA 1965, s 4.

C Purchase by agreement prior to confirmation of the compulsory purchase order

[806]
A landowner threatened with compulsory purchase may, at any time, agree to sell his interest to the acquiring authority. However, unless and until a compulsory purchase order to which the CPA 1965 applies has been confirmed, any acquisition of land comprised in the draft order will not be a compulsory acquisition and the CPA 1965 will not apply[1]. This may raise a number of practical problems, as follows:

(1) Where a purchase is by compulsion, the authorising Act may provide for adverse third party rights to be 'extinguished' or 'overridden'[2]. This may not be the case where an acquisition is by agreement[3].
(2) Where land is subject to compulsory purchase[4], an authority which has effected entry will have power to remain for up to six months, notwithstanding that it has, through mistake or inadvertence, omitted to purchase an estate, right or interest affecting the land[5]. This right is not available where land is not 'subject to compulsory purchase'.
(3) The costs of conveyancing are to be borne by the acquiring authority where land is subject to compulsory purchase[6]. Again, there is no such provision where land is not 'subject to compulsory purchase'.

1 This is so regardless of whether the purchaser has a general power to compulsorily purchase land when authorised by compulsory purchase order: *Catling v Great Northern Rly Co* (1869) 18 WR 121.
2 See, eg, TCPA 1990, s 236 and s 237.
3 See, eg, TCPA 1990, s 236.
4 That is, where its purchase is authorised by a compulsory purchase order (even though the actual purchase may be by agreement): CPA 1965, s 1(3).
5 CPA 1965, s 22; see **D[743]**ff.
6 That is, where its purchase is authorised by a compulsory purchase order (even though the actual purchase may be by agreement): CPA 1965, s 1(3).

D Purchase by agreement after confirmation of the compulsory purchase order

[807]
As mentioned above, the CPA 1965, s 3 provides that it shall be lawful for an acquiring authority to agree with:

(*a*) the 'owners'[1] of any of the land 'subject to compulsory purchase'[2]; and
(*b*) all parties having any estate or interest in any of the land who are enabled[3] to sell and convey or release any of that land to purchase any such interest for a consideration[4] of money or money's worth[5].

1 'Owner' means the persons having power to sell and convey the land to the acquiring authority: CPA 1965, s 1(6).
2 Land 'subject to compulsory purchase' means land in respect of which a compulsory purchase order has been made: CPA 1965, s 1(3).
3 'Enabled' means enabled by the CPA 1965, Sch 1 or by any other enactment. CPA 1965, Sch 1 makes provision for the acquisition, by compulsion or agreement, of interests belonging to persons who would otherwise have no power to sell. The relevant provisions of the CPA 1965 are dealt with more fully in **Division D**, but are rarely used nowadays, as in most, if not all, cases covered by the schedule, the power to convey exists elsewhere in more convenient form.
4 There is a similar provision with respect to 'consideration' including money, in the LCCA 1845, s 6 in respect of land the acquisition of which is authorised by a special Act to which the LCCA 1845 applies. However, there is no provision for 'consideration' under the terms of the LCCA 1845, s 6 to include 'money's worth'.
5 'Money's worth' no longer encompasses a rent-charge paid by the acquiring authority following the repeal of the CPA 1965, s 24 by the Rent Charges Act 1977, s 17(2). Money's worth could however cover, inter alia, exchange land.

[808]

Some provisions of the CPA 1965 will apply to the purchase by agreement of land which is 'subject to compulsory purchase'[1], although not all of the formalities of a compulsory purchase will be applicable and, in particular, there is no requirement to serve a notice to treat[2].

1 See, eg, CPA 1965, s 23, relating to the costs of acquisition.
2 CPA 1965, s 5. A notice to treat is generally regarded as a condition precedent to the exercise of compulsory purchase powers. See **Division D, Chapter 2**.

[809]

In contemplating purchase by agreement in the shadow of a compulsory purchase order both acquiring authorities and landowners may wish to consider the following practical points:

(1) An acquiring authority should beware of finding itself time-barred for exercising its compulsory purchase powers, in the event that negotiations are allowed to slip. To assist negotiations with the acquiring authority whilst retaining the ability to resort to formal procedures if necessary, the landowner may consider agreeing to an extension of time to preserve the validity of a notice to treat beyond its three-year life span[1].
(2) Unless dispossession is inevitable, the landowner also should beware of expressing a willingness on his part to move, as this may prejudice any disturbance claim which is intended to reflect the consequences of a forced move[2].
(3) A landowner can apply for a certificate of alternative development to assist in determining compensation payable, notwithstanding that the acquisition is to proceed by agreement[3].
(4) The landowner should be cautious about allowing entry by agreement, as, once given, this cannot be revoked. Such a concession may, however, be advisable in a falling property market, as compensation will be assessed at, and interest on such compensation will be calculated from, the date of entry[4].
(5) Where the agreement to sell is subject to an assessment of compensation in accordance with the authorising Act, the date for assessment of such

compensation will be the date of possession as opposed to the date of such agreement[5].

1 CPA 1965, s 5(2B); as to which see **Division D, Chapter 2**.
2 A claim for disturbance will be upheld if it is shown that dispossession was inevitable: see *Prasad v Wolverhampton Borough Council* [1983] Ch 333.
3 LCA 1961, s 17. Certificates of alternative development verify what the land could have been used for had it not been required for compulsory purchase: see **Division E**.
4 See **Division D, Chapter 3**.
5 *Marchment v Hampshire County Council* (1982) 43 P & CR 431.

E Formalities regarding sale and purchase of land by agreement

[810]–[820]
An acquisition by agreement must comply with the general law regarding the sale and purchase of land or an interest in land, so that, for example, the requirements of the Law of Property (Miscellaneous Provisions) Act 1989, s 2 will apply, as would be the case in any private transaction[1]. Those requirements are that the contract must be in writing and incorporate all the terms in one document or, where contracts are exchanged, in each document. The terms may be incorporated in a document, either by being set out in it or by reference to some other document. The document incorporating the terms or, where contracts are exchanged, one of the documents incorporating them (but not necessarily the same one) must be signed by or on behalf of each party to the contract.

1 Law of Property (Miscellaneous Provisions) Act 1989, s 2 supersedes the Law of Property Act 1925, s 40.

[821]
Where a compulsory purchase order has been made, a notice to treat has been served and the purchase price is agreed between the parties, then, subject to the Land Compensation Act 1961 (LCA 1961), s 31(5) (withdrawal of notices to treat) there will exist a 'statutory' contract or quasi-contract, which will be enforceable by specific performance[1]. There is some authority for the proposition that such a 'statutory' contract will not need to comply with the requirements of the Law of Property (Miscellaneous Provisions) Act 1989, s 2 and will be binding, even if the agreement as to price was made orally[2]. If the purchase price has only been agreed provisionally or 'subject to contract', however, then there is no enforceable 'statutory' contract[3].

1 *Harding v Metropolitan Rly Co* (1872) 7 Ch App 154; *Grice v Dudley Corpn* [1958] Ch 329.
2 See the judgment of Lord Denning MR in *Munton v Greater London Council* [1976] 1 WLR 649, 32 P&CR 269 in relation to the, now superseded, Law of Property Act 1925, s 40.
3 *Munton v Greater London Council* [1976] 1 WLR 649, 32 P&CR 269; *Dutton's Brewery Ltd v Leeds City Council* (1981) 43 P&CR 160.

F The terms of any agreement

[822]
The statutory provision granting the power to purchase by agreement may expressly apply Pt I of the CPA 1965 to the transaction, with or without

exceptions[1]. Thus, the provisions of Pt I of the CPA 1965 may apply to the sale although not expressly incorporated by the contract itself. Where Pt I of the CPA 1965 is not applied by the Act authorising the purchase, or where particular provisions are expressly excluded, then those advising parties to any purchase by agreement will need to ensure that the terms of the contract are drafted so as to properly protect their client's interests. It may, for example, be appropriate to consider whether Pt I of the CPA 1965 should be expressly applied to the acquisition by the contract itself; again, with or without exceptions.

1 LGA 1972, s 120(3), for example, applies Pt I of the CPA 1965 with the exception of s 31 and the TCPA 1990, s 227(2) applies Pt I with the exceptions of ss 4–8, 10, 31.

[823]
By way of example, the CPA 1965, s 11(1) allows an authority acquiring under compulsory powers, and which has served a notice to treat, to enter on and take possession of the land after giving not less than 14 days' notice to any owner, lessee and occupier. Where there is a purchase by agreement and thus no notice to treat, this provision will not apply. In such circumstances, an authority that has acquired the freehold interest in land by agreement, but which fails to agree terms for entry onto the land with any lessee or other occupier, will have to serve a notice to treat on any such lesser interest.

[824]
The provisions of the LCA 1961 relating to the measure of compensation will, again, not apply to a purchase by agreement, unless applied by a term of the agreement itself. Clearly, any contract will have to be carefully drafted so as to ensure that the interests, in relation to compensation, of both the acquiring authority and the landowner are properly protected. Owners will need to consider, for example, such matters as the valuation date to be applied, any assumptions which should be made as to likely planning permissions in respect of the land to be acquired, and provision for payment in respect of expenses and other losses above the value of the land (ie 'disturbance'). One option available to the parties is to expressly provide within the contract itself that, if compensation is not settled by agreement, then it should be settled by the Upper Tribunal as if the acquiring authority had taken the necessary steps to purchase land compulsorily under the relevant authorising Act and as if a notice to treat had been served on a date specified in the contract. This formula was adopted in *Washington Development Corpn v Bamlings (Washington) Ltd*[1], where it was decided that the date of valuation should be determined in accordance with *Birmingham Corpn v West Midlands Baptist (Trust) Association*[2] as if there had been a compulsory purchase. If the parties to a purchase by agreement wish to see some other date of valuation applied, then this should be expressly provided for in the contract.

1 [1985] 1 EGLR 16.
2 [1970] AC 874, 20 P&CR 1052.

[825]
In *Alfred Golightly & Sons Ltd v Durham County Council*[1], where the owner of land withdrew its objection to a compulsory purchase order, following the

conclusion of an agreement with the acquiring authority, the Lands Tribunal upheld an interpretation of the agreement which gave the owner compensation on a basis more favourable than would have been achieved under the statutory code. A local authority will, however, need to be able to justify agreeing to a purchase price higher than the compensation which would be awarded under the statutory code.

1 (1980) 260 Estates Gazette 1045.

[826]
It is worth emphasising once again, however, that, where the statutory compensation code does not apply, any contract will have to be carefully drafted to ensure that each party's interests are properly protected. If the vendor does enter an enforceable contract, he will be bound by its terms, even if those be less favourable than would be obtained under the statutory code[1].

1 See, eg, *Crabb v Surrey County Council* (1982) 44 P&CR 119.

G No fetter on powers

[827]
An acquiring authority purchasing land by agreement may not contractually bind itself not to exercise specific statutory powers in relation to the land acquired[1]. In *Ayr Harbour Trustees v Oswald*[2], Lord Blackburn put the matter as follows:

> 'I think that where the legislature confer powers on any body to take lands compulsorily for a particular purpose, is on the ground that the using of that land for the purpose will be for the public good. Whether that body be one which is a seeking to make a profit for shareholders, or, as in the present case, a body of trustees acting solely for the public good, I think in case the powers conferred on the body empowered to take the land compulsorily are intrusted to them, and their successors, to be used for the furtherance of that object which the legislature has thought sufficiently for the public good to justify it in intrusting them with such powers; and consequently, that a contract purporting to bind them and their successors not to use those powers is void.'

An acquiring authority may, however, enter into a restrictive covenant so long as it is not incompatible with the purpose for which the land was acquired[3]. Furthermore, in *Dowty Boulton Paul Ltd v Wolverhampton Corpn*[4], Pennycuick V–C made it clear that, where a public authority, by a valid exercise of a statutory power, had created rights over land extending over a term of years, the existence of which to that extent excluded the exercise of certain other statutory powers over the land, it could not subsequently claim that the original exercise of powers was invalid as a fetter upon its future exercise of powers.

1 *Ayr Harbour Trustees v Oswald* (1883) 8 App Cas 623 at 634; *York Corpn v Henry Leetham & Sons Ltd* [1924] 1 Ch 557 at 572; *Southend-on-Sea Corpn v Hodgson (Wickford) Ltd* [1962] 1 QB 416 at 424.
2 (1883) 8 App Cas 623.

3 *Stourcliffe Estates Co Ltd v Bournmouth Corpn* [1910] 2 Ch 12.
4 [1971] 2 All ER 277, [1971] 1 WLR 204, 69 LGR 192.

H Adverse rights over the land acquired

[828]–[1100]
Where an authority acquires land by agreement for statutory purposes, persons entitled to the benefit of restrictive covenants over it cannot assert them in order to prevent the use of the land by the authority for its statutory purposes, or to claim damages[1]. The acquisition does not itself discharge restrictive covenants, however, and persons entitled to the benefit of the such covenants may be entitled to claim compensation under the CPA 1965, s 10 for injurious affection to their own land by reason of the execution of the works[2]. It is permissible for an acquiring authority to grant back an easement upon conveyance, provided that the grant and enjoyment of such is not inconsistent with the purpose for which the land was acquired[3].

1 *Kirby v School Board for Harrogate* [1896] 1 Ch 437; *Long Eaton Recreation Ground Co v Midland Rly Co* [1902] 2 KB 574; *Brown v Heathland Mental Health National Health Service Trust* [1996] 1 All ER 133.
2 *Kirby v School Board for Harrogate* [1896] 1 Ch 437; *Manchester, Sheffield and Lincolnshire Rly v Anderson* [1898] 2 Ch 394; *Re 6, 8, 10 and 12 Elm Avenue, New Milton, ex p New Forest District Council* [1984] 3 All ER 632, [1984] 1 WLR 1398; *Brown v Heathlands Mental Health National Health Service Trust* [1996] 1 All ER 133. For a detailed consideration of the CPA 1965, s 10 see **Division F**.
3 *South Eastern Rly Co v Associated Portland Cement Manufacturers (1900) Ltd* [1910] 1 Ch 12.

Chapter 4

Purchase and blight notices

Contents

[1101]
This section deals with what is sometimes called 'compulsory purchase in reverse'. Compulsory purchase is usually initiated by an acquiring authority in the furtherance of its statutory purposes, but, under the Town and Country Planning Act 1990 (TCPA 1990), two circumstances are defined where an owner of land may be able to force an authority possessing compulsory purchase powers to acquire his land. A landowner may commence 'compulsory purchase in reverse' by serving either a *purchase notice* or a *blight notice*, as appropriate.

A Purchase notices

[1102]
An owner of land may serve a *purchase notice*, where he is refused planning permission or it is granted, subject to conditions, and he considers that the land has become incapable of reasonably beneficial use in its existing state, and that it cannot be rendered capable of beneficial use by carrying out any permitted development.

1 Circumstances in which a purchase notice may be served

Section 137 of the Town and Country Planning Act 1990

[1103]
By s 137(2) of the TCPA 1990, any 'owner' of land or 'person entitled to an interest in land' may, following an adverse planning decision, serve a purchase notice on the council of the district, Welsh county, county borough or London borough council in which the land is situated, requiring that council to purchase his interest in the land[1].

1 Special provisions apply to the service of purchase notices in respect of Crown Land: see TCPA 1990, s 137A.

[1104]
The 'adverse planning decisions', following which an 'owner' of land may serve a purchase notice under s 137, are:

(1) Where, on an application for planning permission to develop any land, permission is refused, or is granted subject to conditions (s 137(1)(*a*)).
(2) Where, by a revocation or modification order under the TCPA 1990, s 97 planning permission is revoked, or is modified by the imposition of conditions (s 137(1)(*b*)). Furthermore, 'any person entitled to an interest' in land may serve a purchase notice in circumstances.
(3) Where a discontinuance order is made under of the TCPA 1990, s 102 or Sch 9, para 1 (s 137(1)(*c*)).

[1105]
In the cases mentioned in s 137(1)(*a*) or (*b*), the 'owner' of the land must claim that the circumstances set out in s 137(3) are satisfied, those being:

(*a*) that the land has become incapable of reasonably beneficial use in its existing state;
(*b*) in a case where planning permission was granted subject to conditions or was modified by the imposition of conditions, that the land cannot be rendered capable of reasonably beneficial use by the carrying out of the permitted development in accordance with those conditions; and
(*c*) in any case, that the land cannot be rendered capable of reasonably beneficial use by the carrying out of any other development, for which planning permission has been granted or for which the local planning authority or the Secretary of State has undertaken to grant planning permission.

[1106]
Similarly, in the case mentioned in s 137(1)(*c*), the 'person entitled to an interest in land' must claim that the circumstances set out in s 137(4) are satisfied, those being:

(*a*) that, by reason of the order, the land has become incapable of reasonably beneficial use in its existing state; and
(*b*) that it cannot be rendered capable of reasonably beneficial use by the carrying out of any development for which planning permission has been granted, whether by that order or otherwise.

Circular 13/83

[1107]
Departmental Circular 13/83 gives advice on the service of a purchase notice, the action to be taken by a council on whom a notice has been served and the action to be taken following the transmission of a purchase notice to the Secretary of State. Although written when the relevant statutory provisions were contained in the Town and Country Planning Act 1971, the circular remains a useful source of guidance on the law and practice relating to purchase notices.

Any 'owner of the land' or 'person entitled to an interest in land'

[1108]
An 'owner' of land is defined by the TCPA 1990, s 336 as meaning:

'a person, other than a mortgagee not in possession, who, whether in his own right or as trustee for any other person, is entitled to receive the rack rent of the land, or where the land is not let at a rack rent, would be so entitled if it were so let.'[1]

A 'person entitled to an interest' in land would include the 'owner' of the land, as well as the owner of any lesser interest in the land. Thus the 'owner' of the land, as so defined, may serve a purchase notice, following any of the three adverse planning decisions set out in s 137(1).

1 See *Rakusen Properties Ltd v Leeds City Council* (1978) 37 P&CR 315 for a consideration of whether the interests of a subsidiary or associated company were sufficient to satisfy s 137.

[1109]
In *Smart and Courtney Dale Ltd v Dover RDC*[1], the Lands Tribunal decided that the words 'the land' in s 137 referred to the totality of the land the subject of the planning refusal, so that a claimant would have to own all of the land in order to qualify as the 'owner of the land' for the purposes of s 137(2)(*a*). If the land the subject of the planning refusal has more than one owner, then all the owners should combine to serve any purchase notice. In *Cook v Winchester City Council*[2] the Lands Tribunal held that a purchase notice must relate to the whole of the land which is the subject matter of the planning refusal. Furthermore, the purchase notice should not relate to more land than was the subject of the planning refusal. Paragraph 7 of Circular 13/83 states that:

'Except in the case of a listed building purchase notice … the land to which a purchase notice relates must be the *identical* area of land which was the subject of the relevant decision or the relevant order. If the notice relates to more land, it is regarded as invalid.'

1 (1972) 23 P&CR 408.
2 (1994) 69 P&CR 99.

Incapable of reasonably beneficial use in its existing state

[1110]–[1120]
Although the Act does not define the phrase 'incapable of reasonably beneficial use', s 137 does make it clear that the issue must be considered with the land 'in its existing state'. Paragraph 13 of Circular 13/83, however, gives the following helpful guidance:

'In considering what capacity for use the land has, relevant factors are the physical state of the land, its size, shape and surroundings, and the general pattern of land-uses in the area; a use of relatively low value may be regarded as reasonably beneficial if such a use is common for similar land in the vicinity. It may sometimes be possible for an area of land to be rendered capable of reasonably beneficial use by being used in conjunction with neighbouring or adjoining land, provided that a sufficient interest in that land is held by the server of the notice, or by a prospective owner of the purchase notice land. Use by a prospective owner cannot be taken into account unless there is a reasonably firm indication that there is in fact a prospective owner of the purchase notice site. (In this paragraph the word "owner" is used to include a person who has a tenancy of the land or some other interest which is sufficient to enable him to use the land.) Profit *may* be a useful comparison in certain circumstances, but the absence of profit (however calculated) is not necessarily material: the concept of reasonably beneficial use is not synonymous with profit.'

Also of assistance is para 16 of the Circular which states:

> 'The Secretary of State considers that, in seeking to satisfy himself whether conditions (*a*) to (*c*) in [s 137(1) of the TCPA 1990] have been fulfilled, he may take into account, among other things, whether there is a reasonable prospect of the server's selling or letting the land for any purpose, were its availability to be made known locally. He would normally expect to see some evidence to show that the server had attempted to dispose of his interest in the land before he could be satisfied that the land had become incapable of reasonably beneficial use.'

[1121]
In *Wain v Secretary of State for the Environment*[1], the Court of Appeal made it clear that s 137 only applies where the whole of the land the subject of the purchase notice has become incapable of reasonably beneficial use. This decision is now reflected in para 17 of Circular 13/83. Whether the land has become incapable of reasonably beneficial use in any particular case is a question of fact for the decision-maker, in other words the Secretary of State where the local authority does not comply with the purchase notice[2]. Paragraph 18 of Circular 13/83 makes it clear that, in s 137, the expression 'has become' incapable of reasonably beneficial use is taken by the Secretary of State to mean 'is' incapable of reasonably beneficial use, so that the claimant is not required to compare the existing state of the land with some earlier state.

1 (1981) 44 P&CR 289. See also *Gavaghan v Secretary of State for the Environment* (1988) 59 P&CR 124.
2 *Brookdene Investments Ltd v Minister of Housing and Local Government* (1970) 21 P&CR 545.

[1122]
Section 138 provides that, in considering the question of whether the land is incapable of reasonably beneficial use in its existing state, no account should be taken of any 'unauthorised' prospective use of the land and this is defined as including a use of the land which would involve the carrying out of 'development'[1] other than that specified in Pt I of Sch 3 to the Act. Part I of Sch 3 to the TCPA 1990 includes matters such as the rebuilding of any building which was in existence on 1 July 1948. Thus, it may be that land, which is incapable of reasonably beneficial use in its existing state, but which includes a ruined building which was in existence on 1 July 1948, will have considerable Sch 3 value. Paragraph 14 of Circular 13/83 states that:

> 'In determining whether the land has become incapable of reasonably beneficial use in its existing state, it may be relevant, where appropriate, to consider the difference (if any) between the annual value of the land in its existing state and the annual value of the land if development of a class specified in [Pt I of Sch 3 to the TCPA 1990] were carried out on the land.

Development of any class not specified in [Sch 3] must not be taken into account.'

However, in a decision on a purchase notice reported at [1986] 2 PAD 143, the Secretary of State has said that:

> 'The Secretary of State now takes the view, notwithstanding para 14 of Circular 13/83, that [Sch 3 to the TCPA 1990] is relevant only as a guide to compensation if a purchase notice should be confirmed, and has no relevance to the issue of whether or not the land in question has reasonably beneficial use.'

Section 138 does mean however that, subject to the Sch 3 exception, even 'development', which does not require planning permission under the TCPA 1990, s 57 should be excluded from consideration.

1 For the meaning of 'development', see the TCPA 1990, s 55.

[1123]

In *R v Minister of Housing and Local Government, ex p Chichester RDC*[1], the Divisional Court held that the term 'incapable of reasonably beneficial use' does not mean the same as 'less useful' to the owner in its present state, than if planning permission had been granted, as this would nearly always be the case on a refusal of permission. Thus, for example, it has been held that the use of a sports field which was refused planning permission for redevelopment, was not 'incapable of reasonably beneficial use in its existing state'[2]. In *Hudscott Estates v Secretary of State for the Environment, Transport and the Regions*[3] the High Court indicated that 'incapable of' bore its ordinary dictionary meaning of 'not susceptible of'.

1 [1960] 1 WLR 587. See also *Adams & Wade v Minister of Housing and Local Government* (1965) 18 P&CR 60 and the judgment of Schieman LJ in *Colley v Secretary of State for the Environment and Canterbury City Council* (1998) 77 P&CR 190.

2 *General Estates Co Ltd v Minister of Housing and Local Government* (1965) 194 Estates Gazette 201.

3 (2000) 82 P & CR 71, [2001] JPL 973.

[1124]

An owner of land does not have to show that the land has become incapable of reasonably beneficial use by reason of the refusal of planning permission[1]. It has been held that mere neglect of the land by the landowner will not be a material consideration in determining whether the land has become incapable of reasonably beneficial use in its existing state[2] and neither will poor site layout of a development[3]. In *Balco Transport Services Ltd v Secretary of State for the Environment and Maidstone BC*[4], the Court of Appeal held that, where the service of a valid 'enforcement notice' under the TCPA 1990 could require the owner or occupier of land to restore it to a state in which it would have a reasonably beneficial use, then the requirements of s 137 will not have been met and a purchase notice served in these circumstances should not be confirmed.

1 See extract from Ministerial decision at [1958] JPL 897.

2 *Leominster Borough Council v Minister of Housing and Local Government* (1971) 218 Estates Gazette 1419.

3 *West Bromwich County Borough Council v Minister of Housing and Local Government* (1968) 206 Estates Gazette 1085.

4 [1985] 3 All ER 689. See also *Purbeck District Council v Secretary of State for the Environment* (1982) 263 Estates Gazette 261.

[1125]
Although there is nothing to prevent an owner of land from lodging an appeal against a refusal of planning permission, as well as a purchase notice, it could be difficult for a such an owner to substantiate a claim that the conditions set out in s 137(1) are fulfilled, if a planning appeal were still outstanding[1].

1 Circular 13/83, para 37.

2 Drafting and serving a purchase notice

[1126]
There is no form of purchase notice prescribed by the TCPA 1990 or subordinate legislation, although the Town and Country Planning General Regulations 1992[1] do provide that a purchase notice must be in writing. A model form purchase notice is provided in Appendix 1 to Circular 13/83[2]. A purchase notice should properly identify the local authority which is being required to purchase the land, the land the subject matter of the notice, the adverse planning decision which has triggered the notice, the grounds in s 137(3) or (4) of the Act which are relied upon, the nature of the owner's interest, and the owner's name and address. A purchase notice should be drafted with care as there is no right to amend it, although the landowner may serve more than one such notice[3]. Whether a subsequent purchase notice implies withdrawal of an earlier notice will be a matter of fact to be determined objectively on the basis of what the owner says and does, and not on the basis of what he thinks[4].

1 SI 1992/1492, reg 12.
2 The model form in Circular 13/83 refers to the provisions of the Town and Country Planning Act 1971 and will therefore need updating for use now.
3 *White v Herefordshire County Council* [2007] EWCA Civ 1204, [2007] All ER (D) 333 (Nov).
4 *White v Herefordshire County Council* [2007] EWCA Civ 1204, [2007] All ER (D) 333 (Nov).

[1127]
A purchase notice must be served on the council of the relevant district, Welsh county, county borough or London borough council[1] within 12 months of the adverse planning decision specified in s 137(1) of the Act, or such longer period as the Secretary of State may allow in any particular case[2]. A purchase notice is served by delivering it at the offices of the council or by sending it by pre-paid post[3].

1 TCPA 1990, s 137(2).
2 Town and Country Planning General Regulations 1992, SI 1992/1492, reg 12. In *Reside v North Ayrshire Council* [2000] PLR 86 the Scottish Court of Session held that, where there had been a planning appeal, the 12-month period ran from the date of an Inspector's decision and not from the date of the Council's original decision to refuse planning permission.
3 Town and Country Planning General Regulations 1992, SI 1992/1492, reg 12.

3 Action following service of a purchase notice on a council

Validity of a purchase notice

[1128]
The council should first consider the validity of any purchase notice served upon it[1]. Such consideration will include examination of whether:

(*a*) there has been an adverse planning decision as required by s 137(1);
(*b*) the purchase notice has been served within 12 months, or such longer period as the Secretary of State may have allowed;
(*c*) the purchase notice has been properly served on the council;
(*d*) that the land to which the purchase notice relates is the identical area of land which was the subject of the adverse planning decision;
(*e*) the person who has served the purchase notice is an 'owner' or, as the case may be, a 'person entitled to an interest in land' within the meaning of the Act; and
(*f*) has the notice described the land and the owner of the land, and has it required the council to purchase the land.

1 Circular 13/83, para 21.

[1129]
DoE Circular 13/83, para 21, advises that authorities should not send to the Secretary of State claims which they consider to be invalid. See **Division G** para **[326]** below.

Another local authority or statutory undertaker

[1130]–[1140]
The council served with the purchase notice may be unwilling to comply with it, but there may be some other local authority or statutory undertaker which would be willing to purchase the land. This may arise where the original adverse planning decision was made because the other authority or undertaker requires the land for its own purposes.

Section 139 of the Town and Country Planning Act 1990

[1141]
Section 139(1) of the TCPA 1990 provides that, where a council receives a purchase notice, it must serve a 'response notice' on the owner who served that purchase notice, stating either:

(*a*) that the council is willing to comply with the purchase notice;
(*b*) that another local authority or statutory undertaker identified in the response notice has agreed to comply with it in their place; or
(*c*) that for reasons specified in the response notice the council is not willing to comply with the purchase notice and that it has not found any other local authority or statutory undertaker who will agree to comply with it in its place, and that it has sent the Secretary of State a copy of the purchase notice and of the response notice.

Such a 'response notice' must be served within three months of the date of service of the purchase notice[1].

1 TCPA 1990, s 139(2).

[1142]
Where the council has served a response notice, stating that it is willing to comply with the purchase notice or that another local authority or statutory undertaker has so agreed, then the body agreeing to comply with the purchase notice is deemed to be authorised to acquire the interest of the owner compulsorily and to have served a notice to treat, in respect of it, on the date of service of the response notice[1]. Following the deemed notice to treat, the server of the purchase notice must make his claim for compensation and the compulsory purchase will follow the normal procedural path. A notice to treat will cease to have effect after three years beginning with the date on which it is served unless[2]:

(*a*) the compensation has been agreed or awarded or has been paid or paid into court;
(*b*) a general vesting declaration has been executed under the Compulsory Purchase (Vesting Declarations) Act 1981, s 4;
(*c*) the acquiring authority have entered on and taken possession of the land specified in the notice; or
(*d*) the question of compensation has been referred to the Upper Tribunal.

1 TCPA 1990, s 139(3). A deemed notice to treat under of the TCPA 1990, s 139(3)(*b*) cannot be withdrawn under the LCA 1961, s 31: see the TCPA 1990, s 139(5).
2 CPA 1965, s 5(2A). This new subsection came into force on 25 September 1991: SI 1991/2067.

[1143]
Where a council proposes to serve a response notice stating that it is not willing to comply with a purchase notice, it must first send to the Secretary of State a copy of the proposed response notice and the purchase notice[1]. Paragraph 27 of Circular 13/83 urges councils to send, to the Secretary of State, the information and documents he requires 'quickly'. Paragraphs 27 and 28 of the circular outline the various documents that the Secretary of State may need to make his decision. Copies of documents sent to the Secretary of State should also be sent to the server of the purchase notice.

1 TCPA 1990, s 139(4). Failure to send a copy of the notice to the Secretary of State under s 139(4) does not, however, amount to a deemed confirmation of the purchase notice at the end of the relevant period: *White v Herefordshire County Council* [2007] EWCA Civ 1204, [2007] All ER (D) 333 (Nov).

4 Action following transmission of the purchase notice to the Secretary of State

[1144]
If the Secretary of State is satisfied that the conditions specified in s 137(3) or (4) are met, in relation to a purchase notice, he must either confirm the notice under s 141(1) of the Act or, if he 'considers it expedient to do so', he may, by s 141(2) of the Act, do the following instead of confirming the notice:

(*a*) in the case of a purchase notice served on account of a refusal of planning permission, grant planning permission for the development in question;
(*b*) in the case of a purchase notice served on account of a planning permission granted on conditions, revoke or amend those conditions so that the

land can be rendered capable of reasonably beneficial use by the carrying out of development;

(*c*) in the case of a purchase notice served on account of a revocation order, cancel the order;

(*d*) in the case of a purchase notice served on account of the modification of planning permission by the imposition of conditions, revoke or amend those conditions, so that the land can be rendered capable of reasonably beneficial use by the carrying out of the development; or

(*e*) in the case of a purchase notice served on account of a discontinuance order, revoke the order or amend the order, so far as is required in order to prevent the land being rendered incapable of reasonably beneficial use.

Furthermore, if the Secretary of State considers that the land could be rendered capable of reasonably beneficial use within a reasonable time by the carrying out of other development for which planning permission ought to be granted, he may, instead of confirming the order, make a direction under s 141(3) that, if a planning application is made for that development, it must be granted[1].

1 TCPA 1990, s 141(3).

[1145]

Before confirming a purchase notice or taking other action under s 141, the Secretary of State must first give notice of his proposed action to the person who served the purchase notice, the council and certain other authorities[1]. Such notice must specify a period of not less than 28 days, during which any of the persons served may require the Secretary of State to give them an opportunity to appear before, and be heard by, a person appointed by the Secretary of State for that purpose[2]. It is usual, in these circumstances, for the Secretary of State to hold a local inquiry, at which the public may attend, rather than a hearing confined to the parties themselves. Although not formally applying to purchase notice inquiries, the Department will normally follow the procedure set out in the Town and Country Planning (Inquiries Procedure) Rules 2000[3], insofar as is appropriate.

1 TCPA 1990, s 140(2).
2 TCPA 1990, s 140(3).
3 SI 2000/1624.

[1146]

If the Secretary of State decides to confirm the purchase notice, he may modify it, either in relation to the whole or any part of the land, by substituting another local authority or statutory undertaker for the council, on whom the notice was served[1]. The Secretary of State may so modify the notice, if it appears to him to be expedient to do so, 'having regard to the probable ultimate use of the land'. Where the Secretary of State confirms a purchase notice under s 141, the authority on which the purchase notice was served or such other authority as may have been substituted, is deemed to be authorised to acquire the interest of the owner compulsorily and to have served a notice to treat in respect of the land on such date as the Secretary of State directs[2].

1 TCPA 1990, s 141(4).
2 TCPA 1990, s 143(1). A deemed notice to treat under the TCPA 1990, s 143(1) cannot be withdrawn under the LCA 1961, s 31: see the TCPA 1990, s 143(8) .

[1147]
There are some fairly tight time limits imposed on the Secretary of State's decision making by the TCPA 1990, s 143(2), (3) failing which, a purchase notice will be confirmed by default. The Secretary of State has a period of either nine months from the date of service of the purchase notice or, if it is earlier, six months from the date when the purchase notice was sent to him, during which, if he neither confirms the notice nor takes such other action as is identified in s 141(2) or (3) nor notifies the owner that he does not propose to confirm the notice, it is deemed to be confirmed[1]. In these circumstances, a notice to treat is deemed to have been served at the end of the nine- or six-month period mentioned above, whichever is the earlier[2].

1 TCPA 1990, s 143(2), (3).
2 TCPA 1990, s 143(2). A deemed notice to treat under the TCPA 1990, s 143(2) cannot be withdrawn under the LCA 1961, s 31: see the TCPA 1990, s 143(8).

[1148]
There is a circumstance, however, in which the Secretary of State is not bound by the time limit identified above. Time does not run for the purposes of s 143(2), if the Secretary of State has before him, at the same time, both a purchase notice and an appeal against refusal of planning permission, an enforcement notice and certain other forms of planning appeal[1]. An outstanding planning appeal will therefore have an effect on the time limit within which the Secretary of State may act under s 143(2) and this may have tactical implications for the server of a purchase notice.

1 TCPA 1990, s 143(4).

[1149]
Once the Secretary of State has issued his decision on a purchase notice, he has no further jurisdiction in the matter and any challenge to his decision is to the High Court under the TCPA 1990, s 288.

5 Power to refuse to confirm a purchase notice where the land has a restricted use by virtue of a previous planning decision

[1150]–[1160]
In the 1960s, a particular problem emerged, with purchase notices being served in respect of open spaces or amenity land within residential developments. On the grant of planning permission for a housing scheme, it was, and, indeed, still is, not unusual for areas of land within or adjoining the development to be reserved as open space or amenity land. In *Adams and Wade Ltd v Minister of Housing and Local Government*[1] the developer of a housing scheme served a purchase notice on the council in respect of such an area of amenity land, comprising a screen of trees alongside an adjoining public road, which had been reserved by a condition attached to the housing permission. The local planning authority rejected the purchase notice, which

was subsequently upheld in the High Court on the grounds that, what is now the TCPA 1990, s 137 clearly applied to the land in its existing state and that there was no statutory provision which permitted amenity benefit to be taken into consideration. The effect of this decision was overruled by what is now the TCPA 1990, s 142[2].

1 (1965) 18 P&CR 60.
2 TCPA 1990, s 142 is the successor to the Town and Country Planning Act 1968, s 32 and, later, of the Town and Country Planning Act 1971, s 184 .

[1161]

Section 142(3) provides that the Secretary of State need not confirm a purchase notice, in respect of land having a 'restricted use by virtue of an existing planning permission', where he considers that, in accordance with that permission, the land ought to remain undeveloped or laid out as amenity land, in relation to the remainder of a larger area for which permission was granted. Section 142(2) defines land as having a 'restricted use by virtue of an existing planning permission', where that land is part of a larger area which has been granted permission, and either:

(*a*) it remains a condition of that permission that the part must remain undeveloped or preserved or laid out as amenity land in relation to the remainder; or
(*b*) the planning permission was granted on an application, which contemplated (expressly or by necessary implication) that the part should not be comprised in the development for which planning permission was sought or should be preserved or laid out as amenity land.

[1162]

It should be noted that s 142 does not prevent the Secretary of State from confirming a purchase notice in relation to 'amenity land', but it does give him a clear discretion not to do so in the circumstances set out in that section. Furthermore, even where a purchase notice is confirmed in relation to 'amenity land', a planning condition restricting the use of that land may have an effect on any compensation to be paid[1].

1 *Birmingham District Council v Morris and Jacombs Ltd* (1976) 33 P&CR 27.

6 Agricultural land

[1163]

Where a notice to treat is deemed to have been served following compliance with, or confirmation of, a purchase notice in respect of part of an agricultural unit, ss 145–147 of the Act make provision for a person, who has a greater interest than as a tenant from year to year of that part, to serve a counter-notice, requiring the council to purchase the 'unaffected area'[1] comprised in the agricultural unit, where that 'unaffected area' is not reasonably capable of being farmed, either by itself or in conjunction with other agricultural land, as a separate agricultural unit.

1 That is, other agricultural land comprised in the same agricultural unit as that to which the purchase notice relates: see TCPA 1990, s 145(1)(*b*).

7 Listed buildings

[1164]
Sections 32–37 of the Planning (Listed Buildings and Conservation Areas) Act 1990 make provision for an 'owner' of a listed building to serve a purchase notice, where consent has been refused in respect of a building or granted, subject to conditions, or is revoked or modified.

[1165]
Sections 32–37 of the Listed Buildings Act are broadly similar in effect to the corresponding sections of the TCPA 1990, although special provision is made in s 32 to permit a purchase notice to be served, in respect of 'any land comprising the building, or contiguous or adjacent to it, and owned with it'[1], where the use of that land is 'substantially inseparable from the building and ought to be treated, together with the building, as a single holding'[2]. Thus, the listed buildings consent application site and the listed buildings purchase notice site need not be identical. Furthermore, by s 35(3), the Secretary of State may not confirm the notice, unless he is satisfied that the 'land'[3] comprises such land contiguous or adjacent to the building as is, in his opinion, required for preserving the building or its amenities or for affording access to it or for its proper control or management.

1 Planning (Listed Buildings and Conservation Areas) Act 1990, s 32(1)(*b*)(i).
2 Planning (Listed Buildings and Conservation Areas) Act 1990, s 32(3).
3 By s 32(5) of the Listed Buildings Act references in ss 33–37 of the Act to the term 'land' are to both the building and the land in respect of which the purchase notice has been served under s 32(1).

[1166]
The time limit for service of a listed buildings purchase notice is the same as for a purchase notice under s 137; that is, 12 months from the date of the decision in respect of which the notice is given or such longer period as the Secretary of State may allow in any particular case[1].

1 Planning (Listed Buildings and Conservation Areas) Regulations 1990, SI 1990/1519, reg 9.

8 Compensation

[1167]
Where a notice to treat is deemed to have been served by an authority, by virtue of ss 139(3) (authority willing to comply with a purchase notice), 143(1) (Secretary of State confirms a purchase notice), or 143(2) (Secretary of State takes no action), then compulsory purchase will proceed in the normal way, including as to the assessment of compensation. By s 5A of the LCA 1961 the valuation date will be the earlier of (a) the date when the acquiring authority enters on and takes possession of the land, and (b) the date when the assessment is made. The rules for the assessment of compensation, generally, are the subject matter of **Division E**, and so are not discussed in detail here. Section 144 of the TCPA 1990 does, however, make special provision in relation to compensation where a compulsory purchase has arisen as a result of a purchase notice. Section 144(1) seeks to avoid double-recovery where

compensation is claimed, as a result of a purchase notice, and also under s 107 of the TCPA 1990, following revocation or modification of planning permission. Section 144(7) makes similar provision where the double-recovery would arise from a claim for compensation under s 115, following a discontinuance order. Section 144(2)–(6), by contrast, establishes a separate right to claim compensation where a purchase notice has not been confirmed, but a direction has been made under s 141(3), requiring planning permission to be granted in the event that an application is made for it[1].

1 The procedure for such a claim is set out in the Town and Country Planning General Regulations 1992, SI 1992/1492, reg 12.

B Blight notices

[1168]
An owner of land may serve a *blight notice* where he has made reasonable endeavours to sell his land but, because of blight caused by planning proposals affecting the land, he has not been able to do so, except at a substantially lower price than might reasonably have been expected.

1 Circumstances in which a blight notice may be served

Section 150 of the Town and Country Planning Act 1990

[1169]
Section 150(1) of the TCPA 1990 provides that:

> 'Where the whole or part of a hereditament or agricultural unit is comprised in blighted land, and a person claims that:
> (*a*) he is entitled to a qualifying interest in that hereditament or unit;
> (*b*) he has made reasonable endeavours to sell that interest or the land falls within paras 21 or 22 (disregarding the notes) of Sch 13 and the powers of compulsory acquisition remain exercisable; and
> (*c*) in consequence of the fact that the hereditament or unit or a part of it was, or was likely to be, comprised in blighted land, he has been unable to sell that interest except at a price substantially lower than that for which it might reasonably have been expected to sell if no part of the hereditament or unit were, or were likely to be, comprised in such land
>
> he may serve on the appropriate authority a notice in the prescribed form requiring that authority to purchase that interest to the extent specified in, and otherwise in accordance with, this Chapter.'

A notice served under s 150 is known as a 'blight notice'[1].

1 TCPA 1990, s 149(5).

[1170]–[1180]
In order to be able to serve a blight notice in respect of land, therefore, a claimant must be able to show that he has a 'qualifying interest' in a 'hereditament or agricultural unit' which has become 'blighted land', that he has

made 'reasonable endeavours to sell' the land and that he has been 'unable to sell', except at a 'price substantially lower' than that which might reasonably have been expected. These concepts are considered below.

[1181]
A blight notice may be served in relation to part of a hereditament or agricultural unit, except where:

(*a*) the claimant is entitled to an interest in the whole of a hereditament or unit and serves the notice in relation to part only of that interest; or
(*b*) the claimant is entitled to an interest in part of a hereditament or unit and serves the notice in relation to less than the whole of that part[1].

1 TCPA 1990, s 150(2), (3).

A qualifying interest in a hereditament or agricultural unit

[1182]
A claimant under s 150 must be entitled to a 'qualifying interest' in the land the subject matter of a blight notice. A 'qualifying interest' is defined[1] in the Act as an interest in the whole or part of:

(*a*) a hereditament the annual value of which does not exceed such amount as may be prescribed[2], where the interest is that of an owner-occupier;
(*b*) a hereditament where the interest is that of a resident owner-occupier of the hereditament; or
(*c*) an agricultural unit where the interest is that of an owner-occupier.

1 TCPA 1990, s 149(2), (3).
2 As of 1 April 2005, the amount prescribed is £29,200 in England (SI 2005/406), and in Wales (SI 2005/367).

[1183]
The term 'hereditament' in the TCPA 1990 is defined as 'a relevant hereditament' within the meaning of the Local Government Finance Act 1988, s 64(4)(*a*)–(*c*) that is, property which can be described as 'lands', 'coal mines' or 'mines of any other description'[1]. An 'agricultural unit' is defined in the TCPA 1990 as land which is occupied as a unit for agricultural purposes, including any dwelling house or other building occupied by the same person for the purpose of farming the land[2]. Certain provisions which relate particularly to agricultural land are considered in paras **[1267]–[1269]**.

1 TCPA 1990, s 171(1). The Local Government Finance Act 1988, s 64(1), defines 'hereditament' as 'anything which, by virtue of the definition of hereditament in s 115(1) of the 1967 Act, would have been a hereditament for the purpose of that Act had this Act not been passed. In the (now repealed) General Rate Act 1967, s 115(1), the term 'hereditament' was defined as 'property which is or may become liable to a rate, being a unit of such property which is, or would fall to be, shown as a separate item in the valuation list'.
2 TCPA 1990, s 171(1).

[1184]
In the case of a hereditament which is shown in a local non-domestic rating list and none of which consists of domestic property or property exempt from local non-domestic rating, the term 'annual value' in s 150 means the value

shown in that list as the rateable value of that hereditament[1]. In the case of a hereditament which is shown in a local non-domestic rating list and which includes domestic property or property exempt from local non-domestic rating, the term 'annual value' means the sum of the value shown in that list as the rateable value of that hereditament and the value certified by the relevant valuation officer under s 171(2) or (3) of the Act[2]. Finally, in the case of any other hereditament, the term 'annual value' in (*a*) above means the value certified by the relevant valuation officer under s 171(2) or (3) of the Act[3].

1 TCPA 1990, s 171(1).
2 TCPA 1990, s 171(1).
3 TCPA 1990, s 171(1).

[1185]
An 'owner-occupier' of a hereditament is a person who has occupied the whole or a substantial part of the hereditament in right of an 'owner's interest' and must have so occupied the hereditament, or that part of it, during the whole of the period of six months ending with the date of service of the blight notice[1]. In circumstances where the whole or a substantial part of the hereditament has, in fact, been unoccupied for a period of not more than 12 months, ending with the date of service of the blight notice, then an 'owner-occupier' is the person who occupied the hereditament, or that part of it, during the whole of a period of six months ending immediately before the period when it was not occupied[2]. A 'resident owner-occupier' of a hereditament is the 'owner-occupier', as described above, of a private dwelling house[3]. An 'owner-occupier' of an agricultural unit must have occupied the whole of it for a similar period as applies in respect of a hereditament, in right of an 'owner's interest' in the whole or part of it[4].

1 TCPA 1990, s 168(1)(*a*). In *Aardvark SRE Ltd v Sedgefield Borough Council* [2008] EWCA Civ 1109, [2009] RVR 93, the Court of Appeal held that an owner was not in occupation and therefore did not have a 'qualifying interest' for the purposes of s 149(2) where the property was let to another party.
2 TCPA 1990, s 168(1)(*b*).
3 TCPA 1990, s 168(3).
4 TCPA 1990, s 168(2).

[1186]
An 'owner's interest', in relation to a hereditament or agricultural unit, means a freehold interest in it or a tenancy of it granted or extended for a term of years certain, not less than three years of which remain unexpired at the date of service of the blight notice[1].

1 TCPA 1990, s 168(4).

Blighted land

[1187]
'Blighted land' is defined in s 149(1) as 'land falling within any paragraph of Sch 13' to the TCPA 1990. The various classes of land identified in Sch 13 are reproduced below and have a common theme in that, in each case, the land is the subject of some public plan or proposal, which is either approved or going through the approval process, and which will ultimately require the

purchase of the land for a public purpose, whether by compulsion or otherwise. It is this threat of purchase for some public purpose which puts off other potential purchasers and thereby blights the land.

[1188]
The classes of 'blighted land' falling within Sch 13 are as follows:

> '**Land allocated for public authority functions in development plans etc.**
> 1A. Land which is identified for the purposes of relevant public functions by a development plan document for the area in which the land is situated.
> 1B. Land in Wales which is identified for the purposes of relevant public functions by a local development plan for the area in which the land is situated.
> . . .
> 5. Land indicated in a plan (other than a development plan) approved by a resolution passed by a local planning authority for the purpose of the exercise of their powers under part III as land which may be required for the purposes of relevant public functions (with the meaning of paragraph 1A or 1B) . . .
> 6. Land in respect of which a local planning authority—
> (*a*) have resolved to take action to safeguard it for development for the purposes of relevant public functions (within the meaning of paragraph 1A or 1B), or
> (*b*) have been directed by the Secretary of State to restrict the grant of planning permission in order to safeguard it for such development.
> **New towns and urban development areas**
> 7. Land within an area described as the site of a proposed new town in the draft of an order in respect of which a notice has been published under paragraph 2 of Schedule 1 to the new Towns Act 1981.
> *Note*
> Land shall cease to be within this paragraph when—
> (*a*) the order comes into operation (whether in the form of the draft or with modifications), or
> (*b*) the Secretary of Sates decides not to make the order.
> 8. Land within an area designated as the site of a proposed new town by an order which has come into operation under section 1 of the New Towns Act 1981.
> 9. Land which is—
> (*a*) within an area intended to be designated as an urban development area by an order which has been made under section 134 of the Local Government, Planning and Land Act 1980 but has not come into effect; or
> (*b*) within an area which has been so designated by an order under that section which has come into effect.
> **Clearance and renewal areas**
> 10. Land within an area declared to be a clearance area by a resolution under section 289 of the Housing Act 1985.
> 11. Land which—
> (*a*) is surrounded by or adjoining an area declared to be a clearance area by a resolution under section 289 of the Housing Act 1985, and

(*b*) is land which a local authority have determined to purchase under section 290 of that Act.

12. Land indicated by information published in pursuance of section 92 of the Local Government and Housing Act 1989 as land which a local authority propose to acquire in exercise of their powers under part VII of that Act (renewal areas).

Highways

13. Land indicated in a development plan (otherwise than by being dealt with in a manner mentioned in paragraph 1A or 1B as—

(*a*) land on which a highway is proposed to be constructed, or

(*b*) land to be included in a highway as proposed to be improved or altered.

14. Land on or adjacent to the line of a highway proposed to be constructed, improved or altered, as indicated in an order or scheme which has come into operation under Part II of the Highways Act 1980 (or under the corresponding provisions of Part II of the Highways Act 1959 or section 1 of the Highways Act 1971), being land in relation to which a power of compulsory acquisition conferred by any of the provisions of Part XII of that Act of 1980 (including a power compulsorily to acquire any right by virtue of section 250) may become exercisable, as being land required for purposes of construction, improvement or alteration as indicated in the order or scheme.

15. Land shown on plans approved by a resolution of a local highway authority as land comprised in the site of a highway as proposed to be constructed, improved or altered by that authority.

16. Land comprised in the site of a highway as proposed to be constructed, improved or altered by the Secretary of State if he has given written notice of the proposal, together with maps or plans sufficient to identify the land in question, to the local planning authority.

17. Land shown on plans approved by a resolution of a local highway authority as land proposed to be acquired by them for the purposes of section 246(1) of the Highways Act 1980.

18. Land shown in a written notice given by the Secretary of State to the local planning authority as land proposed to be acquired by him for the purposes of section 246(1) of the Highways Act 19890 in connection with a highway which he proposes to provide.

New streets

19. Land which—

(*a*) either—

  (i) is within the outer lines prescribed by an order under section 188 of the Highways Act 1980 (orders prescribing minimum width of new streets) or section 159 of the Highways Act 1959 (which is the predecessor of that section); or

  (ii) has a frontage to a highway declared to be a new street by an order under section 30 of the Public Health Act 1925 and lies within the minimum width of the street prescribed by any byelaws or local Act applicable by virtue of the orders; and

(*b*) is, or is part of—

  (i) a dwelling erected before, or under construction on, the date on which the order is made; or

  (ii) the cartilage of any such dwelling.

General improvement areas

20. Land indicated by information published in pursuance of section 257 of the Housing Act 1985 as land which a local authority propose to acquire in the exercise of their powers under the provisions of Part VIII of that Act relating to general improvement areas.

Compulsory purchase

21. Land authorised by a special enactment to be compulsorily acquired, or land falling within the limits of deviation within which powers of compulsory acquisition conferred by a special enactment are exercisable.

22. Land in respect of which—

(*a*) a compulsory purchase order is in force; or

(*b*) there is in force a compulsory purchase order providing for the acquisition of a right or rights over that land;

And the appropriate authority have power to serve, but have not served, notice to treat in respect of the land or, as the case may be, the right or rights.

23. Land—

(*a*) the compulsory acquisition of which is authorised by an order under section 1 or 3 of the Transport and works Act 1992, or

(*b*) which falls within the limits of deviation within which powers of compulsory acquisition conferred by such an order are exercisable, or

(*c*) which is the subject of a proposal, contained in an application made in accordance with rules under section 6 of that Act or in a draft order prepared under section 7(3) of that Act, that it should be such land.

24. Land falls within this paragraph if—

(*a*) the compulsory acquisition of the land is authorised by an order granting development consent, or

(*b*) the land falls within the limits of deviation within which powers of compulsory acquisition conferred by an order granting development consent are exercisable, or

(*c*) an application for an order granting development consent seeks authority to compulsorily acquire the land.

Land identified in national policy statements

25. Land falls within this paragraph if the land is in a location identified in a national policy statement as suitable (or potentially suitable) for a specified description of a development.'

[1189]

The Schedule also contains notes, not reproduced above, which clarify some of the paragraphs. The notes to paras 1–4 of the Schedule are important in making it clear that development plans do not have to have gone through all their statutory procedures in order to fall within Sch 13 and that land, which is subject to proposals for the alteration or replacement of a development plan, may be 'blighted' within the meaning of the Act. In the case of Sch 13, para 1, for example, the reference to a structure plan would include proposals for the alteration or replacement of a structure plan, provided that they had been made available for inspection under the TCPA 1990, s 33(2). Thus, there may still be some early stages of a development plan which are not sufficient to found a blight notice.

[1190]–[1200]
The Lands Tribunal has held that a non-statutory 'Central Area Map' is not a development plan for the purposes of Sch 13 and will not therefore found a valid blight notice, notwithstanding that it might cause genuine planning blight to properties within its area[1]. Similarly, in another case, it was held that a claimant could not rely on a plan which had been drawn up by the borough engineer, outside his delegated powers, and which was not officially approved by the council itself[2].

1 *Comley and Comley v Kent County Council* (1977) 34 P&CR 218.
2 *Page v Gillingham Corpn* (1970) 21 P&CR 973.

[1201]
In *Bolton Corpn v Owen*[1] the House of Lords held that land is not 'allocated' in a development plan for the purposes of the predecessor of para 2 above, just because it is listed in the plan as an area to be redeveloped. For the land to be 'allocated' within the meaning of paras 2 or 4 of the Schedule, it must be clear that it is the authority which is to carry out the redevelopment, if necessary using its compulsory purchase powers, and not private enterprise. If the matter is left open, then the claimant will not have discharged the onus of proof that the site falls within Sch 13. Furthermore, the House of Lords in the *Bolton* case also made it clear that it was not open to the Lands Tribunal to 'speculate' upon the probability that an area would be redeveloped by the authority in the exercise of its powers, rather than by private enterprise. This decision was followed and applied in the more recent Lands Tribunal case of *Elcock and Elcock v Newham London Borough Council*[2]. In *Titterell v Tunbridge Wells BC*[3] the Court of Appeal held that the designation of land as green belt did not bring it within the provisions of Sch 13, as it was not required for the purpose of the exercise of the functions of a government department or local authority. In *Halliday v Secretary of State for Transport*[4] the Lands Tribunal formed the view that Sch 13 does not extend to cover blight caused by the issue of a central government consultation document on options for airport expansion. The Tribunal did observe, however, that Art 8 of the European Convention on Human Rights and Art 1 of the First Protocol to the Convention might be engaged in a suitable case and that this could give rise to a finding that blight did fall within the 1990 Act.

1 [1962] 1 QB 470.
2 (1996) 71 P&CR 575.
3 (1996) 74 P&CR 337.
4 [2003] RVR 12.

[1202]
A blight notice may be successful, even when a road proposal is only shown diagrammatically on a development plan. In *Williams v Cheadle and Gately UDC*[1], the Lands Tribunal, considering a predecessor of Sch 13, para 13, held that a road proposal represented diagrammatically on a development plan was not 'some wild surmise or insubstantial dream, but a proposal which on the evidence before me amounts to a virtual certainty' and was, therefore, 'indicated' on a development plan[2].

1 (1966) 17 P&CR 153.
2 See also *Mercer v Manchester Corpn* (1964) 15 P&CR 321.

[1203]
A resolution authorising an authority to make a compulsory purchase order, in respect of land, is not enough to bring that land within para 22(*a*) of Sch 13[1]. The words 'a compulsory purchase order is in force' in para 22(*a*) means an order which has been made by the acquiring authority, confirmed by the confirming authority and has come into force.

1 *Jones Son & Vernon v Sandwell MBC* (1994) 68 P&CR 563.

Reasonable endeavours to sell

[1204]
Unless the land falls within paras 21 or 22 of Sch 13 (land subject to compulsory purchase), a claimant under s 150 must make 'reasonable endeavours' to sell his interest in the land. Land which does fall within paras 21 or 22 is relieved of this requirement by virtue of s 150(1)(b). Thus, where a compulsory purchase order is in force and the acquiring authority have power to serve, but have not served, a notice to treat, a person entitled to serve a blight notice need no longer show that he has made 'reasonable endeavours' to sell. Where a claimant does have to show 'reasonable endeavours' to sell his interest in the land, however, this means making a genuine effort to sell by putting it on the market. The Lands Tribunal has held that it is not essential to use an estate agent to market the property and, in certain circumstances, a public notice at the property itself may be sufficient[1]. A claimant may not, however, simply take professional advice as to the outcome if he were to try to sell his interest[2]. A claimant who informs a potential purchaser of the prospect of compulsory purchase, but does not disclose that the local authority has made it clear that it has no intention of acquiring the land, does not make reasonable endeavours to sell[3].

1 *Lade and Lade v Brighton Corpn* (1971) 22 P&CR 737. However, see also *WA Whyle v Walsall MBC* (30 September 1996, unreported, Ref 132/95) where a 'For Sale' notice at the property for two months was held to be insufficient. NB where an estate agent or property development business markets an interest in land, that agent or business will be required by the Property Misdescriptions Act 1991 to disclose to a purchaser, inter alia, the 'existence or nature of any planning permission or proposals for development, construction or change of use' (see the Property Misdescriptions (Specified Matters) Order 1992, SI 1992/2834, Sch, para 26), which would appear to cover the proposals of an acquiring authority possessing compulsory purchase powers.
2 *Perkins v West Wiltshire District Council* (1976) 31 P&CR 427.
3 *Glodwick Mutual Insurance and Social Club v Oldham MBC* [1979] RVR 197.

Unable to sell except at a price substantially lower than that which might reasonably have been expected

[1205]
Whether a claimant is unable to sell an interest in land, except at 'a price substantially lower' than that for which it might reasonably have been expected to sell if no part of it had been blighted, is essentially a matter of judgment for the Upper Tribunal. In *Stubbs v West Hartlepool Corpn*[1], for example, the Lands Tribunal held that a lack of offers and of response (apart

from inspections) to advertisements was evidence of a practical disappearance of the market for the land and satisfied the expression 'unable to sell except at a price substantially lower than that for which might it might reasonably have been expected to sell'.

1 (1961) 12 P&CR 365.

[1206]
It is important to note that s 150 does not say that the claimant should have made reasonable endeavours to sell the hereditament or agricultural unit at a substantially lower figure than that at which it was reasonably expected to sell[1]. The requirement is, rather, that the claimant has made reasonable endeavours to sell, but has been unable to do so, except at a price substantially lower than that which might reasonably have been expected.

1 *Stubbs v West Hartlepool Corpn* (1961) 12 P&CR 365.

2 Drafting and serving a blight notice

[1207]
Section 150 requires a blight notice to be served on 'the appropriate authority' in the 'prescribed form'. The 'appropriate authority', for the purpose of a blight notice, is defined by s 169 of the Act as the government department, local authority, National Park authority or any other body or person by whom, under Sch 13, the land is liable to be acquired. The Secretary of State has the power to decide whether the appropriate authority, in relation to any land, is the Secretary of State or a local highway authority or is one of two or more local highway authorities or is one of two or more local authorities[1]. The Secretary of State's decision on such matters is final. It is possible that more than one authority may be 'the appropriate authority', in respect of blighted land. In such circumstances, a blight notice should be served on each such authority[2].

1 TCPA 1990, s 169(2).
2 *R v Secretary of State for the Environment, Dorset County Council and Saunders, ex p Bournemouth Borough Council* [1987] JPL 357.

[1208]
The 'prescribed form', for the purpose of s 150, is that set out at the Town and Country Planning General Regulations 1992, Sch 2 or a form substantially to the like effect[1]. A blight notice should be carefully drafted to refer to the correct paragraphs of Sch 13 as there is no express power to amend such a notice once served, although the Lands Tribunal has allowed amendment by agreement with the appropriate authority[2]. A blight notice should be served in the manner set out in the TCPA 1990, s 329 and may be withdrawn under s 156 of the Act[3].

1 SI 1992/1492, reg 16, Sch 2.
2 See *Smith v Somerset County Council* (1966) 17 P & CR 162. See also *Gennard v Bridgnorth District Council* [2005] RVR 275 for a discussion of the effects of a defect in a blight notice.
3 See para **[1266]**.

[1209]
Special provision is made in relation to blight notices and personal representatives, mortgagees and partnerships[1].

1 TCPA 1990, ss 161–164.

[1209.1]
It now seems reasonably well settled that the sale of the claimant's interests in a property the subject of a blight notice will constitute a deemed withdrawal of that blight notice[1].

1 See *Carrel v London Underground Ltd* [1996] 1 EGLR 179, *Bennet v Wakefield MBC* [1997] RVR 32.

3 Action following service of a blight notice on an 'appropriate authority'

Objecting to a blight notice

[1210]–[1220]
An authority may object to a blight notice served upon it by serving a 'counter-notice' under the TCPA 1990, s 151. A counter-notice must be served within two months, beginning with the date of service of the blight notice[1] and be in the form prescribed[2]. Again, as with a blight notice, a counter-notice should be served in the manner set out in the TCPA 1990, s 329[3].

1 TCPA 1990, s 151(2).
2 Town and Country Planning General Regulations 1992, SI 1992/1492, reg 16, Sch 2.
3 For a decision on alleged defects in a counter-notice, see *Head v Eastbourne Borough Council* [2009] UKUT 271 (LC), [2010] RVR 83.

[1221]
Where a counter-notice has been served under s 151 objecting to a blight notice, the claimant may require the objection to be referred to the Upper Tribunal[1]. If no objection is made to a blight notice within the two-month period or if any objection is made and then withdrawn or if an objection is made but not upheld by the Lands Tribunal, the authority is authorised to compulsorily acquire the claimant's interest and is deemed to have served a notice to treat[2]. A notice of treat which is deemed to have been served in these circumstances may not be withdrawn under the LCA 1961, s 31[3]. By the CPA 1965, s 5(2A)[4], however, where land has become blighted after 25 September 1991, a notice to treat will cease to have effect at the end of the period of three years following service, unless compensation has been agreed or awarded, a general vesting declaration has been executed, the acquiring authority have entered and taken possession of the land or the question of compensation has been referred to the Upper Tribunal.

1 TCPA 1990, s 153(1).
2 TCPA 1990, s 154(2).
3 TCPA 1990, s 167.
4 As amended by the Planning and Compensation Act 1991, s 67.

[1222]
It is vital that any counter-notice is properly drafted and contains all the grounds upon which the authority may wish to object. The House of Lords,

in *Essex County Council v Essex Incorporated Congregational Church Union*[1], held that the Lands Tribunal did not have jurisdiction to consider an objection which had not been specified in an authority's counter-notice and, indeed, that such jurisdiction could not be conferred on the tribunal by the consent of the parties. Furthermore, the Lands Tribunal has held that it is not open to an authority to change its ground of objection, in order to argue that it does not propose to acquire the land, notwithstanding the abandonment of the proposals underlying the blight notice[2]. The Lands Tribunal has held, however, that a single counter-notice may be a valid response to three blight notices[3].

1 [1963] AC 808, 14 P&CR 237. See also *Binns v Secretary of State for Transport* (1985) 50 P&CR 468.
2 *Burn v North Yorkshire County Council* (1991) 63 P&CR 81.
3 *Machin and Machin v Devon County Council* [2007] RVR 81.

The grounds on which objection may be made

[1223]
A counter-notice must specify which one or more of the grounds set out in s 151(4) of the Act, the authority relies upon for its objection to the blight notice[1]. The grounds are as follows:

(*a*) that no part of the hereditament or agricultural unit to which the notice relates is comprised in blighted land;
(*b*) that the appropriate authority does not propose to acquire any part of the hereditament or, in the case of an agricultural unit, any part of the affected area in the exercise of relevant powers, unless forced to do so under the blight notice;
(*c*) that the appropriate authority proposes to acquire a part of the hereditament or, in the case of the agricultural unit, part of the affected area specified in the counter-notice, but does not propose to acquire any other part of the hereditament or area, unless forced to do so under the blight notice;
(*d*) in the case of any land falling within paras 1, 3 or 13 but not 14,15 or 16 of Sch 13, that the appropriate authority does not propose to acquire any part of the hereditament or, in the case of the agricultural unit, any part of the affected area, during the period of 15 years from the date of the counter-notice, or such longer period as may be specified in that notice, unless forced to do so under the blight notice;
(*e*) that, on the date of service of the blight notice, the claimant was not entitled to an interest in any part of the hereditament or agricultural unit to which the notice relates;
(*f*) that, for reasons specified in the counter-notice, the interest of the claimant is not a qualifying interest; and
(*g*) that the conditions specified in paras (*b*) and (*c*) of s 150(1) are not satisfied, that is, that the claimant has made reasonable endeavours to sell and has not been able to sell, except at a price substantially lower than that for which the hereditament or agricultural unit might reasonably have been expected to sell, if no part of it were blighted land.

1 TCPA 1990, s 151(3).

[1224]

Where an authority have served a counter-notice, objecting to a blight notice which was served in respect of proposals for the alteration or replacement of a development plan and that plan comes into force, the authority may, within two months of the plan coming into force, serve a second counter-notice on the claimant, in substitution for the first, specifying different grounds of objection[1].

1 TCPA 1990, s 152.

[1225]

The Court of Appeal held, in *Mancini v Coventry City Council*[1], that the date for determining an authority's intention to acquire the land the subject matter of a blight notice was not the date of the blight notice, but the date of the counter-notice[2]. This may give an appropriate authority an opportunity to revise its plans in circumstances where it does not wish to purchase blighted land. Purchase LJ also went on to say in that decision that 'Nothing in this judgment should be taken to exclude the possibility of contending, in an appropriate case, that the material date might even be postponed to the date of the hearing by the Tribunal.'[3] This possibility was rejected by the Lands Tribunal in *Sinclair v Secretary of State for Transport*[4] in relation to a counter-notice objecting on ground (*a*), although, in *Elcock and Elcock v Newham London Borough Council*[5], the tribunal held that, in order to test the *fides* of an objection under ground (*a*), they could look at subsequent events as an indication of weight to be attached to the grounds contained in the counter-notice.

1 (1985) 49 P&CR 127.
2 See also *Charman v Dorset County Council* (1986) 52 P&CR 88.
3 (1985) 49 P&CR 127 at 141. See also *Kayworth v Highways Agency* (1996) 72 P&CR 433.
4 (1997) 75 P&CR 548.
5 (1996) 71 P&CR 575.

Ground (*a*)

[1226]

This is the relevant ground where the authority consider that the hereditament or agricultural unit does not come within any of the 23 categories of blighted land identified in Sch 13 to the Act[1]. Where this ground is specified in the counter-notice, it is for the claimant to establish that the hereditament or unit, or a part of it, is comprised of blighted land[2]. Where ground (*a*) is advanced by the authority, it is often advisable to include ground (*b*) also, that is, that the authority does not intend to purchase the hereditament or unit.

1 For examples of Lands Tribunal' decisions under this ground of objection see *Jones v Greater Manchester Passenger Transport Executive* [1998] 3 EGLR 121, *Sinclair v Secretary of State for Transport* (1997) 75 P&CR 548, 34 Estates Gazette 92.
2 TCPA 1990, s 153(3), (4).

Ground (*b*)

[1227]

Under this ground, the appropriate authority may object to a blight notice, where they do not intend to purchase any part of the hereditament or 'affected area' of an agricultural unit. For a discussion of what is a 'hereditament' for the purposes of this ground of objection see *Norman v Department of Transport*[1]. Section 171(1) of the TCPA 1990 defines 'the affected area' as so much of an agricultural unit as, on the date of service of the blight notice, consists of land falling within any paragraph of Sch 13 to the Act. It is for the appropriate authority to establish this ground of objection[2] and the evidence of the authority's intention must be clear and unequivocal. The Upper Tribunal will dismiss an objection under this ground, unless it is satisfied that the authority's actions are an effective protection against 'blight'[3]. Furthermore, the Upper Tribunal will examine carefully an authority's intentions, in relation to a hereditament or area the subject matter of a blight notice, and, even if a compulsory purchase order in respect of the land has been revoked, the tribunal will want to know whether there is 'a very real possibility that the council still hankers after obtaining the claimant's [land]'[4]. Where an authority's intentions not to acquire the hereditament or area are real, but not permanent, the authority may be able to take advantage of ground (*d*), that is, that the authority does not propose to acquire for a period of 15 years.

1 (1996) 72 P&CR 210, 24 Estates Gazette 150.
2 TCPA 1990, s 153(3), (4).
3 *Sabey v Hartlepool County Borough Council* (1970) 21 P&CR 448. See also *Glodwick Mutual Insurance and Social Club v Oldham MBC* [1979] RVR 197.
4 *Louisville Investments Ltd v Basingstoke District Council* (1976) 32 P&CR 419.

[1228]
Where an authority is successful under this ground, any compulsory purchase order which it may have made in respect of the land or any special enactment authorising the compulsory purchase of the land within the TCPA 1990, Sch 13, para 21 will cease to have effect[1].

1 TCPA 1990, s 155(1), (2).

Ground (*c*)

[1229]
This ground allows an authority to object to a blight notice on the basis that, although it proposes to acquire a part of the hereditament or 'affected area' under its statutory powers, it does not propose to acquire any other part under those powers. Once again, the onus of establishing this ground of objection is on the authority[1]. If the Upper Tribunal upholds an objection on ground (*c*) alone, it will declare the blight notice valid in respect of that part of the hereditament or area which the authority specified in its counter-notice that it was proposing to acquire, but not in respect of any other part of the hereditament or area.

1 TCPA 1990, s 153(3), (4).

[1230]–[1240]
Section 166 of the Act provides that ground (*c*) does not affect a claimant's right to require an authority to acquire all of the hereditament or 'affected area' under the CPA 1965, s 8. Furthermore, the section also requires the

Upper Tribunal, in determining an objection under ground (*c*), to consider whether, in the case of 'house, building or manufactory', the part proposed to be acquired can be taken without 'material detriment' to the 'house, building or manufactory' or, in the case of a 'park or garden belonging to a house', the part proposed to be acquired can be taken without 'seriously affecting the amenity or convenience' of the house[1]. In *Hurley v Cheshire County Council*[2], the Lands Tribunal held, somewhat tentatively, that, in order to succeed under ground (*c*), the onus was on the authority to show that the required part of a garden could be taken without seriously affecting the amenity or convenience of the house.

1 See, eg, the Lands Tribunal's consideration of these issues in *Smith and Smith v Kent County Council* (1995) 70 P&CR 669, 44 Estates Gazette 141; *Blyth v Humberside County Council* (1996) 73 P&CR 213, Lands Tribunal; *Edwards and Edwards v Surrey County Council* [1999] RVR 223, Lands Tribunal.

2 (1976) 31 P&CR 433. See also *Burns v Sandwell Metropolitan Borough Council* [1998] RVR 97, Lands Tribunal.

Ground (*d*)

[1241]
Under this ground, an authority may object to a blight notice, where it does not propose to acquire any part of the hereditament or 'affected area' during the period of 15 years from the date of the counter-notice, or such longer period as may be specified in the counter-notice. Once again, the burden is on the authority to establish this ground of objection[1]. This ground only applies in the case of blight falling within paras 1, 3 or 13, but not 14, 15 or 16 of Sch 13 to the TCPA 1990. This ground will often be most applicable where an authority's proposals are, as yet, vague and long term, such as may be the case in a structure plan or Pt I of a unitary development plan.

1 TCPA 1990, s 153(3), (4).

[1242]
An authority may not object on ground (*d*) if it does not propose to acquire the hereditament or area at all and could, therefore, object on ground (*b*)[1]. An authority may, however, now rely on ground (*c*) (not proposing to acquire the whole) and ground (*d*), although, at one time, this was not the case[2].

1 TCPA 1990, s 151(6).

2 *Parker and Parker v West Midlands County Council* (1979) 38 P&CR 720.

[1243]
A claimant may be able to renew the 15-year period from time to time, by serving a further blight notice, to which the authority, if they wish to rely on ground (*d*), will again have to respond by a fresh counter-notice disclaiming any intention to acquire within 15 years. A counter-notice upheld on ground (*d*) does not prevent an authority from compulsorily acquiring the hereditament or 'affected area' within the 15-year period, but it does make it more difficult. The Secretary of State has given an assurance that very great weight will be given to a counter-notice upheld on ground (*d*), if a compulsory purchase order is subsequently brought before him for confirmation[1].

1 See HC Debates Standing Committee G, 28 March 1968, col 729.

Ground (*e*)

[1244]
This ground allows the authority to challenge the claimant's *locus standi* to serve the blight notice on the basis that he is not entitled to an interest in any part of the hereditament or agricultural unit. If the authority objects to the blight notice on this ground, it will be for the claimant to establish that he is entitled to an interest in the hereditament or unit and, thus, to establish his *locus standi*[1].

1 TCPA 1990, s 153(3), (4).

Ground (*f*)

[1245]
This ground, again, allows the authority to challenge the claimant's *locus standi* to serve the blight notice, this time on the basis that, although he has an interest in the hereditament or agricultural unit, it is not a 'qualifying interest'[1]. Again, the onus will be on the claimant to establish his *locus standi*, if this ground of objection is raised by the authority[2].

1 See paras **[1182]–[1186]**.
2 TCPA 1990, s 153(3), (4).

Ground (*g*)

[1246]
This ground of objection allows the authority to argue:

(*a*) that the claimant has not made reasonable endeavours to sell his interest in the hereditament or agricultural unit;
(*b*) that he was not unable to sell his interest in the hereditament or unit, as a consequence of the hereditament or unit being comprised in blighted land; and/or
(*c*) that the price at which he could have sold his interest in the hereditament or unit was not substantially lower than that for which it might reasonably have been expected to sell it, if it was not comprised in blighted land.

The onus will be on the claimant to establish that he has complied with paras (*b*) and (*c*) of s 150(1), if this ground of objection is raised by the authority[1]. This issues surrounding this ground of objection are discussed in paras **[1204]–[1206]**.

1 TCPA 1990, s 153(3), (4).

Grounds not included within section 151(4)

[1247]
Section 151(4) does not include any ground which allows an authority to argue that it is not the 'appropriate authority', in relation to the blight notice, although s 169(2) does allow such a question to be 'referred' to the Secretary

of State for determination. There is no set procedure provided by statute under which such a question is to be referred to the Secretary of State, and it is suggested, therefore, that the claimant or the authority simply to write to the Secretary of State, asking him to determine the question. Where a question has been referred to the Secretary of State under s 169(2), the two-month time limit, during which the authority may serve a counter-notice, is suspended until the Secretary of State has determined the question, as are certain other time limits[1]. An authority claiming that it is not the 'appropriate authority' for the purposes a blight notice may also be well advised, on a without prejudice basis, to serve a counter-notice under ground (*b*) at least, objecting that it does not propose to acquire any part of the hereditament or 'affected area'[2].

1 TCPA 1990, s 169(3).
2 See *Church of Scotland General Trustees v Helensburgh Council* (1973) 25 P&CR 105.

[1248]
In *Binns v Secretary of State for Transport*[1], the Lands Tribunal held that it had no jurisdiction to consider a defect in a blight notice. The reasoning behind this decision appears to be that an 'appropriate authority' has no power to object on a ground which is not specified in s 151(4) of the Act and that, based on the decision in the *Essex* case[2], the Lands Tribunal has no jurisdiction to consider a point not specified in a counter-notice, even if it is well founded. Unfortunately, the courts have not indicated what an authority should do in these circumstances and the law in this area remains unsatisfactory.

1 (1985) 50 P&CR 468.
2 *Essex County Council v Essex Incorporated Congregational Church Union* (1963) 14 P&CR 237.

4 Reference of objection to the Upper Tribunal

[1249]
Where a counter-notice has been served under s 151, objecting to a blight notice, the claimant may require the objection to be referred to the Upper Tribunal[1]. Such a reference must, however, be made before the end of two months beginning with the date of the counter-notice[2].

1 TCPA 1990, s 153(1).
2 TCPA 1990, s 153(2).

[1250]–[1260]
It is important to understand the jurisdiction of the Upper Tribunal when considering a reference under s 151. Section 153(3), (4) and (5) provide as follows:

> '(3) On any such reference, if the objection is not withdrawn, the Lands Tribunal shall consider–
> (*a*) the matters set out in the notice served by the claimant, and
> (*b*) the grounds of objection specified in the counter-notice;
> and subject to subsection (4), unless it is shown to the satisfaction of the Tribunal that the objection is not well-founded, the Tribunal shall uphold the objection.

(4) An objection on the grounds mentioned in section 151(4)(*b*), (*c*) or (*d*) shall not be upheld by the Tribunal unless it is shown to the satisfaction of the Tribunal that the objection is well-founded.

(5) If the Tribunal determines not to uphold the objection, the Tribunal shall declare that the notice to which the counter-notice relates is a valid notice.'

[1261]
It can be seen that the Upper Tribunal is confined to consider the matters set out in the blight notice and the grounds of objection specified in the counter-notice. In *Essex County Council v Essex Incorporated Congregational Church Union*[1] the House of Lords held that the Lands Tribunal did not have jurisdiction to consider an objection which had not been specified in an authority's counter-notice and that such jurisdiction could not be conferred by the consent of the parties. Thus, if an authority fail to specify a valid ground of objection, even if one is available, then the blight notice should be upheld[2]. This, together with the inability of an authority to change its ground of objection, makes it very important that any counter-notice is properly drafted[3]. There is, similarly, no express power in the Act for a claimant to amend his blight notice, although, in this case, the Lands Tribunal allowed amendments to be made to such a notice, with the consent of the authority[4].

1 (1963) 14 P&CR 237. See also *Binns v Secretary of State for Transport* (1985) 50 P&CR 468.
2 See also *Lockers Estates (Holdings) Ltd v Oadby UDC* (1970) 21 P&CR 836.
3 *Burn v North Yorkshire County Council* (1991) 63 P&CR 81.
4 *Smith v Somerset County Council* (1966) 17 P&CR 162.

[1262]
Section 153(4) makes it clear that the grounds of objection mentioned in s 151(4)(*b*), (*c*) or (*d*), will not be upheld, unless the tribunal is satisfied that the objection is well founded. In other words, the onus will be in the authority to establish its case. The onus is on the authority in these three grounds of objection because they all relate to matters where the future intentions of the authority are paramount, so that: in relation to ground (*b*), the authority objects on the basis that it does not propose to acquire the hereditament or 'affected area'; in relation to ground (*c*), the authority objects on the basis that it does not propose to acquire all of the hereditament or 'affected area' and, in relation to ground (*d*), the authority objects on the basis that it does not propose to acquire the hereditament or 'affected area' within the next 15 years.

[1263]
By virtue of s 153(3), the remaining grounds of objection (grounds (*a*), (*e*), (*f*) and (*g*)) will be upheld, unless the Upper Tribunal is satisfied that the objection is not well-founded. In other words, it will be for the claimant to establish his case. Thus, the claimant will have to show that: in the case of ground (*a*), that his hereditament or agricultural unit is blighted land within the meaning of Sch 13; in the case of ground (*e*), that he is entitled to an interest in the hereditament or agricultural unit; in the case of ground (*f*), that his interest is a qualifying interest and; in relation to ground (*g*), that he has made reasonable endeavours to sell, but has been unable to sell, except at a

price substantially lower than that for which it might reasonably have been expected to sell.

[1264]
In determining a reference under s 153, the Upper Tribunal may not consider hardship caused to the claimant and the alleviation of that hardship, as these are irrelevant to the question of the validity of an objection in a counter-notice[1].

1 *Mancini v Coventry City Council* (1985) 49 P&CR 127. See also *McDermott and McDermott v Department of Transport* (1984) 48 P&CR 351.

[1265]
It can be seen from s 153(5) above, that, if the tribunal does not uphold the authority's objection, then it must declare the blight notice to be valid. Where a blight notice is upheld by the tribunal, the authority is deemed to be authorised to compulsorily acquire the interest of the claimant in the hereditament or agricultural unit and to have served a notice to treat in respect of it[1] on a date specified in a direction given by the tribunal[2]. Where a notice to treat is deemed to have been served in circumstances where there was no objection to the blight notice or any such objection was withdrawn, then the notice to treat is deemed to have been served two months after the date of service of the blight notice[3].

1 TCPA 1990, s 154(2).
2 TCPA 1990, s 154(3)(*a*).
3 TCPA 1990, s 154(3)(*b*).

[1266]
By s 156 of the Act, a claimant may withdraw a blight notice at any time before compensation has been determined by the Upper Tribunal or, if compensation has been determined, before the end of six weeks, beginning with the date of determination, providing, that is, that the authority has not already exercised its right of entering and taking possession of the land in pursuance of its deemed notice to treat. This provision allows a claimant to 'change his mind' after learning what compensation the Upper Tribunal has awarded. Where a blight notice is withdrawn under this section, any deemed notice to treat served in consequence of the blight notice will be deemed to have been withdrawn and no compensation will be payable.

5 Agricultural land

[1267]
Section 158 of the Act makes special provision, where a claimant serves a blight notice in respect of an interest in the whole or part of an agricultural unit and, on the date of service of the notice, the unit or part contains land which is not blighted, known as 'the unaffected area', as well as land which is blighted, known as 'the affected area'. In these circumstances, a claimant may include in his blight notice:

(*a*) a claim that the 'unaffected area' is not reasonably capable of being farmed as a separate agricultural unit, either by itself or in conjunction with other land in the unit or together with other land occupied by the claimant in which he has an 'owner's interest'[1]; and

(*b*) a requirement that the authority purchase his interest in the whole of the unit or, as the case may be, in the whole of the part of it to which the notice relates.

1 See the TCPA 1990, s 168(4).

[1268]

Where a blight notice includes a claim that the 'affected area' is not capable of being farmed as a separate agricultural unit and requires the authority to acquire the 'unaffected area', an authority may serve a counter-notice under s 159(1), objecting that the claim is not 'justified'[1]. In other words, the authority may argue that the land is capable of being farmed, either by itself or together with other land occupied by the claimant. Furthermore, where a blight notice includes a claim under s 158, an authority must object on this ground if it also wishes to object on ground (*c*) of s 151(4), that is, that it intends to acquire a part of the affected area but not any other part[2]. Indeed, the Upper Tribunal may not uphold an objection on ground (*c*), unless it also uphold an objection under s 159(1)[3].

1 TCPA 1990, s 159(1).
2 TCPA 1990, s 159(2).
3 TCPA 1990, s 159(3).

[1269]

Where the Upper Tribunal upholds an objection, in relation to the ground of objection mentioned in s 159(1), but no other, then it must declare the blight notice valid in relation to the 'affected area', but not the 'unaffected area'[1]. Where the Upper Tribunal upholds an objection, in relation to the ground of objection mentioned in s 159(1) and in relation to ground (*c*) of s 151(4), but no other, then it must declare the blight notice valid only in relation to the part of the affected area specified in the counter-notice[2].

1 TCPA 1990, s 159(5).
2 TCPA 1990, s 159(6).

6 Effect of a blight notice and compensation

[1270]

A blight notice will become effective where either:

(a) no counter-notice objecting to the blight notice has been served in accordance with the Act; or

(b) where such a notice has been served, the objection has been withdrawn or, on a reference to the Upper Tribunal, is not upheld by the tribunal[1].

1 TCPA 1990, s 154(1).

[1271]

Where a blight notice has become effective the authority against whom it has become effective is deemed to be authorised to compulsorily acquire the interest of the claimant and to have served a notice to treat in respect of it[1].

The deemed notice to treat will be taken to have been served either at a date specified in directions given by the Upper Tribunal, where the matter has been referred to the tribunal and any objection not upheld, or, in any other case, at the end of two months starting with the date of service of the blight notice[2].

1 TCPA 1990, s 154(2).
2 TCPA 1990, s 154(3).

[1272]
Specific provision is also made for the effect of a blight notice where the claimant, without referring the matter to the Upper Tribunal, accepts the objection of an authority under ground (c) above, that it intends only to acquire part of the land included in that notice[1].

1 TCPA 1990, s 154(4)-(6).

[1273]
Section 155(1) and (2) of the TCPA 1990 deals with the effect on the powers of compulsory acquisition where an authority has successfully objected to a blight notice under grounds (b) or (d) above, that is, disclaiming any intention to acquire or disclaiming any intention to acquire for 15 years. In short, where land is included in a compulsory purchase order in circumstances where the authority has successfully objected to a blight notice under grounds (b) or (d) above, the powers conferred by that order shall cease to have effect[1].

1 TCPA 1990, s 155(1) and (2).

[1274]
Section 155(3) and (4) of the TCPA 1990 makes provision for the effect of a blight notice where the authority has successfully objected to that notice under ground (c), that is, that it intends to acquire part only of the land. In such circumstances, a compulsory purchase order will cease to have effect in respect of any land other than that which the authority has indicated it intends to acquire.

[1275]
A person may withdraw a blight notice in the circumstances set out in s 156, subject to the appropriate authority not having exercised a right to enter and take possession in pursuance of a deemed notice to treat.

[1276]–[1600]
Compensation for compulsory acquisition pursuant to a blight notice is assessed in accordance with the normal rules, subject to the TCPA 1990, ss 157–160. Any dispute as to compensation is referred to the Upper Tribunal for determination.

Division C

Compulsory purchase orders and procedure

Contents

References in bold are to paragraph numbers.

Chapter 3 Acquisition by a ministerial authority

Chapter 6 Challenging a compulsory purchase order

Chapter 7 Transport and Works Act 1992

Chapter 8 Development consent and the Planning Act 2008

Chapter 1

Introduction

[1]

This Division describes the procedures for the making and confirmation of compulsory purchase orders set out in the Acquisition of Land Act 1981 (ALA 1981) which are applied to most compulsory acquisitions and describes the law on challenging such orders. It also describes the procedures of an application for an order under the Transport and Works Act 1992 which may include power to acquire land compulsorily, and the procedures for obtaining development consent (which may include compulsory acquisition) under the Planning Act 2008. The procedures in the ALA 1981 derive from the Acquisition of Land (Authorisation Procedure) Act 1946 and have been incorporated in a large number of statutes which provide ministers, local authorities, statutory undertakers and other public bodies with powers of compulsory acquisition[1]. The procedures set out in the ALA 1981 apply to all authorising Acts passed before the 1946 Act which authorised compulsory acquisition by local authorities and to all authorising Acts since 1946 which have specifically incorporated its procedures. In a few cases, however, the general procedures of the ALA 1981 have not been applied[2].

1 'Authorising Acts'.
2 See, eg, the Pipelines Act 1962, ss 11–14 (as amended); the Forestry Act 1967, s 40 (as amended); the New Towns Act 1981, ss 10–16 (as amended); and the Housing Act 1985, s 290.

[2]

The ALA 1981 provides that the authorisation for a compulsory purchase to which the Act applies is to be conferred by a 'compulsory purchase order'[1]. Separate procedures are provided for a compulsory purchase by a minister of a Government department (in which case, Sch 1 to the ALA 1981 sets out the procedure to be followed)[2] or a compulsory purchase by other bodies empowered to acquire land compulsorily (in which case, the procedure to be followed is that set out in Pt II of the ALA 1981)[3]. A compulsory purchase order made by a body other than a minister has to be confirmed by the minister identified for that purpose in the authorising Act, referred to as the 'confirming authority'[4]. ODPM Circular 06/2004 provides a key source of guidance to acquiring authorities in England making compulsory purchase orders to which ALA 1981 applies[5].

1 ALA 1981, s 2(1).
2 ALA 1981, s 2(3).
3 ALA 1981, s 2(2).
4 ALA 1981, s 7. In Wales, the confirming authority is the National Assembly.
5 ODPM Circular 06/2004, part I, para 2. The advice in the circular applies to orders listed in part I, para 6 of the circular.

[3]–[150]

Prior to embarking upon the procedures described in this Division, an acquiring authority should ensure that it has followed its own internal procedures to make a compulsory purchase order in respect of all the parcels of land to be included in the order, arriving at a formal resolution or decision. This is a matter for each particular body empowered to acquire land compulsorily and is not addressed in this Division[1].

1 Although it is unusual for a decision to make a compulsory purchase order to be challenged by judicial review, in some circumstances it may be appropriate: see *R v Camden London Borough Council, ex p Comyn Ching & Co Ltd* (1983) 47 P&CR 417. See also *Collis v Secretary of State for Communities and Local Government* [2007] EWHC 2625 (Admin), [2008] RVR 120, a challenge brought under ALA 1981, s 23, where the claimant challenged the confirmation of a compulsory purchase order made under the Housing Act 1985, on the ground that the acquiring authority had no proper authority to make the order because the resolution of the council's committee purporting to authorise it had been defective.

Chapter 2

Acquisition by a non-ministerial authority

Contents

A Introduction

[151]

Guidance on the making and submission for confirmation of compulsory purchase orders by non-ministerial authorities, to which the Acquisition of Land Act 1981 (ALA 1981) applies, may be found in ODPM Circular 06/2004. Acquiring authorities are advised that, in general, compulsory purchase orders should not be made unless there is a compelling case in the public interest for the order[1]. The Government has emphasised the need for the statutory procedures relating to the compulsory acquisition to be completed as quickly as possible in order keep the period of uncertainty and anxiety for owners and occupiers of the subject land to an absolute minimum[2].

1 ODPM Circular 06/2004, para 17. For an explanation on the concept of public interest, see **Division A, Chapter 3**. Although there is no express statutory requirement that there be a compelling case in the public interest, the need for such an overriding justification for compulsory acquisition is well established in decisions of the courts: see, eg, *Chesterfield Properties plc v Secretary of State for the Environment* (1997) 76 P&CR 117 at 129–131 ('it must … be demonstrated that in confirming it [the minister] has concluded that there exists a substantial public interest or interests outweighing the landowner's rights.')

2 ODPM Circular 06/2004, para 28.

B Acquisition by agreement

[152]

ODPM Circular 06/2004 advises acquiring authorities to seek to acquire land by agreement, where practicable, before embarking on compulsory purchase[1]. Having said that, the circular does make it clear that: 'Given the amount of time which needs to be allowed to complete the compulsory purchase process, it may often be sensible for the acquiring authority to initiate the formal procedures in parallel with such negotiations.'[2] It needs to be noted, however, that a confirming authority will not normally agree to cancel an inquiry unless the order, or all outstanding objections to it from statutory objectors, have been withdrawn before the notice of inquiry has been published or in good time for notice of cancellation of the inquiry to be published[3]. Where the acquiring authority can show that reasonable attempts to acquire land by agreement have failed, this can assist in demonstrating to the confirming minister that compulsory acquisition is necessary. To that end it is helpful if negotiations and discussions with landowners are well documented and have been carried out in a helpful, pro-active and transparent manner.

1 ODPM Circular 06/2004, para 24. Note that CPA 1965, s 3 applies only to land acquired by agreement where the land is 'subject to compulsory purchase', defined in CPA 1965, s 1(3) as 'land the compulsory purchase of which is authorised by the compulsory purchase order'. Section 3 does not, therefore, apply in the present context.
2 ODPM Circular 06/2004, para 24.
3 ODPM Circular 06/2004, para 43.

[153]

However, acquiring authorities need to be aware that, if they have engaged in long, close and co-operative discussions with a landowner, that landowner may have a legitimate expectation that he will be consulted prior to an order being made. Where, in such circumstances, an authority has made an order without prior consultation, the courts have indicated that this might amount to a procedural impropriety, although this should be pursued as an objection to the order rather than by way of proceedings for judicial review[1].

1 *R v Central Manchester Development Corpn, ex p Merlin Great Northern Ltd* (1992) 64 P&CR 392. For a modern description of the law on legitimate expectations, see *Nadarajah Senthuran v Secretary of State for the Home Department* [2004] EWCA Civ 950, [2004] 4 All ER 365. See also *HMB Holdings Ltd v Cabinet of Antigua and Barbuda* [2007] UKPC 37, [2007] All ER (D) 53 (Jun), in which the Privy Council considered a legitimate expectation challenge to the Government of Antigua's decision to authorise the compulsory acquisition of the claimant's derelict hotel.

[153.1]

ODPM Circular 06/2004 provides guidance for acquiring authorities urging them to consider offering those with concerns about a compulsory purchase order full access to alternative dispute resolution (ADR techniques)[1]. This guidance is said to echo the spirit of the Government's own pledge to settle legal disputes to which it is a party by means of mediation or arbitration wherever appropriate and the other party agrees. The guidance does not currently indicate that failure to offer ADR will be taken into account in considering costs. It is submitted that the scope for ADR may in practice be limited. If a landowner's objection is to acquisition of his land, it seems unlikely that the objection can be resolved except of course by the landowner recognising the force of the authority's case. If, however, the objector seeks to secure safeguards which are compatible with the principle of the scheme, for example, accommodation works, or is willing and able to redevelop his own property in a manner entirely compatible with the scheme, there may be some scope for ADR.

1 ODPM Circular 06/2004, para 26.

C Planning requirements

[154]

As part of demonstrating that there is a reasonable prospect of the scheme going ahead, the acquiring authority will need to be able to show that it is unlikely to be blocked by any impediments to implementation[1]. So, for example, ODPM Circular 06/2004 requires that 'Where planning permission will be required for the scheme, and has not already been granted, there should be no obvious reason why it might be withheld'[2]. Consequently, Appendix R of ODPM Circular 06/2004 advises that the Statement of Reasons should include 'a statement about the planning position of the order site'[3].

1 ODPM Circular 06/2006, para 22.
2 ODPM Circular 06/2004, para 23.
3 ODPM Circular 06/2004 App R, para (vi).

[154.1]

There is, therefore, no policy requirement that the scheme to be facilitated by the compulsory purchase order already has planning permission. Guidance in the circular relating to specific powers of acquisition provides further advice on planning matters. For orders promoted by RDAs[1] the circular advises that 'it is recognised that it may not always be feasible or sensible … to wait for full planning permission' but that the onus will rest on the RDA to demonstrate 'that there are no planning, or other, barriers to the scheme' and that RDAs should have 'resolved so far as practicable any major planning difficulties before submitting the order for confirmation'[2].

1 At the time of writing, the Government is planning to abolish RDAs by March 2012.
2 ODPM Circular 06/2004, App B, para 12.

[154.2]

Sometimes the inquiry into objections to a compulsory purchase order is heard at the same time as an inquiry dealing with other matters such as a planning appeal[1]. This can provide a convenient way of dealing with any uncertainties that the absence of planning permission might otherwise cause. In such cases, if planning permission is refused following the inquiry, it does not follow that the compulsory purchase order will not be confirmed. The weight to be attached to the refusal will depend upon whether the reasons for the refusal of planning permission represent a significant impediment to the scheme proceeding.

1 For advice on concurrent inquiries, see ODPM Circular 06/2004, para 44.

[154.3]
Where a compulsory purchase order is promoted expressly for the purpose of facilitating a particular scheme which has planning permission, care needs to be taken to ensure that the order lands together with any other land in the control of acquiring authority will be sufficient to enable the scheme in question to be implemented, at least to the extent needed to satisfy the statutory purposes behind the acquisition. If the acquiring authority envisages changes being made to the scheme which will require a variation to the planning permission, it will need to show that there are not likely to be impediments to the grant of such a variation.

[154.4]
In practical terms, whether or not planning permission already exists, planning evidence will often be an important part of the acquiring authority's case. The synergy between the aims of planning policy and the public interest means that showing that the scheme complies with planning policy will often provide powerful evidence to support its public interest credentials. Principles derived from cases concerning the matters which may lawfully be taken into account in determining planning applications apply equally to compulsory acquisition for development purposes provided it is recognised that, because of the serious invasion of property rights involved in compulsory acquisition, a strict approach to the application of those principles is required[1]

1 See the majority judgments in *R (Sainsbury's Supermarkets Ltd) v Wolverhampton City Council* [2010] UKSC 20, [2010] 2 WLR 1173, reversing the Court of Appeal judgment ([2009] EWCA Civ 835, [2009] All ER (D) 339 (Jul)).

D Preparing a compulsory purchase order

1 Form of the order

[155]
The compulsory purchase order is to be in the form prescribed[1] and must describe by reference to a map the land to which it applies[2]. Generally, orders will use Form 1 of the Compulsory Purchase of Land Regulations 2004[3]. However, where the land to be acquired includes part of a common, open space or fuel or field garden allotment, either Form 2 or 3 of the 2004 Regulations will apply[4]. If the order is being made pursuant to the authorising powers in s 290 of the Housing Act 1985, either Form 4, 5 or 6 of the 2004 Regulations will apply[5]. The Government advises acquiring authorities to seek their own legal and professional advice when making compulsory purchase orders, but has indicated that the relevant confirming authority may be willing to provide informal written comments on a draft order, on the basis that such comments are provided 'without prejudice' to the confirming authority's consideration of any order that may subsequently be submitted for confirmation[6].

1 Compulsory Purchase of Land (Prescribed Forms) (Ministers) Regulations 2004, SI 2004/2595, Forms 1–6. The equivalent forms for Wales are contained in the Compulsory Purchase of Land (Prescribed Forms) (National Assembly for Wales) Regulations 2004, SI 2004/2732.

2 ALA 1981, s 10(2).
3 SI 2004/2595.
4 Where the land forms part of a common, open space or fuel or field garden allotment and the order provides for the vesting of exchange land pursuant to the ALA 1981, s 19 or Sch 3, para 6, Form 2 is to be used. Where the land forms part of a common, open space or fuel or field garden allotment but provides for discharging the land from rights, trusts and incidents and not the vesting of exchange land, pursuant to the ALA 1981, s 19 or Sch 3, para 6, Form 3 is to be used: SI 2004/2595, reg 3(*a*)(i) and (ii).
5 Generally, Form 4 will apply, unless that land includes part of a common, open space or fuel or field garden allotment. Where the land forms part of a common, open space or fuel or field garden allotment and the order provides for the vesting of exchange land pursuant to the ALA 1981, s 19 or Sch 3, para 6, Form 5 is to be used. Where the land forms part of a common, open space or fuel or field garden allotment but provides for discharging the land from rights, trusts and incidents and not the vesting of exchange land, pursuant to the ALA 1981, s 19 or Sch 3, para 6, Form 6 is to be used: SI 2004/2595, reg 3(*b*).
6 ODPM Circular 06/2004, paras 32 and 33.

2 Title of the order

[156]
The title of the order should indicate the general area within which the land to be acquired is situated. At the end of the title, the words 'compulsory purchase order' and the year in which it is made should appear[1].

1 Compulsory Purchase of Land (Prescribed Forms) (Ministers) Regulations 2004, SI 2004/2595, Note (*a*) on the use of Forms 1, 2 and 3 and see para **[175]** as to meaning of owners, lessees and occupiers.

3 Identifying the interests in the land

[157]
A compulsory purchase order must include a schedule describing the land to which it relates and the interests of any 'qualifying person' in respect of that land[1]. As a result, one of the first tasks in preparing a compulsory purchase order is to identify all the relevant interests in the land. There are a number of powers which may enable acquiring authorities to obtain information as to ownership[2], and these powers are supplemented by a general power in s 5A of the ALA 1981[3].

1 Compulsory Purchase of Land (Prescribed Forms) (Ministers) Regulations 2004, SI 2004/2595, Forms 1–6.
2 See, eg, the Highways Act 1980, s 297; the Town and Country Planning Act 1990, s 330; and the Local Government (Miscellaneous Provisions) Act 1976, s 16.
3 See ALA 1981, s 5B for offences relating to the provision, or failure to provide, information under s 5A.

4 Preparing the schedule of interests

[158]
Amongst other things, the schedule to the order must:

(*a*) describe the land to which the order relates; and
(*b*) describe the relevant interests in the land.

The description of the land should include an indication of the area of each plot, its nature and its situation, such that the reader is told approximately where the land is situated without needing to refer to the accompanying map[1]. The names and addresses of every qualifying person must also be shown in the schedule[2]. Care should be taken to ensure that the relevant interests in the land are identified correctly. The Government acknowledges that mistakes do happen, and has given guidance on the scope of the confirming authority's power to correct errors and the procedure that should be adopted[3].

1 See ODPM Circular 06/2004, App U, paras 6–10 for more details.
2 See para **[157]**, and ODPM Circular 06/2004, App U, para 15 for more details.
3 See ODPM Circular 06/2004, paras 31, 51 and 52, and ALA 1981, ss 13(1), 13A(5) and 14. See further paras **[196.5]–[196.6]** below.

5 Signing, sealing and dating

[159]
All orders should be made under seal, duly authenticated and dated at the end (after the schedule). They should never be dated before they are sealed and should be sealed and dated on the same day[1]. Where a compulsory purchase order has been sealed on a date subsequent to that which appears on the order, it will be valid, provided that there has been no deliberate attempt to deceive or cause an affected landowner to act to his detriment[2].

1 ODPM Circular 06/2004, App U para 25.
2 *Burke v Secretary of State for the Environment* (1992) 26 HLR 10.

6 The order map

[160]–[169]
Details relating to the preparation of the order map are set out in ODPM Circular 06/2004, Appendix V. The heading of the order map must agree with the description of the map heading stated in the body of the compulsory purchase order and the words 'map referred to in [*order title*]' should be included in the actual heading or title of the map. Land may be identified on the map by colouring or any other method. However, if monochrome copies are to be utilised, the method used must be sufficient to provide clear identification of the relevant plots of land. It is important to use an Ordnance Survey-based map not generally less than 1/1,250 in scale in rural areas. In urban areas, App V of ODPM Circular 06/2004 advises that a smaller scale than 1/500 will be inadequate. The map must show sufficient details to enable it to be related to the description of each plot of land in the schedule to the order. The boundaries between such plots should be clearly marked. There should be no discrepancy between the order schedule and the map.

E Documents to be submitted to the confirming authority

[170]
The guidance requires the following documents to be submitted to the confirming authority:[1]

(*a*) one sealed and four unsealed copies of the order;
(*b*) two sealed copies and four unsealed copies of the map;
(*c*) a general certificate in support of the order;
(*d*) a certificate relating to any listed buildings or land within a conservation area which is included in the order; and
(*e*) two copies of the acquiring authority's statement of reasons, any enclosures thereto and wherever practicable any other documents referred to therein;
(*f*) where the order is made under s 47 of the P(LBCA)A 1990, a copy of the repairs notice served in accordance with s 48 of that Act;
(*g*) where applicable, a copy of any application for a certificate under s 19 ALA 1981 (acquisition of special land)[2].

1 See ODPM Circular 06/2004, App Q.
2 See ODPM Circular 06/2004, App L, paras 17–21 and see paras **[601]–[800]**.

F The general certificate in support of order submission

[171]
The form of this certificate is set out in App T to ODPM Circular 06/2004. It certifies that the relevant procedural steps referred to in paras **[172]–[176]** have been complied with.

G Statement of reasons

[172]–[173]
Paragraphs 35 and 36 of ODPM Circular 06/2004 request all acquiring authorities to serve a statement of reasons for making the order, with the personal notices to owners, lessees and occupiers[1]. This statement should be as comprehensive as possible and may form the basis of the authority's statement of case[2] that is required to be served[3]. Detailed guidance as to the content of the statement of reasons can be found in ODPM Circular 06/2004, App R. Considerable care should be taken in drafting both the statement of reasons and the statement of case[4], since both may be relevant, not only to the strength of the case for confirmation of the order but also to considerations relevant to the assessment of compensation.

1 See para **[175]**. The circular advises that, as far as practicable, this statement should also be sent to any short-term tenant and, where appropriate, to any applicant for planning permission in respect of the land.
2 ODPM Circular 06/2004, para 35.
3 CP(IP)R 2007, r 7.
4 See para **[214]**.

H Notices of the making of the order

1 Notices in newspapers

[174]
The acquiring authority is required to place a notice for two successive weeks in one or more local newspapers circulating in locality in which the land,

which is the subject of the order, is situated[1]. The form of the notice is prescribed[2]. The notice must[3]:

(*a*) indicate that the order has been made and that it is about to be submitted for confirmation;
(*b*) describe the land and state the purpose for which the land is required by the acquiring authority;
(*c*) indicate where, within the locality, a copy of the order and of the map relating to it can be inspected;
(*d*) specify a period of at least 21 days from the first publication of the notice within which objections to the order can be made; and
(*e*) specify the manner in which objections to the order can be made.

In addition, the acquiring authority must fix a notice in the prescribed form to a conspicuous object on or near the land comprised in the order[4].

1 ALA 1981, s 11(1).
2 Compulsory Purchase of Land (Prescribed Forms) (Ministers) Regulations 2004, SI 2004/2595, reg 3(*c*), Schedule, Form 7.
3 ALA 1981, s 11(2).
4 ALA 1981, s 11(3). The requirements of a s 12(3) notice are set out in s 12(4).

2 Notices to 'qualifying persons'

[175]
The acquiring authority must also serve a notice in the prescribed form[1] upon every 'qualifying person', being either: (*a*) an owner[2], tenant (whatever the tenancy period), lessee or occupier of land comprised in the order; (*b*) a person on whom the acquiring authority would be required to serve a notice to treat, if proceeding under s 5(1) of the CPA 1965; or (*c*) a person the acquiring authority thinks is likely to be able to make a claim for injurious affection if the order was confirmed[3]. There are additional requirements where the land is ecclesiastical property[4]. The notice must state the effect of the order and must also indicate that it is about to be submitted for confirmation. In addition, the notice must specify the time within which and the manner in which objections to the order can be made, that time being not be less than 21 days from the service of the notice[5].

1 Compulsory Purchase of Land (Prescribed Forms) (Ministers) Regulations 2004, SI 2004/2595, reg 3(*d*), Schedule, Form 8 or, if the order is made on behalf of a council, Schedule, Form 9.
2 ALA 1981, s 7(1) defines 'owner' as a person, other than a mortgagee not in possession, who is for the time being entitled to dispose of the fee simple of the land, whether in possession or in reversion, and includes a person holding or entitled to the rents and profits of the land under a lease or agreement, the unexpired term of which exceeds three years, and a person who would have the power to sell and convey or release the land to the acquiring authority if a compulsory purchase order were operative. This definition does not include a person who has a mere right, such as an easement of support, over the land comprised in the order; see *Grimley v Minister of Housing and Local Government* [1971] 2 QB 96, [1971] 2 All ER 431. Where a husband is served with a notice, his wife who is the joint owner of the property does not have to be served with a separate notice; see *George v Secretary of State for the Environment* (1979) 38 P & CR 609, 250 Estates Gazette 339.
3 ALA 1981, s 12(2), (2A) and (2B).
4 ALA 1981, s 12(3) provides that where land which is the subject of the order is ecclesiastical property, the Church Commissioners must be served with the notice. 'Ecclesiastical property' is defined by that subsection as meaning land belonging to any ecclesiastical benefice, or

being or forming part of a church subject to the jurisdiction of the bishop or any diocese or the site of such a church, or being or forming part of a burial ground subject to such jurisdiction or being diocesan glebe land within the meaning of the Endowments and Glebe Measure 1976.

5 ALA 1981, ss 10(3), 12(1).

3 Service of notices

[176]

The ALA 1981 provides[1] that any document or notice, which is required to be served pursuant to the ALA 1981, may be served on any person either by delivering it to him, by leaving it[2] at his proper address, or by registered post or recorded delivery[3]. The proper address for service is the last known address[4] of the person to be served or, in the case of a document which is required to be served upon an incorporated company or body service, the registered or principal office of that company or body[5]. In the latter case, service is to be effected by service upon the secretary or clerk of the company[6]. If the authority or minister having jurisdiction to make the order to which the document is related is satisfied that reasonable inquiry has been made and that it is not practicable[7] to ascertain the name or address of an owner, lessee or occupier of land on whom the document is to be served, the document may be served by addressing it to the 'owner', 'tenant', 'lessee' or 'occupier' of the land, by describing the land to which the document relates and by delivering it to some person on the land or, if there is no person on the land to whom it may be delivered, by leaving it or a copy of it on or near the land[8].

1 ALA 1981, s 6(1).

2 A notice must be left in a manner which a reasonable person, minded to bring the document to the attention of the person to whom it is addressed, would adopt; see *Lord Newborough v Jones* [1975] Ch 90, [1974] 3 All ER 17, CA.

3 Service by post other than by way of registered post or recorded delivery will be insufficient, but as this provision is not mandatory, good service may be effected where a notice is served in a different manner and is received; see *Sharpley v Manby* [1942] 1 KB 217, sub nom *Re Shapley's and Manby's Arbitration* [1942] 1 All ER 66, CA; and *Stylo Shoes Ltd v Prices Tailors Ltd* [1960] Ch 396, [1959] 3 All ER 901.

4 Service of the last-known address in England or Wales does not constitute good service if a later address abroad is known; see *R v Farmer* [1892] 1 QB 637, [1891–4] All ER Rep 921, CA.

5 ALA 1981, s 6(3).

6 ALA 1981, s 6(2).

7 The meaning of 'practicable' and the distinction between this phrase and the less stringent 'reasonably practicable' has been considered judicially, although usually in the context of health and safety legislation; see, eg, *Hammond v Haigh Castle & Co Ltd* [1973] 2 All ER 289, [1973] ICR 148; *Owen v Crown House Engineering Ltd* [1973] 3 All ER 618, [1973] ICR 511; *Dedman v British Building and Engineering Appliances Ltd* [1974] 1 All ER 520, [1974] ICR 53, CA.

8 ALA 1981, s 6(4) although this does not apply where the owner, lessee or occupier is a local authority, statutory undertaker or the National Trust. For the meaning of statutory undertaker, see para **[177]**, fn 4.

I Objections and representations

[177]

Objections to a compulsory purchase order may be made in the manner and in the time specified in the notice of the making of the order[1]. An objection should be made in writing and the grounds of the objection should be set out. The confirming authority has the power to require an objector to state his grounds for objection in writing and may disregard that objection if it is satisfied that the objection relates exclusively to matters which can be dealt with by the tribunal by which compensation is to be assessed[2]. The ALA 1981 also provides[3] that statutory undertakers[4] may make representations to the appropriate minister if land comprised in a draft compulsory purchase order includes their land[5]. Particular safeguards apply where the acquisition of this land would cause serious detriment to the carrying on of the undertaking[6].

1 See para **[175]**.
2 ALA 1981, s 13(4).
3 ALA 1981, s 16.
4 ALA 1981, s 8 defines statutory undertakers as any person authorised by any enactment to construct, work, or carry on any railway, light railway, tramway, road transport, water transport, canal or inland navigation undertaking or any dock, harbour, pier or lighthouse undertaking, or any undertaking for the supply of hydraulic power or the Civil Aviation Authority or the Post Office.
5 ALA 1981, s 16(1) (as amended); that land must have been acquired by the statutory undertaker for the purposes of their undertaking.
6 ALA 1981, s 16(2)(*b*).

J Grounds of objection

1 Grounds of objection

[178]
There are many grounds on which an objector may object to a compulsory purchase order. They will inevitably fall to be considered against the reasons why the land in question is needed and the particular justification and evidence advanced by the acquiring authority. Objectors should consider whether to make use of the Freedom of Information Act 2000[1] and the Environmental Information Regulations[2] in order to secure any information they require to advance their objections, but this course would need to be followed in good time to produce any information obtained to the public inquiry.

1 A detailed description of the Act is beyond the scope of this work.
2 SI 2004/ 3391. A detailed description of these regulations is beyond the scope of this work.

[178.1]
It is important to ensure that all relevant arguments are raised in objections[1]. One or more of the following arguments are often employed, although the list is not intended to be exhaustive:

(*a*) there is no need for the scheme for which the land is being acquired;
(*b*) the land being acquired is not needed because there is an alternative means of bringing about the objective of the order;
(*c*) the manner of implementation of the scheme is challenged;
(*d*) retention of the existing use of the land is more important than the purpose for which it is proposed to be acquired;
(*e*) that the underlying scheme is not viable or there are inadequate funds for its implementation; and/or

(*f*) that the order does not meet the statutory purposes for which it was made.

1 In *Moase v Secretary of State for the Environment, Transport and the Regions* [2001] Env LR 227, the Court of Appeal held that it was not open to an objector to raise fresh points of fact before the courts that could have been raised before the inspector at an inquiry. This decision seems to be difficult to square with the case of *South Oxfordshire District Council v Secretary of State for the Environment, Transport and the Regions* [2000] 2 All ER 667, where George Bartlett QC, sitting as a deputy judge of the High Court, held that there was no general rule that a party to a planning appeal decision was to be prevented from raising in a challenge to that decision an argument that had not been advanced in representations made on the appeal. The grounds of objection could in some circumstances have a bearing upon the assessment of compensation: see the remarks of Carnwath LJ in *Moto Hospitality Ltd v Secretary of State for Transport* [2007] EWCA Civ 764, [2007] RVR 247 at [11].

2 No need for the scheme for which the land is being acquired

[179]
It is well established that, in order to dispossess a landowner from his land, an acquiring authority must establish that compulsory acquisition is necessary. Forbes J stated[1] that:

> 'It seems to me that there is a very long and respectable tradition for the view that an authority that seeks to dispossess a citizen of his land must do so by showing that it is necessary, in order to exercise the powers for the purposes of the Act under which the compulsory purchase order is made, that the acquiring authority should have authorisation to acquire the land in question.'

The guidance in ODPM Circular 06/2004 puts it as follows:

> 'A compulsory purchase order should only be made where there is a compelling case in the public interest.'[2]

1 In *Brown v Secretary of State for the Environment* (1980) 40 P&CR 285 at 291. See also **Division A, Chapter 3**.
2 ODPM Circular 06/2004, para 17. See also **Division A**, paras **[352]–[354]**.

[180]–[190]
It follows that, where an acquiring authority fails to establish that the scheme which compulsory acquisition of land seeks to facilitate is necessary, the order will not be confirmed. For example, land may be being compulsorily acquired to provide a public swimming pool. It would be open to an objector to argue that there were already a sufficient number of swimming pools in the local area and, thus, that a further pool was not necessary.

3 Alternatives

[191]
It is commonly argued at compulsory purchase inquiries that the compulsory acquisition of the land in the order is not necessary because there is either an alternative site for the development or an alternative means for achieving the purpose of the order. Some examples are given below:

(*a*) In *Tesco Stores Ltd v Secretary of State for the Environment, Transport and the Regions*[1], it was argued that an alternative to a town centre redevelopment scheme requiring the loss of an existing retail site existed which would enable the store to remain in a smaller replacement store.

(*b*) Where land is being acquired to provide a new road, it could be argued by objectors that an alternative route is more appropriate or that the road does not need to be as wide as that promoted, and that, accordingly, land in the order should be excluded from it.

(*c*) It might also be argued that it is not necessary to acquire the particular type of legal interest sought. For example, it may be in particular circumstances that compulsory acquisition of freehold interest might become unnecessary where an objector offers a leasehold interest to the acquiring authority[2].

1 (2000) 80 P&CR 427. See also *Pascoe v Secretary of State for Communities and Local Government* [2009] EWHC 881 (Admin); *Hall v First Secretary of State* [2007] EWCA Civ 612, [2007] All ER (D) 356 (Jun).

2 Objections of this kind have become increasingly common in the light of the HRA 1998. The basic premise of such objections is the argument that it would not be proportionate to acquire the particular interest in question (eg the freehold) if acquisition of another interest by agreement (eg a lease which the landowner is willing to grant) would suffice to enable the scheme to be implemented. In this context, note the recognition in the circular of the importance of compulsory acquisition in implementing projects and providing a greater overall benefit than piecemeal development, and the question whether, on balance, the scheme is more likely to be delivered if the land is acquired than if it is not: see eg ODPM Circular 06/2004, App B, paras 7, 10 and 14(iv). It should also be remembered that proportionality requires a balancing of the interference with private rights against the benefit to the public interest that the compulsory acquisition seeks to secure. If securing the public interest would be put at risk by the uncertainties which dealing with a private landowner would entail, the compulsory acquisition of his interest will carry a greater justification and is therefore more likely to satisfy the test of proportionality.

4 The manner of implementation

[192]

An objector may seek to challenge the manner in which a scheme is to be implemented. For example, see *Landau v Secretary of State for the Environment*[1], where, although the objector did not question the need to redevelop the area for which his land was being acquired, he nevertheless objected to the compulsory purchase of his land on the ground that he intended to redevelop it himself and thereby achieve the objectives of the compulsory purchase[2].

1 [1992] COD 184, [1991] EGCS 119, CA. This case concerned the adequacy of reasons for the Secretary of State's decision confirming the CPO; it is only referred to here as an example of the type of objection which may be deployed. The facts are outlined in para **[1085]**. See also *Bell v Secretary of State for the Environment* [1989] 13 EG 70; *Singh v Secretary of State for the Environment* (1989) 24 EG 128.

2 Where such claims are made by an objector, the acquiring authority will want to examine questions such as the track record of the objector in delivering comparable development of an appropriate quality, the steps that the objector has taken towards implementing the scheme, his financial position, the timing of the work he proposes to carry out, his track record of working successfully with the public sector, and other practical implications of the objector developing part of the scheme.

5 The existing use of the land is more important than the purpose for which it is proposed to be acquired

[193]
It may be that land in which an objector has an interest has some value to the community as a whole in its existing use. For example, it may be high-quality agricultural land, it may have some historical value or it may be being used to provide much-needed services to a local community. In these circumstances, it is possible to argue that the existing use should carry greater weight than the purpose for which the land is being acquired compulsorily.

[194]
In addressing an objection to an order, objectors and acquiring authorities alike need to take into account the powers which the Secretary of State has to confirm an order with modifications[1].

1 See paras **[195]** and **[257]**.

6 The underlying scheme is not viable or is inadequately funded

[194.1]
Objectors may argue that the acquiring authority has failed to show that they have sufficient resources for the acquisition of the land or to implement the scheme, or that the scheme is not viable and therefore will not be implemented. Government advice[1] is that as much information as possible about the resource implications of both acquiring the land, and implementing the scheme for which the land is required, should be provided. The advice recognises that the scheme may not be intended to be independently financially viable, and that there may be cases where details cannot be finalised until there is certainty about the assembly of the necessary land. Nevertheless, in such cases the acquiring authority should at least provide an indication of how any potential shortfalls are intended to be met. This should include the degree to which other bodies (including the private sector) have agreed to make financial contributions or to underwrite the scheme, and on what basis such contributions or underwriting is to be made. The timing of funding can also be an important issue, particularly where it relates to the acquisition of the land itself. The Government advises that the confirming minister would expect to be reassured that it was anticipated that adequate funding would be available to enable the authority to complete the compulsory acquisition within the statutory period following confirmation of the order.

1 ODPM Circular 04/2006, paras 20–21.

[194.2]
The courts have given confirming ministers considerable discretion in the way in which they approach viability issues, which in turn gives flexibility to a promoting authority in the way in which it advances its case and addresses objections aimed at viability. For example, in *Chesterfield Properties v Secretary of State for the Environment*[1], the court held that the minister had not erred in confirming a compulsory purchase order despite accepting his inspector's

finding that the scheme had marginal viability. The minister was entitled to conclude that there was a substantial public interest in favour of the scheme despite the finding on viability, and that it was in the public interest to allow the scheme to be brought to the market with the benefit of a confirmed compulsory purchase order[2].

1 (1997) 76 P&CR 117.
2 See also *Royal Life Insurance Ltd v Secretary of State for the Environment* [1992] 2 EGLR 23; *Green v Secretaries of State for the Environment and for Transport* [1985] JPL 119; also *Landau v Secretary of State for the Environment* [1991] EGCS 119.

7 The order does not meet the statutory purposes for which it was made

[194.3]
Objectors often allege that the order does not meet the purposes for which it was made, usually for one or more specific reasons set out in the objection. Government guidance advises that acquiring authorities should be sure that the purposes for which it is making the compulsory purchase order sufficiently justify interfering with the rights of those whose land is being acquired[1]. More detailed guidance is given in respect of the factors relevant to particular statutory powers[2]. Where an order is made for a number of statutory purposes, it has been held that the minister may lawfully confirm the order provided at least one relevant statutory purpose is satisfied[3].

1 ODPM Circular 06/2004, paras 13, 14 and 17.
2 ODPM Circular 06/2004, Apps A–K.
3 See *Moggridge v National Assembly for Wales* [2003] EWHC 2188 (Admin), [2004] Env LR 18. NB the power to confirm an order subject to modifications does not enable the confirming authority to add or substitute a new statutory purpose: see paras **[196.5]–[196.6]**.

K Confirming the order

1 Confirming the order where no objections are outstanding

[195]
A confirming authority may confirm a compulsory purchase order with or without modifications if it is satisfied that (*a*) the notice requirements under ss 11 and 12 of the ALA 1981 have been complied with, and (*b*) either no 'relevant objection' is made, or every 'relevant objection' made is either withdrawn or disregarded[1]. For these purposes, a 'relevant objection' is an objection made by a 'qualifying person'[2]. When confirming the order, the confirming authority may not authorise the compulsory purchase of any land which was not included in the draft order, unless all interested persons consent[3]. Once an order has been confirmed, the acquiring authority is required to publish certain notices[4].

1 ALA 1981, s 13 (as substituted by s 100(6) of the PCPA 2004). As to the meaning of 'confirming authority', see ALA 1981, s 7. An objection may be disregarded if it relates exclusively to matters which can be dealt with by the tribunal dealing with compensation (ie the Lands Tribunal): see ALA 1981, s 13(4) and (7).
2 ALA 1981, s 13(6). For the definition of a 'qualifying person' see para **[175]**. NB If a person qualifies only by virtue of s 12(2A)(*b*) and the confirming authority thinks that he is not likely

to have a claim for injurious affection then his objection is not a 'relevant objection' for the purposes of s 13.
3 ALA 1981, s 14.
4 See para **[259]**.

[195.1]
One of the important changes introduced by the Planning and Compulsory Purchase Act 2004 is the power given to acquiring authorities to confirm their own orders in certain specified circumstances[1]. An acquiring authority may confirm its own order where the confirming authority has given notice to that effect, which has not been revoked[2]. The confirming authority may give such notice where: (a) the notice requirements in ss 11 and 12 of the ALA 1981 have been complied with; (b) no objection[3] has been made in relation to the proposed confirmation or all objections have been withdrawn; and (c) the order is capable of being confirmed without modification[4]. An acquiring authority may not confirm its own order in respect of statutory undertakers land or land forming part of a common, open space or fuel or field garden allotment[5], and nor may it confirm an order with modifications or confirm part only of an order[6].

1 ALA 1981, s 14A.
2 ALA 1981, s 14A(1).
3 An objection means an objection made by any person (whether or not a person mentioned in s 12(2)), *including* an objection which is disregarded: see s 14A(4).
4 ALA 1981, s 14A(3).
5 ALA 1981, s 14A(2).
6 ALA 1981, s 14A(5).

2 Confirming the order where objections are outstanding

[196]
Where a 'relevant objection' to the confirmation of a compulsory purchase order is neither withdrawn nor disregarded, it becomes known as a 'remaining objection'[1]. Where there are 'remaining objections' to the confirmation of a compulsory purchase order the confirming authority[2] may either (*a*) proceed under the written representations procedure, or (*b*) proceed by public local inquiry or hearing[3].

1 ALA 1981, s 13A(1).
2 As to the meaning of 'confirming authority', see ALA 1981, s 7.
3 ALA 1981, s 13A(2) and (3).

[196.1]
A confirming authority may proceed under the written representations procedure where:

(*a*) the order is not subject to special parliamentary procedure;
(*b*) the appropriate minister has granted a s 16 certificate[1] in respect of the land of a statutory undertaker; and
(*c*) every person who has made a 'remaining objection' consents in the prescribed manner[2].

The written representations procedure is set out in the Compulsory Purchase of Land (Written Representations Procedure) (Ministers) Regulations 2004[3].

Note that the Government's policy on costs in Department of for Communities and Local Government Circular 03/2009 applies, with adaptations, to the written representations procedure[4].

1 ALA 1981, s 16(2).
2 ALA 1981, s 13A(2).
3 SI 2004/2594 and see also ALA 1981, s 13B. For Wales, see the Compulsory Purchase of Land (Written Representations Procedure) (National Assembly for Wales) Regulations 2004, SI 2004/2730.
4 See DCLG Circular 03/2009, paras 11 and E4.

[196.2]
If the requirements for proceeding under the written representations procedure do not apply, or if the confirming authority decides not to follow the written representations procedure, then if there are 'remaining objections' it must either:

(*a*) cause a local public inquiry to be held[1]; or
(*b*) give persons who have remaining objection the opportunity of appearing before and being heard by a person appointed by the confirming authority for the purpose[2].

The procedure at a public local inquiry is discussed in detail at **Section L** below.

1 A minister has power to arrange for an inquiry by virtue of ALA 1981, s 5.
2 ALA 1981, s 13A(3).

3 Confirmation in stages

[196.3]
Section 13C of the ALA 1981 allows a confirming authority to confirm a compulsory purchase order in stages where:

(*a*) the confirming authority is satisfied that the order ought to be confirmed in so far as it relates to part of the land comprised in the order (the 'relevant part') but has not for the time being determined whether the order ought to be confirmed so far as it relates to the 'remaining part'; and
(*b*) the confirming authority is satisfied that the notice requirements have been complied with[1].

If there is a 'remaining objection'[2] in respect of the order, the confirming authority may only confirm in stages after either following the written representations procedure or the public local inquiry/hearing procedure, unless it is satisfied that all 'remaining objections' relate solely to the 'remaining part' of the land[3]. Guidance on the confirmation of compulsory purchase orders in stages is contained in ODPM Circular 06/2004[4].

1 ALA 1981, s 13C(1) and (2), introduced by P&CPA 2004, Pt 8.
2 See para **[196]** above.
3 ALA 1981, s 13C(3) and (4).
4 ODPM Circular 06/2004 paras 53 and 54 and paras 19–21 of the Annex to the circular.

[196.4]
Section 13C and the guidance given in Circular 06/2004 on its use were considered by the High Court in *R (Neptune Wharf) v Secretary of State for*

Trade and Industry[1]. In the circumstances of that case, the court held that a Direction under s 13C was not required to specify the time by which the confirming authority (in that case the Secretary of State) would decide whether or not to confirm the CPO in respect of the land in question, nor was it procedurally unfair for the confirming authority to make a Direction under s 13C without giving the parties notice of its intention to do so.

1 [2007] EWHC 1036 (Admin), [2007] 3 All ER 676.

4 Confirmation with modifications

[196.5]
The ALA 1981 gives the confirming authority the power to confirm a compulsory purchase order with or without modifications[1]. Although Government advice is that the power will be used sparingly[2], in practice, this power is useful and is quite commonly exercised. A common example is where the acquiring authority no longer needs a plot of land or an interest that was included in the order lands when it was made. In such cases the compulsory purchase order can be confirmed with the relevant plot or interest omitted from it.

1 See ALA 1981, ss 13(1), 13A(5) and 14.
2 ODPM Circular 06/2004, para 51.

[196.6]
The confirming authority's power to modify a compulsory purchase order can also be used to correct errors in the description of the land in the order. There are limitations to the exercise of the power for this purpose. The effect of ALA 1981, s 14 is that an order can only be modified to include any additional land or interests if all the people who are affected give their consent. Government guidance advises that the power can be used to remedy minor slips in the drafting of the order but not to make significant amendments to it[1]. It has been held that the power is not wide enough to allow the confirming authority to add to or substitute the statutory purposes for which the order was made by the acquiring authority[2]. Guidance is also given on the procedure which the acquiring authority should follow where it wishes the confirming authority to make modifications to the order prior to its confirmation[3]. The recommended procedure includes notifying objectors and interested persons of what modifications the acquiring authority proposes.

1 ODPM Circular 06/2004, paras 31, 51 and 52.
2 *Proctor & Gamble Ltd v Secretary of State for the Environment* (1992) 63 P&CR 317, referred to ODPM Circular 06/2004, para 51.
3 ODPM Circular 06/2004, para 52.

L Public local inquiries

1 Acquiring authority's evidence at the inquiry

[196.7]
Acquiring authorities need to consider carefully what evidence will be needed to justify the compulsory purchase order at a public inquiry.

Government guidance[1] provides considerable detail on the kinds of matters that the Secretary of State will take into account when deciding whether or not to confirm a compulsory purchase order. The guidance is obviously not intended to be exhaustive and sometimes the spirit rather than the letter may need to be applied with a degree of common sense. Specific guidance is given in respect of orders promoted under particular powers or by particular acquiring authorities[2]. Even if there are only a limited number of objectors to an order, the confirming authority will need to be satisfied that there is a compelling case in the public interest to justify the confirmation. Accordingly, the acquiring authority should not limit their evidence to that which is necessary to deal with outstanding objections. A positive case in support of the general merits of the compulsory purchase order will usually be needed as well. If the authority's statement of reasons and statement of case have been carefully prepared, it should be possible to identify from them the main parts of the authority's case to which the evidence should relate. A number of witnesses will usually need to be called. Acquiring authorities should carefully study the terms of ODPM Circular 06/2004 to see the factors on which the Secretary of State is likely to need evidence. The guidance makes it clear that it is for the acquiring authority to decide how best to justify its proposals for compulsory acquisition[3].

1 See ODPM Circular 06/2004 (and see paras 13 and 16 of the circular).
2 See ODPM Circular 06/2004, para 13 and Apps A–K.
3 ODPM Circular 06/2004, para 16.

2 Inquiries Procedure Rules

[197]–[198]
The procedure to be followed, once the confirming authority has determined that a public local inquiry should be held into objections, is set out in the Compulsory Purchase (Inquiries Procedure) Rules 2007 (CP(IP)R 2007)[1] in England, and the Compulsory Purchase (Inquiries Procedure) (Wales) Rules 2010 in Wales[2]. Guidance on the 2007 rules is to be found in DCLG Circular 01/2008. Welsh Circular NAFWC 14/2004 gives guidance to acquiring authorities in Wales. This section describes inquiries under the CP (IP)R 2007.

1 SI 2007/3617.
2 SI 2010/3015, which apply in Wales to compulsory purchase orders made by the Welsh ministers and by Welsh local authorities where notice of the inquiry was served after 31 January 2011.

3 Notice of intention to hold an inquiry

[199]
Where the Secretary of State intends to hold a public local inquiry, it must, not later than five weeks after the expiry of the time within which objections to the order had to be made or the submission of the order to it for confirmation (whichever is the later)[1], provide written notice to the acquiring authority[2] and each remaining objector[3] of that intention[4] and shall at the same time give to the acquiring authority notice of the substance of each objection made by a remaining objector and, so far as practicable, of the

substance of other objections[5]. The date of this notice is the reference point for the inquiry timetable and is known as the 'relevant date'[6].

1 CP(IP)R 2007, r 3(3). Note that the Secretary of State is referred to under the CP(IP)R 2007 as 'the authorising authority' whether his role is as a confirming authority or an acquiring authority: see CP(IP)R 2007, r 2. For the time for making objections, see para **[175]**.
2 'Acquiring authority' in the context of acquisition by a non-ministerial authority means a local authority or any person other than a minister who may be authorised to purchase land compulsorily (and who has made and submitted an order to the Secretary of State for confirmation in accordance with the ALA 1981, Pt II): see ALA 1981, s 7 and DCLG Circular 1/2008, para 12.
3 A 'remaining objector' means a person who has a remaining objection within the meaning of ALA 1981, s 13A (or, in the case of ministerial orders, ALA 1981, Sch 1, para 4A(1)): see CP(IP)R 2007, r 2. In simple terms this means, in the context of acquisition by a non-ministerial authority, an objection made by an owner, lessee, tenant or occupier of the land, or someone who would be entitled to a notice to treat if the acquiring authority were proceeding under PCA 1965, s 5(1), or a person who the acquiring authority thinks would be able to make a claim under CPA 1965, s 10 (compensation for injurious affection): see ALA 1981, ss 13(6) and 13A(1).
4 CP(IP)R 2007, r 3(1).
5 CP(IP)R 2007, r 3(4).
6 CP(IP)R 2007, r 2.

4 Secretary of State's power to hold pre-inquiry meetings

[200]–[210]
Before some inquiries are held, a meeting known as a 'pre-inquiry meeting' may be convened to consider arrangements for the inquiry to ensure that it is conducted efficiently and expeditiously[1]. The Secretary of State may cause a pre-inquiry meeting to be held if it appears to him to be desirable to do so[2]. Where he does consider it desirable, he must give notification of his intention to cause a pre-inquiry meeting to be held, and the meeting or, where there is to be more than one, the first pre-inquiry meeting must be held not later than 16 weeks after the relevant date[3]. A notice of intention to cause a pre-inquiry meeting to be held must be published by the Secretary of State not later than three weeks after the relevant date in one or more local newspapers circulating in the locality in which the land is situated[4]. The acquiring authority must send an outline statement to the Secretary of State and each remaining objector not later than eight weeks after the relevant date[5]. The Secretary of State may by written notice require any remaining objector or any other person who has notified of his intention to appear at the inquiry to send within eight weeks of the date of the notice an outline statement; the statement is to be sent to the Secretary of State and any other person specified in the notice[6]. Not less than three weeks' written notice of the meeting is to be given to each remaining objector, any other person whose presence at the meeting seems desirable, and to the acquiring authority[7]. Notice of the time, date and place of the meeting must also be given by the Secretary of State by way of fixing a notice at the site and in at least one place in the locality in which the land is situated where public notices are usually posted, and/or publication of a notice in one or more newspapers circulating in the locality in which the land is situated[8]. An inspector will preside over a pre-inquiry meeting convened by the Secretary of State[9].

1 CP(IP)R 2007, r 2. The minister's power to hold a pre-inquiry meeting will be exercised only in exceptional cases, such as where the draft order raises matters of major public interest, has

national or regional implications, raises issues of particular complexity or involves much third party involvement: see DCLG Circular 1/2008, para 16 and the examples given therein.
2 CP(IP)R 2007, r 4.
3 CP(IP)R 2007, r 4. CP(IP)R 2007, r 5, contains the prescribed procedures for pre-inquiry meetings. See para **[198]** for the meaning of 'relevant date'.
4 CP(IP)R 2007, r 5(1).
5 CP(IP)R 2007, r 5(2). 'Outline statement' is defined as a written statement of the principal submissions which a person proposes to put forward at an inquiry: CP(IP)R 2007, r 2.
6 CP(IP)R 2007, r 5(3).
7 CP(IP)R 2007, r 5(4).
8 CP(IP)R 2007, r 5(5). Acquiring authorities are encouraged to publish notices of pre-inquiries meetings on their websites: DCLG Circular 1/2008, para 17.
9 CP(IP)R 2007, r 6(1). 'Inspector' is defined as a person appointed by the Secretary of State to hold an inquiry or a reopened inquiry: CP(IP)R 2007, r 2.

5 Inspector's power to hold a pre-inquiry meeting

[211]
An inspector has the power to hold a pre-inquiry meeting if he considers it desirable, notwithstanding that the Secretary of State has not caused one to be held[1]. In these circumstances, the inspector must arrange for not less than three weeks' written notice of the meeting to be given to the Secretary of State, the acquiring authority, each remaining objector, any other person known at the date of the notice to be entitled to appear at the inquiry, and any other person whose presence at the meeting appears to him to be desirable[2].

1 CP(IP)R 2007, r 6(3).
2 CP(IP)R 2007, r 6(3).

6 Procedure at a pre-inquiry meeting

[212]
The meeting is to be presided over by the inspector and he is to determine the matters to be discussed and the procedure to be followed[1]. He has the power to require any person present at the meeting to leave, if he is of the opinion that that person is behaving in a disruptive manner. He may refuse to permit that person to return or to attend any further meeting, or he may permit them to return or attend, subject to such conditions as he shall specify[2].

1 CP(IP)R 2007, r 6(4).
2 CP(IP)R 2007, r 6(4)(*a*)–(*b*).

7 Outline statements

[213]
The requirement to serve outline statements appears only to apply where a pre-inquiry meeting is held[1].

1 CP(IP)R 2007, r 5, and DCLG Circular 1/2008, para 17. 'Outline statement' is defined as a written statement of the principal submissions which a person proposes to put forward at an inquiry: CP(IP)R 2007, r 2.

8 The acquiring authority's statement of case

[214]
A 'statement of case' is defined as a written statement containing full particulars of the case which a person proposes to put forward at the inquiry (including, where that person is the acquiring authority, the reasons for making the order), together with any copies of any documents referred to in such a statement (or the relevant extracts from those documents) and a list of any documents to which that person intends to refer or which he intends to put in evidence[1]. Where a pre-inquiry meeting has been held[2], the acquiring authority is required to serve a statement of case upon the Secretary of State and each remaining objector not later than four weeks after the conclusion of that meeting[3]. Where no pre-inquiry meeting has been held, the acquiring authority is required to serve a statement of case upon the Secretary of State and each remaining objector not later than six weeks after the relevant date[4]. Unless every document, or the relevant part of every document, which the acquiring authority intends to refer to or put in evidence at the inquiry has been copied to each remaining objector, the acquiring authority shall send to each remaining objector a notice naming each place where a copy of those documents may be inspected free of charge at all reasonable hours until the date of commencement of the inquiry, and each place so named shall be as close as reasonably possible to the land[5]. The acquiring authority must provide any person who so requests, with a reasonable opportunity to inspect and, where practicable, take copies of any statement or document which (or a copy of which) has been served on or by it[6]. The acquiring authority's statement of case must also indicate the time and place at which this opportunity will be afforded[7]. The Secretary of State or an inspector also has the power to require any person who has served a statement of case to provide such further information about the matters contained in the statement as he may specify[8].

1 CP(IP)R 2007, r 2.
2 See paras **[200]–[212]**.
3 CP(IP)R 2007, r 7(1)(*a*).
4 CP(IP)R 2007, r 7(1)(*b*).
5 CP(IP)R 2007, r 7(2).
6 CP(IP)R 2007, r 6(6).
7 CP(IP)R 2007, r 6(6).
8 CP(IP)R 2007, r 7(5).

9 Statements of case by other parties

[215]
The Secretary of State has the power to require any remaining objector or any other person who has notified him of an intention or wish to appear at the inquiry to serve a statement of case upon him and on any other person[1]. This power must be exercised by means of a notice in writing[2]. Persons so notified who are not remaining objectors are to be supplied with a copy of the acquiring authority's statement of case by the Secretary of State[3] and they are to serve their statements of case within six weeks of the date of that notice[4]. The Secretary of State or an inspector also has the power to require any

person who has served a statement of case to provide such further information about the matters contained in the statement as he may specify[5].

1 CP(IP)R 2007, r 7(3).
2 CP(IP)R 2007, r 7(3).
3 CP(IP)R 2007, r 7(4).
4 CP(IP)R 2007, r 7(3).
5 CP(IP)R 2007, r 7(5). Circular 01/2008, para 20 advises that if any party considers a statement of case produced by another party to be inadequate or incomplete, this should be drawn to the inspector's attention at the earliest opportunity.

10 Inquiry timetable

[216]
Where the Secretary of State or inspector has caused a pre-inquiry meeting to take place[1], the inspector must arrange a timetable for the proceedings at, or at part of, the inquiry. He then has the power to vary that timetable at any time[2]. Where no pre-inquiry meeting has been held, the inspector has the power to set a timetable, but whether he does so is a matter for his discretion[3]. Provision is made for notifying people entitled to appear at the inquiry of the time table for the proceedings and any variation to it[4].

1 See paras **[200]–[212]**.
2 CP(IP)R 2007, r 8(1). The power is subject to CP(IP)R 2007, r 10(1)(*b*), see para **[218]**.
3 CP(IP)R 2007, r 8(1).
4 CP(IP)R 2007, r 8(1) and (3).

11 Appointment of an assessor

[217]
An assessor is a person appointed by the Secretary of State to sit with an inspector at an inquiry or reopened inquiry to advise the inspector on such matters arising as the Secretary of State may specify[1]. They are usually appointed to address matters requiring a particular technical expertise. Where an assessor is appointed, the Secretary of State is required to notify every remaining objector, any person who has sent an outline statement or a statement of case, and the acquiring authority[2] of the name of the assessor and of the matters on which he is to advise the inspector[3].

1 CP(IP)R 2007, r 2.
2 CP(IP)R 2007, r 9.
3 CP(IP)R 2007, r 9.

12 Date and notification of an inquiry

[218]
Where a pre-inquiry meeting is held[1], the date fixed by the Secretary of State for the commencement of the inquiry must be not later than eight weeks after the conclusion of that meeting or the last of any such meetings[2]. Where no pre-inquiry meeting is held, the date fixed for the holding of the inquiry must be not later than 22 weeks after the relevant date[3]. However, the Secretary of State has power to vary the date for the holding of an inquiry where he is

satisfied that, in all the circumstances of the case, it is impracticable to hold an inquiry within either the eight weeks or the 22 weeks, as the case may be[4]. Where this power is exercised, the Secretary of State must hold the inquiry at the earliest practicable date[5]. In any event, unless he has the agreement of the acquiring authority and each remaining objector as to some lesser period of notice, the Secretary of State must give at least six weeks' written notice of the date, time and place fixed by him for the holding of the inquiry to all persons who are entitled to appear at it[6]. The same requirement exists where a date fixed for holding an inquiry is varied[7]. Where the time or place for holding the inquiry is varied the Secretary of State shall give such notice of the variation as appears to it to be reasonable[8]. The inquiry may be held partly in one place and partly in another where the Secretary of State is satisfied that it is reasonable to do so having regard to the nature of the draft order[9]. Further guidance on the fixing of dates for an inquiry is given in DCLG Circular 1/2008[10].

1 See para **[200]–[212]**.
2 CP(IP)R 2007, r 10(1)(*b*).
3 CP(IP)R 2007, r 10(1)(*a*) and, as to relevant date, see paras **[198]–[199]**.
4 CP(IP)R 2007, r 10(1)(*c*).
5 CP(IP)R 2007, r 10(1)(*c*).
6 CP(IP)R 2007, r 10(2).
7 CP(IP)R 2007, r 10(3).
8 CP(IP)R 2007, r 10(4).
9 CP(IP)R 2007, r 10(5). DCLG Circular 1/2008 states that this is only expected to occur where the order relates to a large, linear scheme such as a major road. For non-ministerial orders, PINS are to consult on the arrangements with the acquiring authority: DCLG Circular 1/2008, para 26.
10 See DCLG Circular 1/2008, para 25.

[219]
ODPM Circular 06/2004 advises that an inquiry will typically be held some six months after the submission of the order for confirmation[1]. Once fixed, the date for an inquiry will be changed only for exceptional reasons. As a general rule the date will not be changed because the acquiring authority needs more time to prepare or because a particular advocate may be unavailable[2].

1 ODPM Circular 06/2004, para 42.
2 ODPM Circular 06/2004, para 43.

13 Notice of the inquiry

[220]–[230]
The acquiring authority is under a duty to post a notice of the inquiry in a conspicuous place near the land that is the subject of the order and also in at least one place where public notices are usually posted in the locality, not later than two weeks before the date fixed for the holding of the inquiry[1]. The Secretary of State has the power to vary this requirement[2]. The acquiring authority may also be directed by the Secretary of State to publish a notice of the inquiry in one or more local newspapers not later than two weeks before the date fixed for the holding of the inquiry[3]. Any notice of the inquiry is required to contain a clear statement of the date, time and place of the

inquiry, the powers under which the order has been made and a description of the land sufficient to identify approximately its location without reference to the map referred to in the order[4].

1 CP(IP)R 2007, r 11(2).
2 CP(IP)R 2007, r 11(2)(*a*).
3 CP(IP)R 2007, r 11(2)(*b*).
4 CP(IP)R 2007, r 11(3).

14 Appearances at the inquiry

[231]
The following persons are entitled to appear at an inquiry[1]:

(*a*) any remaining objector[2];
(*b*) the acquiring authority; and
(*c*) any other person who has served an outline statement[3] or a statement of case[4].

An inspector may permit any other person to appear at the inquiry and this permission is not to be unreasonably withheld[5]. Any person who is entitled or permitted to appear may do so in person or be represented by counsel, solicitor or any other person[6]. An inspector may allow one or more persons to appear on behalf of some or all of any persons having a similar interest in the matter under inquiry[7].

1 CP(IP)R 2007, r 14(1) and (2).
2 See paras **[198]–[199]**, fn 3.
3 See para **[213]**.
4 See para **[214]–[215]**.
5 CP(IP)R 2007, r 14(3).
6 CP(IP)R 2007, r 14(4).
7 CP(IP)R 2007, r 14(5).

15 Representation of Government departments

[232]
Where a Government department (other than the department of a minister who is the acquiring authority) has made a statement or representation in writing in support of the order or the draft order and the acquiring authority has included that statement in its statement of case, a representative of the department concerned shall be made available to attend the inquiry[1]. Such a representative shall, at the inquiry, state the reasons for the view expressed by his department and shall give evidence and be subject to cross-examination to the same extent as any other witness[2]. A representative of a Government department shall not be required to answer any question which in the opinion of the inspector is directed to the merits of Government policy[3].

1 CP(IP)R 2007, r 13(1).
2 CP(IP)R 2007, r 13(2).
3 CP(IP)R 2007, r 13(3). See also *Bushell v Secretary of State* [1981] AC 75.

16 Proofs of evidence

[233]
A person entitled to appear at an inquiry to give, or to call another person to give, evidence at the inquiry by reading a statement of that evidence shall send to the inspector and to the acquiring authority, a copy of that statement (known as a 'proof of evidence' together with any relevant supporting documents[1]. A written summary of the statement (known as a 'summary proof') must be provided where the statement contains more than 1,500 words[2]. Proofs of evidence and summary proofs are to be served on the inspector and the acquiring authority on the date provided for by any inquiry time-table where one has been set [3] or, if there is no timetable, not later than three weeks before the date fixed for the holding of the inquiry[4]. Where the acquiring authority provides a proof or a summary proof to an inspector, it is required to send at the same time copies to any remaining objector and to any other person who has sent an outline statement or statement of case[5]. The acquiring authority shall afford to any person who so requests a reasonable opportunity to inspect and, where practicable and on payment of a reasonable charge, take copies of any document sent to or by it[6]. Where summary proofs have been required, only the summary proof shall be read at the inquiry, unless the inspector permits or requires otherwise[7]. Where a summary is read, the proof of evidence to which it relates is to be treated as tendered in evidence unless the person whose evidence the proof contains notifies the inspector that he wishes to rely on his summary proof only, and that person is to be subject to cross-examination on proof of evidence to the same extent as if it were evidence that had been given orally[8].

1 CP(IP)R 2007, r 15(1). Further guidance on statements of evidence and their content is given in DCLG Circular 1/2008, para 32.
2 CP(IP)R 2007, r 15(2).
3 CP(IP)R 2007, r 15(3)(*b*).
4 CP(IP)R 2007, r 15(3)(*a*).
5 CP(IP)R 2007, r 15(6).
6 CP(IP)R 2007, r 16(5).
7 CP(IP)R 2007, r 15(4).
8 CP(IP)R 2007, r 16(5).

17 Procedure at the inquiry

[234]
The general rule is that it is for the inspector to determine the procedure to be followed at an inquiry[1]. However, there are a number of aspects of procedure that are specified by the CP(IP)R 2007. The acquiring authority is to present its case first and to have the final right of reply, unless the inspector, with the consent of that authority, determines otherwise[2]. Other persons entitled or permitted to appear at the inquiry are to be heard in such order as the inspector may determine[3]. Where the inspector has a discretion as to the conduct of the proceedings, this discretion should be exercised in a way that does not infringe common law rules of procedural fairness[4].

1 CP(IP)R 2007, r 16(1).
2 CP(IP)R 2007, r 16(1).

3 CP(IP)R 2007, r 16(1).
4 See, eg, *Nicholson v Secretary of State for Energy* (1977) 76 LGR 693, concerning the discretion of an inspector at a planning inquiry to allow cross-examination, and *R (Gates Hydraulics Ltd) v Secretary of State for Communities and Local Government* [2009] EWHC 2187 (Admin), concerning unfairness where the planning inspector's decision disagreed with matters which had been common ground between the parties at the inquiry.

[235]

Persons entitled to appear at the inquiry[1] are entitled to call evidence, and the acquiring authority and remaining objectors are entitled to cross-examine persons giving evidence, otherwise the calling of evidence and the cross-examination of those giving evidence are at the inspector's discretion[2]. Thus, persons permitted (as opposed to entitled) to appear have no right under the rules to give evidence or to cross-examine[3].

1 See para **[231]**.
2 CP(IP)R 2007, r 16(3).
3 However, common law rules of procedural fairness are relevant to the exercise of an inspector's discretion, see, eg, *Miller (T A) Ltd v Minister of Housing and Local Government* [1968] 2 All ER 633; *Bushell v Secretary of State for the Environment* [1981] AC 75; *Nicholson v Secretary of State for Energy* (1977) 76 LGR 693.

[236]

Where he considers it to be irrelevant or repetitious, the inspector may refuse to permit the giving or production of evidence, the cross-examination of persons giving evidence or the presentation of any other matter[1]. Where the inspector exercises this power and refuses to permit the giving of oral evidence, the person wishing to give that evidence may submit any evidence or other matters in writing to the inspector before the close of the inquiry[2].

1 CP(IP)R 2007, r 16(4). On an inspector's discretion as to what evidence is considered relevant, see *R v Secretary of State for the Environment, ex p Royal Borough of Kensington and Chelsea* [1987] JPL 567.
2 CP(IP)R 2007, r 16(4).

[237]

The inspector has power to require a person appearing or present at an inquiry, who in his opinion, is behaving in a disruptive manner to leave. He may refuse to permit that person to return or may permit him to return only on such conditions as he may specify[1]. Where the inspector exercises this power, the person wishing to give evidence may submit that evidence or other matters in writing to the inspector before the close of the inquiry[2].

1 CP(IP)R 2007, r 16(7).
2 CP(IP)R 2007, r 16(7).

[238]

The inspector may allow any person to alter or add to a statement of case so far as may be necessary for the purposes of the inquiry[1]. Where the inspector does so, he must (if necessary by adjourning the inquiry) give every person entitled to appear at the inquiry an adequate opportunity of considering any new matter of fact or document introduced by the acquiring authority[2].

1 CP(IP)R 2007, r 16(8).
2 CP(IP)R 2007, r 16(8).

[239]
The inspector may from time to time adjourn an inquiry and, if the date, time and place of the adjourned inquiry are announced at the inquiry before the adjournment, no further notice is required[1]. He may also proceed with an inquiry in the absence of any person entitled to appear at it[2].

1 CP(IP)R 2007, r 16(11). On the discretion to adjourn a public inquiry, see *Powell v Secretary of State for Environment, Food and Rural Affairs* [2009] EWHC 643 (Admin); *Orakpo v London Borough of Wandsworth* (1992) 24 HLR 370; *Osreicher v Secretary of State for the Environment* [1978] 1 WLR 810, CA; *Webb v Secretary of State for the Environment* (1990) 22 HLR 274.
2 CP(IP)R 2007, r 16(9).

[240]–[249]
Where any written representation, evidence or other document has been received by the inspector before an inquiry opens or during an inquiry, he may take it into account, as long as he discloses it to the parties at the inquiry[1].

1 CP(IP)R 2007, r 16(10).

[250]
The inspector may direct the acquiring authority to provide facilities so that any person appearing at the inquiry may be afforded a reasonable opportunity to inspect, and where practicable and on payment of a reasonable charge, take copies of, any documents open to public inspection[1].

1 CP(IP)R 2007, r 16(6).

18 Site inspections

[251]
The inspector may make an unaccompanied inspection of the land which is the subject of the order before or during the inquiry, without giving any notice of his intention to do so to the parties to the inquiry[1]. In addition, however, either during an inquiry or after the close of an inquiry, the inspector may inspect the land in the company of a representative of the acquiring authority and any remaining objector[2]. If the acquiring authority or any remaining objector requests such an inspection either before or during an inquiry, the inspector is required to make such an inspection[3]. The date and time when the inspection is proposed to be made must be announced by the inspector during the inquiry[4]. The inspector is not bound to defer the inspection if a representative of the acquiring authority or any statutory objector fails to be present at the time appointed for the inspection[5]. Where the confirming authority takes into account matters noticed on the site inspection which were not in issue at the inquiry, the requirements of procedural fairness may make the compulsory purchase order liable to be quashed[6].

1 CP(IP)R 2007, r 17(1).
2 CP(IP)R 2007, r 17(2).
3 CP(IP)R 2007, r 17(2).
4 CP(IP)R 2007, r 17(3).
5 CP(IP)R 2007, r 17(4).
6 *Fairmount Investments Ltd v Secretary of State for the Environment* [1976] 2 All ER 865, HL; *Hibernian Property Co v Secretary of State for the Environment* (1973) 27 P&CR 197.

19 Procedure after the inquiry

[252]

After an inquiry closes, the inspector must produce a report in writing and submit it to the minister. This report is to include the inspector's conclusions and his recommendations or his reasons for not making any recommendations[1]. There is no general duty upon the inspector to send to the Secretary of State a copy of an objector's final written submissions, provided the inspector's report fairly summarises those submissions and resolves them in his conclusions.[2]

1 CP(IP)R 2007, r 18(1).
2 *Mortell v Secretary of State for Communities and Local Government* [2009] EWCA Civ 1274 at [45].

[253]

Where an assessor was appointed, he may, after the close of the inquiry, submit a report in writing to the inspector in respect of the matters on which he was appointed to advise[1]. Such a report must be appended to the inspector's report, and the inspector must indicate in his own report whether and to what extent he agrees or disagrees with the assessor's report and, where he disagrees, he must indicate his reasons for that disagreement[2].

1 CP(IP)R 2007, r 18(2).
2 CP(IP)R 2007, r 18(3).

[254]

Where:

(*a*) the Secretary of State differs from the inspector on any matter of fact mentioned in or appearing to him to be material to a conclusion reached by the inspector; or
(*b*) the Secretary of State takes into consideration any new evidence or new matters of fact (not being a matter of Government policy),

and is for that reason disposed to disagree with a recommendation made by the inspector, the Secretary of State is not permitted to come to a decision at variance with that recommendation without first notifying the persons who appeared at the inquiry of its disagreement and the reasons for it[1]. Every person so notified must be given an opportunity to make written representations[2]. Written representations are to be made within three weeks of the date of the notification[3]. Where the Secretary of State proposes to disagree with his inspector for reasons that do not require him to notify the parties, he may nevertheless choose to do so[4].

1 CP(IP)R 2007, r 18(4). For a challenge based on the Secretary of State's approach to matters raised after the close of the compulsory purchase inquiry, see *Pascoe v Secretary of State* [2009] EWHC 881 (Admin) at [20]–[36].
2 CP(IP)R 2007, r 18(5)(*a*).
3 CP(IP)R 2007, r 18(5)(*a*).
4 *Alliance Spring Co Ltd v First Secretary of State for Communities and Local Government* [2005] EWHC 18 (Admin), [2005] All ER (D) 112 (Jan) at [14].

[255]

If the reason that the Secretary of State is disposed to disagree with a recommendation made by the inspector falls into category (*b*) above, the persons entitled to appear at the inquiry may, as an alternative to making written representations, request that the inquiry be reopened[1]. Such requests are to be made within three weeks of the date of the notification[2].

1 CP(IP)R 2007, r 18(5)(*b*).
2 CP(IP)R 2007, r 18(5)(*b*).

[256]
Where a request to reopen an inquiry is made, the Secretary of State retains a discretion to do so, save in certain circumstances. Those circumstances are where such a request to reopen an inquiry is made by the acquiring authority or a remaining objector, in which case the Secretary of State must reopen the inquiry to afford an opportunity for persons to be heard on such matters relating to the compulsory purchase order as he may specify[1]. If an inquiry is reopened, the Secretary of State is required to send to all persons entitled to appear at the inquiry who appeared at it a written statement of the matters so specified[2]. In these circumstances, the procedures relating to the setting of the date of and to notification of the inquiry are the same as those generally applicable, with the exception that he must give not less than four weeks' notice of the date, time and place fixed for holding the inquiry, instead of six weeks' notice[3].

1 CP(IP)R 2007, r 18(6). The re-opened inquiry does not have to be before the same inspector.
2 CP(IP)R 2007, r 18(6)(*a*).
3 CP(IP)R 2007, r 18(6)(*b*).

M The decision

1 The decision to confirm or refuse an order

[257]
Having considered the objections and the inspector's report, the Secretary of State may confirm the order with or without modification[1], or he may refuse to confirm the order. When confirming the order the confirming authority may not authorise the compulsory purchase of any land which was not included in the draft order unless all persons interested consent[2].

1 ALA 1981, ss 13(1), 13A(5).
2 ALA 1981, s 14.

2 Notification of the decision

[258]
The Secretary of State is required to give written notification of his decision on the compulsory purchase order together with the reasons for that decision to the acquiring authority, each remaining objector, any person entitled to appear at the inquiry who did appear at that inquiry, the acquiring authority and any other person who appeared at the inquiry and who asked to be notified of the decision[1]. The Secretary of State is not required to send a copy of the inspector's report[2] to all such persons, however, although he is required to provide a copy of the conclusions and of any recommendations made by

the inspector[3]. Any person who is entitled to receive notification of the Secretary of State's decision who makes a written application within four weeks of the date of the Secretary of State's decision to be supplied with a copy of the inspector's report must be provided with such a copy[4].

1 CP(IP)R 2007, r 19(1).
2 In this context the inspector's report is taken to include reference to any report which may have been made by an assessor and has been appended to the inspector's report, but it does not include any other documents so appended: CP(IP)R 2007, r 19(3). Note, however, that any person who has received the inspector's report may make a written request to the Secretary of State for an opportunity to inspect those additional documents within six weeks of the date of publication of the notice of confirmation, and the Secretary of State shall afford that person that opportunity.
3 CP(IP)R 2007, r 19(2).
4 CP(IP)R 2007, r 19(2).

3 Notices after confirmation of order

[259]
Where an order is confirmed by the confirming authority, the acquiring authority is required to publish, in one or more local newspapers, a notice in a prescribed form[1] describing the land, stating that the order has been confirmed, and naming a place where a copy of the order as confirmed and any map referred to in the order may be inspected at all reasonable hours[2]. This notice must also be served upon every owner, lessee and occupier[3].

1 Compulsory Purchase of Land (Prescribed Forms) (Ministers) Regulations 2004, SI 2004/2595, Schedule, Form 10. For Wales, see Compulsory Purchase of Land (Prescribed Forms) (National Assembly for Wales) Regulations 2004, SI 2004/2732.
2 ALA 1981, s 15.
3 ALA 1981, s 15.

N Awards of costs incurred at inquiries

[260]
The Local Government Act 1972 (LGA 1972), s 250, contains a power to make costs awards at public inquiries. LGA 1972, s 250(5) applies to inquiries held under the ALA 1981 in relation to a proposed acquisition of land by an authority other than a minister[1]. Section 250(5) confers a general discretion to 'make orders as to the costs of the parties at the inquiry and as to the parties by whom the costs are to be paid …'. Every such order may be made a rule of the High Court on the application of any party named in the order[2].

1 ALA 1981, s 5(3).
2 LGA 1972, s 250(5).

[261]
The Secretary of State's policy in respect of awards of costs at compulsory purchase inquiries is found in part E of the annex to Department for Communities and Local Government Circular 03/2009 to which reference should be made[1]. If a statutory objector to an order is successful, an award of costs will be made in favour of the objector and against the acquiring authority, unless there are exceptional reasons not to do so. There is no need

to show that the acquiring authority has acted unreasonably in such cases[2]. To qualify for costs under the policy the claimant must have made a formal objection to the order, the order must have been the subject of a local inquiry which the claimant must have attended or been represented at, the claimant must have been heard as a statutory objector, and the claimant must have had his objection sustained by the Secretary of State's refusal to confirm the order[3]. A partially successful objector will usually receive a partial award of costs[4]. Exceptionally an unsuccessful objector may be awarded its costs where it has incurred costs as a result of unreasonable conduct by the other party[5]. In all cases those wishing to seek their costs need to apply for them[6].

1 The Circular applies to compulsory purchase proceedings 'initiated' on or after 6 April 2009. Department of the Environment and Welsh Office Circular 8/93 applies to proceedings initiated before then: Circular 03/2009, para 9. Part E only applies where the acquiring or order making authority is different to the confirming authority: Circular 03/2009, para E2. The guidance on costs applies to written representations cases as well hearings and inquiries: Circular 03/2009, annex, para E4. Paragraph 11 of the circular cancels paras 46, 48 and 49 of Part I of the Memorandum to ODPM Circular 06/2004 (which had applied the guidance in Circular 8/93 to written representations cases).

2 Circular 03/2009, annex, para E1.

3 Circular 03/2009, annex, paras E1, E5 and E7.

4 Circular 03/2009, annex, para E13.

5 Circular 03/2009, annex, para E5.

6 Successful objectors will be invited to make a written costs application when they are notified of the decision on the order. Applications for costs on grounds of unreasonable conduct should be made to the inspector at the inquiry or hearing, or in writing if appropriate: Circular 03/2009, annex, paras E7 and E10.

[262]–[400]

The guidance given in the circular is policy guidance only, and on general principles of administrative law it cannot be allowed to fetter the exercise of the Secretary of State's discretion under LGA 1972, s 250(5). Accordingly, the Secretary of State must always be prepared to award costs in an appropriate case falling within LGA 1972, s 250(5) even if it does not meet his published policy in the circular[1].

1 *Re Findlay* [1985] 1 AC 318 at 335H–336D.

Chapter 3

Acquisition by a ministerial authority

Contents

A Introduction

[401]
This chapter relates to the procedural aspects of compulsory acquisition of land by ministers. The procedures to be followed by a ministerial authority are similar to, but slightly different from, those to be followed by a non-ministerial acquiring authority. Detailed guidance on the making, and submission for confirmation, of compulsory purchase orders by ministerial authorities (to which the Acquisition of Land Act 1981 (ALA 1981), Sch 1 applies) has not been provided in a Government circular; however, in practice, ministerial authorities tend to adhere to the spirit of the guidance set out in ODPM Circular 06/2004[1].

1 Guidance may also be obtained on best practice from the 'Compulsory Purchase Procedure Manual', which is published by the Stationery Office and updated twice a year.

B Preparing the order

1 Preparing the order

[402]
A draft order has to be prepared. The order may be in such form as the minister may determine, but it must describe the land to which it applies by reference to a map. Once it has been prepared, the minister is required to provide notice of it by placing a notice in local newspapers and by serving notice upon owners, lessees and occupiers[1].

1 See paras **[404]** and **[405]**.

2 Identifying the interests in the land

[403]
Early in the process of preparing a compulsory purchase order, the minister should identify the 'qualifying persons'[1] in respect of the land that is to be compulsorily acquired. Generally, such land referencing is carried out by reference to the Land Register. Some authorising Acts provide specific powers which can be used to ascertain this information[1] and these specific powers are supplemented by s 5A of the ALA 1981[3].

1 See para **[175]** above
2 Eg the Highways Act 1980, s 297, the Town and Country Planning Act 1990, s 330 and the Local Government (Miscellaneous Provisions) Act 1976, s 16.
3 See ALA 1981, s 5B for offences relating to the provision, or failure to provide, information under s 5A.

C Notices of preparation of draft order

1 Notices in newspapers

[404]
The minister is required to publish a notice in a prescribed form[1] in two successive weeks in one or more local newspapers circulating in the locality in which the land comprised in the draft order is situated[2]. In addition, the minister must fix a notice in the prescribed form to a conspicuous object on or near the land comprised in the order[3]. The notice must state that the order has been prepared in draft and is about to be made[4]. The notice must describe the land and state the purpose for which the land is required[5]. In addition, the notice must name a place, within the locality, where a copy of the draft order and of the map referred to by the order may be inspected[6], and it must specify the time within which, and the manner in which, objections to the draft order can be made (that time must be not less than 21 days from the first publications of the notice)[7].

1 Compulsory Purchase of Land (Prescribed Forms) (Ministers) Regulations 2004, SI 2004/2595, Schedule, Form 7.
2 ALA 1981, Sch 1, para 2(1).
3 ALA 1981, Sch 1 para 2(3).
4 ALA 1981, Sch 1, para 2(2)(*a*).
5 ALA 1981, Sch 1, para 2(2)(*b*).
6 ALA 1981, Sch 1, para 2(2)(*c*).
7 ALA 1981, Sch 1, para 2(2)(*d*).

2 Notice to 'qualifying persons'

[405]
The minister must also serve a notice in the prescribed form[1] upon every 'qualifying person', being either: (*a*) an owner[2], tenant (whatever the tenancy period), lessee or occupier of land comprised in the order; (*b*) a person on whom the minister would be required to serve a notice to treat, if proceeding under s 5(1) of the CPA 1965; or (*c*) a person the minister thinks is likely to be able to make a claim for injurious affection if the order was made[3]. There are additional requirements where the land is ecclesiastical property[4]. The notice

must state the effect of the draft order[5]. The notice must state that the order is about to be made[6]. In addition, the notice must specify the time within which and the manner in which objections to the draft order can be made (that time must not be less than 21 days from the first publications of the notice)[7].

1 Compulsory Purchase of Land (Prescribed Forms) (Ministers) Regulations 2004, SI 2004/2595, Form 8.
2 ALA 1981, s 7(1) defines 'owner' as a person, other than a mortgagee not in possession, who is for the time being entitled to dispose of the fee simple of the land, whether in possession or in reversion and includes also a person holding or entitled to the rents and profits of the land under a lease or agreement, the unexpired term of which exceeds three years, and a person who would have the power to sell and convey or release the land to the acquiring authority if a compulsory purchase order were operative. This does not include a person who has a mere right, such as an easement of support, over the land comprised in the order; see *Grimley v Minister of Housing and Local Government* [1971] 2 QB 96, [1971] 2 All ER 431. Where a husband is served with a notice, his wife who is the joint owner of the property does not have to be served with a separate notice; see *George v Secretary of State for the Environment* (1979) 38 P&CR 609, 250 Estates Gazette 339.
3 ALA 1981, Sch 1, para 3(2) provides that an occupier who is a statutory tenant within the meaning of the Rent Act 1977, the Rent (Agriculture) Act 1976 or a licensee under an assured agricultural occupancy within the meaning of Pt I of the Housing Act 1988 is deemed to be a tenant for a period less than a month. A tenancy which commences as a weekly tenancy has been held to continue as such, however long it may last, and such a tenant would not be entitled to notice under these provisions; see *EON Motors Ltd v Secretary of State for the Environment* [1981] 1 EGLR 19.
4 ALA 1981, Sch 1, para 3(3) provides that where land which is the subject of the order is ecclesiastical property the Church Commissioners must be served with the notice. 'Ecclesiastical property' is defined by the ALA 1981, Sch 1, para 3(3) as land belonging to any ecclesiastical benefice, or being or forming part of a church subject to the jurisdiction of the bishop of any diocese or the site of such church, or being or forming part of a burial ground subject to such jurisdiction or being diocesan glebe land within the meaning of the Endowments and Glebe Measure 1976.
5 ALA 1981, Sch 1, para 3(1)(*a*).
6 ALA 1981, Sch 1, para 3(1)(*b*).
7 ALA 1981, Sch 1, para 3(1)(*c*).

3 Service of notices

[406]

The ALA 1981 provides[1] that any document or notice, which is required to be served pursuant to the ALA 1981, may be served on any person either by delivering it to him, by leaving it[2] at his proper address, or by registered post or recorded delivery[3]. The proper address for service is the last-known address[4] of the person to be served or, in the case of a document which is required to be served upon an incorporated company or body service, the registered or principal office of that company or body[5]. In the latter case, service is to be effected by service upon the secretary or clerk of the company[6]. If the authority or minister having jurisdiction to make the order to which the document is related is satisfied that reasonable inquiry has been made and that it is not practicable[7] to ascertain the name or address of an owner, lessee or occupier of land on whom the document is to be served, the document may be served by addressing it to the 'owner', 'lessee' or 'occupier' of the land, by describing the land to which the document relates and by delivering it to some person on the land or, if there is no person on the land to whom it may be delivered, by leaving it or a copy of it on or near the land[8].

1 ALA 1981, s 6(1).
2 A notice must be left in a manner which a reasonable person, minded to bring the document to the attention of the person to whom it is addressed, would adopt; see *Lord Newborough v Jones* [1975] Ch 90, [1974] 3 All ER 17, CA.
3 Service by post other than by way of registered post or recorded delivery will be insufficient, but, as this provision is not mandatory, good service may be effected where a notice is served in a different manner and is received; see *Sharpley v Manby* [1942] 1 KB 217, sub nom *Re Shapley's and Manby's Arbitration* [1942] 1 All ER 66, CA; *Stylo Shoes Ltd v Prices Tailors Ltd* [1960] Ch 396, [1959] 3 All ER 901.
4 Service of the last-known address in England or Wales does not constitute good service if a later address abroad is known; see *R v Farmer* [1892] 1 QB 637, [1891–4] All ER Rep 921, CA.
5 ALA 1981, s 6(3).
6 ALA 1981, s 6(2).
7 The meaning of 'practicable' and the distinction between this phrase and the less stringent 'reasonably practicable' has been considered judicially although usually in the context of health and safety legislation; see, eg, *Hammond v Haigh Castle & Co Ltd* [1973] 2 All ER 289, [1973] ICR 148; *Owen v Crown House Engineering Ltd* [1973] 3 All ER 618, [1973] ICR 511; *Dedman v British Building and Engineering Appliances Ltd* [1974] 1 All ER 520, [1974] ICR 53, CA.
8 ALA 1981, s 6(4), although this does not apply where the owner, lessee or occupier is a local authority, statutory undertaker or the National Trust.

D Objections and representations

[407]
Objections may be made in the manner and in the time provided in the notices[1], and must be made in the manner specified[2]. In practice, objections should be made in writing and the grounds of the objection should be set out, as the minister has the power to require an objector to state his grounds for objection in writing and may disregard an objection if he is satisfied that it relates exclusively to matters which can be dealt with by the tribunal by which the compensation is to be assessed[3]. The ALA 1981 also provides[4] that a 'statutory undertaker'[5] may make representations to the minister if its land is included in a draft compulsory purchase order[6]. Examples of potential grounds for objection have been addressed previously[7].

1 See para **[405]**.
2 ALA 1981, Sch 1, para 3(1)(*c*).
3 ALA 1981, Sch 1, para 4(5).
4 ALA 1981, s 16.
5 ALA 1981, s 8 defines statutory undertakers as any person authorised by any enactment to construct, work, or carry on any railway, light railway, tramway, road transport, water transport, canal or inland navigation undertaking or any dock, harbour, pier or lighthouse undertaking, or any undertaking for the supply of hydraulic power or the Civil Aviation Authority or the Post Office.
6 ALA 1981, s 16(1) (as amended); that land must have been acquired by the statutory undertaker for the purposes of their undertaking.
7 See paras **[177]–[194]**.

E Making the order

1 Making the order where no objections are outstanding

[408]
A minister may make a compulsory purchase order with or without modifications if he is satisfied that (*a*) the notice requirements under paras 2 and 3

of Sch 1 to the ALA 1981 have been complied with, and (*b*) either no 'relevant objection' is made, or every 'relevant objection' made is either withdrawn or disregarded[1]. For these purposes, a 'relevant objection' is an objection made by a 'qualifying person'[2]. When making the order, the minister may not authorise the compulsory purchase of any land to which the draft order did not relate, unless all persons interested consent[3]. Once an order has been made, the minister is required to publish certain notices[4].

1 ALA 1981, Sch 1, para 4(1) and (2).
2 ALA 1981, Sch 1, para 4(6). NB If a person qualifies only by virtue of para 3(2A)(b) and the confirming authority thinks that he is not likely to have a claim for injurious affection then his objection is not a 'relevant objection' for the purposes of para 4.
3 ALA 1981, Sch 1, para 5.
4 ALA 1981, Sch 1, para 6.

2 Making the order where objections are outstanding

[409]
Where a 'relevant objection' to the making of a compulsory purchase order is neither withdrawn nor disregarded, it becomes known as a 'remaining objection'[1]. Where there are 'remaining objections' to the making of a compulsory purchase order the minister may either (*a*) proceed under the written representations procedure, or (*b*) proceed by public local inquiry or hearing[3].

1 ALA 1981, Sch 1, para 4A(1).
2 ALA 1981, Sch 1, para 4A(2) and (3).

[409.1]
A minister may proceed under the written representations procedure where:

(*a*) the order is not subject to special parliamentary procedure;
(*b*) the appropriate minister has granted a s 16 certificate[1] in respect of the land of a statutory undertaker; and
(*c*) every person who has made a 'remaining objection' consents in the prescribed manner[2].

The written representations procedure is set out in the Compulsory Purchase of Land (Written Representations Procedure) (Ministers) Regulations 2004[3]. Note that the Government's policy on costs in Department of Communities and Local Government Circular 03/2009 applies, with adaptations, to the written representations procedure.[4]

1 ALA 1981, s 16(2).
2 ALA 1981, Sch 1, para 4A(2).
3 SI 2004/2594. For Wales, see the Compulsory Purchase of Land (Written Representations Procedure) (National Assembly for Wales) Regulations 2004, SI 2004/2730.
4 See DCLG Circular 03/2009, paras 11 and E4.

[409.2]
If the requirements for proceeding under the written representations procedure do not apply, or if the minister decides not to follow the written representations procedure, then if there are 'remaining objections' the minister must either:

(*a*) cause a local public inquiry to be held[1]; or

(*b*) give persons who have remaining objection the opportunity of appearing before and being heard by a person appointed by the confirming authority for the purpose[2].

The procedure at a public local inquiry is discussed in detail at **Section L** below.

1 A minister has power to arrange for an inquiry by virtue of the ALA 1981, s 5.
2 ALA 1981, Sch 1, para 4A(3).

3 Making the order in stages

[409.3]
The new para 4B of Sch 1 to the ALA 1981 allows a minister to make a compulsory purchase order in stages where:

(*a*) the minister is satisfied that the order ought to be made in so far as it relates to part of the land comprised in the order (the 'relevant part') but has not for the time being determined whether the order ought to be made so far as it relates to the 'remaining part'; and
(*b*) the minister is satisfied that the notice requirements have been complied with[1].

If there is a 'remaining objection'[2] in respect of the order, the minister may only make the order in stages after either following the written representations procedure or the public local inquiry/hearing procedure, unless it is satisfied that all 'remaining objections' relate solely to the 'remaining part' of the land[3]. Guidance on the confirmation of compulsory purchase orders in stages is contained in ODPM Circular 06/2004[4].

1 ALA 1981, Sch 1, para 4B(1) and (2).
2 See para **[409]** above.
3 ALA 1981, Sch 1, para 4B(3) and (4).
4 ODPM Circular 06/2004 paras 53 and 54. For the equivalent provisions relating to non-ministerial orders, see paras **[196.3]–[196.4]** above, and *R (Neptune Wharf) v Secretary of State for Trade and Industry* [2007] EWHC 1036 (Admin), [2007] 3 All ER 676.

4 Confirmation with modifications

[410]
The ALA 1981 gives the minister the power to confirm a compulsory purchase order with or without modifications[1]. Government advice in the context of non-ministerial acquiring authorities is that the power will be used sparingly[2], but in practice this power is useful and is quite commonly exercised. A common example is where the minister no longer needs a plot of land or an interest that was included in the order lands when it was made. In such cases the compulsory purchase order can be confirmed with the relevant plot or interest omitted from it.

1 See ALA 1981, Sch 1, para 4(1).
2 ODPM Circular 06/2004, para 51.

[411]–[430]
The minister's power to modify a compulsory purchase order can also be used to correct errors in the description of the land in the order. There are limitations to the exercise of the power for this purpose. The effect of ALA 1981, Sch 1, para 5 is that an order can only be modified to include any additional land or interests if all the people who are affected give their consent. Government guidance in the context of non-ministerial acquiring authorities is that the power can be used to remedy minor slips in the drafting of the order but not to make significant amendments to it[1]. The power is not wide enough to allow the confirming authority to add to or substitute the statutory purposes for which the order was made[2]. By analogy with guidance given on the procedure which a non-ministerial acquiring authority should follow where it wishes the confirming authority to make modifications to the order prior to its confirmation,[3] the confirming authority should notify objectors and interested persons of what modifications it proposes.

1 ODPM Circular 06/2004, paras 31, 51 and 52.
2 *Proctor & Gamble Ltd v Secretary of State for the Environment* (1992) 63 P&CR 317, referred to ODPM Circular 06/2004, para 51.
3 ODPM Circular 06/2004, para 52.

F Public local inquiries

1 Inquiries Procedure Rules

[431]
The procedure to be followed, once the confirming authority has determined that a public local inquiry should be held into objections, is set out in the Compulsory Purchase (Inquiries Procedure) Rules 2007 (CP(IP)R 2007)[1] in England, and the Compulsory Purchase (Inquiries Procedure) (Wales) Rules 2010 in Wales[2]. Guidance on the 2007 rules is to be found in DCLG Circular 01/2008. Welsh Circular NAFWC 14/2004 gives guidance to acquiring authorities in Wales. This section describes inquiries under the CP (IP)R 2007.

1 SI 2007/3617.
2 SI 2010/3015, which apply in Wales to compulsory purchase orders made by the Welsh Ministers and by Welsh local authorities where notice of the inquiry was served after 31 January 2011.

2 Notice of intention to hold an inquiry

[432]
Where the minister intends to hold a public local inquiry, he must, not later than five weeks from the expiry after the time within which objections to the order had to be made[1], provide written notice of that intention[2] to each remaining objector[3]. The date of this notice is the reference point for the inquiry timetable and is known as the 'relevant date'[4].

1 CP(IP)R 2007, r 3(2). For the time for making objections, see para **[175]**.
2 CP(IP)R 2007, r 3(1).

3 A 'remaining objector' means a person who has a remaining objection within the meaning of ALA 1981 Sch 1, para 4A(1): see CP(IP)R 2007, r 2.
4 CP(IP)R 2007, r 2.

3 Minister's power to hold pre-inquiry meetings

[433]
Before some inquiries are held, a meeting known as a 'pre-inquiry meeting' may be convened to consider arrangements for the inquiry to ensure that it is conducted efficiently and expeditiously[1]. The minister may cause a pre-inquiry meeting to be held if it appears to him to be desirable to do so[2]. Where he does consider it desirable, he must give notification of his intention to cause a pre-inquiry meeting to be held, and the meeting or, where there is to be more than one, the first pre-inquiry meeting must be held not later than 16 weeks after the relevant date[3]. A notice of intention to cause a pre-inquiry meeting to be held must be published by the minister not later than three weeks after the relevant date in one or more local newspapers circulating in the locality in which the land is situated[4]. The minister must send an outline statement to each remaining objector not later than eight weeks after the relevant date[5]. The minister may by written notice require any remaining objector or any other person who has notified of his intention to appear at the inquiry to send within eight weeks of the date of the notice an outline statement; the statement is to be sent to the minister and any other person specified in the notice[6]. Not less than three weeks' written notice of the meeting is to be given to each remaining objector, and to any other person whose presence at the meeting seems desirable[7]. Notice of the time, date and place of the meeting must also be given by the minister by way of fixing a notice at the site and in at least one place in the locality in which the land is situated where public notices are usually posted, and/or publication of a notice in one or more newspapers circulating in the locality in which the land is situated[8].

1 CP(IP)R 2007, r 2. The minister's power to hold a pre-inquiry meeting will be exercised only in exceptional cases, such as where the draft order raises matters of major public interest, has national or regional implications, raises issues of particular complexity or involves much third party involvement: see DCLG Circular 1/2008, para 16 and the examples given therein.
2 CP(IP)R 2007, r 4.
3 CP(IP)R 2007, r 4. CP(IP)R 2007, r 5, contains the prescribed procedures for pre-inquiry meetings. See para **[198]** for the meaning of 'relevant date'.
4 CP(IP)R 2007, r 5(1).
5 CP(IP)R 2007, r 5(2). 'Outline statement' is defined as a written statement of the principal submissions which a person proposes to put forward at an inquiry: CP(IP)R 2007, r 2.
6 CP(IP)R 2007, r 5(3).
7 CP(IP)R 2007, r 5(4).
8 CP(IP)R 2007, r 5(5). Acquiring authorities are encouraged to publish notices of pre-inquiries meetings on their websites: DCLG Circular 1/2008, para 17.

4 Inspector's power to hold a pre-inquiry meeting

[434]
An inspector has the power to hold a pre-inquiry meeting if he considers it desirable, notwithstanding that the minister has not caused one to be held[1]. In these circumstances, the inspector must arrange for not less than three

weeks' written notice of the meeting to be given to the minister, each statutory objector, any other person known at the date of the notice to be entitled to appear at the inquiry, and any other person whose presence at the meeting appears to him to be desirable[2].

1 CP(IP)R 2007, r 6(3).
2 CP(IP)R 2007, r 6(3).

5 Procedure at a pre-inquiry meeting

[435]
The meeting is to be presided over by the inspector[1] and he is to determine the matters to be discussed and the procedure to be followed[2]. He has the power to require any person present at the meeting to leave, if he is of the opinion that that person is behaving in a disruptive manner. He may refuse to permit that person to return or to attend any further meeting, or he may permit them to return or attend, subject to such conditions as he shall specify[3].

1 'Inspector' is defined as a person appointed by the minister to hold an inquiry or a reopened inquiry: CP(IP)R 2007, r 2.
2 CP(IP)R 2007, r 6(4).
3 CP(IP)R 2007, r 6(4)(*a*)–(*b*).

6 Outline statements

[436]
The requirement to serve outline statements appears only to apply where a pre-inquiry meeting is held[1].

1 CP(IP)R 2007, r 5, and DCLG Circular 1/2008, para 17. 'Outline statement' is defined as a written statement of the principal submissions which a person proposes to put forward at an inquiry: CP(IP)R 2007, r 2.

7 The minister's statement of case

[437]
A 'statement of case' is defined as a written statement containing full particulars of the case which a person proposes to put forward at the inquiry (including, where that person is the acquiring authority, the reasons for making the order), together with any copies of any documents referred to in such a statement (or the relevant extracts from those documents) and a list of any documents to which that person intends to refer or which he intends to put in evidence[1]. Where a pre-inquiry meeting has been held[2], the minister is required to serve a statement of case upon each remaining objector not later than four weeks after the conclusion of that meeting[3]. Where no pre-inquiry meeting has been held, the minister is required to serve a statement of case upon each remaining objector not later than six weeks after the relevant date[4]. Unless every document, or the relevant part of every document, which the minister intends to refer to or put in evidence at the inquiry has been copied to each remaining objector, the minister shall send to each remaining

objector a notice naming each place where a copy of those documents may be inspected free of charge at all reasonable hours until the date of commencement of the inquiry, and each place so named shall be as close as reasonably possible to the land[5]. The minister must provide any person who so requests, with a reasonable opportunity to inspect and, where practicable, take copies of any statement or document which (or a copy of which) has been served on or by it[6]. The minister's statement of case must also indicate the time and place at which this opportunity will be afforded[7]. The inspector has the power to require the minister to provide such further information about the matters contained in its statement of case as he may specify[8].

1 CP(IP)R 2007, r 2.
2 See paras **[433]–[435]**.
3 CP(IP)R 2007, r 7(1)(*a*).
4 CP(IP)R 2007, r 7(1)(*b*).
5 CP(IP)R 2007, r 7(2).
6 CP(IP)R 2007, r 7(6).
7 CP(IP)R 2007, r 7(6).
8 CP(IP)R 2007, r 7(5).

8 Statements of case by other parties

[438]
The minister has the power to require any remaining objector or any other person who has notified him of an intention or wish to appear at the inquiry to serve a statement of case upon him and on any other person[1]. This power must be exercised by means of a notice in writing[2]. Persons so notified who are not remaining objectors are to be supplied with a copy of the minister's statement of case [3] and they are to serve their statements of case within six weeks of the date of that notice[4]. The minister or an inspector also has the power to require any person who has served a statement of case to provide such further information about the matters contained in the statement as he may specify[5].

1 CP(IP)R 2007, r 7(3).
2 CP(IP)R 2007, r 7(3).
3 CP(IP)R 2007, r 7(4).
4 CP(IP)R 2007, r 7(3).
5 CP(IP)R 2007, r 7(5).

9 Inquiry timetable

[439]
Where the minister or inspector has caused a pre-inquiry meeting to take place[1], the inspector must arrange a timetable for the proceedings at or at part of the inquiry. He then has the power to vary that timetable at any time[2]. Where no pre-inquiry meeting has been held, the inspector has the power to set a timetable, but whether he does so is a matter for his discretion[3]. Provision is made for notifying people entitled to appear at the inquiry of the time table for the proceedings and any variation to it[4].

1 See paras **[433]–[435]**.
2 CP(IP)R 2007, r 8(1).

3 CP(IP)R 2007, r 8(1).
4 CP(IP)R 2007, r 8(1) and (3).

10 Appointment of an assessor

[440]
An assessor is a person appointed by the minister to sit with an inspector at an inquiry or reopened inquiry to advise the inspector on such matters arising as the minister may specify[1]. They are usually appointed to address matters requiring a particular technical expertise. Where an assessor is appointed, the minister is required to notify every remaining objector, and any person who has sent an outline statement or a statement of case[2] of the name of the assessor and of the matters on which he is to advise the inspector[3].

1 CP(IP)R 2007, r 2.
2 CP(IP)R 2007, r 9.
3 CP(IP)R 2007, r 9.

11 Date and notification of an inquiry

[441]
Where a pre-inquiry meeting is held[1], the date fixed by the minister for the commencement of the inquiry must be not later than eight weeks after the conclusion of that meeting or the last of any such meetings[2]. Where no pre-inquiry meeting is held, the date fixed for the holding of the inquiry must be not later than 22 weeks after the relevant date[3]. However, the minister has power to vary the date for the holding of an inquiry where he is satisfied that, in all the circumstances of the case, it is impracticable to hold an inquiry within either the eight weeks or the 22 weeks, as the case may be[4]. Where this power is exercised, the minister must hold the inquiry at the earliest practicable date[5]. In any event, unless the minister has the agreement of each remaining objector as to some lesser period of notice, the he must give at least six weeks' written notice of the date, time and place fixed by him for the holding of the inquiry to all persons who are entitled to appear at it[6]. The same requirement exists where a date fixed for holding an inquiry is varied[7]. Where the time or place for holding the inquiry is varied, the minister shall give such notice of the variation as appears to it to be reasonable[8]. The inquiry may be held partly in one place and partly in another where the minister is satisfied that it is reasonable to do so having regard to the nature of the draft order[9]. Further guidance on the fixing of dates for an inquiry is given in DCLG Circular 1/2008[10].

1 See paras **[433]–[435]**.
2 CP(IP)R 2007, r 10(1)(*b*).
3 CP(IP)R 2007, r 10(1)(*a*) and, as to relevant date, see para **[432]**.
4 CP(IP)R 2007, r 10(1)(*c*).
5 CP(IP)R 2007, r 10(1)(*c*).
6 CP(IP)R 2007, r 10(2).
7 CP(IP)R 2007, r 10(3).
8 CP(IP)R 2007, r 10(4).

9 CP(IP)R 2007, r 10(5). DCLG Circular 1/2008 states that this is only expected to occur where the order relates to a large, linear scheme such as a major road. For non-ministerial orders, PINS are to consult on the arrangements with the acquiring authority: DCLG Circular 1/2008, para 26.
10 See DCLG Circular 1/2008, para 25.

[442]
ODPM Circular 06/2004 advises that an inquiry will typically be held some six months after the submission of the order for confirmation[1]. Once fixed, the date for an inquiry will be changed only for exceptional reasons. As a general rule the date will not be changed because the acquiring authority needs more time to prepare or because a particular advocate may be unavailable[2].

1 ODPM Circular 06/2004, para 42.
2 ODPM Circular 06/2004, para 43.

12 Notice of the inquiry

[443]
The minister is under a duty to post a notice of the inquiry in a conspicuous place near the land that is the subject of the order and also in at least one place where public notices are usually posted in the locality, not later than two weeks before the date fixed for the holding of the inquiry[1]. He must also publish notice of the inquiry in one or more newspapers circulating in the locality in which the land is situated.[2] Any notice of the inquiry is required to contain a clear statement of the date, time and place of the inquiry, the powers under which the order has been made and a description of the land sufficient to identify approximately its location without reference to the map referred to in the order[3].

1 CP(IP)R 2007, r 11(1)(a).
2 CP(IP)R 2007, r 11(1)(*b*).
3 CP(IP)R 2007, r 11(3)(*b*).

13 Representation of the minister at the inquiry

[443.1]
The minister may be represented at the inquiry by counsel or solicitor or by an officer of its department or other person authorised by the minister to represent him[1]. The minister is required to make a representative available at the inquiry to give evidence in elucidation of the statement of case, and such representative shall be subject to cross-examination to the same extent as any other witnesses[2]. The representative shall not be required to answer any question which in the opinion of the inspector is directed to the merits of Government policy[3].

1 CP(IP)R 2007, r 12(1)(*a*).
2 CP(IP)R 2007, r 12(1)(*b*).
3 CP(IP)R 2007, r 12(2). See also *Bushell v Secretary of State for the Environment* [1981] AC 75.

14 Representation of Government departments

[444]
Where a Government department (other than the department of a minister who is the acquiring authority) has made a statement or representation in writing in support of the order or the draft order and the acquiring authority has included that statement in its statement of case, a representative of the department concerned shall be made available to attend the inquiry[1]. Such a representative shall, at the inquiry, state the reasons for the view expressed by his department and shall give evidence and be subject to cross-examination to the same extent as any other witness[2]. A representative of a Government department shall not be required to answer any question which in the opinion of the inspector is directed to the merits of Government policy[3].

1 CP(IP)R 2007, r 13(1).
2 CP(IP)R 2007, r 13(2).
3 CP(IP)R 2007, r 13(3).

15 Appearances at the inquiry

[445]
The following persons are entitled to appear at an inquiry[1]:

(*a*) any remaining objector[2];
(*b*) the minister; and
(*c*) any other person who has served an outline statement[3] or a statement of case[4].

An inspector may permit any other person to appear at the inquiry and this permission is not to be unreasonably withheld[5]. Any person who is entitled or permitted to appear may do so in person or be represented by counsel, solicitor or any other person[6]. An inspector may allow one or more persons to appear on behalf of some or all of any persons having a similar interest in the matter under inquiry[7].

1 CP(IP)R 2007, r 14(1) and (2).
2 See para **[432]**, fn 3.
3 See para **[436]**.
4 See paras **[437]–[438]**.
5 CP(IP)R 2007, r 14(3).
6 CP(IP)R 2007, r 14(4).
7 CP(IP)R 2007, r 14(5).

16 Proofs of evidence

[446]
A person entitled to appear at an inquiry to give, or to call another person to give, evidence at the inquiry by reading a statement of that evidence shall send to the inspector and to the minister, a copy of that statement (known as a 'proof of evidence' together with any relevant supporting documents[1]. A written summary of the statement (known as a 'summary proof') must be provided where the statement contains more than 1,500 words[2]. Proofs of

evidence and summary proofs are to be served on the inspector and the acquiring authority on the date provided for by any inquiry timetable where one has been set [3] or, if there is no timetable, three weeks before the date fixed for the holding of the inquiry[4]. Where the minister provides a proof or a summary proof to an inspector, it is required to send at the same time copies to any remaining objector and to any other person who has sent an outline statement or statement of case[5]. The minister shall afford to any person who so requests a reasonable opportunity to inspect and, where practicable and on payment of a reasonable charge, take copies of any document sent to or by it[6]. Where summary proofs have been required, only the summary proof shall be read at the inquiry, unless the inspector permits or requires otherwise[7]. Where a summary is read, the proof of evidence to which it relates is to be treated as tendered in evidence unless he notifies the inspector that he wishes to rely on his summary proof only, and the person whose evidence the proof contains is to be subject to cross-examination on it to the same extent as if it were evidence that had been given orally[8].

1 CP(IP)R 2007, r 15(1). Further guidance on statements of evidence and their content is given in DCLG Circular 1/2008, para 32.
2 CP(IP)R 2007, r 15(2).
3 CP(IP)R 2007, r 15(3)(*b*).
4 CP(IP)R 2007, r 15(3)(*a*).
5 CP(IP)R 2007, r 15(6).
6 CP(IP)R 2007, r 16(5).
7 CP(IP)R 2007, r 15(4).
8 CP(IP)R 2007, r 16(5).

17 Procedure at the inquiry

[447]
The general rule is that it is for the inspector to determine the procedure to be followed at an inquiry[1]. However, there are a number of aspects of procedure that are specified by the CP(IP)R 2007. The minister is to present its case first and to have the final right of reply, unless the inspector, with the consent of the minister, determines otherwise[2]. Other persons entitled or permitted to appear at the inquiry are to be heard in such order as the inspector may determine[3]. Where the inspector has a discretion as to the conduct of the proceedings, this discretion should be exercised in a way that does not infringe common law rules of procedural fairness[4].

1 CP(IP)R 2007, r 16(1).
2 CP(IP)R 2007, r 16(1).
3 CP(IP)R 2007, r 16(1).
4 See, eg, *Nicholson v Secretary of State for Energy* (1977) 76 LGR 693, concerning the discretion of an inspector at a planning inquiry to allow cross-examination, and *R (Gates Hydraulics Ltd) v Secretary of State for Communities and Local Government* [2009] EWHC 2187 (Admin), concerning unfairness where the planning inspector's decision disagreed with matters which had been common ground between the parties at the inquiry.

[448]
Persons entitled to appear at the inquiry[1] are entitled to call evidence, and the minister and remaining objectors are entitled to cross-examine persons giving evidence, otherwise the calling of evidence and the cross-examination

of those giving evidence are at the inspector's discretion[2]. Thus, persons permitted (as opposed to entitled) to appear have no right under the rules to give evidence or to cross-examine[3].

1 See para **[231]**.
2 CP(IP)R 2007, r 16(3).
3 However, common law rules of procedural fairness are relevant to the exercise of an inspector's discretion: see, eg, *Miller (T A) Ltd v Minister of Housing and Local Government* [1968] 2 All ER 633; *Bushell v Secretary of State for the Environment* [1981] AC 75; *Nicholson v Secretary of State for Energy* (1977) 76 LGR 693.

[449]
Where he considers it to be irrelevant or repetitious, the inspector may refuse to permit the giving or production of evidence, the cross-examination of persons giving evidence or the presentation of any other matter[1]. Where the inspector exercises this power and refuses to permit the giving of oral evidence, the person wishing to give that evidence may submit any evidence or other matters in writing to the inspector before the close of the inquiry[2].

1 CP(IP)R 2007, r 16(4). On an inspector's discretion as to what evidence is considered relevant, see *R v Secretary of State for the Environment, ex p Royal Borough of Kensington and Chelsea* [1987] JPL 567.
2 CP(IP)R 2007, r 16(4).

[450]
The inspector has power to require a person appearing or present at an inquiry, who in his opinion, is behaving in a disruptive manner to leave. He may refuse to permit that person to return or may permit him to return only on such conditions as he may specify[1]. Where the inspector exercises this power, the person wishing to give evidence may submit that evidence or other matters in writing to the inspector before the close of the inquiry[2].

1 CP(IP)R 2007, r 16(7).
2 CP(IP)R 2007, r 16(7).

[451]
The inspector may allow any person to alter or add to a statement of case so far as may be necessary for the purposes of the inquiry[1]. Where the inspector does so, he must (if necessary by adjourning the inquiry) give every person entitled to appear at the inquiry an adequate opportunity of considering any new matter of fact or document introduced by the acquiring authority[2].

1 CP(IP)R 2007, r 16(8).
2 CP(IP)R 2007, r 16(8).

[452]
The inspector may from time to time adjourn an inquiry and, if the date, time and place of the adjourned inquiry are announced at the inquiry before the adjournment, no further notice is required[1]. He may also proceed with an inquiry in the absence of any person entitled to appear at it[2].

1 CP(IP)R 2007, r 16(11). On the discretion to adjourn a public inquiry, see *Powell v Secretary of State for Environment, Food and Rural Affairs* [2009] EWHC 643 (Admin); *Orakpo v London Borough of Wandsworth* (1992) 24 HLR 370; *Osreicher v Secretary of State for the Environment* [1978] 1 WLR 810, CA; *Webb v Secretary of State for the Environment* (1990) 22 HLR 274.
2 CP(IP)R 2007, r 16(9).

[453]
Where any written representation, evidence or other document has been received by the inspector before an inquiry opens or during an inquiry, he may take it into account, as long as he discloses it to the parties at the inquiry[1].

1 CP(IP)R 2007, r 16(10).

[454]
The inspector may direct the minister to provide facilities so that any person appearing at the inquiry may be afforded a reasonable opportunity to inspect, and where practicable and on payment of a reasonable charge, take copies of, any documents open to public inspection[1].

1 CP(IP)R 2007, r 16(6).

18 Site inspections

[455]
The inspector may make an unaccompanied inspection of the land which is the subject of the order before or during the inquiry, without giving any notice of his intention to do so to the parties to the inquiry[1]. In addition, however, either during an inquiry or after the close of an inquiry, the inspector may inspect the land in the company of a representative of the minister and any remaining objector[2]. If the minister or any remaining objector requests such an inspection either before or during an inquiry, the inspector is required to make such an inspection[3]. The date and time when the inspection is proposed to be made must be announced by the inspector during the inquiry[4]. The inspector is not bound to defer the inspection if a representative of the minister or any statutory objector fails to be present at the time appointed for the inspection[5]. Where the minister takes into account matters noticed on the site inspection which were not in issue at the inquiry, the requirements of procedural fairness may make the compulsory purchase order liable to be quashed[6].

1 CP(IP)R 2007, r 17(1).
2 CP(IP)R 2007, r 17(2).
3 CP(IP)R 2007, r 17(2).
4 CP(IP)R 2007, r 17(3).
5 CP(IP)R 2007, r 17(4).
6 *Fairmount Investments Ltd v Secretary of State for the Environment* [1976] 2 All ER 865, HL; *Hibernian Property Co v Secretary of State for the Environment* (1973) 27 P&CR 197.

19 Procedure after the inquiry

[456]
After an inquiry closes, the inspector must produce a report in writing and submit it to the minister. This report is to include the inspector's conclusions and his recommendations or his reasons for not making any recommendations[1]. There is no general duty upon the inspector to send to the Secretary of State a copy of an objector's final written submissions, provided the inspector's report fairly summarises those submissions and resolves them in his conclusions[2].

1 CP(IP)R 2007, r 18(1).
2 *R (Mortell) v Secretary of State* [2009] EWCA Civ 1274 at [45]

[457]
Where an assessor was appointed, he may, after the close of the inquiry, submit a report in writing to the inspector in respect of the matters on which he was appointed to advise[1]. Such a report must be appended to the inspector's report, and the inspector must indicate in his own report whether and to what extent he agrees or disagrees with the assessor's report and, where he disagrees, he must indicate his reasons for that disagreement[2].

1 CP(IP)R 2007, r 18(2).
2 CP(IP)R 2007, r 18(3).

[458]
Where:

(*a*) the minister differs from the inspector on any matter of fact mentioned in or appearing to him to be material to a conclusion reached by the inspector; or
(*b*) the minister takes into consideration any new evidence or new matters of fact (not being a matter of Government policy),

and is for that reason disposed to disagree with a recommendation made by the inspector, the minister is not permitted to come to a decision at variance with that recommendation without first notifying the persons who appeared at the inquiry of his disagreement and the reasons for it[1]. Every person so notified must be given an opportunity to make written representations[2]. Written representations are to be made within three weeks of the date of the notification[3]. Where the minister proposes to disagree with his inspector for reasons that do not require him to notify the parties, he may nevertheless choose to do so[4].

1 CP(IP)R 2007, r 18(3). For a challenge based on the Secretary of State's approach to matters raised after the close of the compulsory purchase inquiry, see *Pascoe v Secretary of State for Communities and Local Government* [2009] EWHC 881 (Admin) at [20] to [36].
2 CP(IP)R 2007, r 18(5)(*a*).
3 CP(IP)R 2007, r 18(5)(*a*).
4 *Alliance Spring Co Ltd v First Secretary of State* [2005] EWHC 18 (Admin), [2005] All ER (D) 112 (Jan) at [14].

[459]
If the reason that the Secretary of State is disposed to disagree with a recommendation made by the inspector falls into category (*b*) above, the persons entitled to appear at the inquiry may, as an alternative to making written representations, request that the inquiry be reopened[1]. Such requests are to be made within three weeks of the date of the notification[2].

1 CP(IP)R 2007, r 18(5)(*b*).
2 CP(IP)R 2007, r 18(5)(*b*).

[460]
Where a request to reopen an inquiry is made, the minister retains a discretion to do so. However, where such a request to reopen an inquiry is made by

a remaining objector, the minister must reopen the inquiry to afford an opportunity for persons to be heard on such matters relating to the compulsory purchase order as he may specify[1]. If an inquiry is reopened, the minister is required to send to all persons entitled to appear at the inquiry who appeared at it a written statement of the matters so specified[2]. In these circumstances, the procedures relating to the setting of the date of and to notification of the inquiry are the same as those generally applicable, with the exception that he must give not less than four weeks' notice of the date, time and place fixed for holding the inquiry, instead of six weeks' notice[3].

1 CP(IP)R 2007, r 18(6). The re-opened inquiry does not have to be before the same inspector.
2 CP(IP)R 2007, r 18(6)(*a*).
3 CP(IP)R 2007, r 18(6)(*b*).

G Notification of the decision

[461]
The minister is required to give written notification of his decision on the draft compulsory purchase order, together with the reasons for that decision, to each statutory objector, any person entitled to appear at the inquiry who did appear at that inquiry, and any other person who appeared at the inquiry and who asked to be notified of the decision[1]. The minister is not required to send a copy of the inspector's report[2] to all such persons, although he is required to provide a copy of the conclusions and of any recommendations made by the inspector[3]. Any person who is entitled to receive notification of the minister's decision, who makes a written application within four weeks of the date of the minister's decision to be supplied with a copy of the inspector's report, must be provided with such a copy[4].

1 CP(IP)R 2007, r 19(1).
2 In this context, the inspector's report is taken to include reference to any report which may have been made by an assessor: CP(IP)R 2007, r 19(2) and (3).
3 CP(IP)R 2007, r 19(2).
4 CP(IP)R 2007, r 19(2).

H Notices after confirmation of the order

[462]
After the minister has confirmed the compulsory purchase order, he must serve a making notice and a copy of the order on all persons upon whom he was required to serve notice of the draft order[1], and affix a making notice to a conspicuous object or objects on or near the land comprised in the order[2]. The making notice must also be published in one or more local newspapers circulating in the locality in which the land comprised in the order is situated[3]. The contents of the making notice and notice to be affixed near the land are specified by statute[4]. The making notice must be in the prescribed form[5].

1 ALA 1981, Sch 1, para 6(1)(*a*).
2 ALA 1981, Sch 1, para 6(1)(*b*).
3 ALA 1981, Sch 1, para 6(3).
4 ALA 1981, Sch 1, para 6(2) and (4).
5 ALA 1981, Sch 1, para 6(5), and the Compulsory Purchase of Land (Prescribed Forms) (Ministers) Regulations 2004, SI 2004/2595, reg 3(*e*), and Schedule, Form 10.

I Awards of costs incurred at inquiries

[463]–[600]

The Local Government Act 1972 (LGA 1972), s 250, which contains a power to make costs awards at public inquiries, does not apply in relation to a proposed acquisition of land by a minister[1]. DCLG Circular 03/2009 does not apply to cases where the minister is the acquiring authority[2]. Nevertheless, where the minister is the acquiring authority his practice is to award costs to successful objectors.

1 ALA 1981, s 5(3).
2 DCLG Circular 03/2009, para E2.

Chapter 4

Special categories of land

Contents

A Introduction

[601]
Where an order includes certain special categories of land, particular procedures may apply. These categories include:

(*a*) land held by a statutory undertakers;
(*b*) land owned by local authority;
(*c*) land owned by the National Trust;
(*d*) land which forms part of a common, open space or allotment;
(*e*) land which includes any listed buildings or which is within a conservation area;
(*f*) land which forms part of a burial ground;
(*g*) land which is ecclesiastical property; and
(*h*) land which forms part of the public highway.

B Land held by statutory undertakers

1 Definition of statutory undertakers

[602]
Certain special procedures apply if a compulsory purchase order includes the operational land1 of body which is defined as or deemed to be a statutory undertaker. A statutory undertaker is defined in the Acquisition of Land Act 1981 (ALA 1981), s 8(1) as any person authorised by any enactment to construct, work or carry on any railway, light railway, tramway, road transport, water transport, canal or inland navigation undertaking or any dock,

harbour, pier or lighthouse undertaking or any undertaking for the supply of hydraulic power, or the Civil Aviation Authority or the Post Office.

1 'Operational land' is land acquired for the purposes of their undertaking: ALA 1981, s 17(1)(*b*).

[603]
Certain other bodies are deemed to be statutory undertakers for the purposes of the ALA 1981 under other enactments:

(*a*) *electricity*: the holder of a licence pursuant to the Electricity Act 1989, s 6 and who is authorised to acquire land compulsorily under s 10 and Sch 3 to that Act is a statutory undertaker for the purposes of the ALA 1981 (Electricity Act 1989, s 112(1), Sch 16, para 2(2)(*g*)).
(*b*) *gas*: a public gas transporter within the meaning of the Gas Act 1986, s 7, as amended by the Gas Act 1995, is a statutory undertaker for the purposes of the ALA 1981 (Gas Act 1995, Sch 4, para 2(1)(xxxi)).
(*c*) *water*: every water undertaker[1] is deemed to be a statutory undertaker and its undertaking is deemed to be a statutory undertaking for the purposes of the ALA 1981 (Water Act 1989, s 190, Sch 25, para 1(1), (2)(xxvii)).
(*d*) *airport operators*: any airport, to which Pt V of the Airports Act 1986 applies, is deemed to be a statutory undertaking and a 'relevant airport operator'[2] is deemed to be a statutory undertaker for the purposes of the ALA 1981 (Airports Act 1986, s 58, Sch 2, para 1(1)).

1 Appointed pursuant to the Water Industry Act 1991, s 6.
2 A 'relevant airport operator' is defined as a person for the time being having the management of an airport: Airports Act 1986, s 82(1).

2 Protection afforded to statutory undertakers

[604]
Statutory undertakers have two forms of protection that can be invoked to protect their undertakings:

(*a*) they can make a *representation* to ensure that their undertaking is excluded from any order[1]; and
(*b*) they can make an *objection* to the order and thereby invoke the 'special parliamentary procedure'[2].

1 See the ALA 1981, s 16.
2 See the ALA 1981, s 17.

Exclusion from compulsory purchase

[605]
Where:

(*a*) the land in the compulsory purchase order includes land acquired by a statutory undertaker for the purposes of its undertaking;
(*b*) it has made a *representation*[1] to the appropriate minister[2] before the expiration of the time within which objections to the order must made, and which has not been withdrawn; and

(*c*) the appropriate minister is satisfied that any of the land within the order is used for the purpose of carrying on the undertaking and that the statutory undertaker holds any interest in the land for that purpose;

then the order may not be confirmed or made so as to authorise the compulsory purchase of any land to which (*c*) applies, except for any land which, due to its nature and situation, the minister certifies[3] can be purchased and not replaced without serious detriment to the carrying on of the undertaking or can be replaced by other land belonging to, or available for acquisition by, the undertakers without serious detriment to the carrying of the undertaking[4].

1 It should be noted that a representation is distinct from an objection to the compulsory purchase order. Where the statutory undertaker objects to an order, the provisions of the ALA 1981, s 17 apply, see para **[606]**.
2 ALA 1981, s 8(3) defines the appropriate minister as meaning the Secretary of State. However, ODPM Circular 06/2004 App L para 6 explains that the appropriate minister is the minister operationally responsible for the undertaker. Thus, the appropriate minister may be a minister other than the minister who is the confirming authority.
3 Where a minister certifies this, he must publish a newspaper notice. The form of such a notice is prescribed by the Compulsory Purchase of Land (Prescribed Forms) (Ministers) Regulations 2004, SI 2004/2595, Form 12.
4 ALA 1981, s 16(1), (2).

Invoking special parliamentary procedure

[606]
Where:

(*a*) the land in the compulsory purchase order includes land acquired by a statutory undertaker for the purposes of their undertaking; and
(*b*) they have made an *objection*[1] to the confirming authority before the expiration of the time within which objections to the order must made, and which has not been withdrawn,

then the order is to be subject to 'special parliamentary procedure'[2], in so far as the order includes land acquired by a statutory undertaker for the purposes of their undertaking[3].

1 As opposed to a representation, see para **[604]**.
2 These are the procedures set out in the Statutory Orders (Special Procedure) Act 1945 (as amended) and addressed in **Chapter 5**.
3 ALA 1981, s 17(1), (2).

[607]
However, this procedure cannot be invoked if the acquiring authority is[1]:

(*a*) a local authority[2];
(*b*) a National Park authority;
(*c*) an urban development corporation,
(*d*) a Welsh planning board;
(*e*) any statutory undertaker[3] (including a housing trust); or
(*f*) a minister.

The details of special parliamentary procedure are contained in **Chapter 5** of this Division.

1 ALA 1981, s 17(3).
2 See definition in the ALA 1981, s 17(4).
3 See definition in the ALA 1981, s 17(4).

C Land owned by a local authority

[608]
If an order includes land which is the property of a local authority, the compulsory purchase order is to be subject to special parliamentary procedure in any case where an objection has been made to the order and that objection has not been withdrawn[1]. However, again, this procedure cannot be invoked if the acquiring authority is[2]:

(*a*) a local authority[3];
(*b*) a National Park authority;
(*c*) an urban development corporation,
(*d*) a Welsh planning board;
(*e*) any statutory undertaker[4] (including a housing trust); or
(*f*) a minister.

1 ALA 1981, s 17(1), (2).
2 ALA 1981, s 17(4).
3 See definition in the ALA 1981, s 17(4).
4 See definition in the ALA 1981, s 17(4).

D National Trust land

[609]
A compulsory purchase order which includes land held by the National Trust inalienably[1] is to be subject to special parliamentary procedure, in respect of such land, in any case where the Trust has made an objection to the order and that objection has not been withdrawn[2].

1 This is defined as meaning land belonging to the National Trust which is inalienable under the National Trust Act 1907, s 21 or the National Trust Act 1939, s 8.
2 ALA 1981, s 18(1), (2).

E Commons, open spaces and allotments

[610]–[620]
Where a compulsory purchase order includes land which forms part of a common[1], open space[2] or fuel or field garden allotment[3], then the order is to be subject to special parliamentary procedure, unless the Secretary of State 'certifies'[4] that he is satisfied that any one of three exceptions is made out[5]. These exceptions are addressed below.

1 A common includes any land subject to be enclosed under the Inclosure Acts 1845–1882 and any town or village green: ALA 1981, s 19(4).
2 Open space is defined as meaning any land laid out as a public garden, land used for the purposes of public recreation or land being a disused burial ground: ALA 1981, s 19(4).

3 Fuel or field garden allotment is defined as meaning any allotment set out as a fuel allotment or a field allotment under an Inclosure Act: ALA 1981, s 19(4).
4 Where a minister certifies this, he must publish a newspaper notice. The form of such a notice is prescribed by the Compulsory Purchase of Land (Prescribed Forms) (Ministers) Regulations 2004, SI 2004/2595, Form 12.
5 ALA 1981, s 19(1).

1 Exchange land

[621]
If the Secretary of State is satisfied that:

(*a*) land has been or will be given in exchange for the common land, open space or allotment which is:
  (i) not less in area,
  (ii) equally advantageous to the persons entitled to use the land;
(*b*) the land has been or will be vested in the persons in whom the land included within the order is vested; and
(*c*) that the land to be given in exchange is subject to the like rights, trusts and incidents as the land included within the order,

he may issue a certificate[1].

1 ALA 1981, s 19(1).

[622]
ODPM Circular 06/2004, App L para 25 advises that in examining exchange land, the Secretary of State may have regard to such matter as relative size and proximity to the land being acquired. The date on which the equality of advantage is to be assessed is the date of exchange, although the Secretary of State may have regard to the prospects of improvement of the exchange land which exist at that date[1]. The Secretary of State will look at the character and features of the exchange land and, whilst it may not offer precisely the same advantages as the land to be acquired, its advantages may be such as to provide an overall equality of advantage[2]. Land which is already in public use for recreation generally cannot be given as exchange land because this would result in a net loss of open space, which would be disadvantageous to the public. However, land temporarily in public use (eg pending development) may be given as exchange land, as this will ensure that its use by the public can be safeguarded for the future.

1 *Greenwich London Borough Council v Secretary of State for the Environment and Secretary of State for Transport* [1994] JPL 607.
2 ODPM Circular 06/2004, App L, para 25.

2 Preserving the land

[623]
If the Secretary of State is satisfied that the land is being purchased in order to secure its preservation or improve its management, he may issue a certificate[1].

1 ALA 1981, s 19(1)(*aa*).

3 Land take is not significant

[624]
If the Secretary of State is satisfied that the land to be acquired:

(*a*) does not exceed 250 square yards; or
(*b*) is required for the widening or drainage of an existing highway or partly for the widening and partly for the drainage of an existing highway,

and that the giving of exchange land is unnecessary, whether in the interests of the persons entitled to use the land or in the interests of the public, he may issue a certificate[1].

1 ALA 1981, s 19(1)(*b*).

[625]
Where the Secretary of State proposes to make a certificate to the effect that one of the three exceptions[1] is made out, he is required to direct the acquiring authority to give public notice of his intention so to do[2]. Notice is to be given in such form as the Secretary of State may direct[3]. The Secretary of State may only give the certificate:

(*a*) after affording opportunity to all persons interested to make representations and objections in relation to the grant of that certificate[4];
(*b*) after considering any representations or objections so made;
(*c*) where he considers it expedient to do so after having had regard to any representations or objections made, after causing a public inquiry to be held[5]; and
(*d*) where an inquiry has been held, after considering the report of the person who held the inquiry[6].

1 See para **[621]**.
2 ALA 1981, s 19(2).
3 ALA 1981, s 19(2A). A notice should be in such terms as are fairly and reasonably necessary to enable members of the public in the area of the land affected to appreciate that they are interested and to make representations as they think fit, and in particular the heading of the notice is of paramount importance: *Wilson v Secretary of State for the Environment* [1974] 1 All ER 428.
4 ALA 1981, s 19(2)(*a*).
5 ALA 1981, s 19(2)(*b*). The discretion as to whether to hold an inquiry or not is relatively wide and, where the issue to decide is relatively straightforward and has been fully covered in written submissions, it is acceptable for the Secretary of State to decide not to hold an inquiry: *Waltham Forest Borough Council v Secretary of State for the Environment and Secretary of State for Transport* [1994] JPL 655.
6 ALA 1981, s 19(2).

[626]
An acquiring authority which will require a s 19 certificate should apply to the relevant Secretary of State as set out in ODPM Circular 06/2004, App L, para 17. If the application is made at the same time as the submission of the compulsory purchase order, the procedures relating to the grant or refusal of a certificate can be run in parallel with those relating to the order generally. Thus, if an inquiry is required in relation to the grant of a certificate, it can be heard alongside any inquiry into the compulsory purchase orders.

F Listed buildings and conservation areas

[627]
Where a compulsory purchase order includes any buildings that are listed[1] or within a conservation area, the acquiring authority must provide a certificate[2] relating to that building, when they submit the order for confirmation[3]. The acquiring authority is also asked to provide particulars of the building concerned and should indicate any action that it has taken or will take in connection with securing any necessary listed building or conservation area consents. A copy of any consent or any application for such a consent should be forwarded to the Department for Culture, Media and Sport with the certificate. The acquiring authority should notify English Heritage as soon as possible, where the submitted order requires the demolition of any building which subsequently becomes included within a conservation area.

1 Ie a building listed under the provisions of the Planning (Listed Buildings and Conservation Areas) Act 1990, s 1.
2 The forms of the certificates are set out in ODPM Circular 06/2004, App S, para 3.
3 ODPM Circular 06/2004, App S, para 2.

G Burial grounds

[628]
A disused burial ground is included within the definition of 'open space' and so is subject to the procedures outlined above[1] relating to exchange land. A burial ground includes any churchyard, cemetery, or other ground, whether consecrated or not, which has been at any time set apart for the purposes of interment[2]. A disused burial ground means any burial ground which is no longer used for interments, whether or not the ground has been partially or wholly closed for burials under the provisions of a statute or Order in Council[3].

1 ALA 1981, s 19(4), see paras **[621]** ff.
2 Open Spaces Act 1906, s 20. As to the meaning of 'set apart for the purposes of interment', see *Nicholl v Llantwit Major Parish Council* [1924] 2 Ch 214; *LCC v Greenwich Corpn* [1929] 1 Ch 305.
3 Open Spaces Act 1906, s 20.

H Ecclesiastical property

[629]
As identified above, there are additional notice requirements to be fulfilled when a compulsory purchase order includes ecclesiastical property[1].

1 See para **[175]**.

I Land which forms part of a public right of way

[630]
Where a public right of way[1] exists over the land included within the compulsory purchase order, the acquiring authority may seek an 'acquisition extinguishment order', so as to extinguish the right of way[2]. The power to

make such an order is subject to the proviso that the acquiring authority be satisfied that a suitable alternative right of way has been or will be provided or that the provision of an alternative is not 'required'[3]. Such orders are subject to confirmation by the Secretary of State[4], and he must consider whether he is satisfied that a suitable alternative right of way has been or will be provided or whether an alternative is not required or not[5].

1 This does not include rights enjoyable by vehicular traffic.
2 ALA 1981, s 32(2).
3 ALA 1981, s 32(2).
4 ALA 1981, s 32(3)(*a*).
5 ALA 1981, s 32(3)(*b*).

[631]
The procedures for the making of an extinguishment order are prescribed in the Highways Act 1980, Sch 6[1]. They are similar to the procedures relating to compulsory purchase orders generally, in so far as they require notices to be served and published, regarding the nature of the order sought and where and how to make relevant objections. The procedures also provide for protection of the apparatus of statutory undertakers[2].

1 Applied by virtue of the ALA 1981, s 32(2).
2 ALA 1981, s 32(6), (6A).

J Crown land

[632]
Land in which the Crown holds an interest is often referred to as 'Crown land'. As a general rule, legislation does not bind the Crown unless the contrary intention appears[1]. For this reason, an interest in land held by the Crown cannot be compulsorily acquired unless the legislation expressly provides the acquiring authority with the power to acquire Crown interests[2]. For this purpose, the Crown includes not only the Sovereign but also Government departments, the Duchy of Cornwall, the Duchy of Lancaster, the Crown Estate Commissioners and other servants or agents. It is submitted that a compulsory purchase order which purports to include a Crown interest by listing it in the schedule to the order and including the parcel on the order map would not for that reason alone be invalid; while the order would have no effect in relation to the Crown interest, it would still be valid and effective to acquire interests in other parcels included in the order[3].

1 A detailed explanation of Crown immunity from legislation is outside the scope of this work.
2 Example of express provisions which are exceptions to the general rule are HA 1980, s 327 and Coast Protection Act 1949, s 32.
3 It might, however, be necessary for the confirming authority to consider in the light of the circumstances of a particular case whether it would be appropriate to confirm the order if control cannot be secured over the Crown land.

[633]–[800]
With regard to interests held by persons or bodies other than the Crown in land in which the Crown holds an interest (for example, where the Crown holds the freehold and others hold leases), a number of enactments make express provision which enables the compulsory acquisition of the non-

Crown interests[1]. It is arguable that non-Crown interests in Crown land may be acquired compulsorily even if the enabling legislation contains no express provision to that effect, but there is no authority which determines this point one way or the other, so doubt must remain[2].

1 For example: TCPA 1990, s 296; P(LBCA)A 1990, s 83; T&WA 1992, s 25; and HA 1996, s 221.

2 Circular 06/04 Appendix N provides advice about compulsory acquisition of interests in Crown land held otherwise than by or on behalf of the Crown. The advice appears to proceed upon the assumption that, in the absence of express provision in the legislation, non-Crown interests in Crown land cannot be acquired compulsorily. As stated above, there is no authority which determines this, and the contrary is arguable.

Chapter 5

Special parliamentary procedure

Contents

A Introduction

[801]
Where special parliamentary procedure applies, a compulsory purchase order is of no effect until it has been laid before Parliament by the confirming authority and has been brought into operation in accordance with the provisions of the Statutory Orders (Special Procedure) Act 1945[1] (SO(SP)A 1945).

1 SO(SP)A 1945, s 1(2).

B Procedural requirements

[802]
A compulsory purchase order may not be laid before Parliament until the procedural requirements of the relevant 'empowering enactment'[1], preliminary to the making or confirmation of the order, have been complied with in respect of:

(*a*) the publication and/or service of notices;
(*b*) the consideration of objections; and
(*c*) the holding of inquiries or other proceedings[2].

1 This means an enactment which has the effect of requiring publication or service of notices, the consideration of objections or the holding of inquiries or other proceedings preliminary to the making or confirmation of the order: SO(SP)A 1945, s 2(3).
2 SO(SP)A 1945, s 2(1).

[803]
In the absence of any such requirements in the relevant 'empowering enactment' the provisions of the SO(SP)A 1945, Sch 1 are to apply. These require the acquiring authority to publish a notice of the order in the *London Gazette* and at least one newspaper circulating in the local area where an order

relates to a particular area[1]. The notice must provide notice of the order as proposed to be made or notice of the order as submitted for confirmation, as appropriate[2]. It must provide for a period of at least 28 days within which objections to the order may be made and it must specify the manner in which objections may be made[3]. If objection is made and not withdrawn, the confirming authority is required to take the objection into consideration and shall require a local inquiry to be held, unless satisfied that, in the special circumstances of the case, the holding of such an inquiry is unnecessary[4]. Notice of an inquiry is to be provided in such manner as the confirming authority may direct and all persons interested shall be permitted to attend and make objections[5]. The costs provisions of the Local Government Act 1972 apply[6].

1 SO(SP)A 1945, Sch 1, para 1.
2 A notice is sufficient if it sets out the purport of the order and specifies a place where copies of the order may be inspected free of charge at all reasonable hours: SO(SP)A 1945, Sch 1, para 5.
3 SO(SP)A 1945, Sch 1, para 2.
4 SO(SP)A 1945, Sch 1, para 3.
5 SO(SP)A 1945, Sch 1, para 4.
6 SO(SP)A 1945, Sch 1, para 4 and see the Local Government Act 1972, s 250(2), (5).

[804]
When the order is laid before Parliament, a certificate must be given by the minister[1] alongside it, specifying the procedural requirements that have to be followed at that these have complied with[2]. Where a local inquiry has not been held, the certificate must contain a statement to that effect[3].

1 Ie the confirming authority.
2 SO(SP)A 1945, s 2(2).
3 SO(SP)A 1945, s 2(2).

C Petitions

[805]
If, within 21 days beginning with the day on which an order was laid before Parliament, a petition is duly presented against the order, the petition is referred to two chairmen; the Lord Chairman of Committees from the House of Lords and the Chairman of the Ways and Means from the House of Commons ('the chairmen')[1]. Petitions fall into two categories:

(*a*) a petition for amendment (that is to say, a petition asking for particular amendments to be made to the order and specifying such amendments)[2]; or
(*b*) a petition of general objection (that is to say, a petition against the order generally)[3].

1 SO(SP)A 1945, s 3(1).
2 SO(SP)A 1945, s 3(2)(*a*).
3 SO(SP)A 1945, s 3(2)(*b*).

[806]
These two categories are separate and a person wishing to object generally to an order and also to ask for specific amendments, in the event that the order

were to be confirmed, must make two separate petitions: one for amendment and one of general objection[1].

1 SO(SP)A 1945, s 3(2).

[807]
As soon as practicable after the end of the 21-day period for the presentation of petitions, the chairmen are to take into consideration all petitions referred to them and if they are satisfied that with respect to any such petition that the provisions of the SO(SP)A 1945 have been complied with, they shall certify that the petition is proper to be received and also certify its designation as either a petition for amendment or a petition of general objection[1]. A petition presented as a petition for amendment, but which includes amendments which would negate the main purpose of the order, is to be certified as a petition of general objection. Alternatively, such a petition may remain a petition for amendment if the petitioner persuades the chairmen that the deletion of some of the amendments which would negate the main purpose of the order would render it a petition for amendment and the chairmen direct that such deletion should be made[2]. In respect of every order laid before Parliament, the chairmen are required to lay a report before both Houses of Parliament, indicating whether any petitions have been presented against it, and, if so, what petitions have been certified as proper to be received and their categorisation as petitions for amendment or petitions of general objection[3].

1 SO(SP)A 1945, s 3(3).
2 SO(SP)A 1945, s 3(4).
3 SO(SP)A 1945, s 3(5).

D After the report as to petitions

[808]
If within the period of 21 days[1] beginning with the date on which the chairmen's report was laid before it ('the resolution period'[2]), either House of Parliament resolves that the compulsory purchase order be annulled, the order thereupon becomes void and no further proceedings may be taken on it[3]. If no resolution annulling the order is passed by either House during this 21-day period, any petitions certified as proper by the chairmen are to be referred to a joint committee of both Houses of Parliament[4]. However, there is power for either House to resolve, within the 21-day period, that any particular petition of general objection should not be so referred[5]. If, during the resolution period, neither House of Parliament has resolved to annul the order and no petitions relating to the order stand to be referred to the joint committee, the order shall come into operation at the end of the resolution period or such later date as may be specified in the order[6].

1 The period of 21 days is not to include any time during which Parliament is dissolved or prorogued or during which both Houses are adjourned for more than four days: SO(SP)A 1945, s 4(1).
2 SO(SP)A 1945, s 4(2).
3 SO(SP)A 1945, s 4(1), although this is without prejudice to any new order which may come forward later.

4 SO(SP)A 1945, s 4(2).
5 SO(SP)A 1945, s 4(2).
6 SO(SP)A 1945, s 4(3).

E The joint committee

[809]
Where petitions are referred to the joint committee, the committee has the power to report the compulsory purchase order with or without amendments or it may, where there is a petition of general objection, report that order be not approved[1]. Even where considering a petition of general objection, the committee has the power to report that the order be amended[2]. The report of the joint committee is then to be laid before both Houses of Parliament[3].

1 SO(SP)A 1945, s 5(1).
2 SO(SP)A 1945, s 5(2).
3 SO(SP)A 1945, s 5(3).

F Operation of orders

[810]–[820]
A compulsory purchase order which is reported by the joint committee without amendment comes into operation on the date it is laid before both Houses of Parliament or such other date as may be specified in the order[1]. Where the joint committee has reported that the order be amended, the minister has three options[2]:

(*a*) he may determine that the order as amended should come into force on such date as he determines;
(*b*) he may withdraw the order; or
(*c*) he may decide to promote a Bill for the confirmation of the order as originally laid before Parliament. In the event that the minister were to decide to adopt this latter course of action, the Bill is to be treated as if it had been through all Parliamentary stages up to, but not including, a Third Reading and there can be no further consideration of the Bill in Committee[3].

1 SO(SP)A 1945, s 6(1).
2 SO(SP)A 1945, s 6(2). For an example of a challenge to the coming into effect of an order modified following the Special Parliamentary Procedure, see *Norris v First Secretary of State* [2006] EWCA Civ 12, [2007] 1 P&CR 72.
3 SO(SP)A 1945, s 6(4).

[821]
Lastly, where the joint committee has reported that the order be not approved[1], the order is not to take effect, unless it is confirmed by Act of Parliament[2]. In such a case, where there are existing petitions for amendment which have been certified as proper[3], the Bill is to be treated as if all stages up to, but not including, a Second Reading have been completed and, after a Second Reading, the Bill is to be passed to committee for the consideration of any relevant petitions for amendment[4]. On the other hand, where no existing

petitions for amendment have been certified as proper, the Bill is to be treated as if it had been through all Parliamentary stages up to, but not including, a Third Reading and there can be no further consideration of the Bill in Committee[5].

1 This can only follow a petition of general objection, see para **[805]**.
2 SO(SP)A 1945, s 6(3).
3 See para **[807]**.
4 SO(SP)A 1945, s 6(5)(*a*).
5 SO(SP)A 1945, s 6(5)(*b*).

G Costs and special parliamentary procedure

[822]–[1000]
A joint committee considering petitions under the special parliamentary procedure has the same powers to award costs as a select committee has, in relation to a provisional order Bill, under ss 9–12 of the Parliamentary Costs Act 2006[1]. Accordingly:

(*a*) petitioners are entitled to recover costs from the promoters, if the committee unanimously report that the promoters have 'unreasonably or vexatiously' subjected the petitioners to expenses[2]; and
(*b*) promoters are entitled to recover costs from petitioners if the opposition is unfounded; however, no landowner, who bona fide opposes, at his sole risk and charge, a Bill which proposes to take a portion of his property, can be made liable to costs in respect of his opposition[3].

The Parliamentary Costs Act 2006 also contains provision for the taxing of costs which apply to the Special Parliamentary Procedure[4].

1 SO(SP)A 1945, s 7(1), as amended by the Parliamentary Costs Act 2006, s 17(3).
3 Parliamentary Costs Act 2006, s 10.
4 Parliamentary Costs Act 2006, s 9.
4 SO(SP)A 1945, s 7(2), as amended by the Parliamentary Costs Act 2006, s 17(4).

Chapter 6

Challenging a compulsory purchase order

Contents

A Restriction on court proceedings

[1001]

A compulsory purchase order or a certificate issued by the Secretary of State, pursuant to the Acquisition of Land Act 1981 (ALA 1981), ss 16–19, may not be questioned in any legal proceedings whatsoever either before or after it has been confirmed, made or given other than in accordance with the provisions of the ALA 1981, ss 23 and 24[1]. As a result, litigants are barred from questioning compulsory purchase orders in proceedings by way of application for judicial review, as well as by way of actions for a declaration, injunction or damages[2]. This is the case even where a litigant may wish to assert that the compulsory purchase order is a nullity due to some fundamental procedural defect[3]. However, it appears that an action for damages will lie against an individual who, in bad faith or by fraud, procures a compulsory purchase order[4]. A party who wishes to challenge a decision not to make or confirm a compulsory purchase order, or not to issue a certificate, may do so in proceedings for judicial review[5]. A party who wishes to challenge the implementation of a valid compulsory purchase order may do so by way of judicial review[6].

1 ALA 1981, s 25. Although it is unusual for a decision to make a compulsory purchase order to be challenged by judicial review, in some circumstances it may be appropriate: see *R v Camden London Borough Council, ex p Comyn Ching & Co Ltd* (1983) 47 P&CR 417. For an example of such a challenge brought under s 23 ALA 1981, see *Collis v Secretary of State* [2007] EWHC 2625 (Admin), [2008] RVR 120.

2 *Tutin v Northallerton Rural District Council* [1947] WN 189, 91 Sol Jo 383, CA.

3 *Smith v East Elloe Rural District Council* [1956] AC 736, CA; *R v Secretary of State for the Environment, ex p Ostler* [1977] QB 122, CA. This is even the case where the applicant had not been notified that a compulsory purchase order was to be made and became aware of its existence only after the time for an application, pursuant to the ALA 1981, s 23 had run out.
4 *Smith v East Elloe Rural District Council, ex p Ostler* [1956] AC 736, CA.
5 See *Islington Borough Council v Secretary of State for the Environment* (1980) 43 P&CR 300. A challenge to a decision to postpone the consideration of confirmation of a compulsory purchase order in respect of part of the land by making a Direction pursuant to ALA 1981, s 13C is brought by way of judicial review: see, eg, *R (Neptune Wharf Ltd) v Secretary of State for Trade and Industry* [2007] EWHC 1036 (Admin), [2007] 3 All ER 676.
6 See, eg, *R (Norris) v First Secretary of State* [2006] EWCA Civ 12, [2007] 1 P&CR 72 at [27]; *R (Iceland Foods Ltd) v Newport City Council* [2010] EWHC 2502 (Admin), a failed challenge based upon the allegation that the acquiring authority had executed and served a general vesting declaration for a purpose different from or collateral to that which underpinned the confirmation of a compulsory purchase order. Where the CPO is executed by means of the General Vesting Declaration, the time for judicial review will start to run from the date the general vesting declaration is executed, and not the date that it takes effect: *R (Iceland Food Ltd) v Newport City Council* [2010] EWHC 2502 (Admin) at [52]–[57].

B Application to the High Court

[1002]
In the following paragraphs of this section, where reference is made to a compulsory purchase order, it can be taken to include reference to a certificate granted pursuant to of the ALA 1981, ss 16–19 also. A 'person aggrieved' may apply to the High Court where they wish to question the validity of a compulsory purchase order within six weeks from the date on which notice of the confirmation or making of the order is first published[1] on the grounds described below.

1 ALA 1981, ss 23(2), (4).

C Person aggrieved

[1003]
The phrase 'a person aggrieved' is not defined in the ALA 1981. However, it has been the subject of interpretation in the courts. Initially, the courts took a fairly restrictive view that only those whose legal rights had been infringed might fall within the scope of the definition[1]. However, the case of *Turner v Secretary of State for the Environment*[2] decided that third parties who have been permitted to appear at an inquiry pursuant to the Inquiries Procedure Rules could be considered to be persons aggrieved; the scope of the definition has broadened over time. Following the *Turner* case, the Court of Appeal has indicated that the phrase should include 'any person who, in the ordinary sense of the word, is aggrieved by the decision'[3]. It is now clear that:

(*a*) a person whose property is directly affected by the order would be a person aggrieved; and
(*b*) a person who has appeared at an inquiry, pursuant to the Inquiries Procedures Rules 1990 and 1994, may also be considered to be a person aggrieved.

Indeed, in *Lomax v Secretary of State for Transport, Local Government and the Regions*[4] the High Court held that two objectors to a compulsory purchase order who had withdrawn their objection by the end of the inquiry were, in the particular circumstances, still 'persons aggrieved' for the purposes of a s 23 challenge.

1 See *Buxton v Minister of Housing and Local Government* [1961] 1 QB 278.
2 (1973) 28 P&CR 123.
3 *Times Investment Ltd v Secretary of State for the Environment* (1990) 61 P&CR 98.
4 [2002] EWHC 921 (Admin).

[1004]

Where, however, a person has no legal interest in the land which is the subject of the compulsory purchase order and has not appeared at an inquiry, such a person may not be considered to be 'aggrieved' by that order. Thus, interest groups who may be concerned with the physical and environmental impact of a development, rather than with issues relating to the compulsory purchase order, might find themselves unable to challenge the making of or confirmation of an order, unless they have appeared at an inquiry. This is because it could be argued that their real concern relates to the grant of planning permission rather than with matters relating to compulsory purchase of land[1].

1 However, in cases where the confirmation of a compulsory purchase order carries with it the 'deemed' grant of planning permission (see the Town and Country Planning Act 1990, s 90), it may be arguable that such groups would be persons aggrieved. See also *A-G of the Gambia v N'Jie* [1961] AC 617 at 634 (person aggrieved are words of wide import); *Martin v Bearsden and Milngavie Council* 1987 SLT 300 (person aggrieved extends beyond persons who have a right to have the order served on them).

D The six-week period

[1005]

The six-week period within which an application must be made begins with and includes the day following the publication of the required notice of the making of or confirmation of the order and will end at midnight on the same day six weeks later[1]. Thus, if a notice confirming a compulsory purchase order is published on a Monday, the six-week period begins with the next day (ie Tuesday) and will run until midnight on the Tuesday in six weeks' time. The period also includes any bank holidays contained within it[2].

1 *Okolo v Secretary of State for the Environment* [1997] 2 All ER 911. The court will not have jurisdiction to consider an application if it is made before the publication of the notice of the making of or confirmation of the order: *Enterprise Inns plc v Secretary of State for the Environment, Transport and the Regions* [2000] JPL 1256.
2 *Stainer v Secretary of State for the Environment* (1992) 65 P & CR 310.

E Grounds for challenge

[1006]

There are two statutory grounds for questioning the validity of a compulsory purchase order contained within the ALA 1981, s 23:

(*a*) that the authorisation of the order is not empowered to be granted under the 1981 Act[1]; or
(*b*) that a 'relevant requirement' has not been complied with[2].

A 'relevant requirement' is defined as any requirement of the ALA 1981, of any regulations made under it, of the Tribunals and Inquiries Act 1992 or of any regulations made under that Act[3].

1 ALA 1981, s 23(1).
2 ALA 1981, s 23(2).
3 ALA 1981, s 23(3).

F Overlap between the grounds

[1007]
The distinction between the first ground (that the order was not empowered to be granted) and the second ground for challenge (that a relevant requirement has not been complied with) is not always clear cut. Megaw LJ stated, in *Gordondale Investments Ltd v Secretary of State for the Environment*[1], that there is:

> 'a real difficulty in seeking to define separate spheres for, or to draw a borderline between, on the one hand, situations in which the order is "not within the powers of this Act" and, on the other hand, situations in which a "requirement of this Act has not been complied with".'

Nevertheless, which of the two grounds is relied upon can be of importance because, where it is alleged that a relevant requirement has not been complied with, the court may only quash an order if the interests of the applicant have been substantially prejudiced[2].

1 (1971) 23 P&CR 334.
2 ALA 1981, s 24(2)(*b*).

[1008]
There have been cases where non-compliance with a relevant requirement has been such as to take the authorisation of an order outside the powers of the ALA 1981 (and its predecessor, the Acquisition of Land (Authorisation Procedure) Act 1946). For example, where the Secretary of State confirmed an order which was required to be subject to special parliamentary procedure, the court considered that, not only had the requirements of the Act not been complied with, but the Secretary of State's action was also beyond his powers[1]. The distinction is further blurred because the courts have held that there is to be implied into the ALA 1981, and the regulations made under it, a requirement that its procedures should be conducted in accordance with the principles of natural justice. A failure to observe the principles of natural justice may result in the subsequent authorisation being outside the powers of the Act[2].

1 *Richardson v Minister of Housing and Local Government* (1956) 8 P&CR 29; *Smith v East Elloe Urban District Council* [1956] AC 736 at 770.
2 *Hibernian Property Co Ltd v Secretary of State for the Environment* (1973) 27 P&CR 197; *Fairmount Investments Ltd v Secretary of State for the Environment* [1976] 2 All ER 865. Fairness does not in general require an inspector to provide a copy of the final written submissions of objectors to

a compulsory purchase order to the Secretary of State with his report, provided that the report fairly summarised the main issues raised by the objectors and resolved them in the inspector's conclusions: *R (Mortell) v Secretary of State for Communities and Local Government* [2009] EWCA Civ 1274, [2010] All ER (D) 131 (May).

G Not empowered to be granted

[1009]
Any applicant to the High Court relying on the first limb of s 23 must establish that the decision was one which could not lawfully have been reached within the powers of the ALA 1981 or the authorising Act. Such a decision is often referred as an 'ultra vires' decision. In reviewing the provisions within the Housing Act 1957 which correspond to those in the ALA 1981, s 23, Lord Denning explained that:

> 'Under this paragraph, it seems to me that the court can interfere with the minister's decision if he has acted on no evidence; or if he has come to a conclusion to which, on the evidence, he could not have reasonably come; or if he has given a wrong interpretation to the words of the statute; or if he has taken into consideration matters which he ought not to have taken into account, or vice versa; or has otherwise gone wrong in law. It is identical with the position when the court has the power to interfere with the decision of a lower tribunal which has erred in point of law.'[1]

In practice, it would appear that the courts have interpreted the actual words of the ALA 1981, s 23 such that the general body of administrative law applicable to the powers of the court to review the decisions of administrative bodies or inferior tribunals is applicable.

1 *Ashbridge Investments Ltd v Minister of Housing and Local Government* [1965] 3 All ER 371 at 374.

H Ultra vires

[1010]–[1020]
It is not intended that this text provide a detailed exposition of the vast body of administrative law that relates to the doctrine of ultra vires. Instead, examples of the general principles, as they have been applied in the context of the compulsory acquisition of land, are provided under the following headings:

(*a*) illegality;
(*b*) irrationality;
(*c*) material and immaterial considerations;
(*d*) procedural impropriety; and
(*e*) other errors of law.

1 Illegality

[1021]
The court will interfere with a decision on the basis of an illegality, where it is apparent that a tribunal has made an error of law. Lord Morris explained

the basis of the court's approach in *Anisminic Ltd v Foreign Compensation Commission*[1]:

> 'If a tribunal while acting within its jurisdiction makes an error of law which it reveals on the face of its recorded determination, then the court, in the exercise of its supervisory function, may correct the error unless there is some provision preventing a review by a court of law.'

Some examples of this category of challenge are given below, as follows:

(*a*) Where the proposed use of the land falls outside the authorising Act;
(*b*) Where the minister has misinterpreted his statutory powers; and
(*c*) Where the confirmation is in breach of the HRA 1998.

1 [1969] 2 AC 147 at 182F–H.

Use of land falling outside the authorising Act

[1021.1]
A clear example of this principle is where the compulsory purchase order is promoted to facilitate a use of the land that falls outside the Act under which it was made. In *London and Westcliff Properties v Minister of Housing and Local Government*[1] the use of the land proposed to be made by the acquiring authority after acquisition would have breached the requirements of the Housing Act 1957 under which the CPO was made. Hence the decision to confirm the order was quashed. The court held that the Act cannot have contemplated acquisition for a purpose outwith the Act itself. Note however that land may be acquired for reasons not directly specified by statute if those reasons are fairly and reasonably incidental to the specified statutory purpose[2].

1 [1961] 1 All ER 610.
2 *Ainsdale Investments Ltd v First Secretary of State* [2004] EWHC 1010 (QB), [2005] RVR 135; *Loweth v Minister of Housing and Local Government* (1970) 22 P&CR 125.

Misinterpretation of statutory powers

[1022]
Other examples of the application of this principle can be found in cases where a minister can be found to have misconstrued the extent of his compulsory purchase powers due to the particular meaning he has attributed to the words of the authorising Act. In *Re Ripon (Highfield) Housing Confirmation Order 1938*[1], the minister had allowed land, which formed part of a park, to be included in an order. The authorising Act prohibited the inclusion of such land. The court held that the minister had misdirected himself as to the meaning of the word 'park' and, accordingly, quashed the order.

1 [1939] 2 KB 838.

[1022.1]
Pascoe v First Secretary of State[1] concerned a CPO made by English Partnerships pursuant to its powers under s 159 of the Leasehold Reform,

Housing and Urban Development Act 1993, which refers to the regeneration of urban land which is 'underused or ineffectively used'. When confirming the CPO, the minister adopted his inspector's reasoning which described the land in question as 'predominantly' underused or ineffectively used. The High Court quashed the minister's decision, holding that he had impermissibly diluted the statutory test that had to be satisfied before the acquiring authority were authorised to acquire land compulsorily for regeneration[2].

1 [2006] EWHC 2356 (Admin). It is the land as a whole that is to be considered: see *McCabe v Secretary of State for Communities and Local Government* [2007] EWHC 959 (Admin), [2007] All ER (D) 75 (Apr).
2 [2006] EWHC 2356 (Admin) at [44].

Breach of the HRA 1998

[1023]
A failure to comply with the requirements of the HRA 1998 would also fall under this head of challenge[1]. HRA 1998, s 6 requires that no public authority may act in a manner incompatible with the ECHR. A confirming authority, such as the Secretary of State, is a public authority to which this obligation applies. A decision under the ALA 1981 to confirm a compulsory purchase order may therefore be challenged on the ground that it breaches the Human Rights of the person aggrieved.

1 For an overview of how the ECHR affects compulsory purchase powers and procedures, see **Division A**, paras **[501]–[650]**.

[1023.1]
Challenges to compulsory purchase orders raising human rights issues will frequently involve either or both Art 1 of the First Protocol to the ECHR[1], and Art 8 of the ECHR[2]. These are qualified rights, which means that they can be interfered with provided there is a sufficient justification in law for doing so. In simple terms in the present context, an interference with them will be lawful if it can be shown that the order was otherwise lawfully made and confirmed, that it serves a legitimate aim in the public interest, and that the interference with the right that would result from the order is proportionate to achieving the aim in question. A compulsory purchase order which meets its statutory purposes will have a legitimate aim in Convention rights terms[3]. However, challenges based on Convention rights frequently involve the argument that the decision to confirm the compulsory purchase order in relation to a particular objector breaches the principle of proportionality[4].

1 The right to peaceful enjoyment of possessions: see **Division A**, para **[503]**. This ground may be raised, for example, by those with an interest in property that is subject to the compulsory purchase order. Legal persons such as a company can have rights under this Article.
2 The right to respect for private and family life: see **Division A**, para **[503]**. This ground may be raised, for example, by those whose homes are to be acquired by the compulsory purchase order, see eg *Mortell v Secretary of State for Communities and Local Government* [2008] EWHC 3022 (Admin), [2010] All ER (D) 131 (May); *Sole v Secretary of State for Trade and Industry* [2007] EWHC 1527 (Admin), (2007) 151 Sol Jo LB 746; *Lisa Smith v Secretary of State for Trade and Industry* [2007] EWHC 1013 (Admin), [2007] All ER (D) 59 (May); *R (Lock) v Secretary of State for the Environment, Transport and the Regions* [2002] 46 EG 203; *Maley v Secretary of State* [2008] EWHC 2652 (Admin), [2008] All ER (D) 98 (Aug) (whether duty to investigate human rights implications).

3 Since the purposes listed in para 2 of Art 1 to the First Protocol to the ECHR and those listed para 2 of Art 8 of the ECHR will usually coincide with the statutory purposes for which the compulsory purchase order was made.
4 See also **Division A**, para **[506.1]**.

[1023.2]
In a number of decisions, the courts have considered whether proportionality in the present context requires the compulsory purchase order to be the least intrusive means of achieving the public benefit sought, or whether the test of proportionality is satisfied provided that the order strikes a fair balance between the public benefit sought and the interference with the rights in question. The latter test (fair balance) is less stringent than the former (least intrusive means). The weight of authority supports the proposition that the fair balance test is the correct test for the proportionality in the context of confirmation of a compulsory purchase order[1]. Moreover, it has been held that the general requirement that there be a compelling case in the public interest to justify confirmation of a compulsory purchase order will usually ensure that the requirements of the ECHR are met[2].

1 *Belfields Ltd v Secretary of State for Communities and Local Government* [2007] EWHC 3040 (Admin), [2007] All ER (D) 367 (Dec) at [20]; *Lisa Smith v Secretary of State for Trade and Industry* [2007] EWHC 1013 (Admin), [2008] 1 WLR 394 at [43]; *Pascoe v First Secretary of State* [2006] EWHC 2356 (Admin), [2006] 4 All ER 1240 at [83]; *Bexley London Borough Council v Secretary of State for the Environment, Transport and the Regions* [2001] EWHC Admin 323, [2001] 18 EGCS 172 at [34]–[35]; see also the approach taken in *Sole v Secretary of State for Trade and Industry* [2007] EWHC 1527 (Admin), (2007) 151 Sol Jo LB 746.
2 See *Bexley London Borough Council v Secretary of State for the Environment, Transport and the Regions* [2001] EWHC Admin 323, [2001] 18 EGCA 172 at [46]; *Tesco Stores Ltd v Secretary of State for Transport and the Regions* (2000) 80 P&CR 427 at 429.

[1023.3]
A question that sometimes arises in proportionality challenges is whether the court is simply reviewing the decision of the confirming authority or whether the court itself is entitled to judge whether the confirmation of the compulsory purchase order is proportionate or not. In *Lisa Smith v Secretary of State for Trade and Industry*[1] the judge accepted that in challenges to the proportionality of a decision it is for the court to determine on an objective basis whether the decision was proportionate. Adopting this approach, even if the decision letter discloses an arguable error in the way in which the Secretary of State has made his decision on a proportionality issue, the court may still itself conclude that the decision was proportionate. Conversely, it would appear that claimants can ask the court to adjudicate on the proportionality of the interference that would be caused by the compulsory purchase order even if the Secretary of State has found such interference to be proportionate and his reasoning discloses no apparent error in the approach which it has taken[2].

1 [2007] EWHC 1013 (Admin), [2008] 1 WLR 394 at [58], following *R (SB) v Governors of Denbigh High School* [2006] UKHL 15, [2007] 1 AC 100 at [30], where it was said that the court was required to adopt an approach that went beyond that traditionally adopted in judicial review, and employ a heightened in intensity of review that enabled it to judge itself, on an objective basis, whether the measure is proportionate or not. By contrast, see *R (Powell) v Secretary of State for Communities and Local Government* [2007] EWHC 2051 (Admin) at [12], where Sullivan J held that the court could intervene only if the balance struck was irrational.

2 On general principles, such a challenge would nevertheless have to be founded on the material before the confirming authority and the relevant reasoning in the inspector's report and the Secretary of State's decision letter: see *Ashbridge Investments v Minister of Housing and Local Government* [1965] 1 WLR 1320 at 1327.

[1023.4]

Challenges based on procedural grounds may raise issues under Art 6 of the ECHR[1]. In *R (Bennett) v Secretary of State for Communities and Local Government*[2] the claimant lived in a house subject to a compulsory purchase order made under the Housing Act 1985 on grounds that it was unfit for human habitation. The claimant alleged that she had been denied a fair hearing because the acquiring authority had failed sufficiently to particularise the respects in which her property was alleged to be inadequate. The court rejected the challenge, holding that sufficient details had been given in the acquiring authority's statement of case, and that the confirming authority's findings were reasonably founded on the evidence[3].

1 Article 6 ECHR is the right to a fair trial. For cases on inquiries procedure generally, see paras **[410]–[610]**.
2 [2007] EWHC 737 (Admin), [2007] All ER (D) 15 (Mar).
3 For other challenges raising Art 6, see, eg, *Belfields Ltd v Secretary of State for Communities and Local Government* [2007] EWHC 3040 (Admin), [2007] All ER (D) 367 (Dec); *R (Powell) v Secretary of State for Communities and Local Government* [2007] EWHC 2051, (Admin), [2007] All ER (D) 137 (Aug).

2 Irrationality

[1024]

A decision which could be described as 'irrational' or 'perverse' will be considered to be ultra vires by the courts. This aspect of the doctrine of ultra vires is often referred to as *Wednesbury* unreasonableness, following the explanation of its operation by Lord Greene MR in the *Associated Picture Houses Ltd v Wednesbury Corpn*[1] case:

> 'The court is entitled to investigate the action of the local authority with a view to seeing whether they have taken into account matters which they ought not to take into account, or, conversely, have refused to take into account or neglected to take into account matters which they ought to have taken into account. Once that question is answered in favour of the local authority, it may still be possible to say that, although the local authority have kept within the four corners of the matters which they ought to consider, they have nevertheless come to a conclusion so unreasonable that no reasonable authority could ever have come to it. In such a case, again, I think the court can interfere.'

1 [1948] 1 KB 223 at 233. In *R v North East Devon Health Authority, ex p Coughlan* [2001] QB 213 Lord Woolf MR held (at [65]) that rationality had two faces: '… one is the barely known decision which simply defies comprehension; the other is a decision which can be seen to have proceeded by flawed logic …'

[1025]

The test that the conclusion must be so unreasonable that no reasonable decision-maker could ever have come to it sets a high threshold. One example of irrationality can be found in the cases in which the courts have examined whether or not there was evidence before the lower tribunal upon which it could have reached the decision it did. The circumstances in which a challenge is successful on this basis are seldom encountered in practice on the compulsory acquisition of land. This is because most of the matters in issue in compulsory purchase proceedings are resolved by the decision-maker balancing conflicting factual and policy evidence. Thus, there is usually some evidence on which the decision can be said to have been rationally based.

[1025.1]
However, an example of a case where a compulsory purchase order was successfully challenged on the basis of irrationality through lack of evidence is that of *Coleen Properties Ltd v Minister of Housing and Local Government*[1]. This was a case where the acquiring authority sought to acquire land, pursuant to powers in Pt II of the Housing Act 1957, consisting of a clearance area and some adjoining land. Under the provisions of the Housing Act 1957, the adjoining land could only be acquired if it was 'land the acquisition of which is reasonably necessary for the satisfactory development or use of the cleared area'. At the inquiry into the orders, the acquiring authority called no evidence to establish that the acquisition of the adjoining land was necessary for the satisfactory development or use of the cleared area but merely asserted that this was the case. The inspector indicated in his report that the acquisition of the adjoining land was not necessary and recommended to the minister that it be excluded from the compulsory purchase order. The minister rejected this recommendation and declared that the adjoining land was necessary for the satisfactory development or use of the cleared area, and confirmed the compulsory purchase order with that adjoining land included within it. The owners of the adjoining land applied to the High Court for an order quashing the part of the compulsory purchase order that related to the adjoining land. The court held that, having regard to the absence of any evidence before the inspector that the land was necessary for the satisfactory development or use of the cleared area and his clear opinion that it was not reasonably necessary, there was no material on which the minister could properly overrule the inspector's recommendation. Accordingly, the court quashed the compulsory purchase order.

1 [1971] 1 All ER 1049.

3 Material and immaterial considerations

[1026]
That the Secretary of State has misdirected himself as to the matters which are relevant to his decision is perhaps the ground most often used to challenge a compulsory purchase order. As Lord Green MR explained, in *Associated Picture Houses Ltd v Wednesbury Corpn*:

> '... a person entrusted with a discretion must, so to speak, direct himself properly in the law. He must call his own attention to the matters which he is bound to consider. He must exclude from his consideration matters which are irrelevant to what he has to consider.'[1]

1 [1948] 1 KB 223 at 229.

[1027]
It can be difficult to ascertain the extent to which a particular consideration may be material or immaterial to a decision and whether the courts will hold a decision to be invalid, even where a consideration is only marginally relevant or irrelevant. The court's approach to this matter has been explained by Glidewell J, who set out the following principles in *Bolton Metropolitan Borough Council v Secretary of State for the Environment*[1]:

> '1. The expressions used in the authorities that the decision maker has failed to take into account a matter which is relevant, which is the formulation for instance in Forbes J's judgment in *Seddon Properties*[2], or that he has failed to take into consideration matters which he ought to take into account, which was the way that Lord Greene put it in *Wednesbury*[3] and Lord Denning in *Ashbridge Investments*[4], have the same meaning …
> 2. The decision maker ought to take into account a matter which might cause him to reach a different conclusion to that which he would reach if he did not take it into account. Such a matter is relevant to his decision making process. By the verb "might," I mean where there is a real possibility that he would reach a different conclusion if he did take that consideration into account.
> 3. If a matter is trivial or of small importance in relation to the particular decision, then it follows that if it were taken into account there would be a real possibility that it would make no difference to the decision and thus it is not a matter which the decision maker ought to take into account.
> 4. As Hodgson J said, there is clearly a distinction between matters which a decision maker is obliged by statute to take into account and those where the obligation to take into account is to be implied from the nature of the decision and of the matter in question. I refer back to the *Creed NZ* case[5].
> 5. If the validity of the decision is challenged on the ground that the decision maker failed to take into account a matter in the second category, it is for the judge to decide whether it was a matter which the decision maker should have taken into account.
> 6. If the judge concludes that the matter was "fundamental to the decision," or that it is clear that there is a real possibility that the consideration of the matter would have made a difference to the decision, he is thus enabled to hold that the decision was not validly made. But if a judge is uncertain whether the matter would have had this effect or was of such importance in the decision making process, then he does not have before him the material necessary for him to conclude that the decision was invalid.
> 7 … Even if the judge has concluded that he could hold that the decision is invalid, in exceptional circumstances he is entitled nevertheless, in the exercise of discretion, not to grant any relief.'

1 (1990) 61 P&CR 343. See also Carnwath LJ's analysis in *Derbyshire Dales District Council v Secretary of State for Communities and Local Government* [2009] EWHC 1729 (Admin), [2010] 1 P&CR 381 at [16]–[28].
2 *Seddon Properties Ltd v Secretary of State for the Environment and Macclesfield Borough Council* (1981) 42 P&CR 26n.
3 *Associated Picture Houses Ltd v Wednesbury Corpn* [1948] 1 KB 223.
4 *Ashbridge Investments Ltd v Minister of Housing and Local Government* [1965] 3 All ER 371.
5 *Creed NZ Inc v Governor-General* [1981] NZLR 172.

[1028]
Set out below are some examples of where 'materiality' has arisen in the context of decisions on compulsory purchase orders under the following headings:

(*a*) alternatives to compulsory acquisition;
(*b*) costs and financial viability;
(*c*) planning considerations; and
(*d*) other examples.

Alternatives to compulsory acquisition

[1029]
The availability of a suitable alternative site to that included in a compulsory purchase order has been held by the courts to be a relevant consideration when determining whether or not to confirm a compulsory purchase order. Consequently, the failure to take this into account may lead to an order being quashed by the courts[1]. In *Brinklow v Secretary of State for the Environment*[2], the Secretary of State regarded the absence of alternative sites as irrelevant. The court held that the absence of alternative sites was a relevant consideration which ought properly to have been taken into account and quashed the compulsory purchase order.

1 See *Brown v Secretary of State for the Environment* (1978) 40 P&CR 285; *Rhodes v Minister for Housing and Local Government* [1963] 1 WLR 208; *London Welsh Association Ltd v Secretary of State for the Environment* [1980] 2 EGLR 17; *R v Secretary of State for Transport, ex p Rothschild* [1989] 1 All ER 933; *Tesco Store Ltd v Secretary of State for the Environment, Transport and the Regions* [2000] 80 P&CR 427; *London Borough of Bexley v Secretary of State for the Environment, Transport and the Regions* [2001] EWHC 323 (Admin).
2 (1976) 241 Estates Gazette 461.

[1029.1]
In *Hall v First Secretary of State*[1] the Court of Appeal considered a challenge to the confirmation of a compulsory purchase order under s 226(1)(*b*) of the Town and Country Planning Act 1990. It was argued that the Secretary of State ought to have, but had not, looked at ways of achieving the objectives of the compulsory purchase order without acquiring the claimant's land, which was used for a scrap metal business. Addressing this argument, Carnwath LJ described the extent of any obligation to explore alternatives in the following way:

> 'To what extent was the Secretary of State under a duty to explore such alternatives, even if not presented by the parties? His primary task under the statute is to consider the issues raised by objections to the CPO, not to search for alternatives. On the other hand, to satisfy himself that there is a "compelling case" for compulsory acquisition, particularly where objectors are unrepresented, fairness may require him to consider at least any obvious alternatives.'

On the facts of the case the court held that the obligation had been discharged, since the relevant alternatives had been considered.

1 [2007] EWCA Civ 612, [2007] All ER (D) 356 (Jun).

[1030]–[1040]
Where an alternative to a compulsory purchase order is put forward at inquiry, the comparative costs of confirming the order or pursuing the alternative may be material to a decision. In *Eckersley v Secretary of State for the Environment*[1], the acquiring authority were seeking a clearance order, pursuant to the Housing Act 1957, in order to demolish some buildings and then to construct a replacement building. It was argued by the applicant that the costs of demolition and rebuilding, as proposed by the acquiring authority, were greater than the costs of repair and rehabilitation of the existing properties. The inspector expressed the view that the comparative costs were irrelevant and the Secretary of State agreed with that view. The Court of Appeal quashed the order on the basis that the Secretary of State had failed to take into account a material consideration.

1 (1977) 34 P&CR 124. See also *London Borough of Bexley v Secretary of State for the Environment, Transport and the Regions* [2001] EWHC 323 (Admin), where the High Court held that the minister was entitled to confirm a CPO in circumstances where it would achieve a better scheme than the alternative scheme put forward by an objector which would not have required the compulsory acquisition of land.

Costs and financial viability

[1041]
The extent to which it is open to objectors to a compulsory purchase order to argue that the project being proposed would not achieve its purpose because it is not financially viable is a matter which has come before the courts from time to time. It has been held to be a matter which the Secretary of State is entitled to take into account in suitable cases and that it can be relevant[1].

1 *Sovmots Investments Ltd v Secretary of State for the Environment* [1977] QB 411 at 424, per Forbes J.

[1042]
In *Prest v Secretary of State for Wales*[1], the objector put forward two alternative sites to that which was included in the compulsory purchase order and offered to sell them to the acquiring authority at agricultural land values. The construction costs in respect of the alternative sites would have been higher, but the lower land acquisition costs might well have reduced the total cost of the acquiring authority's project. The Secretary of State did not take into account the lower land acquisition costs of the alternative sites and the compulsory purchase order was accordingly quashed because he had failed to take into account a material consideration.

1 [1983] 1 EGLR 17.

[1043]
In *Royal Life Insurance Ltd v Secretary of State for the Environment*[1] the applicant had presented evidence at inquiry that the urban regeneration scheme being promoted by the acquiring authority was not financially viable and that an alternative scheme was viable. The acquiring authority, however, refused to adduce evidence on the matter for reasons of 'commercial confidentiality',

but indicated to the inspector that it had satisfied itself on the basis of expert evidence that the scheme was financially viable. The inspector indicated in his report that the financial viability of the scheme had not been tested at the inquiry. The Secretary of State did not take the matter further and confirmed the order on the basis that the purposes of the acquisition were more likely to be achieved if the order was confirmed than if the alternative scheme were to come forward. The court held that neither the authorising Act nor the relevant Government advice (Circular 23/88) made reference to financial viability as a relevant issue. The inspector had indicated that a compelling case for regeneration had been made out. Financial viability was only one of a number of factors to be taken into account. The weight to be given to this issue was a matter for the Secretary of State[2]. Whilst it had not been shown whether the project was viable or not, a compelling case had been made out and, accordingly, the application to quash the compulsory purchase order was refused.

1 (1992) 43 Estates Gazette 145. See also *Chesterfield Properties v Secretary of State for the Environment* (1997) 76 P&CR 117 where it was held that the Secretary of State had lawfully confirmed the order notwithstanding doubts as to whether the scheme was viable.
2 *Green v Secretaries of State for the Environment and Transport* [1985] JPL 119.

[1043.1]
The courts have rejected arguments that matters which are relevant to the grant of planning permission may not be taken into account by the confirming authority in relation to a compulsory purchase order[1], though it may not be appropriate for a confirming authority to usurp planning functions in its determination relating to confirmation[2]. Where land is being acquired for development purposes, the principles derived from cases concerning the matters which may lawfully be taken into account in determining planning applications apply equally to compulsory acquisition, provided it is recognised that, because of the serious invasion of property rights involved in compulsory acquisition, a strict approach to the application of those principles is required.[3]

1 *Hanks v Minister of Housing and Local Government* (1962) 15 P&CR 246.
2 *Vasilou v Secretary of State for Transport* [1991] 2 All ER 77, although it should be noted that the *Hanks* case was not cited to the court.
3 See the majority judgments in *R (Sainsbury's Supermarkets Ltd) v Wolverhampton City Council* [2010] UKSC 20, [2010] 2 WLR 1173, reversing the Court of Appeal judgment [2009] EWCA Civ 835, [2009] All ER (D) 339 (Jul).

Other examples

[1044]
In a case where the CPO was promoted to facilitate the construction of a sewage outfall, it was held that the minister was entitled to take into account the existence of a sewage discharge consent granted by the Environment Agency as proof that relevant pollution control and water standards would be met. Nevertheless, the Court of Appeal held that had the objectors established at the inquiry that the Environment Agency was not enforcing the requirements of the Directive through its administration of the consent

regime, 'that would have been a highly material fact for the inspector to consider when deciding whether a CPO should be confirmed'[1].

1 *Moase v Secretary of State for the Environment, Transport and the Regions* [2001] Env LR 227 at 257. On the discretion of the confirming authority when considering arguments of this kind, see *Moggridge v National Assembly for Wales* [2003] EWHC 2188 (Admin), [2004] Env LR 18 at [34]–[36], adopting the approach in *Chesterfield Properties v Secretary of State for the Environment* (1997) 76 P&CR 117.

4 Procedural impropriety

[1045]
This aspect of the doctrine of ultra vires is something of a hybrid. The term procedural impropriety is generally taken to encompass both 'procedural ultra vires' and breaches of natural justice[1]. A decision will be held to be procedurally ultra vires where the decision-maker has failed to observe procedural rules that are expressly laid down in the relevant enactment which defines the appropriate procedure. The grounds of challenge to the High Court contained in the ALA 1981, s 23(2) cover procedural ultra vires. This is addressed separately below. However, a decision which is contrary to natural justice may be ultra vires[2].

1 See the distinction drawn between these concepts by Lord Diplock in *Council of Civil Service Unions v Minister for the Civil Service* [1985] AC 374 at 411A–B. For cases on inquiries procedure generally, see paras **[410]–[600]**.
2 See para **[1008]**.

5 Abuse of power

[1046]
The phrase 'abuse of power' has been used by the court to embrace a number of cases where intervention in the decision-making process of a lower tribunal is warranted because of the way discretionary power has either been exercised or compromised[1]. Examples of the following categories of 'abuse of power' are set out below, although this list is not intended to be exhaustive:

(*a*) bad faith;
(*b*) ulterior purpose; and
(*c*) fetter upon the decision-maker's discretion.

1 The confirming authority must give genuine consideration to the objections and the inspector's report: *Franklin v Minister of Town and Country Planning* [1948] 1 AC 87; see also *Belfields Ltd v Secretary of State for Communities and Local Government* [2007] EWHC 3040 (Admin), [2007] All ER (D) 367 (Dec); *R (Powell) v Secretary of State for Communities and Local Government* [2007] EWHC 2051 (Admin), [2007] All ER (D) 137 (Aug).

Bad faith

[1047]
It is rare for the court to be asked to quash a decision on the basis that it was taken in bad faith. An example of the potential relevance of bad faith in compulsory purchase proceedings can be found, however, in *Don v*

Secretary of State for the Environment and Manchester City Council[1]. In this case, the applicant applied to the High Court to quash the decision of the Secretary of State to confirm a compulsory purchase order made by the city council on land owned by the applicant where he carried on a market. The city council owned land itself on which a rival market operated nearby. There was a history between the applicant and the city council. In 1967, the city council sought to acquire the applicant's land compulsorily for housing. Nothing came of this. In 1970, the city council wrote to the applicant, saying that it controlled markets in the city and that further markets would be opposed. In 1971, the city council wrote to the applicant saying that it would be opening a further market and that there would be no room for a further market opened by the applicants. In 1979, the city council was prohibited by injunction from entering onto the applicant's land. The applicant alleged that the city council was not acting in good faith, but seeking to stifle opposition. In 1990, the council sought to resurrect the 1967 compulsory purchase order. The matter ended up in court when the city council conceded that they no longer had any rights under the 1967 order. In 1990, the city council made a further compulsory purchase order for the applicant's land, the purposes of which were stated to be the redevelopment of the council's market and a nearby shopping centre. At the public inquiry, the applicants led evidence which, inter alia, challenged the motivation of the city council. The inspector set out the applicant's case on motivation, but made no findings of fact. The court held that the inspector should have decided the issue of motivation, as it was a matter fundamental to the applicant's case. The issue of bad faith went to the vires of the order made by the council.

1 [1994] NPC 18.

Ulterior purpose

[1048]
It is a long-established principle of administrative law that statutory powers given to a body for one purpose may not be used for another purpose. As Denning LJ explained[1]:

> 'the principle is that the legislative power in this country resides in Parliament and not in the government departments … [Powers] must not be used for an ulterior object which is not authorised by law however desirable that object may seem to them to be in the public interest.'

1 *Earl FitzWilliam's Wentworth Estates Co Ltd v Minister of Town and Country Planning* [1951] 2 KB 284 at 313.

[1049]
In *Meravale Builders Ltd v Secretary of State for the Environment*[1] the acquiring authority fell foul of this principle. A compulsory purchase order made under powers in the Housing Act 1957 included land required for highways purposes which were not incidental to the housing scheme. Similarly, a compulsory purchase order made for a sea wall but which included a large

piece of land not for coast protection purposes but to provide a sort of paved promenade was quashed[2].

1 (1978) 36 P&CR 87.
2 *Webb v Minister for Housing and Local Government* [1965] 1 WLR 755.

[1050]–[1060]
This principle can give rise to difficulties for acquiring authorities where they have entered into development agreements with third parties in respect of the land which is the subject of the compulsory purchase order. In *Leggatt v Secretary of State for the Environment*[1], the minister was alleged to have had the ulterior motive of obtaining a large premium from a petroleum company who had an option of the land which was the subject of the order. The courts held that, whilst a premium would be paid, this was incidental to realising the purpose of the order, namely, the construction of a motorway service area. Accordingly, the minister had no ulterior motive.

1 [1991] 1 PLR 103.

[1061]
When confirmed by a minister, a compulsory purchase order authorises the purchase of land for the particular purpose of the authorising Act. If, at some later stage, the acquiring authority's purpose changes, that authority no longer holds good. In Procter and Gamble Ltd v Secretary of State for the Environment[1], a development corporation made a compulsory purchase order for the purposes of regeneration of a large area of land in its urban development area. It subsequently transpired that part of this land would be required for highway improvements, a purpose which had not been expressly identified by the development corporation until after the time for making objections had expired. It was alleged that this was an additional purpose to that of regeneration and that, accordingly, the compulsory purchase order ought to be quashed. The court held that a compulsory purchase order which has been made for one purpose could not be lawfully confirmed for another. In the instant case, however, the inspector had concluded that the highway improvements were necessary in order to achieve the regeneration sought by the order. Accordingly, the purpose for which the order was confirmed was the same as that for which it had been made. There was therefore no ulterior purpose.

1 (1991) 63 P&CR 317.

A fetter upon the decision-maker's discretion

[1062]
Where a decision-maker has been granted a discretion, then it is axiomatic that, in order to exercise that discretion lawfully, a decision-maker must bring it to bear upon each and every case; in other words, each case must be determined on its merits. Where a decision-maker acts in advance of taking a decision and regards itself as bound to come to a particular decision in any

given case because of that action, it can be said to have 'fettered' its discretion unlawfully and the decision is liable to be quashed by the courts[1].

1 See generally, *H Lavender & Son Ltd v Minister of Housing and Local Government* [1970] 1 WLR 1231.

[1062.1]
In *Ayr Harbour Trustees v Oswald*[1], the Harbour Trustees had powers of compulsory acquisition granted to them under a Special Act. During an arbitration with a landowner regarding the compensation payable for acquisition of land, the trustees purported to enter into an agreement with the landowner to limit the future exercise of their statutory powers. The agreement was held to be unlawful since it purported to fetter the statutory powers of the trustees so as to frustrate the purpose for which they were conferred. Lord Fitzgerald said:

> '... having so acquired the land for the purposes expressed in ... their special Act, they have no power in law to preclude themselves or their successors from the exercise of their statutable powers over it.'[2]

An agreement or undertaking by the acquiring authority which does not frustrate the purpose underlying the compulsory purchase order is unlikely to infringe the principle in *Ayr Harbour Trustees.* For example, an acquiring authority may lawfully undertake not to exercise its powers of compulsory acquisition under a confirmed order in respect of land the acquisition of which is no longer needed for the scheme, or over which sufficient rights have been acquired by agreement.

1 (1883) 8 App Cas 623
2 (1883) 8 App Cas 623 at 640; see also at 634 and 638.

I A relevant requirement has not been complied with

[1063]
As described above, the second statutory ground for challenging the validity of a compulsory purchase order is that a 'relevant requirement' has not been complied with[1]. A 'relevant requirement' is defined as any requirement of the ALA 1981 of any regulations made under it, of the Tribunals and Inquiries Act 1992 or of any regulations made under that Act[2]. The court only has power to quash a compulsory purchase order, on the ground that a relevant requirement has not been complied with, where it is satisfied that 'the interests of the applicant have been substantially prejudiced' by that non-compliance[3].

1 ALA 1981, s 23(2).
2 ALA 1981, s 23(3).
3 ALA 1981, s 24(2)(*b*).

[1064]
There are two main categories of challenge on the basis that a relevant requirement has not been complied with:

(*a*) where there has been some procedural error; and

(*b*) where there has been some particular failure in the reasoning of the confirming authority's decision.

1 Procedural error

[1065]
The various procedures to be followed in the process of making and confirming a compulsory purchase order have been explained above. There have been a number of cases where orders have been quashed because of procedural errors that have been made, which have resulted in substantial prejudice to the interests of a participant in those procedures. Some examples follow.

[1066]
Where land was wrongly described in the notice published in a local newspaper[1], such that objectors had not understood that the notice referred to the land in question, the court has held that a relevant requirement had not been complied with and that substantial prejudice arose[2].

1 See para **[174]** and the ALA 1981, s 11(2).
2 *Wilson v Secretary of State for the Environment* [1973] 1 WLR 1083.

[1067]
Where, contrary to the Inquiries Procedure Rules, a local authority refused to allow an objector to see documents to be referred to by the authority prior to the inquiry and the inspector failed to give adequate time for consideration of them once produced, a relevant requirement had not been complied with and substantial prejudice arose.

[1068]
The refusal to grant an adjournment has also been held to give rise to substantial prejudice. In *Webb v Secretary of State for the Environment*[1] the inquiry was held, prior to the hearing of the applicant's appeal against a control order made under the Housing Act 1985, s 379 which related to the same property as that included in the compulsory purchase order. The inspector refused to grant an adjournment pending the resolution of the applicant's appeal. In the event, the applicant won his appeal against the control order. The court held that, in these circumstances, the refusal to adjourn had cause unfairness to the applicant and that substantial prejudice had arisen.

1 (1990) 22 HLR 274.

[1069]
An example of a case where the refusal to grant an adjournment has been held not to give rise to a procedural defect is that of *Orakpo v Wandsworth London Borough Council*[1]. In that case, the acquiring authority made a control order under Pt XI of the Housing Act 1985 and, some three years later, made a compulsory purchase order. At the inquiry into the compulsory purchase order, the applicant's appeal against the control order remained to be heard. However, the inspector refused to grant an adjournment on the basis that the

applicant's record in relation to the property was not satisfactory and that the applicant's appeal was unlikely to succeed. The Court of Appeal considered that this case could be distinguished from the *Webb* case[2] on its facts and that the inspector did not act unreasonably by refusing to adjourn in the circumstances of the case.

1 (1992) 24 HLR 370.
2 See para **[1069]**.

2 No substantial prejudice

[1070]–[1080]
An example of a finding by the court that no substantial prejudice arose is the case of *George v Secretary of State for the Environment*[1]. In that case, a property in the joint ownership of a husband and wife was the subject of a compulsory purchase order. However, only the husband was served with the order and not the wife. The husband objected to the order, but, nevertheless, it was confirmed. The wife then sought to have the order quashed on the basis that she had not been served and only found out about the order after it had been confirmed. Unusually in these sorts of proceedings, at trial, the wife was cross-examined as to the truth of her assertion that she had known nothing of the order. The court held that, whilst a relevant requirement had not been complied with, no substantial prejudice arose[2].

1 (1979) 38 P&CR 609. See also *Lomax v Secretary of State for Transport, Government and the Regions* [2002] EWHC 921 (Admin).
2 Per Denning LJ:

> 'In all probability, she decided not to take any steps of her own, but left it to her husband to do all the fighting, which is a natural thing for a wife to do … It seems to me that there was no prejudice to her whatever' ((1979) 38 P&CR 609 at 617).

[1081]
In *Tsao v Secretary of State for the Environment*[1], a procedural defect occurred in that the acquiring authority only served notice of the making of the order upon the applicant a day after the period for making objections to it had expired. However, the Secretary of State had agreed to treat the applicant as a statutory objector, notwithstanding that his objection was made after the expiration of the period for making objections. The court held that, in these circumstances, no substantial prejudice arose and the application failed.

1 (1995) 28 HLR 259.

3 A failure in the reasoning

[1082]
The Inquiries Procedure Rules impose a duty on the Secretary of State to provide notification of his decision and the reasons therefor in writing[1]. The reasons provided must be adequate and intelligible[2]. The leading authorities regarding the adequacy of reasons were considered by the House of Lords in *South Bucks DC v Porter (No 2)*[3], albeit in the context of a planning decision. Lord Brown summarised the effect of the authorities governing the proper approach to a reasons challenge as follows:

'The reasons for a decision must be intelligible and they must be adequate. They must enable the reader to understand why the matter was decided as it was and what conclusions were reached on the "principal important controversial issues", disclosing how any issue of law or fact was resolved. Reasons can be briefly stated, the degree of particularity required depending entirely on the nature of the issues falling for decision. The reasoning must not give rise to a substantial doubt as to whether the decision-maker erred in law, for example by misunderstanding some relevant policy or some other important matter or by failing to reach a rational decision on relevant grounds. But such adverse inference will not readily be drawn. The reasons need refer only to the main issues in the dispute, not to every material consideration. They should enable disappointed developers to assess their prospects of obtaining some alternative development permission, or, as the case may be, their unsuccessful opponents to understand how the policy or approach underlying the grant of permission may impact upon future such applications. Decision letters must be read in a straightforward manner, recognising that they are addressed to parties well aware of the issues involved and the arguments advanced. A reasons challenge will only succeed if the party aggrieved can satisfy the court that he has genuinely been substantially prejudiced by the failure to provide an adequately reasoned decision.'

1 CP(IR)R 2007, r 19(1).

2 *Re Poyser and Mills Arbitration* [1964] 2 QB 467; *Westminster City Council v Great Portland Estates plc* [1985] AC 661.

3 [2004] 1 WLR 1953, applying in particular *Westminster City Council v Great Portland Estates* (above); *Save Britain's Heritage v Number 1 Poultry Ltd* [1991] 1 WLR 153; *Bolton Metropolitan District Council v Secretary of State for the Environment* (1995) 71 P&CR 309.

[1083]

When considering a reasons challenge the courts will be wary of taking an unduly technical approach to the interpretation of the inspector's report and the minister's decision letter. In *Pascoe v First Secretary of State* [1] Forbes J described the approach to be taken in the following terms:

' … the Inspector's report and Secretary of State's decision letter must be read as a whole, in a reasonably flexible manner and not applying the exacting and precise standards that are applied to a contract or statute.'

1 [2006] EWHC 2356 (Admin), [2006] 4 All ER 1240 at [39].

[1084]

In the context of a challenge to the validity of a compulsory purchase order, the courts have quashed orders where the inspector's report was found to be so lacking in precision and intelligibility that an essential part of the applicant's case had not been put before the Secretary of State for his consideration[1].

1 *W H Gibbs Ltd v Secretary of State for the Environment* (1973) 229 Estates Gazette 103.

[1085]

In *Landau v Secretary of State for the Environment*[1], a development corporation sought to regenerate land within its urban development area. It held a competition for proposals for redevelopment, which was won by a company, NQD. Outline planning permission was granted for the NQD scheme and then the development corporation made a compulsory purchase order for the land in order to implement that scheme. The applicant had also seen that there was potential for redevelopment within the urban development area and had acquired land within it. He prepared four alternative schemes for redevelopment of his land, but, by the time of the compulsory purchase order inquiry, none of them had been granted planning permission. At the inquiry, he sought to have his land excluded from the order so that he could redevelop it himself. The development corporation and NQD presented evidence at the inquiry that, without the acquisition of the applicant's land, there would not be reasonable profit on private investment on the whole unless a substantial grant of public funds were provided. The applicant argued that his scheme did not require any public funds in order to be viable and that, if he were permitted, the public money that would otherwise have been spent on the NQD scheme could be diverted to other public sector projects in the local area. The inspector concluded that the NQD scheme would secure the early and successful regeneration of the urban development area whilst the applicant's schemes were flawed in a number of respects and would put the future of the NQD scheme in doubt because of its effect upon the financial viability of that scheme. The Secretary of State confirmed the order on the basis of the inspector's reasons. Those reasons were criticised before the Court of Appeal as being inadequate, in that it was alleged that they gave no reason for the rejection of the applicant's argument concerning the potential reallocation of public funds. The Court of Appeal held that, because the applicant's alternative scheme was rejected on non-financial grounds, no possibility of the reallocation of public funds arose. As a result, there was no basis for criticism of the adequacy of the reasons because it was not an issue that fell to be determined.

1 [1991] EGCS 119.

[1086]
An example of a successful challenge to the validity of a compulsory purchase order on the basis of inadequate reasons is that of *Don v Secretary of State for the Environment*[1], where an inspector failed to address an allegation raised by an objector at the public inquiry that a compulsory purchase order had been made in bad faith by the acquiring authority.

1 [1994] NPC 18.

J The powers of the court

[1086.1]
ALA 1981, s 24 sets out the powers of the court upon an application made under s 23. There are two distinct discretionary powers. First, the court has power to grant interim relief suspending the operation of the order or certificate[1], pending the final determination of the court proceedings. Second, the court has power to quash the order or certificate being challenged. Both are

discretionary powers, and both can be applied to all or only part of the order or certificate, as explained below.

1 In the case of a challenge brought to a certificate granted under ALA 1981, Pt III (special kinds of land).

1 The discretion to grant interim relief

[1086.2]
ALA 1981, s 24(1) provides that on an application under s 23 the court may make an interim order suspending the operation of the compulsory purchase order or any provision contained therein, or of the certificate, either generally or in so far as it affects any property of the applicant, until the final determination of the proceedings. The power is discretionary but provides a useful safeguard to the landowner where the acquiring authority is minded to implement the order or act upon the certificate notwithstanding the existence of the challenge. Where the ground of challenge relates to the order or certificate as a whole, or the claimant's land cannot easily be severed from the rest of the scheme, it may be more likely that the court would suspend the order or certificate in whole rather than in part. The power is discretionary, and each case will turn upon its own particular facts.

[1086.3]
In *Richardson v Minister of Housing and Local Government*[1] the minister conceded that he had acted unlawfully in making a compulsory purchase order in respect of open space without following the special parliamentary procedure. The court rejected an application that the proceedings be adjourned and the order suspended while the special parliamentary procedure was followed. It held that the claimant had made good his challenge and shown that he had suffered substantial prejudice, and it was appropriate that the order be quashed.

1 (1956) 8 P&CR 29. For an unusual example (not falling within ALA 1981, s 24(2)) of interim relief pending the making of a fresh compulsory purchase order, where an earlier order had been quashed but the local authority nevertheless proceeded with site clearance work in respect of its own property in preparation for the scheme, see *Pascoe v Liverpool City Council* [2007] EWHC 1024 (Admin), [2006] 4 All ER 1240.

2 The discretion to quash

[1086.4]
Where a claimant establishes that the order does not fall within the powers of the Act, or that a relevant requirement has not been complied with and substantial prejudice has been caused thereby, the court nevertheless retains a discretion whether to quash the order or certificate under challenge, and if so how much of it to quash. The court's powers are contained in ALA 1981, s 24(2), which provides that the court:

> '... may quash the compulsory purchase order or any provision contained therein, or the certificate, either generally or in so far as it affects any property of the appellant.'

On the face of the words of the statute, the effect of the exercise of the power to grant relief is therefore to quash all or part of the order or certificate, and not merely to quash the confirming authority's decision[1]. It may, however, be open to argument whether the court could quash a defective decision to confirm thereby enabling the confirming authority to re-take that decision rather than to re-make the compulsory purchase order.

1 Contrast the position in statutory challenges to planning appeal decisions, where the decision letter is quashed and the appeal falls to be redetermined.

[1086.5]
The exercise of the court's discretion to withhold relief where the claimant has otherwise succeeded is an exceptional course to take[1]. Where the claimant has shown that a material consideration was left out of account by the confirming authority, the court should grant relief if, on the facts, the confirming authority might have reached a different decision had the matter in question been considered[2]. In a case where the acquiring authority intended to use the land for a purpose falling outside the scope of the authorising Act, the court held that the minister ought to have refused to confirm the order and therefore the proper course of action was to quash the decision[3]. Similarly, in a case where the claimant had succeeded in showing that the minister had misinterpreted his powers and failed to apply the correct statutory test when confirming an order, the proper cause of action was to quash the whole compulsory purchase order[4].

1 *Pascoe v Secretary of State* [2006] EWHC 2356 (Admin) at [46] per Forbes J, applying *Berkeley v Secretary of State* [2001] 2 AC 603, HL.
2 By analogy with the exercise of discretion in statutory challenges to planning appeal decisions: see *Simplex (GE) Holdings v Secretary of State* (1988) 57 P&CR 306 at 327 and 329.
3 *London and Westcliffe Properties Ltd v Minister of Housing and Local Government* [1961] 1 WLR 519 at 529.
4 *Pascoe v Secretary of State* [2006] EWHC 2356 (Admin), [2006] 4 All ER 1240 at [45]–[49].

K Procedure and applications to the High Court

[1087]
The procedure relating to applications to the High Court, pursuant to the ALA 1981, s 23 is governed by the provisions of Civil Procedure Rules 1998, Pt 8A and Practice Direction 8. The jurisdiction is exercisable by a single judge of the Queen's Bench Division[1].

1 Civil Procedure Rules 1998, Practice Direction 8A, para 22.2.

[1088]
The application must be made by claim form[1] and must state the grounds of the application[2]. The claim form must be filed at the Administrative Court and served within the six-week time period for making the application as specified by the ALA 1981[3]. The claim must be served[4] upon the Secretary of State and upon the acquiring authority[5]. Evidence in support of the application should be by witness statement[6], but affidavit evidence is permissible[7]. The evidence must be filed by the applicant within 14 days after service of the claim form[8]. Copies of the evidence and any exhibits thereto must also be

served upon the Secretary of State and the acquiring authority[9]. Any witness statement or affidavit in opposition to the application must then be filed within 21 days of the service of the applicant's evidence, and such a statement or affidavit, together with any exhibits thereto, must be served upon the applicant[10].

1 A Pt 8 claim form must be used: Civil Procedure Rules 1988, r 8.1(6), Practice Direction 8, para 9.1.
2 Civil Procedure Rules 1998, r 8.2(*b*)(ii).
3 Civil Procedure Rules 1998, Practice Direction 8A, para 22.3 and see ALA 1981, s 23(4) regarding the six-week time limit.
4 As to service, see Civil Procedure Rules 1998, Pt 6.
5 Civil Procedure Rules 1998, Practice Direction 8A, para 22.4.
6 See Civil Procedure Rules 1998, Practice Direction 8A, para 22.7, rr 32.6(1) and 32.8, and Practice Direction 32, paras 17.1 ff.
7 See Civil Procedure Rules 1998, rr 32.15 and 32.16 and Practice Direction 32, paras 2 ff. Note that the additional costs attributable to using an affidavit rather than a witness statement will not be recoverable unless the court orders otherwise: see r 32.15(2).
8 Civil Procedure Rules 1998, Practice Direction 8A, para 22.8.
9 Civil Procedure Rules 1998, Practice Direction 8A, para 22.8(2).
10 Civil Procedure Rules 1998, Practice Direction 8A, para 22.9

L Challenging the refusal to confirm a compulsory purchase order

[1089]–[1250]
The provisions of the ALA 1981, s 23 do not apply where the Secretary of State fails to confirm an order. Accordingly, the jurisdiction of the court to consider and quash the Secretary of State's decision is not precluded by the ALA 1981, s 25[1]. In these circumstances, proceedings are by way of an application for judicial review, pursuant to the Civil Procedure Rules 1998, Pt 54.

1 *Islington Borough Council v Secretary of State for the Environment* (1980) 43 P & CR 300. Judicial review is the appropriate procedure the challenge the making of a Direction under ALA 1981, s 13C: see **[1001]**.

Chapter 7

Transport and Works Act 1992

Contents

A Introduction

[1251]
The Transport and Works Act 1992 (TWA 1992) was enacted to provide a new procedure for obtaining authority to construct transport and other works and for obtaining any required authorisation for the compulsory acquisition of land for those works. Prior to its enactment the promoter of a new railway or tramway had to seek the necessary powers by promoting a private Bill in Parliament.

B The scope of the Act

[1252]
Sections 1 and 3 of the TWA 1992 provide the Secretary of State with the power to make an order authorising certain kinds of works:

(*a*) a railway;
(*b*) a tramway;
(*c*) a trolley vehicle system;
(*d*) a system using a mode of guided transport which has been prescribed by order[1];
(*e*) the construction or operation of an inland waterway;
(*f*) the carrying out of works which interfere with rights of navigation and which are prescribed by order[2];

1 The Transport and Works (Guided Transport Modes) Order 1992, SI 1992/3231 has prescribed the following modes of transport: aerial cableway; lift; magnetic levitation; monorail; road-based with cable guidance; road-based with rail guidance; road-based with side guidance; track-based with side guidance. See also the Transport and Works (Guided Transport Modes) (Amendment) Order 1997, SI 1997/1951.

2 The Transport and Works (Descriptions of Works Interfering with Navigation) Order 1992, SI 1992/3230, as amended by the Transport and Works (Descriptions of Works Interfering with Navigation) (Amendment) Order 1997, SI 1997/2906, has prescribed the following works: barrage; bridge; cable; fountain; land reclamation; navigational aid; observation structure; offshore installation; pier; pipeline; tunnel; utilities structure.

[1253]
The matters which may be included within a TWA order are addressed in s 5 of and Sch 1 to the TWA 1992. These include matters relating to the acquisition of land, whether compulsorily or by agreement, the creation and extinguishment of rights over land, whether compulsorily or by agreement and the abrogation and modification of agreements relating to land.

[1254]
Orders may be promoted by the Secretary of State himself[1] but otherwise are to be made by the submission of an application. Other than where he is the promoter of the order, the Secretary of State is not to make a TWA order except on an application made to him in accordance with rules made by him[2]. The principal rules made are contained in the Transport and Works (Application and Objections Procedure) (England and Wales) Rules 2006[3]. Guidance on the rules is to be found in *A Guide to Transport and Works Act Procedures* 2006, published by the Department for Transport[4].

1 TWA 1992, s 7.
2 TWA 1992, s 6(1).
3 SI 2006/1466. This chapter provides an overview of the main features of the rules rather than a detailed description of every rule.
4 The *Guide* is available from the Department's website at www.dft.gov.uk and contains useful and practical guidance on many aspects of the Transport and Works Act procedures.

C Making an application

1 Pre-application stages

[1255]
At least 28 days before an application is made, an applicant must send to the Secretary of State a draft of the proposed order and a draft of the explanatory memorandum that the applicant intends to submit when making the formal application for an order[1]. Provision is made for the applicant to seek a screening decision from the Secretary of State as to whether or not an environmental impact assessment needs to be carried out to satisfy the requirements of Directive 85/337/EEC (as amended)[2] .Where an environmental impact assessment is or may be required, a scoping opinion as to the information to be provided in an environmental statement for the project may also be sought[3]. Provision is also made for the applicant to request environmental information (as defined under the Environmental Information Regulations 2004[4]) from certain bodies which are not public authorities where it is considered relevant to a screening decision or the preparation of an environmental statement.[4]

1 TW(AOP)(E&W)R 2006, r 5. Rule 5(2) deals with amendments to the draft material prior to the submission of the application.

2 TW(AOP)(E&W)R 2006, r 7. See also *A Guide to Transport and Works Act Procedures 2006*, paras 1.22–1.27.
3 TW(AOP)(E&W) R 2006, r 8.
4 SI 2004/3391.
5 TW(AOP)(E&W)R 2006, r 6.

[1256]
Apart from the requirements of the TW(AOP)(E&W)R 2006, applicants are advised to carry out a thorough consultation with relevant statutory authorities, statutory utilities whose services may be affected, and all other persons likely to be affected by the proposals[1]. Therefore, whilst there is no requirement in the rules for them to be consulted, the Department advises that all persons who must received copies of the applications documents under the rules and all persons who must receive notice of the application should be consulted before an application is made[2]. Guidance indicates that parish councils or community councils ought to be consulted in regard to matters of local interest[3]. There are many other statutory and voluntary groups which applicants are advised to consult where proposals may affect the interest of those groups[4]. Where it is proposed to finance a scheme wholly or partly from public funds, the Department also suggests that the relevant policy Division and the processing unit in the Department be contacted at an early stage[5].

1 See generally, A Guide to Transport and Works Act Procedures 2006, paras 2.1 to 2.18.
2 *A Guide to Transport and Works Act Procedures 2006*, para 2.8
3 *A Guide to Transport and Works Act Procedures 2006*, para 2.6.
4 *A Guide to Transport and Works Act Procedures 2006*, para 2.11 and Annex 4.
5 *A Guide to Transport and Works Act Procedures 2006*, para 2.12.

2 Form of the application

[1257]
Every application for a TWA order under s 1 or s 3 of the TWA 1992 must be made in writing and addressed to the Secretary of State[1]. The application is to state the name of the applicant, the address to which all requests for further information, notices or other documents are to be sent and is to be signed by the applicant[2]. Guidance indicates that the application should be in the form of a letter addressed to the relevant Secretary of State who would be responsible for making the order, or the National Assembly in the case of orders relating solely to Wales, c/o the particular team who will be responsible for processing the application[3]. The letter should state briefly what the draft order is for. There is a requirement to enclose certain documents with the letter[4] and the letter should list the documents enclosed. Three additional copies of the letter and all accompanying documents should be provided[5]. The relevant fee should also be enclosed.

1 TW(AOP)(E&W)R 2006, r 9(1).
2. In the case of a body corporate the signature of a director, the secretary or a duly authorised officer of that body will suffice: TW(AOP)(E&W)R 2006, r 9(3)(*a*). In addition, an authorised agent of the applicant may sign: TW(AOP)(E&W)R 2006, r 9(3)(*b*).
3 *A Guide to Transport and Works Act Procedures 2006*, paras 3.2–3.4. Guidance on the identity of the relevant Secretary of State is given in para 3 of the Introduction to the *Guide*.
4 See below, para **[1258]**.
5 TW(AOP)(E&W)R 2006, r 10(1).

3 Documents accompanying the application

[1258]
The applicant is required to provide the following documents with the application[1]:

(*a*) a draft of the proposed order;
(*b*) a memorandum explaining the purpose and effect of each article and schedule in the draft order;
(*c*) a concise statement of the aims of the proposals to which the application relates;
(*d*) a report summarising the consultations that have been undertaken[2];
(*e*) a declaration as to the status of the applicant if not an individual or a company regulated by the Companies Act 1985;
(*f*) a list of all consents, permissions or licences required under other Acts and which at the date of the application are being sought or which have been obtained or refused[3];
(*g*) any screening decision or direction or scoping opinion made by the Secretary of State;
(*h*) a copy of any direction made by the Secretary of State relaxing the procedural requirements normally applicable under the TW(AOP)R 2006.

An environmental statement must also be supplied with the application where necessary[4].

1 TW(AOP)(E&W)R 2006, r 10(2).
2 The report must confirm that the applicant has consulted all those named in column (2) of the tables in Schs 5 and 6 to the rules where authority is sought for works or other matters described in column (1) of those tables, and if not, why not: see TW(AOP)(E&W)R 2006, r 10(2)(*d*).
3 In respect of each consent, permission or licence the list must specify from whom the consent etc is or was required, the date of the application, or grant or refusal (as the case may be), and the reference number (if any) of the application: see TW(AOP)E&W)R 2006, r 10(2)(*f*).
4 See TWA(APO)(E&W)R, rr 7(12) and 11.

[1258.1]
In addition, the application should contain the applicant's proposals for funding the cost of implementing the order, and in particular, for funding the cost of acquiring land which is blighted within the meaning of section 149 of the Town and Country Planning Act 1990[1].

1 TW(AOP)(E&W)R 2006, r 10(3)(*a*).

[1259]
Where an application is for an order containing proposals to carry out works, the applicant should submit plans and sections and an estimate of the cost of carrying out the works provided for in the proposed order.[1]

1 TWA(AOP)(E&W)R 2006, r 10(3). The estimate should be in the form set out in Sch 3 to the TWA(AOP)(E&W)R 2006, or as nearly in that form as the circumstances permit.

[1259.1]
Where an application is for an order seeking the compulsory acquisition of land, or the right to use land or carry out protective works to buildings, or

the compulsory extinguishment of easements and other private rights over land (including private rights of navigation over water), the applicant shall submit with the application a plan and book of reference[1]. Additional rules apply where the order provides for the extinguishment or diversion of rights of way over a footpath, bridleway, cycle track or byway[2].

1 TW(AOP)(E&W)R 2006, r 10(4).
2 TW(AOP)(E&W)R 2006, r 10(5).

[1259.2]
Where an applicant seeks a direction from the Secretary of State that planning permission shall be deemed to be granted for the development provided for in the proposed order, the application should contain[1]:

(*a*) a request in writing specifying the development for which the request for a direction is sought;
(*b*) a statement of any proposed planning conditions;
(*c*) a statement of any matters that are proposed to be reserved for subsequent approval by the local planning authority;
(*d*) in respect of matters not proposed to be reserved for subsequent approval, such other documents that are necessary to support the request for a direction and which have not otherwise been submitted with the application.

1 TW(AOP)(E&W)R 2006, r 10(6).

[1259.3]
Additional requirements apply where an application seeks a direction from the Secretary of State under s 12(2A) of the Planning (Hazardous Substances) Act 1990, that hazardous substances consent shall be deemed to be granted[1].

1 TA(AOP)(E&W)R 2006, r 10(7).

The draft order

[1260]
Applicants need to consider carefully the powers they need to seek in the draft order. Model clauses have been prepared by the Department to assist in the drafting of orders for railways and tramways[1]. It would be advisable to seek professional help with the drafting of a draft order[2].

1 See the Transport and Works (Model Clauses for Railways and Tramways) Order 2006, SI 2006/1954.
2 The submission of a pre-application draft order pursuant to TWA(AOP)(E&W)R 2006, r 5 is intended to give the relevant Unit the opportunity to comment on the form and content of the draft order. A draft may be submitted to the Unit for initial comments before the rule 5 submission is made, but applicants are encouraged to give a clear explanation of the provisions on which the Unit's advice is particularly sought in these circumstances: see *A Guide to Transport and Works Act Procedures 2006*, paras 1.50–1.51. Annex 3 to the *Guide* contains general pointers on the drafting of TWA orders.

Plans and sections

[1261]
Plans provided should be drawn to a suitable scale, not smaller than 1:2500 and should show clearly existing features and the works described in the draft order[1]. A plan showing the general locations of any works should also be provided drawn to a suitable scale, but not smaller than 1:50000[2]. All plans should contain a reference to the National Grid base[3]. Sections should be produced, on the same horizontal scale as used in the plan showing the works described in the draft order, indicating the levels of the intended works and on a vertical scale not smaller than 1:500[4].

1 TW(AOP)(E&W)R 2006, r 12(1)(*a*).
2 TW(AOP)(E&W)R 2006, r 12(1)(*c*).
3 TW(AOP)(E&W)R 2006, r 12(2).
4 TW(AOP)(E&W)R 2006, r 12(3)(*a*). There are particular requirements in the TW(AOP)(E&W)R 2006, r 12(3)(*b*)–(*e*) for sections relating to bridges, viaducts, aqueducts, gantries, tunnels and other such works.

Land Plans

[1262]
The Land Plans that are required to be prepared in connection with a draft TWA order which seeks the compulsory acquisition of land must be drawn to a suitable scale not smaller than 1:2500. They must show clearly the land over which it is proposed to acquire powers of compulsory acquisition or rights of use, the land over which it is proposed that easements and other private rights shall be extinguished, the land of which the applicant is the sole owner and occupier and land in which there subsists and Crown interest[1].

1 TW(AOP)(E&W)R 2006, r 12(5).

Book of Reference

[1263]
A Book of Reference for certain types of proposal must be submitted with a draft TWA order which seeks the compulsory acquisition of land[1]. There are detailed requirements for the contents of a Book of Reference, and direct reference should be made to the detailed provisions dealing with this[2]. Among other things, the document should include a list of the names of all known owners, lessees, tenants and occupiers of land which it is proposed shall be subject to compulsory acquisition, rights to use land or rights to carry out protective work to buildings, together with those entitled to enjoy easements and other rights over land which it is proposed to extinguish and those who would be served with a notice to treat if the applicant were proceeding under s 5 of the Compulsory Purchase Act 1965[3]. It must also specify any land in which there is a Crown interest, any land which is subject to special parliamentary procedure, which is subject to certain kinds of planning constraints and designations, or which is exchange land or land for which other land is to be given in exchange[4]. Government guidance sets out an example of a Book of Reference[5]. The omission of certain information from

the Book of Reference does not of itself invalidate the application provided the applicant has made diligent inquiry in order to obtain the information in question[6].

1 See para **[1259.1]**.
2 See generally TWA(AOP)(E&W)R 2006, r 12(8). The provisions are too detailed to conveniently summarise here.
3 TWA(AOP)(E&W)R 2006, r 12(8)(*a*)–(*c*).
4 TWA(AOP)(E&W)R 2006, r 12(8)(*e*). See r 12(*e*)(ii)–(xi) for relevant planning constraints and designations.
5 *A Guide to Transport and Works Act Procedures 2006*, Annex 8.
6 TW(AOP)(E&W)R 2006, r 12(11).

4 Service of the application

[1264]
The application and its enclosures must be served upon every local authority in whose area the works are proposed to be situated[1]. Where the proposed works are works which interfere with rights of navigation, Trinity House must be served with a copy of the application[2]. In addition, certain Government agencies and other statutory undertakers are to be served with a copy of the application and its enclosures, as the nature of the works requires[3].

1 TW(AOP)(E&W)R 2006, r 13(1)(*a*) and (*b*) and this includes every relevant coastal authority.
2 TW(AOP)(E&W)R 2006, r 13(2). Trinity House is the General Lighthouse Authority for England, Wales, the Channel Islands and Gibraltar.
3 TW(AOP)(E&W)R 2006, r 13(3) and Sch 5.

5 Notice

[1265]
On, or very shortly after, the date of the application, a notice of the application must be published in the *London Gazette* by the applicant giving the name of the applicant and the address for communication with it, stating to whom the application has been made and whether it is subject to an environmental assessment, summarising the main proposals and specifying the location of the proposed works (if any), and giving the date of expiry of the period within which objections and representations must be made and the address to which they are to be sent[1]. Applicants are also required to publish two notices in a newspaper circulating in the area in which the proposals contained in the application are to have effect; the first at least 14 days before the date of the application and not after, the second no more than seven days after the date of the application[2]. For certain types of proposal certain Government agencies and bodies are required to be served with a copy of the newspaper notice[3]. Site notices are required to be posted in respect of certain types of proposals[4].

1 TW(AOP)(E&W)R 2006, r 14(1).
2 TW(AOP)(E&W)R 2006, r 14(2) and (3). The notice is to be in the form prescribed in Form 1 of Sch 2 to the rules.
3 TW(AOP)(E&W)R 2006, r 14(4), (5) and Sch 6.
4 TW(AOP)(E&W)R 2006, r 14(6)–(9).

6 Notices to owners and occupiers

[1266]
No later than the date of the application all owners, lessees and occupiers listed in the Book of Reference must be served with a formal notice as provided under the rules[1]. Where it has not been possible to ascertain the name of a person with an interest in land but the applicant has noted in the Book of Reference that he believes relevant names have or might have been omitted[2], notice must be served at that land by addressing it to 'owner' or 'occupier'. In addition the notice may be affixed to a building or to a structure on or near the land[3].

1 TW(AOP)(E&W)R 2006, r 15(1) and Form 5, Sch 2.
2 See TWA(AOP)(E&W)R 2006, r 12(10).
3 See TW(AOP)(E&W)R 2006, r 15(2) and Form 5, Sch 2, and TWA 1992, s 66(4).

7 Affidavit of compliance with notice provisions

[1267]–[1278]
Once the applicant has complied with the requirements relating to service of the application and the relevant notice provisions, the applicant is required to submit an affidavit to the Secretary of State indicating that this is the case[1].

1 TW(AOP)(E&W)R 2006, r 10(8).

D Objections and representations

[1279]
Objections and representations made under the rules must[1]:

(*a*) be received by the Secretary of State no later than 42 days[2] after the date of the application;
(*b*) be in writing;
(*c*) state the grounds of the objection or representation;
(*d*) indicate who is making the objection or representation; and
(e) provide an address to which any correspondence relating to the objection or representation can be sent.

Further details relating to the grounds for making an objection to the compulsory purchase elements of a TWA order are set out in **Chapter 2** at para **[178]** and following.

1 TW(AOP)(E&W)R 2006, r 21(1).
2 An objection will be valid if it is submitted after this date in response to information supplied after the date of the application but no later than 42 days after the date on which that information was supplied: see TWA(AOP)(E&W)R 2006, r 21(2).

E Making the order

[1280]–[1290]
The Secretary of State must not make a determination to make or refuse to make an order without first taking into consideration the grounds of any

valid objection[1]. However, where all objections have been withdrawn or the remaining objections appear to be frivolous, trivial or relate to matters which fall to be determined the tribunal concerned with the assessment of compensation, he may determine to make or refuse to make the order[2]. Where valid objections are outstanding, there are three potential procedural routes for the consideration of those objections; by way of written representations[3], by way of a hearing or by way of a public local inquiry. Written representations procedure may be used where there are very few outstanding objections and it is considered practicable to deal with the issues in correspondence. A hearing may be used as an informal alternative to an inquiry but these are normally appropriate where the proposals in the application include the compulsory acquisition of land. In all cases a statutory objector[4] has the right to insist that a public local inquiry or hearing is held[5]. Where a public local inquiry is held the procedure followed is set out in the Transport and Works (Inquiries Procedure) Rules[6]. This procedure is similar to that utilised in respect of compulsory acquisition under the ALA 1981 which is addressed above in para **[197]** and following.

1 TWA 1992, s 10(2).
2 TWA 1992, s 10(3).
3 See TWA(AOP)(E&W)R 2006, rr 23 and 24.
4 TWA 1992, s 11(4): this includes the local authority and any person who would be a statutory objector under the provisions of ALA 1981, s 12: see para **[198]**.
5 TWA 1992, s 11(3) and (4).
6 SI 2004/2018.

F The decision

[1291]
The Secretary of State may determine to make the order as proposed, make the order as proposed with modifications or not make the order[1]. Where the modifications are such that they will make a substantial change to those proposals he is to allow any person likely to be affected by the change to make representations to him and he is to take any representations made as a result into account before making the order[2]. The Secretary of State is required to notify the applicant and every person who took an objection to Inquiry or hearing of his decision and to publish a notice of the determination in the London Gazette[3].

1 TWA 1992, s 13(1).
2 TWA 1992, s 13(4).
3 TWA 1992, s 14(1).

G Special parliamentary procedure

[1292]
Special parliamentary procedure may be invoked in relation to a draft TWA order in the same way as it can under the provisions of the ALA 1981[1].

1 See TWA 1992, s 12(1) and para **[801]** and following.

H Challenging the validity of a TWA order

[1293]–[1300]
Section 22 of the TWA 1992 limits the grounds on which the validity of a TWA order may be challenged in similar terms to s 23 of the ALA 1981. Accordingly, reference should be made to **6[1001]** and following for details relating to challenging the validity of a TWA order.

Chapter 8

Development consent and the Planning Act 2008

Contents

A Introduction

[1301]

The Planning Act 2008 (PA 2008) created a mechanism for granting consent for nationally significant infrastructure projects. Such projects may be authorised by means of a single consent, called a 'development consent', which must be obtained under the Act where development[1] forms or is part of the project in question[2]. An applicant for a development consent may request that the order granting the consent also authorises the compulsory acquisition of land or of interests in or rights over land[3].Such a request is called a 'compulsory acquisition request'[4]. An application for an order granting development consent must be made to the Infrastructure Planning Commission[5]. The Commission is created by the Act itself, and its functions are those given by or under the Act[6]. If no such request is made, the development consent cannot authorise the compulsory acquisition of land unless all those interested in the relevant land consent to the acquisition or prescribed procedures have been followed[7]. A detailed description of the procedures for obtaining development consents is outside the scope of this work, but this chapter provides a brief overview of the principal statutory provisions in order to describe the procedures for authorising compulsory purchase of land.

1 Development is defined under the PA 2008, s 32 as having the same meaning as it has under the TCPA 1990, subject to certain exceptions which are listed in s 32(2) and (3).

2 PA 2008, s 31.

3 PA 2008, s 59(1). It may include the creation of new rights over land: see s 159.

4 PA 2008, s 59(1)(*b*).

5 PA 2008, s 37(2). At the time of writing, the Government proposes to abolish the Independent Planning Commission while retaining the substance of the procedure for scrutinising applications for development consents. However, the legislation to achieve this has not yet been enacted. It is anticipated that, if the proposed changes are enacted, the procedures for including within a development consent authorisation to acquire land compulsorily will remain substantially as described in this chapter.

6 PA 2008, s 1.

7 PA 2008, s 123.

B Overview of provisions relating to development consent

1 The need for 'development consent'

[1302]
The development consent procedure applies where the project involves development as defined under the Act. 'Development' is given a wider meaning under the 2008 Act than under the Town and Country Planning Act 1990[1]. For example, it includes works which would require listed building or conservation area consent[2]. The enlarged definition of development seeks to ensure that the development consent procedure is unified so that the single consent is competent to authorise all the proposed works. As a result, where development consent is needed under the Act, the Act disapplies the requirement for consent under other regimes where this would result in duplication[3]. Consequential amendments are made to other enactments as a result of the new development consent regime[4].

1 PA 2008, s 32.
2 PA 2008, s 32.
3 PA 2008, s 33.
4 PA 2008, s 36 and Sch 2.

[1303]
The Act gives a list of the categories of nationally significant infrastructure projects to which the requirement for development consent applies[1]. The list is subject to certain threshold criteria which must be met if a project within one of the defined categories is to be treated as a nationally significant project[2]. These criteria relate, broadly speaking, to the size, location and capacity of the type of development in question. So for example, the construction or extension of on shore generating stations are nationally significant infrastructure projects provided they are within England and Wales and have a capacity of 50 megawatts. For offshore stations the capacity threshold is 100 megawatts[3]. The Secretary of State may make additions or amendments to the list of types of nationally significant infrastructure projects Act by order[4].

1 PA 2008, s 14(1).
2 PA 2008, ss 14(2) and 15–30.
3 PA 2008, s 15.
4 PA 2008, s 14(3). In certain case the Secretary of State may direct that a particular application for consent or authorisation which has been to a different authority is to be treated as an application for a nationally significant project falling within the Act: see s 35.

2 National policy statements

[1304]
Central to the determination of applications for development consent under the PA 2008 is the consideration of any national policy statement that has effect in relation to the development in question. The Secretary of State may designate a statement as a national policy statement for the purposes of this Act if the statement: (*a*) is issued by the Secretary of State; and (*b*) sets out national policy in relation to one or more specified descriptions of develop-

ment[1]. He may also designate policy as a national policy statement even if it pre-dates the coming into force of the relevant provisions of the PA 2008[2]. No statement of policy can be designated a national policy statement unless a sustainability appraisal of it has been carried out, and it has been subject to the publicity, consultation and parliamentary requirements contained in the Act[3].

1 PA 2008, s 5. National policy statements are not confined to nationally significant infrastructure projects.
2 PA 2008, s 12.
3 PA 2008, s 5(3) and (4). For the detail those requirements, see ss 7–9 of the Act.

[1305]
Subject to certain exceptions, the Act requires the Commission to decide applications in accordance with a relevant national policy statement[1]. The policy set out in a national policy statement may in particular[2]:

(*a*) set out, in relation to a specified description of development, the amount, type or size of development of that description which is appropriate nationally or for a specified area;
(*b*) set out criteria to be applied in deciding whether a location is suitable (or potentially suitable) for a specified description of development;
(*c*) set out the relative weight to be given to specified criteria;
(*d*) identify one or more locations as suitable (or potentially suitable) or unsuitable for a specified description of development;
(*e*) identify one or more statutory undertakers as appropriate persons to carry out a specified description of development;
(*f*) set out circumstances in which it is appropriate for a specified type of action to be taken to mitigate the impact of a specified description of development.

1 PA 2008, s 104.
2 PA 2008, s 5(5).

3 National policy statements and blighted land

[1306]
Where land is in a location identified in a national policy statement as suitable (or potentially suitable) for a specified description of development, it will fall within the blighted land provisions under the TCPA 1990, Sch 13[1].

1 See the amendments made to TCPA 1990, Sch 13 by PA 2008, s 175.

4 Consultation on applications

[1307]
The Act contains express provisions in respect of pre-application consultation[1]. Guidance on how to comply with the provisions may be issued by the Commission or the Secretary of State[2]. Consultation of certain bodies and persons is mandatory[3]. Among those who must be consulted are those who the applicant, after making diligent inquiry, knows to be an owner, tenant, lessee, and occupier of the land, or to have an interest in or the power to

convey or release the land[4]. 'Land' is given the same meaning as under the CPA 1965, s 5(1)[5].

1 See Chapter 2 of the Act, entitled Pre-application Procedure.
2 PA 2008, s 50(1) and (2). Applicants are required to 'have regard' to any such guidance: s 50(3).
3 PA 2008, s 42. This includes consultation with the relevant local authority for the area.
4 PA 2008, s 44(1) and (2).
5 PA 2008, s 44(3).

5 Content of applications and pre-application consultation

[1308]
Applications for orders granting development consent must specify the development to which it relates, be made in the prescribed form, be accompanied by 'the consultation report', and be accompanied by documents and information of a prescribed description[1]. The Commission may give guidance on how the requirements for applications are to be met and such guidance must be published[2]. The consultation report' means a report giving details of what has been done in compliance with certain of the Act's provisions in respect of pre-application consultation in relation to a proposed application that has become the application, any relevant responses, and the account taken of any relevant responses[3]. The public in the vicinity of the proposed development must also be consulted at the pre-application stage[4], and details of the proposal must be publicised[5].

1 PA 2008, s 37(3). For the formal requirements, see the Infrastructure Planning (Applications: Prescribed Forms and Procedure) Regulations 2009, SI 2009/2264.
2 PA 2008, s 37(4) and (6), and see 'Planning Act 2008: Nationally Significant Infrastructure Projects Application form guidance' (DCLG, 2009).
3 PA 2008, s 37(7).
4 PA 2008, s 47.
5 PA 2008, s 48.

6 Consultation of those entitled to claim compensation for injurious affection and diminution in value of retained land

[1309]
The applicant must also consult those who he knows, after making diligent inquiry, would or might be entitled to make a 'relevant claim' if the order were made and the development were fully implemented[1]. A relevant claim means a claim under the CPA 1965, s 10 or a claim under the LCA 1973, Part 1[2].

1 PA 2008, s 44(4), but see the qualifications thereunder.
2 PA 2008, s 44(6). The right to compensation under these provisions is explained in **Division F**.

7 Obtaining information about interests in land

[1310]–[1320]
Provision is made allowing the Commission to authorise applicants or proposed applicants to obtain information about interests in land in order to comply with the consultation procedures[1]. The Commission may also autho-

rise persons to enter land for the purpose of surveying it in connection with an application or proposed application for development consent on that or other land, including where the proposed development consent would include provision for compulsory purchase of that land[2].

1 PA 2008, s 52.
2 PA 2008, s 53.

8 Taking into account consultation responses

[1321]
Where the applicant intends to proceed with the application it must take into account any responses to the consultation that were received within the relevant deadline for such responses, when deciding whether the terms of the application should be the same as those of the proposed application on which consultation took place[1].

1 PA 2008, s 49.

[1322]
Where the Commission duly accepts an application for an order granting development consent, the Act sets out classes of persons who must be notified of the application. The provisions mirror those relating to pre-application consultation in terms of who must be notified[1].

1 PA 2008, ss 55–57.

9 Notice of persons with an interest in land subject to a compulsory acquisition request

[1323]
Where a compulsory acquisition request is made, the applicant must give the Commission notice of those persons who the applicant knows, after diligent inquiry, has in interest in all or part of the land to which the compulsory acquisition request relates. These persons are called 'affected persons' under the Act[1].

1 PA 2008, ss 59(2) and (4).

10 Local impact reports

[1324]
When an application is accepted by the Commission and relevant notification procedures have been followed, the Commission will invite the relevant local authority and the Greater London Authority (where the land in question is in Greater London) to submit a written 'local impact report' to the Commission[1]. A 'local impact report' is a report in writing giving details of the likely impact of the proposed development on the authority's area (or any part of that area)[2].

1 PA 2008, s 60(1) and (2). For the meaning of relevant local authority, see s 102(5).
2 PA 2008, s 60(3).

11 Panel or single commissioner as the examining authority

[1325]
Applications may be handled by a panel or by the single commissioner. Detailed provisions exist governing how the decision allocating the application to one or other is to be made, and regulating the appointment and function of each[1]. Whereas a panel can determine an application where a national policy statement has effect in relation to the development[2], the single commissioner must report his or her findings and recommendations, whether or not a relevant national policy statement is in place[3]. If such a policy statement is in place, the single commissioner's report is made to the Commission who in turn refer it to the Council of the Commission[4] who will determine the application[5]. Where no such policy statement is in place, both the panel and the single commissioner must report to the Secretary of State who will determine the application[6]. This ensures that decisions are taken by central Government where no national policy statement exists.

1 See generally PA 2008, ss 61–85.
2 PA 2008, s 74(1).
3 PA 2008, s 83(1).
4 'The Council' under the Act means the Commission's Council: see PA 2008, s 235(1). For the constitution of the Council, see Sch 1, paras 6–10.
5 PA 2008, ss 84–85.
6 PA 2008, ss 74(2)(*b*), 83(2)(*b*) and 103.

12 Function of the panel or single commissioner

[1326]
It is important to note that the panel or single commissioner has the function of 'examining the application'[1]. This expression connotes a more inquisitorial role than currently exists at planning and CPO inquiries. This inquisitorial role is reflected in the procedural regime created by the Act.

1 PA 2008, ss 74(1)(*a*) and (2)(*a*), 83(1)(*a*).

13 Procedures for examining applications

[1327]
Chapter 4 of the Act applies to the examination of applications by a panel or a single commissioner, who are called 'the examining authority' under this chapter[1]. The Act expressly states that it is for the examining authority to decide how to examine the application[2]. In making its decision, the authority must comply with any relevant provisions of the Act, including any procedural rules published under the Act[3]. It must have regard to any Guidance issued by the Secretary of State or the Commission for the purpose of making such decisions[4].

1 PA 2008, s 86.
2 PA 2008, s 87(1).
3 PA 2008, s 87(2)(*a*), and see the Infrastructure Planning (Examination Procedure) Rules 2010, SI 2010/103.
4 PA 2008, s 87(2)(*b*).

[1328]
The examining authority may in examining the application disregard representations if the examining authority considers that the representations are vexatious or frivolous, relate to the merits of policy set out in a national policy statement, or relate to compensation for compulsory acquisition of land or of an interest in or right over land[1].

1 PA 2008, s 87(3). This qualification reflects the existing procedural rules applicable to compulsory purchase inquiries.

[1329]
The Act introduces a procedure whereby the examining authority makes an initial assessment of the issues involved in the application and then holds a meeting with the applicant and interested parties to enable invitees to make representations on how the application should be examined, and on other matters[1]. At or after the meeting the examining authority makes its decision as to how the application is to be examined[2], though it retains a discretion to make its decision otherwise than in accordance with this procedure[3].

1 PA 2008, s 88.
2 PA 2008, s 89(1), (2) and (5).
3 PA 2008, s 89(3).

[1330]–[1340]
Although the default position under the Act is that applications are to be examined by way of written representations, this is subject to four main exceptions, one of which relates to compulsory acquisition[1]. This is described further below.

1 PA 2008, s 90.

14 Determining applications

[1341]
In deciding the application the Panel or Council must have regard to: (*a*) any national policy statement which has effect in relation to development of the description to which the application relates (a 'relevant national policy statement'); (*b*) any local impact report submitted to the Commission before the relevant deadline; (*c*) any matters prescribed in relation to development of the description to which the application relates; and (*d*) any other matters which the Panel or Council thinks are both important and relevant to its decision[1].

1 PA 2008, s 104(2).

[1342]
Importantly, the Panel or Council must decide the application in accordance with any relevant national policy statement, except to the extent that one or more statutory exceptions to this rule applies[1].

1 PA 2008, s 104(3).

[1343]
These exceptions are[1]:

(*a*) if the Panel or Council is satisfied that deciding the application in accordance with any relevant national policy statement would lead to the United Kingdom being in breach of any of its international obligations;
(*b*) if the Panel or Council is satisfied that deciding the application in accordance with any relevant national policy statement would lead to the Panel or Council, or the Commission, being in breach of any duty imposed on it by or under any enactment.
(*c*) if the Panel or Council is satisfied that deciding the application in accordance with any relevant national policy statement would be unlawful by virtue of any enactment.
(*d*) if the Panel or Council is satisfied that the adverse impact of the proposed development would outweigh its benefits.
(*e*) if the Panel or Council is satisfied that any condition prescribed for deciding an application otherwise than in accordance with a national policy statement is met.

The Act expressly provides that the fact that any relevant national policy statement identifies a location as suitable (or potentially suitable) for a particular description of development does not prevent one or more of the above exceptions from applying[2].

1 PA 2008, s 104(4)–(8).
2 PA 2008, s 104(9).

[1344]
Where the Secretary of State is the decision-maker the Act is far less prescriptive as to the approach to the taken to the decision. In deciding the application the Secretary of State must have regard to: (*a*) any local impact report submitted to the Commission before the relevant deadline; (*b*) any matters prescribed in relation to development of the description to which the application relates; and (*c*) any other matters which the Secretary of State thinks are both important and relevant to the Secretary of State's decision[1].

1 PA 2008, s 105(2).

[1345]
If the application is granted, it may be granted in terms different from those proposed in the application. Where the decision maker proposes terms that are materially different to those applied for, the Secretary of State may make regulations governing the procedure to be followed[1]. Reasons must be given for any decision to grant or refuse an application[2].

1 PA 2008, s 114.
2 PA 2008, s 116.

15 Time periods for decisions

[1346]
The Act provides extendable time limits for concluding the examination of the application and reporting on it[1]. The presumption is that decisions will be made relatively quickly.

1 PA 2008, s 98.

16 Legal challenges

[1347]
Proceedings for questioning a decision granting an order may be made within six weeks of the day on which the order is published or six weeks from the publication of the reasons, if later[1]. Proceedings for questioning a decision to refuse development consent must be brought within six weeks of the publication of the reasons for refusal[2]. Such challenges are to be brought by way of judicial review. The Act also enables proceedings to be brought to question other decisions made under its provisions, and imposes the same six week time period on such challenges[3].

1 PA 2008, s 118(1).
2 PA 2008, s 118(2).
3 See PA 2008, s 118(3)–(7), but note the curiously worded proviso in s 118(9). This appears to be addressing the time period within which challenges need to be made, rather than purporting to oust challenges all together.

C Specific provisions relating to compulsory acquisition

[1348]
In addition to these general provisions relating to development consent, the Act sets contains specific provisions applicable to compulsory acquisition[1]. These are discussed in the following paragraphs.

1 See especially PA 2008, ss 122–134. See also s 135 (Crown Land), ss 136–138 (public rights of way, statutory undertakers), s 139 (common land) and s 144(3) (appropriation of highways). Note also Sch 9, which amends enactments conferring the power to override easements and other rights, such as s 237 of the Town and Country Planning Act 1990.

1 Determining compulsory acquisition requests

[1349]
An order granting development consent may include provision authorising the compulsory acquisition of land[1] only if the decision-maker is satisfied that two conditions are met[2]. The first condition is that either: (*a*) the land is required for the development to which the development consent relates, or (*b*) it is required to facilitate or is incidental to that development, or (*c*) it is replacement land which is to be given in exchange for the order land[3]. The second condition is that there is a compelling case in the public interest for the land to be acquired compulsorily[4]. The second condition puts on a statu-

tory footing the test which is already applicable to compulsory purchase by reason of relevant case law and policy[5].

1 Which may include the creation of new rights in land: see PA 2008, s 159(3).
2 PA 2008, s 122(1).
3 PA 2008, s 122(2). On exchange land, see ss 131 and 132(3).
4 PA 2008, s 122(3).
5 See **Division A, Chapter 2** and Circular 6/2004, para 17.

[1350]–[1360]

So far as the land that may be included in the order is concerned, an order granting development consent may include provision authorising the compulsory acquisition of land only if the decision-maker is satisfied either: (*a*) that the application for the order included a request for compulsory acquisition of the land to be authorised, or (*b*) that all persons with an interest in the land consent to the inclusion of the provision in the order, or (*c*) that the prescribed procedure has been followed in relation to the land[1].

1 PA 2008, s 123. For the prescribed procedure where it is proposed to acquire additional land not shown in the book of reference, see the Infrastructure Planning (Compulsory Acquisition) Regulations 2010, SI 2010/104.

2 Statutory guidance

[1361]

The Secretary of State may make guidance on the making of orders that include the authorisation for the compulsory acquisition of land, to which the Panel or Council must have regard[1]. Guidance relating to procedures on compulsory acquisition has been published[2].

1 PA 2008, s 124.
2 See 'Planning Act 2008 Guidance on Procedures Related to Compulsory Acquisition' (DCLG, February 2010).

3 Compulsory purchase hearings

[1362]

The Act makes express provision for a 'compulsory purchase hearing' to be held, provided that a request for such a hearing is made in accordance with the relevant procedures under the Act. Where the application includes a compulsory acquisition request, the examining authority must fix, and cause each affected person to be informed of, the deadline by which an affected person must notify the Commission that the person wishes a compulsory acquisition hearing to be held. If the Commission receives notification from at least one affected person before the deadline, the examining authority must cause such a hearing to be held.[1]

1 PA 2008, s 92(1)–(3).

[1363]

At a compulsory acquisition hearing, the applicant and each affected person are entitled (subject to the Examining authority's powers of control over the conduct of the hearing) to make oral representations about the compulsory acquisition request[1].

1 PA 2008, s 92(4). An affected person is a person interested in any of the land to which the compulsory purchase request relates: PA 2008, ss 92(5) and 59.

[1364]
Where the oral representation procedure is followed, including the compulsory acquisition hearing, the hearing is to be held in public, but it is for the examining authority to decide how the hearing is to be conducted[1]. In particular, it is for the examining authority to decide whether any person making representations may be questioned and if so, on what and by whom[2].

1 PA 2008, s 94(3).
2 PA 2008, s 94(4).

[1365]
There is a statutory presumption that any such oral questioning will be carried out by the examining authority, unless the authority thinks that oral questioning by another person is necessary in order to ensure adequate testing of any representations, or that a person has a fair chance to put the person's case.[1] The examining authority may appoint an advocate to carry out oral questioning on its behalf.[2]

1 PA 2008, s 94(7).
2 PA 2008, s 101.

[1366]
It is clear that the oral representations procedure is nothing like a public inquiry[1]. Neither the applicant nor an objector with an interest which it is sought to be acquired has the express right under the Act to call witnesses or to cross-examine anyone.

1 Though the examination is a statutory inquiry for the purposes of Sch 7 to the Tribunals, Courts and Enforcement Act 2007 (functions etc of Administrative Justice and Tribunals Council): see PA 2008, s 95(3).

4 Blighted land

[1367]
The Act makes certain amendments to the blighted land provisions under the TCP Act 1990, Sch 13. If either (*a*) the compulsory acquisition of the land is authorised by an order granting development consent, or (*b*) the land falls within the limits of deviation within which powers of compulsory acquisition conferred by an order granting development consent are exercisable, or (c) an application for an order granting development consent seeks authority to compulsorily acquire the land, then the land will fall under Sch 13[1].

1 See PA 2008, s 175. The section also provides that land identified in a national policy statement may fall within Sch 13 (see para **[1306]** above).

5 Procedures for compulsory acquisition

[1368]
Where the order granting development consent authorises the compulsory acquisition of land, the CPA 1965, applies in the same way that it applies to compulsory acquisition under the ALA 1981, Part 1 as if the order granting development consent were a compulsory purchase order under the 1981 Act[1].

1 PA 2008, s 125(2).

[1369]
However, the time limit for the exercise of compulsory purchase powers under the CPA 1965, s 4 and the entitlement to compensation under s 10 for injurious affection are disapplied.[1] These provisions are replaced by the Act's own time limits and provisions for compensation for injurious affection.

1 PA 2008, s 125(3). Paragraph 3(3) of Sch 3 to the 1965 Act is also disapplied (the giving of bonds).

6 Time limits for compulsory acquisition

[1370]–[1380]
Where an order granting development consent authorises the compulsory acquisition of land, steps of a prescribed[1] description must be taken in relation to the compulsory acquisition before the end of either (*a*) the prescribed period, or (*b*) such other period (whether longer or shorter than that prescribed) as is specified in the order granting development consent[2]. If steps of the prescribed description are not taken before the end of the applicable period, the authority to acquire the land compulsorily under the order ceases to have effect[3].

1 'Prescribed' means prescribed by regulations made by the Secretary of State: see PA 2008, s 235(1).
2 PA 2008, s 154(3).
3 PA 2008, s 154(4).

7 Compensation for injurious affection caused by the authorised works

[1381]
The PA 2008 provides that the developer is immune from an action in nuisance arising from the authorised works[1]. However, where this statutory defence to an action in nuisance applies, the person by whom, or on whose behalf, any authorised works are carried out must pay compensation to any person whose land is injuriously affected by the carrying out of the works[2]. Although the wording of the Act is not entirely clear, it appears to be intended that the principles applicable under the CPA 1965, s 10 are to be applied to a compensation for injurious affection under the PA 2008[3]. Any dispute as to compensation is to be referred to the UpperTribunal[4].

1 PA 2008, s 158. The wording of the provision is broad, but it is assumed that it would be construed in accordance with the principle in *Allen v Gulf Oil Ltd* [1981] AC 1001, to the effect

that the nuisance must be the inevitable result of the authorised operations if it is to be immune from action.
2 PA 2008, s 152(3).
3 PA 2008, See s 152(5) and (6). As to compensation under the CPA 1965, s 10, see **Division F**.
4 PA 2008, s 152(4).

8 Depreciation of land value by the use of authorised works

[1382]
The LCA 1973, Pt 1 applies with amendments to provide compensation for the depreciation of land by reason of physical factors arising from the use of the authorised works[1].

1 PA 2008, s 152(7). As to the LCA 1973, Pt 1, see **Division G**.

9 Limits on the scope of orders granting development consent

[1383]
An order granting development consent may not contain any provision the effect of which is to modify the application of a compensation provision[1], except to the extent necessary to apply the provision to the order land[2].

1 Which means a provision of, or made under, an Act which relates to compensation for the compulsory acquisition of land.
2 PA 2008, s 126.

10 Special kinds of land

[1384]
Particular provisions apply imposing constraints on the compulsory acquisition of land of a statutory undertaker, of a local authority, of the National Trust, and on the acquisition of commons, open spaces, and fuel and field garden allotments[1].

1 PA 2008, ss 127–132, which are similar to provisions found in Pt III of the Acquisition of Land Act 1981.

Division D

Implementation of compulsory purchase

Contents

References in bold are to paragraph numbers.

Chapter 4 Acquiring title and completion

Chapter 5 Special cases

Chapter 6 Interests in land

Chapter 1

Introduction

Contents

A The principal statutory provisions

[1]
The confirmation of a compulsory purchase order[1] does not by itself vest title to land in the acquiring authority nor give the acquiring authority the right to possession of that land. The acquiring authority has to make a conscious decision to exercise the powers conferred on it by the compulsory purchase order and the authorising Act (together known as the 'special Act'[2]) to acquire specific land. Moreover, the acquiring authority has a choice of procedures available[3] and it has to decide how it should exercise its powers in order best to meet its objectives.

1 As to which, see **Division C**.
2 See the Compulsory Purchase Act 1965 (CPA 1965), s 1(2), in relation to acquisitions to which the CPA 1965 applies.
3 See para **[21]**.

[2]
There are two statutes that govern the procedure for the exercise of powers of compulsory acquisition, namely, the CPA 1965, which applies to any compulsory purchase to which the Acquisition of Land Act 1981 (ALA 1981), Pt II or Sch 1 applies[1], and the Compulsory Purchase (Vesting Declarations) Act 1981 (CP(VD)A 1981), which applies where any minister or local or other public authority is authorised to acquire land by compulsory purchase order. Neither the CPA 1965 nor the CP(VD)A 1981 authorise the acquisition of land itself, but instead regulate the procedure to be followed in exercising powers to acquire land which have been conferred upon the acquiring authority pursuant to other statutory provisions.

1 ALA 1981, Pt II sets out procedure for acquisition of land by local or other authorities, whereas Sch 1 deals with acquisitions by the minister. See **Division C** generally.

[3]
Until 1965, the Land Clauses Consolidation Act 1845 (LCCA 1845) and the Land Clauses Consolidation Acts Amendment Act 1860 (together known as 'the Lands Clauses Acts') were incorporated into every subsequent Act which authorised the acquisition of land for the purposes of any undertaking[1]. Under the LCCA 1845, it was that Act and the authorising Act which were together known as the 'special Act'. The CPA 1965 part repealed and part consolidated the Lands Clauses Acts and the procedure contained in the CPA 1965 is broadly as before, with one or two exceptions. For example, there is now a right of entry onto land in default of agreement prior to quantification and payment on account of compensation[2], and the acquiring authority now has a limited right of withdrawal[3]. For practical purposes, the Lands Clauses Acts are now largely of historic importance only, as the CPA 1965 applies to most compulsory acquisitions. However, the LCCA 1845 (as amended) does still apply to a limited number of statutes[4] and, for this reason, appropriate references are given in the footnotes to the following chapters of this division.

1 LCCA 1845 (as amended), s 1. Moreover, when the procedure in the Acquisition of Land (Authorisation Procedure) Act 1946 was applicable, the Lands Clauses Acts were incorporated with amendments by s 1(3) and Pt 1 of Sch 2 to the Act of 1946, which Act was the forerunner to the ALA 1981.
2 CPA 1965, s 11(1) (as to which, see paras **[701]–[710]**). Under the LCCA 1845 (as amended), entry onto land could only be made in default of agreement following assessment of compensation, payment into court of security and execution of a bond (as to which, see paras **[721]–[724]**).
3 The LCA 1961, s 31 provides a limited opportunity to withdraw a notice to treat, once it is served (as to which, see para **[341]**).
4 For example, the Military Lands Act 1982 and the Forestry Act 1945.

B The acquiring authority's objectives

[4]
In deciding how to exercise powers of compulsory acquisition, an acquiring authority must consider:

(*a*) how quickly it requires possession of the land; and
(*b*) whether it needs to acquire title to the land as a priority.

Title to the land and the right to possession of the land are not necessarily acquired simultaneously. Where an acquiring authority needs to commence works on site immediately following confirmation of a compulsory purchase order, it may be possible to secure a right of entry in the short term and leave the assessment of compensation and the acquisition of title to that land to a later date. However, an acquiring authority which is assembling a site for commercial redevelopment may require title to the land (rather than mere possession of it) as a priority to enable development by a third party.

[5]
Against these factors, the acquiring authority must consider the date at which compensation is to be assessed under the various procedures. Whilst compensation need not be paid on that date, interest will accrue from that

time. The acquiring authority should also consider staggering entry onto (or the right to enter onto) the land, to enable it to budget for its financial liabilities. Finally, an acquiring authority may consider how the exercise of its powers will be perceived by the public and may want to avoid measures which could be construed as draconian.

[6]
The various means of acquiring title are explained in paras **[7]–[10]**, and the means of obtaining lawful entry are explained in paras **[21]–[26]**. No vesting will take place pursuant to a general vesting declaration made under the CP(VD)A 1981 in relation to land in respect of which a notice to treat has already been served[1] and it is therefore important that an acquiring authority weighs up the merits of the respective procedures before taking any steps under them.

1 CP(VD)A 1981, s 7(1).

C Acquiring title

[7]
An acquiring authority can choose whether to acquire title by:

(*a*) agreement;
(*b*) treating individually with landowners under the CPA 1965; or
(*c*) dispensing with the need to treat with landowners and acquiring title automatically by proceeding under a general vesting declaration.

These possibilities are considered below.

1 Agreement

[8]
If parties are willing, land may be acquired by private agreement[1].

1 As to which, see **B[807]–[809]**. The CPA 1965, s 3 provides that it shall be lawful for an acquiring authority to agree, with the owners of any of the land subject to compulsory purchase and all parties interested in it, to acquire the land for money or money's worth.

2 Service of notice to treat

[9]
Where notice to treat[1] has been served, a quasi-contract for sale is established between landowner and acquiring authority[2] which, subject to a limited right of withdrawal[3], becomes unconditional as soon as compensation is agreed or determined by the Upper Tribunal. Where the parties are unable to agree the amount of compensation, either party has the right to refer the question of disputed compensation to the Upper Tribunal[4] for determination, so triggering the ability to complete the purchase. This is explained in para **[1004]**. Following determination of the compensation payable, either party may seek specific performance of the sale. This procedure does allow for negotiation

with a willing landowner, but also requires the acquiring authority to enter into negotiations with each and every one of those on whom a notice to treat must be served[5].

1 CPA 1965, s 5 (as to which, see paras **[301]–[341]**).
2 See para **[323]**.
3 LCA 1961, s 31 (as to which, see paras **[341]**).
4 CPA 1965, s 6.
5 CPA 1965, s 5 (as to which, see paras **[306]–[309]**).

3 General vesting declaration

[10]–[20]
Where a general vesting declaration is executed in accordance with the CP(VD)A 1981 in relation to land which is the subject of a compulsory purchase order to which the CPA 1965 applies, title to the land (together with rights of entry against all persons interested in it, except certain minor tenants) vests in the acquiring authority on the vesting date[1], which must be at least three months from confirmation of the compulsory purchase order[2]. This is explained in paras **[342]–[361]**. Whilst this procedure is very useful in assembling clean title to a site quickly, as it does not require any negotiations with individual landowners nor any investigation as to title, it can be perceived as draconian. Moreover, compensation is assessed at (and interest accrues from) the vesting date, notwithstanding that entry may not actually be required until later[3].

1 See para **[350]**.
2 See paras **[347]–[348]**.
3 See para **[350]**.

D Means of gaining lawful entry

[21]
An acquiring authority seeking to secure lawful entry onto the land has a choice of procedures available to it, some of which require prior assessment and/or payment on account of compensation[1]. These proceedings are:

(*a*) agreement;
(*b*) service of notice of entry;
(*c*) deposit of moneys and execution of a bond; and
(*d*) general vesting declaration.

1 An undertaker, in relation to a special Act incorporating the LCCA 1845 (as amended), has a more limited choice of procedures available, namely, agreement or advance payment of compensation to the claimant or into court (as to which, see **B[807]–[809]** and paras **[721]–[724]**).

1 Agreement

[22]
The owners[1] and occupiers of land which is the subject of a compulsory purchase order may consent to entry by the acquiring authority prior to quantification and/or payment of compensation due[2]. Once a landowner has

consented to entry, that consent cannot be revoked[3]. Such consent may be presumed from conduct[4].

1 'Owner' means any person with power to sell and convey the land to the acquiring authority: CPA 1965, s 1(6).
2 CPA 1965, s 11(4); unless such consent is obtained, entry may only be made under the CPA 1965 following payment of compensation due (either to those entitled or into court in accordance with the CPA 1965) or otherwise in accordance with the methods of entry authorised by the CPA 1965, ss 11(1)–(3) (as to which, see paras **[701]**ff and paras **[721]**ff). There is a similar provision in the LCCA 1845 (as amended), s 84 as regards entry onto land the acquisition of which is authorised by a special Act to which the LCCA 1845 (as amended) applies. (Entry may also be made following execution of a vesting declaration under the CP(VD)A 1981 (as to which, see para **[350]**)). Where the acquiring authority has failed or omitted to purchase an interest in the land by mistake, it is permitted to stay in possession under the CPA 1965, s 22 (as to which, see para **[743]**.)
3 *Knapp v London, Chatham etc Rly* (1863) 11 WR 890.
4 *Greenhalgh v Manchester and Birmingham Rly* (1838) 3 My & Cr 784.

2 Service of notice of entry

[23]
By the CPA 1965, s 11(1), where an acquiring authority has served a notice to treat[1] in respect of land, it may serve at least 14 days' notice of intended entry on the owner[2], lessee and occupier. The acquiring authority may then enter on and take possession of the land specified in the notice of entry any time after the expiry of the specified notice period[3]. No payment on account of compensation is required prior to entry, but any compensation will be assessed at the date of entry, with interest accruing from that date[4]. Entry can be secured relatively quickly under these provisions. Entry following service of notice to treat and notice of entry is explained in paras **[323]** and **[706]**.

1 CPA 1965, s 5 (as to which, see paras **[301]**ff).
2 For the purposes of the CPA 1965, s 11(1), 'owner' means a person other than a mortgagee not in possession, who is, for the time being, entitled to dispose of the fee simple of land, whether in possession or reversion. This definition includes a person holding and entitled to rents and profits from the land under a lease or agreement with at least three years left to run and any person having power to sell, convey or release land: ALA 1981, s 7(1), as applied by the CPA 1965, s 11(1).
3 CPA 1965, s 11(1). There is no equivalent provision where the acquisition of land is authorised by a special Act to which the LCCA 1845 (as amended) applies. Entry onto land, in that case, without the consent of the owners and occupiers of such land, may only be made where compensation has been assessed and paid (either to those entitled to it or into court): LCCA 1845 (as amended), ss 84, 85 (as to which, see paras **[721]**ff).
4 See paras **[707]**, **[708]**. Having taken possession of the land, the acquiring authority will become liable to make, if so requested, an advance payment of compensation: see paras **[1081]–[1084]** below.

3 Deposit of moneys and execution of a bond

[24]
Where an acquiring authority has, in relation to land within a compulsory purchase order:

(*a*) deposited moneys[1] in court as security for the compensation payable; and (*b*) given or tendered to the owner[2] a bond in respect of the compensation payable, conditioned for payment to the owner or into court[3],

Schedule 3 to the CPA 1965 provides a procedure whereby it may enter on and take possession of such land. This procedure[4], therefore, requires a preliminary assessment of and deposit on account of the compensation payable prior to entry[5], but the owner will retain the right to have compensation finally assessed by the Upper Tribunal. The compensation actually due may therefore differ from the payment on account. This procedure for obtaining entry is explained in paras **[721]**ff, but it is rarely used nowadays, as it is relatively cumbersome.

1 Such sum being the amount claimed by the owner (being each person interested in or entitled to sell and convey the land who has not given his consent to entry: CPA 1965, s 11(2), Sch 3, para 1) or such sum as is determined by a surveyor appointed by two justices of the peace: CPA 1965, s 11(2), Sch 3, para 2.

2 For the purposes of Sch 3 to the CPA 1965, 'owner' means each person interested in or entitled to sell or convey the land who has not given his consent to the entry: CPA 1965, Sch 3, para 1.

3 CPA 1965, s 11(2), Sch 3, para 3. The bond must be in a penal sum equal to the sum deposited in court and must have two sufficient sureties.

4 CPA 1965, s 11(2) and Sch 3. It is submitted that service of a notice to treat under the CPA 1965, s 5 will be required prior to entry under this provision (as to which, see para **[723]**).

5 The LCCA 1845 (as amended), ss 85, 86 makes similar provision, in respect of land which is the subject of a special Act incorporating the LCCA 1845 (as amended).

4 General vesting declaration

[25]

Where a general vesting declaration is executed in accordance with the CP(VD)A 1981, entry onto and possession of such land as is specified in the vesting declaration may be taken by the acquiring authority on the vesting date[1]. The vesting date can, at its earliest, be three months from confirmation of compulsory purchase order[2]. Such rights of entry will be effective against all interests, except a minor tenancy[3] or a long tenancy about to expire[4] and there will be no need to serve any notice to treat and notice of entry[5], except in relation to such minor interests[6]. Exercise of rights of entry pursuant to a general vesting declaration does not require prior assessment of compensation. However, regardless of when entry is actually taken, compensation will be assessed as at the date of vesting[7] with interest accruing from that date. The procedure relating to general vesting declarations is explained in paras **[342]–[361]**.

1 CP(VD)A 1981, s 8(1) (as to which, see para **[350]**). In addition, title to the relevant land will vest in the acquiring authority.

2 See para **[347]**.

3 'Minor tenancy' means a tenancy for a year or from year to year or any lesser interest: CP(VD)A 1981, s 2(1).

4 'Long tenancy which is about to expire' means, in relation to a general vesting declaration, a tenancy granted for an interest greater than a 'minor tenancy', but having, on the vesting date, an unexpired period which is not more than the period specified in the declaration in relation to the land in which the tenancy subsists: CP(VD)A 1981, s 2(2).

5 CPA 1965, ss 5, 11(1) (as to which, see paras **[301]**ff and **[701]**ff).

6 CP(VD)A1981, s 9(2). Indeed, it is possible to simply delay possession until such interests have expired through effluxion of time.

7 LCA1961, s 5A(4): as to the assessment of compensation, see **Division E**.

[26]
The CPA 1965, s 11(4)[1] makes clear that there can be no entry onto land by an acquiring authority except by agreement[2] or as provided in the CPA 1965[3] until the compensation payable for respective interests in that land has been agreed or awarded and paid to the interested persons or paid into court in accordance with the CPA 1965[4]. In any case, an authorising Act[5] granting compulsory purchase powers may make special provision for entry onto the land[6].

1 There is a similar provision in the LCCA 1845 (as amended), s 84, in respect of land the acquisition of which is authorised by a special Act to which the LCCA 1845 (as amended) applies.
2 As to which, see **Division B, Chapter 3**.
3 Ie following service of notice to treat and notice to enter under the CPA 1965, ss 5 and 11 (as to which, see paras **[301]**ff and **[701]**ff), under the alternative procedure specified in the CPA 1965, s 11(2) (as to which, see paras **[721]**ff) or for the purposes of survey under the CPA 1965, s 11(3) (as to which, see para **[726]**).
4 This provision operates without prejudice to the ability to enter onto land under the CP(VD)A 1981 (as to which, see paras **[342]–[361]**) or remain on land where the CPA 1965, s 22 applies (ie where an acquiring authority have omitted an interest by mistake or inadvertence (as to which, see paras **[743]**ff)).
5 Whether it applies the CPA 1965 or the LCCA 1845 (as amended), with any modifications.
6 For example, see the Housing Act 1985, s 584.

E Format

[27]–[300]
Chapter 2 explains how compulsory purchase may be implemented by the acquiring authority once it has been authorised. **Chapter 3** describes the means by which lawful entry over land may be secured. Acquisition of title and completion are described in **Chapter 4**. The special provision made in respect of land affected by leases, rentcharges, mortgages and rights is explained in **Chapters 5** and **6**.

Chapter 2

Commencing implementation of compulsory purchase

Contents

A Notice to treat (Compulsory Purchase Act 1965, section 5)

1 Introduction

[301]
In order to implement a compulsory purchase order, an acquiring authority may serve a 'notice to treat' under the Compulsory Purchase Act 1965 (CPA 1965), s 5[1]. Its purpose is:

(*a*) to inform interested parties that the acquiring authority intends to proceed to exercise its powers of compulsory purchase; and
(*b*) to elicit information as to the interests subsisting in the land and the compensation to be claimed.

The procedure as to, and the effects of, the service of a notice to treat are explained in paras **[302]–[322]** and **[323]** respectively. Rules relating to the abandonment and withdrawal of any notice to treat are described in paras **[328]–[341]**.

1 CPA 1965, s 5 re-enacts the Land Clauses Consolidation Act 1845 (LCCA 1845) (as amended), s 18 which requires service of a notice of intention to enter on lands, the acquisition of which is authorised by a special Act to which the LCCA 1845 (as amended) applies. Case law relevant to the LCCA 1845 (as amended) is still largely applicable to the CPA 1965. Differences in procedure between the CPA 1965 and the LCCA 1845 (as amended) are outlined in **Chapter 1**. The main differences include the ability to withdraw a notice to treat served under the CPA 1965, s 5 (as to which, see para **[341]**) and the fact that compensation is now assessed on entry (as to which, see para **[707]**).

2 Timing of service of notice to treat

Earliest time

[302]
Valid notice to treat cannot be served prior to the confirmation of the relevant compulsory purchase order[1]; it must, however, be served prior to entry[2] onto

the land to be acquired. Failure to do so may result in the acquiring authority being

(*a*) restrained from remaining in possession[3] (although where such entry has been made through mistake or inadvertence it may properly remain on the land for up to six months[4]);
(*b*) sued for trespass[5]; or
(*c*) prosecuted for unauthorised entry[6].

The courts may, however, be reluctant to restrain an acquiring authority from remaining in possession after entry, despite non-compliance with formalities as to service of notice to treat[7].

1 In *Parker (Trustees of the Ware Park Estate) v Hertford BC* (1967) 18 P&CR 315, a notice to treat served by an authority which had compulsory purchase powers, but which did not have the benefit of a confirmed compulsory purchase order, was of no effect. See also *Bostock, Chater & Sons Ltd v Chelmsford Corpn* (1973) 26 P&CR 321.
2 It may, however, be served contemporaneously with the notice of entry, see para **[703]**.
3 *Goodson v Richardson* (1874) 9 Ch App 221; *Ranken v East and West India Docks and Birmingham Junction Rly Co* (1849) 12 Beav 298.
4 CPA 1965, s 22 (as to which, see paras **[743]**ff).
5 *Ramsden v Manchester, South Junction and Altrincham Rly Co* (1848) 1 Exch 723.
6 CPA 1965, s 12 (as to which, see paras **[741]–[742]**).
7 For example, in the case of *Cooke v LCC* [1911] 1 Ch 604, an acquiring authority that took entry without service of notice to treat on a mortgagee was able to regularise its possession by late service of such, without vacating. Further, in the case of *Cohen v Haringey London Borough Council* (1980) 42 P&CR 6, it was held that notice to treat and notice of entry could be validly served after possession had been taken (provided such service was still within the three-year period under the CPA 1965, s 4): see para **[303]**, fn 1, but mesne profits would be payable for the unlawful trespass between the date of entry and expiry of the 14-day period in the (late) notice of entry; the notices could not be backdated.

Latest time

[303]
Notice to treat must be served within the three-year period prescribed in the CPA 1965, s 4[1] or, in the case of a nationally significant infrastructure project authorised pursuant to the PA 2008, steps of a prescribed nature must be taken within the prescribed period or such other period as is specified in the development consent order[2]. Any notice to treat served outside this period will be invalid so that the acquiring authority will no longer have the power to acquire the land and the Upper Tribunal will therefore have no jurisdiction[3] to determine the compensation payable. In calculating this period, the date on which the compulsory purchase order becomes operative will be excluded[4]. Provided notice to treat has been served within the requisite period, entry may be taken subsequently[5] and compensation assessed later[6]. However, service of notice to treat will not preserve powers of acquisition indefinitely. The notice to treat will cease to have effect after three years, unless extended by agreement, possession has been taken of the land, the compensation due has been agreed or determined, a reference has been made to the Upper Tribunal to determine the compensation, or a general vesting declaration has been executed[7].

1 Ie three years from the date when the compulsory purchase order becomes operative upon publication of the first press notice, see **C[259]**. Similar provision exists in the LCCA 1845 (as

amended), s 123, in respect of land the acquisition of which is authorised by a special Act incorporating the LCCA 1845 (as amended), except that the three-year limit will only be applied where the special Act makes no other provision in this regard.

2 PA 2008, s 125(3), which disapplies the CPA 1965, s 4, and s 154(3), (4), which provides for time limits to be prescribed.

3 Land Compensation Act 1961 (LCA 1961), s 1. See *Advance Ground Rents v Middlesborough Borough Council* (1986) 280 Estates Gazette 1015.

4 By analogy with *Goldsmiths' Co v West Metropolitan Rly Co* [1904] 1 KB 1, where the date on which the special Act received royal assent was excluded.

5 *Marquis of Salisbury v Great Northern Rly Co* (1852) 17 QB 840, so long as entry is taken within the time limited by CPA 1965, s 5(2A): see fn 6 below.

6 *R v Birmingham and Oxford Junction Rly Co* (1851) 15 QB 634. Where notice to treat is served out of time, it will not be presumed accepted because the owner has submitted a notice requesting acquisition of whole (as to which, see paras **[381]–[390]**): *Shepherd v Norwich Corpn* (1885) 30 Ch D 553.

7 CPA 1965, s 5(2A) and 5(2B). See paras **[328]**ff.

3 Form of notice to treat

[304]
Every notice to treat must[1]:

(*a*) give particulars of the land to which the notice relates;
(*b*) demand particulars of the recipient's estate and interest in the land, and of the claim made by him in respect of the land; and
(*c*) state that the acquiring authority is willing to treat for the purchase of the land and as to compensation to be made for the damage which may be sustained by reason of execution of the works authorised by the compulsory purchase order.

1 CPA 1965, s 5(2). Similar provision is made in the LCCA 1845 (as amended), s 18, in respect of land, the acquisition of which is authorised by a special Act to which the LCCA 1845 (as amended) applies.

[305]
There is no prescribed form for the notice to treat, although it is usual to attach a plan and a claim form for the purpose of enabling the recipient to state its claim for compensation[1]. What constitutes a valid notice to treat is a matter of interpretation; for example, a letter from the acquiring authority has been held insufficient[2]. It is suggested that an acquiring authority should ensure that:

(*a*) where a document is intended to be a notice to treat, this is made clear on its face by reference to the relevant statutory provisions; and
(*b*) the notice includes an adequate description of the land to which it relates together with a plan[3].

A notice to treat will be invalid if it purports to relate to land which is outside the scope of the relevant compulsory purchase order[4].

1 Failure to supply details of a claim in sufficient time to enable a proper offer of compensation to be made by the acquiring authority may lead to a costs penalty against the claimant: LCA 1961, s 4: see para **[325.1]** below. Standard claim forms usually request submission of a claim within 21 days, that being the period after which an acquiring authority may refer the issue of compensation to the Upper Tribunal for determination, where no claim has been submitted or where the compensation has not been agreed: CPA 1965, s 6.

2 *Parker (Trustees of the Ware Park Estate) v Hertford Borough Council* (1967) 18 P & CR 315. In contrast, in *Hull and Humber Investment Co v Hull Corpn* [1965] 2 QB 145, CA, no point seems to have been taken about a mere letter constituting a notice to treat (the substance of this decision has been reversed by LCA 1961, s 17(9A)).

3 The inclusion of a plan in the case of *Lewis v Hackney London Borough Council* [1990] 2 EGLR 15 saved a notice to treat which failed to describe the property adequately from invalidity. See also *Coats v Caledonian Rly Co* (1904) 6 F 1042, Ct of Sess; *Dowling v Pontypool, Caerlon and Newport Rly Co* (1874) LR 18 Eq 714, which deal with defective plans attached to a notice to treat.

4 *Coats v Caledonian Rly Co* (1904) 6 F 1042, Ct of Sess.

4 Entitlement to notice to treat

The rule

[306]

The acquiring authority must serve notice to treat on 'all the persons interested in, or having power to sell and convey or release, the land, so far as known to the acquiring authority after making diligent inquiry'[1]. With limited exceptions, the CPA 1965 does not provide further clarification as to who is entitled to receive a notice to treat. However, there is authority that, in addition to the freehold owner, the following are so entitled:

(*a*) lessees[2] including those who hold under an agreement equivalent to a lease in equity[3];
(*b*) persons entitled to the property under an enforceable contract for sale[4];
(*c*) mortgagees (including equitable mortgagees)[5];
(*d*) persons entitled to an option to purchase[6];
(*e*) persons who have acquired rights through adverse possession[7];
(*f*) mining lessees who have rights to sink pits in the surface[8];
(*g*) persons with equitable rights[9] (ie under a building agreement[10]), unless those rights would be overreached on conveyance of the legal estate; and
(*h*) where there is a specific power to acquire easements under the authorising Act[11], then such easement will be treated as land in respect of which a notice to treat ought to be served[12].

1 CPA 1965, s 5(1). Similar provision is made in the LCCA 1845 (as amended), s 18 requiring service of notice of intention to enter on all those parties interested in the relevant land or who are enabled by the LCCA 1845 (as amended) to sell and convey or release the same or such of those parties as shall after diligent inquiry be made known to the undertakers. As to differences between provisions of the CPA 1965, s 5 and the LCCA 1845 (as amended), s 18, see para **[3]**. The Church of England (Miscellaneous Provisions) Measure 1978, s 8 provides that where the fee simple of any ecclesiastical property is in abeyance, the fee simple shall for the purposes of compulsory purchase procedure be treated as being vested in the Church Commissioners and any notice to treat shall be served accordingly.

2 There is no requirement to serve notice to treat on tenants who have no greater interest than as tenant for a year or from year to year. Special provision is made for them under the CPA 1965, s 20 (as to which, see paras **[1321]–[1325]**).

3 *Re Kings Leasehold Estates, ex p East of London Rly* (1873) LR 16 Eq 521. See also *Walsh v Lonsdale* (1882) 21 Ch D 9; *Blamires v Bradford Corpn* (1965) 16 P&CR 162; *Sweetman v Metropolitan Rly Co* (1864) 1 Hem & M 543.

4 *Hillingdon Estates Co v Stonefield Estates Ltd* [1952] Ch 627.

5 *Martin v London, Chatham and Dover Rly Co* (1866) 1 Ch App 501; *Cooke v LCC* [1911] 1 Ch 604.

6 *Oppenheimer v Minister of Transport* [1942] 1 KB 242.

7 *Perry v Clissold* [1907] AC 73.

8 *Re Masters and Great Western Rly Co* [1901] 2 KB 84.
9 *Rogers v Kingston-upon-Hull Dock Co* (1864) 34 LJ Ch 165.
10 *Birmingham and District Land Co v London and North Western Rly Co* (1888) 40 Ch D 268.
11 See **B[447]–[468]**.
12 *Hill v Midland Rly Co* (1882) 21 Ch D 143.

[307]
The following persons are not entitled to a notice to treat:

(1) Those who hold no greater interest in the land than a tenancy for a year or from year to year[1].
(2) Licensees[2].
(3) Those with the benefit of easements over, or restrictive covenants against, the land to be acquired. The remedy for any adverse impact on those entitled to the benefit of such rights is a claim for compensation for injurious affection[3].
(4) Commoners[4].
(5) Any person with an interest in land created after the date on which notice to treat was served in respect of the superior interest out of which it was created. Such an interest takes effect, subject to the existing notice to treat, even though, had it existed at the date of service, its owner would have been entitled to receive notice[5].

1 Such tenants may be dealt with under the CPA 1965, s 20 (as to which, see paras **[1321]–[1325]**). Similar provision exists in the LCCA 1845 (as amended), s 121 in relation to acquisitions of land authorised by a special Act to which the LCCA 1845 (as amended) applies. Service of a notice to treat on such a tenant is not necessarily an incorrect practice, but any compensation payable will be assessed in accordance with the CPA 1965, s 20, in any event: *Newham London Borough Council v Benjamin* [1968] 1 WLR 694. The service requirements for notices to treat differ from those relating to notices of confirmation of the compulsory purchase order described in **C[175]**.
2 *Frank Warr & Co Ltd v LCC* [1904] 1 KB 713, CA.
3 CPA 1965, s 10. See **Division F, Chapter 2** and *Macey v Metropolitan Board of Works* (1864) 3 New Rep 669. NB special provision may be made in the authorising Act for acquisition of the benefit of such easements. See, eg, National Parks and Access to Countryside Act 1949, s 103 and paras **[1603]–[1604]**.
4 Where rights of commoners are compulsorily acquired pursuant to the procedure in the CPA 1965, Sch 4 (as to which, see para **[1607]**), there is no need to serve notice to treat on the commoners. See *Lewis v Mid Glamorgan County Council* [1995] 1 All ER 760.
5 *Mercer v Liverpool, St Helens and South Lancashire Rly Co* [1903] 1 KB 652; *Re Marylebone (Stingo Lane) Improvement Act, ex p Edwards* (1871) LR 12 Eq 389. See paras **[369]**ff.

Practical considerations

[308]
'Diligent inquiry' must be made as to the interests in the land[1]. This does not, however, require exhaustive enquiries on the part of the acquiring authority[2]. To avoid challenge, an acquiring authority that wishes to acquire full title would be advised to serve notice to treat on all known legal and equitable interests (other than minor tenants[3]), even where such interests do not sit obviously in any of the categories described[4]. A person who has indicated that he has no interest in land may be estopped from seeking to assert his interest against the acquiring authority subsequently[5]. Special provision is made in the CPA 1965[6] for those who are entitled to notice to treat but are

absent from the United Kingdom or cannot be found after diligent inquiry. Where the acquiring authority has, through mistake or inadvertence, failed to serve notice to treat on a person who should have received one, it may lawfully remain in possession of the land so long as it follows the procedure in CPA 1965, s 22[7].

1 CPA 1965, s 5(1). Similar provision is made in the LCCA 1845 (as amended), s 18 in respect of acquisitions authorised by a special Act to which the LCCA 1845 (as amended) applies.
2 See *R v Secretary of State for Transport, ex p Blackett* [1992] JPL 1041, in which it was held that it was sufficient for the acquiring authority to make enquiries as to the existing interests at the Land Registry; the fact that no information was supplied regarding certain interests which were awaiting first registration did not invalidate the entry made by the acquiring authority against those newly created interests whose owners had not received notice to treat.
3 CPA 1965, s 20 (as to which, see paras **[1321]–[1325]**).
4 See para **[306]**.
5 *Milford Haven UDC v Foster* (1961) 13 P&CR 289.
6 CPA 1965, s 5(3), Sch 2. Provision is made for the assessment of compensation by a surveyor, payment into court of compensation and execution of a deed poll vesting title with the acquiring authority, see paras **[1005]–[1006]**. These provisions cannot be used where interested persons can be traced, but there is on-going debate as to the correct ownership of land: see *Ex p London and South Western Rly Co* (1869) 38 LJ Ch 527.
7 See paras **[743]–[745]**.

[309]

The acquiring authority is not bound to acquire all existing interests in any land subject to compulsory purchase. For example, it can acquire the freehold interest and leave any leasehold interests to determine through effluxion of time[1]. Separate notices to treat may be served in relation to separate plots in common ownership[2] or separate interests in the same land. For example, it is possible to serve one notice to treat relating to the surface of land (omitting minerals) and a further notice to treat (if necessary) relating to the acquisition of subsoil minerals[3]. Further, it is up to the acquiring authority to determine which interests it actually needs[4]. However, it must serve notice to treat on all interests which it requires in order to achieve its objectives[5]. Where a notice to treat has been withdrawn[6], an acquiring authority may serve a fresh notice to treat in respect of the same land, provided the power to compulsorily acquire still exists[7]. However, unless the authorising Act[8] authorises the creation of easements or acquisition of lesser interests than those currently subsisting, the whole of the land or of any interest in it must be acquired, even though no more than an easement is actually required for the purposes of the undertaking[9]. Such lesser interests may, however, be acquired by agreement.

1 *Holloway v Dover Corpn* [1960] 1 WLR 604.
2 *Simpson v the Lancaster and Carlisle Rly Co* (1847) 15 Sim 580.
3 *Errington v Metropolitan District Rly Co* (1882) 19 Ch D 559.
4 *Errington v Metropolitan District Rly Co* (1882) 19 Ch D 559.
5 *Union Railways (North) Ltd and London and Continental Railways Ltd v Kent County Council* [2008] RVR 217, Lands Tribunal, upheld on appeal on different grounds: *Kent County Council v Union Railways (North) Ltd and London and Continental Railways Ltd* [2009] RVR 146, CA.
6 As to which, see para **[341]**.
7 See the CPA 1965, s 4 at para **[303]**; *James Coats v Caledonian Rly Co* (1904) 6 F 1042, Ct of Sess.
8 For example, the Local Government (Miscellaneous Provisions) Act 1976 (LG(MP)A 1976), s 13 enables local authorities authorised by a compulsory purchase order to create new rights over land. See para **[1608]**.

9 *Pinchin v London and Blackwall Rly Co* (1854) 5 De GM & G 851. Where the authorising Act does authorise the creation of easements, then such an easement is to be regarded as land in respect of which notice to be treat should be served: *Ramsden v Manchester, South Junction and Altrincham Rly Co* (1848) 1 Exch 723; *Farmer v Waterloo and City Rly Co* [1895] 1 Ch 527. See also *West Midlands Joint Electricity Authority v Pitt* [1932] 2 KB 1, CA for a case considering the erection of powerlines.

5 Mode of service of notice to treat

[310]–[320]

A notice to treat is only binding where properly served[1]. A notice will be validly served where[2]:

(*a*) it is delivered personally to the recipient;
(*b*) it is left at the recipient's proper address[3]; or
(*c*) it is sent by registered letter or recorded delivery service to the recipient's proper address.

A notice to treat which is to be served on an incorporated company or body is duly served if it is served on the secretary or clerk of the company or body[4].

1 *Shepherd v Norwich Corpn* (1885) 30 Ch D 553.
2 CPA 1965, s 30, which applies the provisions of the Acquisition of Land Act 1981 (ALA 1981), s 6. There is similar provision in the LCCA 1845 (as amended), ss 19, 20 in relation to land the acquisition of which is authorised by a special Act to which the LCCA 1845 (as amended) applies; notices must be delivered personally or left at the last usual place of abode, if any such place can be found after diligent inquiry. Where none can be found, the notice should be left with the occupier or affixed to a conspicuous part of the land. In the case of corporate bodies, notice is to be left at the principal office of business. If none can be found after diligent inquiry, it is to be left with the occupier or affixed upon a conspicuous part of the land.
3 For these purposes, the proper address is, in the case of an incorporated company or body, the registered or principal office of that company or body, or, in any other case, the last known address of the person to be served, unless a different address for service has been provided: ALA 1981, s 6, as applied by the CPA 1965, s 30. In *Staley-Brooks v Secretary of State for Local Government and the Regions* [2002] EWHC 1583, [2002] All ER (D) 159 (Jul) the appellant's property was derelict and boarded-up and the appellant had an arrangement with the Post Office for his mail to be delivered to a neighbouring acquaintance. Notice of confirmation was served on him at the neighbour's property. As the appellant had previously accepted service of communications at that address he could not then complain that service had not been duly effected for the purpose of the ALA 1981, s 6.
4 ALA 1981, s 6(2), as applied by the CPA 1965, s 30.

[321]

Where reasonable inquiry has been made, but it is still not possible to ascertain the ownership of land, the notice to treat may be served by addressing it to the 'owner', 'lessee' or 'occupier' of the land to which it relates (with a description of the land) and by delivering it to some person on the premises; if there is no person on the premises to whom it may be delivered, a copy of it should be affixed to some conspicuous part of the premises[1]. Where the owner can be traced, service of a notice to treat on the occupier of land is not good service on the owner, even where such occupier is the owner's agent[2]. A lessor will not be bound by a notice to treat served on a lessee[3]. Where a property is in multiple occupation, and the owner cannot be found, any notice to treat should be clearly addressed to the owner and served on every occupier[4].

1 ALA 1981, s 6(4), as applied by the CPA 1965, s 30. Unsuccessful steps taken by an acquiring authority to trace a claimant including contact with former solicitors, surveyor and neighbour and placing of notices upon property and in local newspapers and a search of the electoral register were deemed to be reasonable inquiry in the case of *Keith Rhodes v Derby County Council* (2002) ACQ/76/2001, Lands Tribunal (decision 28 February 2002, unreported). See also *In the matter of a Notice of Reference by Southampton City Council* (2002) ACQ/194/2000, Lands Tribunal (decision 20 February 2002 unreported) for adequacy of steps to trace unknown owner.
2 *Shepherd v Norwich Corpn* (1885) 30 Ch D 553. Service on an owner's brother, who had been given authority to act as agent, is likewise not good service on the owner: *Fagan v Knowsley Borough Council* (1985) 50 P&CR 363. However, service on an agent was good service in *Hewitt v Leicester City Council* [1969] 2 All ER 802, 20 P&CR 629.
3 *R v Great Northern Rly* (1876) 2 QBD 151.
4 *Shepherd v Norwich Corpn* (1885) 30 Ch D 553 at 573. See also *Noble's Executors v Ringwood UDC* (1962) 13 P&CR 174.

6 Formalities

[322]
A notice to treat is not registrable at HM Land Registry as an estate contract, as it is only a preliminary stage in the contract of sale[1]. The notice to treat is sometimes, however, registered as a local land charge.

1 *Capital Investments Ltd v Wednesfield UDC* [1965] Ch 774.

7 Effect of notice to treat

[323]
Service of a notice to treat is a condition precedent to the compulsory acquisition of land where an authority elects to proceed under the CPA 1965[1]. It is also an important step for the following reasons:

(1) A relationship analogous to vendor and purchaser is created[2]. The acquiring authority must buy and the owner must sell the interest specified in the notice to treat on an unconditional basis as soon as the compensation (which is in effect the purchase price) is ascertained, either by agreement or following a determination by the Upper Tribunal[3]. Following determination of the compensation, the resulting quasi-contract for sale may be specifically enforced by either party[4]. Until the purchase price is determined, however, there is no enforceable agreement for sale[5].
(2) Proceedings subsequent to service of the notice to treat must relate to the whole of the land which is the subject of that notice[6] except where:
   (*a*) consent is given to deal with part only; or
   (*b*) the notice to treat refers to more than one parcel of land,
   in which case, entry in stages may be possible[7].
(3) Both parties have the right to require compensation to be assessed by the Upper Tribunal in the manner provided by the CPA 1965[8] and, indeed, each person on whom notice to treat has been served is entitled to have compensation assessed in respect of his own interest[9]. Title to the property will not, however, pass to the acquiring authority until conveyance or execution of a deed poll[10].

(4) Once notice to treat has been served, the acquiring authority may serve a notice of entry[11], and enter upon the land without the consent of the landowner and without payment of compensation.

(5) Following service of notice to treat the landowner has the opportunity to:

(*a*) submit a claim for compensation[12]; and/or

(*b*) seek the acquisition of whole, rather than part, of his land[13].

(6) Service of notice to treat 'fixes' the interests in respect of which compensation will be payable. The owner may continue to deal with the property as he would otherwise[14] and may create new interests in the land, but he cannot increase the burden of compensation on the acquiring authority[15]. This is explained more fully in paras **[362]**ff.

(7) Rights and obligations conferred by service of the notice to treat are legal, as distinct from equitable, and bind all persons claiming under the recipient, whether with knowledge of the notice to treat or not[16]. The fact that a purchaser of land already subject to a notice to treat bought the property at a discount reflecting the existence of the notice to treat does not relieve the acquiring authority of its liability to pay the appropriate amount of compensation. A purchaser simply stands in the vendor's shoes and any assertion that he has already received value for money will not succeed[17].

1 Service of notice to treat is only such a condition precedent where the acquiring authority elects to proceed under the CPA 1965. Service of notice to treat has been held not to be an exercise itself of a power of compulsory purchase: *Re Uxbridge and Rickmansworth Rly Co* (1890) 43 Ch D 536; *Guest v Poole and Bournemouth Rly Co* (1870) LR 5 CP 553. However, in *Grice v Dudley Corpn* [1958] 1 Ch 329, Upjohn J held such service could be the exercise of powers of compulsory purchase for some purposes. In particular, service of a notice to treat within the three-year period specified in the CPA 1965, s 4 is enough to keep compulsory purchase powers alive where entry is made after that time, see para **[303]**; *Marquis of Salisbury v Great Northern Rly Co* (1852) 17 QB 840; *Tiverton and North Devon Rly Co v Loosemore* (1884) 9 App Cas 480. If an acquiring authority has failed to serve notice to treat on a person with an interest in the land that has been taken, he can claim compensation under the CPA 1965, s 22: *Kent County Council v Union Railways (North) Ltd and London and Continental Railways Ltd* [2009] RVR 146, CA; see para **[745.1]**.

2 *Adams v London and Blackwall Rly Co* (1850) 19 LJ Ch 557; *Tiverton and the North Devon Rly Co v Loosemore* (1884) 9 App Cas 840.

3 This is subject to a limited right of withdrawal: LCA 1961, s 31 (as to which, see para **[341]**). Following service of notice to treat, either party has the right to refer the issue of compensation to the Upper Tribunal for determination in default of agreement, see para **[1004]**.

4 *Harding v Metropolitan Rly Co* (1872) 7 Ch App 154. It appears that agreement as to price may be either verbal or written, notwithstanding the provisions of the Law of Property (Miscellaneous Provisions) Act 1989, s 2 (which provides that standard agreements for sale must be in writing): *Munton v Greater London Council* [1976] 2 All ER 815 at 818; *Pollard v Middlesex County Council* (1906) 95 LT 870. Where the compensation agreed is subject to contract, this will be insufficient to allow specific performance: *Munton v Greater London Council* [1976] 2 All ER 815. See also *Duttons Brewery Ltd v Leeds County Council* (1982) 43 P & CR 160.

5 *Haynes v Haynes* (1861) 1 Drew & Sm 426.

6 *Stone v Commercial Rly Co* (1839) 4 My & Cr 122; *Thompson v Tottenham and Forest Gate Rly Co* (1892) 67 LT 416. The notice to treat cannot relate to any land outside the scope of the compulsory purchase order: *Coats v Caledonian Rly Co* (1904) 6 F 1042, Ct of Sess. An exception to this arises where the landowner succeeds in requiring the acquiring authority to acquire the whole of his property under the CPA 1965, s 8 (as to which, see paras **[381]–[411]**).

7 See para **[702]**.

8 CPA 1965, s 6 (as to which, see para **[1004]**). See also *Fotherby v Metropolitan Rly Co* (1866) 2 CP 188.
9 *Abrahams v London Corpn* (1868) LR 6 Eq 625.
10 See **Chapter 4**.
11 See paras **[701]–[710]**. There is no equivalent provision for entry for acquisitions to which the LCCA 1845 (as amended) applies. Without consent, entry may only be made under that Act where compensation has been assessed and paid to the appropriate claimant or into court: LCCA 1845 (as amended), ss 84, 85.
12 See para **[325]**.
13 CPA 1965, s 8. See paras **[381]–[390]**.
14 See paras **[362]** ff. Indeed, service of notice to treat will not frustrate an existing contract for the sale of land: *Hillingdon Estates Co v Stonefield Estates Ltd* [1952] Ch 627. A landowner ought to keep his property insured against damage and fire until at least the date when compensation is agreed or determined, or entry is made, and would be advised to ensure that the acquiring authority accepts responsibility for the property before letting any building insurance run out.
15 See *Mercer v Liverpool, St Helens and South Lancashire Rly Co* [1903] 1 KB 652, which held that, where a new interest was created since service of notice to treat, the compensation payable in respect of the original interest(s) is deemed to incorporate compensation for any new interests created. See also *Cardiff Corpn v Cook* [1923] 2 Ch 115.
16 *Mercer v Liverpool, St Helens and South Lancashire Rly Co* [1903] 1 KB 652 held that the right to compensation may be assigned and dealt with as property. A pending claim for compensation following service of a notice to treat is not, however, an attachable debt: *Richardson v Elmitt* (1876) 2 CPD 9.
17 *Landlink Two Ltd and Barclays Bank Ltd v Sevenoaks District Council* (1985) 51 P & CR 100.

8 Action to be taken by owner in response to notice to treat

[324]
An owner of land who receives a notice to treat may:

(*a*) submit a claim for compensation; and/or
(*b*) where his property comprises a house, building or manufactory or a park or garden belonging to a house and part only is included in the notice to treat, follow the procedure to require the acquisition of the whole of his property.

Submitting a claim for compensation

[325]
Every notice to treat must demand particulars of the recipient's interest and estate in the land, and of the claim for compensation to be made by him[1]. A standard claim form is usually attached to the notice to treat. There is, however, no duty on the part of the recipient to submit a claim. While a failure to submit a claim will not disentitle him from receiving compensation or from making a claim at a later date, failure to submit a sufficiently detailed claim promptly may have implications in costs or even lead to withdrawal of the notice to treat, as explained below. If no claim has been submitted at all, or if a claim has been submitted but the parties have not agreed the compensation due within 21 days after service of a notice to treat, the acquiring authority may refer the question of compensation to the Upper Tribunal for determination[2].

1 CPA 1965, s 5(2)(*b*): see paras **[304]–[305]**. The LCCA 1845 (as amended), s 18 contains similar provision.
2 CPA 1965, s 6. Similar provision exists in the LCCA 1845 (as amended), s 21, in relation to acquisitions authorised by a special Act to which the LCCA 1845 (as amended) applies. Under LCA 1961, s 1, either party may make a reference to the Upper Tribunal. As to the Upper Tribunal, see **Division H**.

[325.1]
By virtue of the Land Compensation Act 1961 (LCA 1961), s 4(1)(*b*), where a claimant has failed to make a claim for compensation in sufficient time to enable the acquiring authority make a proper offer, the Upper Tribunal must, unless there are special reasons not to do so, order the claimant to bear his own and the acquiring authority's costs in so far as they were incurred after the time when a proper offer should, in the opinion of the Upper Tribunal, have been made. For this purpose, a claim must be in writing and specify the exact nature of the interest in respect of which compensation is claimed, distinguishing the amounts claimed under separate heads and showing how each head of claim is calculated[1].

1 LCA 1961, s 4(2). See also paras **[1023]–[1028]**.

[325.2]
By virtue of the LCA 1961, s 31, an acquiring authority may withdraw a notice to treat within six weeks of either:

(*a*) receipt of a claim which provides the details required by the LCA 1961, s 4(2); or
(*b*) where no such claim has been made, determination of the compensation by the Upper Tribunal[1].

Compensation may be payable in consequence of withdrawal of a notice to treat[2].

1 As to the Upper Tribunal's jurisdiction and the implications of LCA 1961, s 4, see **Division H**. In the case of *Trustees for Methodist Church Purposes v North Tyneside Metropolitan BC* (1979) 38 P&CR 665, an unquantified claim was submitted after the 21-day period. It was held that this claim did not fulfil the requirements of LCA 1961, s 4 and, accordingly, the acquiring authority was entitled to withdraw from the proposed acquisition after determination of compensation by the Lands Tribunal by virtue of the LCA 1961, s 31(2). See also para **[341]**).
2 LCA 1961, s 31(3).

Seeking acquisition of whole rather than part

[326]
Where a notice to treat relates to part only of a house, building or manufactory or a park or garden belonging to a house, then the recipient of the notice may in certain circumstances require acquisition of the whole of his property[1]. This is explained in paras **[381]**ff.

1 CPA 1965, s 8. A similar provision exists in the LCCA 1845 (as amended), s 92, in respect of land, the acquisition of which is authorised by a special Act incorporating the LCCA 1845 (as amended). The Land Compensation Act 1973 (LCA 1973), ss 53–55 confer similar rights in respect of agricultural land (as to which, see paras **[403]–[404]**).

Seeking professional advice

[327]
A landowner should consider seeking professional advice after receipt of a notice to treat. Costs incurred in preparing and negotiating a claim for compensation may be recoverable by the landowner as part of his compensation in respect of disturbance[1].

1 *LCC v Tobin* [1959] 1 WLR 354 (as to which, see para **[1024]**).

9 Abandonment/withdrawal by acquiring authority

Abandonment

[328]
A notice to treat will cease to have effect three years after its service[1], unless, in relation to the land specified in that notice, either:

(*a*) compensation has been agreed or awarded or paid into court;
(*b*) a general vesting declaration has been executed[2];
(*c*) entry[3] has been taken; or
(*d*) the question of compensation has been referred to the Upper Tribunal.

The three-year period may be extended (more than once, if necessary) where the person who is interested in the land, or has power to sell and convey or release it, agrees[4].

1 CPA 1965, s 5(2A) (as inserted by the Planning and Compensation Act 1991, s 67, from 25 September 1991). There is no equivalent provision in the LCCA 1845, as amended. Different provision may be made in the authorising Act as regards time for exercising compulsory purchase powers. See, eg, *Thicknesse v Lancaster Canal Co* (1838) 4 M & W 472.
2 CP(VD)A 1981, s 4 (as to which, see paras **[342]–[361]**). It should be noted that a general vesting declaration does not however have effect in relation to land in respect of which a notice to treat has already been served: CP(VD)A 1981, s 7(1).
3 For meaning of 'entry', see paras **[727]**ff.
4 CPA 1965, s 5(2B).

[329]
Prior to the enactment in 1991 of the three-year time limit for acting upon a notice to treat, there was a history of cases requiring the acquiring authority[1] to proceed, following service of a notice to treat, within a 'reasonable time' or else forfeit the right to proceed. An acquiring authority which 'slept on its rights' by failing to take steps to acquire a property following service of the notice might be barred from proceeding with the compulsory acquisition[2]. Conversely, a landowner who had acquiesced in any delay might not have been able to prevent the acquiring authority from proceeding[3]. It now appears to be the position that, in relation to compulsory acquisitions to which the CPA 1965 applies, the requirement to proceed within a reasonable time has effectively been superseded by the three-year statutory limit[4]; the historic case law is still applicable in relation to acquisitions to which LCCA 1845 (as amended) applies. Where an acquiring authority communicates an intention to abandon a notice to treat, it may be estopped from proceeding

with the acquisition[5]. A landowner who acknowledges the validity of a notice to treat may be estopped from disputing its validity[6]. The fact that an acquiring authority seeks the acquisition of land for a purpose other than the authorised purpose[7] may amount to an abandonment of its rights and may entitle the owner to disregard the notice to treat[8].

1 Or the promoter in relation to notices served under the LCCA 1845 (as amended), s 18.
2 See *Tiverton and North Devon Rly v Loosemore* (1884) 9 App Cas 480. In *Grice v Dudley Corpn* [1958] Ch 329, a delay of 15 years, amongst other matters, indicated an intention to abandon on the acquiring authority's part. Where the landowner has specific notice prior to the expiry of powers for compulsory purchase that the acquiring authority intend to proceed, the notice to treat will not, however, be treated as abandoned: *Ystalyfera Iron Co v Neath and Brecon Rly Co* (1873) LR 17 Eq 142.
3 *Simpsons Motor Sales (London) Ltd v Hendon Corpn* [1963] Ch 57.
4 CPA 1965, s 5(2A), (2B).
5 *Hedges v Metropolitan Rly Co* (1860) 3 LT 643.
6 This issue was reviewed in *Lynch v London Sewers Comrs* (1886) 32 Ch D 72.
7 Ie as stated in the authorising Act and relevant compulsory purchase order, see **B[30]–[44]**.
8 *Grice v Dudley Corpn* [1958] 1 Ch 329; contrast *Simpsons Motor Sales (London) Ltd v Hendon Corpn* [1963] Ch 57 where it was found that the acquisition was still for the authorised purpose (ie a housing scheme under Housing Act 1985), even though the specific housing scheme was different to that originally proposed. See also *Lewis v Mid Glamorgan County Council* [1995] 1 All ER 760; *Merravale Builders Ltd v Secretary of State for the Environment* (1978) 36 P&CR 87. In *Batson v London School Board* (1903) 67 JP 457, proceedings to acquire the land under the LCCA 1845 were of no effect as the acquiring authority was not authorised to acquire the land for the purposes it had proceeded on. An action for trespass could, accordingly, be brought against it.

[330]–[340]
Where a notice to treat has expired[1], the acquiring authority must immediately notify the person on whom the notice was served and any successors in title[2]. Payment of compensation must be made to any such person for loss or expenses occasioned to him by the giving of the notice and its ceasing to have effect. Where such compensation cannot be agreed, it will be determined by the Upper Tribunal[3]. Any compensation payable carries interest at the prescribed rate[4] from the date of entitlement to notice confirming expiry of the notice to treat to the date of payment[5].

1 Ie after three years from service, unless extended by agreement in accordance with the CPA 1965, s 5(2A), (2B).
2 CPA 1965, s 5(2C).
3 CPA 1965, s 5(2D).
4 LCA 1961, s 32; the rate of interest is currently prescribed in the Acquisition of Land (Rate of Interest After Entry) Regulations 1995, SI 1995/2262, as amended by the Financial Services and Markets Act 2000 (Consequential Amendments and Repeals) Order 2001, SI 2001/364.
5 CPA 1965, s 5(2E).

Withdrawal of notice to treat

[341]
Once served, a notice to treat cannot be withdrawn except:

(*a*) by agreement; or
(*b*) in the following limited circumstances:

(1) An acquiring authority may withdraw a notice to treat within six weeks of delivery of a notice of claim for compensation which meets the requirements of LCA 1961, s 4(2)[1].
(2) Where no proper claim for compensation (ie one which complies with LCA, s 4(2)) has been served, an acquiring authority may withdraw a notice to treat within six weeks of determination of compensation by the Upper Tribunal[2].

provided that possession has not been taken of the land[3]. Failure to deliver a proper claim will, therefore, preserve the right of the acquiring authority to withdraw its notice to treat until determination of the compensation payable by the Upper Tribunal[4]. While the entitlement to withdraw a notice to treat subsists under s 31(2), the acquiring authority cannot be compelled to take the land to which the notice to treat relates nor to pay any compensation awarded in respect of the taking[5].

(3) The acquiring authority may withdraw its notice to treat where a landowner serves a notice requiring acquisition of the whole[5], which would, if upheld, require the acquiring authority to take more land than it requires for its purposes.
(4) The special Act may make provision for withdrawal of notice to treat[6].
(5) The acquiring authority may withdraw its notice to treat where a landowner repudiates its validity in whole or in part[7].

1 LCA 1961, s 31(1) : see also para **[325]**). Where a notice to treat is withdrawn under this sub-section, there may be an entitlement to compensation by virtue of LCA 1961, s 32(3) and interest on the compensation under the Planning and Compensation Act 1991, s 80, Sch 18 at the rate prescribed under the LCA 1961, s 32. In the case of disagreement, the Upper Tribunal will determine the compensation payable: LCA 1961, s 31(4). Compensation will include a sum for any loss flowing directly from receipt of the notice, ie an inability to develop land. See *LCC v Montague Burton Ltd* [1934] 1 KB 360; *Atkins and Atkins v Lymington Corpn* (1962) 14 P&CR 148. In *Duke of Grafton v Secretary of State for Air* (1956) 6 P&CR 374, it was held that such compensation will only extend to reasonable remuneration for sums incurred and should not include surveyors scale fees, unless specifically agreed. Notice to treat may be withdrawn under the LCA 1961, s 31(1), even where entry has been taken and a payment of advance compensation made: *R v Northumbrian Water Ltd, ex p Able UK Ltd* [1996] 2 EGLR 15. NB the LCA 1961, s 31 does not apply to deemed notices to treat, in respect of agricultural land: LCA 1973, s 54(4). See para **[403]**.

2 LCA 1961, s 31(2). Where a notice to treat is withdrawn under this sub-section, there may be an entitlement to compensation by virtue of LCA 1961, s 32(3) and interest on the compensation under the Planning and Compensation Act 1991, s 80, Sch 18 at the rate prescribed under the LCA 1961, s 32. As to the determination of compensation, see fn 1 above.

3 The ability to withdraw the notice to treat after possession has been taken does not apply where withdrawal is pursuant to the LCA 1961, s 31(2).

4 *Trustees for Methodist Church Purposes v North Tyneside MBC* (1979) 38 P&CR 665.

5 LCA 1961, s 31(5).

6 Under the CPA 1965, s 8 (as to which, see paras **[381]–[411]**). Where a notice of intention to enter under the LCCA 1845 (as amended), s 18 has been served, such notice cannot be withdrawn except by consent or where a counter-notice objecting to severance is served under the LCCA 1845 (as amended), s 92. See *Tawney v Lynn and Ely Rly Co* (1847) 4 Ry & Can Cas 615.

7 For example, see Small Holdings and Allotments Act 1908, s 39(8). This should be contrasted with the Town and Country Planning Act 1990 (TCPA 1990), s 143, where the deemed notice to treat following a purchase notice cannot be withdrawn by the acquiring authority (as to which, see **B[1142]**). See also *R v Woods and Forests Comrs, ex p Budge* (1850) 15 QB 761, in which a public body, which had inadequate funds to proceed, following service of notice to treat, was able to, in effect, withdraw.

8 *Wild v Woolwich Borough Council* [1910] 1 Ch 35, CA.

B General vesting declaration

1 Introduction

[342]
A minister or a local or other public authority authorised to acquire land compulsorily by means of compulsory purchase order may elect to execute a general vesting declaration under the CP(VD)A 1981[1], rather than proceed by service of notice to treat under the CPA 1965[2]. The main advantage of this procedure is that title automatically vests in the acquiring authority without any conveyance, thereby conferring an immediate right of entry against all those interested in the land, except certain minor tenants[3]. Good title is therefore acquired without investigation and interests in land are simply converted into rights to compensation. As the general vesting declaration procedure does not rely on any participation by the landowner, onerous formalities as to notification are prescribed. These are explained in paras **[343]**ff. The effect of execution of a general vesting declaration, the special consideration given to minor tenants and the restrictions on acquisition of part are explained in paras **[350]–[361]** and **[406]**ff respectively.

1 CP(VD)A 1981, ss 1(1), (2). The provisions of the CP(VD)A 1981, are also applied (with some modification) to orders made under:
(*a*) the Local Government Planning and Land Act 1980, s 141 (vesting of land in Urban Development Corps) (the CP(VD)A 1981, s 15, Sch 2);
(*b*) the Leasehold Reform, Housing and Urban Development Act 1993, s 161 (vesting of land in the Urban Regeneration Agency); and
(*c*) the Housing Act 1988, s 76 (vesting of land in housing action trusts).

2 The acquiring authority may proceed under the CPA 1965, by means of service of notice to treat: CPA 1965, s 5 (as to which, see paras **[301]–[341]**). Proceeding by agreement is also a possibility (as to which, see **B[807]–[809]** and para **[22]**).

3 Minor tenancies and long tenancies about to expire receive special consideration under the CP(VD)A 1981. See para **[361]**.

2 Procedure

Formalities

Preliminary notice

[343]
Prior to execution of a general vesting declaration and before service of any notice to treat[1], an acquiring authority[2] must give preliminary notice[3] in a prescribed form, containing:

(*a*) a statement as to the effect of the CP(VD)A 1981, ss 3–9[4]; and
(*b*) an invitation to every person who would be entitled to claim compensation, if a general vesting declaration were executed in respect of all land[5] comprised in the compulsory purchase order, to give information in the prescribed form to the acquiring authority as to his name and address and the land in question[6].

1 CP(VD)A 1981, s 3(2). As to service of notice to treat under the CPA 1965, s 5, see paras **[301]–[341]**.

2 'Acquiring authority' means, in relation to the CP(VD)A 1981, a minister or other local or public authority authorised to acquire land by means of a compulsory purchase order: CP(VD)A 1981, ss 1, 2(1).
3 CP(VD)A 1981, s 3(1) and 3(3).
4 CP(VD)A 1981, s 3(3)(*a*). The prescribed information is contained in the Compulsory Purchase of Land (Vesting Declarations) Regulations 1990, SI 1990/497.
5 The term 'land' does not for these purposes include any land in respect of which a notice to treat has already been served: CP(VD)A 1981, s 3(3).
6 CP(VD)A 1981, s 3(3)(*b*) and SI 1990/497. Where notice must be served on any person the acquiring authority may require (on threat of criminal sanctions) the occupier of any premises, or person who receives rent in respect of any premises to provide information about that person: TCPA 1990, s 330, as applied by the CP(VD)A 1981, s 2(3).

[344]
The 'preliminary notice' may be either:

(*a*) the statutory notice of confirmation of the compulsory purchase order[1]; or
(*b*) a notice given subsequently, but in the same manner as if it were such a statutory notice[2].

Such notice must be registered as a local land charge with the local authority[3].

1 The prescribed requirements for publication and service of the notice of confirmation of a compulsory purchase order are set out in the ALA 1981, s 15.
2 The term 'statutory notice of confirmation' means, in relation to a compulsory purchase order, the notice of confirmation served under the ALA 1981, s 15 (as to which, see **C[259]**) or by virtue of any other provision of the relevant enactment corresponding to that section: CP(VD)A 1981, s 3(5). Where the acquiring authority is a minister, 'statutory notice of confirmation' is that notice required to be published or served by him under the ALA 1981, Sch 1, para 6 or by virtue of any other provision of the relevant enactment corresponding to that section.
3 CP(VD)A 1981, s 3(4).

Execution of general vesting declaration

[345]
The acquiring authority may execute a declaration in prescribed form[1] in respect of any of the land which it is authorised to acquire by a compulsory purchase order vesting that land in itself from the end of the period specified in the declaration. The period so specified may not be less than 28 days from the date on which service of the 'notices after execution of declaration' is completed[2].The vesting declaration does not have to relate to all of the land within the compulsory purchase order. The acquiring authority may, for example, choose to limit the extent of the general vesting declaration in response to any information received following service of the preliminary notice, or it may choose to acquire the land it is authorised to acquire in phases.

1 SI 1990/497, Form 1.
2 CP(VD)A 1981, s 4(1). Notices after execution of declaration are made under the CP(VD)A 1981, s 6. The CP(VD)A 1981, s 4(2) provides that a certificate made by the acquiring authority that service of the notice required by the CP(VD)A 1981, s 6 was completed by a certain date, shall be conclusive evidence of the fact so stated. See para **[346]**.

Notices after execution of declaration

[346]
'As soon as may be' after executing a general vesting declaration, the acquiring authority must serve[1] on every:

(*a*) occupier of any land specified in the declaration[2]; and
(*b*) other person who has responded to the acquiring authority's invitation for information attached to the preliminary notice[3],

notices in prescribed form stating that the vesting declaration has been executed[4].

1 CP(VD)A 1981, s 6(1).
2 Except land in which there subsists a minor tenancy or a long tenancy about to expire: CP(VD)A 1981, s 6(1)(*a*). For meaning of 'minor tenancy' or 'long tenancy about to expire', see the CP(VD)A 1981, s 2. See also the CP(VD)A 1981, s 9 at para **[361]** and paras **[1321]–[1325]**.
3 CP(VD)A 1981, s 6(1)(*b*). As to preliminary notices served under the CP(VD)A 1981, s 3, see para **[343]–[344]**.
4 Notices for those purposes are prescribed in SI 1990/497, reg 3(*c*). Service of such notices is governed by the TCPA 1990, s 329: CP(VD)A 1981, s 6(2).

Timing

[347]
The information required in the preliminary notice[1] may be published and served in the notice of confirmation of the compulsory purchase order[2], at the earliest, and must, in any event, be published and served prior to any notice to treat[3]. A general vesting declaration cannot be executed for at least two months beginning with the date of the first publication of the preliminary notice, or such longer period as may be specified in the notice[4]. A vesting declaration cannot of course be executed before the compulsory purchase order has come into operation. This is particularly relevant where the compulsory purchase order is subject to special parliamentary procedure, so that its coming into operation is delayed[5]. The 'vesting date' is the first day after the expiry of the period specified in the vesting declaration[6], which period must be at least 28 days from the date on which service of the notices after execution of the vesting declaration was completed[7]. Notices after execution of declaration must be served 'as soon as may be' after execution of the vesting declaration[8]. Prior to the vesting date, the acquiring authority retains its discretion whether to proceed under the CPA 1965 or by means of general vesting declaration. However, once a notice to treat is served, acquisition of the interest to which such notice relates can only be made pursuant to the CPA 1965 and not by means of the general vesting declaration[9].

1 CP(VD)A 1981, s 3 (as to which, see paras **[343]–[344]**).
2 CP(VD)A 1981, s 3(1)(*a*). Statutory notice of confirmation of a compulsory purchase order is published and served under the ALA 1981, s 15.
3 CP(VD)A 1981, s 3(2).
4 CP(VD)A 1981, s 5(1). See DoE Circular 14/94 'Compulsory Purchase Orders: Procedures', App R, para 5. Such period may be abridged with written consent of every occupier of land specified in the vesting declaration: CP(VD)A 1981, s 5(1). This will involve investigation as to title.
5 CP(VD)A 1981, s 5(2). As regards special parliamentary procedure, see **C[801]–[822]**.

6 CP(VD)A 1981, s 4(3).
7 Service of notices after execution of vesting declaration is dealt with under the CP(VD)A 1981, s 6 (as to which, see para **[346]**).
8 CP(VD)A 1981, s 6.
9 Any vesting declaration will not be effective against interests in respect of which notice to treat has been served: CP(VD)A 1981, s 7(1) and DoE Circular 14/94, App R, para 4.

[348]

The requirement to exercise powers of compulsory purchase within three years from the date of confirmation of the compulsory purchase order[1] applies where the acquiring authority chooses to proceed by general vesting declaration. There are conflicting decisions as to whether the issue of a preliminary notice under the CP(VD)A 1981, s 3[2] constitutes the exercise of powers of compulsory purchase. In *Westminster City Council v Quereshi*[3], such action was held to be sufficient for this purpose, even though the general vesting declaration was not executed until after that date. However, the court took the opposite view in *Co-operative Insurance Society Ltd v Hastings Borough Council*[4] finding that service of a preliminary notice committed the acquiring authority to nothing and therefore was not an exercise of powers of compulsory purchase.

1 CPA 1965, s 4. See para **[303]** and **C[257]–[259]**.
2 As to preliminary notices, see paras **[343]–[344]**.
3 (1990) 60 P&CR 380.
4 [1993] 2 EGLR 19.

Service

[349]

Publication of a preliminary notice[1] is made with, or in a similar manner to, notice of confirmation of the compulsory purchase order[2]. Service of notice after execution of vesting declaration[3] must be delivered personally to, or be left at or sent by registered or recorded postal service to, the usual or last known abode of the recipient. In the case of a company, it must be served on the secretary or clerk at the principal or registered office of the company[4].

1 CP(VD)A 1981, s 3.
2 CP(VD)A 1981, s 3: see requirements for publication and service of notice of confirmation of a compulsory purchase order in the ALA 1981, s 15.
3 CP(VD)A 1981, s 6.
4 TCPA 1990, s 329, as applied by the CP(VD)A 1981, s 6(2).

3 Effect of execution of general vesting declaration

[350]–[360]

On the vesting date[1]:

(1) The land[2] specified in the general vesting declaration vests in the acquiring authority[3] as if a deed poll had been executed in accordance with the CPA 1965[4]. All those with an interest in the land[5] will then have a right to compensation[6].
(2) The acquiring authority is entitled to enter upon and take possession of the land[7], except such land in relation to which there subsists a minor

tenancy or a long tenancy about to expire[8]. Where there is such a short tenancy, there is no right of entry unless notice to treat has been served in respect of such tenancy, and at least 14 days' notice of entry has been served on the occupiers[9].

(3) Notice to treat is deemed to have been served in accordance with the CPA 1965 on the date on which the general vesting declaration was executed[10] on all persons with an interest in the land referred to in the general vesting declaration who should have received such notice (other than minor tenants or those by whom notice to treat had already been received)[11]. Accordingly, the LCA 1961 and the CPA 1965 apply as if notice to treat had been served. In particular, the acquiring authority is liable to pay compensation (and interest) as if it had taken possession of the land following service of a notice to treat and notice of entry under the CPA 1965[12]. However, where a general vesting declaration has been executed:
  (*a*) the provisions in the CPA 1965, regarding untraced and absent owners and interests omitted from purchase, do not apply[13]; and
  (*b*) there is no power under the LCA 1961, s 31 to withdraw the deemed notice to treat[14].

(4) Where any person retains possession of any document relating to title to the land after vesting, he is deemed to have given to the acquiring authority a written acknowledgment of the right of the authority to production of that document and may be obliged to deliver copies of it, except where he retains possession of a document as a mortgagee or trustee of an undertaking for sale[15].

(5) An owner may in certain circumstances request the acquisition of the whole of his property, where part only is included within the general vesting declaration[16]. This will suspend the vesting of the part which is so included until this issue has been resolved[17].

(6) Compensation is assessed at the earlier of the date of vesting or the date when the assessment is made[18].

1 CP(VD)A 1981, s 4(3). For meaning of 'vesting date', see para **[347]**.

2 The term 'land' has the same meaning as in the authorising Act and could thereby potentially include an interest in land: CP(VD)A 1981, s 2(1). See also the CP(VD)A 1981, s 8(2).

3 CP(VD)A 1981, s 8(1). The effect is to vest land or any interest in land and to extinguish the whole or part of any rent-service, rentcharge, chief or other rent, or other payment in incumbrance: s 8(2).

4 As to which, see paras **[1050]–[1062]**.

5 DoE Circular 14/94, App R, para 3 indicates that rights of commoners remain unaffected and should be dealt with by the procedure set out in the CPA 1965, Sch 4 (as to which, see para **[1607]**).

6 The owner of an interest such as an easement or restrictive covenant in land subject to a general vesting declaration will not be able to enforce his rights against an acquiring authority following vesting. See paras **[1605]–[1606]**.

7 CP(VD)A 1981, s 8(1): CPA 1965, s 11(1) is disapplied by the CP(VD)A 1981, s 8(3) and, accordingly, there is no requirement to serve notice to treat and notice of entry.

8 The special provision for such short tenancies is explained in para **[361]**.

9 CP(VD)A 1981, s 9.

10 As to execution of a general vesting declaration, see para **[345]** above.

11 CP(VD)A 1981, ss 7(1), (2). Service of notice to treat under the CPA 1965, s 5 is explained in paras **[301]**ff. The special provision as to minor tenancies and long tenancies about to expire is explained in para **[361]**.

12 As to procedure relating to service of notices to treat and notices of entry under the CPA 1965, s 5, 11, see paras **[301]–[341]** and paras **[701]–[710]**. As to compensation, see **Division E** generally.

13 CP(VD)A 1981, s 10(2). The CPA 1965, Sch 2 applies to untraced and absent owners (as to which, see paras **[1005]–[1006]**). The CPA 1965, s 22 deals with omitted interests (as to which, see paras **[743]–[745]**).
14 CP(VD)A 1981, s 7(3). As to withdrawal of notices to treat, see para **[341]**. The deemed notice to treat may, however, be withdrawn where a landowner, part of whose interest is comprised in the vesting declaration, requires the acquisition of whole under the CP(VD)A 1981, s 12 (as to which, see paras **[381]–[411]**).
15 CP(VD)A 1981, s 14.
16 CP(VD)A 1981, s 12, Sch 1. See para **[406]**.
17 CP(VD)A 1981, s 12, Sch 1, para 6.
18 LCA 1961, s 5A. *Mahboob Hussein v Oldham MBC* (1981) 42 P&CR 388; *Singh v Rochdale MBC* (1992) 65 P&CR 75. See *Park Automobile Co Ltd v Strathclyde Regional Council* (1983) 46 P&CR 433 for a case dealing with a disturbance claim following execution of a general vesting declaration.

4 Minor tenancies and long tenancies about to expire

[361]–[370]
Where a minor tenancy[1] or a long tenancy which is about to expire[2], subsists in land specified in a general vesting declaration, then the right to enter on such land following vesting[3] is not capable of being exercised in relation to that land unless the acquiring authority serves notice to treat in respect of that tenancy, together with 14 days' notice of entry on every occupier of land in which that tenancy subsists[4]. The land in the general vesting declaration therefore vests in the acquiring authority, subject to such tenancy. The acquiring authority will only be able to enter onto the land which is the subject of the tenancy at the earlier of the expiry of the period specified in the notice of entry or the date of expiry of the tenancy[5].

1 The term 'minor tenancy' means a tenancy for a year or from year to year or any lesser interest: CP(VD)A 1981, s 2(1).
2 The term 'long tenancy about to expire' means, in relation to a general vesting declaration, a tenancy granted for an interest greater than a minor tenancy, but having, on the vesting date, a period still to run which is not more than the specified period. For these purposes this means such period longer than one year as may be specified in the declaration in relation to land in which the tenancy subsists: CP(VD)A 1981, s 2(2). In determining, for the purposes of s 2(2), the period a tenancy has left to run, it shall be assumed that the tenant will exercise any option to renew the tenancy and the landlord will exercise any option to terminate the same: CP(VD)A 1981, s 2(2).
3 Such right to enter is conferred by the CP(VD)A 1981, s 8(1), see para **[350]**.
4 CP(VD)A 1981, s 9(2).
5 CP(VD)A 1981, s 9(3). Where proceeding under the CPA 1965, such minor tenants are not entitled to notice to treat (as to which, see paras **[1321]–[1325]**).

C Dealing with land pending compulsory acquisition

1 Introduction

[371]
Prior to the exercise of compulsory purchase powers either by service of a notice to treat or by execution of a general vesting declaration, the fact that an acquiring authority has made and obtained confirmation of a compulsory purchase order imposes no constraint upon an owner's ability to deal with his land as he wishes. If the acquiring authority chooses to exercise its

powers of compulsory purchase by means of the vesting declaration procedure, title and the right to possession pass to the acquiring authority simultaneously following execution of the vesting declaration. At that point, an owner will cease to be able to deal with his land at all. Compensation for the value of the interests acquired will then be assessed at the date of vesting (or the date of assessment, if earlier)[1]. In contrast, if the acquiring authority chooses to follow the notice to treat procedure to exercise its powers, some time may separate the date of service of the notice to treat and the date of entry. Prior to 1970, the date at which compensation was assessed was the date of service of the notice to treat, but in *Birmingham Corpn v West Midlands Baptist (Trust) Association Inc*[2], the House of Lords held that compensation should be assessed at the date of entry. This has subsequently been enacted in the LCA 1961, s 5A. Consequently, the position of an owner of an interest in land in the period between service of notice to treat and entry (or the assessment of compensation, if earlier) needs to be considered in relation to: (*a*) the ability of the owner to deal with his interest, and (*b*) the implications for the assessment of compensation; these aspects are explained separately as follows.

1 LCA 1961, s 5A.
2 [1970] AC 874.

2 Owner's ability to deal with his land after service of notice to treat

[372]
Although service of a notice to treat has the effect of creating a relationship analogous to vendor and purchaser, the interests in the land remain the property of the owners, at law and in equity[1], until the compensation is either agreed or determined by the Upper Tribunal[2], whereupon either the acquiring authority or landowner may seek specific performance of the sale. Notwithstanding service of notice to treat, the landowner can continue to deal with his land as he chooses. Thus:

(1) An owner may sell or assign his interest in the land. A purchaser or assignee will stand in the same position as the original owner, vis-à-vis the acquiring authority[3].
(2) An owner may deal with existing lesser interests. A landlord could, for example, determine a leasehold interest[4].
(3) An owner may enforce the terms of any contract for sale. Such a contract will not be frustrated by service of notice to treat; indeed, the purchaser under such an agreement would be entitled to receive notice to treat[5], as would a person entitled to an interest in land under a building agreement[6].
(4) A landowner will continue to be at risk with respect to the damage or destruction of his premises, until compensation has been determined or entry made, whichever is earlier[7]. It is therefore in the landowner's interest to maintain the value of his property until the risk in respect of it passes to the acquiring authority. Until 1970, it had been considered that risk of damage or destruction would pass to the acquiring authority on service of notice to treat[8], but *Birmingham Corpn v West Midland Baptist*

(Trust) Association Inc[9] this was held by the House of Lords to have been wrongly decided in. A landowner should therefore consider maintaining building insurance until possession is taken by the acquiring authority or compensation determined, or, at least, would be well advised to check that the acquiring authority accepts responsibility for the property prior to discontinuance of insurance. The landowner might also consider maintaining precautions against vandalism[10].

(5) Whereas the right to compensation may be assigned and dealt with as property following receipt of notice to treat, the owner's pending claim for compensation is not an attachable debt[11].

(6) The liability of a lessee under covenants in a lease continues until assignment of the leasehold interest[12] (or entry if earlier). Likewise, a lessor continues to enjoy the benefit of covenants until the transfer of his interest and is entitled to recover damages for any breach of covenant by the lessee before such transfer, but not afterwards[13].

(7) Where a lease contains a proviso that, if any part of the land is compulsorily acquired, the lessor may re-enter and repossess it, service of notice to treat may trigger such proviso[14].

1 *Haynes v Haynes* (1861) 1 Drew & Sm 426. At the time where the quasi-contract for sale created by service of notice to treat becomes unconditional, the owner's interest becomes an interest in personalty rather than realty.

2 Both parties have the right to have compensation determined by the Upper Tribunal under the CPA 1965, s 6, whereupon an unconditional contract of sale is created, which either party may specifically enforce. As to provisions regarding the determination of compensation, see para **[1004]**. See the LCCA 1845 (as amended), s 21, with regard to acquisitions authorised by a special Act to which the LCCA 1845 (as amended) applies.

3 *Dawson v Great Northern and City Rly Co* [1905] 1 KB 260; *Cardiff Corpn v Cook* [1923] 2 Ch 115; *Land Link Two and Barclays Bank v Sevenoaks District Council* (1985) 51 P&CR 100.

4 *Holloway v Dover Corpn* [1960] 1 WLR 604. The LCA 1973, s 50 provides that, after service of a notice to treat, compensation in respect of a landlord's interest shall not be enhanced by the fact that the landlord has obtained vacant possession as a result of fulfilment of any statutory duty to rehouse residential tenants: see *Paul v Newnham London Borough Council* (1989) 61 P&CR 126. This would not, however, prevent a landlord from creating vacant possession value, prior to being served with notice to treat.

5 *Hillingdon Estates Co v Stonefield Estates Ltd* [1952] Ch 627.

6 *Birmingham and District Land Co v London and North Western Rly Co* (1888) 40 Ch D 268. See also *E Johnson & Co (Barbados) Ltd v NRS Ltd* [1997] AC 400 where compulsory purchase procedures commenced after exchange but prior to completion of sale of property and the purchaser refused to complete.

7 *Socratous v Camden London Borough* [1974] RVR 552. In *Lewars v Greater London Council* (1981) 43 P&CR 129, an argument that vandalism to the property at date of possession (which diminished its value) was due to the underlying acquisition scheme and should, therefore, be disregarded was rejected.

8 *Phoenix Assurance Co v Spooner* [1905] 2 KB 753.

9 [1970] AC 874.

10 See, generally, *Otterspool Investments Ltd v Merseyside County Council* (1984) 270 Estates Gazette 46.

11 In *Richardson v Elmit* (1876) 2 CPD 9, creditors could not call on a notice to treat served on a judgment debtor in satisfaction of claim. See also *Dawson v Great Northern and City Rly Co* [1905] 1 KB 260.

12 *Mills v East London Union* (1872) LR 8 CP 79.

13 *Re King; Robinson v Gray* [1963] Ch 459, CA.

14 See *Goodwin Foster Brown Ltd v Derby Corpn* [1934] 2 KB 23 for a discussion of this issue. However, where the lease has a proviso enabling the lessor to re-enter the building for works, the lessor cannot take advantage of this provision to enhance the value of his interest prior to its compulsory acquisition: *Johnson v Edgeware, etc Rly Co* (1866) 35 Beav 480.

3 Implications of notice to treat for assessment of compensation

[373]
Following service of notice to treat, while continued dealings with the land are not prevented, a landowner cannot increase the burden of compensation on the acquiring authority by creating any new interest either in the land included in such notice nor in other land held with that land which is claimed to be injuriously affected by the compulsory acquisition[1]. Where such an interest is created, then the purchaser acquires that new interest subject to the existing notice to treat; he is not entitled to a separate notice to treat and will not necessarily be able to recover full compensation from the acquiring authority[2]. Where a lease expires after service of notice to treat, provided the overall burden of compensation on the acquiring authority is not increased, the freeholder can claim compensation for his interest on the basis of vacant possession[3]. When assessing compensation, no account may be taken of any interest in land or enhancement in the value of any interest in land created by reason of building works, improvements, alterations etc, where such works were not reasonably necessary, but were undertaken with a view to increase compensation[4]. However, where such improvements are not undertaken to improve compensation, they should not be disregarded[5].

1 *Mercer v Liverpool, St Helens and South Lancashire Rly Co* [1903] 1 KB 652.
2 *Mercer v Liverpool, St Helens and South Lancashire Rly Co* [1903] 1 KB 652; *Re Marylebone (Stingo Lane) Improvement Act, ex p Edwards* (1871) LR 12 Eq 389.
3 *Banham v London Borough of Hackney* (1970) 22 P&CR 922; whilst the acquiring authority had to pay more to the freeholder than it would have had the lease continued, it did not have to pay compensation to the tenant. This rule operates, subject to the LCA 1973, s 50, see para **[370]**, fn 2.
4 ALA 1981, s 4.
5 *Neeson v Department of the Environment for Northern Ireland* [1985] RVR 118.

[374]
Prior to 1970, for the purposes of assessing compensation, the interests to be compensated were treated as fixed at the date of service of notice to treat[1] and, as mentioned above, the compensation was assessed at the same date. This approach was followed, for example, in *Square Grip Reinforcement Co (London) Ltd v Rowton Houses Ltd*[2], with the effect that a leasehold property was valued on the basis that a break clause would be exercised a year after service of the notice to treat, notwithstanding that, by the time possession was taken, that break clause had not been exercised and, but for the compulsory acquisition, the lease would have continued for several years further. In contrast, in *Koch v GLC*[4], notice to treat was served in respect of a leasehold interest, but entry was delayed until after the expiry of that lease. The Lands Tribunal awarded a substantial sum as compensation for disturbance, but only nominal compensation in respect of the acquisition of the leasehold interest in the land, as the lessee had enjoyed the lease until its expiry. Similarly, in both *Cleaners (J V) Ltd v County Borough of Luton*[5] and *Holloway v Dover Corpn*[6], there was held to be no entitlement to compensation in respect of a lease subsisting at the date of service of notice to treat which had expired before the date for assessment of compensation.

1 *Penny v Penny* (1867) LR 5 Eq 227 per Wood V-C at 236, as explained in *Rugby Joint Water Board v Shaw-Fox* [1973] AC 202 by Pearson LJ at 216.

2 [1967] Ch 877.
4 (1968) 20 P&CR 472.
5 (1968) 20 P&CR 465.
6 [1960] 1 WLR 604.

[375]
In *R v Kennedy*[1], a landlord served a notice to quit on its tenant after the tenant had been served with a notice to treat by an acquiring authority. Notwithstanding that the lease had 25 years left to run on the date of service of notice to treat, the tenant was only compensated for the three-month period during which he remained in occupation following the landlord's notice to quit, on the basis that he had not submitted a claim for compensation prior to service of the notice to quit.

1 [1893] 1 QB 533.

[376]–[380]
In *Bradford Property Trust Ltd v Hertfordshire County Council*[1], freehold property had been the subject of tenancies when notice to treat was served but by the date of entry the tenancies had terminated. The Lands Tribunal, applying *Birmingham Corpn v West Midlands Baptist (Trust) Association Inc*[2] held that, while the interest to be valued is the interest subsisting at the date of service of notice to treat, that interest should be valued at the date of entry. In *Banham v London Borough of Hackney*[3], the Lands Tribunal held that the true rule emerging from *Birmingham Corpn v West Midlands Baptist (Trust) Association Inc* would seem to be that interests, as well as values, must be taken at the date of valuation or entry, unless the owner had done something which so altered the interests as to increase the compensation burden on the acquiring authority. In *Midland Bank Trust Co Ltd (Executors) v London Borough of Lewisham*[4], the Lands Tribunal held that the valuation of interests on the date of possession was only a sensible proposition if the interests were taken as they existed on the date of possession. In contrast, in *Runcorn Association Football Club Ltd v Warrington and Runcorn Corpn*[5] the Lands Tribunal held that the date of service of notice to treat was the material date for determining the interest to be compensated.

1 (1973) 27 P&CR 228.
2 [1970] AC 874.
3 (1970) 22 P&CR 922. But there must be some doubt about the correctness of this decision in the light of *Bishopsgate Space Management Ltd and Teamworks Karting Ltd v London Underground Ltd* [2004] RVR 89.
4 (1975) 30 P&CR 268.
5 (1982) 45 P&CR 183.

D Restriction on the acquisition of part

1 Introduction

[381]
Where an owner of a house, building or manufactory or of a park or garden belonging to a house is served with notice to treat in relation to part only of his land[1], he can, in certain circumstances, require the acquiring authority

either to take the whole of his interest in the land or to withdraw completely from the proposed acquisition. A person whose land will be divided by the works proposed by the acquiring authority can also in certain circumstances require the authority to take the whole of his land. Similarly, where an acquiring authority propose to take part only of an agricultural unit, a person having an interest in that unit may require the authority to take the whole unit. This is explained in paras **[382]–[405]**. Similar safeguards operate (albeit with more detailed formalities) in relation to general vesting declarations and these are explained at paras **[406]**ff.

1 CPA 1965, s 8 is applied, with the modifications set out in the Local Government (Miscellaneous Provisions) Act 1976 (LG(MP)A 1976), Sch 1, para 7, to the creation of new rights by local authorities, where authorised to do so under the LG(MP)A 1976, s 13. Various other statutes also apply these provisions to the creation of rights over land. See para **[1608]**.

2 Part only of certain premises (Compulsory Purchase Act 1965, section 8(1))

[382]
The CPA 1965, s 8(1) provides that no person[1] shall be required to sell a part[2] only:

(*a*) of any house, building or manufactory; or
(*b*) of a park or garden belonging to a house;

if he is able and willing to sell the whole of the house, building, manufactory, park or garden, unless the Upper Tribunal determines that:

(i) in the case of a house, building or manufactory, the part proposed to be acquired can be taken without material detriment to the house, building or manufactory, or
(ii) in the case of a park or garden, the part proposed to be acquired can be taken without seriously affecting the amenity or convenience of the house[3].

1 'Person' means a person able and willing to convey, whether by virtue of the authorising Act or otherwise: *Governors of St Thomas' Hospital v Charing Cross Rly Co* (1861) 1 John & H 400. A lessee may claim the benefit of this section: *Pulling v London, Chatham and Dover Rly Co* (1864) 33 LJ Ch 505.
2 Where this provision applies, the owner may require the acquiring authority to take the whole, but not a different part to that described in the notice to treat: *Pulling v London, Chatham and Dover Rly Co* (1864) 33 LJ Ch 505.
3 CPA 1965, s 8 is derived from the LCCA 1845 (as amended), s 92, which, although similar, simply requires that no party shall at any time be required to sell or convey to the promoters of any undertaking a part only of any house, building or manufactory if such party is able and willing to sell and convey the whole thereof. Neither the CPA 1965, s 8 nor the LCCA 1845 (as amended), s 92 is affected by the operation of provisions in TCPA 1990 (as amended), s 166 which enable an acquiring authority to oppose a blight notice. See **B[1210]–[1248]**.

[383]
If the Upper Tribunal determines that the part proposed to be acquired can be taken without material detriment or serious affect, then the person interested in the land is required to sell that part only and the Upper Tribunal will award compensation in respect of any diminution in value of the retained land due to the severance of the part acquired, in addition to the value of the

land acquired[1]. If material detriment or a serious effect on amenity or convenience is established, subject to the acquiring authority's right of withdrawal from the proposed acquisition[2], the CPA 1965, s 8 authorises and, indeed, requires the acquiring authority to take such additional land.

1 CPA 1965, s 8(1). See also *Doe d Armistead v North Staffordshire Rly* (1851) 20 LJQB 6249; *Schwinge v London Blackwall Rly Co* (1855) 24 LJ Ch 405 held that a notice to treat was suspended and not destroyed, pending determination of a notice requesting acquisition of whole.
2 As to which, see para **[389]**.

[384]
Where an acquiring authority proposes to exercise its power to create new rights over land, the CPA 1965, s 8 applies with modifications. Where it can be shown that material detriment or serious affect on amenity or convenience would result from the proposed creation of the right, the compulsory purchase order is deemed to authorise the acquisition of the whole of that person's interest in the affected land[1].

1 LG(MP)A 1976, s 13, Sch 1, para 7; the acquiring authority may withdraw the notice to treat within six weeks of such a determination by the Upper Tribunal, see para **[1608]** generally with regard to the acquisition of rights pursuant to the LG(MP)A 1976, s 13 , Sch 1, para 7(3); similar provision is made in the Highways Act 1980, s 252.

Meaning of 'house, building, or manufactory'

[385]
Whilst there are no definitions in CPA 1965, 'house' has been construed widely[1] to include not only a dwelling, but also a shop or inn[2], vacant land[3], dwellings linked by internal communications[4], a substantial place of worship[5], business premises[6], a house including garden and curtilage such as would pass upon conveyance[7], and unfinished houses[8]; 'building' includes blocks of offices[9]. 'Manufactory' has been interpreted to include a building whose main use is manufacturing purposes[10], even where part of the premises is let to another occupier[11] or used for other purposes[12], but does not include a building or land in which some incidental manufacturing is carried on[13]. Manufactory also includes outbuildings, weirs and riverbed associated with the manufactory[14]. Acquisition of subsoil beneath a house, building or manufactory is an acquisition of part for these purposes[15].

1 The majority of cases concern the definition of 'house' as it appears in the LCCA 1845 (as amended), s 92. It is submitted that these cases are relevant to the definition in CPA 1965, s 8(1). *King v Wycombe Rly Co* (1860) 29 LJ Ch 462 held that house includes everything which would ordinarily pass under the word 'house' in a conveyance.
2 *Richards v Swansea Improvement and Tramway Co* (1878) 9 Ch D 425.
3 *Marson v London, Chatham and Dover Rly Co* (1868) LR 6 Eq 101.
4 *Seagenberg v Metropolitan District Rly Co* (1883) 49 LT 554.
5 *LTE v Congregational Union of England and Wales* (1978) 37 P&CR 155.
6 *Ravenseft Properties Ltd v London Borough of Hillingdon* (1968) 20 P&CR 483.
7 *Grosvenor v Hampstead Junction Rly Co* (1857) 1 De G & J 446; *Governors of St Thomas' Hospital v Charing Cross Rly Co* (1861) 1 John & H 400.
8 *Alexander v Crystal Palace Rly Co* (1862) 30 Beav 556.
9 *Greswolde Williams v Newcastle upon Tyne Corpn* (1927) 92 JP 13.
10 *Richards v Swansea Improvement and Tramway Co* (1878) 9 Ch D 425.
11 *Brook v Manchester, Sheffield and Lincolnshire Rly Co* [1895] 2 Ch 571.
12 *Spackman v Great Western Rly Co* (1855) 26 TOS 22.

13 *Reddin v Metropolitan Board of Works* (1862) 4 De GF & J 532.
14 *Furniss v Midland Rly Co* (1868) LR 6 Eq 473.
15 *Sparrow v Oxford, Worcester and Wolverhampton Rly Co* (1852) 2 De G M & G 94.

Meaning of 'park or garden'

[386]
'Park' includes land which is part of a park, garden or pleasureground, or which is otherwise required for the amenity or convenience of any house[1]. The meaning of 'garden' was discussed in *Bomford v Osborne (Inspector of Taxes)*[2].

1 *Re Ripon (Highfield) Housing Confirmation Order 1938* [1939] 3 All ER 548.
2 [1942] AC 14.

Meaning of 'material detriment'

[387]
The meaning of 'material detriment' in the context of CPA 1965, s 8 was considered in *Ravenseft Properties v London Borough of Hillingdon*[1]. The Lands Tribunal concluded that it occurred where, when compared to the property as it previously existed, the retained portion of land was 'less useful or less valuable in some significant degree'. The significance or materiality of the detriment should be considered and determined by reference to its nature and degree. The propositions that material detriment would not occur, unless:

(*a*) there was a severance which could not be adequately compensated; or
(*b*) the retained part was rendered physically or functionally incapable of its previous use,

were rejected. In determining whether a part can be taken without material detriment to the remainder, the Upper Tribunal must take into account, not only the effect of severance, but also the use to be made of the part proposed to be acquired, including the proposed use of the whole land of which the section in question forms a part[3].

1 (1968) 20 P&CR 483.
2 For the purposes of the CPA 1965, s 8(1).
3 LCA 1973, s 58. In *Re Gonty v Manchester, Sheffield and Lincolnshire Rly Co's Arbitration* [1896] 2 QB 439, the manner of acquisition would have been detrimental to the landowner, but for the fact that the railway company had given an undertaking not to deprive the owner of access.

Procedure

[388]
The CPA 1965, s 8 does not prescribe the manner in which an objection to the acquisition of part is to be made. A procedure which evolved in the context of the LCCA 1845 (as amended) is, however, still followed[1]. The person on whom a notice to treat is served in relation to part should consider whether to serve a counter-notice on the acquiring authority requiring the acquisition of whole. It is suggested that a letter to the acquiring authority specifying the land in question and quoting the statutory provisions relied on will be sufficient[2]. There is no time limit imposed by the CPA 1965 for submission of such

a notice, but, in *Glasshouse Properties Ltd v Secretary of State for Transport*[3], the Lands Tribunal held that any notice under the CPA 1965, s 8 must be served before entry[4] is taken. If a notice under the CPA 1965, s 8 is served and the acquiring authority enters part of the land pending determination of the validity of such notice, then it runs the risk of having to buy the whole land without any right of withdrawal.

1 Likewise, the LCCA 1845 (as amended), s 92 does not prescribe any formalities, in respect of acquisitions of land authorised by a special Act incorporating the LCCA 1845 (as amended).
2 Indeed, in the past, verbal notice has been held sufficient: *Binney v Hammersmith* (1863) 8 LT 161.
3 (1993) 66 P & CR 285.
4 As to meaning of 'entry', see paras **[727]–[728]**.

Withdrawal by acquiring authority

[389]
The acquiring authority may abandon its notice to treat on receipt of a counter-notice requiring acquisition of the whole[1]. Further, it would appear that the acquiring authority may withdraw from the purchase following a determination by the Upper Tribunal requiring the acquisition of whole, provided entry has not been taken over any part of that land. Acceptance of a counter-notice by a solicitor on behalf of his client will not preclude the acquiring authority from challenging it subsequently[2], whereas an invalid s 8 notice can be ignored[3]. An acquiring authority is not precluded from serving fresh notices to treat (provided the time for exercise of compulsory purchase powers has not yet expired) following abandonment of the original notice to treat in consequence of service of a s 8 notice[4].

1 *King v Wycombe Rly Co* (1860) 28 Beav 104. See also *Ashton Vale Iron Co Ltd v Bristol Corpn* [1901] 1 Ch 591.
2 The appointment of an arbitrator to determine the compensation payable in respect of a part, following service of counter-notice under the authorising Act requesting acquisition of whole, does not prevent the acquiring authority from withdrawing its notice to treat subsequently: *Grierson v Cheshire Lines Committee* (1874) LR 19 Eq 83.
3 *Treadwell v London and South West Rly Co* (1884) 54 LJ Ch 565.
4 *Harvie v South Devon Rly Co* (1874) 32 LT 1; *Ashton Vale Iron Co Ltd v Bristol Corpn* [1901] 1 Ch 591.

Practical considerations

[390]–[400]
If negotiations on compensation for acquisition of part are commenced but agreement is not reached, this will not prejudice the landowner from serving notice under the CPA 1965, s 8[1]. Before submitting notice under the CPA 1965, s 8, a landowner should consider the value of a claim for compensation in respect of the whole (ie the value of his interest in the whole property, plus disturbance) against the value of a claim for compensation in respect of part only (ie the value of his interest in the part identified in the notice to treat, plus disturbance from that part, plus compensation in respect of severance)[2].

1 *Gardner v Charing Cross Rly Co* (1861) 2 John & H 248.
2 As to the assessment of compensation, see **Division E**.

3 Divided lands (Compulsory Purchase Act 1965, section 8(2) and (3))

[401]
The CPA 1965, s 8(2) provides that, where any land[1] not in a town and not built upon is cut through and divided by works so as to leave less than half an acre on one or both sides, its owner may require the acquiring authority to purchase the remaining land in addition to the land specified in the notice to treat[2]. This provision cannot be invoked where the owner has other land adjoining the divided land, which, together, can be conveniently occupied; in such a case, however, the acquiring authority may be required, at its own expense, to remove any fences and level the site off[3]. This provision is usually relied upon where large estates or farmland are bisected by highways.

1 Such land must not be situated in a town or built upon; a market garden with a cottage is not land which is built upon for these purposes: *Falkner v Somerset and Dorset Rly Co* (1873) LR 16 Eq 458.
2 Similar provision is made in the LCCA 1845 (as amended), s 93, in respect of acquisitions authorised by a special Act to which the LCCA 1845 (as amended) applies.
3 No statutory guidance is given as to procedure. It is submitted that a notice to the acquiring authority invoking this provision and describing the land affected, followed by a reference to the Upper Tribunal, if necessary, will suffice.

[402]
The CPA 1965, s 8(3) provides that where the special Act[1] makes provision for the acquiring authority to make any bridge, culvert or other accommodation work in respect of land which is cut through and divided by the works[2]:

(*a*) the land[3] is intersected so as to leave less than half an acre, or an area of less value than the cost of such accommodation works; and
(*b*) the owner[4] affected has no other adjoining land,

the acquiring authority may require the owner to sell him the whole of that land[5]. Any dispute regarding the value of the land or the costs of any accommodation works is to be determined by the Upper Tribunal at the request of either party[6].

1 'Special Act' means the authorising Act and relevant compulsory purchase order: CPA 1965, s 1(2).
2 For example, see the Railways Clauses Consolidation Act 1845, s 68.
3 There is no requirement under the CPA 1965, s 8(3) for such works to be on open land, in contrast with the provisions of the CPA 1965, s 8(2) (as to which, see para **[401]**, fn 1).
4 The term 'owner' is defined under the CPA 1965, s 1(6).
5 There is similar provision in the LCCA 1845 (as amended), s 94, in respect of land, the acquisition of which is authorised by a special Act to which the LCCA 1845 (as amended) applies.
6 See *Cobb v Mid Wales Rly Co* (1866) LR 1 QB 342 on the issue of costs. See also *Eastern Counties and London and Blackwall Rly Cos v Marriage* (1860) 9 HL Case 32, 31 LJ Ex 73.

4 Agricultural land

Part of an agricultural unit (Land Compensation Act 1973, section 53)

[403]
By the Land Compensation Act 1973 (LCA 1973), s 53 where notice to treat is served in respect of any agricultural land[1] on a person with an interest[2] in other agricultural land comprised in the same agricultural unit[3] as that to

which the notice relates, that person may, within two months of service of the notice to treat, serve a counter-notice on the acquiring authority[4]:

(*a*) stating that the land is not reasonably capable of being farmed either by itself or in conjunction with other relevant land[5] as a separate agricultural unit; and
(*b*) requiring the acquisition of whole[6].

The acquiring authority may accept the counter-notice in writing, or else, within two months following its service, either party may refer the matter to the Upper Tribunal[7]. Where the counter-notice is accepted or upheld by the Upper Tribunal, the acquiring authority is deemed

(*a*) to be authorised[8] to acquire the land to which the counter-notice relates; and
(*b*) to have served notice to treat in respect of it[9].

A claimant may withdraw his counter-notice within six weeks following the Upper Tribunal's determination of compensation payable in respect of the whole[10]. However, there is no ability for the acquiring authority to withdraw the deemed notice to treat in respect of the land to which the counter-notice relates, upon determination of the compensation payable[11]. Special provision applies where the acquiring authority becomes entitled to a leasehold interest, but not the freehold interest[12].

1 The term 'agricultural land' has the meaning given in the Agriculture Act 1947, s 109, as applied by the LCA 1973, s 87.
2 Providing he has an interest in the land greater than as tenant for a year or from year to year (whether in occupation or not).
3 The term 'agricultural unit' means land which is occupied as a unit for agricultural purposes, including any dwelling house or other building occupied by the same person for the purpose of farming: TCPA 1990, s 171(1), as applied by the LCA 1973, s 87.
4 And any other person with an interest in the land to which the counter-notice relates. The LCA 1973, s 55(2). Failure to serve such other persons will not invalidate the counter-notice.
5 The term 'other relevant land' means land comprised in the same agricultural unit as the land to which the notice to treat relates, being land in which the claimant does not have an interest greater than as yearly tenant and which is within another agricultural unit occupied by him on the date of service of notice to treat in which he has an interest greater than as yearly tenant: LCA 1973, s 55(3).
6 LCA 1973, s 53. This provision operates without prejudice to the CPA 1965, s 8(2), (3) or the LCCA 1845 (as amended), ss 93, 94 (as to which, see paras **[401]–[402]**): LCA 1973, s 53(6).
7 LCA 1973, s 54(1). As to commencing proceedings in the Upper Tribunal, see **Division H**.
8 Under the same enactment which authorised the acquisition to which the notice to treat relates: LCA 1973, s 54(2)(*a*).
9 LCA 1973, s 54(2)(6).
10 LCA 1973, s 54(3). The effect of this will be that any deemed notice to treat for these purposes is likewise withdrawn.
11 LCA 1973, s 54(4). The provisions of the LCA 1961, s 31 do not apply in these circumstances. See para **[341]** generally.
12 LCA 1973, s 54(6), (7) (as to which, see para **[1329]**).

Agricultural tenants (Land Compensation Act 1973, section 55)

[404]
Where a person[1] in occupation of an agricultural holding[2] is served with notice of entry[3] in relation to part of its holding, he can, in certain circum-

stances, elect to treat such notice as relating to the entire holding[4]. Such an occupier may, within two months of receipt of notice of entry, serve a counter-notice:

(*a*) claiming that the remainder of the holding is not reasonably capable of being farmed, either by itself or in conjunction with other relevant land[5], as a separate agricultural unit; and
(*b*) electing to treat the notice of entry as a notice relating to the entire holding.

The counter-notice should be served on both the acquiring authority and the landlord[6]. Unless the acquiring authority has confirmed acceptance of the counter-notice[7] in writing within two months after its service, either party may refer it to the Upper Tribunal in writing[8] who will determine its validity[90]. Where the occupier has given up possession of the agricultural holding to the acquiring authority within 12 months of acceptance or declaration of validity of the counter-notice, the notice of entry shall be deemed to extend to the part of the agricultural holding to which the counter-notice relates; the acquiring authority shall be deemed to have taken possession of that part accordingly[10]. Special provision is made where the occupier gives up possession of the whole agricultural holding, but the acquiring authority has not been authorised to acquire the landlord's interest in any part of the holding not included in the original notice of entry[11]. A tenant of agricultural land can, following service of notice to quit, elect to have compensation due to it assessed as if notice under the CPA 1965, s 20 had been served[12].

1 'Person' means a person having no greater interest than as a tenant for a year or from year to year.
2 The term 'agricultural holding' has the same meaning as in the Agricultural Holdings Act 1986, as applied by the LCA 1973, s 87.
3 Under the CPA 1965, s 11(1) (as to which, see paras **[701]–[710]**).
4 LCA 1973, s 55. This provision is similar to that afforded to those with interests other than as minor tenants in agricultural land: LCA 1973, s 53. The LCA 1973, ss 55, 56 apply, regardless of the fact that a notice to treat may have been served in respect of land within the same agricultural holding, where such land was not included in the notice to enter in question: LCA 1973, s 55(4).
5 The term 'other relevant land' means land comprised in the same agricultural unit as the agricultural holding and land comprised in any other agricultural unit occupied by the claimant on the date of service of notice of entry, being land in respect of which he is entitled to a greater interest than as tenant for a year or from year to year: LCA 1973, s 55(3). The term 'agricultural unit' has the meaning in the TCPA 1990, s 171(1), as applied by the LCA 1973, s 87.
6 LCA 1973, s 55(2). Failure to serve the notice on the landlord will not invalidate it.
7 LCA 1973, s 56(1).
8 As to procedure in the Upper Tribunal, see **Division H.**
9 LCA 1973, s 56(1).
10 LCA 1973, s 56(2). Such possession is deemed to have been taken on the day before the expiration of the year of the tenancy which is current when the counter-notice is so accepted or declared.
11 LCA 1973, s 56(3), see para **[1328]**. This provision prevents the landlord from taking action against either the acquiring authority or the occupier. The tenancy is treated as terminated when possession is given up to the acquiring authority; any rights and liabilities of the tenant as against the landlord become those of the acquiring authority. Immediately upon possession, the land to which the counter-notice relates is treated as surrendered to the landlord and any 'vacant possession' value will be reflected in the compensation payable to the landlord.
12 As to which, see paras **[1321]–[1325]**. LCA 1973, s 59. *Dawson v Norwich City Council* (1978) 37 P & CR 516 held that elections under this provision apply, regardless of whether notice to quit is served by an acquiring authority or private landlord.

5 Land subject to mortgages and rentcharges

[405]
Special provision is made in the CPA 1965, s 16 in relation to the compulsory acquisition of part of land which is subject to a mortgage. This is explained at paras **[1043]** and **[1347]**. Special provision is made in the CPA 1965, s 18 in relation to the compulsory acquisition of part of land subject to a rentcharge. This is explained at paras **[1045]** and **[1341]**.

6 General vesting declaration

[406]
The CPA1965, s 8 does not apply where a general vesting declaration under the CP(VD)A 1981 has been executed although provisions apply which have a generally similar effect[1]. Where a general vesting declaration includes part only of any house, building or factory, or a part of a park or garden belonging to a house, any person who is able to sell the whole of the house, building or factory, or park or garden, may, by 'notice of objection to severance', require the acquiring authority to purchase its interest in the whole[2]. 'Notice of objection to severance' must be served within 28 days from service of the 'notice after execution of declaration'[3]. The effect of service of such a notice is that the interest in respect of which it has been served does not automatically vest in the acquiring authority on the vesting date and the acquiring authority cannot enter until the notice has been dealt with[4].

1 CP(VD)A 1981, s 12, Sch 1, para 2(3).
2 CP(VD)A 1981, s 12, Sch 1. This provision is similar to that in the CPA 1965, s 8(1), albeit that the formalities are more detailed.
3 CP(VD)A 1981, s 12, Sch 1, para 2(2). The CP(VD)A 1981, Sch 1, para 10 further provides that notice of objection to severance may also be served within 28 days of the claimant's first knowledge of execution of the general vesting declaration. Notice after execution of declaration is served under the CP(VD)A 1981, s 6 (as to which, see para **[346]**).
4 CP(VD)A 1981, s 12, Sch 1, para 3.

[407]
Within three months from service of the 'notice of objection to severance', the acquiring authority must [1]:

(*a*) withdraw the deemed notice to treat; or
(*b*) serve notice on the claimant that the general vesting declaration is to have effect as if the whole of his interest had been included within both the compulsory purchase order and the general vesting declaration; or
(*c*) refer the notice of objection to severance to the Upper Tribunal and notify the claimant of this[2].

1 CP(VD)A 1981, s 12, Sch 1, para 4.
2 As to commencing proceedings in the Lands Tribunal, see **Division H**.

[408]
Failure on the part of the acquiring authority to take one of the above actions within the three month period will result in the deemed notice to treat being deemed to have been withdrawn[1] so that title to the land would not vest in

the acquiring authority, nor would the acquiring authority obtain any right of lawful entry onto such land[2].

1 CP(VD)A 1981, s 12, Sch 1, para 5.
2 CP(VD)A 1981, s 12, Sch 1, para 6.

[409]

When considering any 'notice of objection to severance', the Upper Tribunal must consider whether the proposed severance could occur (in the case of a house, building, or factory) without material detriment or (in the case of a park or garden) without serious affect on the amenity or convenience of the house[1]. The Upper Tribunal must take into account, not only the effect of severance, but also the proposed use of the parcel and (where the works extend to other land) the effect of the whole of the works, and the use to be made of such other land. Where the Upper Tribunal concludes that there is material detriment or serious affect, then it must determine the area of land which the acquiring authority ought to be required to take, and the general vesting declaration will take effect, subject to this[2].

1 CP(VD)A 1981, s 12, Sch 1, para 8.
2 CP(VD)A 1981, s 12, Sch 1, para 9.

[410]

Where land included in a general vesting declaration is subject to a rentcharge or an unexpired tenancy which also apply to land not included in the vesting declaration, special provision as to extinguishment of the rentcharge or tenancy is prescribed[1].

1 CP(VD)A 1981, s 12, Sch 1, paras 11, 12. Both sections apply the corresponding provision made in the CPA 1965 (ss 18 (as to which, see paras **[1044]–[1046]**), with regard to rentcharges, and 19 (as to which, see para **[1047]**), with regard to unexpired tenancies).

[411]–[700]

Where the general vesting declaration includes part only of any agricultural land, then any person having an interest in that land greater than as a tenant for a year or from year to year may, within two months of the vesting date, serve a counter-notice on the acquiring authority, claiming that the land is not reasonably capable of being farmed either by itself or in conjunction with other relevant land as a separate agricultural unit and requiring acquisition of the whole of his interest[1]. Similar provision is made for occupiers of agricultural holdings where part only is included in a general vesting declaration[2]. This is explained in paras **[403]–[404]**.

1 LCA 1973, s 53(1), (5).
2 LCA 1973, ss 55, 56, as applied by the LCA 1973, s 57.

Chapter 3

Lawful entry

Contents

A Notice of entry (Compulsory Purchase Act 1965, section 11(1))

1 Introduction

[701]
Where the acquiring authority has served notice to treat[1], then it may enter onto land without the consent of the owner and before payment of compensation, provided it has given adequate 'notice of entry'[2].

1 Compulsory Purchase Act 1965 (CPA 1965), s 5. See paras **[301]–[341]**.
2 CPA 1965, s 11(1). This applies only where an acquiring authority elects to proceed by service of notice to treat and notice of entry under the CPA 1965. There are other means of obtaining entry, ie under the alternative procedure specified in the CPA 1965, s 11(2), Sch 3 (as to which, see paras **[721]–[724]**) and by means of general vesting declaration executed under the Compulsory Purchase (Vesting Declarations) Act 1981 (CP(VD)A 1981) (as to which, see paras **[342]–[361]**. The authorising Act may vary the provisions of the CPA 1965 regarding entry. See, eg, the Housing Act 1985, ss 578–584.

2 Form of notice of entry

[702]
Whilst there is no prescribed form of notice of entry, it must[1]:

(*a*) specify the land to which it relates, which must be the whole or part(s) of the land specified in the corresponding notice to treat[2]; and
(*b*) give at least 14 days' notice of intended entry.

Where the notice to treat refers to a number of parcels of land in the same ownership, notice of entry may be served in relation to any one or more of those parcels. In contrast, if notice of entry is served in relation to all (or, at least, more than one), when entry is made on the first parcel, entry is deemed to have been made upon all parcels referred to in that notice, even where actual entry in relation to the remaining parcels takes place later[3]. The compensation consequences of this may be significant.

1 CPA 1965, s 11(1). There is no direct equivalent for acquisitions to which the Land Clauses Consolidation Act 1845 (LCCA 1845) (as amended) applies. The LCCA 1845 (as amended), s 18 provides for service of notice of intention to purchase or take land (which notice is the forerunner to the notice to treat under the CPA 1965, s 5). Except for survey purposes, no entry maybe made under LCCA 1845 (as amended) without consent, unless compensation has been paid to the claimant or into court: LCCA 1845 (as amended), ss 84–86.
2 Notice to treat is served under the CPA 1965, s 5 (as to which, see paras **[301]–[341]**).
3 This was established in *Chilton v Telford Development Corpn* [1987] 3 All ER 992 and it has now been given statutory effect in s 5A(5) and (6) of the LCA 1961.

3 Timing of service of notice of entry

[703]

Notice of entry cannot be served before the corresponding notice to treat[1]. Provided notice to treat has been served prior to the expiry of the three-year period for exercise of compulsory purchase powers[2], it does not matter that entry[3] is taken after that date[4]. In practice, notice to treat is often served at the same time as notice of entry.

1 CPA 1965, s 11(1). For notices to treat, see paras **[301]–[341]**.
2 CPA 1965, s 4. See para **[303]**.
3 For meaning of 'entry', see paras **[727]–[728]**.
4 *Marquis of Salisbury v Great Northern Rly Co* (1852) 17 QB 840. See para **[303]**.

4 Entitlement to notice of entry

[704]

Notice of entry must be served on every owner[1], lessee and occupier of the land[2]. Where the land is ecclesiastical property[3], notice of entry must also be served on the Church Commissioners[4].

1 'Owner' means, in relation to any land, a person other than a mortgagee not in possession who is, for the time being, entitled to dispose of the fee simple in the land, whether in possession or in reversion. The term includes a person holding and entitled to the rents and profits of land under lease or agreement, the unexpired term of which exceeds three years, and a person who would have power to sell and convey or release the land to the acquiring authority if the compulsory purchase order were operative: Acquisition of Land Act 1981 (ALA 1981), s 7(1), as applied by the CPA 1965, s 11(1).
2 Neither 'lessee' nor 'occupier' are defined in the CPA 1965. Requirements for service of the notice of entry should be contrasted with the less specific requirements regarding service of the notice to treat under the CPA 1965, s 5 (see para **[306]**).
3 'Ecclesiastical property' means land belonging to any ecclesiastical benefice or forming part of a church subject to the jurisdiction of the bishop of any diocese or the site of such a church or being or forming part of a burial ground subject to such jurisdiction or being diocesan glebe land within the meaning of the Endowments and Glebe Measure 1976: ALA 1981, s 12(3), as applied by the CPA 1965, s 11(1).
4 CPA 1965, s 11(1). Church Commissioners for England are constituted under the Church Commissioners Measure 1947.

5 Mode of service of notice of entry

[705]

The service requirements for notice of entry are identical to those for notice to treat and are described at paras **[310]–[321]**[1].

1 Service requirements are specified in the ALA 1981, s 6, as applied by the CPA 1965, s 30.

6 Effect of notice of entry and actual entry

[706]

Service of notice of entry enables the acquiring authority to enter[1] onto land to which the notice to treat relates at any time after the date specified[2] in the notice of entry. Expiry of the period referred to in the notice itself does not amount to entry; it simply denotes the earliest date at which entry may be taken[3]. In practice, there may be a considerable delay between service of notice of entry and actual entry. In the event that the owner resists entry following the expiry of the period referred to in the notice of entry, the acquiring authority is entitled to issue a warrant to the sheriff to deliver possession of the land to it[4].

1 For meaning of 'entry', see paras **[727]–[728]**.
2 Such date must be not less than 14 days after service of notice: CPA 1965, s 11(1).
3 *Burson v Wantage* (1974) 27 P&CR 556.
4 CPA 1965, s 13 (as to which, see para **[746]**).

[707]

For the purposes of assessing compensation for the value of the land acquired, the relevant valuation date is the date on which the acquiring authority enters on and takes possession of the land (or the date when the assessment is made, if earlier)[1].

1 LCA 1961, s 5A which effectively enacts the decision of the House of Lords in *Birmingham Corpn v West Midlands Baptist (Trust) Association Inc* [1970] AC 874. Prior to this case, the date of service of notice to treat was considered to be the date for assessment of compensation. See also **Division E [40]–[42]**. Although LCA 1961, s 5A is expressed to apply only to rule 2 of LCA 1961, s 5 (open market value), see **Division E [41]** as to the relevant date for assessing compensation for disturbance.

[708]

Once entry onto land has been taken[1]:

(*a*) the owner may request payment of advance compensation and interest prior to final determination of the compensation due[2];
(*b*) interest will accrue on the compensation from the date of entry onto the land until the date of payment, either to the claimant or into court[3];
(*c*) from the date of entry, the acquiring authority will take responsibility for the property[4] (assuming it has not already acquired title); and
(*d*) as a general rule, the acquiring authority cannot withdraw any notice to treat[5] after entry has been made except by agreement[6].

1 See also paras **[727]–[728]**.
2 Land Compensation Act 1973 (LCA 1973), ss 52, 52A (as to which, see paras **[1081]–[1084]**).
3 CPA 1965, s 11(1); interest will be payable at the rate prescribed under the Land Compensation Act 1961 (LCA 1961), s 32 which is currently set out in the Acquisition of Land (Rate of Interest After Entry) Regulations 1995, SI 1995/2262, as amended by SI 2001/3649.
4 As to which, see para **[370]** subsection (4).
5 Served under the CPA 1965, s 5 (as to which, see paras **[301]–[341]**).
6 LCA 1961, s 31(1). There is a limited entitlement to withdraw notice to treat (notwithstanding that entry has been taken) following the notification of claim (as to which, see para **[341]**). See *R v Northumbrian Water Ltd, ex p Able UK Ltd* [1996] 2 EGLR 15.

7 Withdrawal or abandonment of notice of entry

[709]
Once entry has been taken, then it is not generally possible for the acquiring authority to withdraw from the acquisition, except by agreement[1]. However, until entry is taken, notwithstanding that notice of entry has been served, the acquiring authority may withdraw or abandon its notice to treat as described at paras **[328]–[341]**.

1 LCA 1961, s 31(1) provides a limited statutory right of withdrawal which an acquiring authority may invoke, notwithstanding that it has entered onto the land. See para **[341]**.

8 Action by owner in response to notice of entry

[710]–[720]
Provided that the statutory procedures have been correctly followed[1] there is nothing an owner[2] can lawfully do to prevent entry by the acquiring authority onto his land. The owner's safeguards include:

(*a*) the right to have compensation assessed[3] so that the quasi-contract for sale[4] between the parties created following service of notice to treat becomes unconditional, thereby enabling specific performance and the recovery of compensation and interest; and
(*b*) the right to apply for advance payments of compensation[5].

Where the statutory procedures have not been complied with, entry may not be taken[6]. Where entry onto the land is made without statutory authority, an owner may invoke the statutory remedies in CPA 1965, s 12[7]. These provisions do not preclude civil remedies, such as a claim in damages for trespass or an injunction[8].

1 Ie implementation of compulsory purchase powers has been carried out in accordance with the procedural requirements for service of notice to treat and notice of entry under the CPA 1965. Entry may also be made following execution of a general vesting declaration (as to which, see paras **[342]–[361]**) or in accordance with the alternative procedure specified in the CPA 1965, s 11(2), Sch 3 (as to which, see paras **[721]–[724]**)).
2 See paras **[306]**ff and para **[704]** as to those interests in land which qualify for service with notice to treat and notice of entry.
3 CPA 1965, s 6 (as to which, see para **[323]** and para **[1004]**).
4 See Chapter 2, para **[323]** (1).
5 LCA 1973, ss 52, 52A (as to which, see para **[708]** and paras **[1081]–[1084]**). Such payments carry interest from date of entry.
6 CPA 1965, s 11(4).
7 See paras **[741]–[742]**.
8 See para **[742]**.

B Alternative procedure for obtaining entry (Compulsory Purchase Act 1965, section 11(2) and Schedule 3)

1 Introduction

[721]
As an alternative to gaining entry onto land by means of notice of entry[1], an acquiring authority may, by the CPA 1965, s 11(2), Sch 3 proceed instead by

tender of a performance bond in respect of compensation due for the land taken and payment of moneys into court as security. This alternative procedure is rarely used nowadays, as it is relatively cumbersome and requires quantification of compensation and payment of security prior to entry[2]. The acquiring authority must have sufficient funds available both to make a payment into court as security and to pay the landowner compensation pursuant to the bond, as the security will only be refunded to the acquiring authority when the compensation has been paid.

1 CPA 1965, s 11(1) governs entry following service of notice of entry (as to which, see paras **[701]–[710]**). It is also possible to secure lawful entry by means of general vesting declaration under the CP(VD)A 1981 (as to which, see paras **[342]–[361]**).

2 CPA 1965, s 11(2) and Sch 3 re-enact the LCCA 1845 (as amended), ss 85, 86, which provisions still apply, in relation to acquisitions authorised by a special Act to which the LCCA 1845 (as amended) applies. This remains the only method of entry under the LCCA 1845 (as amended) except where compensation has been paid in full to the landowner or the landowner consents: LCCA 1845 (as amended), s 84. The alternative procedure is the only general statutory procedure requiring quantification and payment on account of compensation prior to entry.

2 Procedure

[722]

In order to effect entry under this procedure[1], the acquiring authority must:

(*a*) pay into court by way of security:
  (i) the compensation[2] claimed by the owner[3], or
  (ii) a sum equal to the value of the owner's interest, as determined by a surveyor appointed by two justices of the peace[4]; and

(*b*) tender or give a bond[5] to the owner in a penal sum equal to the moneys deposited in court and conditioned for payment to the owner or, as the case may be, for payment into court of all compensation which may be awarded or agreed[6], plus interest[7] calculated from date of entry until payment[8].

1 CPA 1965, s 11(2), Sch 3.

2 Compensation should reflect, not only the value of the land to be acquired, but also compensation in respect of severance or other injurious affection: *Field v Carnarvon and Llanberis Rly Co* (1867) LR 5 Eq 190.

3 'Owner' for these purposes means each person interested in or entitled to sell and convey the land *who has not given his consent to entry* (emphasis added): CPA 1965, s 11(2), Sch 3, para 1.

4 CPA 1965, s 11(2), Sch 3, para 2(1). The surveyor must be an able practical surveyor and his appointment must be by two justices of the peace acting together by an instrument in writing, signed by them. Notice of application for an appointment of surveyor need not be given to the landowner: *Bridges v Wiltshire, Somerset and Weymouth Rly Co* (1847) 16 LJ Ch 335.

5 The bond must be under seal where the acquiring authority is a corporation (CPA 1965, s 11(2), Sch 3, para 3(2)) and must be with two sufficient sureties, approved by two justices of the peace, in default of agreement (CPA 1965, s 11(2), Sch 3, para 3(3)). As to form of bond, see *Cotter v Metropolitan Rly Co* (1864) 4 New Rep 454.

6 The compensation actually due may exceed that paid into court by way of security, in which case, an appropriate adjustment will have to be made: *Ashford v London, Chatham and Dover Rly Co* (1866) 14 LT 787.

7 Interest will be calculated under the rate prescribed by the LCA 1961, s 32, which is currently set out in SI 1995/2262, as amended by SI 2001/3649.

8 CPA 1965, s 11(2), Sch 3, para 3(1).

[723]

Whilst it is not an express requirement of the CPA 1965, s 11(2), it is generally accepted that entry cannot be taken by means of this alternative procedure unless a notice to treat has been served[1]. Indeed, no entry may be made onto any parcel of land referred to in any notice to treat, pursuant to this procedure, unless moneys have been paid into court in respect of all parcels referred to in that notice[2], notwithstanding that entry in relation to the whole is not immediately required. Where notice to treat has been served prior to the expiry of the period for exercise of compulsory purchase powers[3], entry by means of the alternative procedure can be made later[4].

1 CPA 1965, s 5 requires service of a notice to treat (as to which, see paras **[301]–[341]**) where the acquiring authority requires to purchase any land subject to compulsory purchase. Under the corresponding provision in the LCCA 1845 (as amended), s 85, there was a difference of judicial opinion as to whether the promoters could proceed with this method of entry, unless notice under the LCCA 1845 (as amended), s 18 had been served: see *Tiverton etc Rly Co v Loosemore* (1884) 9 App Cas 480 at 502–503; *Great Western Rly Co v Swindon and Cheltenham Extension Rly Co* (1854) 9 App Cas 787 at 805. The wording of the CPA 1965, s 11(2) should be contrasted with that in the CPA 1965, s 11(1), which makes provision for service of notice of entry (see paras **[701]–[710]**) and expressly requires service of a notice to treat before entry can be taken.

2 *Barker v North Staffordshire Rly Co* (1848) 2 De G & Sm 55.

3 Three years from the date of the confirmation of the compulsory purchase order: CPA 1965, s 4 (as to which, see para **[303]**).

4 *Marquis of Salisbury v The Great Northern Rly Co* (1852) 17 QB 840.

[724]

Where the bond is fully performed and compensation duly paid to the appropriate owner, the acquiring authority may apply for payment out to it of the moneys[1] held in court as security for that compensation, together with any accumulation[2]. Where, however, the bond has not been fully performed, the High Court may order the money deposited to be applied in the manner it thinks fit[3]. If the purchase is abandoned with the landowner's consent, then the acquiring authority is entitled to repayment of moneys held in court[4]. The rules regulating acquisition of part only of any land[5] apply to entry effected under the alternative procedure as they do where entry is made following service of notice to treat and notice of entry. These are explained at paras **[381]–[411]**. Where the acquiring authority is required to acquire the whole of any interest, entry cannot be made onto part of the land, pursuant to the alternative procedure, unless moneys have been paid into court, in respect of the whole interest, by way of security[6]. Once the compensation has been determined by agreement or otherwise[7], the owner may bring an action for specific performance of the contract for sale[8].

1 CPA 1965, s 11(2) and Sch 3, para 4(3). As to satisfaction of condition of a performance bond, see *Ex p Great Northern Rly Co* (1848) 16 Sim 169.

2 Moneys paid into court can be dealt with under the Administration of Justice Act 1982 and, if so, accumulated accordingly: CPA 1965, s 11(2), Sch 3, para 4(2). These provisions refer to the Administration of Justice Act 1965, which was repealed by the Administration of Justice Act 1982, s 75). See paras **[1063]–[1080]**.

3 CPA 1965, s 11(2) and Sch 3, para 4(4). Payment out will only be made when all conditions of the bond have been fulfilled: *Re London and South Western Railway Extension Act, ex p Stevens* (1848) 2 Ph 772. The conditions of the bond will be met where payment of compensation (as agreed or determined by the Lands Tribunal) is paid into court, even where the owner refuses to accept such moneys: *Re Fooks* (1849) 2 Mac & G 357. See also *Ex p Midland Rly Co* [1904] 1 Ch 61; *Re Mutlows Estate* (1878) 10 Ch D 131.

4 *Ex p Birmingham, Wolverhampton and Dudley Rly Co* (1863) 1 Hem & M 772.
5 CPA 1965, s 8: see also the LCCA 1845 (as amended), s 92.
6 *Giles v London, Chatham and Dover Rly Co* (1861) 30 LJ Ch 603. This is so, even if moneys, in respect of the part the acquiring authority wish to take, have been paid.
7 See para **[1004]**.
8 *Wing v Tottenham and Hampstead Junction Rly* (1868) 3 Ch App 740 held that until all purchase money has been paid, the vendor retains a lien over the property, regardless of the compulsory nature of the acquisition.

C Entry following general vesting declaration

[725]
Where a general vesting declaration is executed in accordance with the CP(VD)A 1981, then entry onto and possession of the land specified in the general vesting declaration may be taken by the acquiring authority on the vesting date[1]. Such rights of entry will be effective against all interests, except a minor tenancy[2] or a long tenancy about to expire[3], and there will be no need to serve any notice to treat nor notice of entry[4] except in relation such minor interests[5]. The exercise of rights of entry pursuant to a general vesting declaration does not require prior assessment of compensation. Regardless of when entry is actually taken, compensation will be assessed as at the date of vesting[6]. The procedure relating to general vesting declarations is explained at paras **[342]–[361]**.

1 CP(VD)A 1981, s 8(1) (as to which, see para **[350]**). In addition, title to the relevant land will vest in the acquiring authority.
2 The term 'minor tenancy' means a tenancy for a year or from year to year or any lesser interest: CP(VD)A 1981, s 2(1).
3 The term 'long tenancy which is about to expire' means, in relation to a general vesting declaration, a tenancy granted for an interest greater than a 'minor tenancy', but having, on the vesting date, an unexpired period which is not more than the period specified in the declaration in relation to the land in which the tenancy subsists: CP(VD)A 1981, s 2(2).
4 CPA 1965, ss 5 and 11(1) (as to which, see paras **[301]–[341]** and **[701]–[710]** respectively).
5 CP(VD)A1981, s 9(2). See para **[361]**.
6 LCA 1961, s 5A(4). This may be contrasted with the situation following service of a notice to treat and notice of entry under the CPA 1965, ss 5 and 11(1) where compensation is assessed at date of entry (or the date of assessment, if earlier): LCA 1961, s 5A(4).

D Other points regarding entry

1 Limited right to enter for survey purposes

[726]
By the CPA 1965, s 11(3) an acquiring authority may enter land which is the subject of a compulsory purchase order to which the CPA 1965 applies for the purpose of:

(*a*) surveying and taking levels of any of the land;
(*b*) probing or boring to ascertain the nature of the soil; and
(*c*) setting out the line of the works,

provided it gives at least three, but no more than 14 days' notice to the owners[1]or occupiers of the land[2].

This power can only be exercised after confirmation of a compulsory purchase order, since, prior to that date, there is no acquiring authority[3] for these purposes[4]. The acquiring authority must compensate the owners or occupiers of land in respect of any damage occasioned as a result of such entry, and any question of disputed compensation may be referred to the Upper Tribunal[5]. Any such compensation will carry interest from the date of entry until the date of payment[6]. Where a local authority proposes to acquire compulsorily interests or rights in land, it can authorise persons to enter onto the relevant land for the purposes of carrying out a survey, provided at least 14 days' notice has been given to any occupier or statutory undertaker[7]. Entry for the purposes of survey only does not constitute entry for the purposes of assessment of compensation payable in respect of landtake[8].

1 The term 'owner' means the person having power to sell and convey the land to the acquiring authority: CPA 1965, s 1(6). This definition follows the LCCA 1845 (as amended), s 3 definition which was held wide enough to include a mortgagee of land with a power of sale: *R v Clerk of the Peace for Middlesex* [1914] 3 KB 259.
2 CPA 1965, s 11(3). There is a similar power in the LCCA 1845 (as amended), s 84, in respect of land authorised to be acquired under a special Act to which the LCCA 1845 (as amended) applies.
3 As defined by the CPA 1965, s 1(3).
4 Where an acquiring authority purports to exercise this power, prior to confirmation of the compulsory purchase order, it is submitted that the owner will be entitled to bring an action in respect of any trespass or nuisance. Where this power is exercised without adequate statutory notice, the owner may likewise bring proceedings to restrain such trespass or nuisance, although, in *Fooks v Wiltshire, Somerset and Weymouth Rly Co* (1846) 4 Ry & Can Cas 210, an injunction (following one day's entry for survey purposes without notice) was refused as the mischief had already ceased.
5 CPA 1965, s 11(3). Such compensation is distinct from compensation payable in respect of the compulsory acquisition itself.
6 Planning and Compensation Act 1991, s 80, Sch 18, Pt 1. Interest will be at the rate prescribed in regulations made under the LCA 1961, s 32.
7 Local Government (Miscellaneous Provisions) Act 1976, s 15.
8 *Courage Ltd v Kingswood DC* (1978) 247 Estates Gazette 307. See also paras **[706]–[708]** and **[727]**.

2 Meaning of entry

Actions constituting entry

[727]
The date of entry onto land is important for the reasons explained in paras **[706]–[708]** and **[730]**. Whilst there is no statutory definition of 'entry', entry will be evidenced by the carrying out of acts which are consistent with ownership[1]. What constitutes entry will depend on the circumstances, but, in the absence of a formal surrender of possession by the owner (for instance through handing over keys), it must involve some physical act in relation to the land[2]. Certain events have been held *not* to constitute entry, including:

(*a*) expiry of the period specified in a notice of entry[3];
(*b*) placing of materials on land with consent of a tenant[4];
(*c*) repeated visits to survey, check measurements and check a bill of quantity[5]; and
(*d*) interference with an easement over land taken[6].

1 *Courage Ltd v Kingswood DC* (1978) 247 Estates Gazette 307.
2 *Welford v Transport for London* [2008] RVR 178, Lands Tribunal. In *Esso Petroleum Company Ltd v Secretary of State for Transport* [2008] RVR 351, the Lands Tribunal held that clearance of trees and vegetation to enable works to take place amounted to entry. See also *BP Oil UK Ltd v Kent County Council* [2003] EWCA Civ 798, [2003] RVR 276 at [17]–[19].
3 *Burson v Wantage RDC* (1974) 27 P&CR 556. Expiry of such period simply indicates the earliest date at which entry may be made. Notice of entry is served under the CPA 1965, s 11(1) (as to which, see paras **[701]–[710]**).
4 *Standish v Liverpool Corpn* (1852) 1 Drew 1, 61 ER 351.
5 *Burson v Wantage RDC* (1974) 27 P&CR 556.
6 The remedy for the owner of an easement in such a case is compensation for injurious affection under the CPA 1965, s 10. See *Clark v London School Board* (1874) 9 Ch App 120.

[728]

The extraction of subsoil for making a tunnel constitutes entry in respect of which the usual formalities are required[1]. Further, the handing over of keys has been held to constitute entry, notwithstanding that physical occupation was not taken until after that time[2].

1 *Farmer v Waterloo and City Rly Co* [1895] 1 Ch 527.
2 *Simmonds v Kent County Council* [1990] 1 EGLR 227.

Scope of entry

[729]

The acquiring authority can enter onto land to carry out its statutory purposes and anything reasonably incidental or consequential to those purposes[1]. The authorising Act may make special provision as regards entry (allowing, for example, entry onto land for the purpose of acquiring an interest in it, ie a right of way or a tunnel[2]), in which case entry can only be made on such conditions as apply to that particular authorisation. If there is no power in the authorising Act and associated compulsory purchase order to acquire an interest less than the whole of any existing interest, steps must be taken to acquire the whole and not part, even though part only is required[3]. Where a single notice to treat and a single notice of entry have been served in relation to more than one parcel of land, entry onto the first parcel is deemed to constitute entry onto all parcels included in the same notices[4]. However, even if a single notice to treat has been served, the acquiring authority has the option to serve notice of entry, and to enter upon, part only of the total area identified in the notice to treat[5].

1 *National Provident Institution v Avon County Council* [1992] EGCS 56 held that there are no rights of entry onto land outside the compulsory purchase order for purposes incidental to the authorised purpose.
2 *Farmer v Waterloo and City Rly Co* [1895] 1 Ch 527. See also *Hill v Midland Rly Co* (1882) 21 CLD 143; *Roderick v Aston Local Board* (1877) 5 Ch D 328; *Great Western Rly Co v Swindon and Cheltenham Extension Rly Co* (1884) 9 App Cas 787.
3 *Errington v Metropolitan District Rly Co* (1882) 19 Ch D 559; *Ramsden v Manchester, South Junction and Altrincham Rly Co* (1848) 1 Exch 723. By way of example, the Highways Act 1980, s 250 enables the compulsory acquisition of rights already in existence, together with the creation of new rights.
4 *Chilton v Telford Development Corpn* [1987] 3 All ER 992. This case turned on the provisions of the New Towns Act 1965, but it is submitted that the same would apply to the CPA 1965.
5 See the judgement of Neil LJ in *Chilton v Telford Development Corpn* [1987] 3 All ER 992.

3 Effect of entry

[730]–[740]

Physical entry upon, and taking possession of, land will trigger the consequences set out in paras **[706]–[708]**. Where proceeding by general vesting declaration pursuant to the CP(VD)A 1981[1], entry is deemed to occur on the vesting date for compensation purposes.

1 As to which, see paras **[342]–[361]**.

4 Unauthorised entry

[741]

If the acquiring authority or its contractors wilfully enter on and take possession of land subject to compulsory purchase in contravention of the provisions of the CPA 1965[1], it will be liable to pay the person in possession of that land[2] compensation in respect of any damage occasioned by such entry, plus a forfeit sum of £10[3]. Such forfeit sums are recoverable summarily as a civil debt[4]. Entry, for these purposes, will only be wilful where there is an absence of honest belief on the part of the acquiring authority that entry was made in accordance with the provisions of the authorising Act[5]. For the avoidance of doubt, this penalty will not bite where the acquiring authority has, in good faith, already paid compensation in respect of the entry in question to the person whom it reasonably believed was entitled to it or into court for the benefit of such person[6]. The acquiring authority will be liable to an additional penalty rate of £25 for each day of continued unauthorised occupation following an adjudication as to the forfeited sum[7]. Such an additional sum is recoverable in the High Court[8].

1 CPA 1965, s 11(4).
2 As distinct from the 'owner', defined in the CPA 1965, s 1(6).
3 CPA 1965, s 12(1). There is similar provision in the LCCA 1845 (as amended), s 89, in respect of unauthorised entry onto land, the acquisition of which is authorised by a special Act to which the LCCA 1845 (as amended) applies.
4 CPA 1965, s 12(2). A right of appeal lies from the magistrates' court to the Crown Court: CPA 1965, s 12(3).
5 *Steele v Midland Rly Co* (1869) 21 LT 387.
6 CPA 1965, s 12(6).
7 CPA 1965, s 12(4).
8 CPA 1965, s 12(5).

[742]

The CPA 1965 does not prohibit a landowner from pursuing other non-statutory remedies including civil actions for trespass[1] or injunctions to restrain continued possession by the acquiring authority, pending compliance with any necessary conditions[2], or actions for possession where the acquiring authority has been acting outside its statutory powers[3]. However, such proceedings will not succeed where consent has been given to entry even if it is subsequently withdrawn[4].

1 *Ramsden v Manchester South Junction and Altrincham Rly Co* (1848) 1 Exch 723; *Armstrong v Waterford and Limerick Rly Co* (1846) 8 LTOS 199.
2 *Ranken v East and West India Docks and Birmingham Junction Rly* (1849) 12 Beav 298. As to grounds for granting an injunction, see, generally, *River Roden Co Ltd v Barking Town UDC*

(1902) 18 TLR 608. An injunction cannot be sought to restrain an acquiring authority from proceeding in anticipation of inadequate funds being available for compensation: *Salmon v Randall* (1838) 3 My & Cr 439.

3 *Batson v London School Board* (1963) 67 JP 457. See also *Martin v London, Chatham & Dover Rly Co* (1866) 1 Ch App 501, where possession was taken without service of notice to treat on an equitable mortgagee.

4 In *Doe d Hudson v Leeds and Bradford Rly Co* (1851) 16 QB 796, consent to enter could not be withdrawn, even though the acquiring authority failed to tender compensation as agreed.

5 Omitted interests

[743]

By the CPA 1965,s 22(1) if, after the acquiring authority has entered onto any of the land subject to compulsory purchase, it appears that, through mistake or inadvertence[1], the acquiring authority has failed or omitted duly to purchase or pay compensation[2] for any estate, right, interest in or charge affecting that land, then, subject to certain conditions, it may remain in undisturbed possession. To benefit from this provision, the acquiring authority must within six months, purchase the relevant interests or pay the appropriate compensation, including full compensation in respect of mesne profits from the date of entry until date of payment[3]. For these purposes, the compensation payable will be assessed at the date of entry, but without regard to any improvements made by the acquiring authority thereafter[4]. This rule applies, regardless of whether the three-year time limit[5] in respect of which compulsory purchase powers may be exercised has expired[6]. A person who has been wrongfully dispossessed may not eject the acquiring authority until the six-month period for payment of compensation has expired[7].

1 *Martin v London, Chatham and Dover Rly Co* (1866) 1 Ch App 501 held that this provision would not apply where a mortgagee's interest was known, but the acquiring authority treated only with the mortgagor in the mistaken belief that the equity of redemption would be sufficient to clear the mortgagee's interest. Where possession is taken without service of notice to treat on a known interest, this provision cannot be relied on: *Stretton v Great Western and Brentford Rly* (1870) 5 Ch App 751.

2 To the person entitled to it or into court.

3 There is similar provision in the LCCA 1845 (as amended), ss 124, 125, in respect of acquisitions of land authorised by an Act to which the LCCA 1845 (as amended) applies.

4 CPA 1965, s 22(4).

5 CPA 1965, s 4; compulsory purchase powers can only be exercised within three years from date of confirmation of the compulsory purchase order.

6 CPA 1965, s 22(2).

7 *Jolly v Wimbledon and Dorking Rly Co* (1861) 31 LJQB 95. See also *Hyde v Manchester Corpn* (1852) 5 De G & Sm 249.

[744]

The CPA1965, s 22(1) raises its own particular difficulties, not least that the period of six months may be insufficient for final determination of the compensation payable. Further, this provision does not afford indefinite protection to an acquiring authority which, prior to entry, was uncertain as to, or disputed, the claimant's title[1].

1 See, eg, *Doe d Hyde v Manchester Corpn* (1852) 12 CB 474; *Marquis of Salisbury v Great Northern Rly Co* (1858) 5 CBNS 174. See also para **[1004]**.

[745]
Where the acquiring authority has taken entry without following the CPA 1965 procedure, it can regularise the position by serving notice to treat and notice of entry, so long as the time for doing so has not expired. In *Cohen v Haringey LBC*[1], the acquiring authority went into possession of a property without having served notice to treat on the mortgagee, as required. The Court of Appeal held that it had regularised its position by late service of a notice to treat and notice of entry albeit without vacating the premises.

1 (1980) 42 P&CR 6. However, in *Ranken v East and West India Docks and Birmingham Junction Rly* (1849) 12 Beav 298, the acquiring authority was restrained by an injunction, where it had failed to treat with a mortgagee. See also *Martin v London, Chatham and Dover Rly Co* (1866) 1 Ch App 501.

[745.1]
The Court of Appeal has held that, if an acquiring authority has taken possession of land but has failed to serve notice to treat on a person who claims to hold an interest in the land, that person can take the initiative and claim compensation under the CPA 1965, s 22[1]. The Upper Tribunal then has jurisdiction to determine whether the person has a sufficient interest to be entitled to compensation.

1 *Kent County Council v Union Railways (North) Ltd* [2009] RVR 146, CA.

6 Failure to give up possession

[746]–[1000]
Where the acquiring authority is authorised under the CPA 1965 to enter on and take possession of any land, but the owner[1] or occupier or any other person refuses to give up possession of it, the acquiring authority may, by virtue of the CPA 1965, s 13, issue a warrant to the sheriff[2] to deliver to it possession of the land[3]. Possession may thus be enforced notwithstanding that the acquiring authority has not yet obtained formal title to the site. Costs accruing by reason of the issue and execution of the warrant will be paid by the person refusing to give up possession and deducted from any compensation otherwise due to him[4]. Where no compensation is payable or the costs exceed the compensation due, recovery of costs may be levied by distress following an application by the acquiring authority to any justice of the peace[5]. Possession may be obtained under this provision notwithstanding protection given to occupiers of property under statutes such as the Protection from Eviction Act 1977[6]. It is doubtful whether the sheriff can be called upon to deliver possession more than once under these provisions in the event that, for example, protesters in relation to the compulsory acquisition once evicted return to the land. In such a case, an acquiring authority will have sufficient locus to bring proceedings for possession under Rule 55 of the Civil Procedure Rules or, alternatively, for injunctive relief to restrain trespass[7]. These provisions operate without prejudice to the acquiring authority's ability to make peaceable entry without the need to call upon the sheriff[8].

1 'Owner' means the person having power to sell and convey the land to the acquiring authority: CPA 1965, s 1(6).

2 'Sheriff' includes an undersheriff or other legally competent deputy and means the sheriff for an area where the land (or part) is situated: CPA 1965, s 13(6).
3 Similar provision is made under the LCCA 1845 (as amended), s 91, in respect of the acquisition of any land authorised by a special Act to which the LCCA 1845 (as amended) applies.
4 CPA 1965, s 13(3).
5 CPA 1965, s 13(4).
6 Protection from Eviction Act 1977, s 9(4)(*e*).
7 See, eg, *Secretary of State v Kreb Dragonrider* (24 October 1996, unreported).
8 *Tiverton and North Devon Rly Co v Loosemore* (1884) 9 App Cas 480.

Chapter 4

Acquiring title and completion

Contents

A Introduction

[1001]

Where the acquiring authority chooses to proceed under the Compulsory Purchase Act 1965 (CPA 1965)[1], both landowner and acquiring authority, in the absence of agreement, are entitled to have the compensation in consequence of the compulsory acquisition determined by the Upper Tribunal[2]. As soon as compensation has been agreed or determined, the landowner and acquiring authority become parties to an unconditional contract for sale[3], which either party has the right to enforce. They will usually simply agree to an appropriate conveyance. The CPA 1965 does, however, make provision for the acquisition of title in the event that the parties are unable to complete by agreement. The acquisition of title is usually dealt with as a separate exercise to obtaining possession of the land under the CPA 1965.

1 Rights of entry may be acquired following service of notice to treat and notice of entry under the CPA 1965, ss 5 and 11(1) (as to which, see paras **[301]–[341]** and **[701]–[710]**) or under the alternative procedure specified in the CPA 1965, s 11(2) and Sch 3 (as to which, see paras **[721]–[724]**).

2 CPA 1965, s 6 and LCA 1961, s 1. This right is triggered following service of notice to treat under the CPA 1965, s 5 (as to which, see para **[323]**ff).

3 As to the quasi-contractual relationship between acquiring authority and landowner, see para **[323]**. Such relationship is subject to a limited statutory right of withdrawal on the part of the acquiring authority: Land Compensation Act 1961 (LCA 1961), s 31 (as to which, see para **[341]**).

[1002]

Where the acquiring authority proceeds by means of general vesting declaration[1], title is transferred automatically without the need for a conveyance, assignment or other formal transfer. If the parties are unable to agree the compensation payable, either of them will then be entitled to refer the question of compensation to the Upper Tribunal.[2] Title and the right to possession are therefore obtained simultaneously under the CP(VD)A 1981.

1 Under the Compulsory Purchase (Vesting Declarations) Act 1981 (CP(VD)A 1981) (as to which, see paras **[342]–[361]**).

2 When a general vesting declaration becomes operative, the provisions of the CPA 1965 apply as if a notice to treat under the CPA 1965, s 5 had been served on all landowners (except certain minor tenants (as to which, see para **[361]**)) on the vesting date: CP(VD)A 1981, s 7 (as to which, see para **[350]**).

[1003]

The mechanism for determination of compensation is explained at para **[1004]** and **[1005]–[1006]**[1]. The mechanism for acquisition of title under the CPA 1965, whether by agreement or otherwise, is explained at paras **[1007]–[1022]** and **[1048]–[1070]**[2]. Special provisions for property subject to mortgages, rentcharges and leases are explained at paras **[1029]–[1047]**. Provision for advance payment of compensation is explained at paras **[1081]–[1084]** and, finally, issues relating to the acquisition of title pursuant to general vesting declarations are drawn together at paras **[1085]–[1087]**.

1 The assessment of compensation is explained in **Division E**. The jurisdiction of the Upper Tribunal is explained in **Division H**.

2 See also **Division B, Chapter 3**.

B Determination of interests to be acquired and assessment of compensation

[1004]

Where a person served with a notice to treat[1] fails:

(*a*) within 21 days from service, to submit particulars of claim[2] or treat with the acquiring authority generally; or

(*b*) to agree with the acquiring authority as to the compensation payable for his interest and/or any damage sustained by him resulting from execution of the works,

a reference to the Upper Tribunal may be made to determine the compensation due[3]. Either party may take the initiative by lodging a notice of reference with the Registrar of the Upper Tribunal[4]. The Upper Tribunal can only determine the compensation to be paid in respect of the interest described in the corresponding notice to treat[5]. The Court retains jurisdiction to make binding decisions on questions of title or contractual rights which may influence the liability for, or quantum of, compensation payable[6].

1 CPA 1965, s 5 (as to which, see paras **[301]–[341]**). Where an acquiring authority proceeds by general vesting declaration, a notice to treat for the purposes of the CPA 1965 is deemed to be served on the vesting date: CP(VD)A 1981, s 7 (as to which, see para **[350]**).

2 Every notice to treat must request details of the landowner's claim: CPA 1965, s 5(2)(*b*). Failure to submit a claim in the appropriate form will not prejudice the landowner's claim for compensation, but may result in a costs penalty in respect of costs accruing from such time as the Upper Tribunal determine a claim should have been lodged to enable the acquiring authority to make a proper offer of compensation: LCA 1961, s 4. See para **[325]**.

3 CPA 1965, s 6. Similar provision exists in the Land Clauses Consolidation Act 1845 (LCCA 1845) (as amended), s 21, in respect of any acquisition of land authorised by a special Act to which the LCCA 1845 (as amended) relates and, indeed, all disputes as to compensation in respect of compulsory acquisition shall be dealt with by the Lands Tribunal: LCA 1961, s 1.

4 As to procedure for making references to the Upper Tribunal, see **Division H**.

5 *Stone v Commercial Rly Co* (1839) 4 My & Cr 122.

6 The jurisdiction of the Upper Tribunal is explained in **Division H**. In *Duttons Brewery Ltd v Leeds CC* (1982) 43 P&CR 160, the court was asked to determine by originating summons whether a binding agreement had been forged between acquiring authority and landowner. In contrast, in *Oppenheimer v Minister of Transport* [1942] 1 KB 242, the court noted that, when the Lands Tribunal was created, a right of appeal was introduced to the Court of Appeal (which did not previously exist in relation to the predecessors of the Lands Tribunal), and it was therefore concluded that the Lands Tribunal had jurisdiction to determine issues of title in so far as it is necessary to do so for the purposes of assessing compensation, subject to the supervision of the Court on appeal. *Oppenheimer* was applied with approval in *Kent County Council v Union Railways (North) Ltd* [2009] RVR 146, CA.

C Untraced and absent owners

[1005]

The CPA 1965, s 5(3), Sch 2[1] applies to any land which is the subject of a compulsory purchase order where the relevant owner is:

(*a*) unable to treat with the acquiring authority on account of absence from the United Kingdom; or
(*b*) cannot be found after diligent inquiry[2].

In such cases, compensation will be:

(*a*) determined by a surveyor[3];
(*b*) paid into court to the credit of the parties interested in the land[4]; and
(*c*) paid out on the successful application of any person so interested in the moneys[5].

1 There is similar provision in the LCCA 1845 (as amended), ss 58 and 76, in respect of land, the acquisition of which is authorised by special Act to which the LCCA 1845 (as amended) applies. There is no need for any similar provision, with regard to acquisitions made pursuant to a general vesting declaration executed under the CP(VD)A 1981, as title vests automatically and, indeed, the CP(VD)A 1981, s 10(2) disapplies the CPA 1965, Sch 2.

2 CPA 1965, s 5(3), Sch 2, para 1(1). This provision does not apply where ownership is in dispute. In such a case, proceedings in court may be necessary to settle any dispute before compensation may be determined: *Ex p London and South West Rly* (1869) 38 LJ Ch 527.

3 CPA 1965, s 5(3), Sch 2, para 1(1). Such surveyor shall be selected from Upper Tribunal members in accordance with Lands Tribunal Act 1949, s 3 (as amended by the Transfer of Functions (Lands Tribunal and Miscellaneous Amendments) Order 2009, SI 2009/1307) and his valuation must be preserved, in case the landowner requires it subsequently: CPA 1965, s 5(3), Sch 2, para 1(3). His expenses will be paid by the acquiring authority: CPA 1965, s 5(3). Sch 2, para 1(4) and there is scope for the absentee landowner to challenge the valuation in the Upper Tribunal: CPA 1965, s 5(3), Sch 1, para 4. The Upper Tribunal has discretion with regard to the costs of an unsuccessful challenge on this issue: CPA 1965, s 5(3), Sch 2, para 4(3). The Upper Tribunal will, if necessary, order payment of further compensation: CPA 1965, s 5(3), Sch 2, para 4.

4 CPA 1965, s 5(3), Sch 2, para 2(1). Descriptions of the land and the payments must be given, so far as the acquiring authority is able.

5 CPA 1965, 5(3), Sch 2, para 3. As to payment out of moneys generally, see paras **[1067]–[1070]**. Moneys in court may also be dealt with under the Administration of Justice Act 1982, s 38 (as to which, see paras **[1063]–[1066]**; the CPA 1965 refers to the Administration of Justice Act 1965, which was repealed by the Administration of Justice Act 1982, s 75). Where money has

remained unclaimed in court for more than 12 years, it may be reclaimed by an acquiring authority which is a local authority under the Local Government (Miscellaneous Provisions) Act 1976, s 29.

[1006]
Following payment into court on account of the compensation, the acquiring authority can execute a deed poll[1] vesting all the estates and interests in the land of the parties for whose use and in respect of which the compensation was paid into court by the acquiring authority[2]. Furthermore, the acquiring authority is entitled to immediate possession of the land as against those parties[3].

1 Provisions regarding execution of deed polls are explained in paras **[1050]–[1062]**.
2 CPA 1965, s 5(3), Sch 2, para 2(2), (3).
3 CPA 1965, s 5(3), Sch 2, para 2(3).

D Conveyance

1 Form

[1007]
Once compensation has been finally agreed or determined and the interests to be acquired are known, any form of conveyance by deed may be agreed between the parties[1]. There are prescribed forms of conveyance in the CPA 1965[2], but, in practice, these are rarely used. Special provision is made where a vendor is under a legal disability which would otherwise prevent him being a party to any conveyance of title[3].

1 The normal covenants for title are usually given. As to implied covenants for title, see the Law of Property (Miscellaneous Provisions) Act 1994, s 1–13. A detailed explanation in this regard is outside the scope of this work. As to proceeding by agreement generally, see **Division B, Chapter 3**.
2 CPA 1965, s 23(6), Sch 5. The prescribed forms of conveyance are similar to those in the LCCA 1845 (as amended), s 81, Schs A, B. The prescribed forms of conveyance do not include any covenants for title.
3 See paras **[1008]–[1021]**.

2 Vendor under a disability

[1008]
Statutory provision is made to prevent the compulsory acquisition of title being impeded by any legal disability on the part of the vendor[1]. Notwithstanding any disability or incapacity which might otherwise prevent a conveyance, persons with an interest in any land which the acquiring authority require are authorised to sell or convey or release such land and enter into all agreements necessary for that purpose[2]. Thus:

(*a*) lessees are released from:
   (i) covenants against assignment, and
   (ii) any subsequent breach of covenant which they are no longer able to perform[3];

(*b*) corporations, tenants in tail or for life, trustees for charitable or other purposes and/or persons entitled to rents and profits from any land[4] are entitled to dispose of their interests[5];

(*c*) any person (with an interest greater than as lessee) may dispose of his interest not only on behalf of himself and any successors in title, but also on behalf of every person entitled in reversion, remainder or expectancy after him[6];

(*d*) trustees for a beneficiary under any disability may dispose of an interest in land as if there were no disability on the beneficiary's part[7]; and

(*e*) the powers conferred by the CPA 1965:

(i) with regard to the release of land from or agreeing to the apportionment of any rentcharge or incumbrance, or

(ii) on any lord of the manor,

may be exercised, regardless of legal disability[8].

1 CPA 1965, s 2, Sch 1. Similar provision exists in the LCCA 1845 (as amended), ss 7–9, in relation to acquisitions authorised by a special Act to which the LCCA 1845 (as amended) applies.

2 CPA 1965, s 2, Sch 1, para 2(1). These provisions take effect, subject to the Law of Property Act 1925, s 42(7), which provides that, where possible, compulsory acquisition of title should not be made by means of payment into court, unless the acquiring authority so elects: CPA 1965, Sch 1, para 1(1).

3 *Slipper v Tottenham and Hampstead Junction Rly Co* (1867) LR 4 Eq 112; *Baily v De Crespigny* (1869) LR 4 QB 180.

4 CPA 1965, s 2, Sch 1, para 2(2).

5 CPA 1965, s 2, Sch 1, para 2(1).

6 CPA 1965, s 2, Sch 1, para 2(3).

7 CPA 1965, s 2, Sch 1, para 2(4).

8 CPA 1965, s 2, Sch 1, para 3. As to powers regarding rentcharges, see paras **[1044]–[1046]**. As to powers exercisable by the lord of the manor, see para **[1607]**.

[1009]

Persons under a disability[1] whose only power of disposal is by virtue of the CPA 1965[2] are entitled to have the compensation due to them:

(*a*) assessed by two surveyors nominated by the acquiring authority and vendor (or, in default of agreement, the Upper Tribunal) or a single surveyor appointed by two justices of the peace[3]; and

(*b*) paid into court for the benefit of those entitled to it, until applied in accordance with the provisions of the CPA 1965, Sch 1[4].

1 For the purposes of the CPA 1965, persons with a legal disability do not include infants, married women, lunatics or defectives: CPA 1965, s 2, Sch 1, para 1(2)(*a*). However, the provisions of the CPA 1965, Sch 1, do not have effect in relation to patients covered by the Mental Health Act 1959, s 104 or the Mental Health Act 1983, s 98: CPA 1965, s 2, Sch 1, para 1(2)(*b*).

2 Ie by virtue of the CPA 1965, s 2, Sch 1.

3 CPA 1965, s 2, Sch 1, para 4(1), (2). *Peters v Lewes and East Grinstead Rly Co* (1881) 18 Ch D 429 held that a trustee of the beneficiary to compensation could not lawfully act as surveyor for these purposes.

4 Where compensation due is quantified as between £20 and £200, it may instead be paid to trustees approved by the acquiring authority; where compensation due is quantified at under £20, it may be paid directly to the person entitled to the rents and profits of the land in respect of which it is payable: CPA 1965, s 2, Sch 1, paras 7, 8. Otherwise, provision is made for the application of any moneys paid in court both where the vendor has no power otherwise to dispose of his interest (CPA 1965, s 2, Sch 1, para 6) and where the vendor is not entitled to dispose of the land absolutely for his own benefit (CPA 1965, s 2, Sch 1, para 9).

[1010]–[1020]
When compensation has been finally determined and paid into court, the landowner (regardless of any disability) must, when required by the acquiring authority, duly convey the land or interest in it[1]. In case of default, the acquiring authority may execute a deed poll[2] vesting the land in itself, following which, it then becomes the legal owner of the relevant interest.

1 CPA 1965, s 2, Sch 1, para 10.
2 CPA 1965, s 2, Sch 1, para 10(2). Provisions regarding deed polls are explained in paras **[1050]–[1062]**.

[1021]
In practice, most persons under a legal disability are able to convey land otherwise than by virtue of the above provisions, which are, therefore, not frequently used. For example, disposals can proceed by agreement with trustees for sale[1], or under the Settled Land Act 1925, or by personal representatives[2]. In such cases, the compulsory acquisition of title is possible without payment of money into court under the provisions of the CPA 1965 and, unless the acquiring authority elects otherwise, these provisions must not be invoked[3].

1 Law of Property Act 1925, s 2.
2 Administration of Estates Act 1925, s 2.
3 CPA 1965, s 2, Sch 1, para 1(1).

3 Deed poll

[1022]
Where the vendor refuses to enter into a conveyance or is unable to make out title, the acquiring authority is entitled to pay the agreed or determined compensation into court and execute a deed poll vesting title to the land in itself. The procedure relating to deed polls[1] is explained in paras **[1050]–[1062]**.

1 CPA 1965, s 9.

E Costs

1 Costs of conveyance

[1023]
The costs of all conveyances of land subject to compulsory purchase[1] must be paid by the acquiring authority[2]. Recoverable costs include all charges and expenses incurred by the acquiring authority or vendor in relation to proving title, any necessary conveyances and assurances, and all other reasonable expenses incidental to investigating, deducing and evidencing title[3]. Where the parties fail to agree such costs, either one may request that they are settled by a taxing master of the Supreme Court[4]. The costs of any taxation shall be borne by the acquiring authority except where one-sixth of the costs claimed is disallowed, in which case the acquiring authority may recover its own costs with respect to the taxation[5].

1 This principle extends to compulsory acquisition completed by agreement (as to which, see **Division B, Chapter 3**). However, the principle may be varied by agreement. Where a sale is completed by agreement, but prior to confirmation of the relevant compulsory purchase order or special Act, this principle does not apply: *Catling v Great Northern Rly Co* (1869) 18 WR 121.
2 CPA 1965, s 23(1). Similar provision is made in the LCCA 1845 (as amended), s 82, in respect of the acquisition of land authorised by a special Act to which the LCCA 1845 (as amended) applies. The landowner does not have a lien in respect of such conveyancing costs over any moneys paid into court as security for compensation, unless the performance bond makes special reference to these and a separate action will have to be brought for their recovery: *Re London and South Western Railway Extension Act, ex p Stevens* (1848) 2 Ph 772; *Neath and Brecon Rly Co* (1874) 9 Ch App 263.
3 The types of recoverable expenditure are listed in detail in the CPA 1965, s 23(2). Such costs also include obtaining letters of administration: *Re Liverpool Improvement Act* (1868) LR 5 Eq 282; the necessary costs of appointing someone to convey: *Re Lowry's Will* (1872) LR 15 Eq 78; and the costs of enrolment of any conveyance: *Ex p Governors of Christ's Hospital* (1864) 12 WR 669.
4 CPA 1965, s 23(3) and (4). Such an order cannot be obtained after payment of costs has already been made; *Re South Eastern Rly Co, ex p Somerville* (1883) 23 Ch D 167. Any order by a taxing master can be appealed against in the courts.
5 CPA 1965, s 23(5). Similar provision is made in the LCCA 1845 (as amended), s 83, in respect of any acquisition of land authorised by a special Act to which the LCCA 1845 (as amended) applies.

2 Professional fees in relation to negotiations

[1024]–[1025]

Expenses incurred by a landowner on obtaining professional advice in preparing and negotiating a claim for compensation before any reference is made to the Upper Tribunal can in certain circumstances be claimed as part of the compensation payable for disturbance[1]. In *LCC v Tobin*[2], the Court of Appeal held that reasonable costs incurred in preparing a claim for compensation could be included in the claim and that such costs should not be treated as part of the costs of the reference to the Upper Tribunal. The costs of obtaining a certificate of alternative development may be recoverable as part of the compensation[3]. Interest accrues on those costs which form part of any compensation for disturbance[4].

1 See **Division E, Chapter 6.**
2 [1959] 1 WLR 354. Applied in *Lee v Minister of Transport* [1966] 1 QB 111 (Court of Appeal). Also applied in *Radnor Trust Ltd v Central Electricity Generating Board* (1961) 12 P&CR 111 (Lands Tribunal). In *Webb v Stockport Corpn* (1962) 13 P&CR 339, the Lands Tribunal restricted such costs to those incurred after the notice to treat. As to costs incurred in connection with a purchase notice served under the Town and Country Planning Act 1990 (TCPA 1990), see *Watkin v Widnes Borough Council* (1962) 13 P&CR 363.
3 *LCA 1961, s 17(9A) (reversing Hull and Humber Investment Co v Hull Corpn* [1965] 2 QB 145). As to certificates of alternative development, see **Division E**, paras **[809]–[828]**.
4 See **Division E**.

3 Stamp duty

[1026]

Stamp duty is payable on the conveyance of any land acquired compulsorily, calculated by reference to the total amount of compensation payable (including that in relation to severance and any injurious affection to the claimant's retained land[1]). As disturbance may form part of the compensation, it too must be stamped[2]. The instrument effecting the disposal must be produced to the Inland Revenue Commissioners by the acquiring authority within 30 days of its execution[3]. Within three months of completion of the purchase, the acquiring authority must also produce the duly stamped instrument to the Commissioners. Any deed poll executed under the CPA 1965 must be stamped as if it were a conveyance[4].

1 The Inland Revenue have not been challenged on this practice, although there is no direct authority for this. By analogy, the case of *Glenrothes Development Corpn v IRC* [1994] STC 74 held that stamp duty was payable on the total consideration for sale, which, in that case, included VAT.
2 *IRC v Glasgow and South Western Rly Co* (1887) 12 App Cas 315.
3 Finance Act 1931, s 28.
4 CPA 1965, s 28(2). As to provisions regarding deed polls, see paras **[1050]–[1062]**.

[1027]
Where the acquiring authority has used the general vesting declaration procedure and compensation has been assessed, stamp duty is payable in respect of the total compensation payable to each owner, on the basis that there has been a separate transaction between the acquiring authority and each owner for the purposes of the Finance Act 1999[1]. Since a general vesting declaration has the effect of a sale, the declaration itself must be produced under the Finance Act 1931, s 28, even where the compensation has not been determined. Where compensation has not yet been determined, stamp duty is payable calculated by reference to the market value immediately prior to execution of the general vesting declaration of the estate or interest which has been so vested[2], notwithstanding that the compensation finally payable may differ.

1 Finance Act 1999, s 112(3) and Sch 13, para 1.
2 Finance Act 1994, s 242.

4 Costs in respect of money paid into court

[1028]
The High Court may order the acquiring authority to pay the costs associated with paying money into court, except where a payment into Court has been made as a result of any wilful refusal on the landowner's part to accept compensation or convey title or any wilful neglect to make out title[1]. The procedure for payments into court is explained in paras **[1063]–[1066]**.

1 CPA 1965, s 26. This provision is rarely used nowadays, as it is not often necessary to make a payment into court. In *Re Jones and Cardiganshire County Council* (1913) 57 Sol Jo 374, it was held that a vendor who had refused to convey property, on account of counsel's advice that the compulsory purchase order might be bad, had wilfully refused for these purposes.

F Mortgages, rentcharges and leases

1 Mortgages

[1029]
Both mortgagor and mortgagee are entitled to notice to treat[1]. The acquiring authority will often treat with the mortgagor for the full value of land and

leave him to pay off or otherwise discharge the mortgage out of the purchase money[2]. If the acquiring authority does proceed in this way, however, it should ensure that the mortgagee's interests are adequately provided for by the mortgagor, or it may find itself restrained from carrying out its purpose on the land until the mortgage is discharged.

1 *Cooke v LCC* [1911] 1 Ch 604. See paras **[306]**ff.
2 The provisions in the CPA 1965, s 14 are optional, but proceeding outside the scope of this provision with the mortgagor alone will be difficult, unless the mortgagor and mortgagee are co-operative. Standard conveyancing practice is outside the scope of this text.

[1030]–[1040]

Alternatively, the acquiring authority may proceed to purchase or redeem the interest of the mortgagee directly[1] by either:

(*a*) immediately tendering or paying to the mortgagee the principal and interest due on the mortgage, together with the mortgagees' costs and charges[2] (if any) plus six months' additional interest on the principal[3]; or
(*b*) giving six months' written notice to the mortgagee that it will pay all the principal plus interest due on the principal, and costs and charges (if any)[4].

1 CPA 1965, s 14. Similar provision is made in the LCCA 1845 (as amended), s 108, in relation to the acquisition of land authorised by the LCCA 1845 (as amended). The CPA 1965, s 14 applies, regardless of whether or not the mortgagee is in possession or is a trustee or whether the mortgage includes land outside the compulsory purchase order or whether the acquiring authority has previously purchased the equity of redemption: CPA 1965, s 14(7).
2 Costs may include reinvestment costs and/or compensation in respect of any lost or reduced interest, which costs may be taxed by the court or determined by the Upper Tribunal respectively: CPA 1965, s 17. Where compensation is paid off before the stipulated time under the CPA 1965, ss 14–16, then any such costs recoverable shall be taxed by the court or determined by the Upper Tribunal in the circumstances described in s 17. Similar provision exists in the LCCA 1845 (as amended), s 114, in relation to acquisitions authorised by a special Act to which the LCCA 1845 (as amended) applies.
3 CPA 1965, s 14(2).
4 CPA 1965, s 14(3).

[1041]

In either case, upon payment of the moneys due, the mortgagee must immediately convey or release his interest in the land to the acquiring authority[1]. In the event of failure to do so or failure to make out good title to the mortgagee's interest, the acquiring authority may pay the moneys due into court[2] and execute a deed poll[3] vesting the mortgagee's interest in itself[4].

1 CPA 1965, s 14(2), (3). Where the acquiring authority has given written notice under s 14(3), the interest maybe acquired, prior to the expiry of the six-month period, where the acquiring authority pays or tenders the moneys due or the person entitled to the equity of redemption has given six months' notice of his intention to redeem, which notice has expired: CPA 1965, s 14(3).
2 CPA 1965, s 14(4). As to payments into court generally, see paras **[1063]–[1080]**.
3 CPA 1965, s 14(5). Similar provision is found in the LCCA 1845 (as amended), s 109, in respect of acquisitions authorised by a special Act to which the LCCA 1845 (as amended) applies. As to execution of deed polls under the CPA 1965, s 9(3), see paras **[1050]–[1062]**.
4 CPA 1965, s 14(6).

[1042]

The CPA 1965, s 15 applies where the compensation in respect of any land to be compulsorily acquired is insufficient to clear the mortgage principal, plus interest and costs. The mortgagee and mortgagor, on the one part, and the acquiring authority, on the other part, must either agree the amount actually payable to the mortgagee or, in default of agreement, refer the question to the Upper Tribunal[1]. When paid, this agreed sum will serve to release the mortgagee's interest in the land to enable the acquiring authority to take the unencumbered title[2]; it will not, however, release the mortgagor from any other bond, covenant or obligation to the mortgagee (other than the right to possession) which may remain outstanding[3].

1 CPA 1965, s 15(1). The acquiring authority is bound to pay the mortgagee's costs under the CPA 1965, s 17 (as to which, see para **[1030]**, fn 2).
2 On payment of such sum, the mortgagee shall convey or release the interest in the land to the acquiring authority: CPA 1965, s 15(3). The acquiring authority may pay moneys into court and execute a deed poll vesting title in itself where the mortgagee fails to do so or fails to make good title: CPA 1965, s 15(3), (4); such payment (whether to the mortgagee or into court) shall be accepted by the mortgagee in full satisfaction of the mortgage: CPA 1965, s 15(6). Similar provision is made in the LCCA 1845 (as amended), ss 110 and 111; in respect of acquisitions authorised by special Act which the LCCA 1845 (as amended) applies.
3 CPA 1965, s 15(7).

[1043]
Where the acquiring authority require part only of any land subject to a mortgage, but the mortgagee considers that the remaining land will not be adequate security for the money charged thereon or is not willing to release part[1], the value of the part to be acquired and any compensation payable for severance must either be agreed between the mortgagor and mortgagee, on the one part, and the acquiring authority, on the other or, in the absence of agreement, determined by the Upper Tribunal. When this sum has been paid to the mortgagee, the mortgage over the part to be acquired is to be conveyed or released to the acquiring authority[2] and a memorandum to this effect endorsed on the mortgage deed[3]. Whilst this exercise will release the part sought by the acquiring authority from the mortgage, the mortgagee will retain his original powers and remedies under the mortgage in relation to the remaining land[4].

1 CPA 1965, s 16. Similar provision is found in the LCCA 1845 (as amended), ss 112, 113, in respect of acquisitions of land authorised by special Act to which the LCCA 1845 (as amended) applies. The CPA 1965, s 16 only applies where the part required is of less value than the principal, plus interest and costs secured thereon. If this is not the case, then the CPA 1965, s 15 applies (as to which, see above).
2 CPA 1965, s 16(2), (3). Failure to release or convey the mortgage or a failure to make out good title will enable the acquiring authority, upon making an appropriate payment into court, to execute a deed poll vesting title of the mortgagee's interest in itself: CPA 1965, s 16(5). As to deed polls, see paras **[1050]–[1062]**. As to payments into court, see paras **[1063]–[1080]**. The sum payable shall include the mortgagees costs in accordance with the CPA 1965, s 17 (as to which, see para **[1030]**, fn 2).
3 CPA 1965, s 16(4).
4 CPA 1965, s 16(6).

2 Rentcharges

[1044]
Where the acquiring authority is unable to agree the compensation payable to any person entitled to a rentcharge[1], in order to secure its release, the

Upper Tribunal must determine the sum due[2] and, on payment or tender of such sum, the owner must release the rentcharge. In the event of failure to do so or failure to make out good title, the acquiring authority may pay the due sum into court and execute a deed poll which extinguishes the rentcharge[3].

1 'Rentcharge' includes any other payment or incumbrance charged on the land not provided for in the foregoing provisions of the CPA 1965: CPA 1965, s 18(6).
2 CPA 1965, s 18(1). Similar provision exists in the LCCA 1845 (as amended), ss 115–118, in respect of acquisitions of land authorised by a special Act to which the LCCA 1845 (as amended) applies.
3 CPA 1965, s 18(3). As to deed polls executed under the CPA 1965, s 9(3), see paras **[1050]–[1062]**. As to payments into court, see paras **[1063]–[1080]**.

[1045]
Where the acquiring authority require part only of any land comprised in a rentcharge, , in the absence of agreement between the person entitled to the rentcharge and the landowner, on the one part, and the acquiring authority, on the other, the apportionment of the rentcharge is to be determined by the Upper Tribunal. Furthermore, if the remaining land subject to the rentcharge is sufficient security in that regard, the person entitled to the rentcharge may, with the consent of the owner of that part of the remaining land, agree to release the rentcharge from part, on condition that the remaining land becomes subject to the whole of the rentcharge[1]. In these circumstances, the owner of the rentcharge will enjoy his original rights under the rentcharge in relation to the remaining land[2]. The acquiring authority will endorse a memorandum of release, at its own expense, on the deed creating or transferring the rentcharge, if so requested[3].

1 CPA 1965, s 18(2).
2 CPA 1965, s 18(4). If the person entitled to the rentcharge fails to release it upon tender of compensation, the acquiring authority can pay the sum into court and execute a deed poll in its favour: CPA 1965, s 18(3).
3 CPA 1965, s 18(5). This memorandum shall be rebuttable evidence of the facts to which it refers.

[1046]
Where the compulsory acquisition of land is made by general vesting declaration[1] and the acquiring authority requires part only of land subject to a rentcharge, similar provision is made for the apportionment of the rentcharge between the part required and the residue, so that the rentcharge can be released from the part required on vesting[2].

1 CP(VD)A 1981. See paras **[342]–[361]**.
2 CP(VD)A 1981, s 12, Sch 1, para 11. See paras **[342]–[361]** generally.

3 Apportionment of rent under leases

[1047]
The acquiring authority must treat directly with any leaseholder[1] to acquire its interest[2]. Where part only of the land comprised in a leasehold interest is required, the rent payable in respect of that interest will be apportioned between the part required and the residue by agreement between the lessor and lessee, on the one part, and the acquiring authority, on the other (or, in

default of agreement, by the Upper Tribunal)[3]. After such apportionment, the lessee will only be liable for the apportioned rent in respect of the part not required by the acquiring authority[4], and the lessor will retain all his original rights and remedies vis-à-vis the lessee in respect of the retained part, except as to amount of rent payable[5]. The lessee is entitled to compensation in respect of the severance of his tenancy[6]. Costs in respect of apportionment of rent under leases are recoverable from the acquiring authority[7]. These provisions are also applied where part of land subject to a lease is comprised in a general vesting declaration[8].

1 Special provision is made in respect of minor tenants under the CPA 1965, s 20 (as to which, see para **[1321]–[1325]**).
2 See paras **[301]–[341]** generally, regarding notices to treat.
3 CPA 1965, s 19(1), (2). Similar provision is made in the LCCA 1845 (as amended), s 119, 120, in respect of acquisitions authorised by a special Act to which the LCCA 1845 (as amended) applies.
4 CPA 1965, s 19(3).
5 CPA 1965, s 19(4).
6 CPA 1965, s 19(5).
7 *Re London, Brighton and South Coast Rly Co, ex p Flower* (1866) 1 Ch App 599.
8 CP(VD)A 1981, s 12, Sch 1, para 12. See paras **[342]–[361]** generally.

G The reluctant vendor or acquiring authority

1 Specific performance

[1048]
Service of notice to treat creates a relationship analogous to vendor and purchaser which becomes unconditional when the compensation has been agreed or determined. The parties then become vendor and purchaser in an unconditional contract for sale and either party may apply to the court for specific performance[1]. Both parties have the right to refer the issue of compensation to the Upper Tribunal for determination[2].

1 As to service of notice to treat under the CPA 1965, s 5, see paras **[301]–[341]**. Where the CP(VD)A 1981 applies (as to which, see paras **[342]–[361]**) title vests in the acquiring authority automatically on the vesting date, and the provisions regarding specific performance are, accordingly, of no relevance.
2 CPA 1965, s 6. See para **[1004]**.

[1049]
Specific performance will only be granted where the vendor can prove good title[1]. Where there is no dispute as to title, the vendor can compel the conveyance/assignment of his interest to the acquiring authority, regardless of the fact that he has already received the compensation, and the acquiring authority cannot refuse to take a conveyance simply to avoid liability for the conveyancing costs[2]. Nor, where there has been part performance, can the acquiring authority refuse to proceed on grounds that it had no authority to enter into an agreement for sale[3]. An acquiring authority must be prepared to execute a conveyance or take an assignment of a lease containing the usual covenants[4]. Any lessee will retain liability for breaches of covenant under the lease, prior to its assignment to the acquiring authority[5]. Generally, interest on the purchase price is payable from the date possession is taken[6].

1 *Wells v Chelmsford Local Board of Health* (1880) 15 Ch D 108.
2 *Re Cary-Elwes Contract* [1906] 2 Ch 143.
3 *Wilson v West Hartlepool Harbour and Rly Co* (1865) 34 LJ Ch 241.
4 *Harding v Metropolitan Rly Co* (1872) 7 Ch App 154.
5 *Mills v East London Union* (1872) LR 8 CP 79.
6 *Inglewood Pulp & Paper Co Ltd v New Brunswick Electric Power Commission* [1928] AC 492 held that this rule was subject to any contrary provision in the relevant statute. See also *Re Piggot and Great Western Rly Co* (1881) 18 Ch D 146. In this case, where the owner remained in possession until the acquiring authority sought to acquire title, interest was only payable from the date title was made out, notwithstanding that the compensation was determined at an earlier date.

2 Deed poll

[1050]–[1060]
There is a statutory alternative to the remedy of specific performance available where the vendor cannot or will not release his interest[1]. Where the owner of any interest, on tender of compensation awarded or agreed in respect of any compulsory acquisition, fails or refuses to accept it or neglects or fails to make out satisfactory title[2], or refuses to convey or release his interest, the acquiring authority may pay the compensation into court[3] and execute a deed poll containing a description of the land in respect of which payment into court was made and declaring the circumstances under which and the names of the parties to whose credit the payment into court was made4[5]. Moneys paid into court may be invested and distributed on application to the court[5]. The deed poll must be made under the acquiring authority's official or common seal and must be stamped as if it were a conveyance[6]. On execution of the deed poll, all the estates and interests in the land of the parties vest absolutely in the acquiring authority[7]. The acquiring authority is then entitled, as against such persons, to immediate possession of the land[8].

1 CPA 1965, s 9.
2 The owner must be given an opportunity to make out good title: *Doe d Hutchinson v Manchester, Bury and Rosendale Rly Co* (1845) 15 LJ Ex 208. Some vendors do not have capacity to enter into a sale and failure to conclude a purchase in such a case is not a wilful refusal to convey, and the party failing to convey should be regarded as under a disability: *Re Leeds Grammar School* [1901] 1 Ch 228. Special provision is made in the CPA 1965, s 2, Sch 1 (as to which, see paras **[1008]–[1021]**). Where the owner cannot be found, the acquiring authority should proceed under the CPA 1965, s 5(3), Sch 2 (as to which, see paras **[1005]–[1006]**).
3 CPA 1965, s 9(1). Costs consequences in respect of payments into court are dealt with under the CPA 1965, s 26 (as to which, see para **[1028]**).
4 CPA 1965, s 9(3). Similar provision exists in the LCCA 1845 (as amended), ss 76, 77 in respect of acquisitions authorised by a special Act incorporating the LCCA 1845 (as amended). The monies to be paid into court pursuant to LCCA 1845, s 76 do not include the interest payable on the compensation (*Rhondda Cynon Taff County Borough Council v Watkins* [2001] All ER (D) 131 (Dec); on appeal [2003] EWCA Civ 129, [2003] 1 WLR 1864). The provisions of the CPA 1965 as to execution of deed polls take effect, subject to the Law of Property Act 1925, s 7(4), under which any power of disposing of a legal estate by a person who is not the estate owner is, when practicable, to be exercised on behalf of the estate owner: CPA 1965, s 28(3).
5 CPA 1965, s 9(5). Moneys which are invested shall be dealt with under the Administration of Justice Act 1982, s 32 (as to which, see paras **[1067]–[1080]**). Where moneys paid into court exceed the sum properly payable in respect of an interest, the acquiring authority only may recover the excess in respect of that interest: *Re County of London (Devon Road, Poplar) Housing Confirmation Order 1945* (1955) 6 P&CR 133.
6 CPA 1965, s 28(1), (2). See paras **[1026]–[1027]**.

7 See *Rhondda Cynon Taff Borough Council v Watkins* [2003] EWCA Civ 129, [2003] 1 WLR 1864. The effect of the LCCA 1845, s 77 is to vest in the acquiring authority *whatever* estates and interests on land the party being compensated had at the time immediately before the deed poll. This included, in the *Watkins* case, a possessory title acquired by the original landowner against the acquiring authority.
8 CPA 1965, s 9(4).

[1061]
The deed poll can only vest the title belonging to any person, in respect of whom money was paid into court, and no more[1]. It confers no right of possession as against third parties who have an interest in the land, but, in respect of which, no compensation was paid into court. A deed poll cannot vest title where the person purporting to sell it has none[2]. Any third party, whose interest is not included in the deed poll, will not be debarred from asserting his rights subsequently[3].

1 See *Douglass v London and North Western Rly Co* (1857) 3 K&J 173.
2 *Wells v Chelmsford Local Board of Health* (1880) 15 Ch D 108.
3 See, eg, *Gedye v Works and Public Buildings Comrs* [1891] 2 Ch 630; *Wells v Chelmsford Local Board of Health* (1880) 15 Ch D 108. See also *Ex p Winder* (1877) 6 Ch D 696, with regard to possessory title.

[1062]
When proceeding by general vesting declaration, title to the land in the vesting declaration vests automatically in the acquiring authority on the vesting date as if a deed poll had been executed[1].

1 CP(VD)A 1981, s 8(1). See paras **[342]–[361]** generally. The vesting declaration is effective against all persons with an interest in the land, except minor tenants and those upon whom a notice to treat has been served.

3 Payment of money into court

[1063]
Money may be paid into court in a number of circumstances, including as security for the payment of compensation[1], and where the landowner is unable or unwilling to convey his interest so that it is necessary to execute a deed poll to ensure title is transferred[2].

1 Where proceeding under the alternative method of entry specified in the CPA 1965, s 11(2), Sch 3 (as to which, see paras **[721]–[724]**).
2 Ie where payments are made into court in respect of persons under a disability (CPA 1965, s 2, Sch 1 (as to which, see paras **[1008]–[1021]**)), commoners (CPA 1965, s 21, Sch 4 (as to which, see para **[1607]**)), absent or untraceable owners (CPA 1965, s 5(3), Sch 2 (as to which, see paras **[1005]–[1006]**)), rentcharges (CPA 1965, s 18(3) (as to which, see paras **[1044]–[1046]**)), refusal of mortgagee to convey (CPA 1965, ss 14(4), 15(3), 16(5) (as to which, see paras **[1029]–[1043]**). As to the costs associated with a payment into court, see para [1028].

[1064]
Moneys paid into court under the provisions of the CPA 1965 are to be paid into the Supreme Court and such payments are governed by the Administration of Justice Act 1982, s 38[1]. Moneys must be paid into an account of a designated bank to the credit of the Accountant General of the Supreme Court. Where money is paid into court in respect of a refusal to

convey title, the moneys must be placed to the credit of the parties interested in the land, with a description of them given, so far as the acquiring authority is able to do so[2]. These provisions, whilst of considerable importance in former times, are rarely used nowadays, as it is unusual to have to make any payments into court; the legal disabilities which render such payments into court necessary are now largely removed[3] and it is possible, in any event, to enter onto land by means of notice to treat and notice of entry without having to pay money into court[4]. However, where payment into court is appropriate, the acquiring authority can be compelled to do so[5].

1 The CPA 1965, s 25 refers to the previous statutory provision, being the Administration of Justice Act 1965, s 4. Similar provision is made in the LCCA 1845 (as amended), ss 69, 74, 76, 79, 86, in respect of acquisitions authorised by a special Act to which the LCCA 1845 (as amended) applies.
2 CPA 1965, s 9(2) (as to which, see para **[1050]**).
3 See paras **[1008]–[1021]**.
4 See paras **[301]–[341]** and paras **[701]–[710]** generally.
5 *Barnett v Great Eastern Rly Co* (1868) 18 LT 408.

[1065]

Moneys paid into court remain impressed with the character of real estate[1], until paid out to the persons absolutely entitled to them upon application[2]. Payment out to a landowner will be made where, in the case of a deed poll having been executed, an interest in the land becomes an interest in compensation or, where money has been paid into court as security for compensation, the acquiring authority has failed to pay that compensation.

1 *Kelland v Fulford* (1877) 6 Ch D 491.
2 CPA 1965, s 25(3). See paras **[1067]–[1070]**.

[1066]

When money is paid into court[1] in respect of any lease or other estate in land which is less than the whole fee simple or any reversion dependant on such lease or estate, the High Court may, on the application of any person interested in that compensation, order that it be 'laid out, invested, accumulated and paid' in such manner as the court considers will give the persons interested in it the same benefit (or as near as possible) as they would otherwise have lawfully had from their interest[2]. This can properly include discharge of mortgages over other land[3], discharge of leasehold interests in other land owned by the claimant[4], repairs to other property[5], payment of an annuity[6] and payment of dividends[7]. Where money paid into court is invested, the acquiring authority may be ordered by the court to pay the costs of such investment or its reinvestment in the purchase of other land[8]. Whilst sometimes more than one application for investment of sums in court may be appropriate[9], usually, the costs of only one such application for reinvestment in land will be allowed, unless it appears to the court that there is benefit in investing in the purchase of more than one parcel of land at different times[10].

1 Indeed, where money ought to have been paid into court, but the acquiring authority has failed to do so, an order for investment of purchase moneys may be made: *Re London, Brighton and South Coast Rly Co, ex p Earl of Abergavenny* (1856) 4 WR 315.
2 CPA 1965, s 25(2). Similar provision is made in the Settled Land Act 1925, s 79, in relation to the purchase of interests less than the fee simple pursuant to that Act.
3 *Re Derby Municipal Estate* (1876) 3 Ch D 289.
4 *Manchester, Sheffield and Co Rly Co, ex p Sheffield Corpn* (1855) 21 Beav 162.

5 *Re Johnson's Settlements* (1869) LR 8 Eq 348.
6 *Re London, Brighton and South Coast Rly Co, ex p Wilkinson* (1849) 3 De G & Sm 633.
7 *Re Dean and Chaplain of Westminster, Re Hampstead Junction Rly Co* (1858) 26 Beav 214.
8 CPA 1965, s 26(2)(*b*). No order for costs in this regard will be made where the money was paid into court as a consequence of the landowner's wilful refusal to accept the purchase moneys or convey his interest or any wilful neglect to make out good title: CPA 1965, s 26(1). Costs which are recoverable are set out in the CPA 1965, s 26(3).
9 *Re Woolley's Trust; Re East and West India Docks and Birmingham Junction Railway Act* (1853) 17 Jur 850.
10 CPA 1965, s 26(4). In *Re Brandon's Estate* (1862) 2 Drew & Sm 162, the court held that the acquiring authority should bear the costs of more than one application to reinvest moneys in court, if there was good reason to do so.

4 Court powers as to distribution of money paid in

[1067]
Money held in court will be paid out upon the successful application of any claimant, according to the respective estates, titles or interests of that claimant[1] and, if before distribution, compensation has been invested under the Administration of Justice Act 1982, s 38[2], payment of any dividends or accumulation thereon may be ordered[3]. Where interest has accrued on the sum paid in, this will be paid out to a successful applicant[4]. The High Court may also order the payment by the acquiring authority of the costs which the claimant has incurred relating to the purchase of new land or the investment of the compensation paid into court or its reinvestment in the purchase of other land[5]; and the term 'costs', for these purposes, includes all reasonable charges and expenses incidental to those matters, and, in addition, the costs of obtaining various orders relating to these and other matters as are set out in the CPA1965, s 26(3)[6]. The High Court is not obliged to order the acquiring authority to pay such costs where money was paid into court as a result of a wilful refusal to accept compensation or convey title or any wilful neglect to make out good title[7].

1 See, eg, *Re County of London (Devons Road) Poplar* (1955) 6 P&CR 133. The CPA 1965 provides no mechanism for determining a claimant's interest and the court will instead use its own machinery to determine the interest of an applicant and the sum due: *Re Perks' Estate* (1853) 1 Sm & G 545.
2 The Administration of Justice Act 1982, s 38 deals with the mode in which money paid into the Supreme Court may be dealt with. See paras **[1063]–[1066]**.
3 Applications to the Court would be governed by the Civil Procedure Rules 1998, Rule 37 and Part 37 of the Practice Directions.
4 CPA 1965, s 25(3).
5 CPA 1965, s 26(2); similar provision exists in the LCCA 1845 (as amended), s 80 in respect of acquisitions authorised by a special Act to which the LCCA 1845 (as amended) applies.
6 Costs of only one reinvestment are usually allowed: CPA 1965, s 26(4) (as to which, see para **[1066]**). The acquiring authority may be ordered to pay the costs of appearance at any application for payment out to persons who no longer have an interest in the land *Ex p London and South Western Rly and Co* (1869) 38 LJ Ch 527, although costs incurred in obtaining a third party's consent to payment out are not necessarily recoverable: *London and South Western Rly Act 1855, ex p Phillips* (1862) 32 LJ Ch 102. As to costs between adverse litigants, see *Armitage v Askham Re London and North Western Rly Co* (1855) 1 Jur NS 227.
7 CPA 1965, s 26(1); 'wilful refusal' means a refusal or neglect without reason (in contrast to the situation in *Re Ryde Comrs, ex p Dashwood* (1856) 26 LJ Ch 229) or the imposition of an improper condition *Re Turner's Estate and the Metropolitan Rly Act 1860* (1861) 5 LT 524. A fair objection, even if it is untenable, will not be a wilful refusal: *Re Windsor, Staines and South Western Railway Act 1850* (1850) 12 Beav 522. See also *Re East India Docks and Birmingham Junction Railway Act, ex p Bradshaw* (1848) 16 Sim 174.

[1068]

In the absence of proof of title, persons in possession of the land (as the owners) and any persons in receipt of rents from any of the land (as being entitled to rents at the time of purchase) are deemed to be entitled to moneys paid into court in respect of such interests, unless the contrary is proved to the court[1]. An application must be made for payment out, and the court will use its own machinery to determine the interest of the party applying[2] and to apportion compensation payable[3]. The court may determine rival applications[4] or wait until the matter is settled elsewhere in other proceedings[5].

1 CPA 1965, s 25(3). There is similar provision in the LCCA 1845 (as amended), in respect of acquisitions authorised by a special Act to which the LCCA 1845 (as amended) applies. Entitlement extends not only to moneys paid in, but also to interest dividends and any annual proceeds from any investment of the moneys in court. In *Re Cook's Estate* (1863) 8 LT 759, the petitioners had possessory title to the land. Compensation was invested with dividends paid to the petitioners, without prejudice to any third party entitlement to the compensation. See *Re Sterry's Estate* (1855) 3 WR 561 as to possessory title.

2 As in *Bogg v Midland Rly Co* (1867) LR 4 Eq 310.

3 *Brandon v Brandon* (1842) 2 Drew & Sm 305. See also *Re Wood's Estate* (1870) LR 10 Eq 572; *Wootton's Estate* (1866) LR 1 Eq 589; *Askew v Woodhead* (1880) 14 Ch D 27; *Re Wilkes' Estate* (1880) 16 Ch D 597 (apportionment of purchase money between tenant for life and remainderman); *Re Robinson's Settlement Trusts* [1891] 3 Ch 129 (apportionment of income from mines); *Ex p The Bishop of London* (1860) 2 De GF & J 14 (apportionment of stamp duty between acquiring authorities).

4 *Re Stead's Mortgaged Estates* (1876) 2 Ch 713.

5 *Galliers v Metropolitan Rly Co* (1871) LR 11 Eq 410; *Cooper v Metropolitan Board of Works* (1883) 25 Ch D 472.

[1069]

A legal or equitable mortgagee may apply for payment out of the compensation due in respect of his mortgage and of arrears of interest of up to six years[1]. Persons may also apply who are entitled in respect of trade claims or loss of profits or goodwill[2] or who have established their title by other proceedings[3]. Once the acquiring authority has paid out compensation in respect of all proper claims, it may itself apply for payment out of any remaining money in court[4]. The court will order a refund of money to the acquiring authority where an excessive amount has been paid in[5]. Where moneys have sat in court for 12 years or more, an acquiring authority which is a local authority may apply to the court for payment out itself[6].

1 *Re Stead's Mortgaged Estates* (1876) 2 Ch D 713.

2 *Cooper v Metropolitan Board of Works* (1883) 25 Ch D 472.

3 *Galliers v Metropolitan Rly Co* (1871) LR 11 Eq 410.

4 *Cooper v Metropolitan Board of Works* (1883) 25 Ch D 472 at 480.

5 *Re County of London (Devons Road, Poplar) Housing Confirmation Order* (1995) 6 P&CR 133.

6 Local Government (Miscellaneous Provisions) Act 1976, s 29.

[1070]–[1080]

A person in possession by virtue of an interest less than fee simple is not entitled to the whole of the moneys paid in, even where the freehold or reversionary freehold owner may not be traced[1].

1 *Gedye v Works and Public Buildings Comrs* [1891] 2 Ch 630. The court has power to award costs (including all reasonable charges and expenses incidental to matters mentioned in the CPA 1965, s 26(3)) in respect of payment out of moneys paid into court.

H Advance payments of compensation

[1081]

The Land Compensation Act 1973 (LCA 1973), s 52 provides that, where an acquiring authority has taken possession of any land or created rights over that land[1], the acquiring authority , if so requested by a person entitled to the compensation, must make an advance payment on account of compensation payable by it in respect of that compulsory acquisition. Such a request may be made regardless of whether the compulsory purchase has been implemented under the CPA 1965 or by means of general vesting declaration under the CP(VD)A 1981[2].

1 LCA 1973, s 52(12). This applies where entry has been taken onto part of the land: LCA 1973, s 52(1A) and (1B).

2 The LCA 1973, s 52 applies simply where possession of land has been taken by the acquiring authority without reference to the procedure invoked.

[1082]

A request for these purposes must[1]:

(*a*) be in writing;
(*b*) give particulars of the claimant's interest in the land (so far as not already given in the notice to treat); and
(*c*) be accompanied by such other particulars as the acquiring authority may reasonably require to enable it to estimate the amount of compensation in respect of which the advance is to be made.

1 LCA 1973, s 52(2).

[1083]

The advance payment must:

(*a*) be 90% of either the amount of compensation agreed between the parties or the amount estimated by the acquiring authority[1];
(*b*) be made within three months from the date of the request; the request may be made prior to entry[2], but the advance payment is not payable unless entry has been taken ;
(*c*) be registered as a local land charge[3];
(*d*) be set off against any compensation payable to the claimant or any successor in title[4]; and
(*e*) carry interest from the date of entry until the date of payment calculated in accordance with the LCA 1961, s 32[5].

Interest on any unpaid balance of the estimated compensation will be topped up on each 12-month anniversary of the advance payment where it exceeds £1,000[6].

1 LCA 1973, s 52(3). The amount paid can be increased if it transpires that it is too low: LCA 1973, s 52(4A).

2 LCA 1973, s 52(4).

3 LCA 1973, s 52(8A).

4 LCA 1973, s 52(9).

5 LCA 1973, s 52A(1). The rate of interest is prescribed in SI 1995/2262, as amended by SI 2001/3649.

6 LCA 1973, s 52A(5).

[1084]
No advance payment may be made where the land is subject to a mortgage the principal of which exceeds the quantum of the advance. The advance payment will be reduced, accordingly, where the principal does not exceed that amount[1]. Payment of an advance under this section is without prejudice to final determination of compensation payable by either the Upper Tribunal or by agreement following negotiations and any excess paid may be recovered or any deficit topped up[2]. Any over or underpayment will carry interest[3]. Any delay in the final payment of compensation may only be compensated for by the payment of interest at the prescribed rate[4].These provisions apply where an acquiring authority, instead of taking possession, serves a notice in respect of land under the Housing Act 1985, s 583 (authorising the existing occupier to continue in occupation) as if possession had been taken on the date the notice was served[5].

1 LCA 1973, s 52(6). With effect from 31 October 2004, s 52(6) has been replaced by ss 52ZA, 52ZB and 52ZC, which make detailed provision for advance payments where land compulsorily acquired is subject to a mortgage: PCPA 2004, s 104 brought into force on 31 October 2004 by SI 2004/2593.
2 LCA 1973, ss 52(5), (9).
3 LCA 1973, ss 52(6), (10).
4 *Mallick v Liverpool City Council* [1999] 2 EGLR 2, CA.
5 LCA 1973, s 52(11).

I Transfer of title following general vesting declarations

[1085]
There is no need for any formal conveyance following execution of a general vesting declaration, as title vests automatically in the acquiring authority. The landowner is deemed to give the acquiring authority an acknowledgment for the production of title documents[1]. Compensation and interest are payable by the acquiring authority as if the acquiring authority had taken possession of the land under the CPA 1965 on the vesting date[2]. It appears to follow that risk in respect of damage or destruction to any property included in a general vesting declaration will pass to the acquiring authority on the vesting date.

1 CP(VD)A 1981, s 14.
2 CP(VD)A 1981, s 10. *Mahboob Hussain v Oldham MBC* (1981) 42 P&CR 388.

[1086]
The time limit within which any claims for disputed compensation can be referred to the Upper Tribunal is six years after the date when the claimant first knew, or could have been reasonably expected to know, of the vesting of his interest in the acquiring authority by virtue of CP(VD)A 1981[1]. Where there has been any overpayment of compensation, the acquiring authority may recover any surplus[2]. Any dispute regarding entitlement or apportionment of compensation are to be referred to the Upper Tribunal[3].

1 CP(VD)A 1981, s 10(3). The effect of this provision is to incorporate the Limitation Act 1980, Pt I into the CP(VD)A 1981. However, where there is a common understanding that compensation will be paid following negotiations without resort to the Upper Tribunal, the acquiring authority may be estopped from relying on the six-year limitation period: *Co-operative Wholesale Society Ltd v Chester le Street District Council* [1998] 3 EGLR 11, CA.

2 CP(VD)A 1981, s 11. Overpayment may arise where an incumbrance comes to light or it transpires the claimant was not entitled to interest in respect of which compensation was paid: CP(VD)A 1981, s 11(2), (3).
3 CP(VD)A 1981, s 11(4).

[1087]–[1100]
Where land has vested by virtue of a general vesting declaration, any person, who, in consequence, is relieved of any liability in respect of a rentcharge, rent payable under a tenancy or mortgage interest etc, but unwittingly continues to make payments in satisfaction or part satisfaction of such liability, shall be entitled to recovery of such overpayment from the appropriate payee[1].

1 CP(VD)A 1981, s 13.

J Adverse possession against an acquiring authority after notice to treat

[1101]–[1300]
In *Rhondda Cynon Taff Borough Council v Watkins*[1], following confirmation of a compulsory purchase order for open space purposes, the acquiring authority, having served notice to treat and notice of entry, took possession of the land in question. The next day, the former owner repossessed the land. The acquiring authority referred the question of compensation to the Lands Tribunal and, following determination of the compensation, the acquiring authority executed a deed poll purporting to transfer title to itself. It then commenced proceedings to obtain possession and the former owner served a defence which contended that: (*a*) he had been in possession of the land adverse to the acquiring authority for more than 12 years, and (*b*) the Council had abandoned the original purpose of the acquisition. The Court of Appeal held that: (*a*) the defendant was entitled to rely on the Limitation Act 1980 to establish adverse possession, and (*b*) he was entitled to raise the question as to the acquiring authority's change of purpose as a defence notwithstanding that the time limit for raising it as a claimant in judicial review proceedings was long past.

1 [2003] EWCA Civ 129, [2003] 1 WLR 1864.

Chapter 5

Special cases

Contents

A Leasehold interests

1 Introduction

[1301]
As a general rule, compulsory purchase procedure treats freehold and leasehold interests alike. Special provision is, however, made where a person has an interest no greater than as a tenant for a year or from year to year; this is explained in paras **[1321]–[1325]**. Apart from that, this Chapter merely summarises what is explained elsewhere and provides references to identify earlier parts of this division which are pertinent to leasehold interests.

2 Application of general rules to leasehold interests

Agreement

[1302]
The acquiring authority and lessee respectively can purchase and assign a leasehold interest by agreement[1]. Unless and until the acquiring authority acquires the reversionary freehold interest, it is bound by a covenant for quiet enjoyment, albeit that the freeholder's remedy for breach of such covenant is compensation, as opposed to damages[2].

1 The Compulsory Purchase Act 1965 (CPA 1965), s 3 enables an 'owner' of land to enter into agreements. An owner means any person having power to sell and convey the land to the acquiring authority: CPA 1965, s 1(6).

2 *Manchester, Sheffield and Lincolnshire Rly Co v Anderson* [1898] 2 Ch 394. See also *Piggott v Middlesex CC* [1909] 1 Ch 134, in which an acquiring authority, which took an assignment of a lease by agreement, was bound by covenants in favour of the landlord in relation to those parts of the leasehold interest not required for the purpose of the undertaking.

Notice to treat and notice of entry

[1303]
Where the acquiring authority proceeds by service of notice to treat[1], any lessee (including one holding under an agreement for lease in equity[2]) is

entitled to receive notice to treat[3], except where his interest is no greater than as tenant for a year or from year to year[4]. The notice to treat must be properly served both on the lessor and lessee; service on one, on behalf of the other, is not acceptable[5].

1 CPA 1965, s 5 (as to which, see paras **[301]–[341]**).
2 CPA 1965, s 1(3).
3 See para **[306]**.
4 See para **[307]**. The CPA 1965, s 20 makes special provision for such tenants (as to which, see paras **[1321]**ff).
5 *R v Great Northern Rly Co, ex p James Baxter* (1896) 2 QBD 151 (as to which, see paras **[310]–[321]**).

[1304]
Following service of notice to treat but prior to entry or determination of compensation payable, the relationship between freeholder and lessee continues broadly as normal. Rent must be paid and covenants in the lease observed[1]. Failure to do so may result in an action for breach of covenant. Any damage to the leasehold premises may reduce compensation payable to the leaseholder[2]. The burden of compensation on the acquiring authority cannot be increased by virtue of any dealings with the interests existing at the time of service of notice to treat[3], and any new lease created will be subject to the notice to treat[4]. A leasehold interest can be determined notwithstanding service of a notice to treat under the usual landlord and tenant relationship. Compensation payable to a residential tenant will not be reduced, nor the compensation to a freeholder increased, as a result of the tenant being rehoused pursuant to a statutory duty with vacant possession value thereby being created[5].

1 *Mills v East London Union* (1872) LR 8 CP 79. See also paras **[369]–[370]**.
2 See paras **[362]ff**.
3 *Holloway v Dover Corpn* [1960] 1 WLR 604. Where a lease is determined following service of notice to treat but before entry is taken or compensation determined, no compensation for compulsory acquisition is payable to the lessee. See also *Rogers v Kingston-upon-Hull Dock Co* (1864) 34 LJ Ch 165. Whilst the landlord could validly determine the lessees' interest prior to compulsory acquisition, the lessee retained a lien over compensation in respect of moneys he would have been entitled to under lease terms with respect to the unexpired residue of lease.
4 See paras **[362]ff**.
5 Land Compensation Act 1973 (LCA 1973), s 50. See paras **[369]–[370]** and *Paul v Newham London Borough Council* (1989) 61 P&CR 126.

[1305]
Where the lease contains a proviso for re-entry upon compulsory acquisition, service of a notice to treat may trigger the re-entry provision[1]. Such a proviso can, however, only be relied upon for its proper purpose and not, for example, simply to defeat the lessee's claim for compensation[2].

1 See, generally, the discussion in *Goodwin Foster Brown Ltd v Derby Corpn* [1934] 2 KB 23.
2 *Johnson v Edgware Rly Co* (1866) 35 Beav 480.

[1306]
Where part only of a house, building or manufactory or of a park or garden belonging to a house which is the subject of a leasehold interest is included in a notice to treat, the lessee can in certain circumstances require that the whole of his land is acquired under the CPA 1965, s 8[1] which is explained in paras **[381]–[411]**. If the lessee is successful, then the whole of his interest will

be acquired. However, if he is not successful or, where such an application has not been made, steps may be necessary to apportion the rent payable by the lessee in respect of the part remaining after the compulsory acquisition[2]. This is explained in para **[1047]**.

1 'Person' for the purposes of the CPA 1965, s 8 includes a lessee: *Pulling v London, Chatham and Dover Rly Co* (1864) 33 LJ Ch 505.
2 CPA 1965, s 19.

[1307]
Notice of entry must be served on every lessee[1] as explained in paras **[701]–[710]**.

1 CPA 1965, s 11(1).

Alternative procedure

[1308]
The alternative procedure for entry described in paras **[721]–[724]** applies to long leasehold interests as it does to freehold interests. Separate provision is made in respect of tenancies for a year or from year to year or less[1].

1 CPA 1965, s 20. See paras **[1321]–[1325]**.

General vesting declarations

[1309]
The provisions regarding general vesting declarations explained in paras **[342]–[361]** apply to long leasehold interests as they do to freehold interests; notice to treat is deemed to have been served[1] on all persons with an interest in land referred to in the general vesting declaration who would have been entitled to receive such a notice under the CPA 1965. On the vesting date, title vests in the acquiring authority, as does the right of entry against all occupiers and persons interested in the land specified in the vesting declaration, except in the case of occupation by virtue of a minor tenancy or a long tenancy about to expire[2]. In such a case, if possession is required immediately, notice to treat and at least 14 days' notice of entry must be given to such persons and the land will vest in the acquiring authority, subject to those interests[3]. Entry may then be made against those occupiers at the expiry of the notice period. Alternatively, possession may be taken at the date of determination of such lessee's interests, if earlier[4]. Where part only of the land subject to a leasehold interest is comprised in a vesting declaration, the lessee may, in some circumstances, require the acquisition of his whole interest[5]. Where unsuccessful or where such an application has not been made, steps may be taken to apportion the rent payable in respect of the part of the leasehold interest not compulsorily acquired[6]. A person, who, after the vesting of his leasehold interest in the acquiring authority, inadvertently continues to pay rent to his former landlord, can recover any overpayment from the appropriate person[7].

1 In accordance with the CPA 1965, s 5 (as to notices to treat, see paras **[301]–[341]**).
2 Compulsory Purchase (Vesting Declarations) Act 1981 (CP(VD)A 1981), ss 8(1), 9. See para **[361]**.

3 CP(VD)A 1981, s 9.
4 CP(VD)A 1981, s 9(3).
5 CP(VD)A 1981, s 12, Sch 1. See paras **[381]–[411]**.
6 CP(VD)A 1981, s 12, Sch 1, para 12.
7 CP(VD)A 1981, s 13.

Acquisition of leasehold only

[1310]–[1320]
The acquiring authority can acquire an existing leasehold interest only in any land, and not the freehold, or vice versa. It is for the acquiring authority to judge which interests it requires for its purposes[1]. However, the acquiring authority cannot, unless the authorising Act[2] specifically authorises it, create a new leasehold interest in land by compulsion where none currently exists; such an interest can only be acquired by agreement[3].

1 *Errington v Metropolitan District Rly Co* (1882) 19 Ch D 559.
2 See **B[466]–[468]**.
3 *Pinchin v London and Blackwall Rly Co* (1854) 5 De GM & G 851; *Ramsden v Manchester, South Junction and Altrincham Rly Co* (1848) 1 Exch 723. See para **[309]**.

3 Special provision for leasehold interests

Minor tenants

[1321]
Special provision is made[1] where any land which is the subject of compulsory purchase is in possession of a person having no greater interest in the land than as tenant for a year or from year to year. Unless proof to the contrary is produced, a claimant of compensation in respect of the unexpired residue of a lease will be presumed to be such a minor tenant[2].

1 CPA 1965, s 20. Similar provision is found in the Lands Clauses Consolidation Act 1845 (LCCA 1845) (as amended), ss 121, 122 in respect of acquisitions authorised by a special Act to which the LCCA 1845 (as amended) applies.
2 CPA 1965, s 20(5).

[1322]
A minor tenant is not entitled to receive notice to treat[1]; instead, where possession is required[2] before the expiry of its interest, the acquiring authority must request possession and tender compensation[3] in respect of:

(*a*) the unexpired term or interest[4] in land;
(*b*) any just allowance which ought to made by an incoming tenant;
(*c*) any loss or injury; and
(*d*) any loss sustained (if appropriate) by severance or injurious affection[5].

The minor tenant must then allow the acquiring authority to take possession. These rules apply to a tenancy which has less than a year to run at the date when possession is required, notwithstanding that, at the date of service of notice to treat, there was an unexpired residue of more than one year[6].

1 Where notice to treat is served on a minor tenant, then he will still be dealt with under the CPA 1965, s 20: *London Borough of Newham v Benjamin* [1968] 1 All ER 1195. Service of notice to

treat alone is not a request for possession for the purposes of the CPA 1965, s 20: *R v Stone* (1866) LR 1 QB 529.
2 A request for possession must be made; the fact that a property in which a minor tenant has an interest is included in a compulsory purchase order does not by itself trigger the right to compensation under the CPA 1965, s 20: *Frisby v Chingford Corpn* (1957) 8 P & CR 423.
3 CPA 1965, s 20(4). Compensation will be determined by the Lands Tribunal in default of agreement.
4 Unexpired term or interest is the period which would elapse between possession and expiry of the tenancy were a notice to quit served on the date of possession: *Greenwoods Tyre Services Ltd v Manchester Corpn* (1972) 23 P & CR 246.
5 CPA 1965, s 20(1), (2).
6 *R v Kennedy* [1893] 1 QB 533.

[1323]
These provisions operate without prejudice, inter alia, to the Landlord and Tenant Act 1954 and any lease terms, the implication being that, where the minor tenant's interest determines through effluxion of time or following service of notice to quit under other provisions, no compensation will be payable in respect of the compulsory acquisition as there is no interest to compulsorily acquire[1]. The acquiring authority can induce the appropriate freeholder to give notice to quit[2] or, where it has acquired the freehold, serve notice to quit itself. Compensation, however, may be payable in respect of the determination of the lease[3]. Where special powers to resume possession are reserved to the freeholder, the acquiring authority cannot exercise such a power after acquiring the reversion for the purpose of obtaining possession without payment of compensation[4], nor may the freeholder exercise such a power, where it is granted for a particular purpose only, in order to sell the unencumbered freehold to the acquiring authority[5].

1 *Syers v Metropolitan Board of Works* (1887) 36 LT 277.
2 As in *Ex p Nadin* (1848) 17 LJ Ch 421. In *Elmslie & Simpson Ltd v Aberdeen DC* [1994] 1 EGLR 33, a landlord which was induced by an acquiring authority to serve notice to quit on a tenant under the terms of the lease reduced a long tenancy to a tenancy for year to year for compensation purposes.
3 Ie under the provisions of the Landlord and Tenant Act 1954 or the lease.
4 *Fleming v Newport Rly* (1883) 8 App Cas 265.
5 *Johnson v Edgware & Co Rly Co* (1866) 35 Beav 480.

[1324]
As occupiers, minor tenants are entitled to notice of entry for survey purposes[1].

1 CPA 1965, s 11(3). See para **[726]**.

[1325]
Where the acquiring authority is proceeding by means of a general vesting declaration, special provision applies to land in which a minor tenancy or a long tenancy about to expire subsists[1].

1 As to which, see para **[361]**.

Apportionment of rent under leases

[1326]
Where part only of the land comprised within an unexpired lease is required by the acquiring authority, provision is made for apportionment of the rent

payable under the lease between the part required and the residue. Apart from recalculation of the rent payable, all other terms, conditions and covenants in a lease remain binding on the lessor and the lessee in respect of the residue. Compensation is be paid to those interested in the part compulsorily acquired[1]. Provisions in this regard are explained in para **[1047]**.

1 CPA 1965, s 19. See the CP(VD)A 1981, s 12, Sch 1, para 12, in respect of general vesting declarations.

Agricultural tenants

[1327]
A person occupying land as an agricultural tenant may object to severance of its agricultural holding[1] on grounds that the residue following the compulsory acquisition of part is not reasonably capable of being farmed by itself or with other land as a separate agricultural unit, so requiring the acquiring authority to take the whole or nothing. This is explained in para **[404]**.

1 LCA 1973, s 55.

[1328]
Where the acquiring authority is required to acquire the whole of an agricultural tenant's holding, but has not been authorised to acquire the corresponding landlord's interest in the same land as it lies outside the compulsory purchase order, the tenancy will be treated as terminated when the tenant gives up possession to the acquiring authority. Immediately upon such possession by the acquiring authority, the part interest outside the compulsory purchase order must be surrendered to the landlord. The landlord cannot take action against either the acquiring authority or tenant, but any rights and liabilities of the tenant arising as a result of the termination are assumed by the acquiring authority. Where there is an increase in the value of the part of the landlord's interest which lies within the compulsory purchase order by virtue of creation of vacant possession value, this must be deducted from any compensation due[1].

1 LCA 1973, s 56(3).

Agricultural land

[1329]
Where part only of any agricultural land is required, the owner can require the acquiring authority to take the whole of its interest in certain circumstances[1]. Where the acquiring authority is so required to acquire the whole of a leasehold interest in agricultural land[2], but not the corresponding interest of the lessor, it must offer to surrender the lease to the lessor on reasonable terms. In default of agreement, the Upper Tribunal will be asked to settle terms of surrender and, unless otherwise agreed, the lessor will be deemed to have accepted a surrender of the lease one month after the Upper Tribunal's determination[3].

1 LCA 1973, s 53 (as to which, see para **[403]**).
2 Meaning an interest greater than an interest for a year or from year to year: LCA 1973, s 53(1).
3 LCA 1973, s 54(6).

B Rentcharges

[1330]–[1340]
Where land subject to a rentcharge[1] is comprised within a compulsory purchase order, there is statutory provision to ensure the release of such land from the rentcharge upon compulsory acquisition[2]. Further, where part only of the land subject to the rentcharge is required, statutory provision is made for the apportionment of the rentcharge between the land required by the acquiring authority and the residue, and the release of the rentcharge over the part so required. The relevant provisions are fully explained in paras **[1044]–[1046]**. Where part only of a rentcharge is extinguished, the person entitled to the rentcharge will maintain the same rights and remedies over the remainder of the land subject to the rentcharge, as he had previously in relation to the whole.

1 'A rentcharge' is a right entitling the beneficiary to receive a periodic sum from the owner of the land. See **B[443]**. New rentcharges cannot (save in limited circumstances) now be created: Rentcharges Act 1977. 'Rentcharge', for these purposes, includes any other payment or encumbrance charged on the land, but not provided for elsewhere in the CPA 1965: CPA 1965, s 18(6). See also the CP(VD)A 1981, s 12, Sch 1, para 11(4).
2 CPA 1965, s 18. Similar provision exists in the LCCA 1845 (as amended), ss 115–118, in relation to acquisitions of land authorised by a special Act to which the LCCA 1845 (as amended) applies.

[1341]
Similar provision is made where the acquiring authority proceeds by general vesting declaration[1]. Where a rentcharge is extinguished (in part) following vesting of land, pursuant to a general vesting declaration, but the landowner has continued inadvertently to make payments pursuant to that rentcharge, such overpayments can be recovered as appropriate[2].

1 CP(VD)A 1981, s 12, Sch 1, para 11. General vesting declarations are executed, pursuant to the CP(VD)A 1981 (as to which, see paras **[342]–[361]**).
2 CP(VD)A 1981, s 13.

C Mortgages

1 Introduction

[1342]
Where land is subject to a mortgage, the mortgagor is able to treat directly with an acquiring authority with regard to the acquisition of its interest. The acquiring authority will not be able to take an unencumbered title to the property unless it has acquired the mortgagee's interest, in addition to the freehold and any other interests. The mortgagee's interest may be purchased or redeemed by agreement or, alternatively, pursuant to statutory provision in the CPA 1965.

2 Notice to treat and notice of entry

[1343]
Whilst not expressly included in the definition of 'owner' in the CPA 1965[1], a mortgagee (legal or equitable) is entitled to be served with a notice to treat[2]

where the acquiring authority proceeds under the CPA 1965[3]. The acquiring authority must treat with the mortgagee directly and formalities as to service of a notice to treat therefore apply to mortgagees as they do to freeholders[4]. A failure, however, to serve a notice to treat on a mortgagee not in possession will not necessarily be fatal to an acquiring authority which has gone into possession and it may be able to regularise its position by late service of notice to treat without vacating, so that lawful possession commenced 14 days thereafter[5] or by reliance upon CPA 1965, s 22[6].

1 CPA 1965, s 1(6); 'owner', for the purposes of the CPA 1965, means any person having power to sell and convey the land to the acquiring authority.
2 *Cooke v LCC* [1911] 1 Ch 604; *Martin v London, Chatham and Dover Rly* Co (1866) 1 Ch App 501.
3 Ie by service of notice to treat and notice of entry under the CPA 1965, ss 5, 11 (as to which, see paras **[301]–[341]** and paras **[701]–[710]**) or following the alternative method of entry specified in the CPA 1965, ss 11(2), Sch 3 (as to which, see paras **[721]–[724]**).
4 See paras **[301]–[341]**.
5 *Cohen v Haringey London Borough Council* (1980) 42 P&CR 6. See also *Cooke v LCC* [1911] 1 Ch 604. See paras **[743]–[745]**.
6 See para **[743]**.

[1344]
Notice of entry[1] must be served on a mortgagee in possession[2] and the provisions explained in paras **[701]–[710]** apply accordingly.

1 Under the CPA 1965, s 11(1) (as to which, see paras **[701]–[710]**).
2 A notice of entry must be served on every owner, lessee and occupier of land, and 'owner', for these purposes, includes a person other than a mortgagee not in possession who would have the power to sell and convey or release the land to the acquiring authority: Acquisition of Land Act 1981, s 7(1), as applied by the CPA 1965, s 11(1). See para **[704]**.

[1345]
Except where a mortgagee is in possession, in which case, entry may only be made following service of notice to treat and notice of entry, an acquiring authority usually proceeds vis-à-vis mortgagees as it would do in any standard conveyance by agreement. The landowner will be asked to:

(*a*) pay off the mortgagee's interest directly out of the compensation he receives from the acquiring authority; and
(*b*) obtain a discharge from the mortgagee.

The acquiring authority will then take a conveyance of the unencumbered fee simple. However, where such agreement cannot be reached or the compensation is inadequate to discharge the mortgage principal, statutory provision is made for the discharge of the mortgage in the manner set out below.

3 Special provision for land subject to mortgages

[1346]
The acquiring authority may redeem a mortgage directly by tendering or paying to the mortgagee the mortgage principal, plus six months' interest and costs and charges[1]. Where compensation in respect of any land subject to a mortgage is insufficient to clear the principal sum plus interest, costs and charges, provision is made for agreeing a compromise figure sufficient to

release the land to be compulsorily acquired from the mortgage and so enable the acquiring authority to take an unencumbered title[2]. This is explained in paras **[1029]–[1043]**. Any rights and remedies the mortgagee has in relation to the mortgagor under the provisions of the mortgage, other than the right to possession, will remain in force in respect of so much of the mortgage debt that has not been satisfied by the payment of compensation[3].

1 CPA 1965, s 14.
2 CPA 1965, s 15.
3 CPA 1965, s 15(7).

[1347]
Where the acquiring authority seek to acquire part only of any land subject to a mortgage, but the mortgagee does not consider that the part not required is sufficient security for the moneys charged in respect of the whole, provision is made for the agreement of compensation and release of the mortgage from the part of the land required by the acquiring authority[1]. The mortgagee will retain powers and remedies in relation to the remaining land and the mortgage terms. Where the mortgage deeds stipulates a penalty in respect of early repayment and the mortgage is discharged in accordance with the statutory provisions above[2], the costs recoverable by the mortgagee will include costs incidental to reinvestment of the principal sum (which costs may be taxed, if not agreed) and/or compensation in respect of any loss of interest upon such reinvestment (which costs may be determined by the Upper Tribunal in the absence of agreement)[3].

1 CPA 1965, s 16. Provision in this regard is explained in para **[1043]**.
2 Ie under the CPA 1965, s 14, 15, 16.
3 CPA 1965, s 17.

4 General vesting declarations

[1348]–[1600]
Where the acquiring authority chooses to proceed by general vesting declaration under the CP(VD)A 1981, a notice to treat is deemed to have been served on all those parties who would have been entitled to a notice to treat had the acquiring authority proceeded under the CPA 1965[1]. The acquiring authority acquires title and the right to enter against all those interested in the land, except minor tenants. Unencumbered title and the right of entry against any mortgagee vest in the acquiring authority and the mortgagees' rights are converted into a claim for compensation[2]. Where, after the vesting of the land, a mortgagee continues inadvertently to make payments in respect of any mortgage interest, these can be recovered as appropriate[3].

1 CP(VD)A 1981, s 7(1).
2 An acquiring authority which takes possession of land without treating with a mortgagee, in respect of the interest, may be restrained by injunction from remaining in possession until such interest had been properly dealt with: *Ranken v East and West India Docks and Birmingham Junction Rly* (1849) 12 Beav 298.
3 CP(VD)A 1981, s 13.

Chapter 6

Interests in land

Contents

A Introduction

[1601]
Land which has the benefit of any rights or easements over other land is known as a 'dominant tenement', whereas land which is burdened by such rights and easements is referred to as a 'servient tenement'. The dominant and servient tenements will not necessarily both be compulsorily acquired; an acquiring authority proceeding to exercise powers of compulsory purchase may:

(*a*) acquire land with the benefit of an existing easement or right over other land (ie the dominant tenement);
(*b*) use land acquired (ie the servient tenement) so as to interfere with an existing easement, restrictive covenant or other right over it; and/or
(*c*) if so authorised, create a new right or interest in the land, without acquiring the land itself.

[1602]
The interests in land which are capable of being compulsorily acquired are considered in **B[406]–[446]**. Paragraphs **[1603]–[1604]** and **[1605]–[1607]**, consider the practical implications for an acquiring authority seeking to acquire or interfere with the benefit of easements or rights in land, whereas paras **[1608]**ff considers the practical implications of acquiring new rights over land. These practical considerations are relevant, regardless of whether the acquiring authority chooses to proceed under the Compulsory Purchase Act 1965 (CPA 1965) or under the Compulsory Purchase (Vesting Declarations) Act 1981 (CP(VD)A 1981).

B Acquisition of land with the benefit of an existing easement or right over other land

[1603]
When an acquiring authority compulsorily purchases a dominant tenement, it automatically acquires the benefit of any easement or right over a servient tenement as would any other purchaser[1]. In these circumstances, the acquiring authority need not identify that easement or other right specifically in its notice to treat. Further, there is no requirement to serve any notice to treat on the owner of the servient tenement.

1 See **B[447]–[449]**.

[1604]
There is no general power to acquire an existing right or easement without acquisition of the dominant tenement[1], although some authorising Acts do make provision for the acquisition of the benefit of a right or interest in land alone, in which case, where proceeding under the CPA 1965, notice to treat must be served in respect of that right or interest and the procedure specified in paras **[301]–[341]** followed with any modifications set out in the authorising Act[2]. However, in practical terms, the acquisition of an existing easement or right may be of no value, unless the land with the benefit of that easement or right is also acquired.

1 *Great West Rly Co v Swindon and Cheltenham Extension Rly Co* (1884) 9 App Cas 787. See also para **[729]**.
2 For example, see the National Parks and Access to the Countryside Act 1949, s 103.

C The use of land acquired so as to interfere with an existing easement or other right over it

[1605]
Unless the authorising Act provides to the contrary, where an acquiring authority compulsorily acquires a servient tenement it remains subject to any existing easement or other right over it for the benefit of other land (ie the dominant tenement). There is no requirement to serve any notice to treat on the owner of the dominant tenement[1], assuming the dominant tenement is not itself required. The owner of the dominant tenement will not, however, be able to enforce such easement or other right against an acquiring authority acting in pursuance of its statutory powers[2]; his rights are instead converted into a claim for compensation under CPA 1965, s 10[3]. Where the acquiring authority later disposes of its interest in the servient tenement to a third party, any such adverse easement or other right may become enforceable again by the dominant tenement against the new owner of the servient tenement, except where this is prevented by express statutory provision[4].

1 *Clark v London School Board* (1874) 9 Ch App 120. See also paras **[306]–[309]** as to entitlement to notice to treat.
2 *Kirby v Harrogate School Board* (1896) 1 Ch 437.
3 As to which, see **Division F, Chapter 2**. *Roberts v Holyhead UDC* (1962) 14 P&CR 358 considered the quantum of compensation payable where a right of access had been interfered with.

Compensation under the CPA 1965, s 10 was considered in *Wrotham Park Settled Estates v Hertsmere BC* [1993] RVR 56. See also *Long Eaton plc Recreation Ground Co v Midland Rly Co* [1902] 2 KB 574.

4 See para **[1606]**.

[1606]

Some Acts provide for the extinction of any adverse easement in or other rights over the servient tenement by the acquiring authority or provide that the acquiring authority and any successor in title to the authority be immune from enforcement of such easement or right[1]. For example, the Town and Country Planning Act 1990 (TCPA 1990), s 237[2] authorises a local authority (or a person deriving title from that authority) to override easements and contractual restrictions affecting land and vested in third parties, provided that such interference is intra vires the purposes of the acquisition. This provision, therefore, operates to confer immunity in respect of interference with easements where the land is disposed of for commercial redevelopment by an acquiring authority[3]. In *Thames Water Utilities v Oxford City Council*[4], the TCPA 1990, s 237 was held to authorise construction of buildings in breach of a restrictive covenant, but not their subsequent use. The decision in *Thames Water Utilities Ltd v Oxford City Council* potentially affected other similar statutory provisions in the Local Government, Planning and Land Act 1980, Sch 28, para 6, the New Towns Act 1981, s 19, the Housing Act 1988, Sch 10, para 5, the Leasehold Reform, Housing and Urban Development Act 1993, Sch 20, para 5 and the Regional Development Agencies Act 1998, Sch 6, para 2. The Planning Act 2008, s 194 and Sch 10 has enacted amendments to all these statutes the intended effect of which is to remove the effect of the decision in *Thames Water Utilities Ltd v Oxford City Council.*

1 See **B[461]**.

2 As to the interpretation of TCPA 1990, s 237, see *R v City of London Corp, ex p the Master, Governors and Commonality of the Mystery of the Barbers of London* (1996) 73 P&CR 59 and *Midtown Ltd v City of London Real Property Company Ltd* [2005] EWHC 33 (Ch), [2005] 1 EGLR 65.

3 The application of this rule was considered in *Dowty Boulton Paul Ltd v Wolverhampton Corpn (No 2)* [1973] Ch 94.

4 [1999] 1 EGLR 167. It is submitted that there must be some doubt as to the correctness of this decision. See also *Marten v Flight Refuelling Ltd* [1962] Ch 115; *Edmunds v Stockport Metropolitan Borough Council* [1990] 1 PLR 1.

[1607]

Where the acquiring authority acquires land compulsorily in which there are rights of common, compensation in respect of the right in the soil must be paid to the lord of the manor (or whoever else is so entitled), in respect of the landtake, and compensation in respect of the commoner's rights must be quantified and paid in the manner set out in the CPA 1965[1]. The acquiring authority should convene a meeting of persons entitled to commonable or other rights by local advertisement, the purpose of which meeting shall be to appoint a committee to undertake negotiations with the acquiring authority as to compensation. In the event that there is a failure successfully to convene a meeting or to agree compensation, then the Upper Tribunal must be asked to determine the compensation payable. Where compensation is determined and paid to a commoners' committee or into court, the acquiring authority may execute a deed poll vesting title in itself and thereby extinguishing rights of common. There is no need to serve notice to treat on any of the commoners where this procedure is used[2]. These provisions take effect, subject to the Inclosure Act 1852, the Inclosure Act 1854, the Commonable Rights Compensation Act 1882 and the Commons Act 1899. Extinction of the rights of commoners will not necessarily enable de-registration of common land as such[3]. Vesting of land under the CP(VD)A 1981 appears to take effect subject to these procedures relating to commoners' rights[4].

1 CPA 1965, s 21 and Sch 4. There is similar provision in the Land Clauses Consolidation Act 1845 (LCCA 1845) (as amended), ss 99 and 107, in relation to acquisitions authorised by a special Act to which the LCCA 1845 (as amended) applies.
2 *Lewis v Mid Glamorgan County Council* [1995] 1 All ER 760.
3 *Lewis v Mid Glamorgan County Council* [1995] 1 All ER 760.
4 DoE Circular 14/94, App R, para 3.

D The creation of new rights in land, where the land itself is not acquired

[1608]–[1900]
Statutes which grant compulsory purchase powers do not entitle an acquiring authority to create new easements or other rights over land in its favour unless the statute says so expressly[1]. Several Acts do, however, make specific provision for the creation of such rights. In particular, the Local Government (Miscellaneous Provisions) Act 1976, s 13 provides that, where a local authority is authorised by a compulsory purchase order to purchase land compulsorily, it is also authorised to purchase such 'new rights' over land as are specified in the order and, for these purposes, 'new rights' means rights which are not in existence when the order specifying them is made. The right to be created is treated as land in respect of which (where the acquiring authority is proceeding under the CPA 1965) notice to treat must be served [2]. The 1976 Act applies the CPA 1965, s 8 (acquisition of part) with modifications appropriate to the acquisition of rights[3]. Other authorising Acts make similar provision and also provide for amendments to the procedure specified in the CPA 1965 and/or the CP(VD)A 1981 accordingly[4].

1 *Sovmots Investments Ltd v Secretary of State for the Environment* [1979] AC 144. See **B[466]–[468]**.
2 As to which, see paras **[301]–[341]**.
3 LG(MP)A 1976, s 13(3).
4 For example, see the Local Government, Planning and Land Act 1980, s 144, the Highways Act 1980, s 250; the Gas Act 1986, s 9(3); the Housing Act 1988, s 78; the Electricity Act 1989, s 10; the Water Resources Act 1991, s 154; and the Water Industry Act 1991, s 155.

Division E

Compensation for compulsory purchase

Contents

All references in bold are to paragraph numbers.

Chapter 4 Disregarding the scheme

Chapter 5 Equivalent reinstatement

Chapter 6 Compensation for disturbance

Chapter 7 Severance and injurious affection

Chapter 8 Deduction for betterment

Chapter 9 Supplementary payments and duty to re-house

Chapter 1

Introduction

Contents

A Introduction

[1]

This Division is concerned with the right to compensation where an interest in land is compulsorily acquired. In certain circumstances, there are rights to compensation for losses resulting from the exercise of statutory powers where no land has been taken from the claimant; these are the subject of **Divisions F** and **G**.

[2]

The rules governing the assessment of compensation for compulsory purchase derive partly from statute and partly from case law[1]. Some of the current statutory provisions originated in the nineteenth century and many of the relevant cases were decided in the context of such earlier statutes. Consequently, an appreciation of the historical development of the principles is of assistance in understanding those which govern the assessment of compensation today. This chapter summarises the historical background, explains the right to compensation, the subject matter of compensation, the nature of compensation and the date at which compensation is assessed. It also provides a brief overview of the principles of compensation in order to set the context for subsequent chapters of this Division which explain the principles in more detail.

1 The Lands Tribunal has commented, 'It is a major shortcoming of current legislation on compensation for compulsory purchase that it contains a series of apparently very specific rules with no statement of the principle or principles on which they are based.' *Waters v Welsh Development Agency* [2001] 1 EGLR 185, Lands Tribunal; upheld [2003] 4 All ER 384, CA and [2004] 1 WLR 1304, HL.

B Historical background

[3]

Prior to 1845, each Act which authorised compulsory purchase contained both the procedural requirements and provisions relating to compensation. The Lands Clauses Consolidation Act 1845 (LCCA 1845) was enacted in order to introduce a degree of uniformity; thereafter, Acts which authorised works for which compulsory acquisition of land was required usually incorporated the LCCA 1845. Although the majority of the LCCA 1845 was concerned with procedure, there were two main provisions relating to compensation. The LCCA 1845, s 63[1] relates to compensation for the compulsory acquisition of a person's interest in land, and the LCCA 1845, s 68[2] came to be interpreted as providing a right to compensation for loss of value caused to land which had not been taken.

1 Re-enacted in substantially the same form as the Compulsory Purchase Act 1965 (CPA 1965), s 7.

2 Re-enacted in substantially the same form as the CPA 1965, s 10 which is explained in **Division F**.

[4]

The LCCA 1845, s 63 identified two kinds of compensation available to an owner whose land was taken:

(*a*) the value of the land taken; and
(*b*) loss of value caused to other land held by him by reason of it being severed from the land taken or otherwise injuriously affected by the exercise of the statutory powers which authorised the works.

The LCCA 1845 did not prescribe the basis of valuation of the land acquired, and rules developed through judicial decisions guided by the principles applicable in the law of tort[1]. The main principles, which had become well established by the beginning of the twentieth century, may be summarised as follows:

(*a*) the value of the land was to be assessed as the value to the owner, and not the value to the acquiring authority[2];
(*b*) an allowance could be made for the fact that the acquisition was compulsory[3];
(*c*) the value to the owner included, not only the value of the land itself, but also all other losses caused to the claimant personally consequent upon being dispossessed[4];
(*d*) the special suitability or adaptability of the land for the purposes of the acquiring authority was to be left out of account[5];
(*e*) an increase in value of the land taken which was attributable to the scheme in connection with which the acquisition was made had to be disregarded[6]; and
(*f*) the compensation was not to be reduced to reflect an increase in value caused to other land held by the claimant[7] by the scheme underlying the compulsory purchase.

1 In *Ricket v Directors etc of the Metropolitan Rly Co* (1867) LR 2 HL 175, Erle CJ said, 'The Company claiming to take land by compulsory process, expel the owner from his property,

and are bound to compensate him for all the loss caused by the expulsion; and the principle of compensation, then, is the same as in trespass for expulsion'.

2 *Stebbing v Metropolitan Board of Works* (1870) LR 6 QB 37; *Cedar Rapids Manufacturing and Power Co v Lacoste* [1914] AC 569, PC, at 576. The value to the owner included the future potential of the land, for example, for building purposes: *R v Brown* (1867) LR 2 QB 630.

3 *Re Athlone Rifle Range* [1902] 1 IR 433. This is what Denning LJ referred to as 'the added sop (which in the old days was always given in these cases) of 10% to soften the blow of compulsory acquisition': *Harvey v Crawley Development Corpn* [1957] 1 QB 485 at 493.

4 *Ricket v Directors etc of the Metropolitan Rly Co* (1867) LR 2 HL 175.

5 *Re Lucas and Chesterfield Gas and Water Board* [1909] 1 KB 16 approved by the House of Lords in *Cedar Rapids Manufacturing and Power Co v Lacoste* [1914] AC 569, PC.

6 *Re South Eastern Rly Co and LCC's Contract, South Eastern Rly Co v LCC* [1915] 2 Ch 252.

7 *Re South Eastern Rly Co and LCC's Contract, South Eastern Rly Co v LCC* [1915] 2 Ch 252.

[5]

Those principles were to some extent codified and to some extent modified by the Acquisition of Land (Assessment of Compensation) Act 1919 (ALACA 1919) which introduced six rules for the assessment of compensation which are similar to the six rules now to be found in the Land Compensation Act 1961 (LCA 1961), s 5[1]:

> 'The main object of the Act of 1919 was undoubtedly to mitigate the evil of excessive compensation which had grown up out of the theory, evolved by the Courts, that because the sale was compulsory the seller must be treated by the assessing tribunal sympathetically as an unwilling seller selling to a willing buyer'[2].

This object was achieved by two of the six rules[3]: r 1 provided that no allowance was to be made on account of the acquisition being compulsory, and r 2 provided that the value of the land was to be taken as the open market value if sold by a willing seller. Rules 3–5 codified principles that had been established in judicial decisions. In addition, the right to claim compensation for disturbance was retained by r 6. Notwithstanding these changes, the underlying objective of the compensation code remained, that is, to provide an amount which reflected the value of the land taken to the owner[4].

1 See **Chapter 2**.

2 Per Scott LJ in *Horn v Sunderland Corpn* [1941] 2 KB 26, CA, at 40. See also the comments at 41.

3 The six rules were similar, though not identical, to those now found in the LCA 1961, s 5; see **Chapter 2**.

4 Per Lord Bridge in *Hughes v Doncaster MBC* [1991] 1 AC 382, HL, at 390G and 392H.

[6]

The period from 1944 to 1954 saw the enactment of various statutory provisions which had the effect of limiting the amount of compensation payable for compulsory acquisition. The Town and Country Planning Act 1944 required that market value be assessed at 1939 levels of value which were lower than those prevailing in 1944 and subsequently; this continued until 1947. The Town and Country Planning Act 1947, which introduced control over development and development plans to guide future land use and development, also included a scheme to nationalise the development value of land. The details of that scheme are outside the scope of this work, but the effect of the scheme upon the assessment of compensation for compulsory purchase was that the value of the land taken reflected only the existing use value (including the right to rebuild and extend within certain limits). The Act also introduced provisions governing situations where planning control affected the value of land[1]. The Town and Country Planning Act 1954 added a refinement which enabled claims for compensation to include, in addition to existing use value, an element of development value. The Town and Country Planning Act 1959 returned the measure of compensation for the land acquired to open market value, as had been provided by the 1919 Act.

1 For example, the rule that any depreciation in the value of land attributable to the threat of compulsory acquisition stemming from the development plan was to be left out of account. This rule is now in the LCA 1961, s 9.

[7]

The LCA 1961 re-enacted in similar terms the six rules which derive from the 1919 Act[1]. It laid down a variety of assumptions to be made in relation to planning permissions, provided for the reference of disputes to the Lands Tribunal, which had been created as a specialist land valuation tribunal in 1950[2], and a variety of other matters. It also included a right to further compensation if planning permission for additional development was granted within ten years; this was repealed in 1967 and re-enacted 1991[3]. The Land Compensation Act 1973 (LCA 1973) (inter alia) amended the law relating to severance and injurious affection[4] and introduced a new right to compensation for the effect on the value of land caused by public works where no land is compulsorily acquired[5]. The LCA 1973 also responded to perceived inadequacies in the compensation code by introducing a system of supplementary payments in respect of home loss and farm loss, and for disturbance where the claimant has no interest in the land taken[6]. The Planning and Compensation Act 1991 (PCA 1991) made a variety of detailed amendments to the LCA 1961, the LCA 1973 and the CPA 1965[7]. A number of detailed amendments were also made by the Planning and Compulsory Purchase Act 2004.

1 See para **[5]**.
2 Lands Tribunal Act 1949; see **Division H**.
3 Repealed by the Land Commission Act 1967, ss 86, 101, Sch 7 and re-enacted as the LCA 1961, s 23 by the PCA 1991, s 66, Sch 14. See para **[829]**.
4 See **Chapter 7**.
5 See **Division F, Chapter 3**.
6 See **Chapter 9**.
7 These amendments had been recommended by the Royal Institution of Chartered Surveyors in their report *Compensation for Compulsory Acquisition* (1989).

C The right of compensation

[8]

Any person from whom an estate or interest in land[1] is acquired compulsorily has a right to claim compensation. Such a person is referred to in this Division as the 'claimant'. This right to compensation is not expressly stated in any statute[2], but is to be implied from the requirement imposed upon acquiring authorities to serve notice to treat upon 'all the persons interested in, or having power to sell and convey or release the land', since the notice to treat must demand particulars of (inter alia) the claim made in respect of the land[3]. Where the acquiring authority follows the general vesting declaration procedure, notice to treat will not be served but the authority is deemed to have served one and is liable pay compensation as if it had and then entered onto the land[4]. It is also to be implied from the many provisions which govern the assessment of compensation. In any event, it is a canon of statutory construction 'that an intention to take away the property of a subject without giving to him a legal right to compensation for the loss of it is not to be imputed to the legislature unless that intention is expressed in unequivocal terms'[5]. There is a right to compensation even where the acquiring authority failed to serve notice to treat[6]. A person who holds a short tenancy will also be entitled to compensation even though he will not receive a notice to treat[7]. A person who has the benefit of a right such as an easement or restrictive covenant over land which is compulsorily acquired will not receive a notice to treat, but, if and when the right is interfered with as a result of the compulsory acquisition of the servient land, he will be entitled to claim compensation[8]. There are also various rights to specific statutory payments which, where they apply, supplement the compensation assessed in accordance with the main principles, such as home loss payments and basic loss payments and occupier's payments, and there is a statutory right to compensation for disturbance even no though no interest in land is held[9]. Acquiring authorities are also under an obligation to rehouse persons displaced[10] and, in certain circumstances, to secure, so far as practicable, that displaced businesses are offered suitable accommodation[11].

1 As to the meaning of 'interest in land' here, see **Division B, Chapter 2**.
2 In contrast, the rights to various forms of supplementary compensation, such as home loss payments and basic loss payments and occupier's payments, are expressly stated; see **Chapter 8**.
3 CPA 1965, s 5. As to notices to treat, see **Division D, Chapter 2**
4 Compulsory Purchase (Vesting Declarations) Act 1981, ss 7, 10. As to vesting declarations, see **Division D, Chapter 2**.
5 Per Lord Atkinson in *Central Control Board (Liquor Traffic) v Cannon Brewery Co Ltd* [1919] AC 744, HL, at 752. As to the position under the Human Rights Act 1998, see **Division A, Chapter 4**.
6 CPA 1965, s 22: see **D [743]**. See also *Kent County Council v Union Railways (North) Ltd and London and Continental Railways Ltd* [2009] RVR 146, in which the Court of Appeal held that, if an acquiring authority fails to serve notice to treat on a person with an interest in land it has taken, that person may claim compensation under CPA 1965, s 22.
7 CPA 1965, s 20. See **D [1321]**.
8 CPA 1965, s 10, which is explained in **Division F, Chapter 2**.
9 See **Chapter 9**.
10 LCA 1973, ss 39–40. They may advance money to enable another dwelling to be purchased or constructed: s 41.
11 Town and Country Planning Act 1990, s 233(5).

D The subject matter of compensation

[9]
The right to compensation described in this Division arises out of the compulsory acquisition of an interest in land. It is, therefore, assumed for the purposes of this Division that the land in respect of which a claim is made, and any features relevant to the assessment of compensation, have been defined sufficiently precisely for compensation to be assessed even though there is no oblig-

ation to prove title to the land until after the assessment of compensation. If the acquiring authority considers that it needs to do so, it has the power to enter and survey the land prior to the formal taking of possession[1]. It is also assumed that any question as to whether the land being acquired comprises part or the whole of the claimant's holding has been determined[2].

1 See the CPA 1965, s 11(3).
2 Where an acquiring authority serve notice to treat in respect of part of a person's holding, it may, in certain circumstances, be required to purchase the whole holding, see **D [326]**.

[10]
In the majority of cases, the acquiring authority will be taking all interests in a particular parcel of land, although, in certain circumstances, it can choose not to acquire a particular interest so long as this is consistent with the purpose for which the land was compulsorily acquired[1]. Defining the interest in respect of which a claim for compensation is made is obviously essential. A claimant may hold any one of a number of possible interests the loss of which entitle him to compensation, such as the freehold in possession, the freehold subject to a lease, a leasehold or an irrevocable licence. Alternatively, the compulsory acquisition may involve the creation of new rights over land in which the claimant has an interest[2]. It also needs to be ascertained whether the acquisition includes the minerals which may be in the land[3]. While the owner of an interest in land upon whom a notice to treat has been served is not prevented from disposing of it or otherwise dealing with it, he cannot increase the burden of compensation payable by creating a new interest in the land, or land held with it, or by carrying out improvements to the land[4]. The principles described in this Division apply to all claims for compensation for compulsory acquisition, whatever the claimant's interest, although the manner in which they apply will depend upon the nature of the interest being acquired[5].

1 See **D [309]**.
2 See **B [466]**.
3 As to the inclusion of minerals in a compulsory purchase, see **B [470]**.
4 As to the effect of a notice to treat, see **D [323]**. This rule stems from judicial decisions, but it is now enacted in the Acquisition of Land Act 1981, s 4.
5 Special provision applies to short leases by virtue of the CPA 1965, s 20: see paras **[32]–[40]**.

[11]–[20]
Where, after the date of the compulsory acquisition, but before the assessment of compensation, evidence becomes available about the subject matter of the acquisition which was not previously available, such evidence may be taken into account in assessing the compensation[1].

1 *Bwllfa and Merthyr Dare Steam Collieries (1891) Ltd v Pontypridd Waterworks Co [1903] AC 426, HL*, in which the House of Lords was concerned with the assessment of compensation for the sterilisation (not acquisition) of minerals. At the time of service of the notice which led to the minerals being sterilised, the price which would have been obtained for them, had they been extracted, was in the future and therefore uncertain. By the time compensation was assessed, the price which would have been obtained for them was known. The House of Lords held that compensation should be assessed on the basis of the facts known at the date of assessment. It is submitted that this principle would not apply in the context of compulsory purchase to factors such as the value of the land taken or the prospect of planning permission being granted in respect of the land taken or the claimant's retained land: see further **E[405]**.

E The nature of compensation

[21]

The right to compensation is 'the right to be put, so far as money can do it, in the same position as if his land had not been taken from him. In other words, (the claimant) gains the right to be receive a money payment not less than the loss imposed on him in the public interest, but, on the other hand, no greater'[1]. Statutory compensation cannot, and must not, exceed the owner's total loss, for, if it does, it will put an unfair burden on the public authority or other promoters who on public grounds have been given the power of compulsory acquisition, and it will transgress the principle of equivalence which is at the root of statutory compensation, the principle that the owner shall be paid neither less nor more than his loss[2].

1 Per Scott LJ in *Horn v Sunderland Corpn* [1941] 2 KB 26 at 42.
2 [1941] 2 KB 26 at 49.

[22]

The assessment of compensation is a question of fact. However, it has been held that, if one of the principles of valuation is ignored, that would amount to an error of law[1]; the same would presumably apply if one of the principles was incorrectly interpreted and applied. The compensation available to a person whose land has been compulsorily acquired may, depending upon the facts of a particular case, be made up of three main elements. These are:

(*a*) the market value of the land taken;
(*b*) any loss caused by reason of losing possession of the land (known as 'disturbance'); and
(*c*) loss of value caused to land held by the claimant by reason of it being severed from the land taken or otherwise detrimentally affected (known as 'severance' and 'injurious affection').

While the process of assessment of the compensation may involve attributing figures to each of these elements of claim, there is an important principle that compensation is a single global figure. Thus Sir Wilfrid Greene MR said in *Horn v Sunderland Corpn*[2], ' … the sum to be ascertained is in essence one sum, namely, the proper price or compensation payable in all the circumstances of the case'. It has also been said that 'A person seeking to obtain compensation under these Acts of Parliament must once and for all make one claim for all damages which can be reasonably foreseen'[3].

1 *Melwood Units Pty Co Ltd v Main Roads Comr* [1979] AC 426, PC.
2 [1941] 2 KB 26 at 34. This rule is particularly significant where a claim is made in respect of both the value of the land taken and disturbance; for example, a claimant cannot claim development value as well as the cost of removal, since, in order to realise the development value, he would have to vacate the land; see further at para **[2021]**. See also *Hughes v Doncaster MBC* [1991] 1 AC 382, HL; *Buildings and Lands Director v Shun Fung Ironworks Ltd* [1995] 2 AC 111, HL.
3 *Chamberlain v West End of London and Crystal Palace Rly Co* (1863) 2 B&S 617.

[23]

In addition to the 'global' sum mentioned by Sir Wilfrid Greene, rights to various supplementary forms of compensation have been introduced by statute, such as home loss payments, farm loss payments and compensation for disturbance where no interest in land is held by the claimant[1]. Furthermore, there is a right to claim supplementary compensation at a later date than the original claim; this arises where, within ten years of the compulsory acquisition, planning permission is granted for additional development[2].

1 See **Chapter 9**.
2 See para **[829]**.

F Principles of compensation in outline

[24]
Compensation in respect of land taken compulsorily is now normally assessed under one or more of the three heads identified in para **[22]**. In certain circumstances, instead of assessing compensation on the basis of the open market value of the land, a claimant may be entitled to compensation based upon the principle of 'equivalent reinstatement'. Each of these possible heads of claim are outlined below and examined in detail in subsequent chapters.

1 Open market value of the land

[25]
The main rules for the assessment of the value of the land taken may be summarised as follows, and each is explained in detail later in this Division:

(*a*) no allowance may be made for the fact that the acquisition is compulsory[1];
(*b*) the value is to be assessed as the amount which the land might be expected to realise if sold in the open market by a willing seller[2]; and
(*c*) no account may be taken of the special suitability or adaptability of the land for any purpose if that purpose is one to which it could be applied only in pursuance of statutory powers or for which there is no market apart from the requirements of any authority possessing purchase compulsory powers[3]:
(*d*) no account may be taken of any increase in value attributable to a use which is contrary to law, which could be prevented by a court, or which is detrimental to the health of the occupants or to public health[4];
(*e*) no account is to be taken of any increase in value attributable to the scheme underlying the acquisition[5]; and
(*f*) in addition to taking account of any actual planning permissions which benefit the land, planning permission may be assumed for the development proposed by the acquiring authority in so far as it relates to the land taken, for purposes which derive from the development plan and for any purposes for which a certificate of appropriate alternative development is granted[6].

1 See para **[406]**.
2 See para **[407]**.
3 See para **[428]**.
4 See para **[444]**.
5 See **Chapter 4**.
6 See **Chapter 3**.

2 Disturbance

[26]
Compensation is payable in respect of losses caused to the claimant as a result of being dispossessed of the land by the compulsory purchase[1].

1 See **Chapter 6**.

3 Equivalent reinstatement

[27]
As an alternative to assessing the open market value of the land, compensation may, in certain circumstances, be assessed on the basis of the cost of equivalent reinstatement of the purpose for which the land was used prior to the compulsory purchase[1]. This can only apply where there is no general demand or market for land for that purpose. There is no right to an award on this basis; it is discretionary.

1 See **Chapter 5**.

4 Severance and injurious affection

[28]
In addition, compensation is payable where the claimant owns other land the value of which is diminished because of severance or other injurious affection caused by the scheme for which the land was acquired[1].

1 See **Chapter 7**.

5 Betterment

[29]
Where the claimant owns other land which increases in value due to the scheme underlying the acquisition, that increase may have to be set off against the compensation due in respect of the land taken[1].

1 See **Chapter 8**.

6 Supplementary payments

[30]
In addition to the right to compensation outlined above, supplementary payments are, in certain circumstances, due, known as home loss payments, basic loss payments and occupier's loss payments, payments for disturbance where the claimant had no interest in the land taken, basic loss payments and occupier's loss payments[1].

1 See **Chapter 9**.

7 Compensation for temporary use

[31]
Where an acquiring authority needs to use land temporarily for some purpose, such as a construction site while permanent works are erected, unless possession of the land required can be obtained by agreement, the acquiring authority will usually have to make a compulsory purchase order and then offer the land back when it is no longer required. [1]Depending upon the scope of the authority's powers, it may be able to obtain sufficient rights over the land without having to acquire all interests. Occasionally, express power is provided to enable land to be used temporarily[2]. The assessment of compensation in respect of such temporary use will differ depending upon the power relied upon by the acquiring authority. If a compulsory purchase order is made, then the starting point will be the amount of compensation for the acquisition assessed in accordance with the principles described in this Division. If the compensation falls to be assessed before the land is handed back, then the figure arrived at will be payable as the compensation for the acquisition; if and when the land is handed back such terms as may be appropriate must be agreed at that stage, and this will have the effect of reducing the net compensation amount paid out by the acquiring authority. Where possession of the land is taken pursuant to a special power to use land temporarily, then the terms of that provision will govern the basis upon which compensation is to be assessed.

1 See **B[64.1]**.
2 For example, the Railways Clauses Consolidation Act 1845, s 43 and the London Docklands Railway (Lewisham) Act 1993, s 23.

8 Short tenancies

[32]
Special provision is made by the CPA 1965, s 20 in relation to tenancies for a year or from year to year. Where such a tenant is required to give up possession before the expiry of his interest, he is entitled to compensation for the value of the expired term, for any just allowance that ought to be made to him by an incoming tenant and for any loss or injury which he sustains[1]. If part only of the land he holds is taken, he is also entitled to compensation for severance[2].

1 CPA 1965, s 20(1). If a tenant claims to hold an interest greater than a tenant at will, he must produce a copy of the lease if requested to do so, otherwise his tenancy will be treated as a tenancy from year to year: s 20(3).
2 CPA 1965, s 20(2).

[33]–[39]
The Lands Tribunal has held that, in assessing compensation under s 20 in respect of a periodic tenancy or a tenancy containing a break clause, it must be assumed that the tenancy would end on the earliest day on which the landlord could bring it to an end. The Lands Tribunal also held in the same case that, for the purposes of assessing any 'loss or damage' sustained by the claimant pursuant to s 20, as a matter of law, no account can be taken of any

possibility which may have existed in fact that the tenancy might have been renewed[1].

1 *Bishopsgate Space Management Ltd and Teamworks Karting Ltd v London Underground Ltd* [2004] RVR 89, Lands Tribunal.

G Date of valuation

[40]

By virtue of the LCA 1961, s 5A, if the value of land is to be assessed under r 2 of the LCA 1961, s 5[1], the date of valuation has now been fixed by statute as explained below[2]. However, for some purposes, it will be helpful to be aware of the law that had developed prior to this enactment and so this is briefly explained in the following two paragraphs.

1 See **E[407]–[427]**.
2 See **E[42.1]**.

[41]

In *Birmingham Corpn v West Midland Baptist (Trust) Association Inc*[1], the House of Lords said that, where compensation is being assessed under r 2 (open market value)[2] and r 6 (disturbance)[3], the date at which compensation should be assessed was either the date on which the acquiring authority take possession of the land or the date when the compensation was assessed, whichever is the earlier. The claim in that case was for compensation assessed under r 5 (equivalent reinstatement); the House of Lords held that compensation under r 5 should be assessed at the date on which reinstatement could reasonably have commenced. It is submitted that this would also have applied to compensation for severance and injurious affection under the CPA 1965, s 7.

1 [1970] AC 874.
2 As to which, see **Chapter 2**. Although this case was concerned with r 5, the House of Lords found it necessary to examine, and express opinions about, the relevant date for the purposes of rr 2 and 6.
3 As to which, see **Chapter 6**. As to the date at which compensation under r 6 should be assessed, see *Optical Express (Southern) Ltd v Birmingham City Council* [2005] RVR 230, Lands Tribunal.

[42]

This decision reversed the rule which had previously been generally applied that compensation should be assessed at the date of the notice to treat. While it settled the question as to the date at which the relevant interests in land should be valued, there appeared to remain uncertainty as to whether the interest to be valued and the surrounding circumstances should be taken at the date of the notice to treat or the date of entry (or the date of assessment of compensation, as the case may be)[1].

1 Cases decided subsequent to the *West Midland Baptist Trust* case in which the interests in land and surrounding circumstances have been taken at the date of entry include: *Banham v London Borough of Hackney* (1970) 22 P&CR 922, Lands Tribunal; *Bradford Property Trust Ltd v Hertfordshire County Council* (1973) 27 P&CR 228, Lands Tribunal; *Metcalfe v Basildon Development Corpn* (1974) 28 P&CR 307, Lands Tribunal; *Midland Bank Trust Co Ltd (Executors) v London Borough of Lewisham* (1975) 30 P&CR 268, Lands Tribunal; *Buckingham Street*

Investments Ltd v Greater London Council (1975) 31 P&CR 453, Lands Tribunal; *Otterspool Investments Ltd v Merseyside County Council* (1984) 25 RVR 99, Lands Tribunal. In contrast, cases in which the interests in land and surrounding circumstances were taken at the date of the notice to treat include: *Lyle v London Borough of Bexley* (1972) 223 Estates Gazette 687, Lands Tribunal; *Toogood v Bristol Corpn* (1973) 26 P&CR 132; *Toogood v Bristol Corpn* (1974) 28 P&CR 473, Lands Tribunal; *Zoar Independent Church Trustees v Rochester Corpn* [1974] QB 246, CA; *Walters, Brett and Park v South Glamorgan County Council* (1976) 32 P&CR 111. Where there is an appeal, the Lands Tribunal has held that the date of valuation is that applicable to the decision appealed against: *Hoveringham Gravels Ltd v Chiltern District Council* [1979] JPL 837.

[42.1]
By virtue of the LCA 1961, s 5A[1], unless there is express provision in any other enactment to the contrary[2], the date at which land compulsorily acquired[3] must be valued pursuant to rule 2[4] of the LCA 1961, s 5 is 'the relevant valuation date'[5]. If the land is the subject of a notice to treat, the relevant valuation date will be the earlier of either the date of entry or the date when compensation is assessed[6]. If the land is the subject of a general vesting declaration, then the relevant valuation date will be the earlier of either the vesting date or the date when compensation is assessed[7]. No adjustment may be made to the valuation in respect of anything which happens after the valuation date[8]. Where the acquiring authority takes possession of part of the land specified in a notice of entry[8] or in respect of which a payment into court[10] has been made, it is deemed to have entered on the whole[11].

1 LCA 1961, s 5A was enacted by the PCPA 2004, s 103 which was brought into force on 31 October 2004 by virtue of the PCPA 2004 (Commencement No 3) Order 2004, SI 2004/2593. This provision had immediate effect upon being brought into force and applies to all valuations carried out after that date notwithstanding that the compulsory purchase order, the notice to treat and entry all occurred prior to the PCPA 2004 coming into force.
2 LCA 1961, s 5A(8).
3 LCA 1961, s 5A(8): this provision does not apply to a valuation of land except where that land has been compulsorily acquired, even if the valuation is required to be made pursuant to r 5 (equivalent re-instatement): see **E[446]**.
4 As to r 2 of LCA 1961, s 5, see **E[407]–[427]**.
5 LCA 1961, s 5A(1).
6 LCA 1961, s 5A(3). The date when compensation is assessed is either the last day of a hearing in the Lands Tribunal or if there has been no oral hearing, the last day for making written submissions: LCA 1961, s 5A(7). As to what constitutes 'entry', see **D[727]–[728]**.
7 LCA 1961, s 5A(4). As to the date of assessment of compensation, see the previous note.
8 LCA 1961, s 5A(2). The purpose and effect of this rather obscure provision is not clear. It may be intended to rule out the use of hindsight when assessing value under r 2: see **E[11]** and **[405]**. In *Essex County Showground Group Ltd v Essex County Council* [2006] RVR 336 at 345, the Lands Tribunal commented that they did not find s 5A(2) 'easy to understand' and that it may not have been intended that events after the valuation date should be made inadmissible in all respects for the purposes of a rule 2 valuation.
9 As to a notice of entry, see LCA 1961, s 5A(9)(*a*).
10 As to payments into Court, see LCA 1961, s 5A(9)(*b*).
11 LCA 1961, s 5A(5). This provision applies for the purposes of calculating interest: s 5A(6).

H Claims

[43]–[400]
There is no statutory requirement that a notice of claim be served in any particular form or within any particular time[1]. Where a notice to treat is served, it normally invites the recipient to respond by providing a notice of

claim; often a form is provided and a response is requested within 21 days. While the right to compensation is not lost if no notice to claim is provided to the acquiring authority, a failure to deliver a notice of claim may have two main consequences:

(*a*) the claimant may have to bear, not only his own costs of any proceedings in the Upper Tribunal, but also those of the acquiring authority[2]; and
(*b*) the acquiring authority may, at any time up to six weeks after the decision of the Upper Tribunal, withdraw the notice to treat, unless it has entered into possession[3].

If compensation is not agreed or determined within six years from the date when the claim arose, enforcement of a claim will become statute-barred[4].

1 *Trustees for the Methodist Church Purposes Trustees v North Tyneside MBC* (1979) 38 P&CR 665 at 670. With regard to the effect of the Limitation Act, see **Division H [24]**.
2 LCA 1961, s 4. See also **Division D [325] and Division H [81]ff**.
3 LCA 1961, s 31(1). *Trustees for the Methodist Church Purposes Trustees v North Tyneside MBC* (1979) 38 P&CR 665. If the notice to treat is withdrawn, compensation may be payable pursuant to s 31(2), (3).
4 See **H [24]**.

Chapter 2

Compensation for land acquired

Contents

A Introduction

[401]

While compensation for compulsory purchase is a single lump sum payment[1] which is intended to reflect the totality of the loss caused to the dispossessed owner, it may be made up of a number of elements, one of which is a figure attributable to the land taken from the claimant. This chapter explains the rules for assessing the amount of compensation payable in respect of the land taken; the structure of this chapter takes as headings the six rules for assessing compensation laid down in the Land Compensation Act 1961 (LCA 1961), s 5, which are supplemented by many judicial decisions.

1 See paras **[21]–[23]**.

[402]
The general effect of these rules is to require that compensation in respect of the land taken is to be assessed at 'open market' value on the basis that the claimant is a 'willing seller'[1]. It is, however, necessary to leave out of account any increase or decrease in value attributable to the purposes for which the land is being acquired[2], and also to leave out of account any special suitability of the land for a purpose to which it could only be put pursuant to statutory powers[3]. In certain limited circumstances, compensation may be assessed on the basis of 'equivalent reinstatement' instead of the open market value of the land taken[4]. Although primarily concerned with the value of the land acquired, these rules may also be relevant to the assessment of compensation under other heads such as disturbance[5].

1 As to the meaning of willing seller, see paras **[408]–[421]**.
2 See para **[424]** and **Chapter 4**.
3 See para **[428]**.
4 See para **[446]** and **Chapter 5**.
5 *Hughes v Doncaster MBC* [1991] 1 AC 382, HL.

[403]
The open market value of land depends upon the amount which a potential purchaser is willing to offer for it; there are many factors which may influence this amount. These factors include the purposes for which potential purchasers will consider the land to be suitable, not only physically, but also in terms of consents required under legislative controls over the use and development of land or under restrictive covenants or similar restrictions[1]. For the purposes of assessing compensation, assumptions may have to be made as to the existence, or the prospects of obtaining, planning permission; special provisions are made for this purpose by the LCA 1961 which are described in **Chapter 3**. Where the claimant owns other land which has increased in value due to the scheme underlying the acquisition, such increase may have to be set off against the compensation payable for the land taken[2].

1 *Abbey Homesteads (Developments) Ltd v Northampton County Council* (1986) 53 P&CR 1, [1986] 1 EGLR 24, CA.
2 See **Chapter 9**.

B What is to be valued: land

[404]
The meaning of 'land' in the context of compulsory purchase has been explained in **Division B, Chapter 2**. Implementation of a compulsory purchase, which is explained in **Division D**, results in an estate or interest in a specific parcel of land being acquired from a person, who then becomes

entitled to claim compensation[1], referred to in this Division as the claimant. Thus, the first step in the process of assessing compensation in respect of the land taken is to identify precisely the parcel of land and the claimant's estate or interest in respect of which his claim is made[2]. The rules described in this Chapter apply whether the acquiring authority is taking from the claimant the whole of the land, or merely a part, such as a stratum[3], or taking the freehold or a lesser interest, or creating a new right over the land[4]; while the method of valuing each of these may differ in detail, the principles described in this chapter are applicable whatever the subject matter of the claim.

1 As to the procedure where a person's interest is omitted from the compulsory acquisition, see **D [743]**.
2 Although it is essential to identify the claimant's estate or interest in order to value it, formal proof of title is normally only examined after compensation has been assessed. It is not normally the Upper Tribunal's role to determine issues of title; this is for the High Court, see **H [9]** but the tribunal may need to determine issue of title for certain purposes: see **D [745.1]**. The estates and interests in respect of which compensation may be claimed are normally those subsisting at the date of the notice treat (where that procedure is followed); see **D [363]–[369]**. It is also necessary to identify all the characteristics and potentialities of the land; see para **[423]**.
3 As to the acquisition of strata only, see **B [469]**. As to the acquisition of minerals, see **B [470]–[480]**.
4 As to the creation of new rights, see **B [466]–[468]**.

[405]

In ascertaining what precisely is to be valued, it may be permissible to take into account facts which only became known after the date of valuation. In *Bwllfa and Merthyr Dare Steam Collieries v Pontypridd Waterworks Co*[1], which concerned a claim for compensation for the sterilisation (not acquisition) of minerals. At the time of service of the notice which led to the minerals being sterilised, the price which would have been obtained for them, had they been extracted, was in the future and therefore uncertain. By the time compensation was assessed, the price which would have been obtained was known. The House of Lords held that compensation should be assessed on the basis of the facts known at the date of assessment. It has been indicated in the Court of Appeal that, for the purposes of assessing compensation under r 5 (equivalent reinstatement)[2], this principle may be applied where the actual costs of reinstatement are known by the time compensation falls to be assessed[3]. This principle has been applied by the Lands Tribunal to ascertaining the planning permissions relevant to valuation of the land[4]. It is submitted, however, that there are limits as to the extent to which it is appropriate to apply the principle established in the *Bwllfa* case. For example, for the purpose of arriving at the open market value of land on a particular date, it would not seem appropriate to use hindsight to take account of factors which would not have been known to a willing buyer and a willing seller at the valuation date. For the purposes of a valuation under r 2, no adjustment may be made in respect of anything which happens after the relevant valuation date[5].

1 [1903] AC 426, HL. It should be noted that this case did not arise out of compulsory acquisition but arose out of a claim for compensation for 'loss' under a statutory provision in the legislation then applicable to the water industry.
2 See para **[446]** and **Chapter 5**.
3 Per Sachs LJ in *West Midlands Baptist (Trust) Association Inc v Birmingham Corpn* [1965] 2 QB 188, CA; this point was not considered when this case went to the House of Lords: sub-nom *Birmingham Corpn v West Midlands Baptist (Trust) Association (Inc)* [1970] AC 874.

4 In *Waterworth v Bolton MBC* (1978) 37 P&CR 104, Lands Tribunal, the claimant claimed compensation for severance; one of the issues was how long after the date of valuation planning permission might have been granted for development. By the time the matter was heard in the Lands Tribunal, planning permission had been granted, and the tribunal took into account the actual grant of permission, notwithstanding that it was after the date of valuation. It is submitted that there must be some doubt as to the correctness of applying the *Bwllfa* principle in these circumstances. Although the matter went to the Court of Appeal, the court found it unnecessary to decide whether the tribunal was correct on this point, sub nom *Bolton MBC v Waterworth* (1981) 42 P&CR 289. In *Essex County Showground Group Ltd v Essex County Council* [2006] RVR 336 at 345, the Lands Tribunal commented that, in determining whether planning permission would be granted, it would seem to be unfair and unreal to exclude from consideration an actual grant of planning permission some months after the valuation date.

5 LCA 1961, s 5A(2): see **[42.1]**.

C Rule 1 'No allowance shall be made on account of the acquisition being compulsory'[1]

[406]

This rule was introduced by the Acquisition of Land (Assessment of Compensation) Act 1919 (ALACA 1919)[2] in order to reverse the rule, which had become established by judicial decisions under the Lands Clauses Consolidation Act 1845 (LCCA 1845), that a figure should be added to the value of the land taken to reflect the fact that the acquisition was compulsory[3]. It has now been re-enacted as r 1 of the LCA 1961, s 5. However, the open market value assessed under r 2 might well not reflect particular qualities of the land which are of value to the owner, such as expensive decorations or a specially planted garden. Furthermore, being compelled to leave one's home or place of business can cause distress. Rule 1 has the effect of eliminating such factors from the compensation. While such factors are difficult to quantify in monetary terms, it came to be recognised that, since the essence of compensation for compulsory purchase is to assess the value to the owner, some provision should be made to take them into account. For this reason, a supplementary payment, known as a home loss payment, was introduced by the Land Compensation Act 1973 (LCA 1973)[4].

1 LCA 1961, s 5.
2 ALACA 1919, s 2.
3 See para **[4]**.
4 See **Chapter 8**. The PCA 2004, s 106 added various other supplementary payments which are also explained in **Chapter 8**.

D Rule 2 'The value of land shall, subject as hereinafter provided, be taken to be the amount which the land if sold on the open market by a willing seller might be expected to realise'[1]

1 Introduction

[407]

Prior to 1919, the value of the land taken was assessed as the value to the owner[2]. Rule 2 was introduced by the ALACA 1919[3], requiring that the land taken be valued at open market value, while preserving the right to claim compensation in respect of losses attributable to the loss of possession of the land, now referred to as 'disturbance'[4]. Since 1919, while the rules still aim to arrive at the value to the owner[5], that is achieved[6] by the combination of rr 2 and 6, in other words, by the sum of the open market value of the land and any amount due in respect of disturbance[7]. Rule 2 was re-enacted by the LCA 1961, s 5. The date at which the open market value should be assessed for the purposes of r 2 is the date on which possession is taken by the acquiring authority or date at which compensation is assessed, whichever is the earlier[8].

1 LCA 1961, s 5, r 2. The Lands Tribunal has pointed out that the definition of open market value in Rule 2 is not the same as the definition of open market value in the RICS Appraisal and Valuation Manual (known as the Red Book): *Yorkshire Traction Co Ltd v South Yorkshire Passenger Transport Executive* [2003] RVR 67 at para 67.
2 See para **[8]**.
3 ALACA 1919, s 2.
4 The right to compensation for disturbance is preserved by r 6, see para **[447]**. As to the assessment of compensation for disturbance, see **Chapter 6**.
5 This was the underlying rationale of the decision in *Hughes v Doncaster Metropolitan Borough Council* [1991] 1 AC 382, HL.
6 Subject to the matters explained in para **[6]**.
7 *Hughes v Doncaster MBC* [1991] 1 AC 382, HL, per Lord Bridge, at 392H.
8 See para **[41]**.

2 The 'willing seller' and the 'open market'

[408]
Since, in the case of a compulsory acquisition, the 'seller' is not willing, and has not placed his property on the open market, r 2 requires an estimate to be made in fictional circumstances. It is the role of the valuer to make that estimate, within the framework laid down by law. The terms 'willing seller' and 'open market' are not defined in the Act, but they have been considered by the courts in a number of cases and guidance can be obtained from the passages cited in the paragraphs which follow.

[409]
In *IRC v Clay*[1] in the Court of Appeal, these concepts were explained by Swifen Eady LJ as follows[2]:

> 'A value, ascertained by reference to the amount obtainable in the open market, shews an intention to include every possible purchaser. The market is to be the open market, as distinguished from an offer to a limited class only, such as members of the family. The market is not necessarily an auction sale. The section means such amount as the land might be expected to realise if offered under conditions enabling every person desirous of purchasing to come in and make an offer, and if proper steps were taken to advertise the property and let all likely purchasers know that the land is in the market for sale …'.

1 [1914] 3 KB 466.
2 [1914] 3 KB 466 at 475.

[410]–[420]
One of the classic descriptions of the concepts of the 'willing seller' and the 'open market' is to be found in the judgment of the Privy Council in *Vyricherla Narayana Gajapatiraju v Revenue Divisional Officer, Vizagapatam*[1]. Having established that there was no material difference between Indian and English law in relation to compensation for compulsory purchase, Lord Romer said:

> 'The compensation must be determined, therefore, by reference to the price which a willing vendor might reasonably expect to obtain from a willing purchaser. The disinclination of the vendor to part with his land and the urgent necessity of the purchaser to buy must alike be disregarded. Neither must be considered as acting under compulsion. This is implied in the common saying that the value of the land is not to be estimated at its value to the purchaser. But this does not mean that the fact that some particular purchaser might desire the land more than others is to be disregarded. The wish of a particular purchaser, though not his compulsion, may always be taken into consideration for what it is worth … It may also be observed in passing that it is often said that it is the value of the land to the vendor that has to be estimated. This, however, is not in strictness accurate. The land, for instance, may have for the vendor a sentimental value far in excess of its "market value". But the compensation must not be increased by reason of any such consideration. The vendor is to be treated as willing to sell at "market price" … It is perhaps desirable in this connection to say something about this expression "market price". There is not in general any market for land in the sense in which one speaks of a market for shares or a market for sugar or any like commodity. The value of any such article at any particular time can readily be ascertained by the prices being obtained for similar articles in the market. In the case of land, its value in general can also be measured by a consideration of the prices that have been obtained in the past for land of similar quality and in similar positions, and this is what must be meant in general by "the market value" … But sometimes it happens that the land to be valued possesses some unusual, and it may be, unique features, as regards its position or potentialities. In such a case the arbitrator in determining its value will have no market value to guide him, and he will have to ascertain as best he may from the materials before him, what a willing vendor might reasonably expect to obtain from a willing purchaser, for the land in that particular position and with those particular potentialities".'

1 [1939] AC 302, PC, per Lord Romer, at 311.

[421]
An 'open market' does not mean a hypothetical market, but the market in which, at the relevant date, the seller could legitimately have sold his property and the buyer could have bought it[1]. The open market value of a parcel of land may be attributable to the price which a speculator is willing to pay notwithstanding that he intends to dispose of it for the best price he can obtain[2]. The absence of reference in r 2 to a willing buyer is of no significance; an open market sale automatically implies both a willing seller and a willing buyer[3]. The personal characteristics of the actual seller are not relevant[4].

Where the sale involved access rights over a railway, the characteristics of the seller as a railway company could be taken into account[5].

1 *Priestman Colliers Ltd v Northern District Valuation Board* [1950] 2 KB 398, 1 P&CR 131.
2 *Blue Jay Investments v Thames Water Authority* [1984] 1 EGLR 187.
3 *Walton v IRC* [1996] STC 68, CA, per Peter Gibson LJ at 83; *Railtrack plc v Guinness Ltd* [2003] EWCA Civ 188, [2003] RVR 280.
4 *Corton Caravans and Chalets Ltd v Anglican Water Services Ltd* [2003] RVR 323.
5 *Railtrack plc v Guinness Ltd* [2003] EWCA Civ 188, [2003] RVR 280.

3 The amount which 'might be expected'

[422]
In *IRC v Clay*[1], Swinfen Eady LJ said:

> '"Expected" refers to the expectations of properly qualified persons who have taken pains to inform themselves of all the particulars ascertainable about the property, and its capabilities, the demand for it, and the likely buyers. The price actually realised by a sale is not necessarily the price which it might have been expected to realise, but if the valuer be competent, and has taken proper pains in the matter, there ought to be little difference between the two figures.'
>
> 'However, it must be recognised that valuation is matter of judgement and "... that there is a range of price, in some circumstances wide, which competent valuers would recognise as the price which property would fetch in the open market"[2].'

1 [1914] 3 KB 466, CA, at 475.
2 *Re Hayes' Will Trusts* [1971] 1 WLR 758 at 768.

4 Characteristics and potentialities of the land

[423]
The land must be valued 'rebus sic stantibus'[1]. In other words, '... the value to be ascertained is the value to the seller of the property in its actual condition at the time of expropriation with all its existing advantages and with all its possibilities ...'[2]. The state of the premises and the likely cost of repair should be taken into account in so far as they might affect the price which a purchaser would be willing to pay[3]. Where the land is subject to a restrictive covenant or other restrictions, these must be taken into account, as should the prospect of having them modified or removed[4]. Compensation is not restricted to the value of the land for its existing use; its potential for development may be taken into account[5].

1 *Penny v Penny* (1868) LR 5 Eq 227, per Wood VC, at 236. In this passage, Wood VC said that it had to be valued rebus sic stantibus at the date of the notice to treat; the date of valuation is no longer the date of the notice to treat (see para **[41]**), but the requirement to value 'rebus sic stantibus' remains.
2 *Fraser v City of Fraserville* [1917] AC 187, PC, per Lord Buckmaster at 194. The citation from the judgment of Lord Buckmaster went on to refer to the rule which excludes any advantage due to the carrying out of the scheme; this rule is referred to in para **[426]** and explained in detail in **Chapter 4**. See also *Cedar Rapids Manufacturing and Power Co v Lacoste* [1914] AC 569, PC; *Re Lucas and Chesterfield Gas and Water Board* [1909] 1 KB 16, PC.

3 *Range v Buckinghamshire County Council* [1985] RVR 54, Lands Tribunal; in assessing the amount likely to be incurred on repairs, it is necessary to have regard to the location and nature of the property. Where possession of land compulsorily purchased was taken in parts and the parties agreed that the valuation date should be the date on which possession was taken of the first part, it was held that deterioration in the condition of the building on the other part of the land which occurred between the valuation date and the date of possession of that part could not be taken into account: *Secretary of State for Transport v Christos and Christos* [2003] RVR 307, [2003] EWCA Civ 1073.

4 *Stebbing v Metropolitan Board of Works* (1870) LR 6 QB 37; *Corrie v MacDermott* [1914] AC 1056; *Abbey Homesteads (Developments) Ltd v Northampton County Council* (1986) 53 P&CR 1. The same applies to restrictions by covenant or statute on the sale, price or rent: *Penny v Penny* (1868) LR 5 Eq 227.

5 *R v Brown* (1867) LR 2 QB 630.

[424]

One of the potentialities of an interest in land may be the possibility of merging it with another interest. The owner of another interest in the same land may be willing to pay more than anyone else for the interest being valued in order to achieve such a merger; this is sometimes referred to as 'the marriage value'. In *Lambe v Secretary of State for War*[1], the Court of Appeal held that, in valuing a freehold reversion, it was legitimate to take into account the fact that the sitting tenant would pay more than anyone else. There must, however, be evidence that merger of the interests would be likely to occur[2].

1 [1955] 2 QB 612, CA; followed in *Hearts of Oak Benefit Society v Lewisham Borough Council* [1979] 1 EGLR 178, Lands Tribunal. However, in *Waters v Welsh Development Agency* [2004] 1 WLR 1304, there was a difference of opinion as to whether *Lambe* was correctly decided. Lord Nicholls said (at para 37) that *Lambe* was correctly decided because the correct test was the price which the acquiring authority would have had to pay in friendly negotiation if it had had no compulsory purchase powers, and this price would have included the marriage value. In contrast, Lord Scott said (at para 99) that *Lambe* had been wrongly decided because, on the facts, the merger value was not an element in the value of the land to the seller for the purposes of r 2 but rather it was an element of value only to a purchaser of the freehold (in this case the Secretary of State) who was the sitting tenant because he happened already to hold the leasehold interest.

2 *Trocette Property Co Ltd v GLC* (1973) 27 P&CR 256, Lands Tribunal, in which it was found, on the evidence, that the GLC, as freeholder, would not have been willing to purchase the leasehold interest in order to achieve development of the land because, as highway authority, they required it for a road scheme. However, compensation was awarded to reflect the loss of marriage value as a result of the operation of the LCA 1961, s 9, see para **[1222]**.

[425]

Another potentiality of land may be the possibility of using or developing it in conjunction with other land. In *Stokes v Cambridge Corpn*[1], land which had been compulsorily acquired was valued on the assumption that planning permission would be granted for industrial development, but the acquiring authority already owned the only land which could provide satisfactory access. The Lands Tribunal held that, in the absence of the compulsory purchase, the owner of the development land would have negotiated with the owner of the access land in order to unlock the development potential, that a figure would have been agreed at one third of the development value and, accordingly, that the development value of the land compulsorily acquired should be reduced by one third to take account of the lack of access. *Stokes v Cambridge Corpn* is often cited as shorthand for the proposition that, where the owner of one parcel of land holds the key to the development of another parcel, this 'ransom' value may be appropriately assessed as a proportion of the development value which the key can unlock. However, *Stokes v Cambridge Corpn* is a principle of valuation and not a rule of law[2]. It is entirely a question of fact whether one parcel holds the, or a, key to the development of another, and a question of fact what, in any particular circumstances, a person would be willing to pay for the key in order to unlock the development value[3].

1 (1961) 13 P&CR 77, Lands Tribunal.
2 *Ward Construction Ltd v Barclays Bank plc* (1994) 68 P&CR 391, CA.
3 *Stokes v Cambridge Corpn* was not followed in *Earl Fitzwilliam's Wentworth Estates v British Railways Board* (1967) 19 P&CR 588, Lands Tribunal, in which the facts were found to be sufficiently different. Other examples of circumstances in which *Stokes v Cambridge Corpn* has been considered include: *Re SJC Construction Co Ltd's Application* (1974) 28 P&CR 200, Lands Tribunal; affd (1975) 29 P&CR 322, CA; *Laing Homes Ltd v Eastleigh Borough Council* (1978) 250 Estates Gazette 350 and 459, Lands Tribunal; *Dicconson Holdings Ltd v St Helens MBC* (1979) 249 Estates Gazette 1075, Lands Tribunal; *Batchelor v Kent County Council* (1989) 59 P&CR 357, CA; *Hertfordshire County Council v Ozanne* (1991) 62 P&CR 1, HL; *Ward Construction Ltd v Barclays Bank plc* (1994) 69 P&CR 391, CA. See also para **[426]** and para **[1209]**.

[425.1]
There is a useful discussion on the character and potentialities of the land in *Ryde International plc v London Regional Transport*[1] where part of the claim was that the developer landowner should have been able to recover the lost 'profit' that would have been made if it had been able to 'refurbish' the property and sell it off as flats. Carnworth LJ made the following comments during the course of an altogether illuminating judgment:

> 'It is irrelevant that, in the real world, [the landowner] would not in fact have sold on a single date, but would have refurbished and marketed the flats as individual units over a period of months. That evidence is only indirectly material, in providing a basis for the assumption to be made about the hypothetical purchaser. It does not of course have to be assumed that the sale would be as a single unit. It is to be assumed that the vendor would market the property in the manner calculated to achieve the best price. However, this does not assist [the landowner] in the present case. The property must be assumed to be sold in its existing state. In this case it is common ground that in order to achieve the agreed "ultimate" price, expenditure would first need to be incurred in refurbishment. That potential was fairly taken into account by assuming a sale to an "entrepreneur" who would carry out the same project.'

Indeed, a consequence of the potential for developer's 'profit' being taken into account by assuming a sale to an 'entrepreneur', who would carry out the redevelopment, was that there was also no claim for such lost 'profit' under r (6) (disturbance).

1 [2004] EWCA Civ 232, [2004] RVR 60.

5 Disregarding the scheme

[426]
Compensation cannot include an increase in the value of the land taken which is attributable to the scheme underlying the acquisition. The case always cited

for this proposition is *Pointe Gourde Quarrying and Transport Co Ltd v Sub-Intendent of Crown Lands*[1], although the principle is of earlier origin. It has been held that this principle also applies to decreases in value attributable to the scheme[2]. Statutory rules have been enacted in the LCA 1961, s 6, which have a similar effect to the *Pointe Gourde* rule, although they have not replaced it. The LCA 1961, s 9 is also aimed at eliminating the effect of the scheme upon the value of the land[3]. These rules, which are often difficult to apply in practice, and which must now all be read in the light of the House of Lords decision in *Waters v Welsh Development Agency*[4], are considered in more detail in **Chapter 4**.

1 [1947] AC 565, PC.
2 *Birmingham City Council v Morris and Jaccombs Ltd* (1976) 33 P&CR 27, CA.
3 See para **[1222]**.
4 [2004] 1 WLR 1304.

6 Evidence of value

[427]
All the available evidence, if relevant, is admissible, but the weight to be attached to it is a matter of fact and valuation judgment[1]. Generally, evidence of open market transactions of comparable property at a comparable date, if available, is likely to be afforded the greatest weight[2]. An analytical approach is usually preferred to a '40 years-man-and-boy' approach[3], but not always[4]. The Upper Tribunal is normally reluctant to attach much weight to a residual valuation as evidence of open market value[5], but, in exceptional cases it has accepted a residual valuation in preference to comparables[6] or for want of better evidence[7]. Agreements of compensation for compulsory purchase are not generally regarded as reliable evidence of open market value[8]. An offer made 'subject to contract' or 'without prejudice' is not binding and may not be taken into account in valuing the land, nor can a party be estopped by such an offer from contending that a different figure is appropriate[9]. In a case in which the prospective compulsory acquisition of land caused a deferral of a rent review, thereby depriving the landowner of the higher rent, the Lands Tribunal held that the higher rent should be taken into account in assessing the value of the land taken under r 2[10].

1 *Garton v Hunter (Valuation Officer)* [1969] 2 QB 37, CA. See also *Griffiths v City and County of Swansea* [2004] RVR 111, LT; [2004] RVR 127, CA (evidence of events after the valuation date are not admissible to prove value) and *Cornwall Coast Country Club v Cardgrange Ltd* [1987] 1 EGLR 146 at 154G–H, Ch D.
2 *Vyricherla Narayana Gajapatiraju v Revenue Divisional Officer, Vizagapatam* [1939] AC 302, PC.
3 *Marson (HM Inspector of Taxes) v Hasler* (1975) 233 Estates Gazette 1183, Lands Tribunal.
4 *Richards v Somerset County Council* [2002] RVR 328, paras 233–234.
5 For example, *Fairbairn Lawson Ltd v Leeds County Borough Council* (1972) 222 Estates Gazette 561; *South Coast Furnishing Co Ltd v Fareham Borough Council* (1976) 242 Estates Gazette 1057; 243 Estates Gazette 53; *Essex Incorporated Congregational Union v Colchester Borough Council* [1983] RVR 267.
6 *Clinker and Ash Ltd v Southern Gas Board* (1967) 18 P&CR 372.
7 *Trocette Property Co Ltd v Greater London Council* (1973) 27 P&CR 256, Lands Tribunal; affd (1974) 28 P&CR 408, CA. As to developer's profit in a residual valuation, see *Richmond Gateways Ltd v Richmond-upon-Thames London Borough Council* [1989] 2 EGLR 182; *Railtrack v Guinness plc* (Lands Tribunal: CON/153/2000); affirmed on other grounds sub nom *Guinness plc v Railtrack plc* [2003] EWCA Civ 188, [2003] RVR 280; *Corton Caravans and Chalets Ltd v Anglican Water Services* [2003] RVR 323; *Tudor Properties Ltd v Bolton Metropolitan Borough*

Council [2000] RVR 94 at 102. See also the discussion of the residual method in the Privy Council decision in *Mon Tresor and Mon Desert Ltd v Ministry of Housing and Lands and Board of Assessment* [2008] UKPC 31, [2009] RVR 217. In *Ridgeland Properties Ltd v Bristol City Council* [2009] UKUT 102 (LC), [2009] RVR 252, the Lands Tribunal (at para 293) drew attention to the need to consider pragmatically and sensibly how much information a developer would expect to require in order to formulate an open market bid, and commented that they had been drawn into a disproportionate amount of detail.

8 *Shaw v London Borough of Hackney* (1974) 28 P&CR 477, Lands Tribunal; *Clegg and Styan (Mortgagee) v Sheffield City Council* (1975) 15 RVR 8. In *Port of London Authority v Transport for London* [2008] RVR 93, Lands Tribunal, the tribunal rejected evidence of settlements reached under other statutory powers which required different 'disregards'. The Upper Tribunal has repeated these views in *Wolff v Transport for London* [2008] RVR 316 and *Toms v Secretary of State for Transport* [2011] UKUT 45 (LC): although in both cases, the context was claims under the LCA 1973, Part 1, similar considerations would apply in the context of a r 2 valuation.

9 *Munton v Greater London Council* (1976) 32 P&CR 269, CA; *Secretary of State for Transport v Christos and Christos* [2003] EWCA Civ 1073, [2003] RVR 307.

10 *Greens Motor Holdings Ltd v Preseli Pembrokeshire District Council* [1991] 1 EGLR 211, Lands Tribunal.

E Rule 3 'The special suitability or adaptability of the land for any purpose shall not be taken into account if that purpose is a purpose to which it could be applied only in pursuance of statutory powers, or for which there is no market apart from ... the requirements of any authority possessing compulsory purchase powers'[1]

1 Introduction

[428]

The effect of this rule was summarised by Parker LJ in *Lambe v Secretary of State for War*[2] in these terms: ' ... if one of the potentialities of the land is such that there is only one purchaser of the land with that potentiality, the added amount which he would pay is to be ignored.' The purpose of this rule is to eliminate from the compensation any increase in value[3] attributable to the special characteristics of the land where:

(*a*) the land has special suitability or adaptability for a particular purpose; and

(*b*) that purpose is either of the following:

  (i) a purpose which could not be carried out without statutory powers, *or*

  (ii) a purpose for which there is no market apart from the special needs of a body having power to purchase land compulsorily.

Each of these limbs of the rule will be explained separately in the paragraphs which follow. Prior to 1991, the rule also eliminated any increase in value attributable to the special needs of a particular purchaser, but the rule was amended to delete the words which had this effect[4].

1 LCA 1961, s 5, r 3. As to the original text of the rule, see note 4 below.

2 [1955] 2 QB 612, CA, at 619. In *Waters v Welsh Development Agency* [2004] UKHL 19, [2004] 1 WLR 1304, there was a difference of opinion as to whether *Lambe* had been correctly decided: see note 1 to para **[424]**. However, this does not appear to effect the description of the effect of r 3 cited here.

3 The rule only applies if it is shown that there is an enhancement of value due to the special suitability or adaptability of the land: *Lambe v Secretary of State for War* [1955] 2 QB 612.

4 Prior to 1991, r 3 contained, where the dots appear in the text of the rule set out above, the following additional words: 'the special needs of a particular purchaser or'. It is generally recognised that these words were included in the rule when it was first enacted in 1919 in order to reverse the effect of the decision in *IRC v Clay; IRC v Buchanan* [1914] 3 KB 466. These words were repealed by the Planning and Compensation Act 1991, s 70 with effect from 25 September 1991. This amendment should be borne in mind when referring to cases which arose prior to that date.

[428.1]

In *Waters v Welsh Development Agency*[1] in the House of Lords, Lord Nicholls commented on r 3 as follows:

> 'Over the years, the courts have interpreted rule 3 narrowly. In an illuminating report the Law Commission said that in practice rule 3 appears to have little remaining purpose. It has become effectively redundant ... Some of the Court decisions restricting the scope of rule 3 are open to criticism. But, like my noble and learned friend Lord Brown of Eaton-under-Heywood, I would let them be. They do not seem to give rise to difficulties in practice. Where rule 3 is not applied the "value to the owner" principle operates... Subject to statutory provision to the contrary it should continue to be applied generally.'

1 [2004] UKHL 19, [2004] 1 WLR 1304 at [39].

2 Special suitability or adaptability of the land for any purpose

[429]

These words refer to the qualities of the land itself and not to the needs of a particular purchaser[1]. The Court of Appeal has adopted the *Oxford English Dictionary* definition of 'special', that is, 'of such a kind as to exceed or excel in some way that which is usual or common, exceptional in character, quality[2] or degree'[3]. Geographical location can give special suitability[4]. The fact that a sitting tenant would be prepared to pay more for the land than anyone else does not give the land special suitability or adaptability for a particular purpose within r 3[5]. The fact that a parcel of land, which has been compulsorily acquired, is the most suitable for a particular purpose, where, on the evidence, other land would also have been suitable, albeit less so, does not make the land acquired specially suitable within the rule[6].

1 *Lambe v Secretary of State for War* [1955] 2 QB 612, CA, at 620. In *Waters v Welsh Development Agency* [2004] UKHL 19, [2004] 1 WLR 1304, there was a difference of opinion as to whether *Lambe* had been correctly decided: see note 1 to para **[424]**. However, this does not appear to effect the proposition for which the case is cited here.

2 The word quality is apt: per Lord Scarman in *Blandrent Investment Developments Ltd v British Gas Corpn* [1979] 2 EGLR 18, HL.

3 *Batchelor v Kent County Council* (1989) 59 P&CR 357, CA, at 362.

4 *Batchelor v Kent County Council* (1989) 59 P&CR 357, CA, at 362, citing *Raja Vyricherla Narayana Gajapatiraju v Revenue Divisional Officer, Vizagapatam* [1939] AC 302, PC. The *Batchelor* case related to land acquired for highway purposes; on the facts found, there was held to be no *special* suitability, because access could have been obtained by other means. Cf *Laing Homes Ltd v Eastleigh Borough Council* (1978) 250 Estates Gazette 350, Lands Tribunal, in which land acquired for a spine road for development was held to be especially suitable.

5 *Lambe v Secretary of State for War* [1955] 2 QB 612 at 620. See the comment on *Lambe* in note 1 above.
6 *Batchelor v Kent County Council* (1988) 59 P&CR 357, CA. See also *Waters v Welsh Development Agency* [2001] 1 EGLR 185, Lands Tribunal; upheld [2003] 4 All ER 384, CA.

[430]–[440]
The purpose must be one to which the land itself can be applied; the special suitability of the products of the land is not sufficient[1]. Thus, for example, land may be especially suitable for a spine road in a development[2], for joint development with other land[3],or for a bridge[4]. The merger of interests in land is not a 'purpose' in this context[5].

1 *Pointe Gourde Quarrying and Transport Co Ltd v Sub-Intendent of Crown Lands* [1947] AC 565, PC, in which a quarry had been acquired compulsorily; r 3 was held not to apply because, although the stone produced from a quarry was particularly suitable for building a naval dockyard nearby, the land comprising the quarry had no special suitability or adaptability within the meaning of the rule.
2 *Laing Homes Ltd v Eastleigh Borough Council* (1978) 250 Estates Gazette 350, Lands Tribunal.
3 *Blandrent Investment Developments Ltd v British Gas Corpn* [1979] 2 EGLR 18, HL, although the rule was held not to apply because there was, on the evidence, a market, see para **[443]**.
4 *Port of London Authority v Transport for London* [2008] RVR 93, Lands Tribunal.
5 *Lambe v Secretary of State for War* [1955] 2 QB 612. See the comment on *Lambe* in para **[429]** note 1.

[441]
There must be evidence that the special suitability or adaptability of the land as defined in the rule enhances the value of the land; it is for the acquiring authority to show that the rule applies[1].

1 *Lambe v Secretary of State for War* [1955] 2 QB 612, CA, at 621. See the comment on *Lambe* in para **[424]** note 1.

3 A purpose which could not be carried out without statutory powers

[442]
For this limb of the rule to apply, the statutory powers must be powers which enable a person entitled to use the land to apply it to a purpose for which statutory powers are necessary[1]. In *Hertfordshire County Council v Ozanne*[2], the claimants contended that a small parcel of land compulsorily acquired should be valued as a 'ransom' strip on the ground that it provided the only means of access to a development site. The acquiring authority contended that r 3 prevented any ransom value being taken into account on the ground that the land could only be put to highway purposes by the exercise of statutory powers to make a stopping up order on other land. The House of Lords held that r 3 did not apply because the power to make a stopping up order in relation to land other than that acquired did not fall within the rule.

1 Per Lord Mackay LC in *Hertfordshire County Council v Ozanne* (1991) 62 P&CR 1 at 6. It was recognised that the effect of r 3 is to eliminate the enhancement of value referred to in the Privy Council case of *Cedar Rapids Manufacturing and Power Co v Lacoste* [1914] AC 569. An example is the construction of a bridge for a highway: *Port of London Authority v Transport for London* [2008] RVR 93.
2 (1991) 62 P&CR 1.

4 A purpose for which there is no market apart from the requirements of any authority possessing compulsory purchase powers

[443]
If there is evidence of a market for the purpose, r 3 will not apply[1].

1 Per Lord Scarman in *Blandrent Investment Developments Ltd v British Gas Corpn* [1979] 2 EGLR 18, HL. See also *Corrie v Central Land Board* (1954) 4 P&CR 276, Lands Tribunal; *Barstow v Rothwell UDC* (1971) 22 P&CR 942, Lands Tribunal; *Rathgar Property Co Ltd v Haringey London Borough Council* (1978) 248 Estates Gazette 693, Lands Tribunal. Cf *Laing Homes Ltd v Eastleigh Borough Council* (1978) 250 Estates Gazette 350, Lands Tribunal, in which there was held to be no market. These cases were decided prior to the amendment to r 3, see para **[428]** note 2. See also *Port of London Authority v Transport for London* [2008] RVR 93.

F Rule 4 'Where the value of land is increased by reason of the use thereof or of any premises thereon in a manner which could be restrained by any court, or is contrary to law, or is detrimental to the health of the occupants of the premises or to public health, the amount of that increase shall not be taken into account'[1]

[444]
Examples of uses which are 'contrary to law' include uses carried on in breach of planning control[2], building regulations or fire regulations[3]. In practice, it seems to be unlikely that such a use will enhance the open market value of land since a purchaser will normally be unwilling to pay a price which reflects a use which can be prevented from continuing. However, there may be instances where a use is contrary to law, but a purchaser would be willing to pay a price which reflects that use because relatively minor works would make it lawful, or because, although in breach of planning control, it is likely that planning permission would be granted.

1 LCA 1961, s 5. The definition of the term 'use' in this context is not to be restricted by its meaning in the context of development control legislation because r 4 originated in 1919 prior to the introduction of planning control: see *Roberts v South Gloucestershire District Council* [2003] 1 P&CR 411, per Carnwath LJ at paras 40–41.

2 *Hughes v Doncaster MBC* [1991] 1 AC 382, HL. One of the issues in this case was concerned with the meaning of 'contrary to law' in the context of the Town and Country Planning legislation, prior to the amendments introduced by the Planning and Compensation Act 1991. At that time, a use which had become 'established', in the sense of becoming immune from enforcement action, was nevertheless termed 'unlawful'; the House of Lords held that a use which was immune from enforcement action was not 'contrary to law' within the meaning of r 4. Since 1991, the same point would not arise, but a use which was carried on in breach of planning control would fall within r 4. See also the comments of Carnwath LJ in *Roberts v South Gloucestershire District Council* [2002] EWCA Civ 1568, [2003] RVR 43, paras 40–41.

3 Examples from a different legislative context are *Tower Hamlets London Borough Council v St Katherine-by-the-Tower Ltd* [1982] RA 261; *Regent Lion Properties Ltd v Westminster City Council* [1989] RA 190.

[445]
In *Hughes v Doncaster Metropolitan Borough Council*[1], the House of Lords held that r 4 operates to eliminate, not only any increase in the open market value of the land assessed under r 2, but also any right to claim compensation for loss due to disturbance of a use which is contrary to law. Thus, for example, where land

which is used in breach of planning control is compulsorily acquired, the person carrying on that use cannot claim compensation for disturbance of the use[2].

1 [1991] 1 AC 382, HL.
2 See, for example, *Hall v Sandwell Metropolitan Borough Council* [2008] RVR 345, in which the Lands Tribunal held that compensation could not be claimed in respect of chattels left on the land when the compulsory purchase took effect because they were there in connection with unlawful activities. In *Samuel Taff v Highways Agency* [2009] UKUT 128 (LC), although the Lands Tribunal held (as mentioned in the preceding paragraph) that this rule did not apply to the assessment of the value of land used as a scrapyard which was a lawful use under the town and country planning legislation but was being carried on without a waste management licence, with regard to the disturbance claim, the tribunal held that the amount could not be increased by reference to business operations which could not lawfully be carried out without a waste management licence.

G Rule 5 'Where land is, and but for the compulsory acquisition would continue to be, devoted to a purpose of such a nature that there is no general demand or market for land for that purpose, the compensation may, if the Lands Tribunal is satisfied that reinstatement in some other place is bona fide intended, be assessed on the basis of the reasonable cost of equivalent reinstatement'[1]

[446]
Where land is compulsorily acquired, the objective of compensation is to put the claimant, so far as money can do it, 'in the same position as if his land had not been taken from him. In other words, (the claimant) gains the right to receive a money payment not less than the loss imposed on him in the public interest, but, on the other hand, no greater'[2]. In the majority of cases, this is achieved by the operation of rr 2 and 6, that is, the payment of a sum comprising the open market value[3] of the land taken, together with any losses caused to the claimant due to disturbance[4]. The claimant can then, if he wishes, acquire other land and reinstate the use to which he had put the land taken from him compulsorily. However, prior to the enactment of the rules for the assessment of compensation in 1919[5], it had been recognised that, where land is put to a use for which there is no market, its open market value cannot be ascertained by reference to sales of similar property, and reinstatement could not be readily achieved merely by the claimant purchasing premises put to a similar use elsewhere[6]. Rule 5 was, therefore, introduced[7] to codify what had previously been the practice; it authorises a sum to be awarded, in appropriate cases, which would enable the claimant to recover the reasonable cost of reinstating the use elsewhere. The application of the rule is not confined to purposes such churches and other non-profit making organisations; it may apply to commercial purposes. This rule is explained in detail in **Chapter 5**.

1 LCA 1961, s 5.
2 *Horn v Sunderland Corpn* [1941] 2 KB 26, per Scott LJ at 42; see para **[21]**.
3 As to open market value, see paras **[408]–[421]**.
4 As to compensation for disturbance, see **Chapter 6**.
5 See para **[5]**.
6 For an explanation of the background of the rule, see the speech of Lord Reid in *Birmingham Corpn v West Midland Baptist Trust Association Inc* [1970] AC 874, HL, 20 P&CR 1052 at 1057.
7 ALACA 1919, s 2, re-enacted by the LCA 1961, s 5.

H Rule 6 'The provisions of rule (2) shall not affect the assessment of compensation for disturbance or any other matter not directly based upon the value of the land'

[447]–[800]
Under the LCCA 1845 and prior to the ALACA 1919, compensation for the value of land compulsorily acquired was assessed as the value of the land to the owner, which included compensation for loss resulting from being disturbed from possession of the land[1]. The ALACA 1919 separated the value of the land, to be assessed at open market value under r 2[2], from compensation for disturbance. As Sir Wilfrid Greene MR explained in *Horn v Sunderland Corpn*[3]:

> 'does not confer a right to claim compensation for disturbance. It merely leaves unaffected the right which the owner would, before the Act of 1919, have had in a proper case to claim that the compensation to be paid for the land should be increased on the ground that he had been disturbed.'

The right to claim compensation for disturbance is explained in detail in **Chapters 6** and **9**.

1 See para **[4]**.
2 As to r 2, see para **[407]**.
3 [1941] 2 KB 26 at 34.

Chapter 3

Assumptions as to planning permission

Contents

A Introduction

[801]

It has been explained above[1] that the open market value of land will often be influenced by its potential for development. Since development is controlled under the town and country planning legislation, the potential for development will depend upon the planning permissions which exist or which are likely to be granted. The Land Compensation Act 1961 (LCA 1961), ss 14–16 require that, for the purposes of assessing compensation, there must be taken into account, not only planning permissions which have actually been granted, but also certain assumptions as to the prospect of planning permission being granted if the land had not been acquired compulsorily[2]. The LCA 1961, ss 17–22 provide a mechanism, an application for a 'certificate of alternative development', for obtaining a determination whether, in the absence of the compulsory purchase, planning permission for development could reasonably have been expected to have been granted[3]. These provisions are explained in this chapter. It should be noted that it does not follow from the requirement that a planning permission, actual or assumed, should be taken into account, that it must also be assumed that such permission would be capable of implementation[4], nor that there would be demand for the development permitted thereby adding value to the land[5].

1 See para **[403]**.
2 LCA 1961, s 14(1). The assumptions apply only to the 'relevant land', ie the land being compulsorily acquired: s 39(1).
3 Regard must be had also to any opinion expressed in such a certificate that planning permission would not have been granted: LCA 1961, s 14(3A).
4 *Manchester Land Securities v Denton UDC* (1970) 21 P&CR 430 at 437; *Pearce and Thorpe v Aughton Parish Council* (1973) 26 P&CR 357 at 392–394.
5 *Viscount Camrose v Basingstoke Corpn* [1966] 3 All ER 161, per Lord Denning: 'Even though the 233 acres are assumed to have planning permission, it does not follow that there would be a demand for it. It is not planning permission by itself which increases value. It is planning permission coupled with demand.' Followed in *Myers v Milton Keynes Development Corpn* [1974] 2 All ER 1096, CA. See also *Halliwell and Halliwell v Skelmersdale Development Corpn*

(1965) 16 P&CR 305; *Bromilow v Greater Manchester Council* (1974) 29 P&CR 517, Lands Tribunal; affd (1978) 31 P&CR 398, CA; *J Davy Ltd v Hammersmith London Borough Council* (1975) 30 P&CR 469.

[802]

The LCA 1961, ss 14–16 provide for the following to be taken into account:

(*a*) existing planning permissions;
(*b*) assumptions not directly derived from the development plan; and
(*c*) assumptions directly derived from the development plan.

Each of these will be explained separately in the paragraphs which follow. It should be noted that, by virtue of s 14(3), these provisions are not to be construed as requiring it to be assumed that planning permission would necessarily be refused for development for which planning permission is not to be assumed pursuant to these provisions. Thus, a claimant may contend that, in the absence of the compulsory purchase, he would have been able to obtain planning permission for development which would have given his land value[1].

1 In *Melwood Units Pty Ltd v Commissioner of Main Roads* [1979] AC 426, the Privy Council held that, even though planning permission would never have been granted for development due to the road scheme for which the land in question had been compulsorily acquired, it was open to the claimant to show that, in the absence of the road proposal, planning permission would have been granted. Applied in *Essex County Showground Group Ltd v Essex County Council* [2006] RVR 336 at 342, Lands Tribunal. See further **Chapter 4** below: 'Disregarding the scheme'.

[802.1]

In a number of decisions between 2003 and 2008, the Lands Tribunal held that the *Pointe Gourde* rule enabled it to be assumed for the purposes of valuing the land taken that planning permission would have been granted on the valuation date, where it was shown by evidence that, on the balance of probabilities, planning permission would have been granted in the absence of the scheme underlying the acquisition[1]. This application of the *Pointe Gourde* rule was upheld by the Court of Appeal[2], but was rejected by the House of Lords in *Transport for London (formerly London Underground Ltd) v Spirerose Ltd*[3]. The House of Lords held that there was no basis in authority or in principle for the conclusion that it is open to the court in effect to establish an assumption that planning permission would be obtained, by analogy with specific statutory rules which create the assumption and that it was not the role of the court to re-write legislation by adding additional assumptions of planning permission. In the light of *Spirerose*, the Upper Tribunal has reiterated the need to apply the statutory provisions systematically rather than to 'leap into the no scheme world and proceed from there[4].

1 *Pentrehobyn Trustees v National Assembly for Wales* [2003] RVR 140; *RMC (UK) Ltd v Greenwich London Borough Council* [2005] RVR 140; *Spirerose Ltd v Transport for London* [2008] RVR 12. The first of these was decided before the House of Lords decision in *Waters v Welsh Development Agency*, and the latter two were decided after *Waters*. In an interim decision published after the House of Lords decision in *Spirerose*, the Lands Tribunal has provided an interesting commentary on the *Spirerose* decision which indicates that the difficulties with this topic may not have been fully resolved: *Persimmon Homes (Midlands) Ltd v Secretary of State for Transport* [2009] UKUT 126 (LC), although in *Thomas Newell Ltd v Lancaster City Council* [2010] UKUT 2 (LC), the tribunal, applying *Spirerose*, concluded (at paras 29–30) that the *Pointe Gourde* rule

cannot be relied upon for an assumption that planning permission would have been granted in the absence of the scheme.
2 *Transport for London v Spirerose Ltd* [2008] EWCA Civ 1230, [2009] 4 All ER 810, [2009] RVR 18, CA.
3 [2009] UKHL 44, [2009] RVR 225, HL. See para **[1208.2]**ff below.
4 *Potter and Potter v Hillingdon London Borough Council* [2010] UKUT 212 (LC), para 73 and *Hornby v Gateshead Borough Council* [2010] UKUT 426 (LC), para 89.

B Existing planning permissions

[803]
Any existing planning permissions in force at the date of service of the notice to treat are to be taken into account[1]. It is immaterial whether or not an existing permission is actual or deemed, conditional or unconditional, full or outline, or granted by a general development order, or whether it relates to the land[2] in question or some larger area[3].

1 This is inferred from the LCA 1961, s 14(2) which refers to any assumed planning permission being in addition to any planning permission which may be in force at the date of service of the notice to treat. As to the meaning of planning permission in this context, see s 39(1).
2 As to the meaning of 'land', see the LCA 1961, s 39(1).
3 LCA 1961, ss 14(4)(*a*)–(*c*). As to the meaning of 'planning permission', see s 39(1). A temporary permission is merely a permanent permission subject to conditions and is to be taken into account notwithstanding it was granted for the period pending compulsory acquisition: *McArdle v Glasgow Corpn* [1971] RVR 357.

C Assumptions not directly derived from the development plan

1 Development included in the existing use

[804]
Prior to 1991, by virtue of the LCA 1961, s 15(3), planning permission was to be assumed for development listed in the TCPA 1990, Sch 3. The Planning and Compensation Act 1991 (PCA 1991) repealed the TCPA 1990, s 114, Sch 3, Pt II, and replaced the LCA 1961, s 15(3). Planning permission is now only to be assumed[1] for:

(*a*) rebuilding a building[2] that was in existence on 1 July 1948 or, if built after that date, in existence at the date when the provisions fall to be applied[3];
(*b*) the carrying out of maintenance, improvement of alterations which affect only the interior or not materially affect the external appearance of the building, or works for making good war damage; or
(*c*) the use of a single dwelling house as two or more dwelling houses[4].

The requirement to assume planning permission for rebuilding a building which was in existence on 1 July 1948 has been held by the Court of Appeal in *Greenweb v London Borough of Wandsworth*[5] to be the result of the clear words of the statutory provisions which were criticised as anomalous. In contrast, the requirement to assume planning permission to rebuild a dwelling can have the result that no compensation is payable; this may occur where there is a deemed compulsory purchase consequent upon service of a purchase notice following refusal of planning permission to rebuild a derelict house[6].

1 Subject to the condition set out in the TCPA 1990, Sch 10.
2 As to the meaning of building, see s 39(1).
3 TCPA 1990, Sch 3, para 12.
4 LCA 1961, s 15(3) as amended applying the TCPA 1990, Sch 3, para 1 and subject to the condition in Sch 10, Sch 2, para 3. This does not apply where an order has been made under the TCPA 1990, s 102 (requiring removal of a building) or s 115 (requiring discontinuance of a use): LCA 1961, s 15(4).
5 [2008] EWCA Civ 910, [2008] RVR 294. This case concerned a parcel of land where there had existed, prior to 1 July 1948, nine houses which were damaged by war time bombing and demolished. From 1979, the land was used as public open space with the benefit of planning permission. Planning permission was refused for the construction of houses. Following service of a purchase notice, compensation had to be assessed as if the land had been compulsorily acquired. A s 17 certificate of appropriate alternative development had been refused by the local planning authority and on appeal under s 18. The land was found by the Lands Tribunal to be worth £15,000 as public open space and £1.6 million on the assumption that planning permission existed for rebuilding the nine houses. The Court of Appeal held that planning permission had to be assumed for rebuilding the houses. Prior to 1988, planning permission was granted by development order for rebuilding war-damaged houses, so a person owning the site of war-damaged houses had the benefit of an actual planning permission and it was logical that, if his land was compulsorily acquired, he should have the benefit of the assumption. The Court of Appeal regarded the retention of the LCA 1961 s 15(3) after 1988 as anomalous and endorsed the recommendation of the Law Commission that it be repealed.
6 The rebuilding to be assumed is limited to the original site or curtilage. Although an adjoining site could be assumed to be incorporated to provide open space, a terrace of houses could not be assumed to be replaced by a single dwelling spread over several plots: *Farley v Bristol Corpn* (1958) 10 P&CR 204 at 208; *Lidle v LCC* (1959) 10 P&CR 421 at 422–423; *Shelton v Birmingham Corpn* (1960) 11 P&CR 193 at 194–195; *Fisher and Cartwright v Birmingham Corpn* (1961) 12 P&CR 387 at 393. Contrast the earlier decision in *Green v Birmingham Corpn* (1951) 2 P&CR 220. See also *Canterbury City Council v Colley* [1993] AC 401, HL, which related to compensation for a discontinuance order. The assumed rebuilding does not have to be an exact replica of the old building: *Re Walker's Settled Estate* [1984] 1 Ch 189 at 194: 'nor would the introduction of alterations and enlargements make any difference in that respect'; *Low v Innes* (1884) 4 De GJ&Sm 289: 'rebuilding does not mean in the same manner, style and shape.' The hypothetical rebuilding must, presumably, conform to all current limitations imposed by statute or deed such as restrictive covenants, building regulations and other health and safety requirements. See also *Old England Properties Ltd v Telford and Wrekin Council* [2000] 3 EGLR 153, Lands Tribunal. The concept of abandonment has no relevance in this context: *Dutton and Black v Blaby District Council* [2006] RVR 203, Lands Tribunal.

2 Development in accordance with the proposals of the acquiring authority

[805]

Where, at the date of the notice to treat, the acquiring authority has not obtained planning permission[1] for the development for which the land is being compulsorily acquired, planning permission is to be assumed which would permit development of the claimant's land (only) in accordance with the acquiring authority's proposals[2]. It is not necessary for the purposes of s 15(1) to make a judgment as to whether such planning permission might reasonably have been expected to be granted. The correct approach is: '(1) determine the nature of the property to be valued … (2) determine the extent of the interest to be valued with the benefit of the planning permission assumed under s 15(1), (3) ascertain the value of that interest'[3]. In *Roberts v South Gloucestershire District Council*[4], land had been acquired for the construction of a road. The process of construction involved excavation of minerals from the claimant's land as part of a cut-and-fill operation. The claimant contended that under s 15(1) he could assume planning permission for mineral extraction. The Court of Appeal held that under s 15(1) he could assume planning permission to construct on his land what the acquiring authority proposed, that is, a road, but he could not assume that such permission extended to adjacent land. The permission was for the 'indivisible process' of building the road. This decision was applied by the Lands Tribunal in *Colneway Ltd v Environment Agency*[5] which concerned land acquired for construction of a flood relief channel involving the extraction of considerable quantities of minerals along the route of the channel. The claimant's contention that s 15(1) entitled him to assume a planning permission for mineral extraction was rejected.

1 As to the meaning of planning permission in this context, see the LCA 1961, s 39(1). A planning permission which does not enure for the benefit of the land is not to be taken into account for this purpose: LCA 1961, s 15(2) and the TCPA 1990, s 75(1).
2 LCA 1961, s 15(1). *Myers v Milton Keynes Development Corpn* (1974) 27 P&CR 518.
3 *Myers v Milton Keynes Development Corpn* (1974) 27 P&CR 518, per Lord Denning at 524.
4 [2003] 1 P&CR 411, CA.
5 [2004] RVR 37.

3 Development in accordance with a 'certificate of appropriate alternative development'

[806]
Where a 'certificate of appropriate alternative development' is issued pursuant to the LCA 1961, ss 17–22, it must be assumed, for the purposes of assessing the value of the land compulsorily acquired, that planning permission would be granted in accordance with the certificate, but subject to any conditions, and at such future time, as are specified in the certificate[1]. The procedure for applying for such a certificate is explained below[2].

1 LCA 1961, s 15(5). The provisions of the LCA 1961 are not to be construed as requiring it to be assumed that planning permission would necessarily be refused for any development for which planning permission is not required to be assumed by virtue of these provisions: LCA 1961, s 14(3).
2 See para **[809]**.

4 Highway land

[807]
Where the compulsory acquisition is for, or in connection with, the construction, alteration or improvement of a highway, it is to be assumed that, if the land was not required for highway purposes, no highway to meet the same, or substantially the same, need would have been constructed[1]. This assumption applies both for the purpose of assessing the value of the land and for the purposes of an application for a certificate of appropriate alternative development[2]. Thus, the land may not be valued on the basis that, in the absence of the scheme, some hypothetical alternative highway would have been constructed to serve the same function as the scheme for which the land is being compulsorily acquired.

1 LCA 1961, s 14(5)–(8), inserted by the PCA 1991, s 64. This also applies where the highway authority is merely considering the use of the land being compulsorily acquired for or in connection with the construction of a highway: s 14(5).
2 LCA 1961, s 14(7). As to certificates of appropriate alternative development, see para **[809]**.

5 Assumptions derived from section 14(3)

[807.1]
Where it can be shown that, in the absence of the compulsory purchase, there would have been a prospect that planning permission would have been granted for development of the land taken, the LCA 1961, s 14(3)[1] enables that prospect to be taken into accounteven if the case does not fall within one of the statutory provisions which expressly provide for assumptions to be made as to the grant of planning permission. However, following the decision of the House of Lords in *Transport for London (formerly London Underground Ltd) v Spirerose Ltd (in admin)*[2], where there is such a prospect, it may not be assumed that planning permission had been granted on or before the valuation date[3]. The value of land with a prospect that planning permission would be granted is likely to be lower than its value if planning permission had already been granted because a purchaser is likely to discount the value to reflect the uncertainties and delay in obtaining permission[4]. In contrast, where a certificate of appropriate alternative development has been granted pursuant to the LCA 1961, s 17, by virtue of s 15(5), it may be assumed that permission existed on the valuation date (or such later date as is specified in the certificate)[5]. Consequently, in any case where there is a prospect that planning permission would have been granted in the absence of the compulsory purchase, it is wise to consider whether an application should be made for a certificate under s 17 before a reference is made to the Lands Tribunal to determine the amount of compensation payable.

1 LCA 1961, s 14(3) provides: 'Nothing in these provisions shall be construed as requiring it to be assumed that planning permission would necessarily be refused for any development which is not development for which, in accordance with those provisions, the granting of planning permission is to be assumed.'
2 [2009] UKHL 44, [2009] 4 All ER 810. See also para **[1208]** below.
3 In contrast, where it can be shown that, in the absence of the compulsory purchase, planning permission would have been granted at some earlier date, the land may be valued as though such permission had been granted: *Jelson v Blaby District Council* [1977] 1 WLR 1020 and *Melwood Units Pty Ltd v Commissioner of Main Roads* [1979] AC 425. See also paras **[1222]–[1224]** below.
4 As to the distinction between valuing a certainty, albeit deferred in time, and valuing a 'hope', see the comments of Lord Denning in *Myers v Milton Keynes Development Corporation* (1974) 27 P&CR 518 at 527, endorsing the approach of the Lands Tribunal in *Camrose v Basingstoke Corporation* cited in the Court of Appeal judgment of that case [1966] 1 WLR 1100 at 1106.
5 As to s 17 certificates, see para **[809]** onwards.

[807.2]
In *Abbey Investments Ltd v London Development Agency*[1], the Upper Tribunal held that the 'cancellation assumption'[2] should be applied to s 14(3) on the valuation date. It is also held (although on the facts it made no difference to the decision) that it was legitimate to take into account the fact that other land in the area had been purchased by the acquiring authority prior to the date of the assumed cancellation notwithstanding that such purchases were made in the 'shadow' of the scheme underlying the compulsory purchase[3].

1 [2010] UKUT 325 (LC).
2 Ie that the proposed acquisition of the claimant's land be assumed to have been cancelled. As to the 'cancellation assumption', see para **[808.1]** note 4.
3 See the reservations expressed on behalf of the acquiring authority in para 48 of the decision.

D Assumptions directly derived from the development plan

[808]
The LCA 1961, s 16 makes provision for assumptions which derive directly from the 'current development plan'. There are four circumstances in which an assumption may be made as to the grant of planning permission which are defined in the LCA 1961, s 16(1)–(4). Where one of the four subsections applies, it is to be assumed for the purpose of valuing the land compulsorily acquired that planning permission would be granted for the form of development specified. This removes any uncertainty which would otherwise exist as to whether and when planning permission would be granted. If section 16 does not apply, then it may still be possible to achieve a similar result by means of a certificate granted under the LCA 1961, s 17[1]. If s 16 does not apply and no certificate is obtained under s 17, it may nevertheless be possible to take account of the prospect of development by virtue of s 14(3)[2].

1 Such a certificate has effect by virtue of s 15(5). See also **[1208.4]–[1208.5]**. As to s 17 certificates, see para **[809]** onwards.
2 See also para **[807.1]**.

[808.1]
The term 'current development plan' means the development plan applicable to the land compulsorily acquired at the date of the notice to treat[1]. The term 'development plan' has the same meaning as in the context of the town and country planning legislation[2]. In *Urban Edge Group Ltd v London Underground Ltd*[3], the acquiring authority contended that s 16 only applied to development plans prepared under the TCPA 1947; while recognising that the drafting of s 16 reflected the drafting of the TCPA 1947, and especially s 5 thereof, the Lands Tribunal rejected this contention. However, the style of modern development plans is such that it may be difficult to conclude that the land compulsorily acquired was 'defined … as the site of proposed development of a description specified … in the plan' or was within an area 'allocated primarily for a use' or uses[4].

1 LCA 1961, s 39(1).
2 The term 'development plan' was defined in the LCA 1961 as having the meaning assigned to it by the TCPA 1947, s 5. The TCPA 1990, s 27 provided that, for the purpose of the LCA 1961, the development plan was (within London) the UDP for the district and (outside London) and s 54 provided that for the purpose of the LCA 1961, the development plan was the structure and local plans. The PCPA 2004, s 38(2), (3) and (7) provides that a reference in the LCA 1961 to the development plan is a reference to the special development strategy and the development plan documents.
3 [2009] UKUT 103 (LC), [2009] RVR 361. See also *Purfleet Farms Ltd v Secretary of State for Transport* [2002] RVR 203, Lands Tribunal (appeal to CA on costs only).
4 These phrases are to be found in LCA 1961, s 16(1)–(4). The difficulty which may be experienced in applying s 16 to modern development plans is illustrated by the discussion in *Urban Edge Group Ltd v London Underground Ltd* [2009] UKUT 103 (LC), [2009] RVR 361 at paras 24–31, in which the Lands Tribunal considered whether the land compulsorily acquired was 'allocated' in the light of certain policies in the Hackney UDP, and decided that it was not. See also *Abbey Investments Ltd v London Development Agency* [2010] UKUT 325 (LC).

[808.2]
The circumstances in which the LCA 1961, s 16(1)–(4) apply may be summarised as follows:

(*a*) Subsection (1) applies where the land acquired 'consists or forms part of an area defined in the current development plan as the site of development of a description specified in relation thereto in the plan'[1]. Where this applies, it is to be assumed that planning permission would be granted for that development.

(*b*) Subsection (2) contains two limbs: the first defines the circumstances to which it applies, and the second provides the criterion for making an assumption. It applies where the land acquired 'consists or forms part of an area allocated primarily for a use specified in the development plan'[2]. Where it applies, it is to be assumed that planning permission would be granted for any development for the purposes of the specified use so long as it is development for which planning permission might reasonably have been expected to be granted[3] if no part of the land had been proposed to be acquired by any authority possessing compulsory purchase powers[4].

(*c*) Subsection (3) also contains two limbs and is similar to sub-s (2) except that it applies where the land acquired 'consists or forms part of an area allocated in the development plan for a range of two or more uses'. Where it applies, it is to be assumed that planning permission would be granted for any development for the purposes of a use within the range of uses specified in the plan so long as it is development for which planning permission might reasonably have been expected to be granted if no part of the land had been proposed to be acquired by any authority possessing compulsory purchase powers[5].

(*d*) Subsection (4) also contains two limbs. It applies where any part of the land acquired is subject to 'comprehensive development'[6]. Where it applies, it is to be assumed that planning permission would be granted for any development within the 'planned range of uses'[7] so long as it is development for which planning permission might reasonably have been expected to be granted if the area had not been designated a comprehensive development area[8].

1 See *Thomas Newell Ltd v Lancaster City Council* [2010] UKUT 2 (LC), [2010] RVR 223, paras 11–17.

2 See *Thomas Newell Ltd v Lancaster City Council* [2010] UKUT 2 (LC), [2010] RVR 223, paras 11–19. See also *Abbey Investments Ltd v London Development Agency* [2010] UKUT 325 (LC), Upper Tribunal.

3 The proper approach is to determine what a reasonable planning authority would have decided: see *Essex County Showground Group Ltd v Essex County Council* [2006] RVR 336 and *Urban Edge Group Ltd v London Underground Ltd* [2009] UKUT 103 (LC), [2009] RVR 361 at paras 49–51.

4 The requirement to assume that no part of the land had been proposed to be acquired by any authority possessing compulsory purchase powers derives from LCA 1961, s 16(7). For a discussion of the corollaries of this requirement, see *Margate Corpn v Devotwill Investments Ltd* [1970] 3 All ER 864, HL, although it should be noted that, in so far as this case was concerned with a highway, the decision preceded the enactment of the LCA 1961, s 14(5)–(8). The same requirement appears in the LCA 1961, s 17; in that context it has been interpreted by the House of Lords as meaning that 'The scheme for which the land is proposed to be acquired, together with the underlying proposal which may appear in any of the planning documents, must be assumed on that date to have been cancelled': *Newell v Secretary of State for the*

Environment [2000] 2 AC 307 at 322H. In *Thomas Newell Ltd v Lancaster City Council* [2010] UKUT 2 (LC), [2010] RVR 223, the Upper Tribunal held that the cancellation assumption applies to s 16(2), but at the valuation date, not the date of publication of the compulsory purchase order as under ss 17 and 22. The tribunal also held that the assumption relates only to the claimant's land and it does not follow that the acquiring authority's scheme or proposals generally have to be disregarded. See also *Abbey Investments Ltd v London Development Agency* [2010] UKUT 325 (LC). For an example of the operation of s 16(7), see *Richardsons Developments Ltd v Stoke-on-Trent Corpn* (1971) 22 P&CR 958. In *Provincial Properties (London) Ltd v Caterham and Warlingham UDC* (1972) 23 P&CR 8, land on a ridge-line within the green belt was zoned for residential use but the Court of Appeal held that both sub-ss (*a*) and (*b*) of s 16(2) had to be complied with and since it was perfectly clear that planning permission would never be granted, the assumption did not apply.

5 See note 4 above.

6 'Land subject to comprehensive development' is defined in the LCA 1961, s 16(8) as an area defined in a development plan as subject to comprehensive development. The TCPA 1990, s 54(5) provides that the term 'comprehensive development area' is to be construed as an action area in a local plan.

7 As to 'planned range of uses' see s 16(5).

8 See s 16(5).

[808.3]

Any planning permission assumed under s 16 is to be assumed to be subject to such conditions as might reasonably have been expected to be imposed and, if the plan indicates that permission would only be given at a future time, then it is to be assumed that permission would be granted at that time[1]. Section 16 is silent about planning obligations under the TCPA 1990, s 106 and similar undertakings, but it is submitted that, where the evidence indicates that planning permission would not have been granted in the absence of a planning obligation, then it should be assumed that an appropriate agreement committing the developer to the obligation would have been entered into[2].

1 Section 16(6).

2 See the decision of the Lands Tribunal in *Purfleet Farms Ltd v Secretary of State for Transport* [2002] RVR 20, LT (appealed unsuccessfully to the Court of Appeal on costs only).

E Certificates of appropriate alternative development

[809]

Where an interest in land[1] is proposed to be acquired by an authority possessing compulsory purchase powers[2], an application for a 'certificate of appropriate alternative development' can be made, either by the person entitled to an interest in land that is proposed to be acquired, or by the authority proposing to acquire that interest[3]. Where a certificate is issued, it is to be assumed, for the purposes of assessing compensation, that planning permission would have been granted for the development specified in the certificate[4].

1 Defined in the LCA 1961, s 39(1).

2 Defined in the LCA 1961, s 39(1).

3 LCA 1961, ss 17(1), s 22(1). The certificate procedure was introduced in the Town and Country Planning Act 1959; see the explanation and advice in Circular 48/59. Where the landowner is abroad or cannot be traced, so that a surveyor is required to value the interest under the Land Clauses Consolidation Act 1845, s 58 or under the Compulsory Purchase Act 1965, Sch 2, para 1(1), the surveyor can also apply for a certificate: LCA 1961, s 19.

4 LCA 1961, s 15(5).

1 Availability of procedure

[810]–[820]

An application for a certificate can only be made in respect of land which an authority proposes to acquire[1], and can only be made where:

(*a*) a notice of acquisition has been published or served in connection with that acquisition[2];
(*b*) a notice of purchase has been served under any enactment and a notice to treat is deemed to have been served[3]; or
(*c*) a written offer to negotiate to purchase has been made by the acquiring authority[4]; or
(*d*) a vesting order has been made in favour of an Urban Regeneration Agency[5].

An application for a certificate cannot be made after a reference to the Lands Tribunal has been made unless either the other party consents in writing or the tribunal grants leave[6].

1 As to land not taken but severed or injuriously affected by the acquisition, see para **[828]**.
2 LCA 1961, s 22(2)(*a*), eg Acquisition of Land Act 1981, ss 11, 12.
3 LCA 1961, s 22(2)(*b*), eg purchase notices served under the TCPA 1990, s 137 and blight notices served under s 149.
4 LCA 1961, s 22(2)(*c*), eg where an agreement for sale is contemplated without resort to the formalities of compulsory acquisition, and the parties wish to ascertain what level of compensation would have been recoverable had the acquisition been compulsory.
5 LCA 1961, s 22(2)(*ca*). This sub-section was added by the Leasehold Reform and Urban Development Act, 1993, s 161(4), Sch 19, para 4, with effect from 10 November 1993, pursuant to SI 1993/2762, in order to extend s 22(1) to vesting orders made by the Urban Regeneration Agency.
6 LCA 1961, s 17(2)(*a*), (*b*). In *Kingsley v Highways Agency* [2010] UKUT 309 (LC), the Upper Tribunal refused to grant leave to the acquiring authority where the landowner had previously been granted a positive certificate and the acquiring authority's purpose in seeking consent to make an application was to obtain a conflicting certificate on the ground that by virtue of s 15(5) the tribunal was obliged to give effect to the first certificate.

2 Procedure for making an application

[821]

An application for a certificate is made to the local planning authority[1] and must:

(*a*) be in writing[2];
(*b*) include a plan or map identifying the land to which the application relates[3];
(*c*) state whether or not there are, in the applicant's opinion, any classes of development which would be appropriate for the land, immediately or at a future time[4];
(*d*) state the applicant's grounds for holding that opinion[5]; and
(*e*) be accompanied by a statement specifying the date on which the application had been, or would be, served on the other party[6].

The phrase 'classes of development' is very general[7] and does not bear the same meaning as in, for example, the Town and Country Planning General

Development Order or the Town and Country Planning (Use Classes) Order nor is it is restricted solely to classes that are likely to be implemented[8]. The costs reasonably incurred in making an application may be recovered as part of the compensation payable[9].

1 LCA 1961, s 17(1). As to the meaning of 'local planning authority', see s 39(1) applying the TCPA 1990, Pt I. Applications in respect of county matters should be made to the county council. Special provision is made in respect of the area of the Norfolk and Suffolk Broads Authority by the LCA 1961, s 17(10), (11).
2 Land Compensation Development Order 1974, SI 1974/539, art 3(1). There is no requirement that it should be accompanied by an environmental assessment, since any certificate granted would not be a development consent within the meaning of the Environmental Assessment Directive 85/337/EEC: *R v North Yorkshire County Council, ex p Brown* [2000] 1 AC 397, [1999] 1 All ER 969, HL.
3 Land Compensation Development Order 1974, SI 1974/539, art 3(1).
4 LCA 1961, s 17(3)(*a*). As to the meaning of 'class' or 'classes' of development, see *Essex Construction Co Ltd v Minister of Housing and Local Government* [1968] RVR 818, High Court and *Sutton v Secretary of State for the Environment* (1984) 50 P&CR 147, High Court. The classes of development and dates at which they are considered appropriate must be specified in the application. 'Immediately' means immediately after the relevant date for the purposes of s 22(2), eg immediately after the proposal to acquire. The 'future' is the future as seen from that same date: *Fox v Secretary of State for the Environment* (1991) 62 P&CR 459, Roch J, at 474. See also para **[824]**.
5 LCA 1961, s 17(3)(*b*).
6 LCA 1961, s 17(3)(*c*).
7 *Essex Construction Co Ltd v Minister of Housing and Local Government* [1968] RVR 818.
8 *Sutton v Secretary of State for the Environment* (1984) 50 P&CR 147. In *Sutton*, the judgment refers to the Town and Country Planning General Development Order 1977. SI 1977/289 or the Town and Country Planning (Use Classes) Order 1972, SI 1972/1385, but it is submitted that the same point would apply equally to later versions of those Orders.
9 LCA 1961, s 17(9A). This provision does not preclude recovery of reasonable expenses of an unsuccessful application, but, if the applicant appeals, only the costs in respect of a successful appeal are recoverable.

3 Determination of an application

[822]
The local planning authority must not determine the application until 21 days have passed from the date of service of the application as specified in the statement accompanying the application, but it must determine the application and issue a certificate within two months[1].

1 LCA 1961, s 17(4) and SI 1974/539, art 3(2). As to the form of the certificate to be issued, see para **[823]**.

4 Form of certificate

[823]
The certificate issued must state that, if the land were not proposed to be acquired by a body possessing compulsory purchase powers, either:

(*a*) planning permission would have been granted for development of one or more of the classes specified in the certificate[1], in addition to the development for which the land is to be acquired[2], setting out any conditions or general requirements that would have been imposed[3] and any future date at which the permission would have been granted[4]; or that (*b*) planning permission would not have been granted for any development of the land apart from the development for which the land is to be acquired[5].

The certificate is to be issued to the applicant[6] and copies must be served on the other parties[7]. If the certificate is not granted in the terms of the application, or if it differs from the terms of written representations made to the local planning authority, it must contain a statement in writing giving the local planning authority's reasons, and it must also give particulars of the manner in which, and the time within which, an appeal may be made to the Secretary of State[8]. A copy of any certificate issued and details of the applicant are to be made available by the local planning authority, on written request, to any person having an interest in the land the subject of the certificate[9].

1 As to the meaning of 'class' or 'classes' of development, see *Essex Construction Co Ltd v Minister of Housing and Local Government* [1968] RVR 818, HC and *Sutton v Secretary of State for the Environment* (1984) 50 P&CR 147, HC. The certificate is not limited to the terms of the application and may state that planning permission would have been granted for development not specified in the application: SI 1974/539, art 3(3).
2 LCA 1961, s 17(4)(*a*).
3 LCA 1961, s 17(5), (6). If conditions are specified by reference to general requirements a copy of the requirements must be supplied with the certificate and every copy of the certificate unless the requirements are already publicly available on deposit: SI 1974/539, art 6. As to the effect of conditions and a tree preservation order, see *Pearce and Thorpe v Aughton Parish Council* (1973) 26 P&CR 357.
4 LCA 1961, s 17 (5).
5 LCA 1961, s 17(4)(*b*).
6 LCA 1961, s 17(4). A copy of a certificate issued by a county planning authority must be sent to the district planning authority, and a copy of a certificate issued by a district planning authority containing a 'county matter' must be sent to the county planning authority: Land Compensation Development Order 1974, SI 1974/539, art 3(4).
7 LCA 1961, s 17(9).
8 SI 1974/539, art 3(3). Failure to include the required particulars will invalidate the certificate: *London and Clydesdale Estates Ltd v Aberdeen District Council* (1979) 39 P&CR 549.
9 SI 1974/539, art 5.

5 Material considerations

[824]
In determining an application for a certificate, it is not open to the local planning authority to certify that planning permission would have been refused for a class of development by reason only that it would not have been in accordance with the development plan[1]. The date at which the facts and circumstances in relation to the land in question, and the relevant planning policies, are to be taken for the purposes of determining an application is the date when the notice of the making of a compulsory purchase order was given, or (as the case may be) the date of the blight or purchase notice, or the date when a written offer to purchase the land is made, or the date when an order vesting land in the Urban Regeneration Agency was made[2]. In determining an application, it must be assumed that the scheme for which the land was proposed to be acquired has been cancelled on that date; it is not correct to assume that the scheme had never been conceived[3].

1 LCA 1961 s 17(7). This is to be contrasted with the obligation of a local planning authority under the TCPA 1990, s 54A to determine planning applications in accordance with the development

plan unless material considerations indicate otherwise. The TCPA 1990, s 54A does not apply to the LCA 1961, s 17 (see the definition of the 'planning Acts' in the TCPA 1990, s 336).

2 LCA 1961, s 22(2). See *Fletcher Estates (Harlescott) Ltd v Secretary of State for the Environment* [1999] QB 114, sub nom *Secretary of State for the Environment v Fletcher Estates (Harlescott) Ltd* (1998) 76 P&CR 382, CA; affirmed by HL on a different point (see note 3 below) [2000] 1 All ER 929, 80 P&CR 95, HL; following *Jelson v Minister of Housing and Local Government* [1970] 1 QB 243; *Fox v Secretary of State for the Environment* (1991) 62 P&CR 459; overruling *Robert Hitchins Builders Ltd v Secretary of State for the Environment* (1978) 37 P&CR 140. In *Transport for London (formerly London Underground Ltd) v Spirerose Ltd* [2009] UKHL 44, [2009] RVR 225 at [58], Lord Neuberger suggested that this issue might be re-visited one day. In contrast, under s 16, the relevant facts and circumstances must be taken as they were on the valuation date: see para **[808.2]**, note 4.

3 *Fletcher Estates (Harlescott) Ltd v Secretary of State for the Environment* [2000] 1 All ER 929, 80 P&CR 1, HL. For the position under s 16, see para **[808.2]**, note 4.

6 Appeals against the certificate

[825]

Where a certificate has been issued[1], or no certificate has been issued within two months of the receipt of the application[2] (or such other period as may be agreed upon[3]), either the person for the time being entitled to the interest in land to which the certificate relates, or the authority proposing to acquire the interest, may appeal in writing[4] to the Secretary of State. An appeal must be made within one month from receipt of the certificate, or from the expiry of the time for determination of the application[5]. Notice of appeal must be given in writing to the Secretary of State, and copies must be sent to the other parties and to the local planning authority which determined it[6]. The appellant must, within one month of giving notice of appeal, or such longer period as the Secretary of State allows[7], send to the Secretary of State:

(*a*) a copy of the application;
(*b*) a copy of the certificate, if one was issued; and
(*c*) a statement of grounds of appeal[8].

Failure to supply the documents in time will result in the appeal being treated as withdrawn[9].

1 LCA 1961, s 18(1).
2 SI 1974/539, art 3(2).
3 The period for determination may be extended by agreement: LCA 1961, s 18(4).
4 SI 1974/539, art 4(1).
5 SI 1974/539, art 4(1).
6 SI 1974/539, art 4(2).
7 SI 1974/539, art 4(3). Any application for an extension of time should be made before the expiry of the specified period: *Ward v Secretary of State for the Environment* [1994] EGCS 164; following *R v Secretary of State for the Environment, ex p Hillingdon London Borough Council* (1991) 64 P&CR 105.
8 SI 1974/539, art 4(3).
9 SI 1974/539, art 4(4).

7 Determination of appeal

[826]

The Secretary of State must consider the appeal as if the application had been made to him in the first instance. He has power to confirm, vary or cancel the certificate, or to issue a different certificate[1]. Before reaching his decision, he must give the parties, if any of them so request it, an opportunity of being heard; this is normally achieved through the holding of a public inquiry[2]. There are no statutory procedural rules for such an inquiry, but normally the procedures of a planning or compulsory purchase inquiry are followed[3]. The decision is not delegated; the inspector appointed to hold the inquiry reports to the Secretary of State with recommendations. The Secretary of State may disagree with his inspector[4]. The Secretary of State has to be satisfied that planning permission would have been granted on a balance of probabilities and does not have to assess more precisely the chances of planning permission being granted for that development[5]. The costs of an appeal may be included in a claim for compensation, but only in so far as the claimant succeeds on any of the issues in the appeal[6].

1 LCA 1961, s 18(2). A certificate issued following an appeal could, therefore, be more unfavourable than the one issued by the local planning authority.
2 LCA 1961, s 18(3).
3 As to the procedures for a compulsory purchase order inquiry, see **C [197]**.
4 *Maidstone Borough Council v Secretary of State for the Environment* [1996] RVR 127.
5 *Porter v Secretary of State for Transport* [1996] 3 All ER 693, CA.
6 LCA 1961, s 17(9A), which reverses the effect of *Hull and Humber Investment Co Ltd v Hull Corpn* [1965] 2 QB 145, CA.

[826.1]
Under the LCA 1961, s 17(4), the question is whether planning permission 'would have been granted' either at the relevant date (which by definition is some date in the past) or at a future date. The question whether planning permission 'would have been granted' must be answered as at the relevant date, in other words, as though the local planning authority had decided a planning application on that date having regard to all policies and other considerations which would have been material on that date. The question must be answered by applying the same test that the local planning authority would have applied to a real planning application on the relevant date[1].

1 By virtue of s 70 of the TCPA 1990, it is a requirement to take account of the development plan and any other material considerations, but the statutory provisions and the policy advice as to the weight to be attached to them has changed over time: (*a*) prior to the Planning and Compensation Act 1991 which enacted the Town and Country Planning Act 1990, s 54A (see PPG1 (1988), para 15 and *Thornville Properties Ltd v Secretary of State for the Environment* [1981] JPL 116); (*b*) after the enactment of the TCPA 1990, s 54A (by the Planning and Compensation Act 1991) (see PPG1 (1992), para 25); (*c*) after the enactment of the Planning and Compulsory Purchase Act 2004, s 38 (PPS1, paras 10–16).

[826.2]
In determining an ordinary planning application, no question of 'burden of proof' in the formal sense arises. The local planning authority's duty is to take into account all material policies and other considerations and to attach appropriate weight to them. Nevertheless, there may be steps which an applicant can take to influence the weight to be attached to a material consideration. For example, if the access to his site does not meet the applicable standards and improvement would require land outside his control, he can overcome what otherwise would be a ground of refusal by signing a planning obligation under TCPA 1990, s 106 binding him to arrange for

improvements. So, in a loose sense, it might be said that there was an 'onus' on him to adduce evidence which would remove or reduce the weight to be attached to a potential ground of refusal. On an appeal against the refusal of planning permission, the inspector or Secretary of State's duty is to determine the planning application on the same approach as the local planning authority is required to follow on the basis of the policies and material considerations as they stand when the decision is taken. While the parties will no doubt ensure that the inspector is informed about all the policies and other material considerations, inevitably, the proceedings will focus upon the reasons given by the local planning authority for refusal. The appellant will know that he must persuade the inspector or the Secretary of State that these should carry little weight. It is therefore up to the appellant to adduce such evidence as he thinks is appropriate for that purpose. Again, in a loose sense, the 'onus' is on the appellant to do so, but that does not affect the approach of the Secretary of State when determining the planning application.

[826.3]

In the context of the LCA 1961, s 17(4), there is no burden of proof in the formal sense on either the applicant/appellant or the local planning authority although the position under s 17(4) is a little different from an ordinary planning application or appeal as revealed by *JD White Ltd v Secretary of State for the Environment*[1], which went to the High Court because the Secretary of State dismissed the appeal even though the Inspector had indicated that he did not have sufficient information to resolve one of the issues. It was held that fairness required that the appellant should have been given the opportunity to adduce further evidence on that issue. This was seen to fit with the purpose and role of s 17. Again, in a loose sense, it might be said that, if the opportunity had been given, the 'onus' would then have been on the appellant to adduce the required information. However, that does not alter the role of the inspector or Secretary of State when determining the question having regard to all material policies and other considerations.

1 [1982] JPL 506, HC.

[826.4]

With regard to the alternative question which arises under the LCA 1961, s 17(4), that is, whether planning permission would have been granted at 'a future date', the date referred to must by definition be subsequent to the relevant date but it may be earlier or later than the date of the local planning authority's decision under s 17 or the Secretary of State's decision on an appeal under s 18. The power to determine whether planning permission would have been granted at a future date is another difference from the determination of an ordinary planning application. Under s 17(4), the question whether permission would have been granted at a future date must still be determined on the relevant date having regard to the policies and other considerations which would have been material on that date. A decision that permission would have been granted at a future date might arise, for example, where the relevant policies state that development will be acceptable but not until a later date, such as after a new road has been constructed or to meet a need which is expected to arise later in the plan period.

8 Right to challenge the Secretary of State's decision on an appeal

[827]
The decision of the Secretary of State on an appeal under the LCA 1961, s 18 may be challenged in the High Court by any person aggrieved by means of an application to the High Court which must be made within six weeks of the date of the decision. Leave to make such an application is not required. The basis upon which a challenge may be made is restricted to the grounds that the decision is not within the powers of the Act, or that there has been a failure to comply with any of the procedural requirements which has resulted in substantial prejudice to the applicant's interests[1]. This is the only procedure for challenging the validity of the Secretary of State's decision[2]. Judicial review may be available if the Secretary of State refuses or fails to give a decision on an appeal[3]. The High Court may suspend the operation of the decision by interim order until the determination of the proceedings[4], and may quash the decision[5].

1 LCA 1961, s 21(1). The procedural requirements are those in the LCA 1961, in a development order (eg the Land Compensation Development Order 1974, SI 1974/539), in the Tribunals and Inquiries Act 1992 or in rules made under that Act. The grounds upon which a decision may be challenged are similar to those available in relation to the right to challenge a decision of the Secretary of State to confirm a compulsory purchase order, as to which, see **C [1006]**. They are also similar to the TCPA 1990, s 288. For an example of the exercise of this jurisdiction, see *Rooff Ltd v Secretary of State for Communities and Local Government* [2011] EWCA Civ 435, [2011] All ER (D) 180 (Apr), in which the Secretary of State's decision under s 18 was quashed on the ground that one paragraph in his inspector's report lacked sufficient clarity of reasoning.
2 LCA 1961, s 21(2).
3 LCA 1961, s 21(3).
4 LCA 1961, s 21(1)(*a*).
5 LCA 1961, s 21(1)(*b*).

9 The status of a certificate of appropriate alternative development

[828]
A certificate of appropriate alternative development concerns only the assumptions that are to be made, for the purposes of assessing compensation, as to the prospects of obtaining planning permission. It does not determine the existence of any market demand for the assumed classes of development[1]. The Lands Tribunal expressed the view in 1977 that the procedure for obtaining a certificate should be used to determine the relevant planning issues in preference to canvassing those matters before the tribunal[2], but in more recent years, it has been willing to determine significant planning issues, for example, in relation to the application of s 16. In any event, not all planning issues which might be relevant to the assessment of compensation are within the scope of s 17. For example, the certificate procedure is not available to ascertain the classes of development which might be permitted for land which has not been compulsorily acquired but has been severed from the land taken or otherwise injuriously affected[3]. Further, s 17(1) is expressed in permissive terms and even if a s 17 certificate has not been obtained, a party cannot be prevented from raising planning issues before the Upper Tribunal. Indeed, planning issues often arise and are determined by the Upper Tribunal. A decision of the Secretary of State, and any

findings of fact relied upon in issuing a certificate, do not raise an issue estoppel in a reference to the tribunal in relation to the assessment of compensation for severance or injurious affection to any of the claimant's land not taken[4]. Where not all of the land the subject of the certificate is in fact acquired the certificate cannot be divided and relied upon in part; the fresh circumstances must be taken into account[5]. A certificate stating that no development would have been permitted but for the acquisition must be taken into account[6], but this does not preclude the assessment of compensation reflecting hope value[7].

1 *Bromilow v Greater Manchester Council* (1975) 31 P&CR 398, where the market demand was found to be limited by an offensive neighbouring trade, and *Porter v Secretary of State for Transport* [1996] 2 EGLR 10.
2 *Williamson and Stevens (executors of Walter Williamson) v Cambridgeshire County Council* [1977] 1 EGLR165.
3 *Abbey Homesteads (Developments) Ltd v Northamptonshire County Council* [1992] 2 EGLR 18; *Portsmouth Roman Catholic Diocesan Trustees v Hampshire County Council* [1980] 1 EGLR 150; *Porter v Secretary of State for Transport* [1996] 2 EGLR 10. However, the background facts may be good evidence for the tribunal in relation to the value of the retained land: *ADP and E Farmers v Department of Transport* [1988] 1 EGLR 209. As to severance and injurious affection, see **Chapter 7**.
4 *BSH Holdings Ltd v West Ashford RDC* (1972) 24 P&CR 392; *Ryefield Securities Ltd v Staffordshire County Council* (1972) 24 P&CR 411; *Porter v Secretary of State for Transport* [1996] 2 EGLR 10, CA, concerning the value of retained land affected by severance or injurious affection.
5 *Hoveringham Gravels Ltd v Chiltern District Council* (1977) 35 P&CR 295, CA.
6 LCA 1961, s 14(3).
7 *Corrin v Northampton Borough Council* [1980] 1 EGLR 148, in which the compensation awarded reflected hope value notwithstanding a 'nil' certificate.

F Planning decisions after acquisition

1 Introduction

[829]
A person whose land has been acquired compulsorily may be entitled to claim additional compensation if, within ten years, planning permission is granted for development of the land taken which causes an increase its value which was not taken into account in the original assessment of compensation[1]. This right, which was originally enacted in 1961, repealed in 1967 and re-enacted in 1991[2], is explained in detail in the paragraphs which follow.

1 LCA 1961, ss 23–29.
2 These provisions were contained in the LCA 1961, Pt IV when it was first enacted but were repealed by the Land Commission Act 1967, and have now been re-enacted by the PCA 1991, s 66, Sch 14.

2 The right to claim additional compensation

[830]–[840]
The right to claim additional compensation arises where[1]:

(*a*) land has been acquired by a body possessing compulsory purchase powers[2], except one of those listed in the next paragraph, whether the land was acquired compulsorily or by agreement; and (*b*) within ten years from the date of completion[3], a planning decision is made granting planning permission for additional development[4] on the land.

1 LCA 1961, s 23(1).
2 As to the meaning of an 'authority possessing compulsory purchase powers', see the LCA 1961, s 39(1). An authority which purchased land by agreement, but for purposes authorised by a local act, was held to be within this definition since the purpose of the acquisition was to provide playing fields, the provision of which was a function of a local authority: *Janes v Bletchley UDC* (1970) 21 P&CR 632. A company having compulsory purchase powers which buys land as part of its business and not for purposes for which it has compulsory powers would be unlikely, it is submitted, to be liable to a claim for any additional development value under these provisions.
3 The date of completion means the date on which the acquisition or sale is completed by the vesting of that interest in the acquiring authority: see the LCA 1961, s 29(1).
4 As to the meaning of 'additional development', see para **[842]**.

[841]
The right does not arise where land has been acquired by agreement or compulsorily:

(*a*) by the Welsh Development Agency[1];
(*b*) by urban development corporations or highway authorities in connection with urban development areas[2];
(*c*) by development corporations or highway authorities in connection with new town areas[3];
(*d*) where a compulsory purchase order includes a direction that minimum compensation be paid because the building had been deliberately allowed to fall into disrepair[4]; and
(*e*) by the Homes and Communities Agency[5].

1 LCA 1961, s 23(3)(*za*); Welsh Development Agency Act 1975, s 21A.
2 LCA 1961, s 23(3)(*a*); Local Government Planning and Land Act 1980, ss 142 or 143.
3 LCA 1961, s 23(3)(*b*); the New Towns Act 1981.
4 LCA 1961, ss 23(3)(*c*), 50; Planning (Listed Buildings and Conservation Areas) Act 1990, ss 142 or 143.
5 LCA 1961, s 23(3)(*d*); Housing and Regeneration Act 2008, Pt I.

3 Planning permission for additional development

[842]
The planning permission which gives rise to this right may be a full or an outline permission, it may be a conditional permission and it may relate to the land originally taken by itself or to an area including that land[1]. It includes[2]:

(*a*) planning permission granted by a development order[3];
(*b*) planning permission granted by the adoption or approval of a simplified planning zone scheme[4];
(*c*) planning permission granted by an order designating an enterprise zone[5];
(*d*) planning permission deemed to be granted on a direction made under the TCPA 1990, s 90[6]; and
(*e*) planning permission deemed to be granted by a local planning authority[7].

1 LCA 1961, s 29(2). There is no express reference to a permission relating to a part only of the land originally taken. By way of contrast, there is specific reference to a part only of the land

for the purpose of a notification that the acquiring authority has ceased to hold an interest in the land: LCA 1961, s 24(6)(*b*).
2 LCA 1961, s 25(1).
3 LCA 1961, s 25(1). The date of the decision is the date when development is initiated.
4 LCA 1961, s 25(1). The date of the decision is the date when the scheme is approved or adopted.
5 LCA 1961, s 25(1). The date of the decision is the date when the designation takes effect.
6 LCA 1961, s 25(1). The date of the decision is the date when the direction is given.
7 LCA 1961, s 25(1). The date of the decision is the date of the occurrence of the event in consequence of which the permission is deemed to be granted.

[843]
'Additional development' of land means any development[1] of land other than:

(*a*) development by a local authority[2] for the purposes of a function for which the land was originally acquired[3];
(*b*) development by an acquiring authority other than a local authority[4] for the purposes of the project for which the land was originally acquired[5];
(*c*) development for which planning permission was in force when the notice to treat was first served or the original contract was made[6]; and
(*d*) development which was assumed for the purposes of a compulsory acquisition or would have been assumed had the acquisition been compulsory and not by agreement[7].

1 'Development' has the same meaning as in the Town and Country Planning Act 1947, s 12, now re-enacted as the TCPA 1990, s 55: LCA 1961, s 39(1).
2 As to the meaning of 'local authority' in this context, see the LCA 1961, s 29(1).
3 LCA 1961, s 29(1)(*a*).
4 As to the meaning of 'local authority', see note 2.
5 LCA 1961, s 29(1)(*b*). See *Kingswood Hall Properties Ltd v NATS (En Route) plc* [1006] RVR 73, Lands Tribunal.
6 LCA 1961, s 29(1)(*c*).
7 LCA 1961, s 29(1)(*d*), (*e*). See *Kingswood Hall Properties Ltd v NATS (En Route) plc* [1006] RVR 73, Lands Tribunal. As to planning assumptions, see paras **[801]–[828]**.

4 Assessment of additional compensation

[844]
The amount of compensation payable is the difference between the amount paid and the amount that would have been payable on the day when the notice to treat was served, or the day when the contract was entered into, on the assumption that the planning decision for additional development had already been made by that date and that the permission had then been in force[1]. The rules in the LCA 1961, Pt I apply[2], as do certain provisions in respect of disturbance, severance and injurious affection[3]. No provision is made for inflation or changes in the level of values between the date at which compensation was originally assessed and the date of claim, and interest is only payable from the date of the planning decision[4].

1 LCA 1961, s 23(1)(*b*), (2).
2 LCA 1961, s 23(6).
3 LCA 1961, s 27, Sch 3; as to disturbance, see **Chapter 6**. As to severance and injurious affection, see **Chapter 7**.
4 LCA 1961, s 23(5). Interest is payable at the rate prescribed under the LCA 1961, s 32, as to which, see **Division D**.

5 Claims and ancillary provisions

[845]–[1200]

In order to facilitate the making of claims, provision is made for local planning authorities to notify persons who have received compensation of any additional planning permissions[1]. A claim must be made within six months of notice of the decision[2] being served by the acquiring authority upon a person who has supplied his address to the acquiring authority in accordance with these provisions, or otherwise, within six months of the decision[3].

1 LCA 1961, ss 24–25. The notice must be in the prescribed form set out in the Land Compensation (Additional Development) (Forms) Regulations 1992, SI 1992/271. The acquiring authority need not notify the original claimant if it has reasonable grounds for believing that the original claimant is dead or has divested himself of his interest: LCA 1961, s 24(3). Where the acquiring authority has ceased to be entitled to any interest in all or part of the land, the acquiring authority must notify the local planning authority; the local planning authority must, within seven days of a planning decision, give the acquiring authority (but not the claimant) notice of the decision: LCA 1961, s 24(6), (7). Since, by virtue of the LCA 1961, s 39, 'local planning authority' has the same meaning as in the TCPA 1990, Pt I, it would be prudent for the acquiring authority to notify all authorities who might satisfy the definition of local planning authority for the land in question. As to Crown development, see the LCA 1961, s 26(2); there is an exemption from giving particulars of the additional development if the minister issues a certificate that, for reasons of national security, the nature of the development shall only be disclosed to the extent specified in the certificate: LCA 1961, s 26(4).

2 Or within six months of the date of a decision on any appeal against the original decision or non-determination: LCA 1961, s 24(4), (5).

3 LCA 1961, ss 24–25.

Chapter 4

Disregarding the scheme

Contents

A Introduction

[1201]
It has been explained above[1] that the measure of compensation for land acquired compulsorily is the open market value on the claimant's interest in the land. This is subject to one important qualification, that is, that any enhancement or diminution in the value of the land acquired compulsorily which is solely attributable to the particular purpose for which it was acquired, and the acquiring authority's need for the land for that purpose, is to be disregarded. Although relatively straightforward in concept, the application of this principle has proved over the last 150 years to be one of the most intractable problems in compensation law.

1 See para **[407]**ff.

[1201.1]
The history of the development and application of this principle is described in detail in a Report on compensation law by the Law Commission[1]. In short, the Lands Clauses Consolidation Act 1845 laid down that the measure of compensation should be the 'value' of the land taken without defining that term[2]. In a series of judicial decisions in the late nineteenth and early twentieth century, the term 'value' came to be interpreted as value to the owner, not value to the acquiring authority. Thus, in *Stebbing v Metropolitan Board of Works*[3], Cockburn CJ said:

> 'When Parliament gives compulsory powers, and provides that compensation shall be made to the person from whom property is taken, for the loss that he sustains, it is intended that he shall be compensated to the extent of his loss; and that his loss shall be tested by what was the value of the thing to him, not by what will be its value to the persons acquiring it.'

As noted above[4], the value to the owner principle as interpreted by judicial decisions was modified to some extent by statutory rules for the assessment of compensation which were introduced by the Acquisition of Land (Assessment of Compensation) Act 1919 and are now to be found in similar form in the Land Compensation Act 1961, s 5[5]. These included rule 3 which was intended to eliminate any value attributable to the acquiring authority's special need to acquire the land[6].

1 'Towards a Compulsory Purchase Code – Compensation' (Final Report): Law Commission No 286).
2 See para **[4]**.
3 (1870) LR 6 QB 37 at 42.
4 See para **[5]**.
5 See para **[407]**ff.
6 See para **[428]**.

[1201.2]

A number of cases arose in which the value of the land acquired was enhanced by the acquiring authority's use (or proposed use) or other land. In *Point Gourde Quarrying and Transport Co Ltd v Sub-Intendent of Crown Lands*[1], the Privy Council held that, in valuing the land acquired, it was necessary to leave out of account any value attributable to the scheme underlying the acquisition. This has come to be known as the *'Pointe Gourde'* rule. An attempt was made to enact this rule. The Land Compensation Act 1961, s 6 and Sch 1 is a complex provision the effect of which, in short, is that any increase (or decrease) in the value of the land acquired which is attributable to the development, or the prospect of development, of land (other than the land acquired) included in same compulsory purchase order (or within certain designated areas) is to be disregarded unless such development would have occurred anyway apart from the compulsory purchase[2]. Following the enactment of this provision, it was initially not clear whether Parliament had intended s 6 to replace the *'Pointe Gourde'* rule or merely supplement it. In due course, the courts concluded that s 6 was not exhaustive and that the *'Pointe Gourde'* rule still applied[3].

1 [1947] AC 565. For a fuller explanation of this case, see para **[1202]**. In *Waters v Welsh Development Agency* [2004] 1 WLR 1304, Lord Scott and Lord Brown thought that the need for the stone from the quarry in *Pointe Gourde* should have been disregarded under r 3 rather than a principle of common law: paras 93 and 142.
2 See **[1210]**ff below.
3 See para **[1203]**.

[1201.3]

In practice, there is often difficulty in identifying 'the scheme' underlying the acquisition, especially where the acquisition was under planning powers[1] to assemble land for others to develop rather than for a specific public project promoted by an undertaker such as a railway or a reservoir. In 2004, a case reached the House of Lords which provided an opportunity for a review of the Lands Compensation Act 1961, s 6 and the *'Pointe Gourde'* rule; this was *Waters v Welsh Development Agency*[2]. At the beginning of his judgment, Lord Nicholls of Birkenhead[3] cited and endorsed a passage from the judgment of Carnwath LJ[4] in the Court of Appeal in which he said that '… there can be few stronger candidates on the statute book for urgent reform, or simple repeal, than [the Land Compensation Act 1961, s 6 and Schedule 1]'.

1 See the comments of Sir Michael Rowe, President of the Lands Tribunal, in *Kaye v Basingstoke Corpn* (1968) 20 P&CR 417 at 455. Examples of planning powers are Town and Country Planning Act 1990, s 226, Leasehold Reform, Housing and Urban Development Act 1993, s 162 (English Partnerships) and Regional Development Agencies Act 1996, s 20 (regional development agencies).
2 [2004] UKHL 19, [2004] 1 WLR 1304.
3 Para 3. See also similar remarks by Lord Brown at para 164.
4 [2003] 4 All ER 384 at 414, para 116.

[1201.4]
In *Waters*, it was held, by a majority[1], that the *'Pointe Gourde'* rule should continue to be applied as a supplement to the statutory provisions. The case turned primarily upon the difficulty of identifying the 'scheme' for the purposes of the rule, and some guidance was given, especially by Lord Nicholls, as to how the extent of the scheme should be identified[2]. Lord Woolf expressed the hope that, in the light of this decision, tribunals and practitioners in future will not find it necessary to refer to any other authority. It remains to be seen whether this hope will be fulfilled. For present purposes, it is considered that readers are likely to be assisted by retention of the text of this chapter concerning the *'Pointe Gourde'* rule, with references inserted to the *Waters* case where appropriate, rather than elimination of the references to all previous cases[3].

1 Lord Scott of Foscote dissenting.
2 See paras **[1207.1]** and **[1207.2]**.
3 The comments in *Waters* on some of the cases referred to in the paragraphs which follow, especially *Myers v Milton Keynes Corpn* should be noted.

[1201.5]
The general principle that any enhancement or diminution in the value of land acquired compulsorily which is solely attributable to the particular purpose for which it was acquired is implemented by four main rules:

- Land Compensation Act 1961, s 5, rule 3.
- *'Pointe Gourde'* rule.
- Land Compensation Act 1961, s 6 and Sch 1.
- Land Compensation Act 1961, s 9.

[1201.6]
The first of those is considered in detail elsewhere[1]. The other three are explained in that order in the following paragraphs of this chapter[2]. In addition, it refers briefly to the provisions which seek to set off any 'betterment' due to the scheme to land owned by a claimant and not compulsorily acquired[3], which may be seen as the 'other side of the coin' in relation to s 6. Finally, this chapter also refers to the special provision relating to motorway service areas.

1 See para **[428]** ff.
2 In the light of the *Waters* case, it may be more appropriate to consider s 6 before *'Pointe Gourde'* rule but the order in which these were dealt with in this work prior to *Waters* has been retained.
3 Betterment is explained in more detail in para **[2901]**ff.

B The '*Pointe Gourde*' rule

1 The rule: an increase in value due to the scheme must be left out of account

[1202]
The '*Pointe Gourde*' rule is that, in valuing land which has been compulsorily acquired, there must be left out of account any increase in value which is attributable to the scheme underlying the acquisition. This rule takes its name from the case of *Pointe Gourde Quarrying and Transport Co Ltd v Sub-Intendent of Crown Lands*[1] decided by the Privy Council in 1947, although it has earlier origins[2]. In *Fraser v City of Fraserville*[3], Lord Buckmaster said:

> '... the value to be ascertained is the value to the seller of the property in its actual condition at the time of expropriation with all its existing advantages and with all its possibilities, excluding any advantage due to the carrying out of the scheme for which the property is compulsorily acquired ... '

The facts of the *Pointe Gourde* case provide a relatively simple illustration of how the rule operates: a quarry was compulsorily acquired in order to supply stone for construction work at a naval base; it was held that the valuation of the quarry could not take account of the fact that the acquiring authority's project created demand for the products of the quarry and consequently increased its value. The purpose of the rule, as explained by Widgery LJ in *Wilson v Liverpool Corpn*[4], is 'to prevent the acquisition of land from being at a price which is inflated by the very project or scheme which gives rise to it'. That case concerned land compulsorily acquired which was made more valuable by the prospect of sewage works and other infrastructure being provided on land adjacent to that taken from the claimant as part of the acquiring authority's scheme; the Court of Appeal held that the Lands Tribunal had been right to leave that increase in value out of account.

1 [1947] AC 565.
2 See the cases cited in the judgment.
3 [1917] AC 187, PC, at 194, applying earlier cases.
4 *Wilson v Liverpool City Council* (1970) 22 P&CR 282 at 293.

[1203]
Although the effect of this rule is similar to the LCA 1961, s 6, which is explained below[1], the Court of Appeal has held that the rule was not replaced when the LCA 1961, s 6 was enacted and that it continues to exist alongside the statute[2]. The continued existence of the rule was confirmed by the House of Lords in *Waters v Welsh Development Agency*[3], in which it was held that the statutory provisions should be applied first and the common law rule applied only where there is a lacuna in the statutory provisions and to ensure fairness. The rule does not apply where the compulsory purchase has caused a change in the nature of the claimant's interest in the land acquired[4].

1 See para **[1210]**.
2 *Viscount Camrose v Basingstoke Corpn* [1966] 1 WLR 1100, CA.
3 [2004] 1 WLR 1304, HL.
4 *Rugby Joint Water Board v Footit* [1973] AC 202. It is a rule of valuation and does not apply to ascertain the interest to be valued.

[1204]
The operation of the *Pointe Gourde* rule was explained by Nourse LJ in *Ward Construction (Medway) Ltd v Barclays Bank plc*[1] as follows:

> 'In order correctly to apply the *Pointe Gourde* principle it is necessary, first, to identify the scheme and, secondly, its consequences. The valuer must then value the land by imagining the state of affairs, usually called the "no-scheme world", which would have existed if there had been no scheme.'

The rule requires that an increase in value be ignored which is entirely due to the scheme; the rule does not diminish or remove any value which the land would have had apart from the scheme[2].

1 (194) 68 P&CR 391 at 396.
2 Per Mann LJ in *Batchelor v Kent County Council* (1989) 59 P&CR 357, CA, at 360–361, explained in (1994) 68 P&CR 391 at 396. See also *Melwood Units Pty Ltd v Main Roads Comr* [1979] AC 426, PC, at 434D–E, approved in *Director of Buildings and Lands Director v Shun Fung Ironworks Ltd* [1995] 2 AC 111, HL. See also *Cronin and Taylor v Swansea City Council* (1972) 24 P&CR 382, Lands Tribunal.

2 Application of the rule to a decrease in value

[1205]
It has been held in the Court of Appeal that the *Pointe Gourde* rule applies equally where the scheme has had the effect of reducing the value of the claimant's land[1]. This has been held to apply where the scheme has created conditions in an area where vandalism thrived, thereby diminishing the value of the property compulsorily acquired[2], and where the scheme limited the potential for development of the land taken[3].

1 *Salop County Council v Craddock* (1969) 213 Estates Gazette 633; *Birmingham City Council v Morris and Jacombs Ltd* (1976) 33 P&CR 27. See also *Melwood Units Pty Ltd v Main Roads Comr* [1979] AC 426, PC.
2 *Gately v Central Lancashire New Town Development Corpn* [1984] JPL 519, Lands Tribunal; *Arrow v Bexley London Borough Council* (1978) 35 P&CR 237, Lands Tribunal; *Lewars v GLC* (1981) 43 P&CR 129, Lands Tribunal.
3 *St Pier Ltd v Lambeth London Borough Council* (1976) 237 Estates Gazette 887, Lands Tribunal for Scotland.

3 'The scheme'

[1206]
In order to apply the *Pointe Gourde* rule, it is necessary to identify 'the scheme' underlying the acquisition[1]. In *Birmingham District Council v Morris and Jaccombs Ltd*[2], Sir John Pennycuick said[3], 'A scheme means, I think, no more than a project on the part of the authority concerned to acquire the land'. In the same case, Ormerod LJ warned[4]:

> 'There is clearly a danger that the word "scheme" is acquiring or will acquire a mystique of its own and be used as a starting point for highly elaborate – I almost said "sophisticated" – argument whereas if one looks at the authorities the scheme referred to is the scheme for which the property is being compulsorily acquired.'

In *Wilson v Liverpool City Council*[5], Lord Denning MR said:

> 'A scheme is a progressive thing. It starts vague and known to few. It becomes more precise and better known as time goes on. Eventually, it becomes precise and definite and known to all. Correspondingly, its impact has a progressive effect on values. At first, it has little effect because it is so vague and uncertain. As it becomes more precise and better known, so its impact increases until it has an important effect. It is this increase, big or small, which is to be disregarded as at the time when the value is to be assessed.'

In the same case, Lord Widgery said[6]:

> 'The extent of the scheme is a matter of fact in every case … The scheme will always exist in some shape or form by the time notice to treat is served … the ultimate question for the valuer is to decide to what extent the … value of the land on the day upon which the valuation is to be made has been increased by reason of the existence of the scheme.'

The principal considerations and cases in identifying the scheme were summarised by Mummery LJ in *Bolton Metropolitan Borough Council v Tudor Properties Ltd*[7], in which he said that the scheme was neither a technical term nor a legally precise concept; it is a question of fact. The Lands Tribunal has said[8] that a scheme must be sufficiently precise to enable an owner, occupier or prospective purchaser to find out what it is. The scheme may have been devised by an authority different from the acquiring authority[9]. It is not necessary for the scheme to have provided for the acquisition of the land; it is enough if the scheme 'underlay' it[10]. Where, in connection with the grant of planning permission for development of land, the local authority had required the developer to enter into a planning agreement reserving an area for school purposes, following service of a purchase notice, this was held to be evidence of the scheme[11]. The scheme cannot be the acquisition itself[12]. A single scheme may underlie two separate compulsory purchase orders[13].

1 *Hertfordshire County Council v Ozanne* [1989] 2 EGLR 18.
2 (1976) 33 P&CR 27, CA.
3 (1976) 33 P&CR 27 at 33–34.
4 (1976) 33 P&CR 27 at 39.
5 (1970) 22 P&CR 282 at 292.
6 (1970) 22 P&CR 282 at 293.
7 (2000) 80 P&CR 537, CA, at 540–541.
8 *Kaye v Basingstoke Corpn* (1959) 20 P&CR 417 at 445.
9 *Bird and Bird v Wakefield Metropolitan District Council* (1978) 37 P&CR 478.
10 *Bird and Bird v Wakefield Metropolitan District Council* (1978) 37 P&CR 478.
11 *Abbey Homesteads (Developments) Ltd v Northamptonshire County Council* (1992) 64 P&CR 377, CA.
12 *J A Pye (Oxford) Ltd v Kingswood Borough Council* [1998] 2 EGLR 159, CA.
13 *Waters v Welsh Development Agency* [2004] UKHL 19, [2004] 1 WLR 1304. Land was compulsorily acquired by the WDA in order to provide a nature reserve to replace features of conservation interest lost or damaged by the construction of Cardiff Bay barrage which had previously been authorised by parliament without providing for the acquisition of land to provide the nature reserve, although such a reserve was recognised to be necessary. The House of Lords took the opportunity to review many of the relevant cases.

[1207]

Where compensation is being assessed in respect of a deemed compulsory purchase in consequence of a purchase notice[1], it can be difficult to identify the 'scheme' underlying an acquisition. In *Toogood v Bristol Corpn*[2], a purchase notice had been served because planning permission had been refused for development on account of a proposed road widening scheme. It was clear that the local authority intended to acquire the land for this purpose if and when funds became available to implement the road proposal; the scheme was, therefore, the road proposal. In contrast, in *Birmingham District Council v Morris and Jacombs*[3], a purchase notice had been served following the grant of planning permission for development subject to a condition which reserved a strip of land for providing access to other land; the Court of Appeal held that the condition did not amount to a scheme. The Lands Tribunal has held that a development plan policy which allocated land for development, subject to a requirement to divert a road through the development, was not a scheme for the purposes of the *Pointe Gourde* rule[4]. In *Richards v Somerset CC*[5], the Lands Tribunal said that, while in relation to a compulsory purchase, there would always be a scheme underlying the acquisition, this is not necessarily so where the acquisition is in consequence of a purchase notice; on the facts of that case, it held that there was no scheme.

1 As to purchase notices, see **Division B, Chapter 4**.

2 (1973) 26 P&CR 132, Lands Tribunal, where the scheme was readily identifiable. Another example of a purchase notice where the scheme was readily identifiable is *Trocette Property Co Ltd v GLC* (1974) 28 P&CR 408, CA, which was concerned primarily with the LCA 1961, s 9, as to which see para **[1222]**. See also *Packwood Poultry Products Ltd v Solihull MBC* (1975) 31 P&CR 315, Lands Tribunal.

3 (1976) 33 P&CR 27, CA; applied in *Lawlor v London Borough of Hounslow* (1980) 41 P&CR 362, Lands Tribunal.

4 *Laing Homes Ltd v Eastleigh Borough Council* (1978) 250 Estates Gazette 350 and 459, Lands Tribunal.

5 [2001] 2 EGLR 135, Lands Tribunal. The claimant owned a small parcel of land on the alignment of the main distributor road within a major housing development. The road had been constructed by developers from each end with the exception of the part across the claimant's land. The claimant served a purchase notice and claimed compensation on the basis that his parcel was a ransom strip which held the key to the development of much of the housing and other development. The tribunal held that there was no scheme underlying the acquisition. Alternatively, if that was wrong, it held that the scheme could not have come into existence until the date of confirmation of the purchase notice.

[1207.1]
In *Waters v Welsh Development Agency*[1] Lord Nicholls had the following to say about identifying the extent of a scheme:

> 'A scheme essentially consists of a project to carry out certain works for a particular purpose or purposes. If compulsory acquisition of the subject land is an integral part of such a scheme, the *Pointe Gourde* principle will apply accordingly. Both elements of a project, the proposed works and the purpose for which they are being carried out, are material when deciding which works should be regarded as a single scheme when applying the *Pointe Gourde* principle to the land … What, then, is the purpose of this principle? Its purpose, in separating "value to the owner" from "value to the purchaser", is to forward Parliament's objective of providing dispossessed owners with a fair financial equivalent for their land. They are to receive fair compensation but not more than fair compensation. This is the over-riding guiding principle when deciding the extent of the scheme.'

This reflects an essentially 'purposive' approach to deciding the extent of the scheme. In other words, the decision-maker should determine the extent of the scheme having regard to the 'purpose' of achieving fair compensation.

1 [2004] UKHL 19, [2004] 1 WLR 2004 at [58] and [61].

[1207.2]
Lord Nicholls went on to provide some guidance as to how the scheme should be identified as follows[1]:

> 'In applying this general principle there is of course no magical detailed formula which will provide a ready answer in every case. That is in the nature of things, circumstances varying so widely. But some pointers may be useful. (1) The Pointe Gourde principle should not be pressed too far. The principle is soundly based but it should be applied in a manner which achieves a fair and reasonable result. Otherwise the principle would thwart, rather than advance, the intention of Parliament. (2) A result is not fair and reasonable where it requires a valuation exercise which is unreal or virtually impossible. (3) A valuation result should be viewed with caution when it would lead to a gross disparity between the amount of compensation payable and the market values of comparable adjoining properties which are not being acquired. (4) When applied as a supplement to the section 6 code, which will usually be the position, the Pointe Gourde principle should be applied by analogy with the provisions of the statutory code. Thus in the class 1 type of case the area of the scheme, should be interpreted narrowly, for instance, so as to embrace the property acquired under the compulsory purchase order and property which would probably have been so acquired had it not been bought by agreement. In other cases, such as case 2, Parliament has spread the "disregard" net more widely. Then it may be appropriate to give the scheme a wider scope. (5) Normally the scope of the intended works and their purpose will appear from the formal resolutions or documents of the acquiring authority. But this formulation should not be regarded as conclusive. (6) When in doubt a scheme should be identified in narrower rather than broader terms.'

1 Para 63, endorsed by Lord Brown at para 152.

[1207.3]
The facts of the *Waters* case were that the construction of a barrage across the mouth of Cardiff Bay had been authorized by the Cardiff Bay Barrage Act 1993. When the bill was before Parliament, it was strongly opposed on grounds related to the likely impact of the barrage upon nature conservation and the Government gave assurances that compensatory provision would be made by the creation of replacement wetland habitats. After construction of the barrage, a suitable site for the replacement wetland habitats was found and purchased compulsorily, which included land owned by the claimants. The question was whether the acquisition was to be regarded as part of the barrage project so that the need for the land in connection with that project should be left out of account. The Lands Tribunal held that it was, and this decision was upheld by both the Court of Appeal and the House of Lords.

[1207.4]
The first case in which the *Pointe Gourde* rule was relevant to be heard by the Lands Tribunal after the House of Lords decision in *Waters v Welsh Development Agency* was *RMC (UK) Ltd and Ace Electrical Distributors v London Borough of Greenwich*[1] which was concerned with the assessment of compensation for the acquisition of parcels of land on Greenwich Peninsula to achieve initially the Millenium Exhibition in the Dome and in the longer term the regeneration of the Peninsula. The Tribunal said[2]: 'To identify the scheme ... and to construct the no-scheme world ... was the conventional application of the *Pointe Gourde* principle prior to *Waters*. Following *Waters*, however, the question to be asked for the purpose of applying *Pointe Gourde* is not "What is the scheme underlying the acquisition?" but "How should the scheme underlying the acquisition be defined as an adjunct of the statutory disregards in order to give the claimant compensation that is neither more nor less than what is fair?"' The Tribunal also said[3]: 'As a matter of approach, therefore, we should seek to confine the scheme to the area of the CPO and should only treat the scheme as extending more widely if this is necessary for a particular reason in establishing fair compensation.'

1 [2005] RVR 140. See also *Persimmon Homes (Wales) Ltd v Rhondda Cynon Taff County Borough Council* [2005] RVR 59, LT.
2 Para 82.
3 Para 84.

4 Relationship of rule to planning assumptions

[1208]
It has been explained above that where an actual planning permission exists, it may be taken into account in valuing the land taken by virtue of the LCA 1961, s 14(2). It is often the case that the acquiring authority has obtained an actual planning permission for its own proposals. Even where planning permission has not been granted for the acquiring authority's proposals, the LCA 1961, s 15(2) enables it to be assumed that planning permission exists for development of the land taken in accordance with the acquiring authority's proposals. In *Myers v Milton Keynes Development Corporation*[1], the Lands Tribunal had thought that there was a conflict between the permission to be assumed under s 15(2) for the proposals of the acquiring authority and the requirement of the *Pointe Gourde* rule to disregard the acquiring authority's scheme. The Court of Appeal held that there was no such conflict. Lord Denning said[2]:

> 'The two can and should be reconciled by tackling the valuation in this way: (1) Determine what was the nature of the property to be valued. In this case it was the freehold of Walton Manor estate. (2) Determine the extent of the interest to be valued. In this case it was the freehold of the Walton Manor estate, with the benefit of planning permission assumed under section 15. (3) Ascertain the value of that interest. It is at this stage, in evaluating the interest, that the *Pointe Gourde* principle applies. "That principle ...," said Lord Cross of Chelsea, " ... does not affect the ascertainment of the interest to be valued but only its value when ascertained": see *Rugby Joint Water Board v Shaw-Fox* [1973] AC 202, 253. It applies so as

to ensure that any increase in value due to the scheme is to be left out of account.'

1 (1974) 27 P&CR 518, CA. See also *Camrose (Viscount) v Basingstoke Corpn* [1966] 1 WLR 1100.
2 At 524.

[1208.1]
In a later passage of his judgment, Lord Denning said[1]:

> 'It is apparent, therefore, that the valuation has to be done in an imaginary state of affairs in which there is no scheme. The valuer must cast aside his knowledge of what has in fact happened in the past eight years due to the scheme. He must ignore the developments which will in all probability take place in the future ten years owing to the scheme. Instead, he must let his imagination take flight to the clouds. He must conjure up a land of make-believe, where there has not been, nor will be, a brave new town but where there is to be supposed the old order of things continuing … In this imaginary state of affairs, the valuer has then to ask himself: what is the appropriate way of valuing the land with this assumed planning permission? …'

This passage was criticised in *Waters v Welsh Development Agency*[2], partly on the basis that the same result could have been achieved by the application of the LCA 1961, s 6 (without reliance on the *Pointe Gourde* principle) and partly on the basis that it was not appropriate for a valuer to allow 'his imagination to take flight to the clouds' to try to envisage how an area would have been planned and developed over a long period of time. However, these criticisms do not affect the passage cited in the preceding paragraph and the general point that the land taken must be valued with the benefit of an actual or assumed permission even though the development so permitted comprised part of the acquiring authority's proposals. It is the effect of the scheme on the value of the land taken with the assumed permission which must be disregarded.

1 At 527.
2 [2004] 1 WLR 1304 at [109] and [148].

[1208.2]
In a number of decisions between 2003 and 2008, the Lands Tribunal held that the *Pointe Gourde* rule enabled it to be assumed for the purposes of valuing the land taken that planning permission would been granted on the valuation date, where it was shown by evidence that, on the balance of probabilities, planning permission would have been granted in the absence of the scheme underlying the acquisition[1]. This application of the *Pointe Gourde* rule was upheld by the Court of Appeal[2], but was eventually rejected by the House of Lords in *Transport for London (formerly London Underground Ltd) v Spirerose Ltd*[3].

1 *Pentrehobyn Trustees v National Assembly for Wales* [2003] RVR 140; *RMC (UK) Ltd v Greenwich London Borough Council [2005] RVR 140; Spirerose Ltd v Transport for London* [2008] RVR 12. The first of these was decided before the House of Lords decision in *Waters v Welsh Development Agency*, and the latter two were decided after *Waters*. In an interim decision published after the House of Lords decision in *Spirerose*, the Lands Tribunal has provided an interesting commentary on the *Spirerose* decision which indicates that the difficulties with this topic may

not have been fully resolved: *Persimmon Homes (Midlands) Ltd v Secretary of State for Transport* [2009] UKUT 126 (LC), although in *Thomas Newell Ltd v Lancaster City Council* [2010] UKUT 2 (LC), the tribunal, applying *Spirerose* concluded (at paras 29–30) that the *Pointe Gourde* rule cannot be relied upon for an assumption that planning permission would have been granted in the absence of the scheme.

2 *Transport for London v Spirerose Ltd* [2008] EWCA Civ 1230, [2009] RVR 18, CA.

3 [2009] UKHL 44, [2009] RVR 225, HL.

[1208.3]

In *Spirerose* the House of Lords held that there was no basis in authority or in principle for the conclusion that it is open to the court in effect to establish an assumption that planning permission would be obtained, by analogy with specific statutory rules which create the assumption and that it was not the role of the court to re-write legislation by adding additional assumptions of planning permission. The *Pointe Gourde* rule was held to be a principle of statutory interpretation mainly designed and used to explain and amplify the expression 'value'. An extension of the *Pointe Gourde* principle which the Court of Appeal had endorsed was considered to be inconsistent with *Rugby Joint Water Board v Shaw-Fox*[1], in which the House of Lords refused to extend the *Pointe Gourde* principle so as to apply it not only to the ascertainment of the value of an interest in land, but also to the ascertainment of the nature and extent of the interest to be valued.

1 [1973] AC 202.

[1208.4]

As the House of Lords pointed out, the LCA 1961 has provided for circumstances such as those which arose in the *Spirerose* case. A claimant can apply under the LCA 1961, s 17 for a certificate of appropriate alternative development. If granted, it may be assumed pursuant to s 15(5), that planning permission existed on the valuation date (or such later date as may be specified in the certificate). If no certificate is obtained under s 17, development value may still be taken in to account by virtue of s 14(3). Consequently, as previously explained[1], in any case where there is a prospect that planning permission would have been granted in the absence of the compulsory purchase, it is wise to consider whether an application should be made for a certificate under s 17 before a reference is made to the Lands Tribunal to determine the amount of compensation payable.

1 See **[807.1]**.

[1208.5]

The decision of the House of Lords in *Spirerose* does not appear to affect the decisions of the Court of Appeal in *Jelson Ltd v Blaby District Council*[1] and of the Privy Council in *Melwood Units Property Ltd v Commissioner for Main Roads*[2]. In both those cases, there was evidence that planning permission would actually have been granted at some time prior to the valuation date in the absence of the scheme[3].

1 (1977) 34 P&CR 77, CA.

2 [1979] AC 426, PC.

3 See the comments on these cases in *Spirerose* by Lord Collins [2009] UKHL 44, [2009] RVR 225 at [105]–[114].

5 The *Pointe Gourde* rule, 'ransom' value and 'special suitability'

[1209]
The relationship between the *Pointe Gourde* rule and the decision in *Stokes v Cambridge Corpn*[1] was considered in *Batchelor v Kent CC*[2], in which Mann LJ said[3]:

> 'I find no difficulty with the relationship. If a premium value is "entirely due to the scheme underlying the acquisition" then it must be disregarded. If it was pre-existent to the acquisition it must in my judgment be regarded. To ignore the pre-existent value would be to expropriate it without compensation and would be to contravene the fundamental principle of equivalence.'

Planning permission had been granted for residential development subject to a condition which prevented the development from being implemented until road improvements had been carried out. Kent County Council acquired land compulsorily from the claimant and constructed a roundabout which gave access to the land with planning permission. Compensation was claimed for the compulsory purchase of the land valued as an access to the land with planning permission. The acquiring authority contended that such value should be disregarded being attributable to the scheme underlying the acquisition. However, the Lands Tribunal had found as a fact that the land acquired to construct the roundabout would, in the absence of the scheme, have been purchased by other developers, so that the land taken had value as an access independently of the scheme[4]. In a sequel to that case, fought between different parties, *Ward Construction (Medway) Ltd v Barclays Bank plc*[5], the Court of Appeal pointed out that, while the *Pointe Gourde* rule is a principle of law, the *Stokes v Cambridge* principle was one of valuation, so that the Lands Tribunal was entitled to reach the conclusion which it did. In certain circumstances, where, on the facts, 'ransom value' potentially exists, it may be eliminated from the assessment of compensation by the operation of r 3 of the LCA 1961, s 5[6].

1 (1961) 13 P&CR 77, Lands Tribunal, see **Chapter 2**.
2 (1989) 59 P&CR 357, CA.
3 (1989) 59 P&CR 357 at 361. This passage was cited with approval by the House of Lords in *Waters v Welsh Development Agency* [2004] UKHL 19, [2004] 1 WLR 1304 at [65] and [157] and in *Bocardo SA v Star Energy Weald Basin Ltd* [2010] UKSC 35, [2010] 3 All ER 975 at [55] and [81].
4 For an example of a case in which it was found on the facts that the land had a ransom value independently of the requirements of the acquiring authority, see *Persimmon Homes (Wales) Ltd v Rhondda Cynon Taff County Borough Council* [2005] RVR 59, LT.
5 (1994) 68 P&CR 391, CA.
6 This rule is explained above in **Chapter 2**. Where r 3 operates so as to exclude any value attributable to the special suitability, it is not then necessary to apply the *Pointe Gourde* rule: *Port of London Authority v Transport for London* [2008] RVR 93, Lands Tribunal.

C Land Compensation Act 1961, section 6

[1210]–[1220]
The LCA 1961, s 6(1) provides that no account is to be taken of any increase or decrease in the value of the relevant interest[1] which is attributable to the circumstances defined in the LCA 1961, Sch 1. Since the provisions set out in Sch 1 are complicated, they are reproduced below in the form of a table,

which operates as follows. The first step is to ascertain whether the land to be valued falls within any of the cases in the first column. Where one of those paragraphs applies, the second step is to identify any development[2] defined in the second column, either already carried out, or in prospect, the carrying out of which would not have been likely if:

(*a*) in relation to land falling within paragraph 1, the acquiring authority had not acquired and did not propose to acquire any land for that purpose; or
(*b*) in relation to land falling within paragraphs 2 to 4B, the area or areas referred to had not been so defined or designated.

Any increase or decrease in the value of the land being acquired as a result of development identified in the second step must then be disregarded. If the circumstances fall outside those defined in the table, then the LCA 1961, s 6 does not apply, although the '*Pointe Gourde*' rule[3] may do so, to a similar effect[4].

	Case	*Development*
1	Where the acquisition is for purposes involving development of any of the land authorised to be acquired[5].	Development of any of the land authorised to be acquired, other than the relevant land, being development for any of the purposes for which any part of the first-mentioned land (including any of the relevant land) is to be acquired.
2	Where any of the relevant land forms part of an area defined in the current development plan as an area of comprehensive development.	Development of any land in that area, other than the relevant land, in the course of the development or redevelopment of the area in accordance with the plan.
3[6]	Where on the date of service of notice to treat any of the relevant land forms part of an area designated as the site of a new town under the New Towns Act 1946[7].	Development of any land in that area, other than the relevant land, in the course of the development of that area as a new town.
3A[8]	Where on the date of service of notice to treat any of the relevant land forms part of an area designated as an extension of the site of a new town by an order under the New Towns Act 1965[9], becoming operative after the date of the commencement of the New Towns Act 1966[10].	Development of any land in that area, other than the relevant land, in the course of the development of that area as part of a new town

	Case	*Development*
4	Where any of the relevant land forms part of an area to which a town development scheme under the Town Development Act 1952 relates, being a scheme which is in operation at the date of Notice to Treat.	Development of any land in that area, other than the relevant land, in the course of town development within the meaning of the Town Development Act 1952.
4A[11]	Where any of the relevant land forms part of an area designated as an urban development area by an order under the Local Government (Miscellaneous Provisions) Act 1980 (LGPLA 1980), s 134.	Development of any land, other than the relevant land, in the course of the development or redevelopment of that area as an urban development area.
4B[12]	Where any of the relevant land forms part of a housing trust action area established under the Housing Act 1988, Pt III.	Development of any land, other than the relevant land, in the course of the development or redevelopment of that area as a housing action trust area

1 That is, the interest in land which has been acquired and is being valued: LCA 1961, s 39(1).
2 Development is to be construed as including clearing the land: LCA 1961, s 6(3).
3 See paras **[1202]–[1209]**.
4 See para **[1221]**.
5 As to the meaning of 'land authorised to be acquired', see the LCA 1961, s 6(3).
6 LCA 1961, s 6(2) applies the provisions in Sch 1, Pt II to this paragraph.
7 Now consolidated into the New Towns Act 1981.
8 Inserted by the New Towns Act 1965. LCA 1961, s 6(2) applies Sch 1, Pt II to this paragraph.
9 Now consolidated into the New Towns Act 1981.
10 Now consolidated into the New Towns Act 1981.
11 Inserted by the LGPLA 1980, s 145(1). LCA 1961, s 6(2) applies Sch 1, Pt III to this paragraph.
12 Inserted by the Housing Act 1988, s 78(3).

[1221]

In *Davy v Leeds Corpn*[1], Viscount Dilhorne[2] commented that the LCA 1961, s 6 is a statutory expression of the *Pointe Gourde* rule, although it now appears to be generally accepted that they are not identical. In *Batchelor v Kent County Council*[3], Mann LJ[4] referred to it as a statutory extension of the *Pointe Gourde* rule. In *Camrose (Viscount) v Basingstoke Corpn*[5], it was contended that the increase in value which is excluded by the LCA 1961, s 6 is only that which is attributable to the purposes for which the 'other land', mentioned in the second column, were to be put, but that an increase in the value of the 'relevant land', that is, the land acquired from the claimant, is not to be ignored. Lord Denning MR said that, although he could see something in the argument, he could not see how any valuer could value on that basis. He went on to provide the following explanation of the LCA 1961, s 6:

'The legislature was aware of the general principle that, in assessing compensation for compulsory acquisition of a defined parcel of land, you do not take into account an increase in value of that parcel of land if that increase was entirely due to the scheme involving the acquisition. That was settled by *Pointe Gourde Quarrying and Transport Co v Sub-Intendent of Crown Lands* ... It is left untouched by s 6(1). But there might be some doubt as to its scope. So the legislature passed s 6(1) and the First Schedule in order to make it clear that you were not to take into account any increase due to the development of the other land, namely, land other than the claimed parcel. I think that the *Pointe Gourde* case covers one aspect; and s 6(1) covers the other ... '

1 (1966) 17 P&CR 83.
2 (1966) 17 P&CR 83 at 91. He was referring to the Town and Country Planning Act 1959, s 9 which was the predecessor of the LCA 1961, s 6.
3 (1989) 59 P&CR 357, CA.
4 (1989) 59 P&CR 357 at 359.
5 [1966] 1 WLR 1100, CA. The view expressed in this case was repeated in *Wilson v Liverpool Corpn* (1970) 22 P&CR 282 at 292. See also *Sprinz v Kingston upon Hull City Council* (1975) 30 P&CR 273, Lands Tribunal, in which the tribunal said that both the rule and s 6 must be applied independently where, on the facts, they are capable of doing so.

D Land Compensation Act 1961, section 9

[1222]
The LCA 1961, s 9[1] provides:

'No account shall be taken of any depreciation of the value of the relevant interest[2] which is attributable[3] to the fact that (whether by way of allocation or other particulars contained in the current development plan, or by any other means) an indication has been given that the relevant land is, or is likely, to be acquired by an authority possessing compulsory purchase powers.[4]'

1 This provision originated in the Town and Country Planning Act 1947, s 51(3).
2 The relevant interest means the interest in land compulsorily acquired: LCA 1961, s 39(2).
3 In *Trocette Property Co Ltd v GLC* (1974) 28 P&CR 408, CA, Megaw LJ said (at 417): 'The phrase "attributable to" is, I think, deliberately used in section 9 in order to ensure greater scope for flexibility in its application than would have been achieved by other phrases such as "caused by".'
4 The term 'authority possessing compulsory purchase powers' is defined in the LCA 1961, s 39(2).

[1223]
There is no definition of the word 'indication', which was probably used to ensure that almost any form of formal, informal, direct or indirect communication would suffice. It has been held that '*it really means very little more or less than the word "sign" - a sign of intention*', which may be judged by the authority's actions; what amounts to an indication is a matter of fact and degree in each case[1]. It would have to be shown that the indication was of such a nature to have affected the value of the land. The phrase 'attributable to' was used to provide greater scope for flexibility in its application than would have been achieved with other phrases, such as 'caused by'[2], but this

does not mean that there can be no causal connection[3]. It is necessary to take into account whatever flowed from the indication, including the reasonable response of the claimants to the indication[4]. It is submitted that the prospect of the land being acquired must stem from a decision or action of the authority in question itself and not merely speculation by one of its officers as to how the authority might decide to act[5].

1 Per Sachs LJ in *Hackney London Borough Council v MacFarlene* (1970) 21 P&CR 342, CA, at 345–346. At 345, Sachs LJ also commented that the provisions of the LCA 1961 should be interpreted liberally. In that case, the local authority's actions in acquiring adjacent land was held to be an indication of its intention to acquire the land being valued.
2 Per Megaw LJ in *Trocette Property Co Ltd v GLC* (1974) 28 P&CR 408, CA, at 417.
3 Per Stephenson LJ in *Jelson Ltd v Blaby District Council* (1977) 34 P&CR 77, CA, at 81.
4 Per Stephenson LJ in *Jelson Ltd v Blaby District Council* (1977) 34 P&CR 77, CA, at 81. See the facts of this case outlined in the next paragraph.
5 This submission is consistent with the Court of Appeal decision in the context of the Town and Country Planning Act 1990 as to the authority of officers to bind a local authority in *Western Fish Products Ltd v Penwith District Council* (1978) 38 P&CR 7, in particular per Megaw LJ, at 28. See also *Richards v Somerset County Council* [2001] 2 EGLR 135, Lands Tribunal.

[1224]
An example of the manner in which the LCA 1961, s 9 can operate is provided by the Court of Appeal decision in *Trocette Property Co Ltd v GLC*[1], in which the claimant held a lease of premises from the GLC which was shortly to expire. Planning permission was granted for redevelopment of the land and the GLC indicated that a new lease would be likely to be granted. The GLC, in their capacity of highway authority, decided to propose a new highway which required the land in question. As a result, they declined to grant a new lease after all. Following service of a purchase notice, it was held that compensation was to be assessed on the basis that, in the absence of the road proposal, the open market value of the claimant's lease would have been enhanced by the prospect of the grant of a new lease enabling the planning permission to be implemented. The likelihood that the land would be required for the road proposal had caused a diminution in its value which had to be disregarded pursuant to the LCA 1961, s 9. Another example is *Jelson Ltd v Blaby District Council*[2], in which planning permission had been granted for development of an area of land excluding a strip which was required for a proposed road. The development was carried out, but the road proposals was then abandoned. Following a purchase notice in respect of the strip, it was held that the value of the strip had been depreciated by the indication that it would be required for a road. In *Hackney London Borough Council v MacFarlene*[3], the local authority had made slum clearance orders in respect of land adjacent to the land being valued, and these were followed at once by compulsory purchase orders; the authority's actions were held to amount to an indication that it also intended to acquire the land being valued. In *Abbey Homesteads (Developments) Ltd v Northamptonshire County Council*[4], the imposition of a restrictive covenant in a planning agreement reserving land for school purposes was held to be an indication within the LCA 1961, s 9. In *Richards v Somerset County Council*[5], it had been indicated in the local plan and other documents that developers would have to provide distributor roads at their own expense in connection with a large area of housing development. In connection with the grant of planning permissions, landowners

and developers entered into s 106 agreements providing for the construction of such roads and their dedication as highways. The Lands Tribunal rejected the claimant's contention that the indication of the intention that the roads should vest in the highway authority after construction amounted to an indication within the meaning of the LCA 1961, s 9.

1 (1974) 28 P&CR 408, CA.
2 (1977) 34 P&CR 77, CA.
3 (1970) 21 P&CR 342, CA.
4 (1992) 64 P&CR 377, CA, applying *Rugby Joint Water Board v Shaw-Fox* [1973] AC 202, HL.
5 [2001] 2 EGLR 135, Lands Tribunal.

[1224.1]
It is not necessary to apply the *Pointe Gourde* rule in addition to LCA 1961, s 9 where it applies[1]. Where the land acquired is part only of the claimant's landholding, the depreciation in value to be ascertained is that sustained by the land acquired separate and distinct from the site as a whole and the land retained[2]. Where, on the facts, an indication of the intention to acquire the land has been given, it does not follow that there will have been a depreciation in the value of the land acquired[3].

1 *English Property Corpn v Royal Borough of Kingston upon Thames* (1998) 77 P&CR 1, CA, at 8–9.
2 *English Property Corpn v Royal Borough of Kingston upon Thames* (1998) 77 P&CR 1, CA, at 8.
3 *Laing Homes Ltd v Eastleigh Borough Council* (1978) 250 Estates Gazette 350, Lands Tribunal.

E Betterment due to the scheme

[1225]
Where the claimant has an interest in other land adjacent to that which is compulsory acquired, and that other land increases in value as a result of the scheme underlying the compulsory acquisition, that increase in value, often referred to as betterment, may have to be deducted from the compensation payable in respect of the land taken[1].

1 LCA 1961, s 7, which applies in the same circumstances as those set out in the table in para **[1210]**. Betterment is explained in **Chapter 9**.

F Special provision for motorway service areas

[1226]–[1600]
Where land is compulsorily acquired[1] for a motorway service area or a lorry area development[2] and the value would be affected by the provision or proposed provision of the motorway, it must be valued on the assumption that traffic from the motorway will not have direct access to the land taken[3].

1 Under the HA 1980, s 239(4)(*c*) or in pursuance of a notice under the Town and Country Planning Act 1990, s 137: HA 1980, s 262(1)–(2).
2 Defined in HA 1980, s 262(4).
3 HA 1980, s 262(3).

Chapter 5

Equivalent reinstatement

Contents

A Introduction

[1601]

It has been explained above[1] that, in the majority of cases, compensation will be assessed by the operation of rr 2 and 6, that is, the payment of a sum comprising the open market value[2] for the land taken and any losses caused to the claimant due to disturbance[3]. The claimant can then, if he wishes, acquire other land and reinstate the use to which he had put the land taken from him compulsorily. However, it has been recognised that, for a certain class of cases, this method could not be relied upon to produce a fair result and the cost of reinstatement would provide a better assessment of the value of the land taken to its owner[4]. Rule 5 was, therefore, introduced[5] to authorise a sum to be awarded, in appropriate cases, which would enable the claimant to reinstate the use elsewhere.

1 See para **[446]**.

2 As to open market value, see paras **[407]–[427]**.

3 As to compensation for disturbance, see **Chapter 6**.

4 For an explanation of the background of the rule, see the speech of Lord Reid in *Birmingham Corpn v West Midland Baptist (Trust) Association Inc* [1970] AC 874, HL, at 893–894, 20 P&CR 1052 at 1057.

5 Acquisition of Land (Assessment of Compensation) Act 1919, s 2, re-enacted by the Land Compensation Act 1961 (LCA 1961), s 5.

B The rule

[1602]

Rule 5 of the six rules set out in the LCA 1961, s 5 provides as follows:

'Where land is, and but for the compulsory acquisition would continue to be, devoted to a purpose of such a nature that there is no general demand or market for land for that purpose, the compensation may, if the Lands Tribunal is satisfied that reinstatement in some other place is bona fide intended, be assessed on the basis of the reasonable cost of equivalent reinstatement.'

[1603]
For r 5 to apply, the following conditions[1] must be satisfied by the claimant[2]:

(*a*) the land must be *devoted to a purpose* of such a nature that there is *no general demand or market* for land for that purpose;
(*b*) the land would *continue to have been devoted to that purpose*, if it had not been compulsorily purchased; and
(*c*) there is a *genuine intention to reinstate* the purpose elsewhere.

The phrases in italics are adopted as headings for the detailed explanation of the rule in the paragraphs which follow. Where those three conditions are met, then there is a discretion to award an amount of compensation which is assessed on the basis of the reasonable cost of reinstating elsewhere the purpose for which the land is used.

1 In *Sparks (Trustees of Hunslet Liberal Club) v Leeds City Council* (1977) 34 P&CR 234, [1977] 2 EGLR 163, the Lands Tribunal set out what it called 'four essentials' in r 5, as follows:
'(1) that the subject land is devoted to the purpose, and but for the compulsory purchase would continue to be so devoted;
(2) that the purpose is one for which there is no general demand or market for the land;
(3) the bona fide intention to reinstate on another site; and
(4) these conditions being satisfied, that the tribunal's reasonable discretion should be exercised in their favour.'
These 'essentials' are referred to in a number of later Lands Tribunal cases. However, for the purposes of explaining and analysing r 5 and the relevant cases in this work, the approach set out in para **[1603]** is preferred.

2 The burden of proof is upon the claimant: per Sir David Cairns in *Wilkinson v Middlesborough Borough Council* (1981) 45 P&CR 142, CA, at 154.

C Devoted to a purpose

[1604]
The purpose to which the land is devoted must be ascertained at the date of the notice to treat[1]. The word 'devoted' is used to mean that the land must be given up wholly or exclusively to a particular purpose[2]. The word 'purpose' is not to be construed as applying only to those activities which the claimant actually carries on; a shop is a shop whatever it sells, a factory is a factory whatever it makes and a clinic used for homeopathy is a clinic for medical purposes generally[3]. While the actual use may be a starting point[4] for identifying the purpose to which premises are devoted, this is not conclusive, since the words 'devoted to a purpose' introduce a 'conception of intention'[5]. Thus, where the land taken is used temporarily for some purpose which would not meet this requirement, it may nevertheless be 'devoted' to some other purpose which does qualify[6]. For example, where premises had been used for charitable purposes but, following war damage, had been largely sub-let for other purposes, the Lands Tribunal held that they were nevertheless still devoted to the charitable purpose[7].

1 Per Buckley LJ in *Trustees of Zoar Independent Church v Rochester Corpn* (1974) 29 P&CR 145 at 151 and 154. The House of Lords decision in *Birmingham Corpn v West Midland Baptist (Trust) Association Inc* [1970] AC 874 was cited in Buckley LJ's judgment, which indicates that he was well aware that the notice to treat was no longer the date of valuation. This contrasts with the valuation date for the purposes of rule 2: LCA 1961, s 5A: see para **[40]** above.

2 *Viscount Vaughan v Cardiganshire Water Board* (1963) 14 P&CR 193, Lands Tribunal, at 199.

3 *Trustees of Manchester Homeopathic Clinic v Manchester Corpn* (1971) 22 P&CR 241, Lands Tribunal, at 250–252; the tribunal also commented that it would be wrong to approach it in terms of town planning use classes.

4 *Kolbe House Society v Department of Transport* (1994) 68 P&CR 569, Lands Tribunal.

5 *Aston Charities Trust Ltd v Stepney Metropolitan Borough* [1952] 2 QB 642, 3 P&CR 82, CA.

6 *Aston Charities Trust Ltd v Stepney Metropolitan Borough* [1952] 2 QB 642, CA.

7 *Aston Charities Trust Ltd v Stepney Metropolitan Borough* [1952] 2 QB 642, CA. See also *Trustees of the Nonentities Society v Kidderminster Borough Council* (1970) 22 P&CR 224, Lands Tribunal.

[1605]

The purpose must be one to which the premises had deliberately and voluntarily been devoted; thus, where church premises, having become surplus to requirements, had been let for another purpose, it was held that they were no longer devoted to church purposes[1]. The purpose for which a building had originally been built is not relevant; thus, it was held that buildings, which were used at the time of the compulsory acquisition as church premises, qualified notwithstanding that they had originally been constructed as dwellings[2]. The purpose to which premises are devoted may be capable of being identified by reference to the purposes of the claimant organisation as expressed in the trust deed or similar document[3].

1 *Trustees of the Central Methodist Church, Todmorden v Todmorden Corpn* (1959) 11 P&CR 32, Lands Tribunal.

2 *London Diocesan Fund v Stepney Corpn* (1953) 4 P&CR 9, Lands Tribunal; *St John's Wood Working Men's Club v LCC* (1947) 150 Estates Gazette 213. See also *Viscount Vaughan v Cardiganshire Water Board* (1963) 14 P&CR 193, Lands Tribunal concerning a cottage used as an office; although r 5 was rejected on other grounds, it was not ruled out on the ground that it was not devoted to office purposes.

3 *Trustees of Zoar Independent Church v Rochester Corpn* (1974) 29 P&CR 145, CA, in which it was held that the question is not whether the former congregation of a church is to be reinstated, but whether the purpose of the church, as defined in its trust deed, was to be reinstated. See also *Kolbe House Society v Department of Transport* (1994) 68 P&CR 569, Lands Tribunal, in which the Lands Tribunal took account of a trust deed which defined a particular category of persons for whom an old persons home was provided.

D No general demand or market

[1606]

The phrase 'no general demand or market for land' refers to land in general, not the subject land alone[1]. In *Harrison & Hetherington v Cumbria County Council*[2], the House of Lords adopted, with a minor qualification, the following passage from the dissenting judgment of Waller LJ in *Wilkinson v Middlesborough Borough Council*[3]:

> '[Rule 5] provides, however, that there must be no general demand or market for *land* for that purpose. This indicates to me that it is not sufficient that there should be a demand for the land in question but that there must be a general demand, ie a demand not [only] for that land but for other land elsewhere for the same purpose. Furthermore, the use of the

word 'market' connotes, in my opinion, something more than the fact that there are potential users of the land for the named purpose; it connotes that there is a buying and selling for that purpose.'

The word 'general' qualifies the word 'demand' and not 'market'[4]. The underlying concept is that there cannot be a market unless both supply and demand exist, but there may be a general demand even when there is no supply and, therefore, no market[5].

1 *Harrison and Hetherington v Cumbria County Council* (1985) 50 P&CR 396, HL, at 399.
2 (1985) 50 P&CR 396 at 399. Lord Fraser would have preferred 'necessarily' instead of 'only'.
3 (1981) 45 P&CR 142, CA, at 148. The House of Lords did not criticise the majority decision.
4 *Harrison and Hetherington v Cumbria County Council* (1985) 50 P&CR 396, HL.
5 *Harrison and Hetherington v Cumbria County Council* (1985) 50 P&CR 396, HL.

[1607]

Since the requirement is that there 'is' no general demand or market, the question as to the existence of either demand or a market must be determined at the date at which compensation falls to be assessed[1]. Latent demand, that is, a demand which does not at present exist, and does not become apparent unless and until land devoted to the purpose is offered for sale, does not amount to general demand for the purposes of the rule[2]. It became established practice in the Lands Tribunal to test general demand and the existence of a market by reference to sale transactions[3]. It is also necessary to consider the geographical extent of the market under scrutiny; the situation of the land for the use must be governed by the nature of the use, and where this involves the resort of people to it, regard will be had to where those people reside[4]. In determining whether there is a general demand or market for a purpose, it is permissible to consider whether there would be such general demand or market if minor alterations or adaptions were to be carried out[5]. Where the claimant holds the freehold of premises and establishes that there is no general demand or market for the freehold for the purpose, evidence that there is a market for a lease may be relevant, but may not carry much weight[6]. The demand or market for a purpose may well be affected by a system of licensing, such as that governing doctors' practices[7].

1 *Harrison and Hetherington v Cumbria County Council* (1985) 50 P&CR 396, HL.
2 *Harrison and Hetherington v Cumbria County Council* (1985) 50 P&CR 396, HL, at 401.
3 *Kolbe House Society v Department of Transport* (1994) 68 P&CR 569, Lands Tribunal, at 588.
4 *Kolbe House Society v Department of Transport* (1994) 68 P&CR 569, Lands Tribunal, at 588, citing Sir David Cairns in *Wilkinson v Middlesborough Borough Council* (1981) 45 P&CR 142, CA, at 154: 'I should not consider that the fact that an isolated transaction had taken place would constitute a "market" '.
5 *Trustees of the Manchester Homeopathic Clinic v Manchester Corpn* (1970) 22 P&CR 241, Lands Tribunal, at 252; cf *London Diocesan Fund v Stepney Corpn* (1953) 4 P&CR 9, Lands Tribunal.
6 *Trustees of Manchester Homeopathic Clinic v Manchester Corpn* (1970) 22 P&CR 241, Lands Tribunal, at 253. It is submitted that such evidence would carry more weight if the interest being acquired is a lease rather than freehold. The tribunal commented that rr 2 and 5 are both concerned with sales; in the sense that compensation requires the capital value to be assessed, that is correct, but the claimant's interest being valued may be a lease or other interest less than the freehold.
7 The implications of a licensing system were considered in *Trustees of Manchester Homeopathic Clinic v Manchester Corpn* (1970) 22 P&CR 241, Lands Tribunal. See also *Rowley v Southampton Corpn* (1959) 10 P&CR 172, Lands Tribunal, in which premises had acquired an established use for offensive trades under planning and other legislation; the claim that there was no market for this activity was rejected on the ground that the premises could be sold on the open market with the benefit of the established use.

E Continuing to be devoted to that purpose

[1608]
The statute provides no guidance as to the timescale to be addressed in considering whether the land would, but for the compulsory purchase, continue to be devoted to the purpose. 'Devoted' does not signify that the land must be committed to that use for any particular length of time, definite or indefinite[1]. Whether the land would have continued to be devoted to the purpose in the absence of the compulsory purchase must be judged on the particular facts of each case. The fact that the claimant holds the premises under a lease which is due to expire shortly does not prevent this requirement from being met if there is evidence that the landlord will permit the premises to continue to be used for that purpose. Thus, the Lands Tribunal held that this requirement was met where purpose-built club premises were held upon a tenancy from year to year; the tribunal was satisfied that the tenancy would have been permitted by the landlord to continue[2].

1 Per Buckley LJ in *Trustees of Zoar Independent Church v Rochester Corpn* (1974) 29 P&CR 145, CA, at 153.
2 *Harpurhey Conservative and Unionist Club and Harpurhey Constitutional Club Ltd v Manchester City Council* (1975) 31 P&CR 300, Lands Tribunal. See also *Runcorn Association Football Club Ltd v Warrington and Runcorn Development Corpn* (1982) 45 P&CR 183, Lands Tribunal, although there must be some doubt as to the correctness of that decision in the light of *Bishopsgate Space Management Ltd and Teamworks Karting Ltd v London Underground Ltd* [2004] RVR 89, Lands Tribunal.

F Genuine intention to reinstate

[1609]
'Intention' in this context is confined to something which the claimant can achieve of his own volition[1]. It is the purpose which must be reinstated, not the precise use which was made of the land compulsorily acquired[2]. This requirement must be determined on the facts of each case. For example, where a theatre had been threatened with closure due to its financial situation, but had been rescued by an arrangement with the local authority which was to take the theatre over, the Lands Tribunal held, on the facts, that the threat of closure had produced a solution which evidenced an intention to continue the use as a theatre, and the change of ownership was not relevant[3]. In contrast, where a church hall had become redundant due to movement of population, the intention to provide a new hall in a different centre of population was held not qualify[4]. Reinstatement is a matter of degree: it might take place a long way off but, having regard to the purpose, could still be regarded as 'reinstatement'; on the other hand, a purpose confined locally to a narrow area might not, if started somewhere else, be said be reinstatement[5]. A claimant is not prevented from meeting this requirement by the fact that he would be unable to reinstate unless he receives compensation assessed under r 5[6].

1 Per Harman LJ in *Festiniog Rly Co v Central Electricity Board* (1962) 13 P&CR 248, CA, at 260.
2 *Zoar Independent Church Trustees v Rochester Corpn* [1975] QB 246, CA.
3 *Trustees of the Nonentities Society v Kidderminster Borough Council* (1970) 22 P&CR 224, Lands Tribunal.

4 *Roberts (Trustees of the St James' Parish Hall Charity, Dover) v Dover Corpn* (1962) 14 P&CR 47, Lands Tribunal; *Central Methodist Church, Todmorden v Todmorden Corpn* (1959) 11 P&CR 32, Lands Tribunal.
5 Per Lord Somerville LJ in *Aston Charities Trust Ltd v Stepney Borough Council* [1952] 2 QB 642, CA, at 647.
6 *Zoar Independent Church Trustees v Rochester Corpn* [1975] QB 246, CA. See also *Trustee of Nonentities Society v Kidderminster Borough Council* (1970) 22 P&CR 224, Lands Tribunal; *Incorporated Society of the Crusade of Rescue and Homes for Destitute Catholic Children v Feltham UDC* (1960) 11 P&CR 158, Lands Tribunal. Cf *Edge Hill Light Rly Co v Secretary of State for War* (1956) 6 P&CR 211, Lands Tribunal.

G Reasonable cost of equivalent reinstatement

[1610]–[1620]
A claim under r 5 is for the 'reasonable cost of equivalent reinstatement'. It has been held that:

> 'The natural meaning of "the basis of reasonable cost of equivalent reinstatement" is that one envisages a reasonable owner reinstating himself in premises reasonably equivalent for his purpose as soon as, in all the circumstances, that is reasonably practicable, and awards him such sum as enables him to do that'[1].

It has been commented that '... "Replacement" would be a more apt word than reinstatement, for reinstatement is one thing that is not going to happen'[2]. The reasonable cost would include the cost of complying with current building control and similar regulations, but it would not be reasonable to include the cost of improvements compared with the premises taken or the cost of replacing outworn facilities[3]. The size of rooms to be provided is primarily a matter for the claimant, subject to the total accommodation not exceeding the premises being taken, but, if advances in design techniques enable equivalent accommodation for the purpose to be provided in a building with a smaller cubic capacity, this should be taken into account[4]. The reasonable cost includes the cost of acquiring substitute premises and the cost of adapting them so that, in the case of a business, the purpose to which the land is devoted may be carried on substantially unaffected[5]. The date for the assessment of compensation under r 5 is the date on which work of reinstatement could reasonably have commenced[6]. Where the reinstatement has been carried out before the compensation is assessed, the actual cost is likely to provide the best evidence[7]. Where the premises compulsorily acquired were in need of major repairs, the Lands Tribunal deducted the cost of the repairs from the cost of the replacement premises[8]. The claimant is under a duty to mitigate his loss[9].

1 Per Lord Reid in *Birmingham Corpn v West Midland Baptist (Trust) Association Inc* [1970] AC 874, HL, at 897B.
2 Per Lord Donovan in *Birmingham Corpn v West Midland Baptist (Trust) Association Inc* [1970] AC 874 at 912E, 20 P&CR 1052 at 1079, HL.
3 *Lane v Dagenham Corpn* (1961) 12 P&CR 374, Lands Tribunal
4 *Trustees of the Zetland Lodge of Freemasons v Tamar Bridge Joint Committee* (1961) 12 P&CR 326, Lands Tribunal.
5 *A and B Taxis Ltd v Secretary of State for Air* [1922] 2 KB 328, CA, at 148; *Trustees of Zetland Lodge of Freemasons v Tamar Bridge Joint Committee* (1961) 12 P&CR 326, Lands Tribunal; *Trustees of Old Dagenham Methodist Church v Dagenham Borough Council* (1961) 179 Estates Gazette 295,

Lands Tribunal. The cost of reinstatement was held not to include VAT where Customs & Excise had given an assurance that vat was not payable (even though they subsequently changed their opinion): *Scout Association Trust Corporation v Secretary of State for the Environment* [2005] EWCA Civ 980, [2005] RVR 303.

6 *Birmingham Corpn v West Midland Baptist (Trust) Association Inc* [1970] AC 874, HL.

7 Per Sachs LJ in *West Midland Baptist (Trust) Association* (1967) 19 P&CR 9 at 29 (affd sub-nom *Birmingham Corpn v West Midland Baptist (Trust) Association* [1970] AC 874, HL), applying *Bwllfa and Merthyr Dare Steam Collieries v Pontypridd Waterworks Co* [1903] AC 426, HL.

8 *Cunningham v Sunderland Borough Council* (1963) 14 P&CR 208, Lands Tribunal. See also the comments of Sachs LJ in *West Midland Baptist Trust v Birmingham Corpn* (1967) 19 P&CR 9, CA. See also *Sparks (Trustees of East Hunslet Liberal Club) v Leeds City Council* (1977) 244 Estates Gazette 56, Lands Tribunal.

9 Lord Reid in *Birmingham Corpn v West Midland Baptist (Trust) Association Inc* [1970] AC 874, HL, at 1056.

H The discretion

[1621]

The rule provides that, if the Lands Tribunal is satisfied[1] that reinstatement elsewhere is genuinely intended, compensation 'may' be assessed on the basis of equivalent reinstatement. Thus, even where the pre-conditions described above are met, an award of compensation under r 5 is a matter of discretion[2]. In exercising the discretion, it is necessary to take into account all material factors, and, in particular, what constitutes equivalent reinstatement and its cost, and a comparison between, on the one hand, compensation assessed under r 5 and, on the other hand, compensation assessed under rr 2 and 6[3]. For this reason, the House of Lords has expressed the view that the question whether r 5 applies in a particular case should not be determined as a preliminary issue[4]. In the case of a business, the relationship between the cost of reinstatement and the total value of the business may be a paramount consideration[5]. However, this factor is likely to be of less significance in relation to a non profit-making organisation[6]. The probable duration of the continuation of the use might well affect the exercise of the discretion[7].

1 Although the rule is expressed in terms which state that it is the Lands Tribunal which must be satisfied, it is submitted that this does not prevent an acquiring authority from agreeing to pay compensation on this basis if it is satisfied that the pre-conditions are met and that the circumstances merit the application of r 5.

2 *Festiniog Rly Co v Central Electricity Generating Board* (1962) 13 P&CR 248 at 256; *Harrison and Hetherington Ltd v Cumbria County Council* (1985) 50 P&CR 396, HL, at 397. In the *Festiniog* case, Harman LJ said that the exercise of the discretion could only be challenged on two grounds: that a relevant consideration had been left out of account, or that an irrelevant consideration taken into account: at 261.

3 *Harrison and Hetherington Ltd v Cumbria County Council* (1985) 50 P&CR 396, HL, at 397. In *Sparks (Trustees of East Hunslet Liberal Club) v Leeds City Council* (1977) 244 Estates Gazette 56, the Lands Tribunal indicated that, where the conditions of r 5 are found to apply, the discretion should be exercised in the claimant's favour; this has not been tested in the Court of Appeal and, it is submitted, may not be correct.

4 *Harrison and Hetherington Ltd v Cumbria County Council* (1985) 50 P&CR 396, HL, at 397.

5 *Festiniog Rly Co v Central Electricity Generating Board* (1962) 13 P&CR 248, CA. For a detailed consideration of the factors taken into account, see the Lands Tribunal decision in this case reported at (1960) 11 P&CR 448.

6 *Sparks (Trustees of East Hunslet Liberal Club) v Leeds City Council* [1977] 2 EGLR 163, Lands Tribunal.

7 Per Buckley LJ in *Trustees of Zoar Independent Church v Rochester Corpn* (1974) 29 P&CR 145 at 154.

I Dwellings adapted for a disabled person

[1622]–[2000]
Where a dwelling has been constructed or substantially modified to meet the special needs of a disabled person[1], and is occupied by that person as his residence immediately before possession is taken by the acquiring authority, or was last so occupied[2], that person may elect to have the compensation assessed as though the dwelling were land devoted to a purpose of such a nature that there is no general demand or market for land for that purpose[3]. Where the claimant so elects, the Upper Tribunal is required to assess the compensation on the basis of equivalent reinstatement; it has no discretion.

1 As to the meaning of disabled person in this context, see the Land Compensation Act 1973 (LCA 1973), s 87(1).
2 LCA 1973, s 45(1)(*b*).
3 LCA 1973, s 45(1)(*a*).

Chapter 6

Compensation for disturbance

Contents

A Introduction

[2001]

While compensation for compulsory purchase is a single lump sum payment[1] which is intended to represent the value of the land to the owner, it may be made up of a number of elements, one of which is intended to compensate for losses caused by reason of being disturbed from possession of the land taken (consequently referred to as 'disturbance') and other losses caused by the compulsory purchase. The right to compensation for such losses came to be established through judicial decisions under the Land Clauses Consolidation Act 1845 (LCCA 1845) prior to the enactment in 1919[2] of the six rules now to be found in the Land Compensation Act 1961 (LCA 1961), s 5[3]; r 6 expressly preserves this right[4]. This chapter explains the principles which govern the right to, and assessment of, compensation for disturbance and other losses not related to the value of the land taken[5]. These principles derive to a large extent from three leading cases which are of such importance that it has been considered appropriate to include several citations from them in this chapter[6].

1 See para **[23]**.
2 Acquisition of Land (Assessment of Compensation) Act 1919, s 2.
3 See para **[4]**.
4 Per Sir Wilfred Greene MR in *Horn v Sunderland Corpn* [1941] 2 KB 26 at 34.
5 The distinction between 'disturbance' and other losses is often blurred; see the passage cited at para **[2007]** from *Horn v Sunderland Corpn*. In certain circumstances, a compulsory purchase may bring a benefit to a claimant, for example, where he is relieved of a lease containing terms which have become onerous (eg an upwards-only rent review in a falling market); it does not appear to have been decided whether such a benefit can be taken into account so as to reduce the amount otherwise due for disturbance.
6 *Horn v Sunderland Corpn* [1941] 2 KB 26, CA; *Harvey v Crawley Development Corpn* [1957] 1 QB 485, CA; *Director of Buildings and Lands v Shun Fung Ironworks Ltd* [1995] 2 AC 111, PC.

[2002]

That disturbance is an element of the value of the land to the owner is a well-established proposition[1]. However, it is inevitable, for practical reasons, that it is assessed separately from the open market value of the land, as Lord Denning explained in *Munton v GLC*[2]:

> 'It was decided in 1845 that the injury was only as to the "value of the land", as it was held that in this sum there was to be included the compensation for disturbance; so that only one sum was to be awarded … But although only one sum is awarded, it is very proper, in assessing it, to divide it into two parts, (i) the land itself, and (ii) disturbance. Starting with the Acquisition of Land Act 1919 and repeated in the Land Compensation Act 1961, Parliament itself has made a division between the two. In s 5(6) it says: "The provisions of rule 2" – that is, about the value of the land – "shall not affect the assessment of compensation for disturbance or any other matter not directly based on the value of the land". Since those Acts, the practice always has been for compensation for disturbance to be assessed separately from the value of the land. That is as it should be. The value of the land can be assessed while the owner is still in occupation, but the compensation for disturbance cannot properly be assessed until he goes out. It is only then that he can tell how much it has cost him to move, such as to get extra premises or to move his furniture. The practice is warranted by two cases in this court: *Harvey v Crawley Development Corpn* [1957] 1 QB 485 and *Lee v Minister of Transport* [1966] 1 QB 111.'

1 *Horn v Sunderland Corpn* [1941] 2 KB 26, CA; *Hughes v Doncaster MBC* [1991] 1 AC 382, HL.
2 (1976) 32 P&CR 269, CA.

[2003]
The underlying rationale of compensation for disturbance is the principle of equivalence. As Lord Nicholls said in *Director of Buildings and Lands v Shun Fung Ironworks Ltd*[1]:

> 'The purpose … is to provide fair compensation for a claimant whose lands have been compulsorily taken from him. This is sometimes described as the principle of equivalence … a claimant is entitled to be compensated fairly and fully for his loss … : a person is entitled to compensation for losses fairly attributable to the taking of his land, but not to any greater amount.'

1 [1995] 2 AC 111, PC.

[2004]
Compensation for 'disturbance' as such arises from loss of occupation of land. In addition, losses may be incurred which do not flow directly from the claimant's loss of occupation of the land, but are nevertheless a consequence of the compulsory purchase[1]. Similarly, a claimant not in occupation may incur losses which are not fully compensated by the open market value of the land alone. Rule 6[2] is expressed in terms which acknowledge this: '… compensation for disturbance *or any other matter not directly based upon the value of the land*'. An example is where a claimant, who had an interest in, but did not occupy, the premises compulsorily acquired, had a service contract with a company which was disturbed from occupation; the Court of Appeal held that he was entitled to compensation[3]. Similarly, a person, whose land is

acquired compulsorily, is entitled to his legal and surveyor's fees in preparing his claim and transferring his property to the acquiring authority, but such items would not fall under the head of 'disturbance'[4]. A person having an interest in, but not occupying, land which is compulsorily acquired can recover the incidental costs of acquiring other land within one year[5]. A property developer who has suffered delays in disposing of his properties as a result of the compulsory acquisition may be able to recover the costs of holding the land for the period of the delay[6]. In addition, it should be noted that all claimants are entitled to reasonable surveyors', legal and other professional fees incurred as a direct consequence of the compulsory purchase[7].

1 *Minister of Transport v Lee* (1965) 17 P&CR 181, especially Davies LJ, at 188.
2 LCA 1961, s 5.
3 *MacDougall v Wrexham Maelor Borough Council* [1993] RVR 141, CA, at 160–164.
4 *LCC v Tobin* [1959] 1 WLR 354. See also *Minister of Transport v Lee* [1965] 2 All ER 986, CA, and the cases cited therein.
5 LCA 1961, s 10A, inserted by the Land Compensation Act 1973 (LCA 1973), s 70, Sch 15, para 2.
6 *Ryde International plc v London Regional Transport* [2001] RVR 59, Lands Tribunal (preliminary issue). However, when the matter returned to the Lands Tribunal, it was found that no loss had been established; see also the Court of Appeal decision at [2004] EWCA Civ 232, [2004] RVR 60.
7 *LCC v Tobin* [1959] 1 WLR 354, CA. Note the distinction explained in this case between the costs of preparing the claim for compensation, which should be claimed as part of the compensation claim, and costs incurred in relation to a reference to the Lands Tribunal which may be awarded in addition to the compensation in an appropriate case (as to which, see **Division H**). See also Circular 63/67.

B The right to compensation for disturbance

[2005]
In order to be entitled to claim compensation for disturbance, a person must:

(*a*) be the occupier of the land taken;
(*b*) have an estate or interest in the land which has been compulsorily acquired;
(*c*) lose possession of the land as a result of the compulsory purchase; and
(*d*) not include in his claim any item which is inconsistent with the basis on which the land taken has been valued, or otherwise duplicates elements of the claim.

Each of these is explained in the paragraphs which follow.

1 Claimant must be the occupier of the land taken

[2006]
Occupation is critical to a claim for disturbance[1]. It is submitted that the claimant would normally have to be in occupation at the date when possession of the land is taken by the acquiring authority, unless, acting reasonably to mitigate his loss, the claimant was justified in moving at an earlier date[2]. A person who does not occupy land which is compulsorily acquired, but has an interest in it, has a statutory right to claim the incidental cost of acquiring other land[3].

1 *Jubb v Hull Dock Co* (1846) 9 QB 443; *Harvey v Crawley Development Corpn* [1957] 1 QB 485, CA; *Cartwright v Sedgley UDC* (1960) 13 P&CR 1, CA; *Kovaks v City of Birmingham District Council* (1984) 272 Estates Gazette 437, Lands Tribunal. The claimant may, nevertheless, be able to claim for matters which are not, strictly, 'disturbance', see para **[2004]**.
2 See para **[2025]**.
3 LCA 1961, s 10A, inserted by the LCA 1973, s 70, Sch 15, para 2.

2 Claimant must have estate or interest in the land

[2007]
In *Horn v Sunderland Corpn*[1], Scott LJ analysed the relevant provisions of the LCCA 1845 and said:

> '… there is in the Act of 1845 no express provision giving compensation for disturbance, or for any of the similar matters to which s 2, r 6, of the Act of 1919 refers, which for brevity I will treat as included in the word "disturbance" … If I am right in saying that the Act expressly grants only two kinds of compensation to an owner who has land taken, (1) for the value of the land, and (2) for injurious affection to his other land[2], it is plain that the judicial eye which has discerned that right in the Act must inevitably have found it in (1), that is, in the fair purchase price of the land taken. That conclusion is consonant with all the decisions, so far as I can discover.'

1 [1941] 2 KB 26 at 43.
2 As to compensation for injurious affection to other land, see **Chapter 7**.

[2008]
It follows, therefore, that disturbance can only be claimed by a person who is able to claim compensation in respect of the estate or interest in the land taken from him. Thus, it has been held that, where premises were in the possession of a legal entity separate from the owner of the land, the owner of the land could not claim disturbance. Where a company occupied land as a yearly tenant, it was held that the owner of the land, who held a majority of the shares in the company, could not claim compensation for depreciation in the value of the shares[1]. However, where the owner of the premises was itself a company, and the premises were occupied by a wholly owned subsidiary which in effect acted as agent for the parent, the parent was held to have retained the right to claim disturbance[2]. Where a business was carried on by a company in premises owned by its subsidiary company, it was held that the parent company held an irrevocable licence to carry on the business which gave it a sufficient interest to claim compensation for disturbance when the premises were compulsorily acquired[3]. Further, where the claimant was using the land taken for a purpose which was contrary to law within the meaning of r 4, the House of Lords held that compensation could not be claimed for disturbance related to that purpose[4].

1 *Roberts v Coventry Corpn* [1947] 1 All ER 308. See also *Brain and Drive Yourself Car Hire Co (London) v LCC* (1957) 9 P&CR 113, Lands Tribunal; *G W Roberts v Bristol Corpn* (1960) 11 P&CR 205, Lands Tribunal; *Greenwoods Tyre Services Ltd v Manchester Corpn* (1972) 23 P&CR 246, Lands Tribunal; *Melias v Manchester Corpn* (1972) 23 P&CR 380, Lands Tribunal; *Taylor v GLC* (1973) 25 P&CR 451, Lands Tribunal.
2 *Smith, Stone & Knight Ltd v Birmingham Corpn* [1939] 4 All ER 116.
3 *DHN Food Distributors Ltd v Tower Hamlets London Borough Council* (1976) 32 P&CR 240, CA.
4 *Hughes v Doncaster MBC* [1991] 1 AC 382, HL.

[2009]
A person who has no interest in the land taken, but is nevertheless in lawful occupation, may be entitled to a payment under the LCA 1961, s 37[1].

1 As to the LCA 1961, s 37, see **Chapter 9**.

3 Loss of possession as a result of the compulsory purchase

[2010]–[2020]
As Romer LJ said in *Harvey v Crawley Development Corpn*[1], '... any loss sustained by a dispossessed owner ... which flows from a compulsory acquisition may be regarded as the subject of compensation for disturbance provided ... that it is the natural and reasonable consequence of the dispossession of the owner'. Where the claimant had mortgaged his house to a building society which was entitled to possession under a court order as a result of arrears of repayments, it was held by the Lands Tribunal that the claimant had not been dispossessed by the compulsory purchase[2]. The Lands Tribunal has held that disturbance may be claimed even where the claimant has initiated the acquisition by service of a purchase notice[3].

1 [1957] 1 QB 485, CA, at 494.
2 *McTaggart v Bristol and West Building Society and Avon County Council* (1985) 50 P&CR 184, Lands Tribunal; the claimant had served a blight notice which was accepted, so that there was a deemed compulsory purchase.
3 *Redfield Hardware Ltd v Bristol Corpn* (1963) 15 P&CR 47, Lands Tribunal. In *Walters, Brett and Pack v South Glamorgan County Council* (1976) 32 P&CR 111, Lands Tribunal, a disturbance claim by a firm of solicitors following service of a blight notice was rejected by the tribunal, but this was because they had vacated the premises prior to confirmation of the blight notice; this case would be decided differently in the light of *Dirctor of Buildings and lands v Shun Fun Ironworks Ltd* [1995] 2 AC 111, PC.

4 Consistency with the basis of valuation of the land taken and avoidance of duplication

[2021]
In *Horn v Sunderland Corpn*[1], compensation was claimed for the land taken, valued on the basis of its suitability for development; it was held that compensation could not be recovered for disturbance of the claimant's agricultural business because he would have had to abandon farming in order to realise the development value of the land. Where land has to be valued on the basis of a cleared site, compensation is not payable for disturbance[2]. Where a claimant held a lease with only ten and a half months' unexpired term when his land was compulsorily acquired, the Lands Tribunal held that his disturbance claim had to be consistent with his interest in land, so that he was able to recover, as disturbance, loss of profits for only ten and a half months[3]. Where a business tenant would, in the absence of the compulsory acquisition, have had a right to apply for a new tenancy under the Landlord and Tenant Act 1954, that (and consequently the possibility that, if the application had been successful, his occupation would have been extended beyond the termination of his current lease) must be taken into account[4]. Where the claimant owned property which he let on residential tenancies, the Court of Appeal held that the basis upon which the value of the land had been assessed, capitalising the

rental income, had in effect compensated him on the basis of total extinguishment so that he could not recover further sums in respect of disturbance[5]. Where development land is compulsorily acquired, the developer cannot claim, in addition to the open market value of the land, loss of profits which he expected to earn by carrying out the development, because the expectation of earning such profits is already reflected in the value of the land[6]. Where the land compulsorily acquired was used for an unlawful purpose which r 4 of LCA 1961, s 5 required to be disregarded, compensation could not be claimed for disturbance in respect of chattels left on the land which had been used in connection with the unlawful use[7].

1 [1941] 2 KB 26.
2 *Northwood v LCC* [1926] 2 KB 411; *Walkes-Hilliman v Greater London Council* (1969) 20 P&CR 736, Lands Tribunal; *Ogunlana v Liverpool City Council* (1983) 265 Estates Gazette 883, Lands Tribunal. The claimant may nevertheless be entitled to a payment under the LCA 1973, s 37, as to which, see **Chapter 9**.
3 *Greenwoods Tyre Services Ltd v Manchester Corpn* (1972) 23 P&CR 246, Lands Tribunal. but not in relation to short tenancies, see: *Bishopsgate Space Management Ltd and Teamworks Karting Ltd v London Underground Ltd* [2004] RVR 89.
4 LCA 1973, s 47 reversing the effect of the Landlord and Tenant Act 1954, s 39.
5 *Mallick v Liverpool City Council* (1999) 79 P&CR 1, CA.
6 *Pastoral Finance Association v The Minister* [1914] AC 1083, PC; *Collins v Feltham UDC* [1937] 4 All ER 189; *Wimpey & Co Ltd v Middlesex County Council* [1938] 3 All ER 781; *D McEwing & Sons Ltd v Renfrewshire County Council* (1959) 11 P&CR 306, Ct of Sess. These cases were reviewed and applied in *Corton Caravans and Chalets Ltd v Anglican Water Services Ltd* [2003] RVR 323. See also para **[2049]**. Contrast *Ryde International plc v London Regional Transport* [2001] RVR 59, Lands Tribunal, in which the Lands Tribunal held on a preliminary issue that a property developer was entitled to recover the costs of holding his land when the sales had been delayed by the compulsory purchase, although, when the matter returned to the Lands Tribunal, there was found to be no loss under this head [2003] RVR 273; see also the Court of Appeal decision at [2004] EWCA Civ 232, [2004] RVR 60. In *Ryde International plc v London Regional Transport* [2004] RVR 60, Court of Appeal, Carnwath LJ pointed out that the decision in *Pastoral Finance Ltd v The Minister* was made under the Australian equivalent of the LCAA 1845 and was therefore an unsafe interpretation of the rules introduced in 1991 now in LCA 1961, s 5. See also *Welford v EDF Energy Networks(LPN) plc* [2006] RVR 245, upheld on appeal [2007] RVR 172, CA.
7 *Hall v Sandwell Metropolitan Council* [2008] RVR 345 (Lands Tribunal). In respect of r 4, see paras **[444]–[445]** above.

C Assessment of disturbance compensation

1 General principles

[2022]
The general principle was described by Scott LJ in *Horn v Sunderland Corpn*[1] as follows:

> '… the principle of compensation will include … personal loss imposed upon the owner by the forced sale, whether it be the cost of preparing the land for the best market available, or incidental loss in connection with the business he has been carrying on, or the cost of reinstatement, because otherwise he will not be fully compensated … But here we come to the other side of the picture. The statutory compensation cannot, and must not, exceed the owner's total loss, for if it does, it will put an unfair burden on the public authority or other promoters who on public grounds have been given the power of compulsory acquisition, and it will transgress the principle of equiv-

alence which is at the root of statutory compensation, the principle that the owner shall be paid neither less not more than his loss. The enunciation of this principle, the most fundamental of all, is easy enough. Its justice is self-evident, but its application to varying facts is apt to be difficult …'

1 [1941] 2 KB 26, CA, at 49.

[2023]
Romer LJ in *Harvey v Crawley Development Corpn*[1] described the scope of compensation for disturbance in these terms:

> '… any loss may be regarded as the subject of compensation for disturbance provided, first, that it is not too remote, and secondly, that it is the natural and reasonable consequence of the dispossession of the owner.'

1 [1957] 1 QB 485, CA, at 494.

[2024]
In *Director of Buildings and Lands v Shun Fung Ironworks Ltd*[1], Lord Nicholls repeated the fundamental principle of equivalence in these terms:

> ' … a claimant is entitled to be compensated fairly and fully for his loss. Conversely, and built into the concept of fair compensation, is the corollary that a claimant is not entitled to receive more than fair compensation: a person is entitled to compensation for losses fairly attributable to the taking of his land, but not to any greater amount. It is ultimately by this touchstone, with its two facets, that all claims for compensation succeed or fail.'

Lord Nicholls went on to acknowledge that the application of the general principle of fair and adequate compensation 'bristles with problems'[2]. He identified three conditions as 'useful guidelines':

(*a*) there must be a causal connection between the compulsory acquisition and the loss claimed;
(*b*) the loss must not be too remote; and
(*c*) the claimant must behave reasonably to eliminate or reduce his loss.

The paragraphs which follow explain Lord Nicholls's three conditions in more detail. It should be noted that it is legitimate to delay assessment of a disturbance claim until the relevant facts are known[3].

1 [1995] 2 AC 111, PC, at 125.
2 [1995] 2 AC 111, PC, at 126.
3 See the remarks of Lord Denning cited in para **[2002]** in the *Munton* case. See also *Wickham Growers Ltd v Southern Water plc* (1996) 73 P & CR 351, Lands Tribunal.

2 Causal connection: pre-acquisition losses

[2025]
The first of Lord Nicholls's conditions has already been explained in general terms[1], but the Privy Council decision in the *Shun Fung* case developed the law to a significant degree by extending the concept of causal connection to losses incurred prior to the acquisition, referred to as the 'shadow period'. Lord Nicholls said[2]:

> 'This claim raises the question whether a loss occurring *before* [compulsory acquisition] can be regarded, for compensation purposes, as a loss *caused* by the [acquisition]. At first sight the question seems to admit of only one answer. Cause must precede effect …'

Having identified the Crown's contention that no losses incurred prior to the taking of possession were recoverable, he continued[3]:

> 'So where can the boundary be drawn sensibly? If the line contended by the Crown is rejected, as it must be for the reasons already spelt out, there is no sensible stopping place short of recognising that losses incurred in anticipation of [compulsory acquisition] and because of the threat which [compulsory acquisition] presented are to be regarded as losses caused by the [compulsory acquisition] as much as losses arising after [compulsory acquisition]. This involves giving the concept of causal connection an extended meaning, wide enough to embrace all such losses.'

He concluded by confirming that the cases of *Aberdeen City District Council v Sim*[4] and *Prasad v Wolverhampton BC*[5] (in which pre-acquisition losses had been awarded as part of disturbance claims) were correctly decided[6].

1 See para **[2009]**.
2 [1995] 2 AC 111, PC, at 135G. It should be noted that, in his speech, Lord Nicholls used the Hong Kong term 'resumption' to refer to compulsory acquisition; this term has been replaced by the latter phrase in square brackets.
3 [1995] 2 AC 111 at 137G.
4 (1982) 264 Estates Gazette 621.
5 [1983] Ch 333, CA.
6 [1983] Ch 333 at 139B. Earlier cases which must now be regarded as incorrect on this point include *Webb v Stockport Borough Council* (1962) 13 P&CR 339; *Square Grip Reinforcement Co (London) Ltd v Rowton Houses Ltd and the LCC* (1967) 18 P&CR 258; *G E Widden & Co Ltd v Kensington and Chelsea Royal London Borough* [1970] RVR 160; *Bostock Chater & Sons Ltd v Chelmsford Corpn* (1973) 26 P&CR 321.

[2026]
The judgment of the Privy Council in the *Shun Fung* case does not identify precisely the earliest date from which losses might in principle be recoverable. However, the facts show[1] that the Government had written a letter in 1981 to indicate its intention to acquire the property in question, but the formal order was not made by the Governor until 1985, with the date for acquisition fixed in 1986. The *Sim* and *Prasad* cases, referred to in the judgment of Lord Nicholls, concerned losses incurred after the compulsory purchase order was made, but prior to the notice to treat. However, in *Shun Fung*, the Privy Council concluded[2] that the claimant could recover losses incurred between the date on which the Government had indicated its intention by letter and the date of taking possession. Thus, while the success of such a claim will depend upon the reasonableness of the claimant's actions, there appears now, in principle, to be no bar to recovering losses incurred even prior to confirmation of the compulsory purchase order. As Lord Denning said in *Wilson v Liverpool Corpn*[3], 'A scheme is a progressive thing. It starts vague and known to few. It becomes more precise and better known as time goes on. Eventually, it becomes precise and definite and known to all'. On the basis of the *Shun Fung* decision, it appears that a claimant must just make a judgment as to what costs it is reasonable to incur in the light of all the circumstances. He will need to take a cautious approach: if he

incurs losses prior to implementation of the compulsory purchase (ie the notice treat or general vesting declaration[4]), and, in the event, the compulsory purchase is not implemented, he will not be entitled to receive any compensation.

1 [1995] 2 AC 111, PC, at 122.
2 [1995] 2 AC 111, PC, at 139B.
3 (1970) 22 P&CR 282, at 292.
4 As to implementation of a compulsory purchase, see **Division D**.

[2026.1]
Pre-acquisition losses may (subject to proof) include a reduction in profits properly attributable to the scheme for which the land was to be acquired, for example, where the location of a shop became unattractive due to a reduction in pedestrian footfall[1].

1 *Optical Express (Southern) Ltd v Birmingham City Council* [2005] RVR 230, LT.

3 Remoteness

[2027]
The concept of remoteness in this context was explained by Lord Nicholls in *Director of Buildings and Land v Shun Fung Ironworks Ltd*[1] as follows:

> 'The adverse consequences to a claimant whose land is taken may extend outwards and onwards a very long way, but fairness does not require that the acquiring authority shall be responsible ad infinitum. There is a need to distinguish between adverse consequences which trigger a claim for compensation and those which do not. A similar problem exists with claims for damages in other fields. The law describes losses which are irrecoverable for this reason as too remote. In *Harvey v Crawley Development Corpn* [1957] 1 QB 485, 493, Denning LJ gave the example of the acquisition of a house which is owner-occupied. The owner could recover the cost of buying another house as his home, but not the cost of buying a replacement house as an investment. The latter would be too remote. The familiar and perennial difficulty lies in attempting to formulate clear practical guidance on the criteria by which remoteness is to be judged in the infinitely different set of circumstances which arise. The overriding principle of fairness is comprehensive, but it suffers from the drawback of being imprecise, even vague, in practical terms. The tools used by lawyers are concepts of chains of causation and intervening events and the like. Reasonably foreseeable, not unlikely, probable, natural are among the descriptions which are or have been used in particular contexts. Even the much maligned epithet "direct" may still have its uses as a limiting factor in some situations.'

1 [1995] 2 AC 111, PC, at 126B.

[2028]
Examples of remoteness were provided by Denning LJ in *Harvey v Crawley Development Corpn*[1]:

> 'Supposing a man did not occupy a house himself but simply owned it as an investment. His compensation would be the value of the house. If he chose to put the money into stocks and shares, he could not claim the

brokerage as compensation. That would be much too remote. It would not be the consequence of the compulsory acquisition but the result of his own choice in putting the money into stocks and shares instead of putting it on deposit at the bank.

If he chose to buy another house as an investment, he would not get the solicitors' costs on the purchase. These costs would be the result of his own choice of investment and not the result of the compulsory acquisition … If an elderly man and his wife owned and occupied a house which was compulsorily acquired and they thought to themselves: "We do not think we need to get another house; we will go into a guest-house", they would not get the costs of moving into a new house when they had not incurred them. Nor would they be able to claim the cost of living in a boarding-house for the rest of their days. They would only get the market value of their home.'

1 [1957] 1 QB 485, CA, at 493.

4 Duty to mitigate loss

[2029]
The claimant's duty to mitigate his loss in this context was explained by Lord Nicholls in *Director of Buildings and Land v Shun Fung Ironworks Ltd*[1] as follows:

> 'The law expects those who claim recompense to behave reasonably. If a reasonable person in the position of the claimant would have taken steps to eliminate or reduce the loss, and the claimant failed to do so, he cannot fairly expect to be compensated for the loss or the unreasonable part of it. Likewise, if a reasonable person in the position of the claimant would not have incurred, or would not incur, the expenditure being claimed, fairness does not require that the authority should be responsible for such expenditure. Expressed in other words, losses or expenditure incurred unreasonably cannot sensibly be said to be caused by, or be the consequence of, or be due to the [compulsory acquisition].'

1 [1995] 2 AC 111, PC, at 126F. As to the general principles applicable to mitigation of loss, see *Geest pc v Lansiquot* [2002] 1 WLR 3111, PC, in which it was said that if a defendant intends to contend that a defendant has failed to mitigate his or her loss, notice of such contention must be given long enough ahead to for the plaintiff to prepare to meet it.

[2030]–[2040]
The Upper Tribunal has endorsed as consistent with *Shun Fung* the approach to mitigation of loss set out in an earlier decision of the Lands Tribunal[1]. The Lands Tribunal has held that the onus of proof is upon the acquiring authority to show that the claimant has failed to mitigate his loss[2]. Even where the claimant was too ill to take steps to mitigate his loss by relocating his business, the Court of Appeal held that he was not entitled to claim compensation on the basis of total extinguishment, because his ill-health was not a consequence of the compulsory purchase[3]. An example of a failure to mitigate loss is where a claimant failed to move to alternative accommodation quickly enough to minimise expenses and other losses[4]. Another example is where the claimant had acquired alternative premises at a significantly greater distance from its principal clients, and claimed for loss of profits reflecting additional costs and lost business. The Tribunal held that the claimant had failed to mitigate its loss by

confining its search to freehold premises and on the evidence there were leasehold premises available in a location more convenient for serving its customers[5].

1 In *Scotia Plastic Binding Ltd v London Development Agency* [2010] UKUT 98 (LC), [2010] RVR 307, para 7, the Upper Tribunal endorsed the three rules set out in *Appleby & Ireland v Hampshire County Council* [1978] RVR 156 at 161.
2 *Lindon Print Ltd v West Midlands County Council* [1987] 2 EGLR 200, Lands Tribunal. Another example is *Welford v EDF Energy Networks (LPN) Ltd* [2006] RVR 245 at paras 106–113.
3 *Bailey v Derby Corpn* [1965] 1 All ER 443, CA.
4 *Bede Distributors Ltd v Newcastle-upon-Tyne Corpn* (1973) 26 P&CR 298, Lands Tribunal.
5 *Scotia Plastic Binding Ltd v London Development Agency* [2010] UKUT 98 (LC), [2010] RVR 307.

D Residential disturbance

[2041]
If a person who occupies his house loses possession of it as a result of compulsory purchase, he can claim compensation for the legal and surveyor's fees incurred in purchasing a replacement house, the cost of moving his furniture, and having his curtains and carpets altered or replaced to fit the replacement house[1]. This even extends to surveyor's fees, legal costs and travelling expenses in relation to a potential replacement house which proved to be unsuitable[2]. The Tribunal has allowed the expenses of translating services where the claimant needed these in connection with the compulsory acquisition[3]. However, an owner can only recover costs of this nature where he has occupied his house and, having been forced out by the compulsory purchase, finds a house elsewhere in which to live[4].

1 Per Denning LJ in *Harvey v Crawley Development Corpn* [1957] 1 QB 485, CA, at 493.
2 *Harvey v Crawley Development Corpn* [1957] 1 QB 485, CA, at 487.
3 *Sadik v London Borough of Haringey* (1978) 37 P&CR 120, Lands Tribunal.
4 Per Denning LJ in *Harvey v Crawley Development Corpn* [1957] 1 QB 485, CA, at 494.

[2042]
A person who pays more for his replacement house than he receives for his house which is compulsorily acquired could not include the additional amount in his claim for compensation, because he is presumed to have obtained value for money[1]. The Lands Tribunal refused to award interest on a bridging loan in circumstances where it took the view that such a loan was not reasonable because the reference to the Lands Tribunal could have been made sooner and an advance payment obtained from the acquiring authority[2]; the corollary appears to be that interest would be recoverable if, in the particular circumstances, it is reasonable for the claimant to take out a bridging loan.

1 Per Denning LJ in *Harvey v Crawley Development Corpn* [1957] 1 QB 485, CA, at 494.
2 *Simpson v Stoke-on-Trent City Council* (1982) 44 P&CR 226, Lands Tribunal.

E Business disturbance

1 Relocation or extinguishment: the principles

[2043]
Where a business is in occupation of land which is compulsorily acquired, compensation may be assessed, depending upon the circumstances, either

upon the basis that the compulsory purchase has the effect of extinguishing the business, or on the basis of the costs of relocating the business. In *Director of Buildings and Lands v Shun Fung Ironworks Ltd*[1], the cost of relocating the business far exceeded the compensation for total extinguishment. The Crown argued that, as a result, compensation for disturbance had to be assessed on the basis of total extinguishment. On this issue, Lord Nicholls said[2]:

> '… their Lordships are unable to accept that a claimant can never be entitled to compensation on a relocation basis if this would exceed the amount of compensation payable on an extinguishment basis. In the ordinary way, the expenses and losses incurred when a business is moved to a new site will be less than the value of the entire business as a going concern. Compensation on a relocation basis will be normally be less than compensation payable on an extinguishment basis. But this will not always be so, and a rigid limitation as contended by the Crown could lead to injustice. Such a limitation finds no support in the statutory provisions, and it would be inconsistent with the purpose for which these provisions exist. A businessman may spend large sums of money setting up a new business. Before the business has time to prove itself, his premises are acquired compulsorily. Having no profit record, the business may be worth little. The compensation payable on extinguishment would be paltry. But a reasonable businessman, spending his own money might consider it worthwhile incurring expenditure in fitting out new premises nearby and continuing his business there. Fairness requires that he should be entitled, in respect of the disturbance of his business, to his reasonable costs incurred in the removal of his business and in setting it up again at the new property. Otherwise he would not be properly compensated for his loss; he would not be placed in a financially equivalent position.
>
> It would be different if no reasonable businessman, forced to quit, would incur the cost of moving the business and setting it up in the new property. In the latter case a claimant would not be entitled to compensation calculated on a relocation basis. He would not be entitled to reimbursement of expenses reasonably incurred.
>
> The conclusion to be drawn, in a case where the cost of moving the business to another site would exceed the present value of the business, is that this is not of itself an absolute bar to the assessment of compensation on the relocation basis. It all depends on how a reasonable businessman, using his own money, would behave in the circumstances …
>
> The same result can be arrived at by reasoning expressed in other language which accords more directly with the basic principle that compensation is payable for the value to the claimant of the land in question … '

1 [1995] 2 AC 111, PC.
2 [1995] 2 AC 111, PC, at 126H–128B.

2 Relocation

General

[2044]
Costs related to relocation of a business can only be claimed if it is the same business which is relocated. Commencement of a business at a distant

locality or after a long time period might not be capable of interpretation as relocating the business which has been dispossessed[1]. There must be evidence that, in the absence of the compulsory acquisition, the claimant would have been entitled to remain in the premises[2].

1 *Director of Buildings and Lands v Shun Fung Ironworks Ltd* [1995] 2 AC 111, PC. See also *Blake v Newcastle-upon-Tyne Corpn* (1966) 198 Estates Gazette 155.
2 *Klein v London Underground Ltd* (1996) 36 RVR 94, LT.

Acquisition of replacement premises

[2045]
The cost of searching for new premises may be claimed as disturbance[1], including the claimant's time spent on the search[2]. However, the purchase price of new premises normally cannot be claimed[3], because there is a rebuttable presumption in law that the purchase price is something for which the claimant has received value for money[4]. For this reason, the Court of Appeal has held that interest charges incurred in financing the cost of constructing alternative premises cannot be recovered as disturbance[5]. If the claimant purchases more expensive premises than those taken, he will not be entitled to compensation for the additional amount, because he is presumed to receive value for money[6]. Where a claimant took premises much larger than he required and sub-let part, the tribunal scaled down his claim for fees and other expenses[7]. A claimant can include in his claim increased operating costs of alternative premises, but only if, first, he had no alternative but to incur such costs, and, secondly, he received no benefit from them which would make them worthwhile[8]. Similarly, it may be possible to include in the claim compensation for better premises if they have been forced upon the claimant[9]. Where a regional development grant was payable to the extent of 22% on certain items included in a claim for disturbance, the Court of Appeal held that the grant should not be deducted from the compensation, on the ground that it would be contrary to public policy to lessen the inducement to re-locate in the area[10].

1 *D Newton & Son v Lincoln City Council* (1985) 275 Estates Gazette 548, Lands Tribunal. However, these may be scaled down or excluded if excessive: *J Bibby & Sons Ltd v Merseyside County Council* (1977) 34 P&CR 101, Lands Tribunal; affd (1979) 39 P&CR 53, CA.
2 *Smith v Birmingham City Council* (1974) 29 P&CR 265, Lands Tribunal. As to personal time, see **[2050]**.
3 *Powner and Powner v Leeds Corpn* (1953) 4 P&CR 167, Lands Tribunal.
4 *Service Welding Ltd v Tyne and Wear County Council* (1979) 38 P&CR 352, CA. See also *Easton v Islington Corpn* (1952) 3 P&CR 145, Lands Tribunal; *Greenberg v Grimsby Corpn* (1961) 12 P&CR 212, Lands Tribunal.
5 *Service Welding Ltd v Tyne and Wear County Council* (1979) 38 P&CR 352, CA. See also *B&T (Essex) v Shoreditch Corpn* (1958) 9 P&CR 471; *Coulson v Borough of Bury St Edmunds* (1969) 210 Estates Gazette 1246; *Simpson v Stoke-on-Trent City Council* (1982) 44 P&CR 226, Lands Tribunal.
6 Per Denning LJ in *Harvey v Crawley Development Corpn* [1957] 1 QB 485, CA, at 494.
7 *J Bibby & Sons Ltd v Merseyside County Council* (1977) 34 P&CR 101, Lands Tribunal; affd (1979) 39 P&CR 53, CA.
8 *J Bibby & Sons Ltd v Merseyside County Council* (1979) 39 P&CR 53, CA.
9 Per Everleigh and Megaw LJJ in *J Bibby & Sons Ltd v Merseyside County Council* (1979) 39 P&CR 53, CA.
10 *Palatine Graphic Arts Co Ltd v Liverpool City Council* [1986] QB 335, CA.

Adaptation and improvement of replacement premises

[2046]
The cost of adaptation of new premises to make them suitable for the claimant's business may be recovered to the extent that the costs make the new premises comparable to those compulsorily acquired[1]. However, the cost of structural additions or improvements will not be recoverable, again on the basis that the claimant receives value for money[2]. In *Tamplins Brewery Ltd v County Borough of Brighton*[3], the local authority had compulsorily acquired land on which a bottling plant was situated which comprised part of a brewery. The brewery constructed a new bottling plant on an alternative site sold to it by the local authority. The Lands Tribunal held that, since the bottling plant was a vital part of a single undertaking, the cost of replacing that plant was the proper measure of compensation, subject to a reduction to reflect the fact that the new plant was better than the old one.

1 *Bresgall & Sons Ltd v Hackney London Borough Council* (1976) 32 P&CR 442, CA; *Service Welding Ltd v Tyne and Wear County Council* (1979) 38 P&CR 352, CA, at 358.
2 *Smith v Birmingham Corpn* (1975) 29 P&CR 265, Lands Tribunal.
3 (1970) 22 P&CR 746, Lands Tribunal, applying *Harvey v Crawley Development Corpn* [1957] 1 QB 485; *Horn v Sunderland Corpn* [1941] 2 KB 26.

Removal and other expenses

[2047]
Subject to the rule that the claimant must mitigate his loss, expenses which are incurred as a direct result of being forced to move will be recoverable; examples include the costs of removal of plant and machinery, new stationery, notification to customers and also losses on the forced sale of stock[1].

1 *Traggett v Surrey Heath Borough Council* (1975) 237 Estates Gazette 423, Lands Tribunal. See also the items which were allowed and those which were not allowed in *DB Thomas & Son Ltd v GLC* (1982) 262 Estates Gazette 991, Lands Tribunal. Translation services were allowed in *Sadik v London Borough of Haringey* (1978) 37 P&CR 120, Lands Tribunal.

Goodwill

[2048]
Goodwill represents the capital value of the business to the owner; it is explained in more detail below under the heading of extinguishment. One of the objectives of relocating a business is to retain its goodwill, but occasionally, notwithstanding relocation, goodwill is partially lost[1]. Loss of goodwill is to be distinguished from temporary loss of profits, which is considered under the next heading. The former represents permanent loss in the capital value to the owner; the latter reflects the temporary effect of the compulsory purchase upon profits.

1 An example is *Handley v Greenwich London Borough* (1970) 21 P&CR 645, Lands Tribunal, in which the tribunal found that 60% of the business would be lost. *LCC v Tobin* [1959] 1 All ER 649, applying *Bwllfa and Methyr Dare Steam Colleries (1891) Ltd v Pontypridd Waterworks Co* [1903] AC 426, HL.

Temporary loss of profits

[2049]
Where a business relocates, a claimant may be able to demonstrate that the profits of the business will be reduced for a temporary period while it re-establishes itself; subject to sufficient supporting evidence, an amount for such temporary loss of profits may be included in the claim[1]. Similarly, where agricultural land was acquired prior to harvesting a cereal crop, the loss of profits on that crop was allowed, but not loss of profits on subsequent years' crops which were taken to be reflected in the value of the land[2]. A developer's loss of profits are not recoverable as disturbance because they are taken to be reflected in the value of the land[3]. Where a claimant held a lease with only ten and a half months' unexpired term, he was able to recover lost profits for ten and a half months only[4]. The Lands Tribunal has rejected a contention that principles relating to the assessment of damages in the law of tort should be applied to the assessment of loss of profits because the principles have been well established for the purposes of assessing compulsory purchase compensation[5].

1 For example, *Bede Distributors Ltd v Newcastle-upon-Tyne Corpn* (1973) 26 P&CR 298, Lands Tribunal.
2 *Watson v Secretary of State for Air* [1954] 3 All ER 582, CA.
3 *Pastoral Finance Association Ltd v The Minister* [1914] AC 1083, PC; *Collins v Feltham UDC* [1937] 4 All ER 189; *Wimpey & Co Ltd v Middlesex County Council* [1938] 3 All ER 781; *D McEwing & Sons Ltd v Renfrewshire County Council* (1959) 11 P&CR 306, Ct of Sess. These cases were reviewed and applied in *Corton Caravans and Chalets Ltd v Anglican Water Services Ltd* [2003] RVR 323. In *Ryde International plc v London Regional Transport* [2004] RVR 60, Court of Appeal, Carnwath LJ pointed out that the decision in *Pastoral Finance Association Ltd v The Minister* was made under the Australian equivalent of the LCAA 1845 and was therefore an unsafe interpretation of the rules introduced in 1991 now in LCA 1961, s 5. See also *Welford v EDF Energy Networks (LPN) plc* [2006] RVR 245, upheld on appeal [2007] RVR 172, CA. See also para **[2021]**.
4 *Greenwoods Tyre Services Ltd v Manchester Corpn* (1972) 23 P&CR 246, Lands Tribunal and see *Bishopsgate Space Management Ltd and Teamworks Karting Ltd v London Underground Ltd* [2004] RVR 89, Lands Tribunal.
5 *Corton Caravans and Chalets Ltd v Anglican Water Services Ltd* [2003] RVR 323, Lands Tribunal.

Personal time

[2050]
It has been held that the claimant's personal time taken up as a result of the works for which land was acquired from him may be the subject of a claim for 'loss or injury' under the LCCA 1845, s 121[1]; it is submitted that the same may apply to a disturbance claim. It has been held that a claimant's personal time spent on searching for alternative premises may be included in a disturbance claim[2]. However, where the claimant is a company, the salaries of directors and employees of a business will not normally be allowed because they will be reflected in any loss of profits of the business for which a claim may be made[3].

1 *Minister of Transport v Pettit* (1968) 20 P&CR 344, CA.
2 *Smith v Birmingham City Council* (1974) 29 P&CR 265, Lands Tribunal.
3 *M&B Precision Engineers v Ealing London Borough Council* (1973) 225 Estates Gazette 1186; however, abnormal overtime, if proved, may be recoverable. Cf *DB Thomas and Sons v GLC* (1982) 262 Estates Gazette 991, [1982] RVR 122, Lands Tribunal, in which directors' time planning removal and formulating claim was allowed in preference to reflecting their time in the loss of profits claim.

Lost rents

[2051]–[2060]
In a case in which the prospect of a compulsory acquisition of land caused a deferral of a rent review, thereby depriving the landowner of the higher rent, the Lands Tribunal held that the higher rent should be taken into account but in connection with the assessment of the value of the land taken under rule 2 of the LCA 1961, s 5[1], not under rule 6. In another case, it was conceded that rents lost due to the difficulty of letting the land to be compulsorily acquired in the shadow of the compulsory purchase could be recovered under rule 6[3]. In *Pattle v Secretary of State for Transport*[2], the Lands Tribunal decided, as a preliminary issue, that in principle a claimant may recover compensation under rule 6 in respect of rents lost in consequence of being prevented by the compulsory acquisition from redeveloping his property. The claimants owned 1.44ha of which 0.045ha was acquired for the construction of a railway. The claimants had obtained planning permission to redevelop the whole of their land by the construction of 20 units for B1 or B2 use. The claimants contended that they did not implement that permission because of the uncertainty created by the acquisition and construction of the railway. The claim was for rents which would have been received before the valuation date if the development had been carried out (less the costs of construction) from the whole of the claimants' land, not just the part compulsorily acquired.

1 *Greens Motor Holdings Ltd v Preseli Pembrokeshire District Council* [1991] 1 EGLR 211, Lands Tribunal.
2 *Castle House Investments Ltd (in voluntary liquidation) v Bradford Metropolitan District Council* [2007] RVR 277.
3 [2009] UKUL 141(LC), [2009] RVR 328, Lands Tribunal. Although the tribunal decided that it was not right to exclude this claim at the stage of preliminary issues, it warned the claimant about the possible difficulties involved in proving the claim: see para 50. In the event, this reference was subsequently settled without returning to the tribunal for determination of the compensation and no appeal was made against the decision. It is submitted that there may be some doubt as to the correctness of this decision.

3 Extinguishment

General

[2061]
Extinguishment of a business may occur, for example, where no suitable alternative premises are available for the business[1]. There must be evidence that, in the absence of the compulsory acquisition, the claimant would have been entitled to remain in the premises[2].The claimant must act reasonably[3]; where the acquiring authority had offered alternative accommodation which was reasonably suitable, the Lands Tribunal refused to award compensation on the basis of extinguishment[4]. In contrast, where the tribunal considered that it was reasonable for the claimant to have rejected alternative accommodation offered by the acquiring authority, compensation for extinguishment was awarded[5].

1 Eg *Helmcourt v Manchester City Council* [1977] RVR 300, Lands Tribunal.
2 *Klein v London Underground Ltd* (1996) 36 RVR 94, Lands Tribunal. However, where the claimant only has a short tenancy to which the CPA 1965, s 20 applies, the likelihood of

renewal of the tenancy cannot be taken into account: *Bishopsgate Space Management Ltd and Teamworks Karting Ltd v London Underground Ltd* [2004] RVR 89.

3 *Director of Buildings and Lands v Shun Fung Ironworks Ltd* [1995] 2 AC 111, PC.

4 *Pettingale v Stockport Corpn* (1961) 12 P&CR 384, Lands Tribunal.

5 *Knott Mill Carpets Ltd v Stretford Borough Council* (1973) 26 P&CR 129, Lands Tribunal.

Goodwill

[2062]

Goodwill is the capital value of a business as a going concern. It is not acquired by the acquiring authority, and it will be lost if the business is extinguished as a result of the compulsory purchase. For the purpose of assessing disturbance compensation, it is not the open market value of the business which must be assessed, but the value to the claimant[1]. A claimant is entitled to compensation for loss of goodwill even if he would have been unable in law to sell his business[2]. In order to ascertain whether, and the extent to which, goodwill has been lost, it is permissible to have regard to facts known at the date of assessment of the compensation, even though such facts only became known after the valuation date[3]. Where the claimant owned property which he used for residential lettings and the assessment of the value of the land was based upon a capitalisation of the rental income, the Court of Appeal held that this in effect compensated him for extinguishment[4].

1 *Remnant v London County Council* (1952) 3 P&CR 185, Lands Tribunal, at 193; *Nielsen v Camden London Borough Council* (1968) 19 P&CR 801, Lands Tribunal; *W Clibbett Ltd v Avon County Council* [1976] RVR 131, Lands Tribunal; *Roy v Westminster City Council* (1975) 31 P&CR 458, Lands Tribunal.

2 *Roy v Westminster City Council* (1975) 31 P&CR 458, Lands Tribunal, concerning a doctor's practice the goodwill of which could not lawfully be sold by virtue of the National Health Service Act 1946, s 35(2).

3 *LCC v Tobin* [1959] 1 All ER 649, applying *Bwllfa and Methyr Dare Steam Colleries (1891) Ltd v Pontypridd Waterworks Co* [1903] AC 426, HL.

4 *Mallick v Liverpool City Council* (1999) 79 P&CR 1.

5 [1995] 2 AC 111.

[2063]

Assessment of the value of goodwill in the hands of the claimant is inevitably somewhat arbitrary. It has been customary to have regard to annual profits over previous years and to capitalise them by applying a number of years' purchase[1]. The Lands Tribunal has often, however, tended to take what it has called a 'robust' approach[2], awarding a figure which, even if not 'plucked out of the air'[3], was not based directly upon a detailed calculation[4]. In *Shun Fung*[5], a discounted cash flow approach was adopted, and this has been followed by the Lands Tribunal[6]. In *Optical Express (Southern) Ltd v Birmingham City Council*[7], the Lands Tribunal preferred to follow the traditional approach of applying a multiplier to an assessment of annual profits. However, the evidence before the tribunal as to how the multiplier should be arrived at was such that the tribunal determined a multiplier significantly higher than figures which could have been derived from previous cases or settlements in the shadow of the same compulsory purchase.

1 See, eg, *Zarraga v Newcastle-upon-Tyne Corpn* (1968) 19 P&CR 609, Lands Tribunal; *Handley v Greenwich London Borough* (1970) 21 P&CR 645, Lands Tribunal.

2 *W Clibbett Ltd v Avon County Council* [1976] RVR 131, Lands Tribunal.
3 This was the phrase used by counsel in *Tragett v Surrey Heath Borough Council* (1975) 237 Estates Gazette 423, Lands Tribunal, at 425.
4 In *Tragett v Surrey Heath Borough Council* (1975) 237 Estates Gazette 423, Lands Tribunal, at 425, the tribunal awarded a figure on the 'robust' approach, but explained that it had been assisted by the evidence in arriving at the right bracket within which its finding should lie. See also *Roy v Westminster City Council* (1975) 31 P&CR 458, Lands Tribunal.
5 [1995] 2 AC 111.
6 *Aslam v South Bedfordshire District Council* [2000] RVR 121.
7 [2005] RVR 230, Lands Tribunal. The Tribunal also made comments about how to arrive at the appropriate figure for annual profits. See also *Crowley (t/a Contraband Discount Stores) v Liverpool PSDA Ltd* [2007] RVR 125.

Extinguishment where claimant over 60

[2064]
Where a person over 60 years old carries on business on land, having an annual value under a prescribed amount[1], from which he is dispossessed by compulsory purchase, compensation for disturbance is to be assessed on the basis of extinguishment if he gives an undertaking not to dispose of the goodwill of the business[2].

1 Ie the amount prescribed for the purposes of the Town and Country Planning Act 1990, s 149(3)(*a*) (blight notices, currently £18,000, see **B [1182]**). See also *Sheffield Development Corpn v Glossop Sectional Buildings Ltd* [1994] RVR 195, CA.
2 LCA 1973, s 46.

Incidental expenses

[2065]
Any incidental losses and expenses which can be proved to result from the extinguishment will be recoverable, such as forced sale of stock.

F Disturbance compenstion and tax

[2066]–[2500]
Since the object of disturbance compensation is to provide the claimant in financial terms with no less, but also no more, than his loss[1], it is sometimes necessary to consider whether a deduction should be made from the compensation to allow for tax. In *West Suffolk County Council v W Rought Ltd*[2], the House of Lords held that an amount representing temporary loss of profits included in an award of disturbance compensation should be reduced to take account of the tax which would have been payable if the profits had been earned. Since 1979, disturbance compensation has been taxable in so far as it includes either taxable income or capital[3]; where tax is payable, it is not appropriate to deduct tax from the award of compensation[4].

1 *Horn v Sunderland Corpn* [1941] 2 KB 26.
2 [1957] AC 403, HL, following *British Transport Commission v Gourley* [1956] AC 185, HL.
3 Capital Gains Tax Act 1979; Taxation of Chargeable Gains Act 1992.
4 *Stoke-on-Trent City Council v Wood Mitchell & Co Ltd* [1979] 2 All ER 65, CA.

Chapter 7

Severance and injurious affection

Contents

A Introduction

[2501]

This chapter is concerned with circumstances where a compulsory acquisition takes part only of a person's land and, in doing so, causes loss of value to other land held by the claimant[1]. It has been explained above[2] that, while compensation for compulsory purchase is to be awarded as a single global figure, it can be made up of a number of elements, one of which can be the loss of value to land which the claimant held with the land compulsorily acquired, caused by the severing of the land taken from the land retained, or by other forms of injurious affection. This head of compensation, known as 'severance and injurious affection' arises under the Compulsory Purchase Act 1965 (CPA 1965), s 7 and may only be claimed by a person from whom an interest in land has been compulsorily acquired. Where a local authority is authorised to purchase new rights over land under the Local Government (Miscellaneous Provisions) Act 1976 (LG(MP)A 1976), s 13[3], the right to compensation under the CPA 1965, s 7 applies with modifications which enable compensation to be claimed, not only for the depreciation in the value of the land over which the right is to be exercised, but also any depreciation to other land held by the claimant[4]. Similar provision is made where other bodies are authorised to acquire new rights[5].

1 In certain circumstances, where an acquiring authority seek to acquire part only of a person's land, he may be able to require the acquiring authority to take the whole of his land, in which case a claim for severance or injurious affection obviously would not arise. This right is explained in **D [326]**.
2 See **Chapter 1**.
3 As to the acquisition of new rights, see **B [466]**.
4 LG(MP)A 1976, s 14.
5 Other examples of powers to create new rights are identified in para **[467]** note 1.

[2502]

This right to compensation under the CPA 1965, s 7 must be distinguished from the right to compensation for injurious affection where no land has been compulsorily acquired from the claimant, which arises under the CPA

1965, s 10 and is explained in **Division F, Chapter 2**. Although both use the term 'injurious affection', the principles which apply are different in a number of significant respects. The CPA 1965, s 7 re-enacted the Lands Clauses Consolidation Act 1845 (LCCA 1845), s 63 in substantially the same form; the interpretation and application of the CPA 1965, s 7 rests upon many judicial decisions made in the context of the LCCA 1845, s 63.

[2503]
Where, following the compulsory acquisition of land, the claimant has other land which has increased in value as a result of the scheme underlying the compulsory acquisition, often referred to as 'betterment', that increase must, in certain circumstances, be deducted from the compensation payable in respect of the land taken. This is explained in more detail in **Chapter 9**.

B The right to compensation

[2504]
The right to compensation under the CPA 1965, s 7 arises where:

(*a*) land has been acquired compulsorily from the claimant;
(*b*) the claimant has an interest in 'other land'[1] which was 'held with'[2] the land compulsorily acquired; and
(*c*) the value of the claimant's other land has been depreciated by either 'severance' or 'injurious affection' as a result of the compulsory purchase.

1 As to the meaning of 'other land' in this context, see para **[2508]**.
2 As to the meaning of 'held with', see para **[2508]**.

1 Severance

[2505]
The terms 'severance' and 'injurious affection' are not defined in the statute. The words of the CPA 1965, s 7 'severing … or otherwise injuriously affecting' suggest that severance was simply identified as one form of injurious affection. The expression severance 'merely signifies that what the promoters have acquired is separated from, in the sense that it can no longer be treated by the landowner as part of, the subjects which, until its purchase, he held with it'[1]. Severance can occur not only in terms of areas of land, but also in terms of horizontal strata, for example, where a railway company was authorised to acquire a right to use the subsoil but not the surface of a property[2]. In such circumstances, if the value of the surface has been depreciated by the taking of the subsoil, compensation may be claimed under the CPA 1965, s 7. Similarly, severance also occurs where an acquiring authority is authorised to acquire a new right[3]; if the value of the land over which the right is taken is thereby depreciated, compensation may be claimed under the CPA 1965, s 7.

1 Per Lord Watson in *Cowper Essex v Acton Local Board* (1889) 14 App Cas 153, HL, at 167. See also the speech of Lord Sumner in *Holditch v Canadian Northern Ontario Rly* [1916] 1 AC 536, PC.
2 *City and South London Rly Co v United Parishes of St Mary, Woolnoth and St Mary, Woolchurch Haw* [1905] AC 1, HL.
3 Ie under the LG(MP)A 1976, ss 13, 14.

2 Injurious affection

[2506]
'Injurious affection' is a term which derives from the LCCA 1845[1] and refers to a factor which depreciates the value of the claimant's land. Injurious affection may be caused by the construction of the works for which the land was compulsorily acquired from the claimant, or by the use of the land acquired or works constructed there. In contrast to the CPA 1965, s 10, the right to compensation for injurious affection under the CPA 1965, s 7 is not limited to circumstances in which a right of action would have existed if the acquiring authority had not been acting under statutory powers[2]. Examples of injurious affection are: where land was taken for a railway with the result that there was a danger of fire occurring on the claimant's retained land[3]; where access to land suitable for building was interrupted[4]; where land was taken for the construction of a road which caused noise, dust, loss of privacy and amenity[5]. Where a new right is acquired compulsorily, compensation will be recoverable for depreciation in the value of the land over which the right is to be exercised, and for depreciation in the value of any other land held by the claimant[6].

1 And the contemporaneous Railways Clauses Consolidation Act 1845. It has an even earlier origin.
2 Where land has been compulsorily acquired and a claimant retains land which is injuriously affected by the works but that land does not qualify as 'other land' for the purposes of the CPA 1965, s 7 (the definition of which is explained at para **[2508]**), he may nevertheless be able to claim compensation under either the CPA 1965, s 10 (as to which see **Division F, Chapter 2**) or under the Land Compensation Act 1973 (LCA 1973), Pt I (as to which see **Division F, Chapter 3**).
3 *Re Stockport, Timperley and Altrincham Rly Co* (1864) 33 LJQB 251.
4 *R v Brown* (1867) LR 2 QB 630. *Waterworth v Bolton Metropolitan Borough Council* (1978) 37 P&CR 104, Lands Tribunal; appeal dismissed (1978) 42 P&CR 289, CA.
5 *Duke of Buccleugh v Metropolitan Board of Works* (1872) LR 5 HL 418, HL. *Oppenheimer v Ministry of Transport* [1942] KB 242.
6 See para **[2501]** note 4.

[2507]
Prior to 1973, compensation could only be claimed in respect of depreciation in value caused by works constructed on, or the use made of, the land compulsorily acquired[1]. The position was changed by the LCA 1973, s 44 which provides that, where land is acquired from a person for the purposes of works which are to be situated partly on the land acquired and partly elsewhere, compensation for injurious affection is to be assessed by reference to the whole of the works and not only that part situated on the claimant's land[2].

1 *Edwards v Minister of Transport* [1964] 2 QB 134, CA, following many earlier cases.
2 LCA 1973, s 44 is also applied by statutes which authorise the creation of new rights, see para **[2501]** note 4.

3 Other land

[2508]
The scope of the right to compensation for severance and injurious affection under the CPA 1965, s 7 is largely defined by the interpretation which the

courts have placed upon the term 'other land'. The fact that land is in common ownership is not sufficient; the other land must be 'held therewith', that is, held with the land taken. The phrase 'held therewith' does not appear in the CPA 1965, s 7, nor in its predecessor the LCCA 1845, s 63; it derives from the LCCA 1845, s 49. The courts have treated the phrases 'other land' and land 'held therewith' as having the same meaning, as appears from the following passages from speeches in *Cowper Essex v Acton Local Board*[1]. Lord Watson said[2]:

> 'The fact that lands are held under the same title is not enough to establish that they are held "with" each other, in the sense of the Act … I shall not attempt to lay down any general rule upon this matter. But I am prepared to hold that, where several pieces of land, owned by the same person, are so near to each other, and so situated that the possession and control of each gives an enhanced value to them all, they are lands held together within the meaning of the Act; so that if one piece is taken compulsorily, and converted to uses which depreciate the value of the rest, the owner has the right to compensation.'

Lord Macnaughten said[3]:

> 'Lands in respect of which a claim for compensation may arise are referred to in the Act, in contradistinction to the lands taken or purchased from the owner thereof, as lands "held therewith" or as "the other lands" of such owner. The Act says nothing about their being held along with the lands taken or purchased for one and the same purpose, nor does it require that they should be in contact with those lands. Apparently it is enough if both parcels of land are held by one and the same owner and if the unity of ownership conduces to the advantage or protection of the property as one holding. That condition seems to be implied. Otherwise the owner could hardly sustain injury by reason of the execution of the works on the land taken.'

The principle was explained in similar terms by Lord Sumner[4]:

> 'The basis of a claim to compensation for lands injuriously affected by severance must be that the lands taken are so connected with or related to the lands left that the owner of the latter is prejudiced in his ability to use or dispose of them to advantage by reason of the severance.'

1 *Cowper Essex v Acton Local Board* (1889) 14 App Cas 153, HL.
2 (1889) 14 App Cas 153, HL, at 167.
3 (1889) 14 App Cas 153, HL, at 175.
4 *Holditch v Canadian Northern Ontario Rly* [1916] 1 AC 536, PC, at 542.

[2509]

Although the land taken must be held by the same person as the other land, it is not necessary that both should be held under the same title[1]. Nor is it necessary that they should be geographically contiguous[2].

1 *Oppenheimer v Minister of Transport* [1942] 1 KB 242, in which the claimant held the freehold in a house and an option to purchase adjoining land which was held to qualify as 'other land'.
2 *Holt v Gas, Light and Coke Co* (1872) LR 7 QB 728.

C Assessment of compensation

[2510]–[2520]

Compensation for severance and injurious affection under the CPA 1965, s 7 is additional to the value of the land taken[1]. The measure of compensation is the amount by which the claimant's other land is depreciated in value[2]. Since it is a separate head of claim, it must be assessed separately from compensation for the value of the land taken[3]. The statutory rules which apply to the assessment of the value of the land taken do not apply to the assessment of the depreciation in value of the claimant's other land under the CPA 1965, s 7[4]. It is legitimate to have regard to the anticipated future use of the land acquired[5], and compensation may include depreciation in the development value of the claimant's other land[6] or loss due to deferment of the development value[7]. Compensation is not to be measured by the cost which the claimant incurs to overcome the consequences of the compulsory acquisition[8].

1 As to the value of the land taken, see **Chapter 2**.

2 *Re Stockport, Timperley and Altrincham Rly Co* (1864) 33 LJQB 251; *Cowper Essex v Acton Local Board* (1889) 14 App Cas 153, HL; *Hoveringham Gravels Ltd v Chiltern District Council* (1977) 35 P&CR 295, CA.

3 *Hoveringham Gravels Ltd v Chiltern District Council* (1977) 35 P&CR 295, CA.

4 Ie the rules in the Land Compensation Act 1961 (LCA 1961), s 5 (as to which, see **Chapter 2**) and ss 14–22 (as to which see **Chapter 3**). In *Hoveringham Gravels Ltd v Chiltern District Council* (1977) 35 P&CR 295, CA, Roskill LJ, giving the judgment of the court, accepted (at 308) a submission that both the *Pointe Gourde* principle and the LCA 1961, s 9 applied (as to which, see **Chapter 4**), although this was not part of the ratio of the decision. However, the LCA 1961, s 9 applies only to depreciation in the value of the 'relevant interest', which is defined in s 39(2) as the interest acquired in pursuance of the compulsory acquisition. In *English Property Corpn v Royal Borough of Kingston upon Thames* (1998) 77 P&CR 1, CA, Morritt LJ said (at 11) that neither the *Pointe Gourde* rule nor s 9 apply to the valuation of the retained land.

5 *Rockingham Sisters of Charity v R* [1922] 2 AC 315, PC.

6 *Hoveringham Gravels Ltd v Chiltern District Council* (1977) 35 P&CR 295, CA.

7 *Waterworth v Bolton Metropolitan Borough Council* (1978) 37 P&CR 104, Lands Tribunal; affd sub nom *Bolton Metropolitan Borough Council Waterworth* (1981) 42 P&CR 289, CA on other grounds.

8 *Cooke v Secretary of State for the Environment* (1973) 27 P&CR 234, Lands Tribunal, in which land had been acquired for a new road which severed part of the claimant's farm land from his farm buildings; the tribunal held that compensation should not be calculated by reference to the cost incurred on providing new farm buildings and extra costs of transportation, but must be based on the depreciation of the value of the land. See also *Frederick Powell & Son Ltd v Devon County Council* [1979] RVR 127, Lands Tribunal, relating to extra costs of developing a smaller area of land.

[2521]

Where time has passed between the date at which compensation falls to be assessed[1] and the determination of the compensation, it may be legitimate to take into account facts about the subject matter of the claim which have only become known subsequently[2]. It is submitted, however, that there are limits as to the extent to which it is appropriate to apply the principle established in the *Bwllfa* case. For example, for the purpose of arriving at the open market value of land on a particular date, it would not seem appropriate to use hindsight to take account of factors which would not have been known to a willing buyer and willing seller at the valuation date.

1 As to the date of valuation, see para **[41]**.

2 *Bwllfa and Merthyr Dare Steam Collieries (1891) Ltd v Pontypridd Waterworks Co* [1903] AC 426, HL. That case was concerned with the assessment of compensation for the sterilisation of

minerals. At the time of service of the notice which led to the minerals being sterilised, the price which would have been obtained for them, had they been extracted, was in the future and therefore uncertain. By the time compensation was assessed, the price which would have been obtained was known. The House of Lords held that compensation should be assessed on the basis of the facts known at the date of assessment. It should be noted that this case did not arise out of compulsory acquisition but arose out of a claim for compensation for 'loss' under a statutory provision in the legislation then applicable to the water industry. This principle has been applied by the Lands Tribunal to compensation for injurious affection under the CPA 1965, s 7: *Waterworth v Bolton MBC* (1978) 37 P&CR 104, Lands Tribunal; affd sub nom *Bolton MBC Waterworth* (1981) 42 P&CR 289, CA on other grounds. It is submitted that there must be some doubt as to the correctness of applying the *Bwllfa* principle in these circumstances.

D Accommodation works and other mitigation

[2522]–[2900]
In order to reduce the amount of compensation which would otherwise be payable in respect of severance, an acquiring authority may carry out works, usually referred to as accommodation works, which lessen the effect of the severance, such as providing a bridge over a road. Similarly, in order to reduce the amount of compensation for injurious affection, the acquiring authority may carry out works such as tree planting or providing a noise barrier. However, an authority cannot be required to take such steps, nor can an authority require a claimant to accept such works on land he retains after the compulsory acquisition, although he is under a duty to mitigate his loss. An acquiring authority may also undertake not to use land which it has compulsorily acquired for certain purposes, so long as the undertaking was compatible with the purposes for which it is authorised to acquire the land[1].

1 *Ayr Harbour Trustees v Oswald* (1883) 8 App Cas 623, HL.

Chapter 8

Deduction for betterment

Contents

A Introduction

[2901]
Where a person, whose land is compulsorily acquired, has other land which has increased in value as a result of the scheme underlying the acquisition, often referred to as betterment, that increase must, in certain circumstances, be deducted from the compensation payable in respect of the land taken. There is no general non-statutory rule to this effect[1], but express statutory provision is made in the Land Compensation Act 1961 (LCA 1961), ss 7–8, the Highways Act 1980, s 261 and sometimes in local Acts. This chapter explains the LCA 1961, ss 7–8 and Highways Act (HA) 1980, s 261.

1 *South Eastern Rly Co v LCC* [1915] 2 Ch 252, CA.

B Land Compensation Act 1961, sections 7–8

1 Application

[2902]
The LCA 1961, s 7 applies to all compulsory acquisitions to which the LCA 1961 applies except where other legislation makes corresponding provision[1].

1 LCA 1961, s 8(5). As to the meaning of corresponding enactment, see s 8(7). Where a local enactment restricts the increase to existing use value, see s 8(6).

2 The deduction

[2903]
By virtue of the LCA 1961, s 7(1), where a person is entitled to compensation for the compulsory acquisition of his land[1], there has to be deducted from the compensation the amount of any increase[2] in the value of any other land[3], to which he is entitled in the same capacity[4] at the date of the notice to treat[5], which arises in the circumstances explained below.

1 Referred to in LCA 1961, s 7 as the 'relevant interest', which is defined in s 39(2).
2 Only an increase arising in the circumstances described below has to be deducted.
3 See para **[2904]**.
4 See para **[2904]**.
5 For 'notice to treat', see the LCA 1961, s 39(2).

3 The other land

[2904]
The LCA 1961, s 7 only applies to 'other land' which[1]:

(*a*) is contiguous[2] or adjacent[3] to the land compulsorily acquired from the claimant; and
(*b*) is held by the claimant in the same capacity[4] as the land compulsorily acquired from him.

1 LCA 1961, s 7(1). It would appear, therefore, that the term 'other land' does not necessarily have the same meaning as that term in the Compulsory Purchase Act 1965 (CPA 1965), s 7 (severance and injurious affection to other land, as to which, see **Chapter 7**). For the definition of 'land', see s 39(1).
2 'Contiguous' means touching: *Spillers Ltd v Cardiff Assessment Committee and Pritchard (Cardiff Revenue Officer)* [1931] 2 KB 21.
3 As to 'adjacent', see *Wellington Corpn v Lower Hutt Corpn* [1904] AC 773, PC; *English China Clays Lovering Pochin & Co Ltd v Plymouth Corpn* [1974] 2 All ER 239, CA.
4 Defined in the LCA 1961, s 39(6).

4 The increase

[2905]
For the LCA 1961, s 7 to apply, the increase in value of the claimant's other land must have arisen in the circumstances set out in the LCA 1961, s 7(2) and Sch 1. Since the provisions set out in Sch 1 are complicated, they are reproduced below in the form of a table[1], which operates as follows. The first step is to ascertain whether the land compulsorily acquired falls within any of the cases in the first column. Where one of those paragraphs applies, the second step is to identify any development[2] defined in the second column, either already carried out, or in prospect, the carrying out of which would not have been likely if[3]:

(*a*) in relation to land falling within paragraph 1, the acquiring authority had not acquired and did not propose to acquire any land for that purpose; or
(*b*) in relation to land falling within paragraphs 2 to 4B, the area or areas referred to had not been so defined or designated.

Any increase in the value of the claimant's other land as a result of development identified in the second step must then be deducted from the compensation otherwise due to him in respect of the land acquired.

	Case	*Development*
1	Where the acquisition is for purposes involving development of any of the land authorised to be acquired[4].	Development of any of the land authorised to be acquired, being development for any of the purposes for which any part of the first-mentioned land (including any of the relevant land) is to be acquired.
2	Where any of the relevant land forms part of an area defined in the current development plan as an area of comprehensive development.	Development of any land in that area, in the course of the development or redevelopment of the area in accordance with the plan.
3	Where on the date of service of notice to treat any of the relevant land forms part of an area designated as the site of a new town under the New Towns Act 1946[5].	Development of any land in that area, in the course of the development of that area as a new town.
3A[6]	Where on the date of service of notice to treat any of the relevant land forms part of an area designated as an extension of the site of a new town by an order under the New Towns Act 1965[7], becoming operative after the date of the commencement of the New Towns Act 1966[8].	Development of any land in that area, in the course of the development of that area as part of a new town.
4	part of an area to which a town development scheme under the Town Development Act 1952 relates, being a scheme which is in operation at the date of Notice to Treat.	Development of any land in that area, in the course of town development within the meaning of the Town Development Act 1952.
4A[9]	forming part of an area designated as an urban development area by an order under the Local Government, Planning and Land Act 1980 (LGPLA 1980), s 134.	Development of any land, in the course of the development or redevelopment of that area as an urban development area.
4B[10]	forming part of a housing trust action area established under the Housing Act 1988, Pt III.	Development of any land, in the course of the development or redevelopment of that area as a housing action trust area

1 This table is the same as that set out in **Chapter 4** (which describes the operation of the LCA 1961, s 6) except that, in accordance with the LCA 1961, s 7(2), the words 'other than the relevant land' have been omitted from the second column in relation to each case.
2 Development is defined in the LCA 1961, s 39(1). Whereas for the purposes of the LCA 1961, s 6, Sch 1, 'development' to be construed as including clearing the land (s 6(3)), no similar provision is made for the purposes of s 7.
3 The conditions (*a*) and (*b*) derive from the LCA 1961, s 6, as applied by the LCA 1961, s 7(2). For an example where these conditions were considered but the LCA 1961, s 7 was held not to apply, see *Laing Homes Ltd v Eastleigh Borough Council* (1979) 250 Estates Gazette 350, Lands Tribunal.
4 'Land authorised to be acquired' is defined for the purposes of the LCA 1961, Sch 1 in s 6(3). See also the definition of 'relevant interest' in s 39(2).
5 Now consolidated into the New Towns Act 1981.
6 Inserted by the New Towns Act 1965.
7 Now consolidated into the New Towns Act 1981.
8 Now consolidated into the New Towns Act 1981.
9 Inserted by the LGPLA 1980, s 145(1).
10 Inserted by the Housing Act 1988, s 78(3).

5 Subsequent compulsory acquisitions

[2906]
Provision is made to ensure that the effects of the LCA 1961, ss 6 and 7 are not applied more than once. The LCA 1961, s 8 provides for two situations:

(*a*) where an increase in value of other land has been deducted from the claimant's compensation pursuant to the LCA 1961, s 7, then, if any of that land is the subject of a further compulsory purchase, that increase must not be disregarded pursuant to the LCA 1961, s 6[1]; and
(*b*) where compensation has been awarded for depreciation in the value of other land due to severance or injurious affection[2] in any of the circumstances listed in column 1 of the table, then, if any of that land is the subject of a further compulsory purchase, that depreciation in value is not to be disregarded pursuant to the LCA 1961, s 6[3].

These provisions also apply to a sale by agreement[4].

1 LCA 1961, s 8(1).
2 Ie pursuant to the CPA 1965, s 7, as to which, see **Chapter 7**.
3 LCA 1961, s 8(2).
4 LCA 1961, s 8(4).

[2907]
The provisions of the LCA 1961, s 8(1) and (2) identified in the previous paragraph only apply where either:

(*a*) the interest acquired by the subsequent acquisition is the same as the interest previously taken into account[1] (whether the acquisition extends to the whole or only part of the land in which the interest previously subsisted)[2]; or
(*b*) the person entitled to the interest acquired is, or derives title to that interest from, the person who, at the time of the previous acquisition, was entitled to the interest previously taken into account[3].

1 The 'interest previously taken into account' is a reference to the interest, the increased or diminished value of which, was taken into account as mentioned in the LCA 1961, s 8(1) or (2): LCA 1961, s 8(3).
2 LCA 1961, s 8(3)(*a*).
3 LCA 1961, s 8(3)(*b*).

C Highways Act 1980, section 261

1 Application

[2908]
The Highways Act (HA) 1980, s 261(1) applies where land has been acquired for highway purposes under s 239 (except sub-s 6), s 240, s 246 or s 250(2)[1], or where rights over land have been acquired under s 250(3)[2]. Section 261(2) applies where compensation is being assessed under s 252(3)(a). Section 261(5) applies where land is acquired between an improvement line and the boundary of a street.

1 HA 1980, s 261(1). As to the interpretation of s 261(1), see *Esso Petroleum Co Ltd v Secretary of State for Transport* [2008] RVR 351, Lands Tribunal, and, in relation to its predecessor, HA 1959, s 222(6)(a), *Portsmouth Roman Catholic Diocesan Trustees Registered v Hampshire County Council* [1980] 1 EGLR 150, Lands Tribunal.
2 HA 1980, s 261(3).

2 Effect

[2909]
Where s 261(1) or (3) apply, the Upper Tribunal is required[1]:

(*a*) to have regard to the extent to which the remaining contiguous lands belonging to the claimant may be benefited by the purpose for which the land (or the right) has been compulsorily acquired;
(*b*) where the land (or the right) has been acquired for highway widening purposes, to set off against the value of the land (or the right) acquired any increase in the value of the claimant's other land by reason of the creation of a frontage to the widened highway; and
(*c*) to take into account, and embody in its award, any undertaking given by the highway authority as to the use to which any part of the land (or the right) taken will be put.

1 HA 1980, s 261(1) and (3). Where two or more rights are acquired together, or rights are acquired as well as land, the Upper Tribunal must consider the compensation payable for all of the rights, or the rights and the land, as the case may be: HA 1980, s 261(4).

[2910]
Where compensation is being assessed under s 252(3)(*a*), the Upper Tribunal is required to take into account and embody in its award, any undertaking given by the highways authority as to rights of user or occupation or other rights which they are willing to accord to the claimant as respects the land referred to in s 252(2)[1].

1 HA 1980, s 261(2).

[2911]
Where land is acquired under s 241 between an improvement line and the boundary of a street, the Upper Tribunal must take into account any benefit accruing to the claimant by reason of the improvement to the street except in so far as it may have been taken into account in assessing compensation previously[1].

1 HA 1980, s 261(5).

[2912]–[3300]
In assessing compensation for the value of land or rights acquired to which the above provisions apply, LCA 1961, s 5[1] has effect subject to these provisions[2].

1 As to which see **Division E, Chapter 2**.
2 HA 1980, s 261(6).

Chapter 9

Supplementary payments and duty to re-house

Contents

A Introduction

[3301]

In order to provide for circumstances in which compensation under the compensation code described in previous chapters of this Division was either not available at all, or was considered to be insufficient, the Land Compensation Act 1973 (LCA 1973), Pt III was enacted introducing three new forms of payment[1]. These are:

(*a*) home loss payments;
(*b*) farm loss payments[2]; and
(*c*) disturbance payments to those displaced from land with no compensatable interest.

In addition, the LCA 1973, Pt III introduced a duty to re-house residential occupiers, together with certain ancillary provisions. Each of these is described in this Division.

1 A number of amendments have been made to the LCA 1973, Pt III by subsequent legislation including the Planning and Compensation Act 1991 (PCA 1991).
2 Farm loss payments cease to be available in consequences of compulsory purchase orders made after 31 October 2005: see para **[3326]**.

[3301.1]

The PCA 1991, s 106 inserted new ss 33A–33K into the LCA 1973, which have created three further forms of supplementary payment intended for circumstances in which the compensation code was regarded as deficient[1]. These are:

(*a*) basic loss payments;
(*b*) occupier's loss payments for agricultural land;
(*c*) occupier's loss payments for non-agricultural land.

Each of these supplementary payments is described in more detail below.

1 For the background to these changes, see **A[172]–[350]**. The Secretary of State will have power to make regulations amending any figure or percentage mentioned in ss 33A-33I: LCA 1973, s 33K.

B Home loss payments

1 Introduction

[3302]
Although the aim of compensation for compulsory acquisition of land is to put the landowner in the same position financially as if no compulsory acquisition had taken place[1], it came to be recognised that compensation assessed under rr 1, 2 and 6 did not always achieve this[2]. The LCA 1973[3], ss 29–33 were enacted in order to provide for additional payments, known as home loss payments, to be made to certain persons who are displaced from their dwellings in order to reflect, first, the personal inconvenience and distress suffered as a result of the loss of their homes, and, second, the fact that open market value does not always equate to the value of the property to the owner[4]. Home loss payments may be claimed, not only following compulsory acquisition of land, but also where displacement occurs pursuant to a number of other statutory proceedings. Consequently, the authority responsible for making the payment will depend upon the cause of the dispossession[5]. This chapter explains the entitlement to, and amount of, home loss payments.

1 See para **[21]**.
2 Land Compensation Act 1961 (LCA 1961), s 5, as to which, see **Chapter 2**.
3 As amended, inter alia, by the PCA 1991.
4 The Urban Motorways Committee recommended that an additional head of compensation should be payable in recognition of the personal disturbance that compulsory purchase procedure inflicts upon those required to move: New Roads in Towns, DoE HMSO 1972 para 12.18–19. This rationale was repeated in the White Paper '*Development and Compensation – Putting People First*' (1972), which preceded the LCA 1973 and in Circular 73/73, para 21, which followed the Act in order to explain it (cancelled by Circular 28/83). The amendments were explained in Circular 15/91 'Planning and Compensation Act 1991: Land Compensation and Compulsory Purchase'.
5 See para **[3303]**, condition (iv).

2 Entitlement to home loss payments

[3303]
To qualify for a home loss payment, a claimant must show that he fulfils the following conditions:

(*a*) he has been in occupation of the dwelling[1], or a substantial part of it, as his only or main residence[2];
(*b*) his occupation is by virtue of[3]:
  (i) an interest in the dwelling[4], or
  (ii) a right to occupy the dwelling as a statutory tenant[5],
  (iii) a right under a contract[6],
  (iv) a right to occupy under an employment contract[7], or

   (v) a right to occupy under a licence pursuant to certain statutory provisions[8];
(*c*) he has been in such occupation for a year ending with the date of displacement[9]; and
(*d*) he is displaced[10] from his dwelling in consequence of:
   (i) the compulsory acquisition of an interest in the dwelling[11],
   (ii) the making or acceptance of a housing order, resolution or undertaking[12] in respect of the dwelling,
   (iii) the carrying out of any improvement[13] to the dwelling or redevelopment[14] of land where the land has been previously appropriated by a local authority or compulsorily acquired and is for the time being held by the authority for the purposes for which it was acquired[15],
   (iv) the carrying out of any improvement to the dwelling or a redevelopment on the land by a housing association which has previously acquired the land and which is registered as a social landlord[16] at the date of displacement[17], or
   (v) the making of a possession order under the Housing Act 1985[18].

1 'Dwelling' means a building or part of a building occupied (or if not occupied) last occupied or intended to be occupied as a private dwelling. For the purposes of the LCA 1973, s 29 dwelling does not include any garden, outhouses and appurtenances belonging to or usually enjoyed with that building or part: LCA 1973, s 87(1).
2 LCA 1973, s 29(2)(*a*).
3 LCA 1973, s 29(2)(*b*).
4 LCA 1973, s 29(4)(*a*).
5 For these purposes, 'statutory tenant' means a tenant within the meaning of the Rent (Agriculture) Act 1976 or the Rent Act 1977; LCA 1973, s 29(4)(*b*)(i).
6 For these purposes, a contract means a contract to which the Rent Act 1977, s 19 applies, or would have applied but for an exclusion under s 19(3)–(5) or s 144 of that Act; LCA 1973, s 29(4)(*b*)(ii).
7 LCA 1973, s 29(4)(*d*).
8 For these purposes, this includes protected occupiers covered by the Rent (Agriculture) Act 1976, secure tenants under Pt IV of the Housing Act 1985, assured agricultural tenants within the meaning of Pt I of the Housing Act 1988 or introductory tenants within Chapter 1 of Pt V of the Housing Act 1996; LCA 1973, s 29(4)(*e*).
9 LCA 1973, s 29(2).
10 The word 'displaced' has overtones of compulsion: *Ingle v Scarborough Borough Council* [2002] EWCA Civ 290, [2002] HLR 671. See also *Evis v Commission for New Towns* (5 July 2001, unreported), Lands Tribunal (not yet reported).
11 LCA 1973, s 29(1)(*a*). In this case, the home loss payment is payable by the acquiring authority; LCA 1973, s 29(1) (i). For these purposes, 'acquiring authority' means the person or body of persons by whom an interest in land is proposed to be acquired; LCA 1961, s 39(1), as applied by the LCA 1973, s 87(1).
12 'Housing order or undertaking' means (1) a demolition or closing order, or an obstructive building order under the slum clearance provisions in Pt IX of the Housing Act 1985 (2) a closing order under the Housing Act 1985, s 368(4) for inadequate fire escape from multi-occupied housing, or (3) an undertaking accepted under the Housing Act 1985, ss 211, 264 or 368, LCA 1973, s 29(7). (This ground also includes improvement notices served under Pt VII of the Housing Act 1985 in respect of any dwelling prior to 1 April 1990); LCA 1973, s 29(1)(*b*). In this case, the home loss payment is payable by the authority who made the order accepted the undertaking or served the notice, LCA 1973, s 29(1)(*e*)(ii).
13 'Improvement' for the purposes of the LCA 1973, s 29 includes alteration and enlargement; LCA 1973, s 29(7A).
14 'Redevelopment' for the purposes of the LCA 1973, s 29 includes a change of use; LCA 1973, s 29(7A). Redevelopment may also include demolition preceding the construction of new buildings; *R v Corby District Council, ex p MacLean* [1975] 1 WLR 735, DC, High Court. In *R v Cardiff City Council, ex p Cross* [1982] RVR 270, CA, it was held that there was no displacement

for redevelopment of premises where a tenant was displaced from an unfit house owned by the local authority and re-housed by them, because the unfit premises retained their character as a dwelling and there was no change of use. However in *GLC v Holmes* [1986] QB 989, CA, it was held that a mobile home owner, displaced from a local authority-owned caravan park which it intended to sell for housing development, who was re-housed by that local authority, was entitled to a home loss payment as the council still held the land for the purpose for which it was acquired and the displacement was an essential step in the council's redevelopment process.

15 LCA 1973, s 29(1)(*c*). In this case, the home loss payment is payable by the authority carrying out the improvement or redevelopment; LCA 1973, s 29(1)(*e*)(iii).

16 Within the meaning of the Housing Act 1985, s 5(4), (5).

17 LCA 1973, s 29(1)(*d*). In this case the home loss payment is payable by the housing association carrying out the improvement or redevelopment; LCA 1973, s 29(1)(*e*)(iv).

18 Provided the possession order is made on ground 10 or 10A in Pt II to Sch 2 of the Housing Act 1985; LCA 1973, s 29(1)(*e*). In this case the home loss payment is payable by the landlord; LCA 1973, s 29(1)(*e*)(v).

[3304]

Failure to fulfil the condition (*c*) above will not necessarily be fatal to a claim for a home loss payment. A person who, at the date of displacement, satisfies all the conditions except the period of occupation, may aggregate his period of qualifying occupation with that of any predecessor(s)[1]. Likewise, a claimant can aggregate the period of time in which he has been in occupation of different dwellings[2] within a single building for these purposes[3]. If condition (*c*) above cannot be satisfied, but all the other conditions are satisfied, the claimant may be awarded a discretionary payment to the same value as the home loss payment[4].

1 LCA 1973, s 32(3), (3A).

2 Being dwellings consisting of a room or rooms not constructed or structurally adapted for use as a separate dwelling; LCA 1973, s 32(5).

3 LCA 1973, s 32(5).

4 LCA 1973, s 29(2).

[3305]

A person who satisfies all the conditions set out in para **[3303]** except condition (*b*) may nonetheless qualify for a home loss payment where he is:

(*a*) a beneficiary under a trust in respect of an interest in a dwelling vested in trustees (other than a sole tenant for life within the meaning of the Settled Land Act 1925)[1];

(*b*) a deserted spouse who has acquired matrimonial home rights under Pt IV of the Family Law Act 1996[2], who has no independent interest in the dwelling. In this case the home loss payment will always be £1500[3]; and

(*c*) the beneficiary of a deceased occupant who would have been entitled to a home loss payment, provided that such beneficiary was also in occupation of the property or a substantial part of it as his only or main residence for at least one year ending with the displacement of the deceased[4].

1 LCA 1973, s 29(8).

2 LCA 1973, s 29A(1).

3 See para **[3310]**.

4 LCA 1973, s 32(4).

[3306]
Home loss payments may also be made to persons residing in caravans on caravan sites who are displaced in similar circumstances, provided no suitable alternative is made available[1].

1 LCA 1973, s 33.

[3307]
There is no entitlement to a home loss payment in consequence of the compulsory acquisition of an interest in a dwelling if the claimant gives up occupation before the date on which the acquiring authority is authorised to acquire the interest[1]. Claimants should accordingly be cautious of agreeing to move before the relevant compulsory purchase order has been confirmed. There is also no entitlement to a home loss payment in consequence of acceptance of an undertaking or carrying out of any improvement to the dwelling, unless the displacement is permanent[2].

1 LCA 1973, s 29(3).
2 LCA 1973, s 29(3A).

[3308]
Where the displacement results from compulsory purchase, the acquiring authority will be obliged to pay the home loss payment as soon as it is authorised to acquire an interest compulsorily, notwithstanding that it has not actually required the occupant to give up his occupation[1]. There is specific provision[2] enabling discretionary home loss payments to be paid to landowners who sell their interest by agreement to an acquiring authority possessing powers of compulsory purchase. Any claimant who would be entitled to a home loss payment if the displacement was by virtue of compulsory acquisition should therefore ensure that such entitlement is reflected in the compensation package finally agreed[3].

1 LCA 1973, s 29(3): for example, by service of notice to treat and notice of entry under the Compulsory Purchase Act 1965, ss 5, 11 as to which, see **D [301]**ff.
2 LCA 1973, s 32(7).
3 LCA 1973, s 32(7B). Discretionary payments may also be made where a landlord obtains possession of a dwelling subject to a secure tenancy within the meaning Pt IV of the Housing Act 1985 (1) by agreement and (2) notice of proceedings for possession could be or has been served specifying ground 10 or 10A in Pt II of Sch 2 to that Act or the landlord has applied or could apply for approval for the purposes of ground 10A of a development scheme including the dwelling or part of it, as if an order had indeed been made.

[3309]
Where an authority with powers of compulsory acquisition acquires an interest in a dwelling by agreement, and such agreement, as a consequence, results in the displacement of a third party, that third party is entitled, subject to satisfaction of the conditions described in para **[3303]** to claim a home loss payment[1]. Where two or more persons are entitled to a home loss payment in respect of the same dwelling, the payment to be made on each claim is to be equal to the whole amount of the home loss payment, divided by the number of such persons[2].

1 LCA 1973, s 29(6).
2 LCA 1973, s 32(6).

3 Amount of home loss payment

[3310]–[3320]
Home loss payments are calculated on one of two alternative bases:

(*a*) where a claimant occupies the dwelling by virtue of an 'owners interest'[1], in which case the home loss payment is 10% of the market value of his interest in the dwelling, subject to maximum and minimum limits which were originally enacted as £1,500 and £15,000 respectively but have subsequently been increased[2]; and
(*b*) in any other case, the amount as originally enacted was £1,500 which has subsequently been increased[3].

1 'Owner's interest' means the interest of a person other than a mortgagee not in possession who is for the time being entitled to dispose of the fee simple of the land whether in possession or in reversion, and includes a person holding or entitled to the rents and profits of the land under a lease the unexpired term whereof exceeds three years and a person who would have power to sell and convey or release the land to an acquiring authority were the compulsory purchase order operative; Acquisition of Land Act 1981, s 7(1) as applied by the LCA 1973, s 30(7).
2 LCA 1973, s 30(1); Home Loss Payments (Prescribed Amounts) (England) Regulations 2004, SI 2004/1631, revoked with effect from 1 September 2005 and replaced by Home Loss Payments (Prescribed Amounts) (England) Regulations 2005, SI 2005/1635. Where the date of displacement is on or after 1 September 2005, the minimum is £3,800 and the maximum is £38,000. From the same date, the prescribed amount is £3,800.
3 LCA 1973, s 30(2). As to subsequent increases, see the Regulations cited in note 2 above. A payment to a deserted spouse under the LCA 1973, s 29A will always be calculated on this basis.

[3321]
In order to determine the amount of a home loss payment in respect of an owner's interest[1], the market value of his interest in the dwelling is taken to be equivalent to the value agreed or determined for the purposes of any compulsory acquisition[2] or, where there is no compulsory acquisition, the value of the interest as if a notice to treat had been served on the date of displacement[3].

1 LCA 1973, s 30(1). 'Owner's interest' is defined at para **[3310]**, fn 1. For these purposes, the dwelling is be taken to include any garden, yard, outhouses and appurtenances belonging to or usually enjoyed with that dwelling; LCA 1973, s 30(4).
2 See **Division E**.
3 LCA 1973, s 30(3). Notice to treat is served pursuant to the Compulsory Purchase Act 1965, s 5, as to which, see **D [301]** ff.

4 Advance payment of home loss payment

[3322]
The acquiring authority may at any time, and, in certain circumstances, must make an advance payment on account of the home loss payment[1]. The amount of an advance payment is the lesser of the full amount due or 10% of the market value of the property[2]. Where the market value of the property has not been agreed, the advance payment is limited to 10% of the authority's estimate of the market value[3]. Where the home loss payment, when finally agreed or determined, differs from any advance payment made, any overpayment must be refunded, or any shortfall made good[4].

1 LCA 1973, s 32(2A).
2 LCA 1973, s 32(2B).
3 LCA 1973, s 32(2B).
4 LCA 1973, s 32(2C).

5 Procedure

Claims

[3323]
A claim for a home loss payment must be made in writing giving such particulars as the authority responsible for the payment[1] reasonably requires for the purpose of assessing entitlement to and quantum of the home loss payment[2]. There is no prescribed form. A claim must be made within six years of date of the displacement[3].

1 As to which, see para **[3302]**.
2 LCA 1973, s 32.
3 LCA 1973, s 32(7A).

[3324]
The payment must be made on or before the later of:

(*a*) the date of displacement;
(*b*) the expiry of three months following the claim; and
(*c*) where the payment is calculated by reference to an owners interest[1], the date on which the market value of the interest in the dwelling is finally agreed or determined[2].

Discretionary payments may be made at any time.

1 See para **[3310]** fn 1.
2 LCA 1973, s 32(2).

Disputes

[3325]
Any dispute as to the amount of a home loss payment is to be determined by the Upper Tribunal[1].

1 LCA 1973, s 30(3). As to proceedings in the Upper Tribunal, see **Division H**.

C Farm loss payments

[3326]–[3346]
In consequence of a compulsory purchase order made (or made in draft) before 31 October 2004, a farmer who was an owner occupier could, in certain circumstances, claim, in addition to compensation payable in respect of land acquired from him compulsorily[1], a payment pursuant to the LCA 1973, ss 34–36, known as a farm loss payment, provided that he continued his farming business elsewhere. These provisions have, however, been repealed so that they are not available in consequence of compulsory

purchase orders made (or made in draft) after 31 October 2004[2]. From that date, they have been replaced by 'occupier's loss payments: agricultural land', which are explained below[3].

1 As to which, see **D [1327]**ff.
2 LCA 1973, ss 34–36 have been repealed with effect in relation to any compulsory purchase order made or made in draft before the commencement of Sch 7, para 7(3), ie 31 October 2004: PCPA 2004, s 118 and Sch 7 and s 120 and Sch 9.
3 See para **[3811]** below.

D Disturbance payments

1 Introduction

[3347]
A person who lawfully occupies, but does not have an interest in, the land compulsorily acquired is not entitled to compensation for disturbance[1]. The LCA 1973, ss 37–38 were enacted in order to provide for payments to be made to such persons in order to cover costs such as relocation and loss of business goodwill. They are also available as a result of certain other statutory procedures. The paragraphs which follow explain the entitlement to, and assessment of, such disturbance payments.

1 See **Chapter 6**.

2 Entitlement to disturbance payments

[3348]
To qualify for a disturbance payment under these provisions, a person must be displaced from land lawfully possessed at the appropriate date[1]. No such payments will be made in respect of land used for agriculture[2]. For these purposes, a person is displaced if he is displaced from land in consequence of[3]:

(*a*) the compulsory acquisition of land[4], providing he has no interest in land the acquisition or extinguishment of which would entitle him to compensation under any other enactment[5];
(*b*) the making or acceptance of a housing order or undertaking[6] in respect of a house or building on the land[7], providing he is entitled to a payment under the Housing Act 1985, s 584A(1)[8];
(*c*) the carrying out of any improvement to a house or building on the land or of redevelopment[9] of land, where the land has been previously appropriated by a local authority or compulsorily acquired, and is for the time being held by the authority for the purposes for which it was acquired[10];
(*d*) the carrying out of any improvement[11] to a house or building on the land by a housing association which has previously acquired the land and which is registered as a social landlord[12] at the date of displacement[13].

1 LCA 1973, s 37.
2 LCA 1973, s 37(7). Dispossessed farmers may qualify for farm loss payments, as to which, see **[3326]**.
3 The meaning of 'displaced in consequence of' was considered in *Prasad v Wolverhampton Borough Council* (1983) 265 Estates Gazette 1073, CA, and could include dispossession in anticipation of compulsory purchase.

4 LCA 1973, s 37(1)(*a*). This ground applies where the compulsory acquisition is by an authority possessing compulsory purchase powers and, in this case, the payment must be made by the acquiring authority; LCA 1973, s 37(1)(i). In *R v Islington Borough Council, ex p Knight* [1984] 1 All ER 154, it was held that no disturbance payment could be made where a tenancy is surrendered, as there has been no acquisition of land.
5 LCA 1973, s 37(2)(*b*).
6 'Housing order or undertaking' means for these purposes (*a*) a demolition or closing order or an obstructive building order under the slum clearance provisions in Pt IX of the Housing Act 1985; (*b*) a closing order under the Housing Act 1985, s 368(4) for inadequate fire escape from multi occupied housing or (*c*) an undertaking accepted under s 368 of the Housing Act 1985; LCA 1973, s 29(7) as applied by the LCA 1973, s 37(9). In this case, displacement must be permanent; LCA 1973, s 37(3A). Payments are to be made by the authority who made the order, accepted the undertaking or served the notice; LCA 1973, s 37(i)(ii).
7 This ground also covers improvement notices served in respect of a house on the land pursuant to Pt VII of the Housing Act 1985 before 1 April 1990.
8 LCA 1973, s 37(2)(*c*). The Housing Act 1985, s 584A(1) makes provision for compensation in respect of closing and demolition orders.
9 'Redevelopment' for these purposes includes a change of use; LCA 1973, s 29(7A) as applied by the LCA 1973, s 37(9).
10 LCA 1973, s 37(1)(*c*). In this case, home loss payments are payable by the authority carrying out the improvement or redevelopment; LCA 1973, s 37(1)(iii).
11 'Improvement' includes alteration and enlargement; LCA 1973, s 29(7A) as applied by LCA 1973, s 37(9).
12 Within the meaning of the Housing Act 1985, s 5(4)(5).
13 LCA 1973, s 37(1)(*d*). In this case, the payment is made by the housing association carrying out the improvement or redevelopment; LCA 1973, s 37(1)(iv). A claim will only be successful under this ground if the date of displacement was after 31 July 1974; LCA 1973, s 37(2)(*d*).

[3349]
A claimant must be in lawful possession[1] of the property, at certain key dates, namely:

(*a*) in any case where land has been acquired under a compulsory purchase order, he must be in possession at the time when notice was first published of the making of the compulsory purchase order prior to its submission for confirmation, or, where no such confirmation is required, the preparation of the order in draft[2];
(*b*) in any case where land is acquired under an Act specifying the land as subject to compulsory acquisition, he must be in possession at the time when the provisions of the Bill for that Act specifying the land were first published[3];
(*c*) in any case of land acquired by agreement, he must be in possession at the date of agreement[4]; or
(*d*) in the case of displacement in consequence of an order, undertaking or improvement notice, he must be in possession at the time when the order was made, the undertaking was accepted or the notice was served[5].

1 LCA 1973, s 37(2)(*a*).
2 LCA 1973, s 37(3)(*a*).
3 LCA 1973, s 37(3)(*b*).
4 LCA 1973, s 37(3)(*c*).
5 LCA 1973, s 37(3).

[3350]–[3360]
A licensee in possession with the consent of the landlord, but without any greater interest in the property, qualifies as being in lawful possession[1]

whereas a squatter without possessory title would not[2]. Where a mortgagee is entitled by a court order to possession prior to the mortgagee lodging a claim for a disturbance payment, the defaulting mortgagor is not dispossessed as a consequence of the acquisition for these purposes[3].

1 *Wrexham Maelor Borough Council v MacDougall* [1993] RVR 141, CA. See also *Smith and Waverley Tailoring Co v Edinburgh District Council* [1980] RVR 23, Lands Tribunal for Scotland in which a yearly tenant whose lease terminated prior to dispossession was entitled to a disturbance payment.
2 *Rivers v Dorset County Council* [1995] RVR 177, Lands Tribunal.
3 *McTaggart v Bristol and West Building Society and Avon County Council* (1985) 50 P&CR 184, Lands Tribunal.

[3361]
A person who is entitled to a disturbance payment under these provisions, or to compensation under the Landlord and Tenant Act 1954[1], s 37 for disturbance, may elect under which statutory regime to claim, but he cannot recover compensation for disturbance more than once[2]. An authority may make discretionary payments equivalent to disturbance payments where a person is displaced from land but certain of the qualifying criteria noted above are not met[3].

1 Section 37 of the 1954 Act allows for compensation to be paid in respect of certain failures to extend protected business tenancies.
2 LCA 1973, s 37(4).
3 LCA 1973, s 37(5).

3 Amount of disturbance payment

[3362]
A disturbance payment is to be equal to[1]:

(*a*) the reasonable expenses of the person entitled to payment in removing from the land in respect of which it is displaced; and
(*b*) if he was carrying on a trade or business on that land, the loss he will sustain by reason of disturbance of the trade or business consequent upon his having to quit the land.

1 LCA 1973, s 38(1).

Removal expenses

[3363]
Reasonable expenses could cover the cost of removal expenses, telephone connections, refitting of domestic appliances, loss of earnings from time off work[1] or an increase in travel costs attributable to the acquisition[2]. In some circumstances, it may include the cost of new curtains[3], although new carpets have been disallowed elsewhere[4].

1 *Nolan v Sheffield MDC* (1979) 38 P&CR 741, Lands Tribunal.
2 *Barker v Hull City Council* [1985] 2 EGLR 200, Lands Tribunal.
3 *Allen v Doncaster MBC* (1997) 73 P&CR 98, Lands Tribunal.
4 See *Nolan v Sheffield MDC* (1979) 38 P&CR 741, Lands Tribunal; *Goss v Paddington Churches Housing Association* (1982) 261 Estates Gazette 373, Lands Tribunal.

[3364]
It has been held in Scotland that a disturbance payment should be calculated on its own merits and should include those expenses which, as a matter of circumstance and degree, were reasonably incurred as a direct and natural consequence of the removing, in addition to the expenses strictly referable to the removal itself[1].

1 *Glasgow Corpn v Anderson* 1976 SLT 225, Ct of Sess.

Business losses

[3365]
In estimating the loss to trade or business for the purposes of (*b*) above in para **[3342]**, regard must be had to the period for which the land occupied by the claimant may have reasonably been expected to be available for the purpose of that trade or business and as to the availability of other suitable land for that purpose[1]. Where the interest acquired is either that of a landlord or a tenant of business premises to which the Landlord and Tenant Act 1954, Part II applies, the right of the tenant to apply for a new tenancy is to be taken into account[2]. Subject to that consideration, the factors which are relevant to the assessment of compensation for disturbance described in **Chapter 6 of this Division** would appear to be equally applicable to the assessment of compensation under this provision. The Lands Tribunal has held that compensation may include pre-acquisition losses[3].

1 LCA 1973, s 38(2). This provision is subject to the LCA 1973, s 46, which provides that, in relation to land used for business or trade, compensation is to be assessed on the basis of total extinguishment of business, provided that the claimant is over 60 at the date of possession, the rateable value of the premises does not exceed £18,000 and the goodwill has not been disposed of elsewhere; LCA 1973, s 46(7), see para **[2604]**.
2 LCA 1973, s 47 which reversed the effect of the Landlord and Tenant Act 1954, s 39.
3 *Roberts v Ashford Borough Council* [2005] RVR 388.

[3366]
Where the displacement is from a dwelling which has been modified to meet the requirements of a disabled occupier, then, in certain circumstances, the disturbance payment must include an amount equal to any reasonable expenses in re-providing such of those modifications as are reasonably required for the disabled person[1]. Costs in respect of temporary relocation may be recoverable if reasonable[2].

1 LCA 1973, s 38(3).
2 *Davies v Newham London Borough Council* [1998] RVR 11, Lands Tribunal.

4 Procedure

Claims

[3367]
No procedure as to claims for disturbance payments is prescribed. It is suggested that any claims should be made in writing to the appropriate

authority, accompanied by sufficient details to enable the authority to assess entitlement and amount.

Disputes

[3368]
Any dispute as to the amount of a disturbance payment is to be determined by the Upper Tribunal[1].

1 LCA 1973, s 38(4). *Gozra v Hackney Borough Council* (1988) 57 P&CR 211, CA, held that the Lands Tribunal had jurisdiction to determine a dispute in respect of the quantum of a discretionary payment notwithstanding the statutory empowerment in this regard in respect of disturbance payments only. This should be contrasted with the Scottish case of *City of Glasgow District Council and Yoker Housing Associationv Mackie* (1991) 65 P&CR 94, Ct of Sess, which held that judicial review would have been the appropriate remedy in respect of a claim for a discretionary payment. As to the Upper Tribunal, see **Division H**.

Interest

[3369]
Disturbance payments carry interest at the statutory rate from the date of displacement to the date of payment[1].

1 LCA 1973, s 37(6). Interest is calculated as prescribed under the LCA 1961, s 32.

E The duty to re-house

1 Introduction

[3370]–[3380]
The right to compensation for compulsory purchase assessed under the compensation code described in earlier chapters of this Division does not remedy the immediate predicament of a dispossessed home owner who is left without anywhere to live. LCA 1973, ss 39–42 were, therefore, enacted to impose statutory duties on the relevant authority to provide suitable alternative residential accommodation on reasonable terms. The 'relevant authority' is usually the local housing authority[1], and not the authority whose actions have lead to the dispossession of the land owner, although, where the relevant authority differs from the authority responsible for dispossession it can recover its costs from the latter.

1 In certain circumstances, it will be the new towns residuary body or the Homes and Communities Agency: LCA 1973, s 39(7), (8) and (9).

2 Circumstances in which the statutory duty to re-house arises

Relevant circumstances

[3381]
It is the duty[1] of the relevant authority[2] to re-house any person:

(*a*) who is displaced from residential accommodation in consequence of:
   (i) the acquisition of land by an authority with compulsory purchase powers[3],
   (ii) the making or acceptance of a housing order or undertaking[4] in respect of a house or building on the land[5], or
   (iii) the carrying out of any improvement[6] to a house or building on, or the redevelopment[7] of, the land for the purposes for which the land was previously appropriated by local authority or compulsorily acquired[8]; and

(*b*) for whom no suitable alternative accommodation[9] on reasonable terms can be found.

1 LCA 1973, s 39.
2 'Relevant authority' means the local housing authority within the meaning of the Housing Act 1985, except where the property is in an area designated as a new town, in which case it will be the new town development corporation, the new towns residuary body, or the Homes and Communities Agency, as appropriate; LCA 1973, s 39(7), (8) and (9).
3 LCA 1973, s 39(1)(*a*).
4 'Housing order or undertaking' for these purposes has the same meaning as in the LCA 1973, s 29 (as to which, see para **[3303]**); LCA 1973, s 39(9).
5 LCA 1973, s 39(1)(*b*).
6 'Improvement' for these purposes has the same meaning as in the LCA 1973, s 29 (as to which, see para **[3303]**) LCA 1973, s 39(9).
7 'Redevelopment' for these purposes has the same meaning as in the LCA 1973, s 29 (as to which, see para **[3303]**); LCA 1973, s 39(9).
8 LCA 1973, s 39(1)(*c*).
9 *R v Bristol Corpn, ex p Hendy* (1973) 27 P&CR 180, CA, deals with the adequacy of alternative accommodation offered following displacement from unfit premises. The case of *R v East Hertfordshire District Council, ex p Smith* (1991) 23 HLR 26, CA, considered the reasonableness or otherwise of temporary accommodation being offered to a displaced gipsy family.

[3382]

There is a statutory duty to re-house certain caravan dwellers displaced in similar circumstances to those described above from caravan sites in which they have been residing where neither suitable alternative accommodation nor a suitable alternative site on reasonable terms is available[1].

1 LCA 1973, s 40.

Qualifying date

[3383]

A person will not be treated as displaced from property unless he was residing in the dwelling in question at:

(*a*) (in a case where land is acquired pursuant to a compulsory purchase order) the time when the notice was first published of the making of the order prior to its submission for confirmation or where the draft order did not require confirmation, the date of the preparation of the order[1];

(*b*) (in a case of land acquired under an Act specifying the land as subject to compulsory acquisition) the time when the provisions of the bill of the Act specifying the land were first published[2];

(*c*) (in a case of land acquired by agreement) the time of the agreement[3]; and (*d*) (in a case of land subject to a housing order or undertaking) the date the order was made or the undertaking accepted[4].

1 LCA 1973, s 39(6)(*a*).
2 LCA 1973, s 39(6)(*b*).
3 LCA 1973, s 39(6)(*c*).
4 LCA 1973, s 39(6).

Exceptions

[3384]
There is no duty to re-house the following:

(*a*) Trespassers or those permitted to remain on land pending improvements to or demolition of, any house or building[1].
(*b*) Those who, in certain circumstances, have been advanced money for the purpose of enabling them to obtain accommodation in substitution for that from which they have been displaced[2].
(*c*) Those temporarily displaced in consequence of acceptance of an undertaking or the carrying out of any improvement to a house or building. In such circumstances, entitlement depends on permanent displacement[3].
(*d*) Those who have sold their interests to an acquiring authority pursuant to service of a blight notice on that authority[4].

1 LCA 1973, s 39(3).
2 LCA 1973, s 39(4). These circumstances include advances under: (1) LCA 1973, s 41, as to which, see para **[3385]**; (2) the Small Dwellings Acquisition Act 1899–1923 or the Housing (Financial Provisions) Act 1958, s 43 or the Housing Act 1985, s 435; or (3) by a development corporation or the Commission for New Towns otherwise than under the LCA 1973, s 41.
3 LCA 1973, s 39(6A).
4 LCA 1973, s 39(2). Blight notices are served pursuant to the Town and Country Planning Act 1990, s 149, as to which, see **B [1102]**ff.

Money advance in lieu of re-housing

[3385]
Where an owner occupier[1] of a dwelling is displaced in the circumstances described above and wishes to acquire or construct[2] another dwelling in substitution for the one from which he is displaced, the relevant authority[3] may advance money to him for the purpose of enabling him to acquire or construct that other dwelling[4]. The advance is to be made on terms providing for the repayment of the principal sum at the end of an (extendible) fixed period, or upon notice, or upon the happening of a specific event (such as the death of the borrower) and any other terms the authority considers reasonable having regard to the circumstances[5]. The principle of the advance, together with the interest, is to be secured by way of a mortgage of the borrower's interest in the dwelling and the principal must not exceed the value which the relevant authority attributes to such interest[6].

1 'Owner occupier' in relation to any dwelling means a person who occupies it in right of a freehold interest or a leasehold interest with no less than three years unexpired as at either the date of displacement or, where improvement or redevelopment is carried out on the land, the date of appropriation by the local authority, as to which, see para **[3303]**; LCA 1973, s 41(9).

2 Construction may include acquisition of a building and conversion of it into a dwelling; LCA 1973, s 41(10).
3 'Relevant authority' means the local housing authority under the Housing Act 1985 or the development corporation or Commission for New Towns as appropriate; LCA 1973, s 39(7).
4 LCA 1973, s 41(2). The acquiring authority must be satisfied that the dwelling acquired or constructed will be fit for human habitation as a dwelling; LCA 1973, s 41(6).
5 LCA 1973, s 41(3).
6 LCA 1973, s 41(5).

[3386]
Since the relevant authority, which is required to re-house the claimant, is not necessarily the authority whose action caused the displacement, there is provision to ensure that, in such a case, the displacing authority must indemnify the relevant authority against any net loss that the relevant authority incurs[1]. An indemnity is also required where an advance of money is made in the circumstances described above[2].

1 LCA 1973, s 42. 'Net loss' for these purposes is defined in the LCA 1973, s 42(2).
2 LCA 1973, s 42(3).

[3387]–[3800]
There is a discretionary power to pay to a person who qualifies to be rehoused under the LCA 1973, s 39[1], but who has no greater interest than as tenant for a year or from year to year in the dwelling, and who wishes to acquire another dwelling in substitution, reasonable expenses in connection with that acquisition other than the purchase price[2], provided such premises are acquired within one year following displacement and are reasonably compatible with that from which he is displaced[3].

1 As to which, see para **[3381]**.
2 LCA 1973, s 43(1).
3 LCA 1973, s 43(2).

F Basic loss payments

1 Introduction

[3801]
The LCA 1973, s 33A provides a right to a supplementary payment called a 'basic loss payment' in addition to other rights to compensation. It applies to the compulsory acquisition of all types of property but is excluded where certain types of notices or orders have been served. Where the property acquired comprises partly a dwelling and the claimant is entitled to a home loss payment[1], the claimant is only entitled to a basic loss payment to the extent that the amount exceeds the home loss payment. The amount of such a payment is modest, being 7.5% of the value of the property acquired, but capped at a maximum of £75,000.

1 As to home loss payments, see para **[3302]** above.

2 Entitlement to basic loss payment

[3802]
The acquiring authority is liable to make a basic loss payment to a claimant who qualifies for one[1]. To qualify for a basic loss payment, a claimant must fulfil three conditions[2]:

(*a*) he must have a 'qualifying interest in land';
(*b*) his interest must have been acquired compulsorily[3]; and
(*c*) where he is entitled to a home loss payment, his entitlement to a basic loss payment is limited to the extent to which the basic loss payment exceeds to home loss payment.

1 LCA 1973, s 33A(3).
2 LCA 1961, s 33A(1).
3 As to 'acquired compulsorily', see **[3804]** below.

[3803]
A 'qualifying interest' is a freehold interest or an interest as a tenant. The tenant must have held that interest for not less than a year prior to the earliest of[1]:

(*a*) where a notice of entry has been served pursuant to CPA 1965, s 11[2], the date on which the acquiring authority takes possession of the land;
(*b*) where the acquiring authority has relied on the procedure in CPA 1965, Sch 3[3], the date on which the acquiring authority enters onto the land;
(*c*) where a vesting declaration is made[4], the vesting date;
(*d*) the date on which compensation is agreed;
(*e*) the date on which the compensation is determined by the Upper Tribunal[5].

1 LCA 1973, s 33A(4)(a).
2 As to the taking of possession pursuant to a notice of entry, see **Division D**.
3 As to the taking of entry under CPA 1965, Sch 3, see **Division D**.
4 As to the procedure for vesting declarations under the CP(VD)A 1981, see **Division D**.
5 As to determination of compensation by the Upper Tribunal, see **Division H**.

[3804]
The compulsory acquisition of an interest in land includes acquisition of an interest in consequence of a blight notice or a purchase notice[1]. Compulsory acquisition of an interest is treated as including acquisition by agreement in the shadow of a compulsory purchase order[2].

1 LCA 1973, s 33A(5). As to blight notices and purchase notices, see **Division B**.
2 LCA 1973, s 33J and see CPA 1965, s 3. However, the right to a basic loss payment does not apply to a 'pre-commencement acquisition', that is, where the interest was acquired prior to the commencement of the PCPA 2004, Pt 8 (31 October 2004): PCPA 2004, s 106(2) and (3).

[3805]
The right to a basic loss payment is excluded[1] where, at the relevant time[2], any of the following have been served[3]:

(*a*) a notice under the TCPA 1990, s 215 (power to require proper maintenance of land);

(*b*) a notice under HA 2004, s 11 (improvement notice relating to category 1 hazard);
(*c*) a notice under HA 2004, s 12 (improvement notice relating to category 2 hazard);
(*d*) a notice under P(LBCA)A 1990, s 48 (repairs notice on listed building);
(*e*) an order under HA 2004, s 20 (prohibition order relating to category 1 hazard);
(*f*) an order under HA 2004, s 21 (prohibition order relating to category 2 hazard);
(*g*) an order under HA 2002, s 43 (emergency prohibition orders);
(*h*) an order under HA 1985, s 265 (demolition order relating to category 1 or 2 hazard).

1 LCA 1973, s 33D(1)–(3).
2 If the compulsory purchase order falls within the ALA 1981, s 2(2), the relevant time is the date of confirmation; if the order falls within ALA 1981, s 2(3), the relevant time is the date on which the order is made: LCA 1973, s 33D(6).
3 LCA 1973, s 33D(4) and (5). There is power to amend this list by regulation: s 33D(7).

3 Amount of basic loss payment

[3806]
The amount of a basic loss payment is the lower of[1]:

(*a*) 7.5% of the value of his interest;
(*b*) £75,000.

1 LCA 1973, s 33A(2). There is power to amend these figures by regulation: LCA 1973, s 33K.

[3807]
The value of an interest for this purpose is its value for the purpose of deciding the amount of compensation payable in respect of the acquisition[1]. However, where the land taken comprises partly a dwelling in respect of which the claimant is entitled to a home loss payment, the value of the dwelling is excluded[2]. Where compensation is assessed under rule 5 (equivalent reinstatement)[3], the value of the interest for the purpose of assessing a basic loss payment is nil[4]; the effect of this provision is that no basic loss payment is payable where compensation is assessed under rule 5.

1 LCA 1973, s 33A(6), but this is subject to s 33A(7) and (8).
2 LCA 1973, s 33A(7).
3 See **Chapter 5 of this Division**.
4 LCA 1973, s 33A(8).

4 Claims and payment

[3808]
A claim for payment must be made in writing to the acquiring authority giving such particulars as the authority may reasonably require for determining entitlement or for calculating the amount[1].

1 LCA 1973, s 33E(2) and (3).

[3809]
Any dispute as to the amount of a payment is to be referred to the Upper Tribunal[1]. For the purposes of the Limitation Act 1980, a claimant's right to recover a payment is taken to have accrued on the last day of the period specified in LCA 1973, s 33A(4)[2].

1 LCA 1973, s 33I(1). As to the Upper Tribunal, see **Division H**.
2 LCA 1973, s 33E(4)(a). See **[3803]**.

[3810]
Provision is made in the event of insolvency[1] or death[2] of a claimant.

1 LCA 1973, s 33F.
2 LCA 1973, s 33G.

G Occupier's loss payments: agricultural land

1 Introduction

[3811]
The LCA 1973, s 33B provides a right to a supplementary payment called in the Act an 'occupier's loss payment: agricultural land', in addition to other rights to compensation. It applies to the compulsory acquisition of agricultural land. The amount of such a payment is modest being 2.5% of the value of the property acquired but capped at a maximum of £25,000.

2 Entitlement to occupier's loss payment: agricultural land

[3812]
The acquiring authority is liable to make an occupier's loss payment: agricultural land to a claimant who qualifies for one[1]. To qualify for an occupier's loss payment: agricultural land, a claimant must fulfil the following conditions[2]:

(*a*) he must have a 'qualifying interest in land' for the purposes of s 33A[3],
(*b*) the land must be agricultural land,
(*c*) his interest must have been acquired compulsorily[4], and
(*d*) he must have occupied the land for the period specified in s 33A(4)[5].

1 LCA 1973, s 33B(4).
2 LCA 1973, s 33A(1).
3 See para **[3803]** above.
4 In contrast to LCA 1973, s 33A, s 33B does not define this term, but by virtue of s 33J it is treated as including acquisition by agreement in the shadow of a compulsory purchase order. PCPA 2004, s 107(2) and (3) prevent this provision from applying to acquisitions by agreement prior to the commencement of PCPA 2004, Pt 8 (31 October 2004).
5 See para **[3804]**.

[3813]
The right to an occupier's loss payment: agricultural land is excluded[1] where, at the relevant time[2], any of the following have been served[3]:

(*a*) a notice under TCPA 1990, s 215 (power to require proper maintenance of land);

(*b*) a notice under HA 2004, s 11 (improvement notice relating to category 1 hazard);
(*c*) a notice under HA2004, s 12 (improvement notice relating to category 2 hazard);
(*d*) a notice under P(LBCA)A 1990, s 48 (repairs notice on listed building);
(*e*) an order under HA 2004, s 20 (prohibition order relating to category 1 hazard);
(*f*) an order under HA 2004, s 21 (prohibition order relating to category 2 hazard) ;
(*g*) an order under HA 2002, s 43 (emergency prohibition orders);
(*h*) an order under HA 1985, s 265 (demolition order relating to category 1 or 2 hazard).

1 LCA 1973, s 33D(1)–(3).
2 If the compulsory purchase order falls within the ALA 1981, s 2(2), the relevant time is the date of confirmation; if the order falls within ALA 1981, s 2(3), the relevant time is the date on which the order is made: LCA 1975, s 33D(6).
3 LCA 1973, s 33D(4) and (5). There is power to amend this list by regulation: s 33D(7).

3 Amount of occupier's loss payment: agricultural land

[3814]
The amount of an occupier's loss payment: agricultural land is the greatest of the following amounts[1]:

(*a*) 2.5% of the value of the claimant's interest;
(*b*) the 'land amount'[2];
(*c*) the 'buildings amount'[3].

1 LCA 1973, s 33B(2). There is power to amend these figures by regulation: LCA 1973, s 33K.
2 See **[3816]**.
3 See **[3817]**.

[3815]
The value of an interest for this purpose is its value for the purpose of deciding the amount of compensation payable in respect of the acquisition[1]. However, where the land taken comprises partly a dwelling in respect of which the claimant is entitled to a home loss payment, the value of the dwelling is excluded[2]. Where compensation is assessed under rule 5 (equivalent reinstatement)[3], the value of the interest for the purpose of assessing an occupier's loss payment is nil[4]; the effect of this provision is that no payment is payable where compensation is assessed under rule 5.

1 LCA 1973, s 33B(5), but this is subject to s 33B(6) and (7).
2 LCA 1973, s 33B(6).
3 See **Chapter 5 of this Division**.
4 LCA 1973, s 33B(7).

[3816]
The 'land amount' is the greater of £300 and the amount calculated as follows[1]:

> Where the area of land acquired does not exceed 100 hectares: £100 per hectare or part of a hectare.

Where the area of land acquired exceeds 100 hectares: £100 per hectare for the first 100 hectares and £50 per hectare for the next 300 hectares or part of a hectare.

1 LCA 1973, s 33B(8).

[3817]
The 'buildings amount' is £25 per square metre (or part of a square metre) of the gross floor space of any buildings on the land[1].

1 LCA 1973, s 33B(9). The gross floor space must be measured externally: s 33B(10).

4 Claims and payment

[3818]
A claim for payment must be made in writing to the acquiring authority giving such particulars as the authority may reasonably require for determining entitlement or for calculating the amount[1].

1 LCA 1973, s 33E(2) and (3).

[3819]
Any dispute as to the amount of a payment is to be referred to the Upper Tribunal[1]. For the purposes of the Limitation Act 1980, a claimant's right to recover a payment is taken to have accrued on the date of his displacement from the land[2].

1 LCA 1973, s 33I(1). As to the Upper Tribunal, see **Division H**.
2 LCA 1973, s 33E(4)(*b*).

[3820]
Provision is made in the event of insolvency[1] or death[2] of a claimant.

1 LCA 1973, s 33F.
2 LCA 1973, s 33G.

H Occupier's loss payment: other land

1 Introduction

[3821]
The LCA 1973, s 33B provides a right to a supplementary payment called in the Act an 'occupier's loss payment: other land' in addition to other rights to compensation. It applies to the compulsory acquisition of any land other than agricultural land. The amount of such a payment is modest being 2.5% of the value of the property acquired but capped at a maximum calculated by reference to the area of the land and floor space of any buildings.

2 Entitlement to occupier's loss payment: other land

[3822]
The acquiring authority is liable to make an occupier's loss payment: other land to a claimant who qualifies for one[1]. To qualify for an occupier's loss payment: other land, a claimant must fulfil the following conditions[2]:

(*a*) he must have a 'qualifying interest in land' for the purposes of s 33A[3],
(*b*) the land must not be agricultural land,
(*c*) his interest must have been acquired compulsorily[4], and
(*d*) he must have occupied the land for the period specified in s 33A(4)[5].

1 LCA 1973, s 33C(4).
2 LCA 1961, s 33C(1).
3 See **[3803]** above.
4 In contrast to s 33A, s 33C does not define this term, but by virtue of s 33J it is treated as including acquisition by agreement in the shadow of a compulsory purchase order. PCPA 2004, s 107(2) and (3) prevent this provision from applying to acquisitions by agreement prior to the commencement of PCPA 2004, Pt 8.
5 See **[3804]**.

[3823]
The right to a occupier's loss payment: other land is excluded[1] where, at the relevant time[2], any of the following have been served[3]:

(*a*) A notice under the TCPA 1990, s 215 (power to require proper maintenance of land);
(*b*) a notice under HA 2004, s 11 (improvement notice relating to category 1 hazard);
(*c*) a notice under HA2004, s 12 (improvement notice relating to category 2 hazard);
(*d*) a notice under P(LBCA)A 1990, s 48 (repairs notice on listed building);
(*e*) an order under HA 2004, s 20 (prohibition order relating to category 1 hazard);
(*f*) an order under HA 2004, s 21 (prohibition order relating to category 2 hazard);
(*g*) an order under HA 2002, s 43 (emergency prohibition orders);
(*h*) an order under HA 1985, s 265 (demolition order relating to category 1 or 2 hazard).

1 LCA 1973, s 33D(1)–(3).
2 If the compulsory purchase order falls within the ALA 1981, s 2(2), the relevant time is the date of confirmation; if the order falls within ALA 1981, s 2(3), the relevant time is the date on which the order is made: LCA 1973, s 33D(6).
3 LCA 1973, s 33D(4) and (5). There is power to amend this list by regulation: s 33D(7).

3 Amount of occupier's loss payment: other land

[3824]
The amount of an occupier's loss payment: other land is the greatest of the following amounts[1]:

(1) 2.5% of the value of the claimant's interest;
(2) the 'land amount'[2];
(3) the 'buildings amount'[3].

1 LCA 1973, s 33C(2). There is power to amend these figures by regulation: LCA 1973, s 33K.
2 See **[3826]**.
3 See **[3827]**.

[3825]
The value of an interest for this purpose is its value for the purpose of deciding the amount of compensation payable in respect of the acquisition[1]. However, where the land taken comprises partly a dwelling in respect of which the claimant is entitled to a home loss payment, the value of the dwelling is excluded[2]. Where compensation is assessed under rule 5 (equivalent reinstatement)[3], the value of the interest for the purpose of assessing an occupier's loss payment is nil[4]; the effect of this provision is that no payment is payable where compensation is assessed under rule 5.

1 LCA 1973, s 33C(5), but this is subject to s 33B(6) and (7).
2 LCA 1973, s 33C(6).
3 See **Chapter 5 of this Division**.
4 LCA 1973, s 33C(7).

[3826]
If the whole of the land in which the claimant has an interest is acquired, the 'land amount' is the greater of £2,500 or £2.50 per square metre (or part) of the area of the land acquired[1]. If only part of the claimant's land is acquired, the £2,500 is replaced by £300[2].

1 LCA 1973, s 33C(8).
2 LCA 1973, s 33C(9).

[3827]
The 'buildings amount' is £25 per square metre (or part) of the gross floor area of any buildings on the land acquired[1].

1 LCA 1973, s 33C(10) and (11).

4 Claims and payment

[3828]
A claim for payment must be made in writing to the acquiring authority giving such particulars as the authority may reasonably require for determining entitlement or for calculating the amount[1].

1 LCA 1973, s 33E(2) and (3).

[3829]
Any dispute as to the amount of a payment is to be referred to the Upper Tribunal[1]. For the purposes of the Limitation Act 1980, a claimant's right to recover a payment is taken to have accrued on the date of his displacement from the land[2].

1 LCA 1973, s 33I(1). As to the Upper Tribunal, see **Division H**.
2 LCA 1973, s 33E(4)(*b*).

[3830]

Provision is made in the event of insolvency[1] or death[2] of a claimant.

1 LCA 1973, s 33F.
2 LCA 1973, s 33G.

Division F

Compensation where no land taken

Contents

References in bold are to paragraph numbers.

Chapter 1

Introduction

Contents

A Introduction

[1]
This chapter explains the scope of **Division F**. This division describes the entitlement to compensation where no land has been compulsorily acquired from the claimant, but the value of his land has, nonetheless, been depreciated as the result of works authorised by statute. It is also concerned with measures which are intended to mitigate the effects of such works. The scope of each of the four chapters of this division is as follows:

(1) Introduction providing an outline of the subject matter of the chapters which follow.
(2) Compensation under the Lands Clauses Consolidation Act 1845 (LCCA 1845), s 68 and the Compulsory Purchase Act 1965 (CPA 1965), s 10 for injurious affection caused by the carrying out of works authorised by statute.
(3) Compensation under the Land Compensation Act 1973 (LCA 1973), Pt I for depreciation in the value of land caused by the use of public works.
(4) Powers under the LCA 1973, Pt II and other provisions to provide mitigation for public works.

B Injurious affection where no land taken

[2]
There is a right to compensation in certain circumstances where no land has been compulsorily acquired from the claimant, but where the value of his interest in land has been depreciated as a result of works authorised by statute. This right was originally enacted as the LCCA 1845, s 68 which has now been re-enacted in substantially the same form as the Land Compulsory Purchase Act 1965 (CPA 1965), s 10(1). The CPA 1965, s 10(2) expressly preserves the interpretation placed by the courts upon the LCCA 1845, s 68, and so the scope of both s 68 and s 10 is governed by numerous cases, many dating back to the nineteenth century. Although the term 'injuriously

affected', which appears in both the CPA 1965, ss 7 and 10, is not defined, it is well established that it refers to circumstances where land is affected in such a way that its value is depreciated. This right to compensation is explained in **Chapter 2**.

C Depreciation in the value of land due to the use of public works

[3]
A claimant is entitled to compensation under the LCA 1973, Pt I where his interest in land has been depreciated in value by physical factors caused by the use of public works and it applies not only to new works, but also to the alteration of existing ones. These provisions were enacted in order to provide a right to compensation for injurious affection in some (but not all) of the circumstances where compensation was not otherwise recoverable[1]. Where land has been compulsorily acquired, a claimant is entitled to compensation under the LCCA 1845, s 63 or the CPA 1965, s 7[2] for severance or injurious affection, that is, depreciation of the value of any land which he held with the land taken caused not only by the execution of the authorised works but also by the subsequent use of those works. The LCCA 1845, s 68 and the CPA 1965, s 10, which apply where no land has been taken from the claimant, only provide compensation for loss of value attributable to the execution of works, and not their use. Thus the LCA 1973, Pt I provides compensation for loss attributable to the use of public works constructed elsewhere than on land acquired from the claimant; this is explained in **Chapter 3**.

1 See para **[105]**.
2 As to compensation as a result of compulsory purchase for severance and injurious affection under the LCCA 1845, 63 or the CPA 1965, s 7, see **Division E**.

D Mitigation measures

[4]–[100]
The LCA 1973, Pt II introduced arrangements for mitigating the effect of public works, including the soundproofing of buildings, landscaping and temporary relocation, with ancillary powers to acquire land and execute works for these purposes. Some of the provisions originally enacted in the LCA 1973 have been repealed and re-enacted in other legislation. This is explained in **Chapter 4**.

Chapter 2

Injurious affection where no land has been taken

Contents

A Introduction

[101]
This chapter explains the right to compensation where land has been 'injuriously affected' by works authorised by statute, even though no land has been taken from the claimant. The term 'injurious affection' derives from the Lands Clauses Consolidation Act 1845 (LCCA 1845)[1] and, in particular, two sections:

(1) Section 63, which relates to the assessment of compensation where land has been compulsorily acquired from the claimant and the value of other land held by the claimant with the land taken has been depreciated by severance or injuriously affection. Section 63 was the predecessor of the Compulsory Purchase Act 1965 (CPA 1965), s 7[2].
(2) Section 68, which, as interpreted by the courts, gives a right to compensation in certain circumstances in respect of the execution of works where no land had been taken from the claimant. Section 68 was the predecessor of the CPA 1965, s 10.

Although the term 'injuriously affected' is not defined by statute for the purposes of either the LCCA 1845 or the CPA 1965, it has been interpreted as referring to circumstances where land is affected in such a way that its value is depreciated. While both the LCCA 1845, ss 63 and 68 provide rights to compensation where land has been 'injuriously affected', as do s 7 and the CPA 1965, s 10, that is where the similarity ends; the principles which are described in this chapter apply only to the LCCA 1845, s 68 and the CPA 1965, s 10[3].

1 The term 'injurious affection' probably has an even earlier origin. The term also appeared in the Railways Clauses Consolidation Act 1845, s 6 (repealed) which was similar to the LCCA 1845, s 68. Parts of the LCCA 1845 were repealed by the CPA 1965, s 39(4), Sch 8. Other parts, including ss 63 and 68 which are referred to in this paragraph, remain in existence and apply where the CPA 1965 does not. For most purposes, the provisions of the LCCA 1845 have been superseded by those of the CPA 1965.

2 See **Division E**.
3 This distinction was recognised in *Cowper Essex v Acton Local Board* (1889) 14 App Cas 153, HL, at 161–162, where Lord Halsbury LC said:

> 'It may seem at first sight a little strange that what is injuriously affecting in one case should not be in the other. But it is possible to explain the apparent contradiction by the consideration that the injurious affecting by the use, as distinguished from the construction, is a particular injury suffered by the proprietor from whom some portion of his land is taken different in kind from that which is suffered by the rest of Her Majesty's subjects.'

See also *Wildtree Hotels Ltd v London Borough of Harrow* [1998] 3 All ER 638, CA, per Pill LJ at 642; [2000] 3 All ER 289, HL.

[101.1]

The CPA 1965, s 10 does not apply to nationally significant infrastructure projects authorised pursuant to the PA 2008[1]. However, there is instead a right to compensation for injurious affection in circumstances where the grant of development consent for such a project has provided the promoter with a defence of statutory authority to a claim for nuisance, and the principles applicable to the assessment of compensation which have developed under the CPA 1965, s 10 are applicable to the assessment of compensation under the PA 2008[2].

1 PA 2008, s 125(3).
2 PA 2008, s 152(1)–(6).

[102]

The CPA 1965, Pt I, in which s 10 appears, applies where land has been acquired by compulsory purchase under the Acquisition of Land Act 1981, Pt II or Sch 1[1] for the carrying out of works, or has been acquired by agreement for such purposes under the shadow of such compulsory purchase powers[2]. Although parts of the LCCA 1845 have been repealed, other parts, including s 68, were retained; this Act applies where land is acquired compulsorily or by agreement in circumstances where the CPA 1965 is not applicable[3]. It is, therefore, necessary in this chapter to refer to both provisions, but there is no material distinction between them. Since 1 April 1974, the CPA 1965 Pt I has applied to all purchases of land by agreement made by local authorities[4]. In respect of land acquired prior to 1 April 1974, a local authority may resolve, subject to the Secretary of State's confirmation by order, that the LCCA 1845, s 68 or the CPA 1965, s 10, as the case may be, is to apply to that land. The effect is to enable the local authority to carry out works on the land, notwithstanding that such works are in breach of a restrictive covenant, subject to the payment of compensation[5].

1 CPA 1965, s 1(1). See **Division C**.
2 CPA 1965, s 3. See further para **[106]**.
3 LCCA 1845, s 1.
4 Local Government Act 1972, s 120(3).
5 Local Government (Miscellaneous Provisions) Act 1976, s 14. As to the application of the LCCA 1845, s 68 and the CPA 1965, s 10 to restrictive covenants, see para **[124]**.

[103]

Although the words of the LCCA 1845, s 68 suggest that it was drafted as a procedural provision, the courts have interpreted it as creating a right to compensation. As Lord Wilberforce explained in *Argyle Motors (Birkenhead) Ltd v Birkenhead Corpn*[1], the LCCA 1845, s 68:

> 'has, over 100 years, received through a number of judicial decisions, some in this House, and by no means easy to reconcile, an interpretation which fixes upon it a meaning having little perceptible relation to the words used. This represents a century of judicial effort to keep the primitive wording – which itself has an earlier history – in some sort of accord with the realities of the industrial age … '

In essence, the LCCA 1845, s 68 and the CPA 1965, s 10 provide rights to compensation where an action for damages would have provided a remedy but for the defence of statutory immunity (subject to a number of qualifications described in the paragraphs which follow). While the context of the LCCA 1845, s 68 and the CPA 1965, s 10 is that of compulsory acquisition, the right to compensation does not arise out of the process of compulsory acquisition, but out of the execution of works which would have given rise to a cause of action in tort if they had not been authorised by statute.

1 [1975] AC 99 at 129A–F.

[104]
Compensation may be claimed for physical damage to land or interference with rights which benefit the land. With regard to such rights, it has been explained in **Division D**[1] that, where land is compulsorily acquired, the person entitled to the benefit of easements, restrictive covenants and other rights would not receive a notice to treat. If such rights are interfered with, however, that person may be entitled to compensation under the LCCA 1845, s 68 or the CPA 1965, s 10[2].

1 See **D[307]** and **[1605]**.
2 As to the rights which qualify for compensation under the LCCA 1845, s 68 and the CPA 1965, s 10, see para **[124]**.

[105]
The rights to compensation under the LCCA 1845, s 68 and the CPA 1965, s 10 are limited in a number of ways, largely determined in the nineteenth century, which are described in this chapter. The courts were clearly conscious of the need to limit the scope of claims; thus, for example, Lord Cranworth said in *Ricket v Metropolitan Rly Co*[1]:

> 'The very existence of a railway must cause loss to many persons in its neighbourhood. Every inn or posting house at which post horses were kept suffered, as is well known, grievous loss by the first establishment of a railroad in its neighbourhood; in fact, the business of such a house was often utterly destroyed. But it was never contended that this was an injury to the house … for which compensation could be demanded … Such a claim, if sustainable, would admit of no limit. The railroad would, it is true, chiefly affect the custom of posting houses near to it, but it would or might diminish the quantity of posting to an almost indefinite extent, and I can discover no limit to the claims which, on the doctrine asserted, might successfully be made.'

The courts have declined to extend the scope of the rights, taking the view that this is a matter for Parliament. For example, in *Argyle Motors (Birkenhead)*

Ltd v Birkenhead Corpn[2], in which the House of Lords rejected a claim for compensation for loss of business profits, Lord Wilberforce commented[3]:

> '... though it might be said that generous policy of compensation would favour compensation for losses caused to individuals through works of social benefit, a policy to this effect, however just it might appear in a particular case, involves too great a shift in financial burden and too many adjustments or qualifications (if it were to be workable) to be suitable for introduction by judicial decision.'

Parliament did extend the rights to compensation by enacting the Land Compensation Act 1973 (LCA 1973), Pt I, which is described in the next chapter of this division, providing a right to compensation for the effects of the use of public works, whereas, as explained below, the LCCA 1845, s 68 and the CPA 1965, s 10 only provide compensation for the effects of the execution of works. However, the rights to compensation have not been extended to personal loss such as loss of profits.

1 (1867) LR 2 HL 175 at 198–199.
2 [1975] AC 99.
3 [1975] AC 99 at 130F. See also the comments of Viscount Dilhorne at 134G.

B The right to compensation

[106]
By the LCCA 1845, s 68 and the CPA 1965, s 10, compensation may be claimed[1] in respect of any land[2] or any interest in land[3] which is injuriously affected by the execution of works[4] authorised by statute where the claimant is not otherwise entitled to compensation. Compensation under this section does not depend upon the works being carried out on land which has been compulsorily acquired[5]; compensation may therefore be payable even where such land was acquired by agreement[6]. The right to compensation may, however, be excluded by the authorising Act[7].

1 Under the LCCA 1845, s 68, compensation may be claimed from the 'promoters of the undertaking', defined in s 2. Under the CPA 1965, s 10 compensation may be claimed from the 'acquiring authority'; this term is used notwithstanding that s 10 provides compensation in circumstances where no land has been taken from the claimant. 'Acquiring authority' is defined in the CPA 1965, s 1(3), 'unless the context otherwise requires', as the person authorised by the compulsory purchase order to purchase the land. For the purposes of s 10, it must mean the person or body authorised by statute to execute the works which give rise to the claim. For the purposes of the Town and Country Planning Act 1990, Pt IX, s 245(4)(*b*) expressly provides that references in the CPA 1965, s 10 to the acquiring authority are to be construed as references to the person by whom the buildings or works in question are constructed. Although the right to compensation does not depend upon making an objection to the orders or other statutory procedures which authorised the works, the making or absence of an objection may be relevant to the factual context of a claim: see the comments of Carnwath LJ in *Moto Hospitality Ltd v Secretary of state for Transport* [2007] EWCA Civ 764 at [11].
2 By the CPA 1965, s 1(3), '"land" includes anything falling within any definition of that expression in the enactment under which the purchase is authorised'.
3 Interests in land which qualify for compensation under the LCCA 1845 and the Compulsory Purchase Act 1968, s 10 are considered in para **[124]**.
4 Defined in the CPA 1965, s 1(4) as 'the works or undertaking, of whatever nature, authorised to be executed by the special Act'. The 'special Act' is defined in s 1(2) as 'the enactment under which the purchase is authorised and the compulsory purchase order'. Where road improve-

ments were implemented pursuant to orders made under the Highways Act 1980 and with the use of compulsory purchase powers, the Lands Tribunal held that 'the special Act' comprised the Highways Act 1980 and the orders: *Wagstaff and BP Oil (UK) Ltd v Department of the Environment, Transport and the Regions* [1999] 2 EGLR 108, Lands Tribunal. Where loss was caused to a motorway service area as a result of the stopping up of motorway slip roads, the Lands Tribunal held that the 'works' comprised the whole of the authorised works including the stopping up and the special Act comprised all of the relevant provisions enabling such works to be carried out: *Moto Hospitality Ltd v Secretary of State for Transport* [2006] RVR 280, Lands Tribunal; affirmed by the Court of Appeal [2007] EWCA Civ 764 on this point although the appeal was allowed on a different point.

5 Although both the LCCA 1845, s 68 and the CPA 1965, s 10 refer to land 'taken for or injuriously affected by …', the words 'taken for or' were considered by Scott LJ to be superfluous: *Horn v Sunderland Corpn* [1941] 2 KB 26, CA, at 43. However, the LCCA 1845 and the CPA 1965 only apply where the acquiring authority used, or could have used, compulsory purchase powers, or, in relation to a local authority, where either the Local Government Act 1972, s 120(3) or the Local Government (Miscellaneous Provisions) Act 1976, s 14 applies, see para **[102]**.

6 *Kirby v Harrogate School Board* [1896] 1 Ch 437. However, the body which acquired the land did have compulsory powers which could have been exercised if the seller had been unwilling.

7 *Ferrar v London Sewers Comrs* (1869) LR 4 Exch 227.

[107]

The CPA 1965, s 10(1) re-enacts the LCCA 1845, s 68 in similar terms, but the CPA 1965, s 10(2) acknowledges the interpretation by the courts of the LCCA 1845, s 68, by providing that the CPA 1965, s 10 is to be construed as affording the same right as the LCCA 1845, s 68 has been construed as affording. The scope of this right has been developed by numerous cases, many in the nineteenth century, some of which are not easy to reconcile[1]. It is now established that a claim may only be made under the LCCA 1845, s 68 or the CPA 1965, s 10 in respect of loss of value of the claimant's land which meets the requirements explained in the paragraphs which follow, often now referred to as the 'McCarthy' Rules[2].

1 See the comments of Lord Wilberforce in the *Argyle Motors* case cited in para **[103]**and see Lord Hoffmann's statement of the 'basic principles' in *Wildtree Hotels v Harrow London Borough Council* [2000] 3 All ER 1 HL, at 293H–294B.

2 This term is adopted for convenience although it is not entirely accurate; it derives from *Metropolitan Board of Works v McCarthy* (1874) LR 7 HL 243, HL; however, although reference can be found to them in that case, they are not listed in any of the speeches as a set of rules. They were referred to as the 'McCarthy' Rules by Sir Christopher Slade in *Clift v Welsh Office* [1998] 3 All ER 852, CA, at 858J. The rules derive from a number of cases. The rules may be modified by the Act which authorises the works.

1 The 'McCarthy' Rules

Rule 1
The loss must result from an act made lawful by statute

[108]

The LCCA 1845, s 68 and the CPA 1965, s 10 only apply where the acts which caused the loss of value to the claimant's land are specifically authorised by statute, either expressly or by implication[1]. Where an authority acts outside its statutory powers[2], or acts negligently[3], the claimant's remedy is an action for damages, and not a claim for compensation under these provisions[4]. The court will be reluctant to allow an authority to rely upon its own negligence or excess of powers to escape liability to pay compensation[5].

1 In *Hammersmith and City Rly Co v Brand* (1869) LR 4 HL 171 an Act had authorised the construction of a railway, the use of which caused vibration on the plaintiff's land. Lord Chelmsford said at 202:

> '... we do not expect to find words in an Act of Parliament expressly authorising an individual or a company to commit a nuisance or to do damage to a neighbour ... if such locomotives cannot possibly be used without occasioning vibration ... it must be taken that power is given to cause that vibration without liability to an action.'

This case arose in the context of the Railways Clauses Consolidation Act 1845, s 6 (repealed), which was similar to the LCCA 1845, s 68. As a result of the operation of r 4, it was held that compensation was not payable, see para **[125]**. The term in s 10 'the special Act' is not confined to the Act by virtue of which land has been compulsorily acquired but includes all relevant statutory powers including stopping up orders: *Moto Hospitality Ltd v Secretary of State for Transport* [2007] EWCA Civ 764, upholding the decision of the Lands Tribunal on this point although the appeal was allowed on a different issue.

2 In *Clowes v Staffordshire Potteries Waterworks Co* (1872) 8 Ch App 125, a company authorised by statute to construct a waterworks caused pollution to a stream. It was held that the pollution was *avoidable* and was not, therefore, authorised by the Act, and, accordingly, the claimant's remedy was in tort.

3 In *Geddis v Bann Reservoir (Proprietors)* (1878) 3 App Cas 430, HL, Lord Blackburn said:

> ' ... no action will lie for doing that which the legislature has authorised, if it be done without negligence ... but an action does lie for doing that which the legislature has authorised, if it be done negligently. And I think that if by a reasonable exercise of the powers ... the damage could be prevented, it is ... negligence not to make such reasonable exercise ...'

4 *Imperial Gas Light and Coke Co (Directors etc) v Broadbent* (1859) 7 HL Cas 600; *Caledonian Rly Co v Colt* (1860) 3 Macq 833.

5 *Colac Corpn v Summerfield* [1893] AC 187, PC; *Uttley v Todmorden Local Board of Health* (1874) 44 LJCP 19.

Rule 2
The loss must be such that in the absence of statutory powers it would have given rise to a cause of action

[109]

An authority will only be liable to pay compensation under the LCCA 1845, s 68 or the CPA 1965, s 10 for acts which would have created liability to damages if done without statutory authority[1]. Thus a claim for loss of privacy was held to be outside the LCCA 1845, s 68 because it was not actionable in tort[2].

1 Per Lord Chelmsford in *Hammersmith and City Rly Co v Brand* (1869) LR 4 HL 171, HL, at 201; *Ricket v Metropolitan Rly* (1867) LR 2 HL 175; *Biscoe v Great Eastern Rly Co* (1873) LR 16 Eq 636; *Metropolitan Board of Works v McCarthy* (1874) LR 7 HL 243; *Fleming v Newport Rly Co* (1883) 8 App Cas 265.

2 *Re Penny and South Eastern Rly Co* (1857) 7 E & B 660.

[110]–[120]

In *Clift v The Welsh Office*[1], a claim for compensation had been made arising out of the construction of a dual carriageway in place of a single carriageway highway. The Court of Appeal upheld the Lands Tribunal's decision that compensation under the CPA 1965, s 10 was not payable in respect of the dust and noise caused by the works because such effects were not actionable in nuisance as a result of the rule established by *Andreae v Selfridge & Co Ltd*[2]. The Court of Appeal upheld the Tribunal's decision that the rule in *Andreae v Selfridge* did not apply to physical damage caused to the claimants' house, which would have been actionable as a private nuisance, so that an award of compensation could be made in respect of such damage. The Court of Appeal also upheld the Tribunal's decision that interference with the claimant's access would have been actionable as public nuisance because the claimants had suffered special damage, and consequently that compensation was payable[3]. In *Wildtree Hotels Ltd v Harrow London Borough* Council[4], the House of Lords held that the rule in *Andrea v Selfridge* prevented recovery of compensation in respect of noise, dust and vibration resulting from road works.

1 [1997] RVR 12, Lands Tribunal, upheld by [1998] 4 All ER 852, CA. The passage at the end of the Court of Appeal's judgment should be noted concerning *Wildtree Hotels Ltd v London Borough of Harrow*, see further para **[128]**.
2 [1938] Ch 1, CA. *Andrea v Selfridge & Co Ltd* laid down the rule that temporary construction works which cause noise, dust etc do not give rise to an actionable nuisance so long as all proper and reasonable steps are taken to ensure that no undue inconvenience is caused.
3 See now *Westminster City Council v Ocean Leisure Ltd* [2005] 1 P&CR 450, CA.
4 [2000] 3 All ER 289, HL. Lord Hoffmann did not entirely rule out the possibility of such a claim being made successfully, but regarded it as almost impossible: at 299G and 300C.

Rule 3
The loss must arise from physical interference with the land or with a right enjoyed with it, and must result in depreciation of the value of the claimant's land

[121]
In *Argyle Motors (Birkenhead) Ltd v Birkenhead Corpn*[1], Lord Wilberforce said:

> ' … it is well established that the only compensation which can be obtained under this section is "in respect of lands", ie in respect of some loss of value of land, or (what is a branch under this same heading) in respect of some damage to lands … '

It appears from the judicial decisions that compensation may be claimed in respect of two kinds of damage only, actual physical damage, and interference with rights which benefit land.

1 [1975] AC 99, HL, at 129G.

Physical damage

[122]
In *Ricket v Metropolitan Rly Co*[1], Lord Cranworth said:

> 'The injury must be actual injury to the land, as by loosening the foundations of the buildings on it … '

1 Per Lord Cranworth in *Ricket v Metropolitan Rly Co* (1867) LR 2 HL 175 at 198. For examples of cases involving physical damage, see *Biard v Deal Corpn* (1961) 12 P&CR 398, Lands Tribunal; *Flanagan v Stoke-on-Trent City Council* (1982) 262 Estates Gazette 1201, Lands Tribunal.

Interference with rights

[123]
The passage cited above from Lord Cranworth in the case of *Ricket*[1] continued by giving examples of obstructing a building's light or drains or

making it inaccessible. In *Metropolitan Board of Works v McCarthy*[2], Lord Chelmsford said:

> 'Where by the construction of works there is a physical interference with any right, public or private, which an owner of a house is entitled to make use of, in connection with the house, and which gives it marketable value apart from any particular use to which the owner may put it, if the house, by reason of the works, is diminished in value, there arises a claim for compensation. I think the rule thus stated may be accepted with this necessary qualification, that where the right which the owner of the house is entitled to is one which he possesses in common with the public, there must be something peculiar to the right in its connection with the house to distinguish it from that which is enjoyed by the rest of the world.'

1 (1867) LR 2 HL 175 at 198.
2 (1874) LR 7 HL 243 at 256.

[124]
The underlying rationale of the right to compensation for interference with such rights in relation to land is that, although they are not acquired by the promoter[1], they cannot be enforced against the promoter if his works interfere with the rights, because his works are authorised by statute. Examples of legal rights interference with which have been held to entitle a claimant to compensation include the following:

(*a*) rights of support[2];
(*b*) easements[3];
(*c*) profits a prendre[4];
(*d*) rights of riparian owners[5];
(*e*) rights of access to a highway[6];
(*f*) restrictive covenants[7]; and
(*g*) rights of ancient lights[8].

1 See **D[307]** and **D[1605]**. Where a promoter acquired by agreement the reversion of land subject to a lease which contained a covenant for quiet enjoyment, the lessee could not enforce the covenant, but was entitled to compensation for breach of the covenant under the LCCA 1845, s 68: *Manchester, Sheffield and Lincolnshire Rly Co v Anderson* [1898] 2 Ch 394.
2 *Metropolitan Board of Works v McCarthy* (1874) LR 7 HL 243; *Fletcher v Birkenhead Corpn* [1907] 1 KB 205; *Till v Finchley Borough Council* (1954) 4 P&CR 362 (removal of support by demolition of adjoining building).
3 *Glover v North Staffordshire Rly Co* (1851) 16 QB 912; *Clark v London School Board* (1874) 9 Ch App 120; *Duke of Bedford v Dawson* (1875) LR 20 Eq 353; *Bush v Trowbridge Waterworks* (1875) LR 19 Eq 291; *London School Board v Smith* [1895] WN 37; *Ford v Metropolitan Rly* (1886) 17 QBD 12; *Furness Rly Co v Cumberland Building Society* (1884) 52 LT 144; *Barnard v Great Western Rly* (1902) 86 LT 798. In *Re Masters and Great Western Rly Co* [1901] 2 KB 84, the Court of Appeal held that a right to sink a coal shaft in land which had been acquired by the railway company was an interest in land for the purposes of the LCCA 1845, s 68.
4 A profit a prendre is an interest in land. Where a sporting right amounts to an interest in land, interference may give rise to compensation under the LCCA 1845, s 68 or the CPA 1965, s 10, as the case may be. However, there is no right to compensation if the sporting right is merely a licence: *Bird v Great Eastern Rly Co* (1865) 34 LJCP 366.
5 *R v Great Northern Rly Co* (1849) 14 QB 25 (access to an ancient ferry); *Macey v Metropolitan Board of Works* (1864) 33 LJ Ch 377 (right of access of riparian owner to the foreshore); *Metropolitan Board of Works v McCarthy* (1874) LR 7 HL 243 (right of access of riparian owner to the foreshore); *A-G of Straits Settlement v Wemyss* (1888) 13 App Cas 192 (access to the sea); *Hewett v Essex County Council* (1928) 138 LT 742 (construction of bridge prevented access by

vessels to a wharf); *Mortimer v South Wales Rly Co* (1859) 1 E & E 375 (interruption of flow of water in a river).

6 *Caledonian Rly Co v Walker's Trustees* (1882) 7 App Cas 259 (works caused access to be less direct and steeper), in which Lord Selborne LC commented at 285 that the right of access must be proximate, and not remote or indefinite. Other examples include: *Chamberlain v West End of London etc Rly* (1862) 2 B & S 605; affd (1863) 2 B & S 617 (access partially obstructed); *R v Wallasey Local Board* (1869) LR 4 QB 351 (level of street raised obstructing access to house); *R v St Luke's Vestry* (1871) LR 7 QB 148 (level of street lowered); *Re Wadham and North Eastern Rly Co* (1885) 16 QBD 227; *Wright v Air Council President* (1929) 143 LT 43 (street stopped up); *Metropolitan Board of Works v Howard* (1889) 5 TLR 732 (closure of bridge); *R v Great Northern Rly Co* (1849) 14 QB 25 (obstruction of access to ferry); *Beckett v Midland Rly Co* (1867) LR 3 CP 82 (access reduced in width); *Flanagan v Stoke on Trent City Council* [1982] JPL 520 (claimant deprived of easy access to shop); *Clift v Welsh Office* [1998] 4 All ER 852, CA (effect of additional traffic on roads giving access); *Moto Hospitality Ltd v Secretary of State for Transport* (highway improvements which reduced the traffic flow to a motorway service area but did not directly affects its access roads held by the Court of Appeal not to give rise to a right to compensation) [2007] EWCA Civ 764. The interference with the right must be the result of the execution of the works authorised by the special Act and not a separate stopping-up order: *Jolliffe v Exeter Corpn* [1967] 1 WLR 993, 18 P&CR 343, CA; distinguished in *Wagstaff and BP Oil (UK) Ltd v Department of the Environment, Transport and the Regions* [1999] 2 EGLR 108, Lands Tribunal and in *Moto Hospitality Ltd v Secretary of State for Transport* [2006] RVR 280, Lands Tribunal; affirmed by the Court of Appeal [2007] EWCA Civ 764 on this point although the appeal was allowed on a different point.

7 *Long Eaton Recreation Grounds Co v Midland Rly Co* [1902] 2 KB 574; *Wrotham Park Settled Estates v Hertsmere Borough Council* [1993] 2 EGLR 15, CA. However, see also *Thames Water Utilities Ltd v Oxford City Council* [1999] 1 EGLR 167, in which it was held that there was a right to compensation under the CPA 1965, s 10 in consequence of works which conflict with a restrictive covenant or other right, but not in consequence of a use which has such effect. This led the court to hold that the protection afforded to a local planning authority and persons acquiring title from it by the TCPA 1990, s 237 extended to works but not a use. It is submitted that there may be some doubt as to the correctness of this decision. As to quantum of damage for breach of a restrictive covenant, see para **[130]**.

8 *Eagle v Charing Cross Rly Co* (1867) LR 2 CP 638; *Re London, Tilbury and Southend Rly Co and Gower's Walk Schools Trustees* (1889) 24 QBD 326, CA; *Courage & Co v South Eastern Rly Co* (1902) 19 TLR 61.

[125]

Examples of circumstances in which it has been held that insufficient rights existed to qualify for compensation include: interference with an underground flow of water[1], loss of privacy through overlooking[2], diminution in the use of a ferry due to the construction of a bridge[3] and loss of the right to sell refreshments in a theatre[4].

1 *New River Co v Johnson* (1860) 29 LJMC 93.

2 *Re Penny and South Eastern Rly Co* (1857) 7 E & B 660, 26 LJQB 225.

3 *Hopkins v Great Northern Rly Co* (1877) 2 QBD 224.

4 *Frank Warr & Co Ltd v London County Council* [1904] 1 KB 713, CA, applying *Edwardes v Barrington* (1901) 85 LT 650, HL; followed in *Walton, Harvey Ltd v Walker and Homfrays Ltd* [1931] 1 Ch 274, CA.

Other forms of loss

[126]

Compensation is only recoverable in respect of depreciation in the value of the claimant's interest in land. In *Argyle Motors (Birkenhead) Ltd v Birkenhead Corpn*, Lord Wilberforce said:

> '... it is well established that ... compensation cannot be obtained for any loss which is personal to the owner, or which is related to some particular user of the land.'

Compensation is not, therefore, recoverable, for example, for injury to the claimant's trade, unless it can be shown that the loss of profits affects the value of the claimant's interest in the land[1]. In *Ricket v Metropolitan Rly Co*[2], the streets adjoining the claimant's public house had been obstructed with hoardings, resulting in loss of business profits; it was held that no compensation was payable because the value of the claimant's land had not been affected. In contrast, in *Metropolitan Board of Works v McCarthy*[3], the construction of the Victoria Embankment beside the River Thames resulted in the blocking up of access between the river and the claimant's dock; it was held that the claimant was entitled to compensation because the value of his business premises had been depreciated.

1 *Argyle Motors (Birkenhead) Ltd v Birkenhead Corpn* [1975] AC 99, HL, at 130H–131A.
2 (1867) LR 2 HL 175, following *Wilkes v Hungerford Market Co* (1835) 2 Bing NC 281.
3 (1874) LR 7 HL 243. See also *Chamberlain v West of London and Crystal Palace Rly Co* (1863) 2 B & S 617.

[127]
In *Wildtree Hotels Ltd v London Borough of Harrow*[1], the Court of Appeal rejected the contention that compensation was payable under the CPA 1965, s 10, in respect of noise, dust and vibration or any other matter not affecting the value of the land when the works are complete.

1 [1999] QB 634, [1998] 3 All ER 638, CA; on appeal [2000] 3 All ER 289, HL. The decision was by a majority of Gibson and Pill LJJ with Ward LJ dissenting. The court distinguished cases, such as *Lingké v Christchurch Corpn* [1912] 3 KB 595, decided under the Public Health Act 1875, on the basis that the right to compensation was wider under that legislation than under the LCCA 1845, s 68. See also *Clift v Welsh Office* [1998] 4 All ER 852, CA.

Temporary loss

[128]
In *Wildtree Hotels Ltd v London Borough of Harrow*[1], the House of Lords held that a claim for compensation could be made in respect of temporary loss. Lord Hoffmann explained[2] that, whereas, in considering damage whose effects would last for a long time, such as deprivation of a right of way, it would obviously be sensible to take a valuation date and capitalise the value of the future loss at that date, in respect of past damage, it is permissible to calculate the effect which it had had upon the value of the land in the sense of reducing its letting value in the open market while the damage occurred. In *Clift v Welsh Office*[3], which also related to a claim for compensation for loss alleged to have been caused by the carrying out of road works, the Court of Appeal held that compensation was payable for actual physical damage caused during temporary building operations and for loss attributable to the effect on the claimant's access to his property, but rejected a claim in respect of noise and dust during the works[4].

1 [2000] 3 All ER 289, HL. See also *Westminster City Council v Ocean Leisure Ltd* [2005] 1 P&CR 450, CA.

2 At 303D.
3 [1997] RVR 12, Lands Tribunal, upheld by [1998] 4 All ER 852, CA.
4 A note at the end of the Court of Appeal's judgment records that the court was aware of the *Wildtree Hotels* case, considered simultaneously by a differently constituted Court of Appeal, which recognised that both decisions might need to be revisited if there was an appeal: see [1998] 4 All ER 852 at 863H, CA. As to compensation for noise, dust and vibration, see para **[110]**.

Rule 4
The loss must arise from the execution of the authorised works and not from their use

[129]
A claimant under the LCCA 1845, s 68 or the CPA 1965, s 10 is entitled only to compensation for loss attributable to the execution of the works, and not from their use[1]. There have been a number of cases concerning the enforcement of restrictive covenants in which it has been suggested that a person having the benefit of a restrictive covenant may claim compensation in respect, not only of the execution of the works, but also of their use[2]. In *Thames Water Utilities v Oxford City Council and Oxford United Football Club Ltd*[3], these and many other cases were reviewed. The court concluded that compensation under the CPA 1965, s 10 does not extend to the use of works after construction and that the suggestions to the contrary in certain cases were incorrect, but were not part of the ratio of those decisions.

1 *Hammersmith and City Rly Co v Brand* (1869) LR 4 HL 171, decided in the context of the Railways Clauses Consolidation Act 1845, s 6 which was similar to the LCCA 1845, s 68; *London, Brighton etc Rly v Truman* (1885) 11 App Cas 45; *Cowper-Essex v Acton Local Board* (1889) 14 App Cas 153, HL. Distinguished in *Fletcher v Birkenhead Corpn* [1907] 1 KB 205, CA, under the Waterworks Clauses Act.
2 *Re Simeon* [1937] Ch 525; *Re Elm Avenue* [1984] 1 WLR 1398; *Brown v Heathlands NHS Trust* [1996] 1 All ER 133.
3 [1999] 1 EGLR 167. It is submitted that there must be some doubt as to the correctness of this decision. This case arose out of the TCPA 1990, s 237, which extinguishes rights over land in certain circumstances and provides a right to compensation under the CPA 1965, s 10 instead. So far as s 237 is concerned, and a number of other similar statutory provisions, the effect of the *Thames Water* decision has been reversed by the Planning Act 2008, s 194 and Sch 10: see **Division D [1606]**.

C Assessment of compensation

[130]–[140]
Compensation is to be assessed in accordance with the rules which apply to damages in tort[1]. The claimant is entitled to compensation for all the loss which is the direct and foreseeable consequence of the act[2]. Where there has been physical damage, compensation may be assessed as the cost of repair or the effect on the value of the land[3]. Following principles established in the law of tort, the cost of repair is to be assessed according to the rule that compensation should put the injured party in the same position as if the wrong had not been committed and should be assessed at the earliest date when this could be undertaken, rather than the date when the damage occurred[4]. Where there is no physical damage (for example, where the execution of the works interferes with a restrictive covenant benefiting the

claimant's land), the measure of damages is the diminution in the value of the claimant's land as a result of the execution of the works[5]. There is no entitlement to a 'ransom element' even if the claimant could have used the restrictive covenant to extract a share of the development value in the absence of the compulsory purchase powers[6]. Where the value of the claimant's land is increased as a result of the works, such betterment cannot be set off against a claim for compensation under the LCCA 1845, s 68, unless there is an express statutory provision requiring this[7].

1 *Clift v Welsh Office* [1998] 4 All ER 852, CA, at 856H; *Re Clark and Wandsworth District Board of Works* (1868) 17 LT 549.
2 This part of the decision in *Re London, Tilbury and Southend Rly Co and Gower's Walk Schools Trustees* (1889) 24 QBD 326, CA, at 329, was cited with approval in *Horton v Colwyn Bay Urban Council* [1908] 1 KB 327, CA. However, in the *Tilbury* case, the Court of Appeal awarded compensation for interference with both ancient and modern lights (the latter not in themselves being a legal right) because it was foreseeable that interference with the ancient lights would also amount to interference with the modern lights. See also Lord Nicholls of Birkenhead in *Director of Buildings and Lands v Shun Fung Ltd* [1995] 2 AC 111, PC, at 126D.
3 *Clift v Welsh Office* [1998] 4 All ER 852, CA, at 858h. The parties had agreed the cost of repair, which had been paid and other physical damage which was not agreed was claimed as the effect on value; the measure of damage was not in issue in the Court of Appeal.
4 *Dodd Properties (Kent) Ltd v Canterbury City Council* [1980] 1 All ER 928.
5 Another example is *Hewett v Essex County Council* (1928) 138 LT 742, which arose out of the construction of a bridge which caused obstruction to a wharf; compensation was held to be recoverable for loss of value to the wharf but not for the cost of constructing a new wharf and other consequential losses. The assessment of value does not involve the same approach as for assessing the value of land compulsorily acquired which reflects its value to the owner: see the comments of Pill LJ in *Wildtree Hotels Ltd v Harrow London Borough* [1998] 3 All ER 638, CA, at 652B. As to remoteness, see *Wagstaff and BP Oil (UK) Ltd v Department of the Environment, Transport and the Regions* [1999] 2 EGLR 108, [1999] RVR 325 and *Moto Hospitality Ltd v Secretary of State for Transport* [2007] EWCA Civ 764.
6 *Wrotham Park Settled Estates v Hertsmere Borough Council* [1993] 2 EGLR 15, CA. But note that in *Eagle v Charing Cross Rly Co* (1867) LR 2 CP 638, it was held that, in estimating the amount of compensation for injuriously affecting ancient lights, the fact that, by reason of outside and accidental circumstances, the saleable value of the premises were not diminished is not to be taken into account.
7 *Senior v Metropolitan Rly Co* (1863) 2 H&C 258; *Eagle v Charing Cross Rly Co* (1867) LR 2 CP 638.

[141]

Measures taken by the acquiring authority to mitigate the claimant's loss are not to be taken into account. In *Joliffe v Exeter Corpn*[1], the acquiring authority built a new by-pass, which caused the road in which the claimant's filling station was located to become a cul-de-sac. The acquiring authority leased other land to the claimant on either side of the new by-pass and he set up a filling station there. The Court of Appeal held[2] that the fact that the authority had rented land to the claimant did not affect the claimant's entitlement to compensation, if there was any, although, on the facts of that case, there was held to be no entitlement to compensation.

1 [1967] 1 WLR 993, 18 P&CR 343, CA.
2 [1967] 1 WLR 993 at 997D, 18 P&CR 343 at 347.

[142]

It is not clear either from the LCCA 1845 or the CPA 1965, or the decided cases, at what date compensation should be assessed. Although interest runs from the date of the claim, this right was introduced in 1973[1] and does not assist in the interpretation of either the LCCA 1845 or the CPA 1965, neither of which provided for interest on compensation. Both the LCCA 1845, s 68 and the CPA 1965, s 10 refer to a claim for 'compensation in respect of land … which has been … injuriously affected by the execution of the works'. This suggests that the date of assessment should be the date on which the injurious affection occurs. In *Wildtree Hotels Ltd v London Borough of Harrow*[2], the parties had agreed that the valuation date should be the completion of the works, which may have provided a practical solution in the circumstances of that case. However, where the claim results from a single event, such as the closure of an access, it may be more appropriate to take the date on which that event occurs, even though that might be some time before completion of the works as a whole.

1 LCA 1973, s 63.
2 [1999] QB 634, [1998] 3 All ER 638, CA; on appeal [2000] 2 All ER 289, HL. Compensation was claimed (inter alia) for temporary loss while the works were in progress; had that element of the claim not been rejected by the Court of Appeal, it might have been difficult to apply the agreed valuation date. See the comments on this point of Ward LJ, who gave a dissenting judgment.

D Claims

[143]
Notice of claim should be given in writing, stating the exact nature of the interest in respect of which compensation is claimed, stating the amount and details of the compensation claimed, distinguishing between separate heads of claim and showing how the amount under each head is calculated[1]. Any question of disputed compensation is to be referred to the Upper Tribunal[2]. Although the LCCA 1845 and the CPA 1965 do not lay down any time limit for making a claim[3], particulars should be provided in sufficient time to enable the authority to make an offer; otherwise, if the matter is referred to the Upper Tribunal, the tribunal may order the claimant to bear the costs of proceedings[4]. In *Turner v Midland Rly Co*[5], it was held that recovery of compensation under the LCCA 1845, s 68 was subject to a limitation period of six years from the date of the award of compensation. However, in *Hillingdon London Borough Council v ARC Ltd*[6], the Court of Appeal, distinguishing *Turner*, held that a reference to the Lands Tribunal to determine the amount of compensation under the CPA 1965, s 11(3)[7] was an action to recover such a sum within the meaning of the Limitation Act 1980, s 9(1), which applies to 'any sum recoverable by virtue of any enactment', and, accordingly, that the limitation period of six years runs from the event giving rise to the claim for compensation. The same would appear to apply now to the LCCA 1845, s 68 and the CPA 1965, s 10[8].

1 Land Compensation Act 1961 (LCA 1961), s 4(1)(*b*), (2).
2 LCA 1961, s 1.
3 By the Lands Tribunal Act 1949, s 3(6)(*a*)(ii), rules may be made to regulate the proceedings before the Upper Tribunal and, in particular, the time within which any proceedings before the tribunal are to be instituted. However, the Tribunal (Lands Chamber) Rules 2010, SI 2010/2600 (as to which, see **Division H**), do not contain any provision which limits the time within which a reference must be made under the LCCA 1845, s 68 or the CPA 1965, s 10.
4 LCA 1961, s 4(1).
5 [1911] 1 KB 832, QBD.

6 [1999] Ch 139, CA upholding the decision of the Lands Tribunal at [1998] 1 WLR 174.
7 This provision entitles a person to compensation for damage caused by surveying and taking levels, and contains provision for disputes to be referred to the Upper Tribunal.
8 The Court of Appeal, in the *Hillingdon* case, agreed with the two grounds on which the Chancery Division had distinguished *Turner*, namely, because it had been based on a concession and was not therefore binding and because the wording of the statute of limitations then applicable was different: see [1997] 3 All ER 506, Ch D, at 512G–514C, and [1999] Ch 139, CA.

[144]
The normal rule for the assessment of compensation for compulsory purchase is that only one claim may be made:

> 'A person seeking to obtain compensation under these Acts of Parliament must once and for all make one claim for all damages which can reasonably be foreseen.'[1]

However, under the LCCA 1845, s 68 and the CPA 1965, s 10, where, following settlement of a claim, additional and unforeseen loss results from the execution of the works, it appears that further claims may be made[2]. A claim under the LCCA 1845, s 68 or the CPA 1965, s 10 may be assigned[3].

1 *Chamberlain v West End of London etc Rly* (1863) 2 B&S 617, per Erle CJ at 638. See also *Croft v London and North Western Rly* (1863) 3 B&S 436; *Mercer v Liverpool, St Helens etc Rly Co* [1904] AC 461; *Rockingham Sisters of Charity v R* [1922] 2 AC 315. See also **Division E**.
2 Support for this proposition can be found in *Lawrence v Great Northern Rly* (1851) 16 QB 643; *Lancashire and Yorkshire Rly Co v Evans* (1851) 15 Beav 322 and in *Re Ware and Regent's Canal Co* (1854) 23 LJ Ex 145. A different view was taken in *Re Brogden and Llynvi Valley Rly* (1860) 30 LJCP 61; *Stone v Yeovil Corpn* (1876) 2 CPD 99.
3 *Dawson v Great Northern and City Rly Co* [1905] 1 KB 260.

E Interest

[145]–[300]
Compensation under the LCCA 1845, s 68 and the CPA 1965, s 10 carries interest from the date of the claim until payment[1].

1 LCA 1973, s 63. The rate is that prescribed from time to time for the purposes of the LCA 1961, s 32, see **D[708]**.

Chapter 3

Compensation for the use of public works

Contents

A Introduction

[301]

Under the Land Compensation Act 1973 (LCA 1973), Pt I, compensation is payable by the 'responsible authority'[1] in certain circumstances where the value of the claimant's interest in land[2] has been depreciated by 'physical factors'[3] caused by the use of 'public works'[4] following either their construction or their alteration or a change in their use[5]. These provisions were enacted[6] in order to provide a right to compensation in circumstances where neither the Compulsory Purchase Act 1965 (CPA 1965), s 7[7] nor s 10[8] apply, and where no action in nuisance can be brought[9]. They apply to the Crown except any aerodrome occupied by a Government department[10].

1 See para **[322]**.
2 See para **[307]**.
3 See para **[303]**.
4 See para **[304]**.
5 LCA 1973, s 1. As to alteration or change of use of public works, see para **[305]**.
6 The right to compensation came into effect in relation to public works completed on or after 17 October 1969: LCA 1973, s 1(8).
7 Because s 7 only applies where land has been compulsorily acquired from the claimant; see **Division E**.
8 Because s 10 only applies to the execution of the works, and not their subsequent use; see **Division F, Chapter 2**.
9 Because the use of the works is immune from such action being authorised by statute, see para **[306]**.
10 LCA 1973, s 84(1).

B The right to compensation

[302]

The right to compensation[1] applies where:

(*a*) the value of the claimant's interest in land has been depreciated[2];
(*b*) the depreciation is caused by 'physical factors'[3];
(*c*) the physical factors are caused directly by the use of 'public works'[4];
(*d*) the use of the public works is immune from an action in nuisance[5];
(*e*) the claimant's interest qualifies[6];
(*f*) the claimant makes his claim at the correct time and in the correct manner[7]; and
(*g*) the compensation claimed exceeds £50[8].

These and other factors are explained in the paragraphs which follow.

1 LCA 1973, s 1.
2 As to the assessment of compensation, see para **[323]**.
3 As to 'physical factors', see para **[303]**.
4 As to 'public works', see para **[304]**.
5 As to immunity from actions, see para **[306]**.
6 As to the interests which qualify for compensation, see para **[307]**.
7 As to the time and procedure for claims, see para **[310]**.
8 LCA 1973, s 7.

C Physical factors

[303]

The physical factors are defined[1] as noise, vibration, smell, fumes, smoke, artificial lighting[2], and the discharge on to the land in respect of which the claim is made of any solid or liquid substance. The source of the physical factors must be situated on or in the public works, the use of which is alleged to be their cause, with the exception that, where the physical factors are caused by an aircraft arriving at or departing from an aerodrome, the aerodrome is to be treated as the cause of the physical factors, whether or not the aircraft is within the boundaries of the aerodrome[3].

1 LCA 1973, s 1(2).
2 *Blower v Suffolk County Council* (1994) 67 P&CR 228, Lands Tribunal.
3 LCA 1973, s 2(5). Compensation is not payable in respect of physical factors caused by accidents involving vehicles on a highway or involving aircraft: LCA 1973, s 1(7).

D Public works

[304]

'Public works' are defined[1] as:

(*a*) any highway[2];
(*b*) any aerodrome; and
(*c*) any works or land, other than a highway or aerodrome, provided or used in the exercise of statutory powers.

The depreciation of value must be caused directly by the use of the public works[3] and not, for example, by an increase in traffic on a side road, even if it is attributable to the public works[4]. The right to compensation is triggered by the commencement of use of the works, referred to as the 'relevant date'[5], which is defined, in the case of a highway, as the date on which it is first open to public traffic and, in the case of other public works, as the date on which they are first used after completion. The responsible authority[6] is required to keep a record and, on demand, furnish a statement in writing of the relevant date for the purposes of this Act[7].

1 LCA 1973, s 1(3). This applies to the Crown apart from aerodromes occupied by Government departments: LCA 1973, s 84(1).
2 As to the application of these provisions to a highway which has not always been a highway maintainable at the public expense, see LCA 1973, s 19(3). In *O'Connor and O'Connor v Wiltshire County Council* [2007] EWCA Civ 426, [2007] RVR 179, the Court of Appeal held that these provisions applied to a highway constructed by a consortium of developers pursuant to a s 106 agreement notwithstanding that the highway had not been formally adopted. Where a highway has been constructed in sections, the 'highway' for the purposes of claiming compensation is the section which causes the noise which founds the claim: *Price v Caerphilly County Borough Council* [2005] RVR 103.
3 *Barb and Barb v Secretary of State for Transport* [1978] RVR 182, Lands Tribunal; *Marchant v Secretary of State for Transport* [1979] RVR 113, Lands Tribunal; *Maile v West Sussex County Council* [1984] 1 EGLR 194, Lands Tribunal; *Dhenin v Department of Transport* (1990) 60 P&CR 349; *Hallows v Welsh Office* [1995] 1 EGLR 191, Lands Tribunal.
4 *Williamson v Cumbria County Council* (1994) 68 P&CR 367, Lands Tribunal; *Hickmott v Dorset County Council* (1975) 30 P&CR 237, Lands Tribunal; affd (1977) 35 P&CR 195, CA; *Shepherd v Lancashire County Council* (1976) 33 P&CR 296, Lands Tribunal; *Stuart and Stuart v British Airports Authority* [1983] RVR 161, Lands Tribunal.
5 LCA 1973, s 1(9).
6 See para **[322]**.
7 LCA 1973, s 15. With regard to an aerodrome, a certificate from the Secretary of State that runway or apron alterations have been carried out and the date of first use is conclusive evidence of these facts: LCA 1973, s 15(2). The issue of such a certificate may be open to challenge by judicial review: see *R v Secretary of State for the Environment, Transport and the Regions, ex p Plymouth City Airport Ltd* (2001) 82 P&CR 285, CA.

E Alterations to public works and changes of use

[305]
Compensation may also be claimed in relation to existing public works where[1]:

(*a*) in the case of a highway, a carriageway[2] has been altered after it has been open to traffic;
(*b*) in the case of other public works, the works have been reconstructed, extended or otherwise altered[3] after they have been first used; or
(*c*) in any case other than a highway or aerodrome, there has been a change in the use[4] of the works.

However, compensation is only payable in respect of depreciation of the value of the claimant's interest in land, in so far as such depreciation is attributable to the alteration or change of use[5].

1 LCA 1973, s 9(1).
2 The only alterations to the carriageway of a highway which qualify are where the location, width or level is altered (other than by resurfacing), or where an additional carriageway is provided: LCA 1973, 9(5). See *Broom and Broom v Department of Transport* [1993] RVR 218, Lands Tribunal.

3 In the case of an aerodrome, the only alterations which qualify are 'runway or apron alterations': LCA 1973, s 9(3). 'Runway and apron alterations' are defined in s 9(6) as: (*a*) construction of a new runway, major realignment of an existing runway, or the extension or strengthening of an existing runway, or (*b*) substantial addition to, or alteration of, a taxiway or apron whose only or main purpose is the provision of facilities for a greater number of aircraft. Where runway or apron alterations have been carried out in phases, it is a question of fact whether they are to be treated for the purposes of these provisions as one alteration or separate alterations: *Davies v Mid-Glamorgan County Council* [1979] 2 EGLR 158, 251 Estates Gazette 65, Lands Tribunal. In *R (on the application of Plymouth City Airport Ltd) v Secretary of State for Transport, Environment and the Regions (Thomas intervening)* [2001] EWCA Civ 144, 82 P&CR 265, it was held that s 9(6) was concerned with the purpose of the works and does not require proof that the number of aircraft using the airport has actually increased as a result of the works. As to the meaning of 'a greater number of aircraft', see *Brunt v Southampton International Airport Ltd* [2005] EWCA Civ 93, [2005] RVR 120, in which it was held that s 9(6) requires a numerical comparison between the number of aircraft for which facilities existed prior to the works and after the works, and the fact that an increase in a particular type of aircraft was not relevant.

4 For the avoidance of doubt, the LCA 1973, s 9(7) provides that this does not include intensification of an existing use.

5 LCA 1973, s 9(2) and (with regard to highways) (5) and see *Williamson v Cumbria County Council* (1994) 68 P&CR 367, Lands Tribunal.

F Immunity from action in nuisance

[306]

In respect of public works other than highways, compensation is not payable unless immunity from an action in nuisance is conferred on the use of the works by statute, expressly or by implication[1]. Where the nuisance arises from the use of a highway, statutory immunity from an action in nuisance is irrelevant. Where the responsible authority contends that it does not have statutory immunity from an action in nuisance in respect of works which are the subject of a claim, and no compensation is paid, then the authority cannot rely on a defence of statutory immunity in respect of the same matters in a subsequent action for nuisance[2].

1 LCA 1973, s 1(6). In the case of aircraft, the aerodrome must be immune from an action by virtue of the Civil Aviation Act 1982, s 77(2). There is immunity from an action in nuisance where the source of the nuisance is authorised by statute: *Hammersmith and City Rly Co v Brand* (1869) LR 4 HL 171. A detailed explanation of this principle is outside the scope of this work. In *Vickers v Dover DC* [1993] 1 EGLR 193, Lands Tribunal, a claim under the LCA 1973, Pt I was rejected because the statute which permitted the council to carry out the works could not be interpreted as authorising a nuisance, so the claimant's remedy was an action for tort.

2 LCA 1973, s 17.

G Interests qualifying for compensation

[307]

The claimant must have acquired his interest before the relevant date[1], that is, the date on which the public works were first used or, in the case of a highway, first open to traffic[2]. In addition, certain requirements must be satisfied as to the claimant's interest on the date of the claim, depending on whether the land is a dwelling or not.

1 LCA 1973, s 2(1). This does not apply, where the interest is 'acquired by inheritance' before the relevant date, if the deceased had acquired his interest before the relevant date: LCA 1973, s 11. As to legacies, intestate succession etc, see s 11. As to the 'relevant date', see para **[304]**.

2 An interest purchased before the relevant date qualifies, notwithstanding that it was purchased after the works had commenced and with knowledge of the works: *Fallows v Gateshead Metropolitan Council* (1993) 66 P&CR 460, Lands Tribunal. An interest acquired or disposed of, or a tenancy granted, pursuant to a contract is to be treated as acquired or disposed of or granted when the contract was made: LCA 1973, s 19(2).

1 Dwellings

[308]
In the case of a dwelling, the interest must be an 'owner's interest', defined[1] as the freehold or a tenancy of which not less than three years remain unexpired at the date of the claim. Where his interest entitles the claimant to occupy the land, the claimant must be occupying it as his residence[2]. There are special provisions in relation to tenants who are entitled to enfranchisement under the Leasehold Reform Act 1967, Pt I[3], or who are participating in collective enfranchisement or entitled to individual lease extension under the Leasehold Reform, Housing and Urban Development Act 1993, Pt I[4].

1 LCA 1973, s 2(2)(*a*), (4).
2 LCA 1973, s 2(2)(*b*).
3 LCA 1973, s 12.
4 LCA 1973, s 12A inserted by the Leasehold Reform, Housing and Urban Development Act 1993, s 187(1), Sch 21, para 5. By the Leasehold Reform, Housing and Urban Development Act 1993 (Commencement and Transitional Provisions No 1) Order 1993, SI 1993/2134, Sch 1, para 9, the LCA 1973, s 12A applies to claims where the relevant date falls before 1 November 1993. As to ecclesiastical property, see the LCA 1973, s 13.

2 Non-residential property

[309]
Where the claimant's land is not a dwelling, the claimant must be an 'owner-occupier'[1] and the land must either be an agricultural unit or have an annual value which is less than the 'prescribed amount'[2].

1 LCA 1973, s 2(3)(*a*). 'Owner-occupier' is defined by the LCA 1973, s 2(5), in relation to land in hereditament, as the person who occupies the whole or a substantial part in right of an owner's interest and, in relation to an agricultural unit, means a person who occupies the whole of that unit and who is entitled to an owner's interest in the whole or any part. As to 'owner's interest', see s 2(4).
2 LCA 1973, s 2(3), (5), (6): the 'prescribed amount' and other terms are imported from the blight provisions in the Town and Country Planning Act 1990 (TCPA 1990). Currently £18,000: Town and Country Planning (Blight Provisions) Order 1990, SI 1990/465.

H Claims

[310]–[320]
A claim cannot, in general, be made before the 'first claim day', which is defined[1] as the day next following the expiration of twelve months after the 'relevant date'[2]. The only exception is where the claimant has, during the 12 months between the relevant date and the first claim date, made a contract to dispose of his interest in the land or (if it is not a dwelling) to grant a tenancy of it; in such a case, the claimant may make a claim before the first claim date, provided he has not yet disposed of the interest or granted the tenancy[3]. Only

one claim can be made, in respect of the same land (or any part of it) and the same public works, except that, in relation to a dwelling, claims can be made in respect of the fee simple and a tenancy[4].

1 LCA 1973, s 3(2).
2 As to the 'relevant date', see para **[304]**. Where works have been carried out in phases, it is a question of fact as to whether they comprise one alteration or separate alterations for the purposes of these provisions: Davies v Mid-Glamorgan County Council [1979] 2 EGLR 158, 251 Estates Gazette 65, in which the Lands Tribunal held that runway and apron alterations at an airport carried out in three phases should be treated as a single scheme so a claim could be made after the third phases had been completed.
3 LCA 1973, s 3(3), but compensation is not payable before the first claim day.
4 LCA 1973, s 8(1); see *Bannocks v Secretary of State for Transport* [1995] RVR 57, Lands Tribunal.

[321]
Notice of the claim must be served on the responsible authority[1] and the notice must set out the particulars of the claim as specified in the LCA 1973, s 3(1)[2], otherwise the Upper Tribunal will not have jurisdiction to entertain the claim[3]. Where the land is jointly owned, all of the joint owners must make the claim[4]. The claim must be made within six years of the first claim date[5]. Where a claim has been made, the responsible authority is entitled to enter the land to survey and value it[6]. Claims may be made by mortgagees and trustees[7].

1 As to the 'responsible authority', see para **[322]**.
2 LCA 1973, s 3(1) requires the notice to contain particulars of the following:
(*a*) the land in respect of which the claim is made;
(*b*) the claimant's interest and the date on which, and the manner in which, it was acquired;
(*c*) the claimant's occupation of the land (except where the interest qualifies for compensation without occupation);
(*d*) any other interest in the land so far as known to the claimant;
(*e*) the public works to which the claim relates;
(*f*) the amount of compensation claimed; and
(*g*) the land contiguous or adjacent to the land in respect of which the claim is made, being land to which the claimant was entitled in the same capacity (within the meaning of s 6) on the relevant date.
3 *Fennessy v London City Airport Ltd* [1995] 2 EGLR 167, [1995] 31 EG 76, Lands Tribunal. In this case, the Lands Tribunal held that it had no jurisdiction to hear a claim where the particulars specified the claim as being for 'an amount in excess of £50 to be agreed'. The tribunal distinguished its earlier decision in *Litherland v Trafford Borough Council* [1993] RVR 29.
4 *Williams v British Gas Corpn* (1980) 41 P&CR 106, Lands Tribunal.
5 LCA 1973, s 19(2A). When the LCA 1973 was first enacted, claims had to be made within two years of the first claim date, but this was changed by the Local Government, Planning and Land Act 1980, s 112.
6 LCA 1973, s 3(4); any person who wilfully obstructs a person exercising this power is guilt of an offence.
7 LCA 1973, s 10(1), (4). The LCA 1973, s 10(2), (3) make provision for the treatment of compensation where the land is subject to a trust for sale or is settled land under the Settled Land Act 1925.

I Responsible authority

[322]
Compensation is payable by the 'responsible authority' which, in respect of a highway, is the appropriate highway authority and, in relation to other public works, is the person managing them[1]. This includes the Crown, except in relation to aerodromes occupied by Government departments[2].

1 LCA 1973, s 1(4).
2 LCA 1973, s 84(1).

J Assessment of compensation

[323]
In assessing the depreciation of the value of the claimant's interest, account has to be taken of the use of the public works, as it exists on the first claim day[1], and of any intensification which may then be reasonably expected of the use of those works[2]. Account is also to be taken of the benefit of any sound-proofing works carried out or available under various enactments[3]. The value of the claimant's interest must be assessed[4]:

(*a*) by reference to the nature of the interest[5] and the condition of the land as it subsisted on the date of service of the claim[6]; and
(*b*) in accordance with rr 2–4 of the Land Compensation Act 1961, s 5[7].

1 As to the 'first claim day', see para **[310]**.
2 LCA 1973, s 4(2).
3 LCA 1973, s 4(3). This applies where soundproofing works may be carried out, or grants paid, under the LCA 1973, ss 20, 23 and 27, the Airports Authority Act 1965, s 15, the Civil Aviation Act 1971, s 29A, the Civil Aviation Act 1982, s 79 or any corresponding local enactment or under a scheme operated by the manager of an aerodrome. See **Division F, Chapter 4**.
4 LCA 1973, s 4(4).
5 If the interest is subject to a mortgage or a contract of sale or a contract for the grant of tenancy, the interest must be valued as if it was not subject to such mortgage or contract: LCA 1973, s 4(4)(*c*).
6 LCA 1973, s 4(4)(*a*), which is subject to s 4(5), which relates to changes after the relevant date.
7 LCA 1973, s 4(4)(*b*): in short, open market value, but excluding certain factors. For an explanation of the rules provided by the Land Compensation Act 1961, s 5, see **Division E**. The LCA 1973, s 4(4)(*b*) is subject to the LCA 1973, s 5, which relates to assumptions as to planning permission.

[324]
Certain assumptions must be made as to planning permissions which would or would not be granted in respect of the claimant's land; the effect of these provisions is that, with limited exceptions, the value of the land is to be assessed on the basis of its existing use and existing buildings[1]. The limited exceptions are: first, in some circumstances, the assessment can take account of the rebuilding, maintenance, alteration and improvement of buildings[2]; and, second, the splitting of a single dwelling house into two or more separate dwelling houses may also be taken into account[3]. Any unimplemented planning permission is to be ignored[4].

1 LCA 1973, s 5.
2 LCA 1973, s 5(2)(*a*), incorporating the TCPA 1990, Sch 3, para 1, subject to the conditions in Sch 10 thereto.
3 LCA 1973, s 5(2)(*b*), incorporating the TCPA 1990, Sch 3, para 2. The exceptions in s 5(2)(*a*), (*b*) do not apply where an order has been made, under the TCPA 1990, s 102 or Sch 9, para 1, requiring the removal of any building or the discontinuance of any use on the land.
4 LCA 1973, s 5(4).

[325]
Any increase in the value of the claimant's interest in:

(*a*) the land to which the claim relates[1]; or

(*b*) other contiguous[2] or adjacent[3] land, to which he is entitled in the same capacity[4] on the relevant date[5],

which is attributable to the existence of or the use or prospective use of the public works is to be set off against his claim[6].

1 LCA 1973, ss 4, 5 do not apply to the assessment of the increase in value of this land.
2 'Contiguous' is not defined in this Act, but is usually interpreted as meaning 'touching': eg *Haynes v King* [1893] 3 Ch 439; *Spiller's Ltd v Cardiff Revenue Officer etc* [1931] 2 KB 21 at 43.
3 'Adjacent' is not defined in this Act, but is usually interpreted as meaning close to: eg *Wellington Corpn v Lower Hutt Corpn* [1904] AC 773, PC; *English Clays Lovering Pochin & Co Ltd v Davis (Valuation Officer)* [1966] RA 475, 12 RRC 307; *English Clays Lovering Pochin & Co Ltd v Plymouth Corpn* [1974] 2 All ER 239, CA.
4 'In the same capacity' means that the claimant must be entitled to both beneficially or to both as trustee of the same trust or to both as personal representative of one person: LCA 1973, s 6(5).
5 As to the 'relevant date', see para **[304]**.
6 LCA 1973, s 6.

[326]
Any question of disputed compensation is to be referred the Upper Tribunal[1]. In addition to compensation, the claimant is entitled to reasonable valuation or legal expenses in connection with the claim[2].

1 LCA 1973, s 16. As to the procedures in the Upper Tribunal, see **Division H**.
2 LCA 1973, s 3(5), without prejudice to the powers of the Upper Tribunal in respect of the costs of proceedings before the tribunal.

K Interest on compensation

[327]
Interest is payable from the date of service of the notice of claim or, if the notice of claim is served before the first claim day[1], the first claim day[2].

1 As to the first claim day, see para **[310]**.
2 LCA 1973, s 18. The rate of interest is that prescribed from time to time for the purposes of the LCA 1961, s 32, as to which, see **D[708]**.

L Effect of compulsory purchase of claimant's land

[328]–[470]
Compensation is not payable, in respect of the same depreciation, both under the LCA 1973, Pt I and any other enactment[1], and there are detailed provisions to prevent this[2]. Where land is compulsorily acquired[3] for the carrying out of public works (as defined for the purposes of the LCA 1973) and the claimant retains land which constitutes 'other land' for the purposes of the CPA 1965, s 7 (or the Lands Clauses Consolidation Act 1845 (LCCA 1845), s 63)[4], then no claim, in respect of that land, may be made under the LCA 1973, Pt I after the notice to treat has been served or, if the land is acquired by agreement, the date of the agreement[5]. However, this does not preclude the payment of compensation, which is assessed otherwise than under the LCA 1973, s 44, in respect of public works situated elsewhere than on the land acquired[6]. Where land is compulsorily acquired after a claim under the LCA

1973, Pt I has been made and the compensation for the acquisition has to be assessed without regard to the depreciation in value caused by the works, the compensation for the acquisition must be reduced by an amount equal to the compensation payable on the claim under the LCA 1973[7].

1 LCA 1973, s 8(7).
2 Ie the LCA 1973, s 8(1)–(6).
3 See the LCA 1973, s 8(3).
4 These provisions give rights to compensation where the compulsory acquisition of land injuriously affects other land held by the claimant; the term 'other land' has acquired a particular meaning through judicial decisions, see **Division E**.
5 LCA 1973, s 8(2). This provision assumes that compensation for compulsory purchase will include compensation for loss which would in the absence of the compulsory purchase have been recoverable under the LCA 1973, Pt I. Since s 8(2) has the effect of depriving the owner of a right to compensation under the LCA 1973, there are provisions for depositing the particulars of the land and the nature and extent of the works with the district or borough council and they will be registered as a local land charge under s 8(4), (4A).
6 LCA 1973, s 8(5). Under the CPA 1965, s 7 (and the LCCA 1845, s 63), compensation for injurious affection is only payable in relation to the use of works in so far as they are situated on the land taken from the claimant. The LCA 1973, s 44 was enacted to enable a claimant to obtain compensation under the CPA 1965, s 7 for the effects of the use of such works wherever situated, see **Division E**. The purpose of the LCA 1973, s 8(5) appears to be to preserve the right to compensation under the LCA 1973, Pt I where a claim can be made under the LCCA 1845, s 68 or the CPA 1965, s 10: as to which, see **Division F, Chapter 2**.
7 LCA 1973, s 8(6); if the acquisition extends to part only, an apportionment has to be made.

Chapter 4

Mitigation of the effects of public works

Contents

A Introduction

[471]

This chapter explains the statutory provisions which enable bodies responsible for public works to provide mitigation for their injurious effects. These provisions fall under the following heads, each of which is explained in the paragraphs which follow:

(*a*) soundproofing of buildings affected by noise caused by public works other than aerodromes[1];
(*b*) soundproofing of buildings affected by noise caused by aerodromes[2];
(*c*) payments in respect of caravans and other structures affected by noise caused by public works[3];
(*d*) acquisition of land for mitigating the adverse effects of public works[4];
(*e*) execution of works to mitigate the adverse effects of public works[5];
(*f*) payments for temporary accommodation for occupiers of dwellings during the carrying out of public works[6]; and
(*g*) in relation to highways, the acquisition of land, the execution of works and the making of agreements to mitigate their adverse effects[7].

These provisions were originally enacted in the Land Compensation Act 1973 (LCA 1973), Pt II, but those relating to highways were repealed and re-enacted in the Highways Act 1980 (HiA 1980). The meaning of 'public works', for the purposes of these provisions, is derived from the LCA 1973, Pt I[8], but with qualifications applicable to certain of these provisions, which are identified in the paragraphs which follow. The bodies which have powers and duties described in this chapter under the LCA 1973, Pt II, are referred to as 'responsible authorities', the meaning of which is also derived from the LCA 1973, Pt I[9], but is also applied, with qualifications, to the provisions referred to in this chapter, as identified in the paragraphs which follow; in relation to the powers under HiA 1980 described in this chapter, the bodies are highway authorities as defined in HiA 1980[10]. The LCA 1973, Pt II applies to the Crown[11].

1 See para **[472]**.
2 See para **[473]**.
3 See para **[480]**. The power to make regulations for this purpose has never been exercised.
4 The LCA 1973, s 1(3) defines 'public works' as any highway, any aerodrome and any other works or land provided or used in the exercise of statutory powers. This is applied with qualifications to ss 20, 20A, 26–28, see para **[481]**.
5 See para **[472]**.
6 See para **[473]**.
7 See paras **[474]–[479]**.
8 Ie the LCA 1973, s 1(3).
9 Defined in the LCA 1973, s 1(4) as, in relation to a highway, the highway authority or, in relation to other public works, the person managing the works.
10 HiA 1980, ss 1–3.
11 LCA 1973, s 84.

B Soundproofing of buildings affected by noise caused by public works other than aerodromes

[472]

The Secretary of State has power[1] to make regulations, by means of statutory instrument[2], which require or enable a responsible authority[3] to insulate buildings against noise caused or expected to be caused by the construction or use of public works[4] other than aerodromes[5], or to make grants in respect of the costs of such insulation. Such regulations may contain a range of ancillary provisions relating, for example, to the level of noise at which the power or duty is triggered, the classes of works or buildings to which the power or duty may arise, the nature of the works and the level of grants[6]. Two sets of regulations have been made under this section: the Noise Insulation Regulations 1975[7] and the Noise Insulation (Railways and Other Guided Transport Systems) Regulations 1996[8], which are explained separately as follows.

1 LCA 1973, s 20(1).
2 LCA 1973, s 20(8).
3 For the purposes of s 20, 'responsible authority' has the same meaning as in the LCA 1973, s 1(4) (ie the highway authority or the person managing the works) except that, in relation to a highway, the term includes any authority having power to make an order in respect of that highway under the Road Traffic Regulation Act 1984, ss 1 or 6: s 20(12). For the application of the LCA 1973 to the Crown, see s 84(1).
4 For the purposes of s 20, 'public works' has the same meaning as in the LCA 1973, s 1(3) (ie a highway or other works or land provided or used under statutory powers) except that it does not include an aerodrome: s 20(12).
5 Soundproofing of buildings affected by aerodromes was excluded from s 20 because it was originally dealt with separately by the LCA 1973, s 21. That provision was repealed by the Airports Authority Act 1975, Sch 6. As to the current provisions applicable to aerodromes, see para **[479]**.
6 See the LCA 1973, s 20(2)–(7).
7 SI 1975/1763, as amended by the Noise Insulation (Amendment) Regulations 1988, SI 1988/2000.
8 SI 1996/428.

1 The Noise Insulation Regulations 1975

[473]
These regulations[1] relate to noise from highways and contain:

(*a*) a duty to carry out or pay a grant towards insulation work;
(*b*) a power to carry out or pay a grant towards insulation work; and
(*c*) a power to carry out or pay a grant towards insulation against construction noise.

Each of these is outlined in the paragraphs which follow.

1 SI 1975/1763, as amended by SI 1988/2000. For a general explanation of the regulations, see DoE Circular 114/75.

Duty to carry out or pay a grant towards insulation work

[474]
The highway authority is under a duty[1] to carry out or pay a grant towards the cost of insulating eligible buildings, where a highway[2] has been constructed or an additional carriageway has been, or is to be, constructed and the use of the highway causes, or is expected to cause, noise 'at a level not less than the specified level'[3].

1 SI 1975/1763, reg 3(1), (3). As to eligible buildings, see para **[477]**.
2 This includes a highway which was not but has become maintainable at the public expense: reg 4(3).
3 This means that the relevant noise level (defined in reg 2(1) as the level of noise expressed as a level of L 10 (18 hour) measured one metre from the most exposed windows or doors) must be at least 1dB(A) above the prevailing noise level, not less than 68 dB(A) L10 (18 hour) and the traffic must make an effective contribution to the relevant noise level of at least 1dB(A): reg 3(2). As to the ascertainment of levels of noise, see reg 6, which refers to the technical memorandum 'Calculation of Road Traffic Noise' (1975), referred to as 'the 1975 Code', or, for schemes after 1 December 1987, the 1988 Code.

Power to carry out or pay grant towards insulation work

[475]
Where a highway[1] has been constructed or an additional carriageway constructed and the duty mentioned above has not arisen, or where a highway has been altered, if the use of the highway causes, or is expected to cause, noise 'at a level not less than the specified level'[2], the highway authority has power to carry out or pay grant towards insulating eligible buildings[3].

1 See para **[474]**, note 2.
2 See para **[474]**, note 3.
3 SI 1975/1763, reg 4(2). As to eligible buildings, see para **[477]**.

Power to carry out or pay grant towards insulation against construction noise

[476]
Where works to construct or alter a highway cause, or are expected to cause, noise which, in the opinion of the highway authority, seriously affects, or will

seriously affect, for a substantial period, the enjoyment of an 'eligible building'[1] adjacent to the construction site, in respect of which no duty or power as mentioned above has arisen, the highway authority has power to carry out or pay a grant towards the cost of insulation work[2].

1 As to eligible buildings, see para **[477]**.
2 SI 1975/1763, reg 5.

[477]
'Eligible buildings' comprise dwellings and other buildings used for residential purposes within 300 metres from the nearest point of the highway, but exclude any building first occupied after the relevant date[1], any part of a building in respect of which a grant has already been paid or is payable, or which is the subject of compulsory purchase, a closing order or certain other designations[2]. The amount of grant is equal to the actual cost of carrying out the work or the reasonable cost, whichever is the less[3]. Ancillary provisions deal with such matters as the nature and extent of the work to be undertaken[4], the conditions of carrying out the work or making a grant, and the offer and acceptance of insulation work or grants.

1 The 'relevant date' is the date when the highway or altered highway is first open to public traffic: reg 2(1).
2 SI 1975/1763, reg 7. See also reg 4(4).
3 SI 1975/1763, reg 11.
4 SI 1975/1763, reg 9, Sch 1.

2 The Noise Insulation (Railways and Other Guided Transport Systems) Regulations 1996

[478]
These regulations[1] apply where a railway, tramway or other guided transport system is provided or altered in the exercise of statutory powers. The regulations impose a duty[2] and create powers[3] with ancillary provisions, in very similar terms to those described above[4], in relation to highways.

1 SI 1996/428, as amended by SI 1998/1701, which added procedures for predicting noise levels generated by Eurostar and similar trains. The procedures are described in 'Calculation of Railway Noise 1995 (Supplement 1)', The Stationery Office (ISBN 0 11 551873 8).
2 SI 1996/428, reg 4.
3 SI 1996/428, reg 5.
4 Ie in paras **[473]–[477]**.

C Soundproofing of buildings affected by noise caused by aerodromes

[479]
The Secretary of State has power[1] to make[2] a scheme requiring the person managing an aerodrome to make grants towards the cost of insulating buildings from noise and vibration attributable to the aerodrome. Although no schemes have been made under this provision, schemes have been made under earlier legislation, in relation to Heathrow[3] and Gatwick[4] Airports, which have effect as if made under this provision[5].

1 Civil Aviation Act 1982, ss 79, 80.
2 By statutory instrument: Civil Aviation Act 1982, s 79(1).
3 Heathrow Airport–London Noise Insulation Grants (Schools) Scheme 1977, SI 1977/1319, amended by SI 1979/414. Heathrow Airport–London Noise Insulation Grants Scheme 1980, SI 1980/153, as amended by SI 1981/652.
4 Gatwick Airport–London Noise Insulation Grants Scheme 1980, SI 1980/154, as amended by SI 1981/653.
5 By virtue of the Interpretation Act 1978, s 17(2)(*b*).

D Payments in respect of caravans and other structures affected by noise caused by public works

[480]–[490]

The Secretary of State has power[1] to make regulations, by statutory instrument[2], which empower responsible authorities[3] to make payments in respect of dwellings which are not buildings[4] and which are, or are likely to be, affected by noise caused by the construction or use of public works[5]. Such regulations may only apply to a dwelling occupied as a person's only or main residence. The regulations may include a range of ancillary provisions[6]. Although inserted into the LCA 1973 in 1991, this power has never been exercised.

1 LCA 1973, s 20A, inserted by the Planning and Compensation Act 1991, s 70, Sch 15, para 5, with effect from 25 September 1991. No regulations have been made under this section.
2 LCA 1973, s 20A(3).
3 For the purposes of the LCA 1973, s 20A, 'responsible authority' has the same meaning as in the LCA 1973, s 1(4) (ie the person managing the works or the highway authority, which includes an authority having power to make an order under the Road Traffic Regulation Act 1984, ss 1 or 6): LCA 1973, s 20(12). See also s 84(1).
4 For example, caravans would fall within this provision.
5 For the purposes of s 20A, 'public works' has the same meaning as in the LCA 1973, s 1(3) (ie an aerodrome or other works or land provided or used under statutory powers) *except that* it does not include a highway or any works forming part of a statutory undertaking as defined in the Town and Country Planning Act 1990 (TCPA 1990), s 336(1): LCA 1973, ss 20(12), 20A(4).
6 LCA 1973, s 20A(2).

E Acquisition of land for mitigating the effect of public works

[491]

A responsible authority[1] has three distinct powers to acquire land for the purpose of mitigating the effects of public works. First, it has power[2] to acquire land by agreement in order to mitigate any adverse effect which the existence or use of any public works[3] has or will have on the surroundings of the works. Second, a responsible authority has power[4] to acquire by agreement land, the enjoyment of which is seriously affected either by the construction or alteration[5] of, or by the use[6] of, public works, where the vendor's interest is a 'qualifying interest'[7]. Third, a responsible authority[8], which proposes to carry out the construction or alteration of public works on 'blighted land'[9], has the power[10] to acquire land, the enjoyment of which will, in its opinion, be seriously affected by the carrying out or the use of the works, so long as the vendor's interest in that land is a 'qualifying interest'[11]. These powers only apply where the responsible authority has statutory powers to acquire land (whether compulsorily or by agreement), but would not, in the absence of the LCA 1973, s 26, have had power to acquire land for these purposes[12]. Where land has been acquired under the LCA 1973, s 26, the responsible authority has power to dispose of it[13].

1 For the purposes of the LCA 1973, s 26, 'responsible authority' has the same meaning as in the LCA 1973, s 1(4) (ie the highway authority or the person managing the works): LCA 1973, s 26(6).
2 LCA 1973, s 26(1).
3 For the purposes of the LCA 1973, s 26(1), 'public works' has the same meaning as in the LCA 1973, s 1(3) (ie an aerodrome or other works or land provided or used under statutory powers) *except that* it does not include a highway or any works forming part of a statutory undertaking as defined in the TCPA 1990, s 336(1): LCA 1973, s 26(6).
4 LCA 1973, s 26(1).
5 This only applies to works constructed or altered after 17 October 1972: LCA 1973, s 26(3), (4).
6 This only applies to works first used after 17 October 1971: LCA 1973, s 26(3).
7 'Qualifying interest' has the same meaning as in the TCPA 1990, s 149(2) (ie, in short, an owner-occupier of a hereditament having an annual value below a prescribed amount, or an owner-occupier of an agricultural unit).
8 For the purposes of the LCA 1973, s 26(2A), the responsible authority must also be the 'appropriate authority' within the meaning of the TCPA 1990, s 169(1) (ie, in short, the body likely to acquire the land): LCA 1973, s 26(6).
9 For the purposes of the LCA 1973, s 26(2A), 'blighted land' has the same meaning as in the TCPA 1990, s 149(1) (ie, in short, land affected by planning proposals of public authorities and other bodies): LCA 1973, s 26(2B).
10 LCA 1973, s 26(2A), inserted by the Planning and Compensation Act 1991, s 62. For a general explanation of this provision, see DoE Circular 15/91, paras 1–3.
11 See note 7.
12 LCA 1973, s 26(5).
13 LCA 1973, s 27(3)(*b*).

F Execution of works to mitigate the adverse effects of public works

[492]

A responsible authority[1] has power[2] to carry out works on land belonging to them or purchased under the LCA 1973, s 26, for the purpose of mitigating any adverse effect which the construction, alteration, existence or use of any public works[3] will have on their surroundings. This may include the planting of trees, the laying out of grassland or any other works[4]. A responsible authority also has power[5] to develop or redevelop any land belonging to them or acquired under the LCA 1973, s 26 for the purpose of improving the surroundings of public works.

1 For the purposes of the LCA 1973, s 27, 'responsible authority' has the same meaning as in the LCA 1973, s 1(4) (ie the highway authority or the person managing the works): LCA 1973, s 27(5). The LCA 1973, s 27 only applies to a responsible authority which is a body incorporated by or under any enactment, and only has effect to extend the powers of that body: LCA 1973, 27(4).
2 LCA 1973, s 27(1).
3 For the purposes of the LCA 1973, s 27, 'public works' has the same meaning as in the LCA 1973, s 1(3) (ie, an aerodrome or other works or land provided or used under statutory powers) *except that* it does not include a highway: LCA 1973, s 27(5).
4 LCA 1973, s 27(2).
5 LCA 1973, s 27(3).

G Power to pay expenses of persons moving temporarily during construction of works

[493]

A highway authority or, as the case may be, a responsible authority[1] has power[2] to pay reasonable expenses[3] incurred by the occupier of a dwelling for the purpose of providing suitable alternative residential accommodation for himself and his household for the whole or part of the duration of works comprising the construction or improvement of a highway, or the construction or alteration of other public works[4]. This applies where the dwelling is adjacent to the site on which the works are being carried out and where the carrying out of the works affects the enjoyment of the dwelling, and where continued occupation of the dwelling is not reasonably practicable.

1 For the purposes of the LCA 1973, s 28, 'responsible authority' has the same meaning as in the LCA 1973, s 1(4) (ie the highway authority or the person managing the works): LCA 1973, s 28(4).
2 LCA 1973, s 28(1), (2). An agreement for this purpose must be entered into before the expenses are incurred: LCA 1973, s 28(3).
3 The amount payable can relate only to expenses which exceed what the occupier would have incurred if the dwelling had continued to be occupied: LCA 1973, s 28(3).
4 For the purposes of the LCA 1973, s 28, 'public works' has the same meaning as in the LCA 1973, s 1(3): LCA 1973, s 28(4).

H Powers of highway authorities

[494]

A highway authority has three distinct powers[1] to acquire land in order to reduce the adverse effects of constructing or improving a highway. It also has power[2] to execute works for such purposes and, in addition, has power[3] to enter into agreements with landowners to restrict or regulate the use of land, for the purpose of mitigating the adverse effects of a highway. These provisions were originally enacted as the LCA 1973, ss 22–25, but were repealed and re-enacted in substantially the same terms in HiA 1980.

1 HiA 1980, s 246, see paras **[495]–[497]**. The power in s 248 to acquire land in advance of requirements does not apply to s 246.
2 HiA 1980, s 282, see para **[498]**.
3 HiA 1980, s 253, see para **[499]**.

1 Acquisition of land to mitigate the adverse effects of a highway

[495]

A highway authority has power[1] to acquire land, compulsorily or by agreement, for the purpose of mitigating the adverse effects which the existence or use of a highway constructed or improved by it[2] has or may have upon its surroundings. This power may only be exercised compulsorily if the acquisition is begun[3] before the date on which the highway (or improved highway, as the case may be) is first opened to traffic and the power to acquire by agreement may only be exercised if the acquisition is begun[4] within one year of the opening date[5]. The highway authority may also use this power to acquire land to exchange for a common, open space or allotments[6].

1 HiA 1980, s 246(1). As to compensation, see s 246(6).
2 See also s 246(7).
3 Ie the date of publication of notice: HiA 1980, s 246(4)(*a*).
4 Ie the date of the agreement: HiA 1980, s 246(4)(*b*).
5 HiA 1980, s 246(3).
6 HiA 1980, s 246(5).

2 Acquisition of land seriously affected by a highway

[496]
A highway authority has power[1] to acquire, by agreement (but not compulsorily), land which is seriously affected by the carrying out of works for the construction or improvement of a highway, or the use of a highway, if the vendor's interest is a 'qualifying interest'[2]. This power is only exercisable if the acquisition is begun before the highway is first opened to traffic or, where it is the use which causes the adverse effect, one year after the opening date[3].

1 HiA 1980, s 246(2).
2 'Qualifying interest' has the same meaning as in the TCPA 1990, s 149(2) (ie, in short, an owner-occupier of a hereditament having an annual value below the prescribed amount or an owner-occupier of an agricultural unit).
3 HiA 1980, s 246(3).

3 Acquisition of land which will be seriously affected by proposed highway works on blighted land

[497]
A highway authority has power[1] to acquire, by agreement, land, the enjoyment of which will be seriously affected by the construction of a highway or by its use, where the highway is proposed to be constructed on blighted land[2]. It has been held by the Court of Appeal that a highway authority must ask itself two separate questions: the first being whether, in its opinion, the enjoyment of the land would be seriously affected by the carrying out of the works or the use of the highway; and the second being whether (once the first criterion was met) it should exercise their discretion to acquire the land by agreement[3].

1 HiA 1980, s 246(2A), inserted by the Planning and Compensation Act 1991, s 62.
2 'Blighted land' has the same meaning as in the TCPA 1990, s 149(1) (ie, in short, land affected by planning proposals of public authorities and other bodies): HiA 1980, s 246(2B).
3 *R v Secretary of State for Transport, ex p Owen* [1995] RVR 117, CA.

4 Execution of works for mitigating adverse effects of highways

[498]
A highway authority has power[1] to execute works for mitigating any adverse effect which the construction, improvement, existence or use of a highway has or will have on its surroundings. Such works may be carried out on land belonging to it, land acquired under the HiA 1980, s 26, land for which it is the highway authority or any highway which it is authorised to construct or improve. Such works may include the planting of trees, the laying out of grasslands or any other works[2]. It may[3] also develop or redevelop any land

belonging to it or acquired under the HiA 1980, s 246, for the purpose of improving the surroundings of a highway in any manner it thinks desirable.

1 HiA 1980, s 282(1).
2 HiA 1980, s 282(2).
3 HiA 1980, s 282(3).

5 Agreements as to use of land near highways

[499]–[1000]
A highway authority has power[1] to enter into an agreement with any person having an interest in land adjoining, or in the vicinity of, a highway, for restricting or regulating its use temporarily or permanently for the purpose of mitigating any adverse effect which the construction, improvement, existence or use of a highway has or may have upon its surroundings. Such an agreement could include provision for the planting of trees or restricting the removal of trees[2]. It could also contain incidental and consequential provisions[3] and it would be binding upon persons deriving title from the parties[4].

1 HiA 1980, s 253(1). This provision is without prejudice to the TCPA 1990, s 106: HiA 1980, s 253(5).
2 HiA 1980, s 253(1).
3 HiA 1980, s 253(2).
4 HiA 1980, s 253(3). An agreement is a local land charge: s 253(4).

Division G

Compensation for decisions, controls and works

Contents

References in bold are to paragraph numbers.

Chapter 3 Compensation for decisions relating to mineral planning permissions

Chapter 4 Compensation for the exercise of powers under the Highways Act 1980

Chapter 5 Compensation for the exercise of powers relating to water supply, sewage disposal, land drainage, pollution control and public health

Chapter 6 Compensation under the legislation relating to the gas, electricity and telecommunications industry

Chapter 1

Introduction

Contents

A Introduction

[1]
This chapter explains the scope of **Division G** and provides a general introduction to its subject matter. This division draws together a large number of rights to compensation which arise, not as a result of compulsory purchase of land, but as a consequence of decisions or actions of bodies acting under statutory powers which affect the value or use of land. These rights fall broadly into two categories:

(*a*) where a body has power to take a decision which restricts the manner in which land may be used or developed, for example, where a planning permission is revoked or a building line designated; and
(*b*) where a body has power to enter onto land without acquiring it and to carry out works or place pipes, cables or apparatus there temporarily or permanently, or to carry out inspections or surveys[1].

The majority of the bodies which have these powers are local authorities or other public bodies, but the water and sewerage undertakers and the public utilities, now in the private sector, have powers which fall into category (*b*) above. We have endeavoured to gather the rights to compensation relating to the ownership or use of land contained in the legislation most frequently encountered, but we do not claim the division to be comprehensive. The legislation in relation to (for example) telecommunications, coal mining subsidence and oil exploration is not within the scope of this work. In addition to the circumstances in which rights to compensation arise, there are many circumstances in which local authorities and other bodies have power to take decisions which do not give rise to rights to compensation, notwithstanding that the decision can affect the value of land significantly, for example, the refusal of planning permission, the listing of buildings or the stopping up or diversion of highways[2].

1 Such rights are sometimes referred to as 'quasi easements', but the use of the term easement in *Halsbury's Laws* in relation to statutory powers to lay pipes and cables was criticised in the Court of Appeal: *Newcastle-under-Lyme Corp v Wolstanton Ltd* [1947] Ch 427, CA, per Morton LJ at 456, adopting remarks in the court below by Evershed J.

2 As to the implications of the Human Rights Act upon compensation law, see **Division A, Chapter 4**.

[2]

The rights to compensation described in this Division are grouped as follows:

Chapter 2: the town and country planning legislation (except in relation to mineral working);

Chapter 3: the town and country planning legislation relating to mineral working;

Chapter 4: the Highways Act 1980 (HiA 1980);

Chapter 5: the legislation relating to water supply, sewage disposal, land drainage, pollution control and public health;

Chapter 6: the legislation relating to the public utilities.

[3]

Throughout this division, the text describes each right to compensation in turn, the basis for the assessment of the compensation, the procedures for claiming it and for settling disputes, together with other ancillary provisions. This format has been adopted because the statutory provisions are specific to each right and differ widely. For example, in some cases, the time limit for making claims is specified, in other cases, it is not; in some cases, the form in which a claim should be made is prescribed, in other cases, it is not. In some cases, disputes are to be referred to the Upper Tribunal, in other cases, to arbitration, and, in a few cases, other means of determination are to be followed. Of particular significance is the variety of expressions used to describe the bases on which compensation is to be assessed. The format of the text is reflected in the headings which are used consistently; in the following paragraphs of this chapter, each of these headings is introduced generally.

B Rights to compensation

[4]

Each right to compensation stems from the exercise of a statutory power. Where a body has acted outside its powers or has acted negligently, then the remedy is an action for damages and not one of the rights to compensation described in this division[1]. This division identifies the right to compensation, but does not elaborate upon the powers the exercise of which give rise to the right, since this would be outside the scope of this work[2]. In the majority of cases, a claimant must have an interest in land, but, in some cases, occupation[3] is sufficient and, in other cases, it is sufficient merely to have suffered loss or damage[4]. In some cases, the meaning of an interest in land is expressly extended to include an interest in the minerals in on or under the land[5]. In some cases, express provision is made in relation to mortgagees[6]. In a few cases, a claim may be made in respect of damage to chattels[7].

1 *Imperial Gas, Light and Coke Co v Broadbent* (1859) 7 HL Cas 600; *Caledonian Rly Co v Colt* (1860) 3 Macq 833; *Uttley v Tordmorden Local Board of Health* (1874) 44 LJCP 19; *Colac Corpn v Summerfield* [1893] AC 187.
2 In most cases, a cross-reference to another work is provided.
3 Eg the Town and Country Planning Act 1990 (TCPA 1990), s 186(2), the HiA 1980, s 122(2) and the Water Resources Act 1991 (WRA 1991), Sch 9, para 1.
4 Eg the Water Industry Act 1991 (WIA 1991), Sch 12, para 1(2)(*b*).
5 Eg the TCPA 1990, s 107(1).
6 Eg the TCPA 1990, s 117(3).
7 Eg the TCPA 1990, s 325(6), the Ancient Monuments and Archaeological Areas Act 1979 (AMAAA 1979), s 46 and the HiA 1980, ss 292, 294(4).

C Assessment of compensation

[5]

In relation to each right, the statute provides the basis upon which compensation is to be assessed. The differences are remarkable and may be a potential source of confusion. The following words and phrases are used, sometimes alone, sometimes in conjunction with others:

(*a*) depreciation in the value of land;
(*b*) injurious affection;
(*c*) damage;
(*d*) loss;
(*e*) injury;
(*f*) disturbance;
(*g*) expenditure; and
(*h*) full compensation.

Each of the above words and phrases is commented upon in the paragraphs which follow. In addition, in certain circumstances, where a statutory undertaker is entitled to compensation, the undertaker may opt for the compensation to be assessed on a special basis[1]. In some cases, provision is made that the compensation is to be reduced on account of benefits to the claimant resulting from the same cause as the claim, such as an increase in the value of other land held by him[2]. In some cases, compensation is limited where the damage giving rise to the claim is attributable in whole or part to the default or negligence of the claimant[3]. In some cases, it is expressly provided that the damage in respect of which compensation may be claimed must be directly attributable to the exercise of the body's power[4]; in any event, the common law principles relating to remoteness of damage apply[5].

1 Eg the TCPA 1990, s 279.
2 Eg the WRA 1991, Sch 21, para 3(4) and the HiA 1980, s 307(6).
3 Eg the HiA 1980, ss 96(8), 283(4) and the Public Health Act 1936 (PHA 1936), s 278.
4 Eg the TCPA 1990, s 107(1) and the Planning (Listed Buildings and Conservation Areas) Act 1990 (P(LBCA)A 1990), s 28(1).
5 *Hobbs (Quarries) Ltd v Somerset County Council* (1975) 30 P&CR 286, Lands Tribunal.

1 Depreciation in the value of land

[6]
Several of the enactments expressly provide for compensation in respect of depreciation in the value of the claimant's interest in land attributable to the decision or action in question[1]. This is a relatively straightforward concept and the principles applicable will usually be similar to those described in the context of compensation for compulsory acquisition[2]. Indeed, in many cases where depreciation in the value of land is the basis of compensation, ancillary provisions expressly apply the rules in the Land Compensation Act 1961 (LCA 1961), s 5, which apply to compulsory acquisition of land[3]. In some cases, the statute identifies specific assumptions that must be made for valuation purposes[4].

1 Eg the TCPA 1990, ss 115(2), 250(1), the Planning (Hazardous Substances) Act 1990 (P(HS)A 1990), s 16(2), the WRA 1991, Sch 21, para 2(1), the HiA 1980, ss 28(1), 109(2), 110(4), 126(2).
2 See **Division E**.
3 Eg the TCPA 1990, s 117(1), the HiA 1980, s 307(3) or the WRA 1991, Sch 21, para 3(2). As to compensation in the context of compulsory purchase, see **Division E**.
4 Eg the TCPA 1990, s 107(4) and the AMAAA 1979, s 7(6).

2 Injurious affection

[7]
This term is used both in the context of compensation for compulsory purchase[1] and in the context of compensation for the effect of works where no land has been taken[2]; in both those contexts, it means the diminution in the value of land. It is similarly used in the context of several of the rights described in this division[3], especially under the HiA 1980. In certain cases, however, the phrase is used in the context of a person being injuriously affected[4].

1 Compulsory Purchase Act 1965 (CPA 1965), s 7, see **Division E**.
2 CPA 1965, s 10; see **Division F, Chapter 2** and see the comments of Lord Hoffmann in *Wildtree Hotels v Harrow London Borough Council* [2000] 3 All ER 1, HL, at 294D .
3 Eg the TCPA 1990, s 203 and model tree preservation order; the WRA 1991, Sch 9, paras 1, 2(2), 2(3), Sch 21, para 2(3); the WIA 1991, Sch 11, para 8(3), Sch 12, para 2(3); the HiA 1980, ss 73(9), 74(8), 79(11).
4 For example, the WRA 1991, Sch 9, paras 1, 2(1), which provide that a claim may be made by all owners and other persons interested in the land *and all other persons injuriously affected*; the measure of compensation may, nevertheless, be the effect on the value of the person's interest in land.

3 Damage

[8]
It has been said that the term 'damage' has more than one meaning and great care must be exercised in examining the context in which it appears[1]. This word is frequently used on its own[2] and as part of the phrase 'loss or damage', which is commented upon separately below. In the contexts in which it appears in the legislation covered in this division, damage normally means depreciation in the value of land[3] and this is often made clear by the express application of the rules in the LCA 1961, s 5[4]. However, in some

contexts, the term could be interpreted as the cost of repairing physical damage[5]. In certain cases, the damage is defined, for example, as damage due to disturbance[6], damage due to the execution of works[7], damage due to extinguishment of an access to a watercourse[8], damage due to being deprived of an interest in land[9] or anticipated future loss[10]. Unless the meaning of damage is clear from its context, it may be interpreted as having the same meaning as in the Land Clauses Consolidation Act 1845 (LCCA 1845), s 68 and the Compulsory Purchase Act 1965 (CPA 1965), s 10, in respect of which limitations upon the scope of the right to compensation, known as the 'McCarthy' Rules, have been held to apply[11].

1 *Swansea Corpn v Harpur* [1912] 3 KB 493, CA per Fletcher Moulton LJ at 505.
2 Eg the Reservoirs Act 1975, s 18(1)(*a*); the WRA 1991, Sch 21, para 4(1); the WIA 1991, Sch 12, paras 4(1), 5(1).
3 Eg the HiA 1980, ss 122(2), 307(3).
4 Eg the HiA 1980, s 307(3) which applies (inter alia) to, ss 231, 256(5), 288(2).
5 Eg the WIA 1991, Sch 12, para 5(1). See the comments of Lord Cranworth on the meaning of damage in the context of the Railways Clauses Consolidation Act 1845 in *Ricket v Metropolitan Rly Co* (1867) LR 2 HL 175, HL at 198 and of Fry LJ in *R v Poulter* (1867) 20 QBD 132, CA at 138.
6 HiA 1980, s 28(1).
7 HiA 1980, s 77(2).
8 HiA 1980, s 109(2).
9 HiA 1980, s 256(5).
10 Eg the WRA 1991, Sch 9, para 4(2).
11 See *Argyle Motors (Birkenhead) Ltd v Birkenhead Corpn* [1975] AC 99, HL. For compensation under the LCCA 1845, s 68, the CPA 1965, s 10 and the 'McCarthy' Rules, see **Division F, Chapter 2**.

4 Loss

[9]
This word is occasionally used on its own[1], but more often as part of the phrase 'loss or damage', which is commented upon below. When used on its own, it appears to include depreciation in the value of land[2].

1 Eg the HiA 1980, ss 79(12), 286(3).
2 Because the LCA 1961, s 5 is expressly applied in those cases.

5 Loss or damage

[10]–[20]
This phrase is frequently used to describe the basis of compensation[1]. It usually includes depreciation in the value of land, and this is sometimes expressly provided[2], and sometimes implied as a result of the express application of the rules in the LCA 1961, s 5[3], but not always[4]. Sometimes, depreciation in value is expressly excluded[5]. It may include disturbance and other loss not related to the value of land, such as loss of trade[6]. In some cases, specific provision is made as to a matter which is included[7], but sometimes matters are expressly excluded[8] and, in other cases, the phrase 'loss or damage' is used without more[9].

1 Eg the TCPA 1990, ss 107(1), 186(2), 204(2), and model tree preservation order. As to the meaning of loss and damage used separately, see above.

2 Eg the TCPA 1990, s 107(4) and the AMAAA 1979, s 7(6).
3 Eg the P(LBCA)A 1990, s 29(3) and the HiA 1980, s 28(1).
4 Eg the TCPA 1990, s 186(2).
5 Eg the LDA 1991, Sch 11, para 8(2).
6 TCPA 1990, s 107(1) and *Hobbs (Quarries) Ltd v Somerset County Council* (1975) 30 P&CR 286, Lands Tribunal.
7 Eg the P(LBCA)A 1990, s 29(3).
8 Eg the TCPA 1990, ss 171C, 330.
9 P(HS)A 1990, s 19, the WRA 1990, Sch 21, para 1(2)(*b*), the WIA 1991, Sch 12, paras 1(2)(*b*), 6(1).

6 Injury

[21]
This term is used on its own in a few statutory provisions[1]. The distinction between loss, damage and injury is not clear. In some contexts, damage and injury have been held to mean the same[2]. In some contexts, it may be limited to circumstances where there would have been a right of action in the absence of statutory powers[3]. The cases suggest that, when determining whether there has been any injury, it is necessary to take into account the overall net effect of the exercise of the powers on the person affected. Where the value of an interest in land has been affected, the Tribunal has approached this on a before and after valuation basis[4]. It has been held that there is no injury if the value of the land is not diminished by the exercise of the powers[5]. The cases also suggest that regard should be had to the exercise of the powers in the locality as a whole and not just as they directly affect an individual.

1 Eg the WRA 1991, Sch 21, para 5(1) and the LDA 1991, ss 14(5), 22(7), 29(5).
2 See the comments of Lord Cranworth on the meaning of damage in the context of the Railways Clauses Consolidation Act 1845 in *Ricket v Metropolitan Rly Co* (1867) LR 2 HL 175, HL, at 198 and of Fry LJ in *R v Poulter* (1867) 20 QBD 132, CA, at 138.
3 *Marriage v East Norfolk Rivers Catchment Board* [1949] 2 KB 456, KB and see the comments of the Lands Tribunal in *St John's College, Oxford v Thames Water Authority* [1990] 1 EGLR 229.
4 *Matthews v Environment Agency* [2002] 3 EGLR 168, Lands Tribunal; *Penty v GLC* [1982] 2 EGLR 196, Lands Tribunal; *Welsh National Water Development Authority (formerly Gwynedd River Authority) v Burgess* (1972) 24 P&CR 150, Lands Tribunal; (1974) 28 P&CR 378, CA. See also: *Stuckey v North Somerset Drainage Board* (1960) 11 P&CR 224, Lands Tribunal.
5 *Glazebrook v Gwynedd River Board* (1964) 15 P&CR 75, Lands Tribunal.

7 Disturbance

[22]
In a number of cases, disturbance is expressly included[1] and sometimes impliedly included[2]. Disturbance refers to circumstances where a person's occupation or use of land is disturbed or removed[3]. The principles of compensation for disturbance have been developed by the courts in the context of compulsory purchase[4]. Thus, where, in relation to a right to compensation described in this division, compensation is to be assessed for disturbance, reference should be made to the description of the principles in **Division E**. A claim for disturbance may include loss of profits.

1 Eg the TCPA 1990, s 115(2) and the Reservoirs Act 1975, s 18(1)(*b*).
2 TCPA 1990, s 107(1).
3 Eg the TCPA 1990, s 115(2), the P(HS)A 1990, s 16(2), the Reservoirs Act 1975, s 18(1)(*b*), the WRA 1991, Sch 21, para 2(2) and the WIA 1991, Sch 12, para 2(3).

4 See the LCA 1961, s 5, r 6 which preserves the pre-existing right to compensation for disturbance. As to compensation for disturbance in the context of compulsory purchase, see **Division E**.

8 Expenditure

[23]
In some contexts, an express right is given to claim for expenditure which:

(*a*) may have been incurred before the decision giving rise to compensation was made and is rendered abortive by the decision[1]; or
(*b*) may have been incurred in order to comply with the decision[2].

1 Eg the TCPA 1990, s 107(1), the P(LBCA)A 1990, s 28(2)(*a*) and the AMAAA 1979, s 9(1)(*a*).
2 Eg the TCPA 1990, ss 115(3), 223(1) and the P(HS)A 1990, s 16(3).

9 Full compensation

[24]
This phrase originated in the public health legislation[1] and has found its way into the legislation which was enacted when the water industry was privatised[2]. It is not clear that the word 'full' adds anything[3]. It has been held (in the context of the public health legislation) that compensation can only be recovered where a right of action would have been available if the cause of the claimant's loss had not been authorised by statute[4]. Such compensation extends to personal losses such as loss of profits.

1 PHA 1936, s 278, which re-enacted, in similar terms, the Public Health Act 1875, s 308.
2 Eg the WIA 1991, Sch 12, para 4(1), the WRA 1991, Sch 20, para 6(1) and the LDA 1991, s 14(5).
3 Although see *Taylor v North West Water* [1995] 1 EGLR 266 at 273.
4 See **Chapter 5**. For a wide ranging review of the terms "full compensation for any loss, injury or damage" in Scotland referring to a number of English cases including consideration of the relevance of the *'Pointe Gourde'* rule, see *Logan v Scottish Water* [2006] RVR 160, Court of Session on appeal from the Scottish Lands Tribunal.

D Procedure

[25]
In relation to each right, the procedures for making claims and resolving disputes are identified. The provisions are far from consistent across the range of statutes referred to; indeed, they are not even consistent within a single statute. For example, as mentioned above, in some cases, there are time limits for making claims, in other cases, there are none. In some cases, the form of claim is prescribed, whereas, in most cases, it is not. There is a variety of mechanisms for determining disputed claims. In some cases, the mechanism for quantifying the compensation is separate from the mechanism for establishing liability[1]. It has been held that a reference to the Lands Tribunal (whose jurisdiction is now exercised by the Upper Tribunal) to determine the amount of compensation was an action to recover a sum 'recoverable by virtue of any enactment' within the meaning of the Limitation Act 1980, s 9(1) and, accordingly, that the limitation period of six years runs from the event giving rise to the claim for compensation[2].

1 In the context of the PHA 1936, s 278 (and its predecessor), it has been held that the arbitrator's jurisdiction extends only to quantifying the compensation, but liability is a matter for the courts, see **Chapter 5**.

2 *Hillingdon London Borough Council v ARC Ltd* [1999] Ch 139, CA; affg [1998] 1 WLR 174; this was decided in the context of the CPA 1965, s 11, but the same would appear to apply to other forms of compensation. As to the jurisdiction of the Upper Tribunal, see **Division H**.

E Interest on compensation

[26]

Prior to 1991, there was no general right to interest[1], although it was expressly provided for in a few cases[2]. The Planning and Compensation Act 1991 (PCA 1991), s 80[3] introduced a right to interest on compensation payable under the provisions listed in Sch 18 (as amended). While this extended to many of the rights to compensation referred to in this Division, not all of them were included in Sch 18; the position has, therefore, been noted in relation to each right separately. The rate of interest is that prescribed from time to time for the purposes of the LCA 1961, s 32. The PCA 1991, Sch 18 contains provisions for payments on account of compensation and interest, and for the recovery of sums paid, if, in due course, it is agreed or determined that such sums were not payable. Where a matter has been referred to the Upper Tribunal on a reference by consent, the tribunal has a discretion to award interest on a simple or compound basis and from such date as it considers just in the circumstances of each case[4].

1 *Loromah Estates Ltd v Haringey London Borough* (1978) 38 P&CR 234, Lands Tribunal; *Knibb v National Coal Board* [1986] 2 EGLR 11, CA; *Hobbs (Quarries) Ltd v Somerset County Council* (1975) 30 P&CR 286, Lands Tribunal.

2 Eg the National Parks and Access to the Countryside Act 1949, s 72(5) and the Wildlife and Countryside Act 1981, s 30(7).

3 As to commencement, see the Planning and Compensation Act 1991 (Commencement No 1 and Transitional Provisions) Order 1991, SI 1991/2607, art 4, Sch 2, paras 24–25.

4 Arbitration Act 1996, s 49 applied by the Tribunal Procedure (Upper Tribunal) (Lands Chamber) Rules 2010, SI 2010/2600, r 30. Prior to the coming into force of those rules, the Lands Tribunal Rules 1996, SI 1996/1022, r 32 (inserted by SI 1997/1965) (now revoked) applied s 49 (and various other sections) of the Arbitration Act 1996 to all proceedings.

F Other provisions

[27]–[300]

In some cases, there are further ancillary provisions, concerning such matters as apportionment of compensation and recovery of compensation consequent upon events at a later date, which apply to some of the rights described in this division[1].

1 Eg the TCPA 1990, ss 109, 110.

Chapter 2

Compensation for planning decisions

Contents

A Introduction

[301]

This chapter explains the rights to compensation which arise in consequence of decisions and orders made under the legislation relating to town and country planning, except for those relating to mineral working, which are explained separately in **Chapter 3**. These chapters do not attempt to provide a full exposition of town and country planning law, and are confined to compensation issues. In addition to the rights described here, further rights existed prior to 16 November 1990, but were repealed by the Planning and Compensation Act 1991 (PCA 1991)[1].

1 PCA 1991, s 31. These repeals included compensation for restrictions on new development where there was an unexpended balance of development, compensation for decisions restricting development other than new development and compensation for refusal of consent to alter etc a listed building.

B Revocation and modification of planning permission

1 The right to compensation

[302]

A right to compensation arises where a planning permission is revoked or modified[1]. A person interested in the land[2] or in the minerals in, on or under it, who has suffered loss as a result of the revocation or modification is entitled to claim compensation from the local planning authority[3] who granted the planning permission, even where it was the Secretary of State who revoked or modified it[4]. It would appear that a claimant must have an interest in land at the time when the order, where it was made by the local planning authority, is confirmed or, in the case of an order made by the Secretary of State, at the time when the order was made. A claim may be made by a mortgagee of an interest, without prejudice to a claim by the person entitled to the interest[5], but compensation is not payable in respect of the interest of the mortgagee[6].

1 For the power of a local planning authority to revoke or modify a planning permission, see the Town and Country Planning Act 1990 (TCPA 1990), s 97; for the Secretary of State's power, see s 100. As to the application of these provisions to statutory undertakers, see the TCPA 1990, s 279(1)(*b*). This right to compensation also applies where the planning permission revoked or modified was granted by a discontinuance order under the TCPA 1990, s 102(2): TCPA 1990, ss 102(3), 107(5). Compensation in respect of revocation and modification of mineral planning permissions is explained separately in **Chapter 3** of this Division.

2 The phrase 'a person interested in the land' has no technical meaning and is not to be construed in the strict conveyancing sense; it includes a person with a contractual right to use the land: *Pennine Raceway Ltd v Kirklees Metropolitan Borough Council* [1983] QB 382, CA.

3 TCPA 1990, s 107(1).

4 TCPA 1990, s 1, Sch 1, para 16(1).

5 TCPA 1990, s 117(3)(*b*).

6 TCPA 1990, s 117(3)(*c*). The compensation must be paid to the mortgagee or the first mortgagee, as the case may be, who must apply it as if it were proceeds of sale: TCPA 1990, s 117(3)(*d*).

2 Assessment of compensation

[303]

Compensation is payable in respect of:

(*a*) expenditure incurred in carrying out work[1] which is rendered abortive by the revocation or modification, but this does not include work carried out before the planning permission was granted[2]; and

(*b*) any other loss or damage which is directly attributable to the revocation or modification[3]. This includes depreciation of the value of an interest in land, but does not include loss resulting from anything done or omitted to be done before the grant of the planning permission (other than the depreciation in value of land)[4].

1 TCPA 1990, s 107(1)(*a*) Expenditure incurred in the preparation of plans or upon other similar matters preparatory to the work is taken to be expenditure incurred in carrying out the work: TCPA 1990, s 107(2).

2 TCPA 1990, s 107(3)(*a*).

3 TCPA 1990, s 107(1)(*b*). As to the assessment of compensation when the planning permission revoked was subject to a time limit, see *Harrison v Gloucester County Council* (1954) 4 P&CR 99, Lands Tribunal. As to the phrase 'directly attributable', see *William Henry Bond, Holme Sand & Ballast and Hanson Quarry Products Ltd v Dorset County Council* [2010] UKUT 364.

4 TCPA 1990, s 107(3)(*b*). In *Loromah Estates Ltd v London Borough of Haringey* (1978) 38 P&CR 234, Lands Tribunal, the contention that compensation should include interest on money borrowed by a developer to purchase another property for development, pending payment of compensation, was rejected. Statutory undertakers are entitled to compensation assessed on a special basis: TCPA 1990, s 280(1)(*a*), see para **[421]**.

[304]

For the purposes of calculating compensation, in respect of depreciation of the value of an interest in land, it is to be assumed that planning permission would be granted for rebuilding and maintenance, improvement or alteration within certain limits and subject to conditions[1], and, where it relates to a building used as a single dwelling house at the material date, for its use as two or more dwelling houses[2]. The rules in the Land Compensation Act 1961 (LCA 1961), s 5 apply, subject to any necessary modifications[3]. If the interest is subject to a mortgage, compensation for depreciation in the value of the interest is to be assessed as if the interest were not subject to the mortgage[4]. Compensation for loss of business profits can be claimed under these provisions, so long as it is not too remote[5]. In *Hobbs (Quarries) Ltd v Somerset CC*[6], the Lands Tribunal awarded compensation for loss of profits which would have been made if the quarry had secured a contract (which, on the evidence, was found to be highly likely) to supply minerals for the construction of a motorway and rejected the local authority's contention that compensation should be limited to depreciation in the value of the land because that basis would only have compensated the claimants if there had been another quarry to purchase where they could have earned equal profits.

1 TCPA 1990, Sch 3, para 1, Sch 10: TCPA 1990, s 107(4)(*a*). In *Canterbury City Council v Colley* [1993] AC 401, [1993] 1 All ER 591, HL, it was held that this provision must be interpreted literally even though this eliminated the claim. In that case, planning permission had been granted for the rebuilding of a house which had been demolished; the planning permission was revoked leading to a claim for compensation. It was held that the compensation had to be assessed assuming planning permission for rebuilding, so that the value as a result of the order was higher than without it, with the result that no compensation was payable.

2 TCPA 1990, Sch 3, para 2: TCPA 1990, s 107(4)(*b*). The material date is 1 July 1948 or the date by reference to which the Schedule falls to be applied in a particular case (unless an enforcement notice has been served before that date): TCPA 1990, Sch 3, para 12.

3 TCPA 1990, s 117(1).These rules apply to the assessment of compensation for the compulsory acquisition of an interest in land; they are explained in **Division E**. A claim was held to be valid notwithstanding s 4 of the LCA 1961, s 5 (which excludes any value attributable to uses contrary to law or detrimental to health): *Bolton v North Dorset District Council* (1997) 74 P&CR 73, Lands Tribunal. In *William Henry Bond, Holme Sand & Ballast and Hanson Quarry Products Ltd v Dorset County Council* [2010] UKUT 364, LC, the Upper Tribunal decided on a preliminary issue that LCA 1961, s 9 did not apply to the assessment of compensation under TCPA 1990, s 107, and accordingly it was not possible to take into account the likelihood that the mineral operator's lease which was nearing termination would, in the absence of the order, have been renewed.

4 TCPA 1990, s 117(3)(*a*).

5 Examples of cases where claims were held to be too remote are *Halford v Oxfordshire County Council* (1952) 2 P&CR 358 and *Evans v Cheshire County Council* (1952) 3 P&CR 50.

6 (1975) 30 P&CR 286, Lands Tribunal. Another example of an award for loss of profits is *Pennine Raceway Ltd v Kirklees Metropolitan Borough Council* [1984] RVR 85, Lands Tribunal. See also *Pennine Raceway Ltd v Kirklees Metropolitan Borough Council* (1982) 42 P&CR 421, Lands

Tribunal; on appeal (1983) 45 P&CR 313, CA. In *Pennine Raceway Ltd v Kirklees Metropolitan Borough Council (No 2)* (1989) 58 P&CR 482, CA, it was held that compensation should be paid in full without deduction of tax, unless it was certain that the compensation would not be taxable in the hands of the claimant. Another example of a loss of profits claim is *Cawoods Aggregates (South Eastern) Ltd v Southwark London Borough* (1982) 264 Estates Gazette 1087, Lands Tribunal.

3 Procedure

[305]
A claim must be made[1] within 12 months from the date of the decision, in respect of which the claim is made, although the Secretary of State has power to extend the time for making the claim[2]. The claim must be in writing and served on the local planning authority by delivering it to their offices or by sending it by prepaid post[3]. Any question of disputed compensation is to be referred to the Upper Tribunal[4]; the LCA 1961, ss 2 and 4 then apply, subject to any necessary modifications[5].

1 A claim is 'made' when it is received: *Camden London Borough v ADC Estates Ltd* (1990) 61 P&CR 48, CA.
2 Town and Country Planning General Regulations 1992, SI 1992/1492, reg 12(1). There is no particular form for the claim, so long as it is an unequivocal claim and not merely an intention to make a claim: *Texas Homecare Ltd v Lewes District Council* (1986) 51 P&CR 205, Lands Tribunal.
3 Town and Country Planning General Regulations 1992, SI 1992/1492, reg 12(2).
4 TCPA 1990, s 118(1). As to references to the Upper Tribunal, see **Division H**.
5 TCPA 1990, s 118(2). As to the LCA 1961, ss 2, 4, see **Division H**.

4 Interest on compensation

[306]
Interest is payable on compensation due, from the date of the order, except in relation to revocation or modification orders made before 25 September 1991[1].

1 PCA 1991, s 80, Sch 18, see para **[26]**.

5 Apportionment and registration of compensation

[307]
Where compensation in excess of £20 becomes payable and it appears to them to be practicable to do so, the local planning authority must apportion the compensation between parts of the land and give particulars of the apportionment to the claimant and to other persons interested in the land[1]. Regulations may be made[2] providing for a right to refer any question of disputed apportionment to the Upper Tribunal[3], but no such regulations have been made. The local planning authority is required to give notice that compensation has become payable to the Secretary of State, together with details of any apportionment, and the Secretary of State must give notice to the council of the district or borough[4]. Such a notice is a local land charge and must be registered[5].

1 TCPA 1990, s 109(1), (2).
2 TCPA 1990, s 109(3).
3 As to the jurisdiction of the Upper Tribunal, see the TCPA 1990, s 109(4), (5).
4 TCPA 1990, s 110(1)–(3), (5).
5 TCPA 1990, s 110(4).

6 Recovery of compensation on subsequent development

[308]
Compensation which has been paid, in respect of the revocation or modification of a planning permission, can later be recovered before any development of a residential, commercial or industrial character or the winning or working or minerals is carried out on the same land. The carrying out of such development is prohibited until the recoverable amount has been repaid or secured to the satisfaction of the Secretary of State[1], unless, in the opinion of the Secretary of State, having regard to the probable value of the development, it is not reasonable that any amount be recovered[2]. Where the development would be on land identical with, or includes the whole of, the land comprised in the notice, the amount which may be recovered is the whole of the compensation paid and, where the development would be on part only of that land, an apportionment must be made[3]. The Secretary of State may 'remit'[4] all or part of the amount recoverable, where he is satisfied that, having regard to the probable value of any proper development of the land, no such development is likely to be carried out, unless he does so[5].

1 TCPA 1990, 111(1). This does not apply to development authorised by a modified planning permission: TCPA 1990, s 111(4). Nor does it apply to the types of development specified in the TCPA 1990, Sch 3, paras 1 (subject to Sch 10), 2: TCPA 1990, s 111(5).
2 TCPA 1990, s 111(3).
3 TCPA 1990, s 112(1). For various ancillary provisions, see the TCPA 1990, s 112(4)–(13).
4 Presumably, this means 'cancel'.
5 TCPA 1990, s 112(2), (3).

C Withdrawal of planning permission granted by a development order

1 The right to compensation

[309]
A right to compensation arises where planning permission granted by a development order is withdrawn and an application for planning permission for development formerly permitted by the order is refused or granted, subject to conditions different from those in the order[1]. Such withdrawal of planning permission may occur, either if the order is repealed or modified[2], or where a local planning authority or the Secretary of State exercise their power to issue a direction under the Town and Country Planning (General Permitted Development) Order 1995[3], art 4 withdrawing permitted development rights granted under art 3. Where an art 4 direction is made by the local planning authority, but is not confirmed by the Secretary of State, a claim may be made in respect of the period during which the direction had the effect of preventing development[4].

1 TCPA 1990, s 108(1). As to the nature of the planning application which can trigger the right to compensation, see *Strandmill Ltd v Epping Forest District Council* [1992] 2 PLR 154, Lands Tribunal.
2 Where the order is repealed or modified, the right to compensation arises only if the application for planning permission is made within 12 months of the date on which the permission granted by the order is withdrawn: TCPA 1990, s 108(2).
3 SI 1995/418.
4 *Bolton v North Dorset District Council* (1997) 74 P&CR 73, Lands Tribunal.

2 Assessment, procedure and ancillary provisions

[310]–[320]
In such cases, the provisions described above[1] relating to the assessment of compensation[2], procedure, interest[3], apportionment and subsequent recovery of compensation for revocation or modification of a planning permission granted by the order, apply as if the planning permission had been granted by the local planning authority and had subsequently been revoked by an order under the TCPA 1990, s 97[4]. Where an art 4 direction is made by a local planning authority, but then is not confirmed by the Secretary of State, the date for assessing compensation is the date of the Secretary of State's decision not to confirm the order[5].

1 See paras **[303]–[308]**.
2 For examples of compensation under these provisions, see *Slot v Guilford Borough Council* [1993] 1 EGLR 213; *Pennine Raceway Ltd v Kirklees Metropolitan Borough Council* [1984] RVR 85, Lands Tribunal. Where land had been divided into 15 fenced plots, it was held that it should be valued as such: *Carter v Windsor and Maidenhead Royal Borough Council* (1988) 57 P&CR 480.
3 Interest runs from the date of refusal of planning permission or the grant, subject to conditions. See also para **[306]**.
4 TCPA 1990, s 108(1). For an example, see *Jones v Stockport Metropolitan Borough Council* (1983) 45 P&CR 419, Lands Tribunal.
5 *Bolton v North Dorset District Council* (1997) 74 P&CR 73, Lands Tribunal.

D Discontinuance orders

1 The right to compensation

[321]
A right to compensation arises where a local planning authority makes an order[1] which:

(*a*) requires any use of land to be discontinued;
(*b*) imposes conditions on the continuation of a use; or
(*c*) requires any buildings or works on land to be altered or removed.

A claim may be made against the local planning authority by any person who has suffered damage of the type described in the next paragraph in consequence of such an order[2]. A claim may be made by a mortgagee of an interest without prejudice to a claim by the person entitled to the interest[3], but compensation is not payable in respect of the interest of the mortgagee[4].

1 Under the TCPA 1990, s 102. The right to compensation for discontinuance orders in respect of minerals and waste are explained separately below: see **Division G, Chapter 3**.
2 TCPA 1990, s 115(1).

3 TCPA 1990, s 117(3)(*b*).
4 TCPA 1990, s 117(3)(*c*). The compensation must be paid to the mortgagee or the first mortgagee, as the case may be, who must apply it as if it were proceeds of sale: TCPA 1990, s 117(3)(*d*).

2 Assessment of compensation

[322]
Compensation is payable in respect of damage in consequence of the order by[1]:

(*a*) depreciation of the value of an interest in the land or minerals in, on or under the land[2]; or
(*b*) disturbance[3] in the enjoyment of the land or minerals.

In addition, any person who carries out works in compliance with the order is entitled to recover compensation for any expenses he has reasonably incurred in so doing[4]. The rules in the LCA 1961, s 5 apply to the assessment of depreciation in the value of land or minerals with any necessary modifications[5]. It is not clear whether, in order to make a claim for disturbance in this context, the claimant must have an interest in land. The amount of compensation is to be reduced by the value to the claimant of any timber, apparatus or other materials removed for the purpose of complying with the order[6]. If the interest is subject to mortgage compensation is to be assessed as if the interest were not subject to the mortgage[7]. Statutory undertakers are entitled to compensation assessed on a special basis[8]. The date for the assessment of the compensation is the date of confirmation of the order[9].

1 TCPA 1990, s 115(2).
2 In assessing compensation, it is legitimate to take into account risks which would affect a purchaser's mind as to the extent of existing user rights: *Blow v Norfolk County Council* [1966] 3 All ER 579, CA. For an example of the effect of conditions on a planning permission where a use was the subject of a discontinuance order, see *Williamson v Mid Suffolk District Council* [2006] RVR 210, Lands Tribunal.
3 As to compensation for disturbance in the context of a compulsory purchase, see **Division E**.
4 TCPA 1990, s 115(3).
5 TCPA 1990, s 117(1). As to the LCA 1961, s 5, see **Division E**.
6 TCPA 1990, s 115(4).
7 TCPA 1990, s 117(3)(*a*).
8 TCPA 1990, s 280(1)(*b*). See para **[421]**.
9 *K & B Metals v Birmingham City Council* (1976) 33 P&CR 135, Lands Tribunal.

3 Procedure

[323]
A claim must be made[1] within 12 months from the date of the decision, in respect of which the claim is made, although the Secretary of State has power to extend the time for making a claim[2]. The claim must be in writing and served on the local planning authority by delivering it to their offices or by sending it by prepaid post[3]. Any question of disputed compensation is to be determined by the Upper Tribunal[4]; the Land Compensation Act 1961 (LCA 1961), ss 2 and 4 then apply, subject to any necessary modifications[5].

1 A claim is 'made' when it is received: *Camden London Borough Council v ADC Estates Ltd* (1990) 61 P&CR 48, CA.

2 Town and Country Planning General Regulations 1992, SI 1992/1492, reg 12.
3 TCPA 1990, s 115(2) and the Town and Country Planning General Regulations 1992, SI 1992/1492, reg 12. There is no particular form for the claim, so long as it is an unequivocal claim and not merely an intention to make a claim: *Texas Homecare Ltd v Lewes District Council* (1985) 51 P&CR 205, Lands Tribunal. See also *International Ferry Traders Ltd v Adur District Council* [2004] EWCA Civ 288, [2004] RVR 65.
4 TCPA 1990, s 118(1). As to the application of the Limitation Act 1980, see *Hillingdon London Borough Council v ARC Ltd* [1999] Ch 139, CA. As to references to the Upper Tribunal, see **Division H**.
5 TCPA 1990, s 118(2). As to the LCA 1961, ss 2, 4, see **Division H**.

4 Interest on compensation

[324]
Interest is payable on compensation due, from the date on which the damage is suffered or the expenses are incurred[1].

1 PCA 1991, s 80, Sch 18, see para **[26]**.

E Purchase notices

1 The right to compensation

[325]
Where a purchase notice[1], which has been duly served, is either accepted or confirmed[2], compensation is assessed as if the land had been compulsorily acquired[3]; compensation for compulsory purchase is explained in **Division E**. A right to compensation also arises where a purchase notice is not confirmed, but the Secretary of State directs[4] that planning permission be granted[5]. A claim may be made against the local planning authority by a person entitled to an interest in the land in respect of which the purchase notice was served[6].

1 In certain circumstances, a person may serve a 'purchase notice' requiring a local planning authority to purchase his interest in land on the ground that it is incapable of reasonably beneficial use. As to service, acceptance, confirmation and the effect of purchase notices, see **Division B, Chapter 4**.
2 As to service and confirmation of purchase notices, see **Division B, Chapter 4**.
3 Where compensation is payable following a revocation or modification order in respect of expenditure incurred in carrying out works, compensation payable in respect of the purchase notice must be reduced by that amount: TCPA 1990, s 144(1).
4 Under the TCPA 1990, s 141(3).
5 Under the TCPA 1990, s 144(2).
6 TCPA 1990, s 144(2).

2 Procedure

[325.1]
Where compensation is claimed following acceptance or confirmation of a purchase notice, the procedure for pursuing a claim is the same as that for compensation in consequence of compulsory purchase: see **Divisions D and E**. Where compensation is claimed in consequence of a decision by the

Secretary of State under TCPA 1990, s 144(2) to grant planning permission, the claims procedure is the same as that described in para **[323]** above.

3 Assessment of compensation

[326]–[327]
Where compensation is claimed following acceptance or confirmation of a purchase notice, compensation is assessed on the basis applicable if the land had been acquired compulsorily: see Division E. Where compensation falls to be assessed in consequence of a decision by the Secretary of State under TCPA 1990, s 144(2) to grant planning permission, the measure of compensation is the difference between the value of the land with the benefit only of the permission which the Secretary of State has directed should be granted[1] and its value on the assumption that planning permission would be granted for development within TCPA 1990, Sch 3[2].

1 Referred to as its 'permitted development value': TCPA 1990, s 144(6).
2 TCPA 1990, s 144(2). Its 'Sch 3 value': the value of the interest calculated on the assumption that planning permission would be granted for development as described in s 144(6).

F Stop notices

1 The right to compensation

[328]
A right to compensation arises in certain circumstances where a stop notice has been served. A stop notice may be served in conjunction with an enforcement notice; this procedure enables a local planning authority to require that the activity specified in the stop notice should cease prior to the expiry of the time for compliance with the enforcement notice. Compensation may be payable in respect of a prohibition contained in a stop notice where[1]:

(*a*) the enforcement notice is quashed;
(*b*) the enforcement notice is varied in such a way that the activity which is the subject of the stop notice ceases to be prohibited;
(*c*) the enforcement notice is withdrawn otherwise than in consequence of the grant of planning permission; or
(*d*) the stop notice is withdrawn,

except where the enforcement notice has been quashed or varied because an appeal against it has succeeded solely on the ground that planning permission ought to be granted. Compensation is not payable if the activity prohibited by the stop notice constitutes or contributes to a breach of planning control at any time when the stop notice is in force[2]. A claim may be made against the local planning authority by a person who has an interest in the land or occupies it when the notice is first served[3].

1 TCPA 1990, s 186(1).
2 TCPA 1990, s 186(5)(*a*).
3 TCPA 1990, s 186(2). *International Ferry Traders Ltd v Adur District Council* [2004] EWCA Civ 288, [2004] RVR 65, CA.

2 Assessment of compensation

[329]

Compensation is payable in respect of any loss or damage directly attributable[1] to the prohibition contained in the stop notice[2]. The claim may include any loss or damage suffered as a result of breach of contract caused by the taking of action necessary to comply with the prohibition[3]. The compensation cannot include any amount in respect of loss or damage which could have been avoided if the person had provided information required by the local planning authority[4] or otherwise co-operated with the local planning authority when responding to the notice[5]. Compensation cannot include any amount attributable to the claimant's impecuniosity[6].

1 This is not qualified by the concept of reasonable foreseeability: see *J Sample (Warkworth) Ltd v Alnwick District Council* (1984) 48 P&CR 474, Lands Tribunal.
2 TCPA 1990, s 186(2). An example of such a claim is *Robert Barnes & Co Ltd v Malvern Hills District Council* [1985] 1 EGLR 189, Lands Tribunal.
3 TCPA 1990, s 186(4).
4 Ie under the TCPA 1990, ss 171C, 330 or under the Local Government (Miscellaneous Provisions) Act 1976, s 16: TCPA 1990, s 186(5)(*b*).
5 TCPA 1990, s 186(5)(*b*).
6 *Graysmark v South Hams District Council* [1989] 1 EGLR 191, CA.

3 Procedure

[330]–[340]

A claim must be made[1] within 12 months from the date of the decision[2] in respect of which the claim is made, although the Secretary of State has power to extend the time for making the claim[3]. It must be in writing and served on the local planning authority by delivering it to their offices or by sending it by prepaid post[4]. Any question of disputed compensation is to be determined by the Upper Tribunal[5]; the LCA 1961, ss 2 and 4 will then apply[6].

1 A claim is 'made' when it is received: *Camden London Borough v ADC Estates Ltd* (1990) 61 P&CR 48, CA.
2 The 'date of the decision' is the phrase used in, reg 12(2) of SI 1992/1492; in relation to compensation for a stop notice, it must refer to the decision to quash, vary or withdraw the enforcement notice: see *R v Secretary of State for the Environment, ex p Hillingdon London Borough Council* (1992) 64 P&CR 105, QBD.
3 Town and Country Planning General Regulations 1992, SI 1992/1492, reg 12. There is no power to extend the time if the application for the extension is made after the expiry of the six months: *R v Secretary of State for the Environment, ex p Hillingdon London Borough Council* (1992) 64 P&CR 105, QBD.
4 Town and Country Planning General Regulations 1992, SI 1992/1492, reg 12. There is no particular form for the claim, so long as it is an unequivocal claim and not merely an intention to make a claim: *Texas Homecare Ltd v Lewes District Council* (1985) 51 P&CR 205, Lands Tribunal. See also *International Ferry Traders Ltd v Adur District Council* [2004] EWCA Civ 288, [2004] RVR 65.
5 TCPA 1990, s 186(6); this is subject to any regulations which provide otherwise, but none have been made. For references to the Upper Tribunal, see **Division H**.
6 TCPA 1990, s 186(7). As to the LCA 1961, ss 2, 4, see **Division H**.

4 Interest on compensation

[341]

Interest is payable on compensation due, from the date of the stop notice[1].

1 PCA 1991, s 80, Sch 18, see para **[26]**.

G Tree preservation orders

1 Introduction

[342]
Tree preservation orders give rise to two separate rights to compensation:

(*a*) where any consent required by a tree preservation order is refused or granted, subject to conditions; and
(*b*) where a direction is made requiring the replanting of trees which have been felled.

These are explained separately as follows.

Compensation for the refusal of consent or the grant of consent, subject to conditions, under a tree preservation order

The right to compensation

[343]
A right to compensation may arise where any consent required by a tree preservation order is refused[1], or where consent is granted subject to conditions. This right to compensation is not provided for in the statute itself, but in each tree preservation order[2]. Regulations set out a model order[3]; these paragraphs describe the right provided under the model order. An order must be in the same form as the model order or in a form substantially to the same effect[4].

1 Where the local planning authority has failed to make a decision, there is a deemed refusal which triggers the right to claim compensation: *Duncan and Prudential Assurance Co Ltd v Epping Forest District Council* [2004] RVR 213, Lands Tribunal.
2 TCPA 1990, s 203.
3 Town and Country Planning (Trees) Regulations 1999, SI 1999/1892 (as amended by SI 2001/1149), reg 2, Schedule. Article 4 of the model order deals with the grant and refusal of consent, and art 9 provides for compensation.
4 Town and Country Planning (Trees) Regulations 1999, reg 2.

Assessment of compensation

[344]–[345]
Compensation is payable in respect of any loss or damage in consequence of a refusal of consent or imposition of a condition[1]. This has been held to include:

(*a*) the depreciation in the value of the claimant's land[2];
(*b*) the costs of remedial works to property damaged by a tree where consent to fell had been refused[3];
(*c*) the costs of investigations carried out in order to ascertain the risks posed by a tree where consent for its felling had been refused[4];
(*d*) costs incurred by the claimant as a result of a condition imposed on the grant of consent, which required the use of an approved contractor[5];

(*e*) interest charges and professional fees incurred where a developer was required to stop work on development in order to obtain consents required under the order[6]; and
(*f*) the costs of pursuing an appeal against the refusal of consent[7].

1 The test is whether the loss was such as may fairly and reasonably be considered to arise naturally: *Factorset Ltd v Selby District Council* [1995] 2 PLR 11. For a discussion of the relevant principles, see *Cardigan Timber Co v Cardiganshire County Council* (1957) 9 P&CR 158, Lands Tribunal.
2 *Bell v Canterbury City Council* (1988) 56 P&CR 211, CA.
3 *Buckle v Holderness Borough Council* (1996) 71 P&CR 428, Lands Tribunal.
4 *Fletcher v Chelmsford Borough Council* (1992) 63 P&CR 312, Lands Tribunal. The claimant had commissioned a report into the effects of a protected tree on the foundations of his house.
5 *Deane v Bromley Borough Council* (1992) 63 P&CR 308, Lands Tribunal. The condition required pruning to be carried out by an approved contractor and the claimant was able to show that he could have done the work more cheaply himself.
6 *Factorset Ltd v Selby District Council* (1995) 2 PLR 11, Lands Tribunal.
7 *Buckle v Holderness Borough Council* (1996) 71 P&CR 428, Lands Tribunal. The Lands Tribunal held that the appeal was a reasonable attempt by the claimant to mitigate his loss.

Procedure

[346]
A claim for compensation must be made[1] within 12 months from the date of the decision or, where there is an appeal, from the date of the decision on the appeal; there is no provision for extending that time[2]. Any question of disputed compensation is to be referred to the Upper Tribunal[3]; the LCA 1961, ss 2 and 4 will then apply, with any necessary modifications[4].

1 A claim is 'made' when it is received: *Camden London Borough v ADC Estates Ltd* (1990) 61 P&CR 48, CA. There is no particular form for the claim, so long as it is an unequivocal claim and not merely an intention to make a claim: *Texas Homecare Ltd v Lewes District Council* (1986) 51 P&CR 205, Lands Tribunal. See also *International Ferry Traders Ltd v Adur District Council* [2004] EWCA Civ 288, [2004] RVR 65.
2 Model order, art 9.
3 TCPA 1990, s 205(1). As to references to the Upper Tribunal, see **Division H**.
4 TCPA 1990, s 205(2). As to the LCA 1961, ss 2, 4, see **Division H**.

Interest on compensation

[347]
Interest is payable on compensation due, from the date of refusal of consent or the imposition of the conditions[1].

1 PCA 1991, s 80, Sch 18, see para **[26]**.

Compensation for a direction requiring replanting of trees

The right to compensation

[348]
A right to compensation arises where a direction is made by the local planning authority or the Secretary of State requiring the replanting of woodland which has been felled in the course of forestry operations permitted by a tree

preservation order and the Forestry Commissioners have decided not to make a grant or loan under the Forestry Act 1979, s 1, on the ground that the direction frustrates the use of the woodland for the growing of timber or other forest products commercially[1].

1 TCPA 1990, s 204(1). The Forestry Commissioners must on request give a certificate as to their decision not to make a grant or loan and the reasons for the decision: s 204(3).

Assessment of compensation

[349]
Compensation is payable in respect of loss or damage caused or incurred in consequence of the direction[1].

1 TCPA 1990, s 204(2).

Procedure

[350]–[360]
A claim must be made[1] within 12 months of the date of the direction or, where an appeal has been made, within 12 months of the date of the Secretary of State's decision on the appeal[2], although the Secretary of State has power to extend this time. It must be in writing and served[3] on the local planning authority[4]. Any question of disputed compensation is to be determined by the Upper Tribunal[5]; the LCA 1961, ss 2 and 4 will then apply[6].

1 A claim is 'made' when it is received: *Camden London Borough v ADC Estates Ltd* (1990) 61 P&CR 48, CA.
2 TCPA 1990, s 204(4).
3 As to service, see the TCPA 1990, s 329.
4 TCPA 1990, s 204(4). There is no particular form for the claim, so long as it is an unequivocal claim and not merely an intention to make a claim: *Texas Homecare Ltd v Lewes District Council* (1986) 51 P&CR 205, Lands Tribunal. See also *International Ferry Traders Ltd v Adur District Council* [2004] EWCA Civ 288, [2004] RVR 65.
5 TCPA 1990, s 205(1). As to references to the Upper Tribunal, see **Division H**.
6 TCPA 1990, s 205(2). As to the LCA 1961, ss 2, 4, see **Division H**.

Interest on compensation

[361]
Interest is payable on compensation due, from the date of the decision[1].

1 PCA 1991, s 80, Sch 18, see para **[26]**.

H Refusal of tree-felling licence

1 The right to compensation

[362]
A right to compensation arises[1] where an application for a tree-felling licence is refused, unless the owner gives notice to the Forestry Commissioners requiring them to buy the trees[2].

1 Forestry Act 1967 (FoA 1967), s 10(4)(*a*).
2 FoA 1967, s 14(3), (4).

2 Assessment of compensation

[363]
Compensation is payable in respect of depreciation in the value of the trees which is attributable to the deterioration in the quality of the timber in consequence of the refusal of consent[1]. However, no account is to be taken of deterioration in quality of the timber attributable to neglect after refusal of the licence[2]. The value of the trees is to be ascertained at the date of the claim[3].

1 FoA 1967, s 11(1). As to the subsequent grant of a licence, see s 11(5). Examples of claims are *Cardigan Timber Co v Cardiganshire County Council* (1957) 9 P&CR 158 (Lands Tribunal); *Winders v Forestry Commission* (1958) 9 P&CR 500 (Lands Tribunal).
2 FoA 1967, s 11(4)(*a*).
3 FoA 1967, s 11(4)(*b*).

3 Procedure

[364]
Claims may be made from time to time in respect of deterioration in the trees after the refusal of the felling licence up to one year after the eventual felling of the trees, but claims can only relate to deterioration occurring during the ten years prior to the date of the claim[1]. A claim must be made in the form prescribed[2]. Any dispute as to compensation may be referred to the Upper Tribunal[3].

1 FoA 1967, s 11(3).
2 FoA 1967, s 11(2) and the Forestry (Felling of Trees) Regulations 1979, SI 1979/791, reg 5, Sch 1, form 1.
3 FoC 1967, s 11(6) and 31.

4 Interest on compensation

[365]
Interest is payable on compensation due, from the date of the claim[1].

1 PCA 1991, s 80, Sch 18, see para **[26]**.

I Revocation or modification of listed building consent

1 The right to compensation

[366]
A right to compensation arises where a local planning authority or the Secretary of State revokes or modifies a listed building consent[1]. Compensation may be claimed by a person interested in the building[2], except where no one who was potentially affected objected to the order[3]. A claim may be made by a mortgagee of an interest, without prejudice to a claim by

the person entitled to the interest mortgaged[4], but compensation is not payable in respect of the interest of the mortgagee[5].

1 Planning (Listed Buildings and Conservation Areas) Act 1990 (P(LBCA)A 1990), ss 23, 26. The legislation empowers local planning authorities to acquire listed buildings compulsorily in certain circumstances: see **Division B**. Compensation for compulsory purchase is explained in **Division E**.
2 As to a 'person interested in the building', see *Pennine Raceway Ltd v Kirklees Metropolitan Borough Council* [1983] QB 382, CA.
3 P(LBCA)A 1990, s 28(1).
4 P(LBCA)A 1990, s 31(3)(*b*).
5 P(LBCA)A 1990, s 31(3)(*c*).

2 Assessment of compensation

[367]
Compensation is payable in respect of:

(1) Expenditure incurred in carrying out works[1] which are rendered abortive by the order, but this does not include works carried out before the grant of the consent which has been revoked or modified[2].
(2) Any other loss or damage which is directly attributable to the revocation or modification[3]. This includes depreciation in the value of an interest in land, but does not include loss resulting from anything done or omitted to be done before the grant of planning permission (other than the depreciation in value of land)[4].

The rules in the LCA 1961, s 5 apply, with any necessary modifications[5]. If the interest is subject to a mortgage, compensation for depreciation in value of the interest is to be assessed as if the interest is not subject to a mortgage[6].

1 Expenditure incurred in the preparation of plans or other similar matters is deemed to be expenditure incurred in carrying out the work: P(LBCA)A 1990, s 28(4).
2 P(LBCA)A 1990 28(3)(*a*).
3 P(LBCA)A 1990, s 28(2).
4 P(LBCA)A 1990, s 28(3)(*b*). As to loss of business profits, see para **[304]**.
5 P(LBCA)A 1990, s 31(1).
6 P(LBCA)A 1990, s 31(3)(*a*). The compensation must be paid to the mortgagee or the first mortgagee, as the case may be, who must apply it as if it were the proceeds of sale: s 31(3)(*d*).

3 Procedure

[368]
A claim must be made[1] within six months of the date of the decision, in respect of which the claim is made, although the Secretary of State has power to extend this time[2]. A claim must be in writing and served[3] on the local planning authority[4]. Any question of disputed compensation is to be referred to the Upper Tribunal[5]; the LCA 1961, ss 2 and 4 then apply, with any necessary modifications[6].

1 A claim is 'made' when it is received: *Camden London Borough v ADC Estates Ltd* (1990) 61 P&CR 48, CA.
2 Town and Country Planning (Listed Buildings and Conservation Areas) Regulations 1990, SI 1990/1519, reg 9(2)(*b*).
3 As to service, see the TCPA 1990, s 329, applied by the P(LBCA)A 1990, s 89.

4 There is no particular form for the claim, so long as it is an unequivocal claim and not merely an intention to make a claim: *Texas Homecare Ltd v Lewes District Council* (1986) 51 P&CR 205, Lands Tribunal. See also *International Ferry Traders Ltd v Adur District Council* [2004] EWCA Civ 288, [2004] RVR 65. As to the meaning of local planning authority for this purpose, see the P(LBCA)A 1990, s 30.
5 P(LBCA)A 1990, s 31(4). As to references to the Upper Tribunal, see **Division H**.
6 P(LBCA)A 1990, s 31(5). As to these sections, see **Division H**.

4 Interest on compensation

[369]
Interest is payable on compensation, due from the date of the order[1].

1 PCA 1991, s 80, Sch 18, see para **[26]**.

J Building preservation notices

1 The right to compensation

[370]–[380]
A right to compensation arises where a local planning authority serves a building preservation notice[1] but the notice ceases to have effect without the building being listed[2]. Any person with an interest in land when the notice is served is entitled to compensation from the local planning authority[3].

1 P(LBCA)A 1990, s 3. The purpose of a building preservation notice is to preserve an unlisted building while it is decided whether it should be listed.
2 P(LBCA)A 1990, s 29(1).
3 P(LBCA)A 1990, s 29(2).

2 Assessment of compensation

[381]
Compensation is payable in respect of any loss or damage directly attributable to the effect of the notice[1]. The claim may include loss and damage caused by a breach of contract resulting from the necessity to discontinue or countermand building works on account of the notice[2]. The rules in the LCA 1961, s 5 apply, with any necessary modifications[3]. If the interest is subject to a mortgage, compensation for depreciation in value of the interest is to be assessed as if the interest is not subject to a mortgage[4].

1 P(LBCA)A 1990, s 29.
2 P(LBCA)A 1990, s 29(3).
3 P(LBCA)A 1990, s 31(1). As to the LCA 1961, s 5, see **Division E**.
4 P(LBCA)A 1990, s 31(3)(*a*). The compensation must be paid to the mortgagee or the first mortgagee , as the case may be, who must apply it as if it were the proceeds of sale: s 31(3)(*d*).

3 Procedure

[382]
A claim must be made[1] within six months of the date of the decision in respect of which the claim is made, although the Secretary of State has power

to extend this time[2]. It must be in writing and served[3] on the local planning authority[4]. Any question of disputed compensation is to be referred to the Upper Tribunal[5]; the LCA 1961, ss 2 and 4 then apply, with any necessary modifications[6].

1 A claim is 'made' when it is received: *Camden London Borough v ADC Estates Ltd* (1990) 61 P&CR 48, CA.
2 Town and Country Planning (Listed Buildings and Conservation Areas) Regulations 1990, SI 1990/1519, reg 9(2)(*b*).
3 As to service, see the TCPA 1990, s 329, applied by the P(LBCA)A 1990, s 89.
4 There is no particular form for the claim, so long as it is an unequivocal claim and not merely an intention to make a claim: *Texas Homecare Ltd v Lewes District Council* (1986) 51 P&CR 205, Lands Tribunal. See also *International Ferry Traders Ltd v Adur District Council* [2004] EWCA Civ 288, [2004] RVR 65. For the meaning of local planning authority for this purpose, see the P(LBCA)A 1990, s 30.
5 P(LBCA)A 1990, s 31(4). As to references to the Upper Tribunal, see **Division H**.
6 P(LBCA)A 1990, s 31(5). As to the LCA 1961, ss 2, 4, see **Division H**.

4 Interest on compensation

[383]
Interest is payable on compensation due, from the date of the notice[1].

1 PCA 1991, s 80, Sch 18, see para **[26]**.

K Ancient monuments

1 Introduction

[384]
There are three rights to compensation arising out of decisions relating to ancient monuments[1]:

(*a*) where, in certain circumstances, scheduled monument consent is refused or granted, subject to conditions;
(*b*) where works to an ancient monument have been authorised, but then cease to be; and
(*c*) where the Secretary of State undertakes works and causes damage.

Each of these is explained separately in the paragraphs which follow.

1 As to the meaning of 'monument', see the Ancient Monuments and Archaeological Areas Act 1979 (AMAAA 1979), s 61(7), (8), (13). In addition to the provisions described here, the legislation empowers local authorities to acquire ancient monuments compulsorily in order to secure their preservation; compensation for compulsory purchase is described in **Division E**.

Compensation in respect of refusal of consent or grant, subject to conditions

The right to compensation

[385]
A right to compensation arises where scheduled monument[1] consent is refused, or granted subject to conditions[2], for:

(*a*) works[3] which are reasonably necessary for carrying out development, for which planning permission had been granted otherwise than by a development order before the monument was scheduled;
(*b*) works which do not constitute development or for which planning permission is granted by a development order[4]; and
(*c*) works which are reasonably necessary for the continuation of the monument in its use (apart from a use subject to legal restrictions) immediately before the application for consent was made[5].

A claim may be made by any person who has an interest in the whole or any part of the monument[6]. Where an interest is subject to a mortgage, a claim may be made by any mortgagee, without prejudice to a claim by the owner of the interest[7], but no compensation is payable in respect of the interest of the mortgagee[8]. Any compensation is payable to the mortgagee or, as the case may be, the first mortgagee, who must apply it as though it were proceeds of sale[9].

1 That is, a monument included in a schedule prepared by the Secretary of State under the AMAAA 1979, s 1. The Act provides protection for such monuments and consent is required for works which damage or destroy them.
2 AMAAA 1979, s 7.
3 As to the meaning of works, see the AMAAA 1979, s 61(1).
4 This does not apply if the works might result in total or partial demolition of the monument, unless those works are for agriculture or forestry: AMAAA 1979, s 7(4).
5 AMAAA 1979, s 7(1), (2). No compensation is payable under (*c*) unless compliance with the conditions would make it impossible to use the monument for such use: AMAAA 1979, s 7(5). Any use in contravention of legal restrictions applying to the use of the monument is to be disregarded: AMAAA 1979, s 7(2).
6 AMAAA 1979, s 7(1). There is no definition of 'interest' for this purpose.
7 AMAAA 1979, s 27(3)(*b*).
8 AMAAA 1979, s 27(3)(*c*).
9 AMAAA 1979, s 27(3)(*d*).

Assessment of compensation

[386]
Compensation is payable for[1]:

(*a*) any expenditure incurred; or
(*b*) any other loss or damage sustained in consequence of the refusal of consent or the grant, subject to conditions[2].

Where the claim relates to works necessary for carrying out development, compensation can only relate to loss sustained by virtue of the fact that any development for which planning permission has been granted could not be carried out without infringing the requirement for consent[3]. In assessing compensation for depreciation in the value of an interest, it is to be assumed that any subsequent application for consent would be determined in the same way, unless, on refusing consent, the Secretary of State undertook to grant consent for different works[4]. The rules in the LCA 1961, s 5 apply, with any necessary modifications[5]. Where an interest in land is subject to a mortgage, compensation for depreciation in the value of that interest is to be assessed as if it is not subject to a mortgage[6].

1 AMAAA 1979, s 7(1).
2 It has been held in Scotland under this provision that the date for assessing compensation is the date of refusal of consent: *Currie v Secretary of State for Scotland* [1993] 2 EGLR 221, Lands Tribunal for Scotland.
3 AMAAA 1979, s 7(3).
4 AMAAA 1979, s 7(6).
5 AMAAA 1979, s 27(1). As to the LCA 1961, s 5, see **Division E**.
6 AMAAA 1979, s 27(3)(*a*).

Procedure

[387]
A claim must be made[1] within six months of the date of refusal or the grant subject to conditions, although the Secretary of State has power to extend that time[2]. A claim must be in the prescribed form (or substantially to the like effect) and delivered or sent by recorded delivery service to the person against whom the claim is made[3] who is (in England) the Historic Buildings and Monuments Commission for England or (elsewhere) the Secretary of State[4]. Any question of disputed compensation is to be referred to the Upper Tribunal[5]; the LCA 1961, ss 2 and 4 will then apply, with any necessary modifications[6].

1 A claim is 'made' when it is received: *Camden London Borough v ADC Estates Ltd* (1990) 61 P&CR 48, CA.
2 Ancient Monuments (Claims for Compensation) (England) Regulations 1991, SI 1991/2512, reg 2(2)(*a*).
3 SI 1991/2512, reg 2(1). The form is in the Schedule.
4 AMAAA 1979, s 7(1).
5 AMAAA 1961, s 47(2). As to references to the Upper Tribunal, see **Division H**.
6 AMAAA 1979, s 47(3). As to the LCA 1961, ss 2, 4, see **Division H**.

Recovery of compensation on subsequent grant of consent

[388]
Where compensation has been paid under the provisions described above and the Secretary of State subsequently grants scheduled monument consent for any of the works for which compensation in excess of £20 was paid, the Secretary of State may direct that the consent may not be implemented unless the compensation is repaid[1].

1 AMAAA 1979, s 8, which sets out how the recoverable amount is to be assessed.

Compensation in respect of works previously authorised

The right to compensation

[389]
A right to compensation arises where any works affecting an ancient monument, which were previously authorised, cease to be so authorised as a result of revocation or modification of the consent or a direction made by the Secretary of State[1]. Where an interest is subject to a mortgage, a claim may be made by any mortgagee, without prejudice to a claim by the owner of the

interest[2], but no compensation is payable in respect of the interest of the mortgagee[3]. Any compensation is payable to the mortgagee or, as the case may be, the first mortgagee, who must apply it as though it were proceeds of sale[4].

1 AMAAA 1979, s 9(1), (2). A claim under s 9(2)(*a*) can only be made if an application for scheduled monument consent is refused or granted, subject to conditions different from the previous consent: AMAAA 1979, s 9(3).
2 AMAAA 1979, s 27(3)(*b*).
3 AMAAA 1979, s 27(3)(*c*).
4 AMAAA 1979, s 27(3)(*c*), (*d*).

Assessment of compensation

[390]–[400]
Compensation is payable in respect of:

(*a*) expenditure incurred in carrying out works[1] which are rendered abortive by the fact that any further works have ceased to be so authorised; or
(*b*) any other loss or damage directly attributable to removal of authorisation for the works.

The rules in the LCA 1961, s 5 apply, with any necessary modifications[2]. Where an interest in land is subject to a mortgage, compensation for depreciation in the value of that interest is to be assessed as if it is not subject to a mortgage[3].

1 AMAAA 1979, s 9(1). This includes expenditure on the preparation of plans or other similar matters: AMAAA 1979, s 9(4). However, it does not include expenditure on any works carried out before the scheduled monument consent was granted or other loss arising out of anything done or omitted to be done before the consent was granted (other than loss due to depreciation in the value of an interest in land): AMAAA 1979, s 9(5).
2 AMAAA 1979, s 27(1). As to the LCA 1961, s 5, see **Division H**.
3 AMAAA 1979, s 27(3)(*a*).

Procedure

[401]
A claim must be made[1] within six months of the revocation or grant, subject to conditions, or, as the case may be, the direction, although the Secretary of State has power to extend that time[2]. A claim must be in the prescribed form (or substantially to the like effect) and delivered or sent by recorded delivery service to the person against whom the claim is made[3] which is (in England) the Historic Buildings and Monuments Commission or (elsewhere) the Secretary of State[4]. Any question of disputed compensation is to be referred to the Upper Tribunal[5]; the LCA 1961, ss 2 and 4 will then apply, with any necessary modifications[6].

1 A claim is 'made' when it is received: *Camden London Borough v ADC Estates Ltd* (1990) 61 P&CR 48, CA.
2 Ancient Monuments (Claims for Compensation) Regulations 1991, SI 1991/2512, reg 2(2)(*b*).
3 SI 1991/2512, reg 2(1). The form is set out in the Schedule.
4 AMAAA 1979, s 9(1).
5 AMAAA 1961, s 47(2). As to references to the Upper Tribunal, see **Division H**.
6 AMAAA 1979, s 47(3). As to the LCA 1961, ss 2 and 4, see **Division H**.

Compensation for damage caused by the exercise of powers

The right to compensation

[402]
Compensation is payable[1] where damage is caused to land or to chattels on land as a result of the exercise of various powers which authorise entry onto land for survey and investigation[2]. A claim may be made by any person having an interest in the land or the chattels[3].

1 AMAAA 1979, s 46.
2 The powers are those under the AMAAA 1979, ss 6, 6A, 26, 38, 39, 40, 43, which all relate to entry and investigation: AMAAA 1979, s 46(3).
3 AMAAA 1979, s 46(1).

Assessment of compensation

[403]
Compensation is recoverable in respect of the damage caused[1].

1 AMAAA 1979, s 46(1).

Procedure

[404]
A claim must be made[1] within six months of the date on which the damage occurred, although the Secretary of State has power to extend that time[2]. A claim must be in the prescribed form (or substantially to the like effect) and delivered or sent by recorded delivery service to the person against whom the claim is made[3] which is (in England) the Historic Buildings and Monuments Commission or (elsewhere) the Secretary of State[4]. Any question of disputed compensation is to be referred to the Upper Tribunal[5]; the LCA 1961, ss 2 and 4 will then apply, with any necessary modifications[6].

1 A claim is 'made' when it is received: *Camden London Borough v ADC Estates Ltd* (1990) 61 P&CR 48, CA.
2 Ancient Monuments (Claims for Compensation) Regulations 1991, SI 1991/2512, reg 2(2)(*c*).
3 SI 1991/2512, reg 2(1). The form is set out in the Schedule.
4 AMAAA 1979, s 9(1).
5 AMAAA 1961, s 47(2). As to references to the Upper Tribunal, see **Division H**.
6 AMAAA 1979, s 47(3). As to the LCA 1961, ss 2, 4, see **Division H**.

Interest on compensation

[405]
Interest is payable on compensation due under these provisions[1].

1 This applies to compensation under the AMAAA 1979, ss 7 (from the date of refusal or imposition of conditions), 9 (from the date on which the works cease to be authorised), 46 (from the date of entry): PCA 1991, s 80, Sch 18, see para **[26]**.

L Advertisements

1 The right to compensation

[406]
A right to compensation arises where, for the purposes of complying with an order made under regulations controlling the display of advertisements, a person carries out works for removing an advertisement which was displayed on 1 August 1948 or for discontinuing the use of a site for the display of advertisements which was used on that date[1]. A claim may be made by the person who incurred expense in carrying the works.

1 TCPA 1990, s 223(1).

2 Assessment of compensation

[407]
Compensation is payable for any expenses reasonably incurred in carrying out the works[1].

1 TCPA 1990, 223(1).

3 Procedure

[408]
A claim must be made[1] within six months of completion of the works. It must be made in writing to the local planning authority and must contain such information as the local planning authority consider to be required to enable them to deal with the claim[2]. Any question of disputed compensation is to be referred to the Upper Tribunal, unless otherwise provided in regulations[3]; the LCA 1961, ss 2 and 4 will then apply, with any necessary modifications[4].

1 A claim is 'made' when it is received: *Camden London Borough v ADC Estates Ltd* (1990) 61 P&CR 48, CA.
2 Town and Country Planning (Control of Advertisement) Regulations 1992, SI 1992/666, reg 20.
3 TCPA 1990, s 223(2). As to references to the Upper Tribunal, see **Division H**.
4 TCPA 1990, s 223(3). As to the LCA 1961, ss 2, 4, see **Division H**.

4 Interest on compensation

[409]
Interest is payable on compensation due, from the date on which the expenses were incurred[1].

1 PCA 1991, s 80, Sch 18, see para **[26]**.

M Statutory undertakers

1 The rights to compensation

[410]–[420]
Statutory undertakers[1] have rights to compensation in the following circumstances[2]:

(*a*) where planning permission to develop operational land[3] is refused, or granted subject to conditions, in circumstances where planning permission would have been granted by a development order, but for a direction that such permission is not to apply to that development, and it is not development which has received parliamentary approval[4];
(*b*) where planning permission granted to a statutory undertaker is revoked or modified[5];
(*c*) where any right belonging to a statutory undertaker is extinguished[6];
(*d*) where any right belonging to an operator of a telecommunications code system[7] is extinguished or any requirement is imposed upon the operator of such a system[8]; and
(*e*) where works are carried out for removing or resiting statutory undertakers' apparatus and the undertakers have the right to carry out those works[9].

1 'Statutory undertaker' is defined in the TCPA 1990, s 262(1) as persons authorised by any enactment to carry on any railway, light railway, tramway, road transport, water transport, canal, inland navigation, dock, harbour, pier or lighthouse undertaking, or an undertaking for the supply of hydraulic power and a relevant airport operator within the meaning of the Airports Act 1986. This definition is extended for certain purposes (including the rights to compensation described here) by s 262(3)–(7) to include any public gas transporter, water or sewerage undertaker, the Environment Agency, the Post Office, the Civil Aviation Authority and electricity undertakers holding a licence under the Electricity Act 1989, s 6.
2 For this purpose the conditions in the TCPA 1990, ss 91, 92 are to be disregarded.
3 'Operational land' is defined by the TCPA 1990, s 263.
4 TCPA 1990, s 279(1)(*a*) which applies to any decision made in accordance with, s 266. However, with regard to land acquired after 7 January 1947, a direction can be made by the Secretary of State and the minister that this is not to apply: TCPA 1990, s 279(5). As to the grounds on which such a direction may be made, see the TCPA 1990, s 279(6).
5 TCPA 1990, s 279(1)(*b*) which applies where an order under s 97 as modified by s 269 has been made. With regard to land acquired after 7 January 1947, see the previous note.
6 TCPA 1990, 279(2) which applies to rights extinguished under s 271.
7 An operator of a telecommunications code system is an operator whose licence granted under the Telecommunications Act 1984, s 7 applies the 'Telecommunications Code': Telecommunications Act 1984, s 10.
8 TCPA 1990, s 279(3) which applies where a right has been extinguished under s 272.
9 TCPA 1990, s 279(4) which applies where undertakers have the right to carry out works under s 273.

2 Assessment of compensation

[421]
Compensation is assessed on a special basis comprising the aggregate[1] of:

(*a*) 'a business adjustment', that is, the amount of any expenditure reasonably incurred in acquiring land, providing apparatus, erecting buildings or doing work for the purpose of any adjustment of the carrying on of the undertaking or, as the case may be, the running of the telecommunications code system, rendered necessary by the proceeding giving rise to compensation[2];

(*b*) loss of profits[3]; and

(*c*) where the compensation arises out of a requirement to remove apparatus, the cost of complying with that requirement.

1 TCPA 1990, s 280(1), (2). This also applies where land is compulsorily acquired: s 280(1)(*c*); as to compensation for compulsory acquisition, see **Division E**.
2 'Proceeding giving rise to compensation' is defined in the TCPA 1990, s 280(8).
3 As to the assessment of loss of profits, see para **[423]**.

[422]

Where a business adjustment is made, the compensation has to be reduced by:

(*a*) an amount which appears reasonable to offset:
 (i) the estimated value of any property which ceases to be used in consequence of the adjustment, and
 (ii) the estimated amount of any increase in net receipts[1] from carrying on the undertaking in the period after the adjustment has been completed (in so far as it has not been taken into account in assessing any loss of profits)[2]; and

(*b*) an amount which appears appropriate having regard to any increase in the capital value of the statutory undertakers' immoveable property directly attributable to the proceeding giving rise to the adjustment[3].

1 For 'increase in net receipts', see the TCPA 1990, s 280(7).
2 TCPA 1990, s 280(4).
3 TCPA 1990, s 280(5).

[423]

Loss of profits is assessed as follows:

(*a*) where a business adjustment is made, the loss of profits is the estimated amount of any decrease in net receipts[1] directly attributable to the proceeding giving rise to the compensation both pending the adjustment and after it[2]; or

(*b*) where a business adjustment is not made, the loss of profits is the amount which appears reasonable compensation for any estimated decrease in net receipts directly attributable to the proceeding giving rise to the compensation[3].

1 For decrease in net receipts, see the TCPA 1990, s 280(7).
2 TCPA 1990, s 280(3)(*a*).
3 TCPA 1990, s 280(3)(*b*).

3 Procedure

[424]

No procedure or time limit[1] for making claims is laid down by the Act[2]. A claim should be made to the local planning authority which made the decision or took the action. Compensation is, in default of agreement, to be assessed by the Upper Tribunal[3]; the LCA 1961, ss 2 and 4 then apply, with any necessary modifications[4].

1 Claims would, however, be subject to the Limitation Act 1980, s 9. See *Hillingdon London Borough Council v ARC Ltd* [1999] Ch 139, CA.
2 Although there is no particular form for a claim, it must be an unequivocal claim and not merely an intention to make a claim: *Texas Homecare Ltd v Lewes District Council* (1986) 51 P&CR 205, Lands Tribunal. See also *International Ferry Traders Ltd v Adur District Council* [2004] EWCA Civ 288, [2004] RVR 65.
3 TCPA 1990, s 282(1). As to references to the Upper Tribunal, see **Division H**.
4 TCPA 1990, s 282(2).

4 Interest on compensation

[425]
Interest is payable on compensation due, from the date on which the right is extinguished or the requirement imposed[1].

1 PCA 1991, s 80, Sch 18, see para **[26]**.

N Revocation or modification of hazardous substances consent

1 Introduction

[426]
There are two rights to compensation in relation to hazardous substances consents:

(*a*) where an existing consent is revoked or modified; and
(*b*) where, on an application to continue a consent upon a change of control of the land, the consent is modified or revoked.

Each of these is explained separately as follows.

Revocation or modification

The right to compensation

[427]
A right to compensation arises where an order[1] is made by a hazardous substances authority[2] revoking or modifying a hazardous substances consent[3]. A claim may be made against the authority by any person who has suffered damage[4] or has carried out works in compliance with the order[5]. A claim may be made by a mortgagee of an interest without prejudice to a claim by the person entitled to the interest[6], but compensation is not payable in respect of the interest of the mortgagee[7].

1 Under the Planning (Hazardous Substances) Act 1990 (P(HS)A 1990), s 14.
2 P(HS)A 1990, ss 1, 3, 39(1).
3 P(HS)A 1990, ss 4, 39(1).
4 P(HS)A 1990, s 16(2).

5 P(HS)A 1990, s 16(3).
6 TCPA 1990, s 117(3)(*b*), applied by the P(HS)A 1990, s 16(5).
7 TCPA 1990, s 117(3)(*c*), applied by the P(HS)A 1990, s 16(5). The compensation must be paid to the mortgagee or the first mortgagee , as the case may be, who must apply it as if it were proceeds of sale: TCPA 1990, s 117(3)(*d*).

Assessment of compensation

[428]
Compensation is payable in respect of:

(*a*) depreciation in the value of an interest in land[1] or in minerals on or under it;
(*b*) disturbance[2] in the enjoyment of land or minerals[3]; and
(*c*) any expenses reasonably incurred in carrying out works in compliance with the order[4].

The compensation is to be reduced by the value of any timber, apparatus or other materials removed for the purpose of complying with the order[5]. The rules in the LCA 1961, s 5 apply for the purposes of assessing depreciation in the value of land, subject to any necessary modifications[6]. If the interest is subject to a mortgage, compensation for depreciation in the value of the interest is to be assessed as if the interest were not subject to the mortgage[7].

1 P(HS)A 1990, s 39(2).
2 As to compensation for disturbance in the context of compulsory acquisition, see **Division E**.
3 P(HS)A 1990, s 16(2).
4 P(HS)A 1990, s 16(3).
5 P(HS)A 1990, s 16(4).
6 TCPA 1990, s 117(1), applied by the P(HS)A 1990, s 16(5).These rules apply to the assessment of compensation for the compulsory acquisition of an interest in land; they are explained in **Division E**. A claim was held to be valid, notwithstanding r 4 of the LCA 1961, s 5 (which excludes any value attributable to a use which is contrary to law or detrimental to health): *Bolton v North Dorset District Council* (1997) 74 P&CR 73, Lands Tribunal.
7 TCPA 1990, s 117(3)(*a*), applied by the P(HS)A 1990, s 16(5).

Procedure

[429]
Although the Act provides that claims are to be made within the time and in the manner to be prescribed[1], no regulations have yet been made governing such matters[2]. Any question of disputed compensation is to be referred to the Upper Tribunal[3]; the LCA 1961, ss 2 and 4 then apply, subject to any necessary modifications[4].

1 P(HS)A 1990, s 16(2).
2 Nor are there any which have effect by virtue of the Planning (Consequential Provisions) Act 1990, s 2(2). Claims would, however, be subject to the Limitation Act 1980, s 9. See *Hillingdon London Borough Council v ARC Ltd* [1999] Ch 139, CA.
3 TCPA 1990, s 118(1), applied by the P(HS)A 1990, s 16(5). As to references to the Upper Tribunal, see **Division H**.
4 TCPA 1990, s 118(2), applied by the P(HS)A 1990, s 16(5). As to the LCA 1961, ss 2, 4, see **Division H**.

Revocation or modification on an application to continue consent

The right to compensation

[430]–[440]
A right to compensation arises where an application[1] has been made to continue a hazardous substances consent as a result of a change of control of the land and the hazardous substances authority either revokes or modifies the consent. A claim may be made against the authority by the person in control of the whole of the land before the change in control[2].

1 Under the P(HS)A 1990, s 17.
2 P(HS)A 1990, s 19. There appears to be no right to compensation where the Secretary of State revokes or modifies the consent under s 20.

Assessment of compensation

[441]
Compensation is payable in respect of any loss or damage sustained which is directly attributable to the revocation or modification[1].

1 P(HS)A 1990, s 19.

Procedure

[442]
The time within which a claim must be made[1], and the manner in which a claim must be made are not prescribed by the Act, nor is there any power to make regulations for this purpose[2]. Nor is there any provision in the Act as to how questions of disputed compensation are to be determined.

1 The Limitation Act 1980, s 9 would apply: *Hillingdon London Borough Council v ARC Ltd* [1999] Ch 139, CA.
2 Although there is no particular form for the claim, it must be an unequivocal claim and not merely an intention to make a claim: *Texas Homecare Ltd v Lewes District Council* (1985) 51 P&CR 205, Lands Tribunal. See also *International Ferry Traders Ltd v Adur District Council* [2004] EWCA Civ 288, [2004] RVR 65.

Interest on compensation

[443]
Interest is payable on compensation, due from the date of the order[1].

1 PCA 1991, s 80, Sch 18, see para **[26]**.

O Extinguishment of right to use vehicles on highway

1 The right to compensation

[444]
A right to compensation arises where the Secretary of State, on the application of a local planning authority, makes an order[1] extinguishing a right of way over

a highway with vehicles. A claim may be made against the local planning authority by any person who has at the time when the order comes into force an interest in land having lawful access to the highway where the rights of way are restricted[2]. A claim may be made by a mortgagee or an interest, but without prejudice to a claim being made by the person entitled to the interest[3], but compensation is not payable in respect of the interest of the mortgagee[4].

1 Under the TCPA 1990, s 249.
2 TCPA 1990, s 250(1).
3 TCPA 1990, s 250(5)(*b*).
4 TCPA 1990, s 250(5)(*c*). The compensation must be paid to the mortgagee or the first mortgagee , as the case may be, who must apply it as though it were proceeds of sale: s 250(5)(*d*).

2 Assessment of compensation

[445]
Compensation is payable in respect of[1]:

(*a*) depreciation in the value of an interest in land which is directly attributable to the order; and
(*b*) any other loss or damage attributable directly to the order.

For the purposes of assessing depreciation in the value of an interest in land, the rules in the LCA 1961, s 5 apply for the purposes of assessing the value of land with any necessary modifications[2]. Where an interest is subject to a mortgage, depreciation in the value of the interest is to be assessed as if it were not subject to a mortgage[3].

1 TCPA 1990, s 250(1).
2 TCPA 1990, s 250(4). As to the LCA 1961, s 5, see **Division E**.
3 TCPA 1990, s 250(5)(*a*).

3 Procedure

[446]
A claim must be made[1] within 12 months of the date of the order, although the Secretary of State has power to extend that time[2]. Any question of disputed compensation is to be referred to the Upper Tribunal[3]; the LCA 1961, ss 2 and 4 then apply, with any necessary modifications[4].

1 A claim is 'made' when it is received: *Camden London Borough v ADC Estates Ltd* (1990) 61 P&CR 48, CA.
2 Town and Country Planning General Regulations 1992, SI 1992/1492, reg 12. There is no particular form for the claim, so long as it is an unequivocal claim and not merely an intention to make a claim: *Texas Homecare Ltd v Lewes District Council* (1985) 51 P&CR 205, Lands Tribunal. See also *International Ferry Traders Ltd v Adur District Council* [2004] EWCA Civ 288, [2004] RVR 65.
3 TCPA 1990, s 250(6). As to references to the Upper Tribunal, see **Division H**.
4 TCPA 1990, s 250(7).

4 Interest on compensation

[447]
Interest is payable on compensation due, from the date of the order[1].

1 PCA 1991, s 80, Sch 18, see para **[26]**.

P Rights of entry

1 The rights to compensation

[448]
Rights to compensation arise where rights of entry are exercised:

(*a*) for the purpose of surveying land in connection with the various functions of a local planning authority[1];
(*b*) for the purpose of surveying land in connection with a proposal to include a building in a list of buildings of historic or architectural interest[2];
(*c*) for the purpose of surveying land in connection with an application for a hazardous substances notice or a hazardous substances contravention notice[3]; and
(*d*) for the purpose of inspecting land with a view to obtaining information for the Historic Buildings and Monuments Commission[4].
(*e*) various purposes under the Countryside and Rights of Way Act 2000 (CROW 2000)[5]; and
(*f*) various purposes under the Wildlife and Countryside Act 1981[6].

A claim may be made against the body exercising the power by any person suffering damage.

1 Under the TCPA 1990, s 324.
2 Under the P(LBCA)A 1990, s 88.
3 Under the P(HS)A 1990, s 36.
4 Under the National Heritage Act 1983 (NHA 1983), s 36.
5 Section 40.
6 Section 51.

2 Assessment of compensation

[449]
Compensation is payable in respect of any damage to land or to chattels[1]. Compensation is payable under CROW 2000, s 41 and WCA, s 51 in respect of damage sustained by any person.

1 In relation to rights of entry exercised under the TCPA 1990, s 324: s 325(6). In relation to rights of entry exercised under the P(LBCA)A 1990, s 88: s 88B(7). In relation to rights of entry under the P(HS)A 1990, s 36: s 36B(6). In relation to rights of entry exercised under the NHA 1983, s 36: s 36(8).

3 Procedure

[450]–[460]
The time within which a claim must be made[1] and the manner in which a claim must be made under the TCPA 1990, the P(LBCA)A 1990 or the P(HS)A 1990 are not specified by those Acts. For the purposes of claims in England only under the NHA 1983, s 36(8), a claim must be made within six months from the date of the damage and must be in the form prescribed or in a form substantially to the like effect[2]. Any question of disputed compensation is to

be referred to the Upper Tribunal; the LCA 1961, ss 2 and 4 will then apply, with any necessary modifications[3]. There is no provision for the payment of interest under these provisions[4]. Any dispute as to compensation under CROW 2000 s 41(1) or WCA 1981 s 51(5) is to be referred to arbitration[5].

1 The Limitation Act 1990, s 9 would apply: *Hillingdon London Borough Council v ARC Ltd* [1999] Ch 139, CA.
2 Ancient Monuments (Claims for Compensation) (England) Regulations 1991, SI 1991/2512, reg 3, made under the NHA 1983, s 36(9). The form is set out in the Schedule.
3 TCPA 1990, s 118, applied (in relation to rights of entry under the TCPA 1990, s 324) by s 325(7), (in relation to rights of entry under the P(LBCA)A 1990) by s 88B(7) and (in relation to rights of entry under the P(HS)A 1990) by s 36B(6). In relation to rights of entry exercised under the NHA 1983, s 36: s 36(10). As to reference to the Upper Tribunal, see **Division H**.
4 Ie it is not listed in the PCA 1991, s 80, Sch 18.
5 CROW 2000 s 41(2): WCA 1981 s 51(5).

Q Access to the countryside

1 The right to compensation

[461]
A right to compensation arises where an access order (that is, an order which entitles any person to enter on land without being treated as a trespasser[1]) comes into operation[2]. A claim may be made against the local planning authority, in respect of land included in the order and any other land held therewith[3], other than excepted land, by any person interested in the land[4]. A claim may be made by a mortgagee, but a mortgagee[5] is not entitled to compensation, in respect of his interest, as such[6].

1 For the power to make an access order, see the National Parks and Access to the Countryside Act 1949 (NPACA 1949), s 65.
2 NPACA 1949, s 70.
3 Compensation cannot be claimed in respect of land held with the land over which the order allows access, unless such access would have been actionable apart from the order: NPACA 1949, s 70. As the meaning of land 'held with', see the text in relation to the CPA 1965, s 7 (severance and injurious affection) in **Division E**.
4 As to 'excepted land', see the NPACA 1949, s 60(5).
5 NPACA 1949, s 107(5)(*b*).
6 NPACA 1949, s 107(5)(*c*).

2 Assessment of compensation

[462]
Compensation is payable for depreciation in the value of the land[1]. The date for the assessment of compensation can be no later than the date of the coming into operation of the order[2]. The assessment must take into account the actual effect of the order over a period of five years, the fact and date of any revocation of the order, and the fact and date of any changes to the land over the five year period[3]. Rules 2–4 of the LCA 1961, s 5 apply to the assessment of the depreciation in value of land[4]. Compensation is to be assessed as if the interest was not subject to a mortgage[5].

1 NPACA 1949, s 70.
2 NPACA 1949, s 71(2).

3 NPACA 1949, s 71(1)–(4).
4 NPACA 1949, s 107(4). As to the LCA 1961, s 5, see **Division E**.
5 NPACA 1949, s 107(5)(*a*).

3 Procedure

[463]
No claim can be paid for five years after the coming into operation of the order, except on the grounds of hardship[1], so that its effects may be assessed[2]. In the meantime, a claim may be recorded with the local planning authority, which must be done by serving it in writing on the local planning authority within six months of the coming into operation of the order[3]. An application for payment of compensation must be served on the local planning authority in the prescribed manner within six months of the end of the five-year period[4]. If the land is subject to a mortgage, the compensation is to be paid to the mortgagee, who must deal with it as though it was proceeds of sale[5]. Any dispute as to compensation is to be referred to the Upper Tribunal[6].

1 In exceptional circumstances, payments on account may be made within the five years: NPACA 1949, s 73.
2 NPACA 1949, s 71(1).
3 NPACA 1949, s 72(1). The manner in which this is to be done is prescribed by the National Parks and Access to the Countryside Regulations 1950, SI 1950/1066, reg 23.
4 National Parks and Access to the Countryside Regulations 1950, SI 1950/1066, reg 24.
5 NPACA 1949, s 107(5)(*d*).
6 NPACA 1949, s 107(2). LCA 1961, s 4 in relation to costs applies: NPACA 1949, s 107(3): see **Division H**.

4 Interest

[464]–[800]
Interest is payable on any compensation due, from the date on which the order came into operation[1].

1 NPACA 1949, s 72(5). See para **[26]**.

Chapter 3

Compensation for decisions relating to mineral planning permissions

Contents

A Introduction

1 Scope

[801]
This chapter explains the rights to compensation which arise from the exercise by mineral planning authorities of certain of their powers in relation to development consisting of the winning and working of minerals and the deposition of mineral waste. These powers may be summarised as follows:

(*a*) power to make a revocation or modification order[2];
(*b*) power to make a discontinuance order[3];
(*c*) power to make a prohibition order[4];
(*d*) power to make a suspension order[5]; and
(*e*) power to impose conditions on interim development order permissions[6].

1 Under the Town and Country Planning Act 1990 (TCPA 1990), s 97.
2 Under the TCPA 1990, s 102.
3 Under the TCPA 1990, Sch 9, para 3(1).
4 Under the TCPA 1990, Sch 9, para 5.
5 Under the Environment Act 1995 (EA 1995), Sch 13.

2 Background

[802]
Three enactments, together with associated regulations introduced between 1981 and 1995 in response to the recommendations of the Stevens Committee[1] in 1976, have put in place a special regime applicable to mineral development. These enactments were:

(1) The Town and Country Planning (Minerals) Act 1981, which placed a duty on mineral planning authorities to review existing mineral sites and to make orders to bring mineral planning permissions up to date[2]. In order to encourage mineral planning authorities to use these powers to require higher environmental standards, especially in the restoration of sites, the rights to compensation, which would otherwise have been payable, were removed or reduced, so long as restrictions were not placed on the winning and working of the mineral. These provisions are now in the TCPA 1990, Sch 9 and regulations made thereunder.
(2) The Planning and Compensation Act 1991 (PCA 1991), in which:
  (*a*) section 21 and Sch 1 amended a number of the provisions of the TCPA 1990, relating to mineral development and compensation for restrictions on mineral development; and
  (*b*) section 22 and Sch 2 provided for the review of permissions granted between 1943 and 1948 under an interim development order (known as 'old mining permissions')[3].
(3) The EA 1995, s 96, Schs 13, 14, which provided for the review of planning permissions granted between 1948 and 1982 and for the periodic review of all permissions granted thereafter[4].

1 '*Planning Control over Mineral Working*' (HMSO, 1976).
2 For a general explanation of the operation of these provisions, see MPG 4. For a brief history of the legislative provisions see *Earthline Ltd v Secretary of State for Transport, Local Government and the Regions and West Berkshire County Council* [2002] EWCA Civ 1599, [2003] 1 P&CR 393, Sullivan J.
3 For a general explanation of the operation of these provisions, see MPGs 8 and 9.
4 For a general explanation of the operation of these provisions, see MPG 14.

B Revocation and modification orders

1 The right to compensation

[803]
The right to compensation, which arises where a planning permission is revoked or modified, is described above[1]. Where an order is made, which modifies a planning permission for development consisting of the winning and working of minerals or involving the depositing of mineral waste, the right to compensation is removed if the following conditions are all met[2]:

(*a*) the order does not:
  (i) impose any restriction on working rights[3], or
  (ii) modify or replace any restriction on working rights, subject to which the planning permission was granted[4], other than a restoration or aftercare condition[5]; and
(*b*) the planning permission was granted:
  (i) at least five years before the order was made; or
  (ii) before 22 February 1982; and
(*c*) within five years before the date on which the order was made,
  (i) the mineral planning authority have not made any other modification order or discontinuance order or prohibition order; and
  (ii) no application to determine conditions was finally determined[6].

1 See **Division G, Chapter 2**. The right to compensation in respect of a modification order under the TCPA 1990, s 107 is subject to s 116, which empowers the Secretary of State to make regulations which modify s 107. This power has been exercised in relation to (inter alia) modification orders relating to the working of minerals and deposition of mineral waste by the making of the Town and Country Planning (Compensation for Restrictions on Mineral Working and Mineral Waste Deposition) Regulations 1997, SI 1997/1111.
2 SI 1997/1111, reg 3.
3 As to the definition of 'restriction on working rights', see para **[804]**.
4 Or which has been imposed by an earlier modification, discontinuance or prohibition order: reg 3(2)(*a*)(ii).
5 As to the definition of 'restoration condition' and 'aftercare condition', see paras **[805]** and **[806]**.
6 That is, under the PCA 1991, Sch 2, para 2 or under the EA 1995, Sch 13 or 14.

2 Definitions

[804]
A 'restriction on working rights' means[1] a restriction which has the effect that one or more of the following is restricted or reduced:

(*a*) the size of the area which may be used for the winning and working of minerals or the depositing of mineral waste;
(*b*) the depth to which operations for the winning and working of minerals may extend;
(*c*) the height of any deposit of mineral waste;
(*d*) the rate at which any particular mineral may be extracted;
(*e*) the rate at which any particular mineral waste may be deposited;
(*f*) the period at the expiry of which any winning or working of minerals or depositing of mineral waste is to cease; or
(*g*) the total quantity of minerals which may be extracted from, or of mineral waste which may be deposited, on the land.

1 SI 1997/1111, reg 2(1).

[805]
A 'restoration condition'[1] is a condition requiring that, after the winning and working of minerals is completed or the depositing of refuse or waste materials has ceased, the site is be restored by the use of subsoil, topsoil and soil-making material.

1 TCPA 1990, s 336(1), Sch 5, para 2.

[806]
An 'aftercare condition'[1] is a condition requiring that such steps shall be taken as may be necessary to bring the land to the standard required for whichever of the following uses is specified in the condition, namely:

(*a*) use for agriculture;
(*b*) use for forestry; or
(*c*) use for amenity,

or a condition which requires a scheme to be approved by the mineral planning authority for that purpose.

1 TCPA 1990, s 336(1), Sch 5, para 2.

3 Buildings, plant and machinery

[807]
Compensation is not payable in respect of buildings, plant and machinery, unless the claimant can prove that they cannot be put to a reasonably beneficial use, except at the loss claimed[1]. The Upper Tribunal may direct that the claim for expenditure or loss in respect of buildings, plant or machinery, be severed from the remainder of the claim and dealt with at a later date[2].

1 TCPA 1990, s 107(3A), inserted by the Town and Country Planning (Minerals) Regulations 1995, SI 1995/2863, reg 3, Schedule, para 2.
2 TCPA 1990, s 107(3B), inserted by SI 1995/2863, reg 3, Schedule, para 2.

4 Ancillary provisions

[808]
Where, notwithstanding the restrictions on compensation described above, compensation is payable for modification of a planning permission, the provisions which govern procedure, interest, apportionment and registration and recovery of compensation on later development described above[1], in relation to revocation and modification of planning permissions, generally apply.

1 See **Division G, Chapter 2**. Where the revocation or modification order is made pursuant to the Conservation (Natural Habitats etc) Regulations 1994, SI 1994/2716, reg 55, provision is made by reg 57 that the order is to take effect on the date on which it is made and not (as under the TCPA 1990, s 97) when it is confirmed by the Secretary of State. This will be relevant, inter alia, to the date as at which compensation is to be assessed.

C Discontinuance orders

1 The right to compensation

[809]
The right to compensation where a discontinuance order is made is described above[1]. A Mineral Planning Authority may make a discontinuance order[2] requiring that:

(*a*) any use of land for winning or working of minerals, or for the depositing of refuse or waste minerals should be discontinued or that any conditions be imposed upon continued working or depositing; or
(*b*) any buildings or works on land so used be altered or removed; or
(*c*) any plant or machinery be altered or removed.

Where such an order is made, the right to compensation is removed[3] where all of the following conditions are met:

(*a*) the order does not:
 (i) impose any restriction on working rights[4], or
 (ii) modify or replace any such restriction, subject to which the planning permission was granted[5], other than a restoration or aftercare condition[6]; and

(*b*) the order:
  (i) imposes a condition on the continuance of the use of the land, or
  (ii) requires the alteration or removal of any buildings, works, plant or machinery used in connection with the development; and
(*c*) the development was begun at least five years before the order was made; and
(*d*) within five years of the order,
  (i) the mineral planning authority have not made any other modification, discontinuance or prohibition order, and
  (ii) no application to determine conditions[7] was finally determined.

1 See para **[321]**. The right to compensation for a discontinuance order under the TCPA 1990, s 115 is subject to s 116, which empowers the Secretary of State to make regulations modifying s 115. This power has been exercised in the form of the Town and Country Planning (Compensation for Restrictions on Mineral Working and Mineral Waste Depositing) Regulations 1997, SI 1997/1111.
2 The power of a mineral planning authority to make such an order is in the TCPA 1990, Sch 9, para 1(1).
3 TCPA 1990, s 116 and the Town and Country Planning (Compensation for Restrictions on Mineral Working and Mineral Waste Depositing) Regulations 1997, SI 1997/1111, reg 4.
4 For the definition of 'restriction on working rights', see para **[804]**.
5 Or which was imposed by an earlier modification, discontinuance or prohibition order: reg 4(2)(a)(ii).
6 For the definition of 'restoration condition' and 'aftercare condition', see paras **[805]** and **[806]**.
7 That is, under the PCA 1991, Sch 2, para 2 or under the EA 1995, Schs 13, 14.

2 Ancillary provisions

[810]–[820]
Where, notwithstanding the restrictions on compensation described above, compensation is payable in respect of a discontinuance order, the provisions which govern procedure and interest described above[1] in relation to discontinuance orders generally apply.

1 See paras **[324]–[325]**.

D Prohibition orders

1 The right to compensation

[821]
A right to compensation arises where a mineral planning authority makes an order[1] which:

(*a*) prohibits the resumption of winning and working minerals or depositing mineral waste; or
(*b*) imposes a requirement:
  (i) to alter or remove plant or machinery;
  (ii) to take specified steps to remove or alleviate any injury to amenity[2];
  (iii) to comply with any permission attached to the permission; or
  (iv) imposes a restoration condition[3].

1 Such an order may be made where winning and working of minerals or the deposition of mineral waste appears to have occurred, but permanently ceased: TCPA 1990, Sch 9, para 3(1).

2 Ie caused by the winning, working or depositing, but not injury due to subsidence caused by underground mining operations: TCPA 1990, Sch 9, para 3(3)(b).
3 TCPA 1990, Sch 9, para 3(3)(*d*) and see para **[805]**.

2 Assessment of compensation

[822]
Compensation is payable pursuant to the making of a prohibition order subject to two conditions being satisfied[1]:

(a) the development to which the order relates was begun at least five years before the order was made; and
(b) that the mineral planning authority did not make any other prohibition, discontinuance or modification order in respect of the land within the previous five years.

Where these conditions are met, the provisions of the TCPA 1990 s 15 apply, subject to modifications[2]. In these circumstances compensation is payable[3] for:

(a) expenditure incurred in carrying out work which is rendered abortive by the provisions of the order[4]; or
(b) any other loss or damage directly attributable to the provisions of the order[5].

However, in calculating the amount of any loss or damage attributable to the order, no account is to be taken of the value of any mineral which cannot be won or worked, the value of any mineral waste which cannot be deposited, the value of any void which cannot be filled, or the cost of complying with any restoration or aftercare condition in consequence of the order[6].

1 SI 1997/1111, reg 5(1) and (2).
2 SI 1997/1111, reg 5(1) and (3).
3 TCPA 1990, s 115(2) as modified by SI 1997/1111, reg 5(3).
4 This includes any expenditure on the preparation of plans for any work or upon other similar preparatory matters: TCPA s 115(3), as modified by SI 1997/1111, reg 5(3).
5 This includes work carried out for the purpose of alleviating or removing any injury to amenity caused by the winning and working of minerals on the land to which a prohibition order relates (unless included in another claim for compensation): TCPA 1990 s 15(3A), as modified by SI 1997/1111, reg 5(3).
6 See paras **[805]** and **[806]**.

[823]
Having assessed the amount of compensation, a deduction must be made as follows[1]:

(*a*) if the claimant is the only person entitled to claim compensation in respect of the order, £7,800 must be deducted from the claim; or
(*b*) if the claimant is not the only such person, the claimant's interest in the land and minerals must be assessed as a proportion of the total value of the land and minerals, and that proportion of £7,800 must be deducted from his claim.

1 SI 1997/1111, regs 5(1)(*b*), 7.

3 Ancillary provisions

[824]
The provisions which govern procedure and interest described in **Chapter 2**[1] in relation to discontinuance orders apply to claims for compensation arising out of prohibition orders[2].

1 See paras **[324]–[325]**.
2 SI 1997/1111, reg 5.

E Suspension orders

1 The right to compensation

[825]
A right to compensation arises where a mineral planning authority makes a suspension order[1] which requires steps to be taken for the protection of the environment while mineral working is suspended, that is, steps for:

(*a*) preserving the amenities of the area;
(*b*) protecting the area from damage; or
(*c*) preventing any deterioration of the condition of the land.

1 Mineral planning authorities have power to make suspension orders under the TCPA 1990, Sch 9, para 5 and supplementary suspension orders under Sch 9, para 6.

2 Assessment of compensation

[826]
Compensation is payable[1] for:

(*a*) expenditure[2] rendered abortive by a suspension order; and
(*b*) any other loss and damage which is directly attributable to the order[3].

However, in calculating the amount of any loss or damage, no account is to be taken of the value of any minerals which cannot be won or worked, of the value of any mineral waste which cannot be deposited or of the value of any void which cannot be filled in consequence of the order[4].

1 SI 1997/1111, reg 6(2), which modifies the TCPA 1990, s 115, by substituting sub-ss (2) and (3) and inserting sub-ss (3A) and (3B), and reg 6(1)(*b*), which applies the TCPA 1990, ss 115 (as modified) and 117. As to mortgagees, see s 117(3).
2 This includes expenditure on the preparation of plans and upon other similar preparatory matters: TCPA 1990, s 115(3A), inserted by SI 1997/1111, reg 6(2).
3 Works carried out to remove or alleviate injury to amenity is to be treated as loss or damage directly attributable to the order: TCPA 1990, s 115(3) as substituted by SI 1997/1111, reg 6(2).
4 See the provisions identified in note 1.

[827]
Having assessed the amount of compensation, a deduction must be made as follows[1]:

(*a*) if the claimant is the only person entitled to claim compensation in respect of the order, £7,800 must be deducted from the claim; or (*b*) if the claimant is not the only such person, the claimant's interest in the land and minerals must be assessed as a proportion of the total value of the land and minerals, and that proportion of £7,800 must be deducted from his claim.

1 SI 1997/1111, regs 6(1)(*b*), 7. This deduction has the effect of imposing on the claimant(s) the first £7,800 of any claim.

3 Ancillary provisions

[828]
The provisions which govern procedure and interest described in **Chapter 2**[1] in relation to discontinuance orders apply to claims for compensation for a suspension order.

1 See paras **[324]–[325]**.

F New conditions on old mining permissions

1 The right to compensation

[829]
A right to compensation arises where a mineral planning authority determines conditions which are to apply to a relevant planning permission relating to an active Phase I or Phase II site[1] and gives notice that[2]:

(*a*) the effect of the conditions, other than any restoration or aftercare conditions[3], as compared with the effect of the conditions to which the planning permission was subject immediately prior to the making of the authority's determination, is to restrict working rights[4] in respect of the site; and
(*b*) the effect of that restriction of working rights would be to prejudice adversely to an unreasonable degree:
  (i) the economic viability of operating the site, or
  (ii) the asset value of the site.

The right to compensation also arises: (i) where the Mineral Planning Authority gives notice that in its opinion the economic viability or the asset value would *not* be prejudiced to an unreasonable degree but an appeal is made and allowed[5]; and (ii) where the conditions were determined upon a reference to the Secretary of State and he gives notice that in his opinion such prejudice would arise[6].

1 'Relevant planning permission' is defined by the EA 1995, Sch 13, para 1(1) as any planning permission granted after 30 June 1948 for minerals development. It does not include 'old mining permissions' (for which see the PCA 1991, s 22(1), applied by the EA 1995, Sch 13, para 1(1)). Nor does it include a planning permission granted by development order. For the definition of 'Phase I' and 'Phase II' sites, see the EA 1995, Sch 13, para 2.
2 EA 1995, Sch 13, para 15(1)(*b*), (2), (3), read with para 10(2).
3 By the EA 1995, s 96(2), Sch 13 has effect as if it were included in Pt III of the TCPA 1990, so that 'restoration condition' and 'aftercare condition' have the meanings given to them in the TCPA 1990, Sch 5, para 2(2), (3): see the TCPA 1990, s 128(3) and see paras **[805]** and **[806]**.
4 Defined in the EA 1995, Sch 13, para 1(6) in the same way as for modification orders as set out in para **[804]**.

5 EA 1995, Sch 13, paras 15(2)(c)(ii) and 15(3)(a)(ii).
6 EA 1995, Sch 13, para 15(3)(b).

2 Assessment of compensation

[830]–[840]
Compensation is to be assessed as if a modification order had been made in respect of development other than for the winning and working of minerals or deposition of mineral waste[1].

1 EA 1995, Sch 13, para 15(4)–(6). As to compensation for modification orders generally, see paras **[302]–[308]**.

3 Ancillary provisions

[841]–[1100]
The provisions which govern procedure, interest, apportionment and registration and recovery of compensation on subsequent development which are described in **Chapter 2**[1], in relation to revocation and modifications orders, generally apply[2].

1 See paras **[305]–[308]**.
2 EA 1995, Sch 13, para 15(5), (6).

Chapter 4

Compensation for the exercise of powers under the Highways Act 1980

Contents

A Introduction

[1101]

This chapter describes the rights to compensation which arise from the exercise by local authorities[1] and highway authorities[2] of certain of their powers under the Highways Act 1980 (HiA 1980)[3], the basis of assessment and the procedure for claims. Highway authorities also have powers to acquire land compulsorily and to carry out works to mitigate the effects of the construction and use of highways; these are explained elsewhere in this work[4]. In addition to the rights described in this chapter, a right to compensation arises where a right of way with vehicles over a highway is extinguished under the Town and Country Planning Act 1990 (TCPA 1990)[5]. It should be noted that, although there are numerous rights to compensation arising under the HiA 1980, there is no general right to compensation where highways are stopped up or diverted, although, in some circumstances, stopping up or diversion may give rise to a claim under the Land Clauses Consolidation Act 1845 (LCCA 1845) or the Compulsory Purchase Act 1965 (CPA 1965), s 10[6]. The rights described in this chapter stem from the exercise of powers which fall into the following broad categories:

(*a*) directions and other matters affecting specific properties;
(*b*) orders affecting public rights which have consequences for individuals;
(*c*) the carrying out of works in connection with highways; and
(*d*) entry onto land.

1 Defined in the HiA 1980, s 329.
2 Defined in the HiA 1980, Pt I. This includes the Secretary of State in certain circumstances: HiA 1980, s 23.
3 This chapter deals with the rights to compensation once the powers have been exercised and not the scope of the powers or the procedure for their exercise. Powers similar to some of those in the HiA 1980 may also be found in other legislation, such as local Acts and Transport and Works Act orders, which authorise specific works; see, for example, the model clauses in the Transport and Works Act (Model Clauses for Railways and Tramways) Order 1992, SI 1992/3270.
4 Powers of compulsory purchase are explained in **Division B**. Compensation for compulsory purchase is explained in **Division E**. Powers to mitigate the effect of highways is explained in **Division F, Chapter 4**.
5 TCPA 1990, s 250. This right is described in paras **[444]–[447]**.
6 See **Division F, Chapter 2**.

B Prescription of an improvement line

1 The right to compensation

[1102]
A right to compensation arises where a highway authority prescribes an improvement line in relation to one or both sides of a street[1]. A claim may be made against the highway authority by any person whose property is injuriously affected by the prescribing of the line[2]. A claim may be made by a mortgagee, but not in respect of his interest as such[3]. Compensation, in respect of an interest subject to a mortgage, is to be paid to the mortgagee (or, as the case may be, the first mortgagee) and must be applied as if it were proceeds of sale[4].

1 Under the HiA 1980, s 73. The purpose of an improvement line is to enable the street to be widened at a later date, and the effect of such a line is to prohibit the erection of any building or any permanent excavation in front of the line. As to the meaning of 'street', see s 329. As to the meaning of 'building', see s 73(13).
2 HiA 1980, s 73(9).
3 HiA 1980, s 309(*b*).
4 HiA 1980, s 309(*d*).

2 Assessment of compensation

[1103]

Compensation is payable in respect of any injurious affection (that is, depreciation in value) of the claimant's property[1]. The measure of compensation is the depreciation in value of the claimant's land; it would not extend to personal losses[2]. Rules 2–4 of the Land Compensation Act 1961 (LCA 1961), s 5 apply to the assessment of the depreciation in the value of the land[3]. Compensation is not recoverable in respect of any building erected, contract made or other things done after a plan showing the proposed improvement line has been deposited in accordance with the prescribed procedure for making an order[4]. In determining the amount of compensation payable, any benefit to the claimant, by reason of the improvement of the street, and any undertaking given by the authority to improve the street must be taken into account[5]. Where an interest in land is subject to a mortgage, compensation is to be assessed as if there were no mortgage[6].

1 HiA 1980, s 73(9).
2 *Argyle Motors (Birkenhead) Ltd v Birkenhead Corpn* [1975] AC 99, HL. Although decided in the context of the LCCA 1845, s 68, the same would appear to apply to s 73.
3 HiA 1980, s 307(3). As to the LCA 1961, s 5, see **Division E**.
4 HiA 1980, s 73(10), Sch 9, para 5.
5 HiA 1980, s 307(5). Such an undertaking becomes binding on the authority if it is embodied in the Upper Tribunal's award.
6 HiA 1980, s 309(*a*).

3 Procedure

[1104]

The statute does not prescribe a time within which claims must be made[1], nor the procedure for making claims[2]. Any dispute arising on a claim for compensation is to be determined by the Upper Tribunal; the LCA 1961, s 4 (as to costs) will then apply[3].

1 However, the Limitation Act 1980, s 9 will apply. A reference to the Upper Tribunal to resolve a dispute as to compensation is an action to recover compensation for the purposes of s 9: *Hillingdon London Borough Council v ARC Ltd* [1999] Ch 139, CA, at 280.
2 Although there is no particular form for the claim, it must be an unequivocal claim and not merely an intention to make a claim: *Texas Homecare Ltd v Lewes District Council* (1985) 51 P&CR 205, Lands Tribunal. See also *International Ferry Traders Ltd v Adur District Council* [2004] EWCA Civ 288, [2004] RVR 65.
3 HiA 1980, s 307(1), (2), see **H[81]**.

4 Interest on compensation

[1105]

Interest is payable on compensation due, from the date of the claim[1].

1 Planning and Compensation Act 1991 (PCA 1991), s 80, Sch 18. See para **[26]**.

C Prescription of a building line

1 The right to compensation

[1106]
A right to compensation arises where a highway authority prescribes a building line[1]. A claim may be made by any person whose property is injuriously affected[2]. A claim may be made by a mortgagee, but not in respect of his interest as such[3]. Compensation, in respect of an interest subject to a mortgage, is to be paid to the mortgagee (or, as the case may be, the first mortgagee) and must be applied as if it were proceeds of sale[4].

1 That is, a line in front of which no new building or permanent excavation may take place: HiA 1980, s 74. As to the meaning of 'building', see ss 73(13), 74(13).
2 HiA 1980, s 74(8).
3 HiA 1980, s 309(*b*), (*c*).
4 HiA 1980, s 309(*d*).

2 Assessment of compensation

[1107]
Compensation is payable in respect of any injurious affection (that is, depreciation in value) of the claimant's property[1]. Compensation is not recoverable in respect of anything done after a plan showing the proposed building line has been served on him[2]. In determining the amount of compensation payable, any benefit to the claimant by reason of the improvement made or about to be made to the street must be taken into account[3]. Rules 2–4 of the LCA 1961, s 5 apply, insofar as the compensation is calculated by reference to the depreciation in the value of an interest in the land[4]. Where an interest in land is subject to a mortgage, compensation is to be assessed as if there were no mortgage[5].

1 HiA 1980, s 74(8).
2 Except for completing a building or contract commenced before that date: HiA 1980, s 74(9)(*b*).
3 HiA 1980, s 307(6).
4 HiA 1980, s 307(3). As to the LCA 1961, s 5, see **Division E**.
5 HiA 1980, s 309(*a*).

3 Procedure

[1108]
The claim must be made[1] within six months of the date on which the line was prescribed or, if the claimant was a person on whom notice was required to be served, six months from the date on which he was served with notice[2]. Any dispute arising on a claim for compensation is to be determined by the Upper Tribunal; the LCA 1961, s 4 (as to costs) will then apply[3].

1 A claim is 'made' when it is received: *Camden London Borough v ADC Estates Ltd* (1990) 61 P&CR 48, CA.
2 HiA 1980, s 74(9)(*a*). Although there is no particular form for the claim, it must be an unequivocal claim and not merely an intention to make a claim: *Texas Homecare Ltd v Lewes District Council* (1985) 51 P&CR 205, Lands Tribunal. See also *International Ferry Traders Ltd v Adur District Council* [2004] EWCA Civ 288, [2004] RVR 65.
3 HiA 1980, s 307(1), (2), see **Division H[81]**.

4 Interest on compensation

[1109]
Interest is payable on compensation due, from the date of the claim[1].

1 PCA 1991, s 80, Sch 18. See para **[26]**.

D Directions to prevent obstructions to view

1 The right to compensation

[1110]–[1120]
A right to compensation arises where a highway authority serves notice directing an owner or occupier of land to alter a wall, fence or vegetation, in order to prevent danger from obstruction to view[1]. A claim may be made by any person sustaining direct loss and any person having an interest in the land which is injuriously affected[2]. A claim may be made by a mortgagee, but not in respect of his interest as such[3]. Compensation, in respect of an interest subject to a mortgage, is to be paid to the mortgagee (or, as the case may be, the first mortgagee) and must be applied as if it were proceeds of sale[4].

1 Under the HiA 1980, s 79.
2 HiA 1980, s 79(11).
3 HiA 1980, s 309(*b*).
4 HiA 1980, s 309(*d*).

2 Assessment of compensation

[1121]
Compensation is payable in respect of:

(*a*) loss in direct consequence of any direction in the notice;
(*b*) for injurious affection[1]; and
(*c*) any expenses reasonably incurred in complying with any directions made in the notice[2].

Rules 2–4 of the LCA 1961, s 5 apply, insofar as the compensation is calculated by reference to the depreciation in the value of an interest in the land[3]. Where an interest in land is subject to a mortgage, compensation is to be assessed as if there were no mortgage[4].

1 HiA 1980, s 79(11).
2 HiA 1980, s 79(12).
3 HiA 1980, s 307(3). As to the LCA 1961, s 5, see **Division E**.
4 HiA 1980, s 309(*a*).

3 Procedure

[1122]
A claim must be made[1] within six months of service of the notice upon the claimant[2]; the manner of making a claim is not prescribed[3]. Any dispute in

relation to compensation is, if the parties agree, to be determined by arbitration, or otherwise, by the county court[4].

1 A claim is 'made' when it is received: *Camden London Borough v ADC Estates Ltd* (1990) 61 P&CR 48, CA.
2 HiA 1980, s 79(11).
3 Although there is no particular form for the claim, it must be an unequivocal claim and not merely an intention to make a claim: *Texas Homecare Ltd v Lewes District Council* (1985) 51 P&CR 205, Lands Tribunal. See also *International Ferry Traders Ltd v Adur District Council* [2004] EWCA Civ 288, [2004] RVR 65.
4 HiA 1980, s 308. This applies even if the amount claimed exceeds the county court's jurisdiction: s 308(2).

4 Interest on compensation

[1123]
Interest is payable on compensation due in respect of loss from the date of the notice, in respect of injurious affection from the date of the claim or, where the claim relates expenses incurred, from the date of the notice[1].

1 PCA 1991, s 80, Sch 18. See para **[26]**.

E Directions requiring the angles of new buildings on corners to be rounded off

1 The right to compensation

[1124]
A right to compensation arises where a local authority or highway authority require[1] that a new building on the corner of two streets be rounded off or splayed[2]. A claim may be made against the authority which made the direction by any person suffering loss. A claim may be made by a mortgagee, but not in respect of his interest, as such[3]. Compensation, in respect of an interest subject to a mortgage, is to be paid to the mortgagee (or, as the case may be, the first mortgagee) and must be applied as if it were proceeds of sale[4].

1 HiA 1980, s 286.
2 HiA 1980, s 286(3).
3 HiA 1980, s 309(*b*), (*c*).
4 HiA 1980, s 309(*d*).

2 Assessment of compensation

[1125]
Compensation is payable in respect of any loss sustained through the exercise of these powers[1]. Rules 2–4 of the LCA 1961, s 5 apply, insofar as the compensation is calculated by reference to the depreciation in the value of an interest in the land[2]. Where an interest in land is subject to a mortgage, compensation is to be assessed as if there were no mortgage[3].

1 HiA 1980, s 286(3).
2 HiA 1980, s 307(3). As to the LCA 1961, s 5, see **Division E**.
3 HiA 1980, s 309(*a*).

3 Procedure

[1126]
The statute does not prescribe a time within which claims must be made[1], nor the procedure for making claims[2]. Any dispute, in relation to compensation, is, if the parties agree, to be determined by arbitration, or otherwise, by the county court[3]. There is no provision for the payment of interest on compensation under these provisions[4].

1 However, the Limitation Act 1980, s 9 will apply. A reference to the Upper Tribunal to resolve a dispute as to compensation is an action to recover compensation for the purposes of s 9: *Hillingdon London Borough Council v ARC Ltd* [1999] Ch 139, CA.
2 Although there is no particular form for the claim, it must be an unequivocal claim and not merely an intention to make a claim: *Texas Homecare Ltd v Lewes District Council* (1985) 51 P&CR 205, Lands Tribunal. See also *International Ferry Traders Ltd v Adur District council* [2004] EWCA Civ 288, [2004] RVR 65.
3 HiA 1980, s 308. This applies, even if the amount claimed is above the county court jurisdiction: s 308(2).
4 Ie this section is not listed in the PCA 1991, Sch 18. As to an arbitrator's power to award interest, see the Arbitration Act 1996, s 49. See para **[26]**.

F Directions requiring gas and water supplies to be moved

1 The right to compensation

[1127]
A right to compensation arises where a local authority exercises its powers[1] to order gas and water pipes to be moved[2]. A claim may be made against the local authority by any person suffering loss. A claim may be made by a mortgagee, but not in respect of his interest as such[3]. Compensation in respect of an interest subject to a mortgage is to be paid to the mortgagee (or, as the case may be, the first mortgagee) and must be applied as if it were proceeds of sale[4].

1 By virtue of the HiA 1980, s 288, the power under the Public Health Act 1875, s 153 to direct water and gas supplies to be moved is applied where a local authority exercises its powers under the HiA 1980, s 294 or any of the powers listed in Sch 22. This does not apply where the code in the Public Utilities Street Works Act 1950, Pt II applies.
2 HiA 1980, s 288(2).
3 HiA 1980, s 309(*b*), (*c*).
4 HiA 1980, s 309(*d*).

2 Assessment of compensation

[1128]
Compensation is payable in respect of damage suffered as a result of the execution of works under these powers[1]. The measure of damage is the depreciation in the value of claimant's land and rr 2–4 of the LCA 1961, s 5 apply to the assessment of such depreciation[2]. Where an interest in land is subject to a mortgage, compensation is to be assessed as if there were no mortgage[3].

1 HiA 1980, s 288(2).
2 HiA 1980, s 307(3). As to the LCA 1961, s 5, see **Division E**.
3 HiA 1980, s 309(*a*).

3 Procedure

[1129]
The statute does not prescribe a time within which claims must be made[1], nor the procedure for making claims[2]. Any dispute in relation to compensation is, if the parties agree, to be determined by arbitration, or otherwise, by the county court[3]. There is no provision for the payment of interest on compensation under these provisions[4].

1 However, the Limitation Act 1980, s 9 will apply. A reference to the Upper Tribunal to resolve a dispute as to compensation is an action to recover compensation for the purposes of s 9: *Hillingdon London Borough Council v ARC Ltd* [1999] Ch 139, CA.
2 Although there is no particular form for the claim, it must be an unequivocal claim and not merely an intention to make a claim: *Texas Homecare Ltd v Lewes District Council* (1985) 51 P&CR 205, Lands Tribunal. See also *International Ferry Traders Ltd v Adur District Council* [2004] EWCA Civ 288, [2004] RVR 65.
3 HiA 1980, s 308. This applies, even if the amount claimed is above the county court jurisdiction: s 308(2).
4 Ie this section is not listed in the PCA 1991, Sch 18. As to an arbitrator's power to award interest, see the Arbitration Act 1996, s 49. See para **[26]**.

G Exchange of land to adjust boundaries of highways

1 The right to compensation

[1130]–[1140]
A right to compensation arises where a highway authority, for the purpose of straightening or otherwise adjusting the boundaries of a highway, enters into an agreement providing for an exchange of land with a landowner and the former highway land provided in exchange is not owned by the highway authority[1]. A claim may be made against the highway authority by any person deprived of an estate, interest, right or charge as a result of the exchange[2].

1 HiA 1980, s 256.
2 HiA 1980, s 256(4).

2 Assessment of compensation

[1141]
Compensation is payable in respect of damage suffered by any person as a result of being deprived of an estate, interest, right or charge in the exchange land[1]. Rules 2–4 of the LCA 1961, s 5 apply, insofar as the compensation is calculated by reference to the depreciation in the value of an interest in the land[2]. Where an interest in land is subject to a mortgage, compensation is to be assessed as if there were no mortgage[3].

1 HiA 1980, s 256(5).
2 HiA 1980, s 307(3).
3 HiA 1980, s 309(*a*). As to the LCA 1961, s 5, see **Division E**.

3 Procedure

[1142]
The statute does not prescribe a time within which claims must be made[1], nor the procedure for making claims[2]. Any dispute in relation to compensation is, if the parties agree, to be determined by arbitration, or otherwise, by the county court[3]. There is no provision for the payment of interest on compensation under these provisions[4].

1 However, the Limitation Act 1980, s 9 will apply. A reference to the Upper Tribunal to resolve a dispute as to compensation is an action to recover compensation for the purposes of s 9: *Hillingdon London Borough Council v ARC Ltd* [1999] Ch 139, CA.
2 Although there is no particular form for the claim, it must be an unequivocal claim and not merely an intention to make a claim: *Texas Homecare Ltd v Lewes District Council* (1985) 51 P&CR 205, Lands Tribunal. See also *International Ferry Traders Ltd v Adur District Council* [2004] EWCA Civ 288, [2004] RVR 65.
3 HiA 1980, s 308. This applies, even if the amount claimed is above the county court jurisdiction: s 308(2).
4 Ie this section is not listed in the PCA 1991, Sch 18. As to an arbitrator's power to award interest, see the Arbitration Act 1996, s 49. See para **[26]**.

H Removal of apparatus of public utility undertakers and removal of public sewers

1 The right to compensation

[1143]
A right to compensation arises where any apparatus of public utility undertakers[1] or any public sewer is removed pursuant to an order made by a highway authority[2]. A claim may be made against the highway authority by an owner or occupier of premises to which a supply was given from that apparatus or, as the case may be, to which the sewer was connected[3].

1 HiA 1980, s 329.
2 Under the TCPA 1990, ss 271, 272 or 273, as applied to the HiA 1980, ss 14, 16 or 18 by s 21. Statutory undertakers are entitled to compensation under the TCPA 1990, ss 279–282, as described in para **[410]**.
3 HiA 1980, ss 21(4), (4A) for sewers.

2 Assessment of compensation

[1144]
Compensation is payable in respect of expenditure reasonably incurred for the purpose of making a connection with other apparatus[1].

1 HiA 1980, s 21(4), (4A).

3 Procedure

[1145]
The statute does not prescribe a time within which claims must be made[1], nor the procedure for making claims[2]. Any dispute arising on a claim for

compensation is to be determined by the Upper Tribunal; the LCA 1961, s 4 (as to costs) will then apply[3]. There is no provision for the payment of interest on compensation under these provisions[4].

1 However, the Limitation Act 1980, s 9 will apply. A reference to the Upper Tribunal to resolve a dispute as to compensation is an action to recover compensation for the purposes of s 9: *Hillingdon London Borough Council v ARC Ltd* [1999] Ch 139, CA.
2 Although there is no particular form for the claim, it must be an unequivocal claim and not merely an intention to make a claim: *Texas Homecare Ltd v Lewes District Council* (1985) 51 P&CR 205, Lands Tribunal. See also *International Ferry Traders Ltd v Adur District Council* [2004] EWCA Civ 288, [2004] RVR 65.
3 HiA 1980, s 307(1), (2).
4 Ie this section is not listed in the PCA 1991, Sch 18. See para **[26]**.

I Creation, diversion or extinguishment of public paths and rail crossings

1 The right to compensation

[1146]
A right to compensation arises[1] where a local authority[2] makes any of the following orders:

(*a*) a public path creation order[3];
(*b*) a public path extinguishment order[4];
(*c*) a public path diversion order[5];
(*d*) a rail crossing extinguishment order[6]; or
(*e*) a rail crossing diversion order[7].

Compensation may be claimed from the local authority by a person who has an interest in land, which is defined, for this purpose, as including any estate in or right over land, whether exercisable by virtue of ownership, licence or agreement, and includes sporting rights[8]. Where the path does not cross the claimant's land, compensation is only payable if the creation, diversion or extinguishment (as the case may be) would have been actionable if done otherwise than under statutory power[9]. A claim may be made by a mortgagee, but not in respect of his interest as such[10]. Compensation, in respect of an interest subject to a mortgage, is to be paid to the mortgagee (or, as the case may be, the first mortgagee) and must be applied as if it were proceeds of sale[11].

1 HiA 1980, s 28(1), which applies to public path creation orders. Section 121 applies s 28 to the other orders listed in this paragraph.
2 HiA 1980, s 26 uses the term 'local authority', other sections use the term 'council'; both are defined in the HiA 1980, s 329. The Secretary of State has power to make orders under ss 26(2) and 120; when he does so, the local authority is that nominated by the Secretary of State: HiA 1980, s 28(3).
3 That is, an order creating a footpath or bridleway under the HiA 1980, s 26.
4 That is, an order stopping up a footpath or bridleway under the HiA 1980, s 118.
5 That is, an order diverting a footpath or bridleway under the HiA 1980, s 119.
6 That is, an order stopping up a footpath or bridleway which crosses a railway under the HiA 1980, s 118A.
7 That is, an order diverting a crossing of a railway: HiA 1980, s 119A.
8 HiA 1980, s 28(5).
9 HiA 1980, s 28(4).
10 HiA 1980, s 309(*b*), (*c*).
11 HiA 1980, s 309(*d*).

2 Assessment of compensation

[1147]
Compensation may be claimed in respect of:

(*a*) depreciation in the value of an interest[1] in land; and
(*b*) damage resulting from disturbance[2] in the enjoyment of land

in consequence of the coming into operation of one of the orders listed above[3]. Rules 2–4 of the LCA 1961, s 5 apply, insofar as the compensation is calculated by reference to the depreciation in the value of an interest in the land[4]. Where an interest in land is subject to a mortgage, compensation is to be assessed as if there were no mortgage[5].

1 As to the meaning of 'interest', see the HiA 1980, s 28(5).
2 As to disturbance in the context of compulsory acquisition, see **Division E**.
3 HiA 1980, ss 28(1), 121.
4 HiA 1980, s 307(3). As to the LCA 1961, s 5, see **Division E**.
5 HiA 1980, s 309(*a*).

3 Procedure

[1148]
A claim must be made[1] within six months from the coming into force of the order[2]. A claim must be made in writing and served on the authority by delivering it at or sending it by prepaid post to the office of the authority addressed to the chief executive[3]. Any dispute arising on a claim for compensation is to be determined by the Upper Tribunal; the LCA 1961, s 4 (as to costs) will then apply[4].

1 A claim is 'made' when it is received: *Camden London Borough v ADC Estates Ltd* (1990) 61 P&CR 48, CA.
2 Public Path Orders Regulations 1993, SI 1993/11, reg 5 and Rail Crossings Extinguishment and Diversion Orders 1993, SI 1993/9, reg 6.
3 SI 1993/11, reg 5 and SI 1993/9, reg 6. Although there is no particular form for the claim, it must be an unequivocal claim and not merely an intention to make a claim: *Texas Homecare Ltd v Lewes District Council* (1985) 51 P&CR 205, Lands Tribunal. See also *International Ferry Traders Ltd v Adur District Council* [2004] EWCA Civ 288, [2004] RVR 65.
4 HiA 1980, s 307(1), (2).

4 Interest on compensation

[1149]
Interest is payable on compensation, from the date of the claim[1].

1 PCA 1991, s 80, Sch 18 (referring to the HiA 1980, ss 28, 121). See para **[26]**.

J Stopping up of private means of access

1 The right to compensation

[1150]–[1160]
A right to compensation arises where a private means of access to premises is stopped up or restrictions on its use are imposed by a highway authority[1].

A claim may be made against the highway authority by any person having an interest in or in possession of land. A claim may be made by a mortgagee, but not in respect of his interest as such[2]. Compensation, in respect of an interest subject to a mortgage, is to be paid to the mortgagee (or, as the case may be, the first mortgagee) and must be applied as if it were proceeds of sale[3].

1 Under the HiA 1980, s 124 or s 125 (extending the HiA 1980, ss 14 and 18 and the TCPA 1990, s 248): HiA 1980, s 126. As to restrictions on use of a private means of access, see the HiA 1980, 126(2).
2 HiA 1980, s 309(*b*), (*c*).
3 HiA 1980, s 309(*d*).

2 Assessment of compensation

[1161]
Compensation is payable in respect of[1]:

(*a*) depreciation of the value of any interest in the premises; or
(*b*) damage by reason of being disturbed[2] in the enjoyment of the premises.

In determining the amount of compensation, it is necessary to take into account any new means of access to the premises, provided by the authority from whom the compensation is claimed[3]. Rules 2–4 of the LCA 1961, s 5 apply, insofar as the compensation is calculated by reference to the depreciation in the value of an interest in the land[4]. Where an interest in land is subject to a mortgage, compensation is to be assessed as if there were no mortgage[5].

1 HiA 1980, s 126(2).
2 As to disturbance in the context of compulsory acquisition, see **Division E**.
3 HiA 1980, s 307(4).
4 HiA 1980, s 307(3). As to the LCA 1961,s 5, see **Division E**.
5 HiA 1980, s 309(*a*).

3 Procedure

[1162]
The statute does not prescribe a time within which claims must be made, nor the procedure for making claims[1]. Any dispute arising on a claim for compensation is to be determined by the Upper Tribunal; the LCA 1961, s 4 (as to costs) will then apply[2].

1 However, the Limitation Act 1980, s 9 will apply. A reference to the Upper Tribunal to resolve a dispute as to compensation is an action to recover compensation for the purposes of s 9: *Hillingdon London Borough Council v ARC Ltd* [1999] Ch 139, CA. Although there is no particular form for the claim, it must be an unequivocal claim and not merely an intention to make a claim: *Texas Homecare Ltd v Lewes District council* (1985) 51 P&CR 205, Lands Tribunal. See also *International Ferry Traders Ltd v Adur District council* [2004] EWCA Civ 288, [2004] RVR 65.
2 HiA 1980, s 307(1), (2): see **Division H**.

4 Interest on compensation

[1163]
Interest is payable on compensation, from the date of the claim[1].

1 PCA 1991, s 80, Sch 18. See para **[26]**.

K Alteration of levels of highways

1 The right to compensation

[1164]
A right to compensation arises where a highway authority alters the level of a highway maintainable at the public expense[1]. A claim may be made against the highway authority by any person who sustains damage by reason of the execution of the works. A claim may be made by a mortgagee, but not in respect of his interest as such[2]. Compensation, in respect of an interest subject to a mortgage, is to be paid to the mortgagee (or, as the case may be, the first mortgagee) and must be applied as if it were proceeds of sale[3].

1 HiA 1980, s 77.
2 HiA 1980, s 309(*b*), (*c*).
3 HiA 1980, s 309(*d*).

2 Assessment of compensation

[1165]
Compensation is payable in respect of damage sustained by reason of the execution of the works[1]. This includes structural injury to premises, but does not include loss of trade caused by the diversion of traffic[2]. The measure of compensation is the depreciation in the value of the land and rr 2–4 of the LCA 1961, s 5 apply to the assessment of such depreciation[3]. Where an interest in land is subject to a mortgage, compensation is to be assessed as if there were no mortgage[4].

1 HiA 1980, s 77(2).
2 *Bigg v London Corpn* (1873) LR 15 Eq 376, applying *Ricket v Metropolitan Rly Co* (1867) LR 2 HL 175, which was a decision under a local Act which gave power to alter the level or stop up a street. See also *Argyle Motors (Birkenhead) Ltd v Birkenhead Corpn* [1975] AC 99, HL, decided in the context of the LCCA 1845, s 68.
3 HiA 1980, s 307(3). As to the LCA 1961, s 5, see **Division E**.
4 HiA 1980, s 309(*a*).

3 Procedure

[1166]
The statute does not prescribe a time within which claims must be made[1], nor the procedure for making claims[2]. Any dispute, in relation to compensation, is, if the parties agree, to be determined by arbitration, or otherwise, by the county court[3].

1 However, the Limitation Act 1980, s 9 will apply. A reference to the Upper Tribunal to resolve a dispute as to compensation is an action to recover compensation for the purposes of s 9: *Hillingdon London Borough Council v ARC Ltd* [1999] Ch 139, CA.
2 Although there is no particular form for the claim, it must be an unequivocal claim and not merely an intention to make a claim: *Texas Homecare Ltd v Lewes District Council* (1985) 51 P&CR 205, Lands Tribunal. See also *International Ferry Traders Ltd v Adur District Council* [2004] EWCA Civ 288, [2004] RVR 65.
3 HiA 1980, s 308. This applies, even if the amount claimed is above the county court jurisdiction: s 308(2).

4 Interest on compensation

[1167]
Interest is payable on compensation due, from the date of the claim or, where the claim relates to damage sustained, from the date of the damage[1].

1 PCA 1991, s 80, Sch 18. See para **[26]**. As to an arbitrator's power to award interest, see the Arbitration Act 1996, s 49.

L Planting of trees, laying out of grass verges, erection of fences etc

1 The right to compensation

[1168]
A right to compensation arises where a local authority, highway authority, community or parish council exercises its powers[1] to plant trees and shrubs, to lay out verges, to erect fences and to maintain the trees, shrubs and verges[2]. A claim may be made by any person whose property is damaged. A claim may be made by a mortgagee, but not in respect of his interest as such[3]. Compensation, in respect of an interest subject to a mortgage, is to be paid to the mortgagee (or, as the case may be, the first mortgagee) and must be applied as if it were proceeds of sale[4].

1 Under the HiA 1980, s 96, which also applies to land which is not highway: s 96(3). As to the exercise of this power by local authorities, see s 96(4), and by community or parish councils, see s 96(5).
2 HiA 1980, s 96(7).
3 HiA 1980, s 309(*b*), (*c*).
4 HiA 1980, s 309(*d*).

2 Assessment of compensation

[1169]
Compensation is payable in respect of any damage caused to property in the exercise of those powers[1], but no compensation is payable if the damage is caused by the negligence of the claimant and it is to be reduced proportionately if he has contributed to the damage by his negligence[2]. The measure of compensation is the depreciation in the claimant's land and rr 2–4 of the LCA 1961, s 5 apply to the assessment of such depreciation[3]. Where an interest in land is subject to a mortgage, compensation is to be assessed as if there were no mortgage[4].

1 HiA 1980, s 96(7).
2 HiA 1980, s 96(8) . For an example of a case under earlier legislation in which a driver was alleged to have caused the danger, but was held not to have been at fault, see *Hale v Hants and Dorset Motor Services Ltd* [1947] 2 All ER 628.
3 HiA 1980, s 307(3). As to the LCA 1961, s 5, see **Division E**.
4 HiA 1980, s 309(*a*).

3 Procedure

[1170]–[1180]
The statute does not prescribe a time within which claims must be made[1], nor the procedure for making claims[2]. Any dispute in relation to compensation is, if the parties agree, to be determined by arbitration or otherwise by the county court[3]. There is no provision for the payment of interest on compensation under these provisions[4].

1 However, the Limitation Act 1980, s 9 will apply. A reference to the Upper Tribunal to resolve a dispute as to compensation is an action to recover compensation for the purposes of s 9: *Hillingdon London Borough Council v ARC Ltd* [1999] Ch 139, CA.
2 Although there is no particular form for the claim, it must be an unequivocal claim and not merely an intention to make a claim: *Texas Homecare Ltd v Lewes District Council* (1985) 51 P&CR 205, Lands Tribunal. See also *International Ferry Traders Ltd v Adur District Council* [2004] EWCA Civ 288, [2004] RVR 65.
3 HiA 1980, s 308. This applies, even if the amount claimed is above the county court jurisdiction: s 308(2).
4 Ie this section is not listed in the PCA 1991, Sch 18. See para **[26]**. As to an arbitrator's power to award interest, see the Arbitration Act 1996, s 49.

M Diversion of a navigable watercourse

1 The right to compensation

[1181]
A right to compensation arises where works for the diversion of a navigable watercourse are carried out under an order made by a highway authority[1], except where the works are on land or in the exercise of rights which have been compulsorily acquired[2]. A claim may be made against the highway authority by any person having an interest in land or a right of access to the watercourse. A claim may be made by a mortgagee, but not in respect of his interest as such[3]. Compensation, in respect of an interest subject to a mortgage, is to be paid to the mortgagee (or, as the case may be, the first mortgagee) and must be applied as if it were proceeds of sale[4].

1 HiA 1980, ss 108(1), 109(1).
2 HiA 1980, s 109(2).
3 HiA 1980, s 309(*b*), (*c*).
4 HiA 1980, s 309(*d*).

2 Assessment of compensation

[1182]
Compensation is payable in respect of:

(*a*) depreciation of the value of an interest in land; and
(*b*) damage by reason of the fact that the claimant's right of access to the watercourse has been extinguished or interfered with[1].

In determining the amount of compensation, it is necessary to take into account any new means of access to the premises of the claimant or to the watercourse provided by the authority from whom the compensation is claimed[2]. Rules 2–4 of the LCA 1961, s 5 apply, insofar as the compensation is calculated by reference to the depreciation in the value of an interest in the land[3]. Where an interest in land is subject to a mortgage, compensation is to be assessed as if there were no mortgage[4].

1 HiA 1980, s 109(2). The distinction between (*a*) and (*b*) is not clear. One would assume that the right of access referred to would be from the claimant's land, in which case, the loss of such access would be reflected in the value of his land, which fall under (*a*). This suggests that (*b*) may intended to extend the compensation beyond depreciation in the value of land.
2 HiA 1980, s 307(4).
3 HiA 1980, s 307(3). As to the LCA 1961, s 5, see **Division E**.
4 HiA 1980, s 309(*a*).

3 Procedure

[1183]
The statute does not prescribe a time within which claims must be made[1], nor the procedure for making claims[2]. Any dispute arising on a claim for compensation is to be determined by the Upper Tribunal; the LCA 1961, s 4 (as to costs) will then apply[3]. There is no provision for the payment of interest on compensation under these provisions[4].

1 However, the Limitation Act 1980, s 9 will apply. A reference to the Lands Tribunal to resolve a dispute as to compensation is an action to recover compensation for the purposes of s 9: *Hillingdon London Borough Council v ARC Ltd* [1999] Ch 139, CA.
2 Although there is no particular form for the claim, it must be an unequivocal claim and not merely an intention to make a claim: *Texas Homecare Ltd v Lewes District Council* (1985) 51 P&CR 205, Lands Tribunal. See also *International Ferry Traders Ltd v Adur District Council* [2004] EWCA Civ 288, [2004] RVR 65.
3 HiA 1980, s 307(1), (2).
4 Ie this section is not listed in the PCA 1991, Sch 18. See para **[26]**.

N Works on watercourses

1 The right to compensation

[1184]
A right to compensation arises where a non navigable watercourse is diverted or where works are carried out on any navigable or non-navigable watercourse[1], except where the works are carried out on land or in the exercise of rights which have been compulsorily acquired[2]. A claim may be made against the highway authority by any person having an interest in land or with a right of access to the watercourse. A claim may be made by a mortgagee, but not in respect of his interest as such[3]. Compensation, in respect of an interest subject to a mortgage, is to be paid to the mortgagee (or, as the case may be, the first mortgagee) and must be applied as if it were proceeds of sale[4].

1 Under the HiA 1980, s 110(1).
2 HiA 1980, s 110(4).
3 HiA 1980, s 309(*b*), (*c*).
4 HiA 1980, s 309(*d*).

2 Assessment of compensation

[1185]
Compensation is payable in respect of:

(*a*) depreciation of the value of an interest in land; or
(*b*) damage by reason of the fact that the claimant's right of access to the watercourse has been extinguished or interfered with[1].

In determining the amount of compensation payable, it is necessary to take into account any new means of access to the premises of the claimant or to the watercourse, provided by the authority from whom the compensation is claimed[2]. Rules 2–4 of the LCA 1961, s 5 apply, insofar as the compensation is calculated by reference to the depreciation in the value of an interest in the land[3]. Where an interest in land is subject to a mortgage, compensation is to be assessed as if there were no mortgage[4].

1 HiA 1980, s 110(4). The distinction between (*a*) and (*b*) is not clear. One would assume that the right of access referred to would be from the claimant's land, in which case, the loss of such access would be reflected in the value of his land, which fall under (*a*). This suggests that (*b*) may intended to extend the compensation beyond depreciation in the value of land.
2 HiA 1980, s 307(4).
3 HiA 1980, s 307(3). As to the LCA 1961, s 5, see **Division E**.
4 HiA 1980, s 309(*a*).

3 Procedure

[1186]
The statute does not prescribe a time within which claims must be made[1], nor the procedure for making claims[2]. Any dispute arising on a claim for compensation is to be determined by the Upper Tribunal; the LCA 1961, s 4 (as to costs) will then apply[3]. There is no provision for the payment of interest on compensation under these provisions[4].

1 However, the Limitation Act 1980, s 9 will apply. A reference to the Upper Tribunal to resolve a dispute as to compensation is an action to recover compensation for the purposes of s 9: *Hillingdon London Borough Council v ARC Ltd* [1999] Ch 139, CA.
2 Although there is no particular form for the claim, it must be an unequivocal claim and not merely an intention to make a claim: *Texas Homecare Ltd v Lewes District Council* (1985) 51 P&CR 205, Lands Tribunal. See also *International Ferry Traders Ltd v Adur District Council* [2004] EWCA Civ 288, [2004] RVR 65.
3 HiA 1980, s 307(1), (2).
4 Ie this section is not listed in the PCA 1991, Sch 18. See para **[26]**.

O Temporary diversions

1 The right to compensation

[1187]
A right to compensation arises where a highway authority (or, in the case of a highway maintainable by another person, that person) constructs a temporary highway on land, in order to widen or repair the existing highway[1]. A claim may be made against the highway authority by an owner or occupier

of the property who has sustained damage. A claim may be made by a mortgagee, but not in respect of his interest as such[2]. Compensation, in respect of an interest subject to a mortgage, is to be paid to the mortgagee (or, as the case may be, the first mortgagee) and must be applied as if it were proceeds of sale[3].

1 HiA 1980, s 122.
2 HiA 1980, s 309(*b*), (*c*).
3 HiA 1980, s 309(*d*).

2 Assessment of compensation

[1188]
Compensation is payable in respect of any damage sustained in consequence of the construction of the temporary highway[1]. The measure of compensation is the depreciation in the value of the claimant's land and rr 2–4 of the LCA 1961, s 5 apply to the assessment of such depreciation[2]. Where an interest in land is subject to a mortgage, compensation is to be assessed as if there were no mortgage[3].

1 HiA 1980, s 122(2).
2 HiA 1980, s 307(3). As to the LCA 1961, s 5, see **Division E**.
3 HiA 1980, s 309(*a*).

3 Procedure

[1189]
The statute does not prescribe a time within which claims must be made[1], nor the procedure for making claims[2]. Any dispute, in relation to compensation, is, if the parties agree, to be determined by arbitration, or otherwise, by the county court[3]. There is no provision for the payment of interest on compensation under these provisions[4].

1 However, the Limitation Act 1980, s 9 will apply. A reference to the Lands Tribunal to resolve a dispute as to compensation is an action to recover compensation for the purposes of s 9: *Hillingdon London Borough Council v ARC Ltd* [1999] Ch 139, CA.
2 Although there is no particular form for the claim, it must be an unequivocal claim and not merely an intention to make a claim: *Texas Homecare Ltd v Lewes District Council* (1985) 51 P&CR 205, Lands Tribunal. See also *International Ferry Traders Ltd v Adur District Council* [2004] EWCA Civ 288, [2004] RVR 65.
3 HiA 1980, s 308. This applies, even if the amount claimed is above the county court jurisdiction: s 308(2).
4 Ie this section is not listed in the PCA 1991, Sch 18. See para **[26]**. As to an arbitrator's power to award interest, see the Arbitration Act 1996, s 49.

P Obtaining materials for repair of highways and bridges

1 The right to compensation

[1190]–[1200]
A right to compensation arises where a highway authority exercises its powers[1] to gather and carry away stones, and to search for, dig, get and

carry away materials for the repair of highways and bridges. A claim may be made against the highway authority by any person interested in the land on which these powers are exercised[2]. A claim may be made by a mortgagee, but not in respect of his interest as such[3]. Compensation, in respect of an interest subject to a mortgage, is to be paid to the mortgagee (or, as the case may be, the first mortgagee) and must be applied as if it were proceeds of sale[4].

1 HiA 1980, s 45.
2 HiA 1980, s 45(10).
3 HiA 1980, s 309(*b*), (*c*).
4 HiA 1980, s 309(*d*).

2 Assessment of compensation

[1201]

Compensation is payable in respect of any damage to the land as a result of the carriage of those materials and, where materials are taken or stone quarried[1], for the value of those materials[2]. The measure of compensation for damage is the depreciation in the value of the claimant's land and rr 2–4 of the LCA 1961, s 5 apply to the assessment of such depreciation[3]. With regard to stones or other materials removed, it is not clear whether the compensation should be assessed on their value in situ or as dug, but the former would seem more logical. Where an interest in land is subject to a mortgage, compensation is to be assessed as if there were no mortgage[4].

1 Under the HiA 1980, s 45(6) or (8).
2 HiA 1980, s 45(10).
3 HiA 1980, s 307(3). As to the LCA 1961, s 5, see **Division E**.
4 HiA 1980, s 309(*a*).

3 Procedure

[1202]

The statute does not prescribe a time within which claims must be made[1], nor the procedure for making claims[2]. Any dispute, in relation to compensation, is, if the parties agree, to be determined by arbitration, or otherwise, by the county court[3]. There is no provision for the payment of interest on compensation under these provisions[4].

1 However, the Limitation Act 1980, s 9 will apply. A reference to the Upper Tribunal to resolve a dispute as to compensation is an action to recover compensation for the purposes of s 9: *Hillingdon London Borough Council v ARC Ltd* [1999] Ch 139, CA.
2 Although there is no particular form for the claim, it must be an unequivocal claim and not merely an intention to make a claim: *Texas Homecare Ltd v Lewes District Council* (1985) 51 P&CR 205, Lands Tribunal. See also *International Ferry Traders Ltd v Adur District Council* [2004] EWCA Civ 288, [2004] RVR 65.
3 HiA 1980, s 308. This applies, even if the amount claimed is above the county court jurisdiction: s 308(2).
4 Ie this section is not listed in the PCA 1991, Sch 18. See para **[26]**. As to an arbitrator's power to award interest, see the Arbitration Act 1996, s 49.

Q Execution of private street works

1 The right to compensation

[1203]
A right to compensation arises[1] where a street works authority[2] carries out street works under the private street works code[3]. A claim may be made by any person who sustains damage as a result of the execution of the works. A claim may be made by a mortgagee, but not in respect of his interest as such[4]. Compensation, in respect of an interest subject to a mortgage, is to be paid to the mortgagee (or, as the case may be, the first mortgagee) and must be applied as if it were proceeds of sale[5].

1 HiA 1980, s 231.
2 HiA 1980, s 203(3).
3 HiA 1980, s 203. The 'private street works code' comprises the HiA 1980, ss 205–218, under which the highway authority can carry out works on a highway, which is not maintainable at the public expense, and recover the cost from frontagers.
4 HiA 1980, s 309(*b*), (*c*).
5 HiA 1980, s 309(*d*).

2 Assessment of compensation

[1204]
Compensation is payable in respect of any damage sustained by reason of the execution of the works[1]. The measure of compensation is the depreciation in the value of the claimant's land and rr 2–4 of the LCA 1961, s 5 apply to the assessment of such depreciation[2]. Where an interest in land is subject to a mortgage, compensation is to be assessed as if there were no mortgage[3].

1 HiA 1980, s 231. The code is defined in s 203(1).
2 HiA 1980, s 307(3). As to the LCA 1961, s 5, see **Division E**.
3 HiA 1980, s 309(*a*).

3 Procedure

[1205]
The statute does not prescribe a time within which claims must be made[1], nor the procedure for making claims[2]. Any dispute, in relation to compensation, is, if the parties agree, to be determined by arbitration, or otherwise, by the county court[3].

1 However, the Limitation Act 1980, s 9 will apply. A reference to the Upper Tribunal to resolve a dispute as to compensation is an action to recover compensation for the purposes of s 9: *Hillingdon London Borough Council v ARC Ltd* [1999] Ch 139, CA.
2 Although there is no particular form for the claim, it must be an unequivocal claim and not merely an intention to make a claim: *Texas Homecare Ltd v Lewes District Council* (1985) 51 P&CR 205, Lands Tribunal. See also *International Ferry Traders Ltd v Adur District Council* [2004] EWCA Civ 288, [2004] RVR 65.
3 HiA 1980, s 308. This applies, even if the amount claimed is above the county court jurisdiction: s 308(2).

4 Interest on compensation

[1206]
Interest is payable on compensation due, from the date of the claim or, where the claim relates to damage sustained, from the date of the damage[1].

1 PCA 1991, s 80, Sch 18. See para **[26]**.

R Carrying out of experiments for improving highways

1 The right to compensation

[1207]
A right to compensation arises where the minister exercises his powers[1] to carry out or arrange for experiments or trials for improving the construction of highways, road ferries or subways or the effect of various classes of vehicle on various types of highway[2]. A claim may be made against the highway authority by any person whose property is damaged. A claim may be made by a mortgagee, but not in respect of his interest as such[3]. Compensation, in respect of an interest subject to a mortgage, is to be paid to the mortgagee (or, as the case may be, the first mortgagee) and must be applied as if it were proceeds of sale[4].

1 HiA 1980, s 283.
2 HiA 1980, s 283(4).
3 HiA 1980, s 309(*b*), (*c*).
4 HiA 1980, s 309(*d*).

2 Assessment of compensation

[1208]
Compensation is payable in respect of any damage caused to property, unless the damage is caused by the negligence of the claimant, and compensation is to be reduced proportionately, if he has contributed to the damage by his negligence[1]. The measure of damage is the depreciation in the value of the claimant's land and rr 2–4 of the LCA 1961, s 5 apply to the assessment of such depreciation[2]. Where an interest in land is subject to a mortgage, compensation is to be assessed as if there were no mortgage[3].

1 HiA 1980, s 283(4).
2 HiA 1980, s 307(3). As to the LCA 1961, s 5, see **Division E**.
3 HiA 1980, s 309(*a*).

3 Procedure

[1209]
The statute does not prescribe a time within which claims must be made[1], nor the procedure for making claims[2]. Any dispute, in relation to compensation, is, if the parties agree, to be determined by arbitration, or otherwise, by the county court[3]. There is no provision for the payment of interest on compensation under these provisions[4].

1 However, the Limitation Act 1980, s 9 will apply. A reference to the Upper Tribunal to resolve a dispute as to compensation is an action to recover compensation for the purposes of s 9: *Hillingdon London Borough Council v ARC Ltd* [1999] Ch 139, CA.
2 Although there is no particular form for the claim, it must be an unequivocal claim and not merely an intention to make a claim: *Texas Homecare Ltd v Lewes District Council* (1985) 51 P&CR 205, Lands Tribunal. See also *International Ferry Traders Ltd v Adur District Council* [2004] EWCA Civ 288, [2004] RVR 65.
3 HiA 1980, s 308. This applies, even if the amount claimed is above the county court jurisdiction: s 308(2).
4 Ie this section is not listed in the PCA 1991, Sch 18. See para **[26]**. As to an arbitrator's power to award interest, see the Arbitration Act 1996, s 49.

S Provision of barriers, rails, footbridges, drains, picnic sites and other facilities

1 The right to compensation

[1210]–[1220]
Rights to compensation arise where a highway authority, local authority or the minister[1] exercise their powers to provide the following facilities in respect of highways:

(*a*) walls, fences, barriers, rails etc[2];
(*b*) footbridges over highways[3];
(*c*) drains and related works[4];
(*d*) works to protect highways against snow, flooding, landslide and other hazards of nature[5]; and
(*e*) picnic sites and public conveniences[6].

A claim may be made against the body exercising the power by any person who sustains damage. A claim may be made by a mortgagee, but not in respect of his interest as such[7]. Compensation, in respect of an interest subject to a mortgage, is to be paid to the mortgagee (or, as the case may be, the first mortgagee) and must be applied as if it were proceeds of sale[8].

1 Defined: HiA 1980, s 329(1).
2 HiA 1980, ss 66(8), 67(4).
3 HiA 1980, ss 70(6).
4 HiA 1980, s 100(3).
5 HiA 1980, s 102(3).
6 HiA 1980, s 112(6).
7 HiA 1980, s 309(*b*).
8 HiA 1980, s 309(*d*).

2 Assessment of compensation

[1221]
Compensation is payable in respect of damage sustained by reason of the execution of works under these powers. The measure of damage is the depreciation in the value of the claimant's land[1] and rr 2–4 of the LCA 1961, s 5 apply to the assessment of such depreciation[2]. Where an interest in land is subject to a mortgage, compensation is to be assessed as if there were no mortgage[3].

1 Per Lord Radcliffe in *Ching Garage Ltd v Chingford Corpn* [1961] 1 All ER 671, HL, at 677H, applying *Caledonian Rly Co v Walker's Trustees* (1882) 7 App Cas 259.
2 HiA 1980, s 307(3). As to the LCA 1961, s 5, see **Division E**.
3 HiA 1980, s 309(*a*).

3 Procedure

[1222]
The statute does not prescribe a time within which claims must be made[1], nor the procedure for making claims[2]. Any dispute, in relation to compensation, is, if the parties agree, to be determined by arbitration, or otherwise, by the county court[3]. There is no provision for the payment of interest on compensation under these provisions[4].

1 However, the Limitation Act 1980, s 9 will apply. A reference to the Upper Tribunal to resolve a dispute as to compensation is an action to recover compensation for the purposes of s 9: *Hillingdon London Borough Council v ARC Ltd* [1999] Ch 139, CA.
2 Although there is no particular form for the claim, it must be an unequivocal claim and not merely an intention to make a claim: *Texas Homecare Ltd v Lewes District Council* (1985) 51 P&CR 205, Lands Tribunal. See also *International Ferry Traders Ltd v Adur District Council* [2004] EWCA Civ 288, [2004] RVR 65.
3 HiA 1980, s 308. This applies, even if the amount claimed is above the county court jurisdiction: s 308(2).
4 Ie these sections are not listed in the PCA 1991, Sch 18. See para **[26]**. As to an arbitrator's power to award interest, see the Arbitration Act 1996, s 49.

T Discharge of water

1 The right to compensation

[1223]
A right to compensation arises where a highway authority exercises its power[1] to discharge, into any inland or tidal water, surface water from a highway through drains constructed in land or pursuant to rights acquired by the authority. A claim may be made against the highway authority by any owner or occupier of land who suffers damage[2]. A claim may be made by a mortgagee, but not in respect of his interest as such[3]. Compensation, in respect of an interest subject to a mortgage, is to be paid to the mortgagee (or, as the case may be, the first mortgagee) and must be applied as if it were proceeds of sale[4].

1 HiA 1980, s 299(1).
2 HiA 1980, s 299(2).
3 HiA 1980, s 309(*b*), (*c*).
4 HiA 1980, s 309(*d*).

2 Assessment of compensation

[1224]
Compensation is in respect of damage by reason of the exercise of this right[1]. The measure of compensation is the depreciation in the value of the claimant's land and rr 2–4 of the LCA 1961, s 5 apply to the assessment of

such depreciation[2]. Where an interest in land is subject to a mortgage, compensation is to be assessed as if there were no mortgage[3].

1 HiA 1980, s 299(2).
2 HiA 1980, s 307(3). As to the LCA 1961, s 5, see **Division E**.
3 HiA 1980, s 309(*a*).

3 Procedure

[1225]
The statute does not prescribe a time within which claims must be made[1], nor the procedure for making claims[2]. Any dispute, in relation to compensation, is, if the parties agree, to be determined by arbitration, or otherwise, by the county court[3]. There is no provision for the payment of interest on compensation under these provisions[4].

1 However, the Limitation Act 1980, s 9 will apply. A reference to the Upper Tribunal to resolve a dispute as to compensation is an action to recover compensation for the purposes of s 9: *Hillingdon London Borough Council v ARC Ltd* [1999] Ch 139, CA.
2 Although there is no particular form for the claim, it must be an unequivocal claim and not merely an intention to make a claim: *Texas Homecare Ltd v Lewes District Council* (1985) 51 P&CR 205, Lands Tribunal. See also *International Ferry Traders Ltd v Adur District Council* [2004] EWCA Civ 288, [2004] RVR 65.
3 HiA 1980, s 308. This applies, even if the amount claimed is above the county court jurisdiction: s 308(2).
4 Ie this section is not listed in the PCA 1991, Sch 18. See para **[26]**. As to an arbitrator's power to award interest, see the Arbitration Act 1996, s 49.

U Entry on to premises for survey and maintenance

1 The right to compensation

[1226]
A right to compensation arises where a highway authority exercises its powers[1] to enter premises to survey or maintain structures or works. A claim may be made against the highway authority by any person having an interest in the land or in any chattels on the land[2]. A claim may be made by a mortgagee, but not in respect of his interest as such[3]. Compensation, in respect of an interest subject to a mortgage, is to be paid to the mortgagee (or, as the case may be, the first mortgagee) and must be applied as if it were proceeds of sale[4].

1 Under the HiA 1980, ss 289 (for surveys) or 291 (for maintenance of structures and works).
2 HiA 1980, s 292(1). Where works are carried out under the HiA 1980, s 289(3) in any street, certain provisions of the New Roads and Street Works Act 1991 apply, including s 82, which provides for liability for damage and loss caused.
3 HiA 1980, s 309(*b*), (*c*).
4 HiA 1980, s 309(*d*).

2 Assessment of compensation

[1227]
Compensation is payable[1] in respect of:

(*a*) any damage caused by the exercise of these powers to the land or to any chattels; or
(*b*) disturbance[2] in the enjoyment of the land or chattels caused by the exercise of these powers.

Rules 2–4 of the LCA 1961, s 5 apply, insofar as the compensation is calculated by reference to the depreciation in the value of an interest in the land[3]. Where an interest in land is subject to a mortgage, compensation is to be assessed as if there were no mortgage[4].

1 HiA 1980, s 292. In respect of works under s 289(3) in any street, the New Roads and Street Works Act 1991, s 82 (liability for damage and loss caused) applies.
2 As to disturbance in the context of compulsory acquisition, see **Division E**.
3 HiA 1980, s 307(3). As to the LCA 1961, s 5, see **Division E**.
4 HiA 1980, s 309(*a*).

3 Procedure

[1228]
The statute does not prescribe a time within which claims must be made[1], nor the procedure for making claims[2]. Any dispute arising on a claim for compensation is to be determined by the Upper Tribunal; the LCA 1961, s 4 (as to costs) will then apply[3].

1 However, the Limitation Act 1980, s 9 will apply. A reference to the Upper Tribunal to resolve a dispute as to compensation is an action to recover compensation for the purposes of s 9: *Hillingdon London Borough Council v ARC Ltd* [1999] Ch 139, CA.
2 Although there is no particular form for the claim, it must be an unequivocal claim and not merely an intention to make a claim: *Texas Homecare Ltd v Lewes District Council* (1985) 51 P&CR 205, Lands Tribunal. See also *International Ferry Traders Ltd v Adur District Council* [2004] EWCA Civ 288, [2004] RVR 65.
3 HiA 1980, s 307(1), (2): see **Division H**.

4 Interest on compensation

[1229]
Interest is payable on compensation under these provisions[1]. In the case of damage, interest runs from the date of entry; in the case of disturbance, interest runs from the date of the claim.

1 PCA 1991, s 80, Sch 18. See para **[26]**.

V Entry, examination and laying open of premises

1 The right to compensation

[1230]–[1240]
A right to compensation arises where a highway authority exercises its powers[1] to enter, examine or lay open any premises for the purpose of surveying, making plans, executing, maintaining or examining works, ascertaining the course of sewers or drains, ascertaining or fixing boundaries, or ascertaining whether any vegetation is diseased or insecurely rooted[2]. A

claim may be made against the highway authority by any person having an interest in the land or chattels on the land or who is in possession of the land. A claim may be made by a mortgagee, but not in respect of his interest as such[3]. Compensation, in respect of an interest subject to a mortgage, is to be paid to the mortgagee (or, as the case may be, the first mortgagee) and must be applied as if it were proceeds of sale[4].

1 Under the HiA 1980, ss 101, 154(2) and those listed in Sch 22: HiA 1980, s 294.
2 HiA 1980, s 294(4).
3 HiA 1980, s 309(*b*), (*c*).
4 HiA 1980, s 309(*d*).

2 Assessment of compensation

[1241]
Compensation is payable in respect of[1]:

(*a*) any damage to land or to chattels; or
(*b*) disturbance[2] caused to any person interested in the land or in the chattels.

The measure of compensation for damage to land is normally the depreciation in its value[3] and rr 2–4 of the LCA 1961, s 5 apply to the assessment of such depreciation[4]. Where an interest in land is subject to a mortgage, compensation is to be assessed as if there were no mortgage[5].

1 HiA 1980, s 294(4).
2 As to disturbance in the context of compensation for compulsory acquisition, see **Division E**.
3 It could be envisaged that the exercise of these powers could cause direct physical damage to the land for which the cost of repair might provide a better measure.
4 HiA 1980, s 307(3). As to the LCA 1961, s 5, see **Division E**.
5 HiA 1980, s 309(*a*).

3 Procedure

[1242]–[1600]
The statute does not prescribe a time within which claims must be made[1], nor the procedure for making claims[2]. Any dispute, in relation to compensation, is, if the parties agree, to be determined by arbitration, or otherwise, by the county court[3]. There is no provision for the payment of interest on compensation under these provisions[4].

1 However, the Limitation Act 1980, s 9 will apply. A reference to the Upper Tribunal to resolve a dispute as to compensation is an action to recover compensation for the purposes of s 9: *Hillingdon London Borough Council v ARC Ltd* [1999] Ch 139, CA.
2 Although there is no particular form for the claim, it must be an unequivocal claim and not merely an intention to make a claim: *Texas Homecare Ltd v Lewes District Council* (1985) 51 P&CR 205, Lands Tribunal. See also *International Ferry Traders Ltd v Adur District Council* [2004] EWCA Civ 288, [2004] RVR 65.
3 HiA 1980, s 308. This applies, even if the amount claimed is above the county court jurisdiction: s 308(2).
4 Ie this section is not listed in the PCA 1991, Sch 18. See para **[26]**. As to an arbitrator's power to award interest, see the Arbitration Act 1996, s 49.

Chapter 5

Compensation for the exercise of powers relating to water supply, sewage disposal, land drainage, pollution control and public health

Contents

A Introduction

[1601]
This chapter describes rights to compensation which arise under legislation concerned with water supply, sewage disposal, pollution control, land drainage and public health. The majority of the powers which give rise to these rights are exercisable by water and sewerage undertakers and the Environment Agency, but a few are in the hands of other bodies. These bodies have, in addition to the powers referred to in this chapter, power to acquire land compulsorily; compensation for compulsory purchase is the subject of **Division E**.

B Inspection of reservoirs

1 The right to compensation

[1602]
A right to compensation arises where a person duly authorised in writing by an enforcement authority[1] enters upon land on which a reservoir is situated, which is not in the occupation of the undertakers[2], for the purposes of carrying out a survey or inspection or to carry out measures in the interests of safety[3]. A claim may be made by any person interested in such land which

is damaged or who is disturbed in his enjoyment of such land. Compensation is payable by the enforcement authority.

1 Reservoirs Act 1975, ss 2(6), 2(1), as amended, ie the councils of counties, metropolitan districts and London boroughs.
2 Reservoirs Act 1975, s 1(4).
3 For the power to enter for such purposes, see the Reservoirs Act 1975, s 17. The right to compensation is provided by s 18.

2 Assessment of compensation

[1603]
Compensation is payable in respect of:

(*a*) damage to the land[1]; and
(*b*) disturbance[2] in the enjoyment of the land[3].

1 Reservoirs Act 1975, s 18(1)(*a*).
2 As to compensation for disturbance in the context of compulsory acquisition, see **Division E**.
3 Reservoirs Act 1975, s 18(1)(*b*).

3 Procedure

[1604]
The time within which a claim must be made and the manner of making a claim are not specified in the Act[1]. Any dispute as to a right to compensation or as to the amount payable is to be determined by the Upper Tribunal[2].

1 However, the Limitation Act 1980, s 9 will apply; see *Hillingdon London Borough Council v ARC Ltd* [1999] Ch 139, CA. Although there is no particular form of claim, it must be unequivocal and not merely an intention to make a claim: *Texas Homecare Ltd v Lewes District Council* (1985) 51 P&CR 205, Lands Tribunal. See also *International Ferry Traders Ltd v Adur District Council* [2004] EWCA Civ 288, [2004] RVR 65.
2 Reservoirs Act 1975, s 18(2). As to references to the Upper Tribunal, see **Division H**.

4 Interest on compensation

[1605]
Interest is payable on compensation due, from the date of entry[1].

1 Planning and Compensation Act 1991 (PCA 1991), s 80, Sch 18. See para **[26]**.

C Works by the Environment Agency

1 Introduction

[1606]
Rights to compensation arise where[1] the Environment Agency[2] exercises its powers to:

(*a*) lay pipes in streets[3];
(*b*) lay pipes in private land[4];

(*c*) carry out works to control pollution[5];
(*d*) discharge water from a pipe, well, borehole or other work in to a watercourse[6];
(*e*) carry out flood defence and drainage work[7];
(*f*) carry out works for providing a flood warning system[8]; and
(*g*) dispose of spoil from flood defence works[9].

The provisions which govern the right to compensation, assessment of the amount and the procedure for determining claims are set out in the WRA 1991, Sch 21, grouped under the following four headings.

1 Water Resources Act 1991 (WRA 1991), s 177, Sch 21, paras 1 (in respect of street works), 2 and 3 (in respect of pipe-laying on private land), 4 (in respect of discharges) and 5 (in respect of flood defence and drainage).
2 Environment Act 1995, s 1.
3 WRA 1991, s 159.
4 WRA 1991, s 160.
5 WRA 1991, s 161–162.
6 WRA 1991, s 163–164.
7 WRA 1991, s 165.
8 WRA 1991, s 166.
9 WRA 1991, s 167.

Compensation in respect of street works powers

The right to compensation

[1607]
A right to compensation arises where the Environment Agency exercises its powers under the WRA 1991, ss 159 (pipe-laying in streets) and 162 (prevention of pollution). A claim may be made against the Environment Agency by any person sustaining loss or damage as a result of the exercise of those powers[1].

1 WRA 1991, Sch 21, para 1(2)(*b*).

Assessment of compensation

[1608]
Compensation is payable in respect of any loss caused or damage done in the exercise of the powers[1].

1 WRA 1991, Sch 21, para 1(2)(*b*).

Procedure

[1609]
The time within which a claim must be made and the manner of making a claim are not specified by the Act[1]. Any dispute as to whether compensation is payable or as to the amount is to be referred to arbitration[2]. There is no provision governing the payment of interest on compensation under these provisions[3].

1 However, the Limitation Act 1980, s 9 will apply; see *Hillingdon London Borough Council v ARC Ltd* [1999] Ch 139, CA. Although there is no particular form of claim, it must be unequivocal and not merely an intention to make a claim: *Texas Homecare Ltd v Lewes District Council* (1985) 51 P&CR 205, Lands Tribunal. See also *International Ferry Traders Ltd v Adur District Council* [2004] EWCA Civ 288, [2004] RVR 65.
2 WRA 1991, Sch 21, para 1(3).
3 Ie they are not listed in the PCA 1991, s 80, Sch 18. See para **[26]**. As to an arbitrator's power to award interest, see the Arbitration Act 1996, s 49.

Pipe-laying works on private land

The right to compensation

[1610]–[1620]
A right to compensation arises where the Environment Agency exercises its powers under the WRA 1991, ss 160 (pipe-laying) and 162(3) (prevention of pollution)[1]. A claim may be made against the Environment Agency by a person having an interest in the 'relevant land' (that is, the land where the power is exercised) and any person having an interest in other land which is damaged or injuriously affected[2].

1 WRA 1991, Sch 21, para 2(6). A claim may be made by a mortgagee without prejudice to a claim by the person entitled to the interest mortgaged, but compensation is not payable, in respect of the interest, if the mortgagee. Any compensation is to be paid to the mortgagee (or first mortgagee, as the case may be), who must apply it as though it were proceeds of sale: Sch 21, para 3(3).
2 WRA 1991, Sch 21, para 2.

Assessment of compensation

[1621]
Compensation is payable in respect of:

(*a*) depreciation in the value of an interest in the relevant land[1];
(*b*) depreciation in the value of any land held with the relevant land[2];
(*c*) disturbance[3] on the relevant land; and
(*d*) damage or injurious affection to land other than the relevant land[4].

For the purpose of assessing compensation for depreciation in the value of an interest in land, the rules in the Land Compensation Act 1961 (LCA 1961), s 5 apply, with any necessary modifications[5]. Where an interest in land is subject to a mortgage, compensation is to be assessed as if it were not subject to a mortgage[6]. The amount of compensation is to be reduced to reflect any enhancement attributable to the works in the value of an interest in contiguous or adjacent land held by the claimant in the same capacity[7].

1 WRA 1991, Sch 21, para 2(1).
2 WRA 1991, Sch 21, para 2(1) as extended by para 2(5).
3 WRA 1991, Sch 21, para 2(2). Disturbance relates to personal losses resulting from being disturbed in the enjoyment of land. This applies if the person would have been entitled to compensation for disturbance if his land had been compulsorily acquired: Sch 21, para 2(2)(*c*). As to disturbance in the context of compulsory acquisition, see **Division E**.
4 WRA 1991, Sch 21, para 2(3).
5 WRA 1991, Sch 21, para 3(2). These rules are described in **Division E**.
6 WRA 1991, Sch 21, para 3(3)(*a*).
7 WRA 1991, Sch 21, para 3(4).

Procedure

[1622]
The time within which a claim must be made and the manner in which a claim must be made are not specified in the Act[1]. Any question of disputed compensation is to be referred to the Upper Tribunal; the LCA 1961, ss 2 and 4 will then apply, with any necessary modifications[2].

1 However, the Limitation Act 1980, s 9 will apply; see *Hillingdon London Borough Council v ARC Ltd* [1999] Ch 139, CA. Although there is no particular form of claim, it must be unequivocal and not merely an intention to make a claim: *Texas Homecare Ltd v Lewes District Council* (1985) 51 P&CR 205, Lands Tribunal. See also *International Ferry Traders Ltd v Adur District Council* [2004] EWCA Civ 288, [2004] RVR 65.
2 WRA 1991, Sch 21, para 3(1). As to references to the Upper Tribunal, see **Division H**.

Interest on compensation

[1623]
Interest is payable on compensation under (*a*)–(*d*) above from the date of the claim, except where the claim relates to expenditure under (*c*) or (*d*) above, in which case interest runs from the date on which the expenditure was incurred[1].

1 PCA 1991, s 80, Sch 18. See para **[26]**.

Discharges of water

The right to compensation

[1624]
A right to compensation arises where the Environment Agency exercises its powers under the WRA 1991, s 163 to discharge water. A claim may be made against the Environment Agency by any person sustaining loss or damage[1].

1 WRA 1991, Sch 21, para 4(1)(*b*).

Assessment of compensation

[1625]
Compensation is payable in respect of any loss caused or damage done in the exercise of these powers[1]. This includes any expenditure which a water undertaker, sewerage undertaker or public authority reasonably incurs, which is attributable to the discharge of water under these powers[2].

1 WRA 1991, Sch 21, para 4(1).
2 WRA 1991, Sch 21, para 4(2).

Procedure

[1626]
The time within which a claim must be made and the manner of making a claim are not specified by the Act[1]. Any dispute as to whether compensation is payable or as to the amount is to be referred to arbitration[2].

1 However, the Limitation Act 1980, s 9 will apply; see *Hillingdon London Borough Council v ARC Ltd* [1999] Ch 139, CA. Although there is no particular form of claim, it must be unequivocal and not merely an intention to make a claim: *Texas Homecare Ltd v Lewes District Council* (1985) 51 P&CR 205, Lands Tribunal. See also *International Ferry Traders Ltd v Adur District Council* [2004] EWCA Civ 288, [2004] RVR 65.
2 WRA 1991, Sch 21, para 4(3).

Interest on compensation

[1627]
Interest is payable on compensation, from the date of the damage or loss[1].

1 PCA 1991, s 80, Sch 18. See para **[26]**. As to an arbitrator's power to award interest, see the Arbitration Act 1996, s 49.

Flood defence and drainage works

The right to compensation

[1628]
A claim may be made against the Environment Agency by any person sustaining injury as a result of the exercise of the power:

(*a*) under the WRA 1991, s 165(1) or (3) (works for flood defence and drainage); and
(*b*) where the injury could have been avoided if the Environment Agency had taken reasonable care, under the WRA 1991, s 167(1)(*b*) (deposition of excavated material on the banks of a watercourse)[1].

1 WRA 1991, Sch 21, para 5(1), (3).

Assessment of compensation

[1629]
Compensation is payable in respect of any injury sustained by reason of the exercise of the powers[1].

1 WRA 1991, Sch 21, para 5(1). This applies only to injury resulting from the exercise of the powers in s 165(1)–(3). Where powers are exercised under s 167(1)(*b*), compensation is at the discretion of the Agency, unless the injury could have been avoided by reasonable care: WRA 1991, Sch 21, para 5(3).

Procedure

[1630]–[1640]
The time within which a claim must be made and the manner in which a claim must be made are not specified by the Act[1]. In case of dispute, the amount of compensation is to be determined by the Upper Tribunal[2].

1 However, the Limitation Act 1980, s 9 will apply; see *Hillingdon London Borough Council v ARC Ltd* [1999] Ch 139, CA. Although there is no particular form of claim, it must be unequivocal and not merely an intention to make a claim: *Texas Homecare Ltd v Lewes District Council* (1985)

51 P&CR 205, Lands Tribunal. See also *International Ferry Traders Ltd v Adur District Council* [2004] EWCA Civ 288, [2004] RVR 65.
2 WRA 1991, Sch 21, para 5(2): as to the Upper Tribunal, see **Division H**.

Interest on compensation

[1641]
Interest is payable on compensation, from the date of the claim[1].

1 PCA 1991, s 80, Sch 18. See para **[26]**.

D Works by water and sewerage undertakers

1 Introduction

[1642]
Rights to compensation arise where[1] water and sewerage undertakers[2] exercise their powers to:

(*a*) lay pipes in streets[3];
(*b*) lay pipes in private land[4];
(*c*) carry out works in a street to prevent water in a waterworks being polluted[5];
(*d*) carry out works in connection with metering[6]; and
(*e*) carry out work to fit stopcocks[7].

In addition, rights to compensation arise where a sewerage undertaker exercises any of its powers under 'the relevant sewerage provisions'[8]. The provisions which govern the right to compensation, assessment of the amount and the procedure for determining claims are set out in the WIA 1991, Sch 12, grouped under the following five headings.

1 Water Industry Act 1991 (WIA 1991), s 180, Sch 12, paras 1 (in respect of street works), 2 and 3 (in respect of pipe-laying on private land), 4 (in respect of sewerage works), 5 (in respect of metering works) and 6 (in respect of discharges of water).
2 Defined in the WIA 1991, s 6.
3 WIA 1991, s 158.
4 WIA 1991, s 159.
5 WIA 1991, s 161.
6 WIA 1991, s 162.
7 WIA 1991, s 163.
8 Defined in the WIA 1991, s 219(1) as the WIA 1991, ss 102–109, 111–141 (except for the provisions relating to regulations under s 138), 160, 171, 172(4), 178, 184, 189, 196, 204, Sch 12, para 4.

Compensation in respect of street works powers

The right to compensation

[1643]
A right to compensation arises where a water or sewerage undertaker exercises its powers under the WIA 1991, ss 158 (pipe-laying), 161 (prevention of pollution in waterworks) and 162 (works in connection with metering). A

claim may be made against the undertaker by any person sustaining loss or damage from the exercise of these powers[1].

1 WIA 1991, Sch 12, para 1(2)(*b*). The Act does not require that the claimant should have an interest in land.

Assessment of compensation

[1644]
Compensation is payable in respect of any loss caused or damage done in the exercise of the powers[1].

1 WIA 1991, Sch 12, para 1(2)(*b*).

Procedure

[1645]
The time within which a claim must be made and the manner of making a claim are not specified by the Act[1]. Any dispute as to whether compensation is payable or as to the amount is to be referred to arbitration[2]. There is no provision governing the payment of interest on compensation under these provisions[3].

1 However, the Limitation Act 1980, s 9 will apply; see *Hillingdon London Borough Council v ARC Ltd* [1999] Ch 139, CA. Although there is no particular form of claim, it must be unequivocal and not merely an intention to make a claim: *Texas Homecare Ltd v Lewes District Council* (1985) 51 P&CR 205, Lands Tribunal. See also *International Ferry Traders Ltd v Adur District Council* [2004] EWCA Civ 288, [2004] RVR 65.
2 WIA 1991, Sch 12, para 1(3).
3 Ie they are not listed in the PCA 1991, s 80, Sch 18. See para **[26]**. As to an arbitrator's power to award interest, see the Arbitration Act 1996, s 49.

Pipe-laying works on private land

The right to compensation

[1646]
A right to compensation arises where a water or sewerage undertaker exercises its powers under the WIA 1991, ss 159 (pipe-laying), 161(2) (prevention of pollution of water in a waterworks) and 163 (fitting of stopcocks), which all relate to private land[1]. A claim may be made by a person having an interest in the 'relevant land'[2] (that is, the land where the power is exercised) and any person having an interest in other land which is damaged or injuriously affected[3].

1 Where a water undertaker entered onto land and laid pipes having failed to give the notice required by WIA 1991, s 159, the landowner successfully claimed damages for trespass but the measure of damages was held to be only the loss of the opportunity to seek by negotiation to obtain a higher figure of compensation than might have been awarded by the Lands Tribunal: *Severn Trent Water Ltd v Barnes* [2004] EWCA Civ 570, [2005] RVR 181.
2 WIA 1991, Sch 12, para 2(5).
3 WIA 1991, Sch 12, para 2. A claim may be made by a mortgagee without prejudice to a claim by the person entitled to the interest mortgaged, but compensation is not payable in respect of

the interest of the mortgagee. Any compensation is to be paid to the mortgagee (or first mortgagee, as the case may be), who must apply it as though it were proceeds of sale: Sch 12, para 3(3).

Assessment of compensation

[1647]
Compensation is payable in respect of:

(*a*) depreciation in the value of an interest in the relevant land[1];
(*b*) depreciation in the value of any land held with the relevant land[2];
(*c*) disturbance[3] on the relevant land; and
(*d*) damage or injurious affection to land other than the relevant land[4].

For the purpose of assessing compensation for depreciation in the value of an interest in land, the rules in the LCA 1961, s 5 apply, with any necessary modifications[5]. Where an interest in land is subject to a mortgage, compensation is to be assessed as if it were not subject to a mortgage[6]. The amount of compensation is to be reduced to reflect any enhancement in the value of an interest in contiguous or adjacent land held by the claimant in the same capacity which is attributable to the works[7].

1 WIA 1991, Sch 12, para 2(1). For examples of awards of compensation for the effects of pipe-laying, see (in the context of the Public Health Act 1936 (PHA 1936), s 278); *Griffiths v Swansea Corpn* (1960) 11 P&CR 470, Lands Tribunal; *Weston v Bedford RDC* (1960) 11 P&CR 475, Lands Tribunal and (in the context of the Water Act 1945) *King v West Dorset Water Board* (1963) 14 P&CR 166, Lands Tribunal. The Lands Tribunal has held that in assessing compensation under Sch 12, para 2(1) it is not to be assumed that the undertaker's powers do not exist: *Kettering Borough Council v Anglian Water Services plc* [2001] 2 EGLR 157.
2 WIA 1991, Sch 12, para 2(1), as extended by para 2(5).
3 WIA 1991, Sch 12, para 2(2). Disturbance relates to personal losses resulting from being disturbed in the enjoyment of land. This applies if the person would have been entitled to compensation for disturbance if his land had been compulsorily acquired: Sch 12, para 2(2)(*c*). As to disturbance in the context of compulsory acquisition, see **Division E**.
4 WIA 1991, Sch 12, para 2(3). The measure of compensation for injurious affection is the depreciation in the value of the land.
5 WIA 1991, Sch 12, para 3(2). These rules are described in **Division E**.
6 WIA 1991, Sch 12, para 3(3)(*a*).
7 WIA 1991, Sch 12, para 3(4).

Procedure

[1648]
The time within which a claim must be made and the manner in which a claim must be made are not specified in the Act[1]. Any question of disputed compensation is to be referred to the Upper Tribunal; the LCA 1961, ss 2 and 4 will then apply, with any necessary modifications[2].

1 However, the Limitation Act 1980, s 9 will apply; see *Hillingdon London Borough Council v ARC Ltd* [1999] Ch 139, CA. Although there is no particular form of claim, it must be unequivocal and not merely an intention to make a claim: *Texas Homecare Ltd v Lewes District Council* (1985) 51 P&CR 205, Lands Tribunal. See also *International Ferry Traders Ltd v Adur District Council* [2004] EWCA Civ 288, [2004] RVR 650.
2 WIA 1991, Sch 12, para 3(1). As to references to the Upper Tribunal, see **Division H**.

Interest on compensation

[1649]
Interest is payable on compensation, from the date of the claim or, where the claim relates to expenditure, from the date of that expenditure[1].

1 PCA 1991, s 80, Sch 18. See para **[26]**.

Sewerage works

The right to compensation

[1650]–[1660]
A right to compensation arises where a sewerage undertaker exercises any of its powers under 'the relevant sewerage provisions'[1]. A claim may be made by any person sustaining damage by reason of the exercise of any of the powers of a sewerage undertaker, so long as the claimant himself is not at fault[2].

1 For the definition of 'relevant sewerage provisions', see para **[1642]**.
2 WIA 1991, Sch 12, para 4(1).

Assessment of compensation

[1661]
Full[1] compensation is payable in respect of any damage done in the exercise of the sewerage undertaker's powers[2].

1 The word 'full' is used in the WIA 1991, Sch 12, para 4(1), although it is not clear that it adds anything. Although see *Taylor v North West Water* [1995] 1 EGLR 266 at 273.
2 WIA 1991, Sch 12, para 4(1). This terminology derives from the PHA 1936, s 278 and its predecessor, see para **[1725]**.

Procedure

[1662]
Where the amount claimed exceeds £5,000, any question as to the fact of damage, liability or the amount of compensation is to be referred to arbitration[1]. Where the compensation claimed is less than £5,000, any dispute as to the fact of damage or as to the amount of compensation is to be referred to the Director[2]. There is no provision governing the payment of interest on compensation under these provisions[3].

1 WIA 1991, Sch 12, para 4(2).
2 WIA 1991, Sch 12, para 4(3). The WIA 1991, s 30A provides for the determination of certain disputes by the Director. The Director is defined as the Director General of Water Services: s 1.
3 Ie they are not listed in the PCA 1991, s 80, Sch 18. See para **[26]**. As to an arbitrator's power to award interest, see the Arbitration Act 1996.

Metering works

The right to compensation

[1663]
A claim may be made by any person sustaining damage caused by a person authorised by an undertaker to carry out works in connection with metering[1].

1 WIA 1991, Sch 12, para 5(1).

Assessment of compensation

[1664]
Compensation is payable in respect of any damage[1].

1 WIA 1991, Sch 12, para 5(1). This applies only to injury resulting from the exercise of the powers in s 165(1)–(3). Where powers are exercised under s 167(1)(*b*), compensation is at the discretion of the Agency, unless the injury could have been avoided by reasonable care: WRA 1991, Sch 21, para 5(3).

Procedure

[1665]
The time within which a claim must be made and the manner in which a claim must be made are not specified by the Act[1]. Any dispute as to whether compensation is payable or the amount of compensation is to be determined by arbitration[2]. There is no provision governing the payment of interest on compensation under these provisions[3].

1 However, the Limitation Act 1980, s 9 will apply; see *Hillingdon London Borough Council v ARC Ltd* [1999] Ch 139, CA. Although there is no particular form of claim, it must be unequivocal and not merely an intention to make a claim: *Texas Homecare Ltd v Lewes District Council* (1985) 51 P&CR 205, Lands Tribunal.
2 WIA 1991, Sch 12, para 5(2).
3 Ie they are not listed in the PCA 1991, s 80, Sch 18. See para **[26]**. As to an arbitrator's power to award interest, see the Arbitration Act 1996, s 49.

Discharges of water

The right to compensation

[1666]
A claim may be made against the water or sewerage undertaker where loss or damage results from the exercise of its power[1] to discharge water while carrying out works[2]. This includes any expenditure incurred by another water or sewerage undertaker or a public authority, which is reasonably necessary as a result of the discharge of the water[3].

1 Under the WIA 1991, s 165.
2 WIA 1991, Sch 12, para 6(1)(*b*).
3 WIA 1991, Sch 12, para 6(2).

Assessment of compensation

[1667]
Compensation is payable in respect of loss or damage done in the exercise of the powers[1].

1 WIA 1991, Sch 12, para 6(1)(*b*).

Procedure

[1668]
The time within which a claim must be made and the manner in which a claim must be made are not specified by the Act[1]. Any dispute as to whether compensation is payable or the amount of compensation is to be determined by arbitration[2].

1 However, the Limitation Act 1980, s 9 will apply; see *Hillingdon London Borough Council v ARC Ltd* [1999] Ch 139, CA. Although there is no particular form of claim, it must be unequivocal and not merely an intention to make a claim: *Texas Homecare Ltd v Lewes District Council* (1985) 51 P&CR 205, Lands Tribunal. See also *International Ferry Traders Ltd v Adur District Council* [2004] EWCA Civ 288, [2004] RVR 65.
2 WIA 1991, Sch 12, para 6(3).

Interest on compensation

[1669]
Interest is payable on compensation, from the date of the loss or damage[1].

1 PCA 1991, s 80, Sch 18. See para **[26]**. As to an arbitrator's power to award interest, see the Arbitration Act 1996, s 49.

E Drought orders

1 Introduction

[1670]–[1680]
Rights to compensation arise where the Environment Agency makes a drought order. There are two types of drought order: an 'emergency' drought order; and an 'ordinary' drought order[1]. Compensation is recoverable in relation to:

(*a*) an ordinary drought order; and
(*b*) the exercise of certain powers ancillary to both types of drought order, as described below.

1 WRA 1991, s 79, Sch 9.

Ordinary drought orders

The rights to compensation

[1681]
Rights to compensation arise[1] as follows:

(*a*) where water is taken from its source otherwise than in accordance with a restriction or obligation which has been suspended or modified, a claim may be made by the owner of the source or any person interested in the source or injuriously affected by the taking of the water[2];

(*b*) where water is discharged or not discharged otherwise than in accordance with a restriction or obligation which has been suspended or modified, the owner of the place of discharge and any person interested in the place of discharge or injuriously affected by the discharge or lack of discharge[3];

(*c*) where a prohibition or limitation is placed upon the taking of water from a source, a claim may be made by any person to whom the restriction applies[4]; and

(*d*) where consent to discharge sewage or trade effluent is suspended, varied or made, subject to conditions, a claim may be made by a person who has been making such discharge pursuant to the consent[5].

1 WRA 1991, s 79, Sch 9, para 2.
2 WRA 1991, Sch 9, para 2(2). The term 'interested in' is used in the Act without definition; it is not clear whether it means anything different from having a legal interest.
3 WRA 1991, Sch 9, para 2(3).
4 WRA 1991, Sch 9, para 2(4).
5 WRA 1991, Sch 9, para 2(5).

Assessment of compensation

[1682]
Compensation is payable in respect of loss or damage. Where the claim is made while the drought order is still in effect, compensation may include a sum representing future loss and damage for each day on which the order is likely to have effect[1]. In relation to compensation for the taking of water from a source, the assessment of compensation may reflect the amount of water available from the source to the claimant, having regard to an equitable apportionment between those entitled to use the source[2]. In relation to discharges, the assessment of compensation may reflect the amount of water which would have been available to the claimant under the drought conditions if the applicant for the drought order had never carried on its undertaking[3].

1 WRA 1991, Sch 9, para 4(2).
2 WRA 1991, Sch 9, para 4(3).
3 WRA 1991, Sch 9, para 4(4).

Procedure

[1683]
A claim must be made within six months of the end of the period during which the drought order has effect[1]. A claim must state the grounds and the amount claimed, and must be served upon the applicant for the drought order for the purposes of carrying out or maintaining any works[2]. Any question as to the right to compensation or the amount is, in default of agreement, to be referred to the Upper Tribunal[3].

1 WRA 1991, Sch 9, para 4(1).
2 WRA 1991, Sch 9, para 3(1).
3 WRA 1991, Sch 9, para 3(2): as to references to the Upper Tribunal, see **Division H**.

Interest on compensation

[1684]
Interest is payable on compensation, from the date of the drought order or the prohibition or limitation on taking water[1].

1 PCA 1991, s 80, Sch 18. See para **[26]**.

Entry, occupation or use of land

Right to compensation

[1685]
A right to compensation arises where, following a drought order, entry is made onto a person's land or such land is occupied and used by the Environment Agency or water undertaker[1]. A claim may be made, against the body which exercise the right, by all owners and occupiers of the land and all other persons injuriously affected[2].

1 Pursuant to the WRA 1991, s 78.
2 WRA 1991, s 79, Sch 9, para 1.

Assessment of compensation

[1686]
Compensation is payable in respect of loss or damage sustained by reason of the entry, occupation or use of the land[1].

1 WRA 1991, Sch 9, para 1.

Procedure

[1687]
No time limit is specified for claims under this provision[1]. A claim must state the grounds and the amount claimed, and must be served upon the applicant for the drought order[2]. Any question as to the right to compensation or the amount is, in default of agreement, to be referred to the Upper Tribunal[3].

1 However, the Limitation Act 1980, s 9 will apply; see *Hillingdon London Borough Council v ARC Ltd* [1999] Ch 139, CA.
2 WRA 1991, Sch 9, para 3(1).
3 WRA 1991, Sch 9, para 3(2): as to references to the Upper Tribunal, see **Division H**.

Interest on compensation

[1688]
Interest is payable on compensation, from the date of entry, occupation or use of the land[1].

1 PCA 1991, s 80, Sch 18. See para **[26]**.

F Rights of entry by the minister, Environment Agency, water undertakers and local authorities

1 The rights to compensation

[1689]
Rights to compensation arise:

(*a*) where the Environment Agency (or, in the case of s 169, the minister[1]) exercises a right of entry under the WRA 1991, s 169 (enforcement), s 170 (carrying out works), s 171 (surveying) or s 172 (miscellaneous)[2]; and
(*b*) where a water undertaker or, in certain cases, a local authority exercises a right of entry under the WIA 1991, ss 71–84 (prevention of contamination, temporary hose-pipe bans and control over private supplies) or ss 162–172 (metering, stopcocks, water sources, discharges, works, surveys and miscellaneous)[3].

1 Ie the Minister of Agriculture, Fisheries and Food and the Secretary of State for the Environment Transport and the Regions: s 221.
2 WRA 1991, s 173, Sch 20.
3 WIA 1991, Sch 6.

2 Assessment of compensation

[1690]–[1700]
Full compensation is payable in respect of loss or damage caused by the exercise of the power (or in certain cases, the failure to exercise the power), except for loss or damage sustained due to the default of the claimant and loss or damage for which compensation is recoverable under other provisions[1].

1 WRA 1991, Sch 20, para 6(1), (2) and the WIA 1991, Sch 6, para 11(1), (2). This terminology derives from the PHA 1936, s 278 and its predecessor; see para **[1725]**. The equivalent Scottish statutory provision was examined in some detail by the Court of Session in *Logan v Scottish Water* [2006] RVR 160, in which it was held that 'full compensation' was for loss, injury or damage caused in a direct sense by the exercise of the statutory power. It was also held that the *Pointe Gourde* principle (as to which see **Division E**) did not apply and on the facts of the case, the claimant was not entitled to recover loss of development value or ransom value.

3 Procedure

[1701]
The time within which a claim must be made and the manner of making a claim are not specified by the Acts[1]. Any dispute as to entitlement to

compensation or the amount is to be referred to arbitration[2]. Interest is not payable on compensation under these provisions[3].

1 However, the Limitation Act 1980, s 9 will apply; see *Hillingdon London Borough Council v ARC Ltd* [1999] Ch 139, CA. Although there is no particular form of claim, it must be unequivocal and not merely an intention to make a claim: *Texas Homecare Ltd v Lewes District Council* (1985) 51 P&CR 205, Lands Tribunal. See also *International Ferry Traders Ltd v Adur District Council* [2004] EWCA Civ 288, [2004] RVR 65.
2 WRA 1991, Sch 20, para 6(3); the WIA 1991, Sch 6, para 11(3).
3 Ie it is not listed in the PCA 1991, s 80, Sch 18. See para **[26]**. As to the power of an arbitrator to award interest, see the Arbitration Act 1996, s 49.

G Compulsory works orders

1 The right to compensation

[1702]
A right to compensation arises where, on the application of a water undertaker, the Secretary of State makes a compulsory works order, which authorises engineering or building operations on land, which is not the subject of compulsory acquisition[1]. A compulsory works order may also authorise the compulsory acquisition of land, for which compensation would be assessed in accordance with the rules described in **Division E**. These paragraphs apply to works on land not compulsorily acquired. A claim may be made by any person entitled to an interest in the 'relevant land'[2] (that is, the land where the operations are carried out) or in other land[3]. A claim may be made by a mortgagee of an interest, without prejudice to a claim by the owner of the interest, but is not payable in respect of the interest of the mortgagee[4].

1 WIA 1991, s 167. A compulsory works order is a mechanism by which a water undertaker may be authorised to carry out building or engineering operations or to discharge water into inland waters or underground strata; it can include powers of compulsory acquisition, but the rights to compensation described here are those applicable where loss or damage is suffered apart from compulsory acquisition.
2 WIA 1991, Sch 11, para 8(9).
3 WIA 1991, Sch 11, para 8(2), (3).
4 WIA 1991, Sch 11, para 8(8)(*b*), (*c*). Compensation is to be paid to the mortgagee (or first mortgagee, as the case may be), who must deal with it as though it were proceeds of sale: Sch 11, para 8(8)(*d*).

2 Assessment of compensation

[1703]
Compensation, in relation to the relevant land, is payable in respect of loss or damage attributable to the operations, for which compensation for disturbance would have been payable if the land had been compulsorily acquired[1], but compensation is not payable for depreciation in the value of the land[2]. In relation to other land, compensation is payable for damage or injurious affection attributable to the operations[3], which may include depreciation in value. In addition, compensation is payable to any person sustaining loss or damage attributable to the discharge of water[4]. Where an interest in land is subject to a mortgage, compensation is to be assessed as if the interest is not

subject to a mortgage[5]. In assessing compensation in respect of depreciation in the value of an interest in land, the rules in the LCA 1961, s 5 apply[6].

1 As to disturbance in the context of compulsory acquisition, see **Division E**.
2 WIA 1991, Sch 11, para 8(2).
3 WIA 1991, Sch 11, para 8(3).
4 WIA 1991, Sch 11, para 8(4), (5).
5 WIA 1991, Sch 11, para 8(8).
6 WIA 1991, Sch 11, para 8(7). As to the LCA 1961, s 5, see **Division E**.

3 Procedure

[1704]
The time within which a claim must be made and the manner of making a claim are not specified by the Act[1]. Any question of disputed compensation is to be referred to the Upper Tribunal; the LCA 1961, ss 2 and 4 then apply, with any necessary modifications[2]. Interest is not payable on compensation under these provisions[3].

1 However, the Limitation Act 1980, s 9 will apply; see *Hillingdon London Borough Council v ARC Ltd* [1999] Ch 139, CA. Although there is no particular form of claim, it must be unequivocal and not merely an intention to make a claim: *Texas Homecare Ltd v Lewes District Council* (1985) 51 P&CR 205, Lands Tribunal. See also *International Ferry Traders Ltd v Adur District Council* [2004] EWCA Civ 288, [2004] RVR 65.
2 WIA 1991, Sch 11, para 8(6). As to the Upper Tribunal and LCA 1961, ss 2, 4, see **Division H**.
3 Ie Sch 11 is not listed in the PCA 1991, Sch 18. See para **[26]**.

H Land drainage

1 Introduction

[1705]
Rights to compensation under the Land Drainage Act 1991 (LDA 1991) arise under the following three heads:

General powers of drainage boards and local authorities

The rights to compensation

[1706]
Rights to compensation arise where a drainage board or local authority:

(*a*) exercises its power[1] to maintain or improve existing works or to construct new works; and
(*b*) exercises its power[2] to deposit excavated material on the banks of a watercourse, but does so without reasonable care.

A claim may be made against the body exercising the power by any person sustaining injury[3] as a result[4].

1 Under the LDA 1991, s 14.
2 Under the LDA 1991, s 15.

3 This is limited to injury which would have given rise to a cause of action in the absence of statutory powers: *Marriage v East Norfolk Rivers Catchment Board* [1949] 2 KB 456, KB,

4 LDA 1991, ss 14(5) and 15(4)(*b*). Where this power is exercised with reasonable care, compensation may be claimed, but it is at the discretion of the board or authority: s 15(4)(*a*). The Act does not state that a claimant must have an interest in land. For an example of a claim under the predecessor of this provision (Land Drainage Act 1976, s 17), see *Marine Industrial Transmissions Ltd v Southern Water Authority* [1989] RVR 221, Lands Tribunal.

Assessment of compensation

[1707]
Full compensation is payable in respect of injury sustained by reason of the exercise of the powers[1].

1 LDA 1991, ss 14(5), 15(4). This terminology is similar to the PHA 1936, s 278 and its predecessor, see para **[1725]**.

Drainage works carried out by landowners

The right to compensation

[1708]
Where the minister makes an order[1] to enable a person interested in land to carry out drainage works on other land which would be entered upon, cut through or interfered with, any person interested in the land affected by the order who has suffered injury[2] may claim compensation[3].

1 Under the LDA 1991, s 22.
2 As to the meaning of injury, see para **[1706]**, note 3.
3 LDA 1991, s 22(7).

Assessment of compensation

[1709]
Compensation is payable in respect of any injury[1] suffered in respect of that interest by reason of the works[2].

1 As to the meaning of injury, see para **[1706]**, note 3.
2 LDA 1991, s 22(7).

Orders requiring the cleansing of ditches

The rights to compensation

[1710]–[1720]
Rights to compensation arise where:

(*a*) an order has been made requiring the owner or occupier of land, through which a ditch passes, to carry out remedial work to the ditch and that order having not been complied with, the minister or drainage body carry out the work[1]; and
(*b*) an order is made by the Agricultural Lands Tribunal[2] requiring work to be carried out on a ditch[3].

A claim may be made by any person sustaining injury[4] by reason of the exercise of these powers, unless the power was exercised in order to carry out work which the claimant had been required to undertake himself, pursuant to an order under the LDA 1991, s 28[5].

1 Under the LDA 1991, s 29(2). The 'minister' is defined in ss 29(8), 72(1), and 'drainage body' in s 72(1).
2 See the LDA 1991, s 31.
3 LDA 1991, s 30. The Tribunal has a right of entry under s 31(4), which also gives rise to a right to compensation: s 31(5).
4 As to the meaning of injury, see para **[1706]**, note 3.
5 LDA 1991, s 29(5), applied to s 30 by s 30(3) and to s 31 by s 31(5).

Assessment of compensation

[1721]
Full compensation is payable in respect of any injury sustained by reason of the exercise of the powers[1].

1 LDA 1991, s 29(5). This terminology is similar to the PHA 1936, s 278 and its predecessor, see para **[1725]**.

Procedure

[1722]
The time within which a claim must be made and the manner in which a claim must be made are not specified in the Act[1]. Disputes as to the amount of compensation are to be referred to the Upper Tribunal[2], but liability is a matter for the courts[3].

1 However, the Limitation Act 1980, s 9 will apply; see *Hillingdon London Borough Council v ARC Ltd* [1999] Ch 139, CA. Although there is no particular form of claim, it must be unequivocal and not merely an intention to make a claim: *Texas Homecare Ltd v Lewes District Council* (1985) 51 P&CR 205, Lands Tribunal. See also *International Ferry Traders Ltd v Adur District Council* [2004] EWCA Civ 288, [2004] RVR 65.
2 LDA 1991, ss 14(6), 22(7), 29(6) respectively. As to references to the Upper Tribunal, see **Division H**.
3 *Lingké v Christchurch Corpn* [1912] 3 KB 595, CA; *Leonidis v Thames Water Authority* (1979) 251 Estates Gazette 669.

Interest on compensation

[1723]
Interest is payable on compensation, from the date of the claim[1].

1 PCA 1991, s 80, Sch 18. See para **[26]**.

I Public Health Acts

1 The rights to compensation

[1724]
Rights to compensation arise:

(*a*) where a local authority[1] exercises any of its powers under the PHA 1936[2], except in cases where such an authority has a discretionary power to pay compensation if it thinks fit[3];
(*b*) where a local authority exercises any of its powers under the Public Health (Control of Diseases) Act 1984[4]; and
(*c*) where a local authority exercises any of its powers under the Building Act 1984[5].

A claim may be made by any person, who has sustained damage of a type described in the next paragraph, in relation to a matter as to which he himself has not been in default.

1 As to 'local authority', see the PHA 1936, s 1(2).
2 PHA 1936, s 278(1). The powers of a local authority under the PHA 1936 were originally very wide and included water supply and sewage disposal. Many such powers have now no longer in the hands of local authorities and have been removed from the PHA 1936, and are covered in other legislation. The scope of the PHA 1936, s 278 has been considered in a number of cases in the courts.
3 PHA 1936, s 278(3).
4 Public Health (Control of Diseases) Act 1984, s 57.
5 Building Act 1984, s 106.

2 Assessment of compensation

[1725]
Full[1] compensation is payable in respect of damage sustained by reason of the local authority's exercise of its powers[2]. This extends only to damage in respect of which the claimant would have had a cause of action, had it been caused by a private individual[3]. It is not confined to depreciation in the value of land and may extend to personal loss[4].

1 'Full' is the word used in the PHA 1936, s 278(1), Building Act 1984, s 106; Public Health (Control of Diseases) Act 1984, s 57, but it is not clear whether it adds anything.
2 PHA 1936, s 278(1).
3 *Lingké v Christchurch Corpn* [1912] 3 KB 595, CA per Vaughan Williams LJ at 604, relying on *Ricket v Metropolitan Rly Co* (1867) LR 2 HL 175 (decided in the context of the Land Clauses Consolidation Act 1845, s 68).
4 *Lingké v Christchurch Corpn* [1912] 3 KB 595, CA; *Leonidis v Thames Water Authority* (1979) 251 Estates Gazette 669, in which a number of earlier cases were reviewed.

3 Procedure

[1726]
The time within which a claim must be made and the manner in which a claim is to be made are not specified in these Acts[1]. Where the compensation claimed exceeds £50, any dispute as to the fact of damage or the amount of compensation is to be determined by arbitration[2], but liability is determined by the courts[3]. Where the compensation claimed is less than £50, questions as to the fact of damage, the amount of compensation and liability are to be determined by a court of summary jurisdiction, which also has jurisdiction for the recovery of any amount awarded[4].

1 However, the Limitation Act 1980, s 9 will apply; see *Hillingdon London Borough Council v ARC Ltd* [1999] Ch 139, CA. Although there is no particular form of claim, it must be unequivocal

and not merely an intention to make a claim: *Texas Homecare Ltd v Lewes District Council* (1985) 51 P&CR 205, Lands Tribunal. See also *International Ferry Traders Ltd v Adur District Council* [2004] EWCA Civ 288, [2004] RVR 65.
2 PHA 1936, s 278(2); Building Act 1984, s 57; Public Health (Control of Diseases) Act 1984, s 106.
3 *Lingké v Christchurch Corpn* [1912] 3 KB 595; *Leonidis v Thames Water Authority* (1979) 251 Estates Gazette 669, in which a number of earlier cases were reviewed.
4 PHA 1936, s 278(2); Building Act 1984, s 57; Public Health (Control of Diseases) Act 1984, s 106.

4 Interest on compensation

[1727]
There is no provision governing the payment of interest on compensation under the PHA 1936[1], but the PCA 1991 provides for interest to be payable on compensation under the Public Health (Control of Diseases) Act 1984 and the Building Act 1984[2].

1 This provision is not listed in the PCA 1991, s 80, Sch 18. As to an arbitrator's power to award interest, see the Arbitration Act 1996, s 49.
2 PCA 1991, s 80, Sch 18. See para **[26]**.

J Waste management licences

1 The right to compensation

[1728]
A waste regulation authority may grant a waste management licence[1] subject to conditions which require the holder to carry out works on land outside his control. Any person whose consent would be required to enable such a condition to be complied with can be compelled to grant rights for this purpose to the holder of the licence[2]. Any person who has granted, or joined in granting, such rights is entitled to compensation from the holder of the licence[3]. The scope of the right to compensation is defined by regulations[4]. The entitlement to compensation arises on the date of the grant of the rights or, where there is an appeal, the final determination of the appeal[5].

1 Environmental Protection Act 1990 (EPA 1990), s 35(1)–(3). A general explanation of the waste management licensing system is outside the scope of this work; it will be found in *Garner's Environmental Law*.
2 EPA 1990, s 35(4).
3 EPA 1990, s 35A(2). No compensation is payable in respect of the interest of a mortgagee: Waste Management (Consultation and Compensation) Regulations 1999, SI 1999/481, reg 7(5)(*b*). Where an interest is subject to a mortgage, the compensation must be paid to the mortgagee, who must apply it as though it were proceeds of sale: reg 8(1).
4 EPA 1990, s 35A(3). In exercise of this power, the Secretary of State has made the Waste Management Licences (Consultation and Compensation) Regulations 1999, SI 1999/481.
5 Waste Management Licences (Consultation and Compensation) Regulations 1999, SI 1999/481, reg 5.

2 Assessment of compensation

[1729]
Compensation is recoverable as a consequence of the grant in respect of[1]:

(*a*) depreciation in the value of any 'relevant interest'[2] to which the grantor is entitled;
(*b*) depreciation in the value of any other interest in land to which the grantor is entitled:
(*c*) loss or damage in respect of which he would have been entitled to compensation for disturbance if the interest had been compulsorily acquired;
(*d*) damage to, or injurious affection of, any interest to which the grantor is entitled, which is not a relevant interest; and
(*e*) loss, in respect of work[3] carried out, which is rendered abortive.

1 Waste Management Licences (Consultation and Compensation) Regulations 1999, SI 1999/481, reg 4.
2 Ie an interest in land out of which rights have been granted: Waste Management Licences (Consultation and Compensation) Regulations 1999, SI 1999/481, reg 2.
3 This includes the preparation of plans or other preparatory matters: Waste Management Licences (Consultation and Compensation) Regulations 1999, SI 1999/481, reg 7(4).

[1730]–[1740]
The date of assessment of compensation is, presumably, the date of entitlement. The rules in the LCA 1961, s 5 apply as if the interest had been compulsorily acquired[1]. No account is to be taken of any improvement carried out or building erected on the claimant's land, if the Upper Tribunal is satisfied that it was carried out or built unnecessarily or with a view to increasing the compensation[2]. Where the interest is subject to a mortgage, compensation is to be assessed as if it was not[3]. Compensation is to include reasonable legal and valuation expenses[4].

1 For the assessment of compensation for compulsory acquisition, see **Division E**.
2 Waste Management Licences (Consultation and Compensation) Regulations 1999, SI 1999/481, reg 7(3).
3 Waste Management Licences (Consultation and Compensation) Regulations 1999, SI 1999/481, reg 7(5)(*a*).
4 Waste Management Licences (Consultation and Compensation) Regulations 1999, SI 1999/481, reg 7(6).

3 Procedure

[1741]
An application for compensation must be made within 12 months from the date of entitlement to compensation or six months of the date when the rights are first exercised[1]. The application must be made in writing, containing or accompanied by the particulars specified in the regulations[2]. Any question of disputed compensation is to be referred to the Upper Tribunal[3]; the LCA 1961, ss 2–4 then apply[4]. The parties may agree that the compensation is to be paid as a single sum or by instalments[5].

1 Waste Management Licences (Consultation and Compensation) Regulations 1999, SI 1999/481, reg 6(1).
2 Waste Management Licences (Consultation and Compensation) Regulations 1999, SI 1999/481, reg 6(2).
3 Waste Management Licences (Consultation and Compensation) Regulations 1999, SI 1999/481, reg 8(3).
4 Waste Management Licences (Consultation and Compensation) Regulations 1999, SI 1999/481, reg 8(4). As to references to the Upper Tribunal, see **Division H**.

5 Waste Management Licences (Consultation and Compensation) Regulations 1999, SI 1999/481, reg 8(2).

4 Interest

[1742]–[2100]
Interest is payable on compensation under this provision[1].

1 PCA 1991, s 80, Sch 18. See para **[26]**.

Chapter 6

Compensation under the legislation relating to the gas, electricity and telecommunications industry

Contents

A Introduction

[2101]

This chapter identifies the rights to compensation which arise where the public utilities exercise powers to install pipes, cables or apparatus, or to carry out other works on land outside their control, which is not the subject of compulsory acquisition[1]. These rights are sometimes referred to as quasi easements, although the use of the term 'easement' in this context has been criticised in the courts[2]. While it is convenient for present purposes to group these utilities together, the legislation relating to each is very different, reflecting the different requirements of each and the different origin of each, prior to privatisation. The operators in each industry have powers of compulsory purchase of land, including the creation of new rights; these are briefly identified as well as their additional powers to install pipes, cables and apparatus without compulsory purchase of land or rights. It should be noted that the Utilities Act 2000 will amend, inter alia, the Gas Act 1986 and the Electricity Act 1989.

1 For powers of compulsory acquisition, see **Division B**; for procedures before compulsory acquisition, see **Division C**; for procedures to implement compulsory acquisition, see **Division D**; and for compensation for compulsory acquisition, see **Division E**.

2 The use of the term easement in *Halsbury's Laws* to describe statutory powers to lay pipes and cables was criticised in the Court of Appeal: *Newcastle-under-Lyme Corpn v Wolstanton Ltd* [1947] Ch 427, CA per Morton LJ at 456, adopting remarks in the court below by Evershed J.

B Gas

[2102]

Public gas transporters[1] have the power to acquire land, including new rights over land, compulsorily[2]; compulsory purchase is explained in other divisions[3]. They do not have powers to lay pipes or place apparatus on land outside their control in the absence of the landowner's agreement, other than by means of compulsory purchase of the land or rights in, under or over the land. The Acquisition of Land Act 1981 applies to a compulsory purchase by a public gas transporter. This however is subject, in the case of the acquisition of a right by the creation of a new right, to Schedule 3 of the ALA[4]. The Compulsory Purchase Act 1965 will also apply, subject, in the case of the compulsory acquisition of a right by the creation of a new right, to both general[5] and specific[6] adaptions. The relevant statutory provisions which apply to the compensation of land will also apply, with the necessary modifications, to the compulsory acquisition of a right by the creation of a new right[7].

1 Gas Act 1986, Pt I, as amended by the Gas Act 1995.
2 Gas Act 1986, s 9, Sch 3, Pt I as amended by the Gas Act 1995, s 10(1), Sch 3, para 56.
3 See para **[2101]**, note 1.
4 Gas Act 1986, Sch 3, Pt II, para 4.
5 Gas Act 1986, Sch 3, Pt II, para 5.
6 Gas Act 1986, Sch 3, Pt II, para 6.
7 Gas Act 1986, Sch 3, Pt II, para 13.

C Electricity

[2103]

A public electricity supplier, a person authorised by licence to transmit electricity and any other licence holder, if his licence so provides, has power to acquire land, including new rights over land, compulsorily[1]. In addition, these bodies have power to acquire 'wayleaves', either by agreement, or compulsorily[2]. A wayleave is a consent for the licence holder to install and keep installed, an electric line on, under or over the land and to have access to it for maintenance[3]. It is a contractual licence and not an easement. The ALA 1981 applies to a compulsory purchase by a licence holder of land or rights[4]. Schedule 3 to the ALA applies in the case of a compulsory acquisition of a right by the creation of a new right[5]. Where the rights in question belong to another licence holder, however, s 16 of, and para 3 of Sch 3 to, the ALA (statutory undertaker's land excluded from compulsory purchase) do not apply[6].

1 Electricity Act 1989, s 10, Sch 3 Pt I. See para **[2101]**, note 1.
2 Electricity Act 1989, s 10, Sch 4, paras 6–7.
3 Electricity Act 1989, Sch 4, para 6(1).
4 Electricity Act 1989, Sch 3, Pt II, para 5(1). See **Division C**.
5 Electricity Act 1989, Sch 3, Pt II, para 5(1).
6 Electricity Act 1989, Sch 3, Pt II, para 5(2).

[2103.1]

The CPA 1965 applies to the compulsory purchase of a right by the creation of a new right subject to both general[1] and specific[2] amendments. The relevant statutory provisions which apply to the compensation of land will also apply, with the necessary modifications, to the compulsory acquisition of a right by the creation of a new right[3].

1 Electricity Act 1989, Sch 3, Pt II, para 6.
2 Electricity Act 1989, Sch 3, Pt II, para 7.
3 Electricity Act 1989, Sch 3, Pt II, para 14. For an example of a Lands Tribunal decision assessing compensation for the compulsory acquisition of rights over land for a 400kV electric line, see *Turris Investments Ltd v Central Electricity Generating Board* [1981] 1 EGLR 186.

[2104]
Where a wayleave is granted to a licence holder, the occupier of the land and the owner of the land (if different) may recover from the licence holder compensation in respect of the grant. Compensation is payable in respect of all the loss (that is not too remote) that flows from the grant[1]. If damage is caused to any land or moveables in the exercise of any right conferred under a wayleave, any person interested in the land or moveables may recover compensation from the license holder in respect of the damage. Similarly, where the exercise of the right causes disturbance to any person's enjoyment of any land or moveables, that person may recover compensation from the licence holder[2].

1 Electricity Act 1989, Sch 4, para 7(1); see also *Macleod v National Grid Co plc* [1998] 2 EGLR 217 and *Welford v EDF Energy Networks plc* [2006] RVR 245, Lands Tribunal; affirmed [2007] EWCA Civ 293, [2007] RVR 172.
2 As to the assessment of disturbance in the context of compulsory purchase, see **Division E** and *Welford v EDF Energy Networks plc* [2006] RVR 245, Lands Tribunal; affirmed [2007] EWCA Civ 293, [2007] RVR 172.

[2104.1]
Compensation may be recovered as a lump sum or as instalments[1]. Any question of disputed compensation is to be referred to the Lands Tribunal; the LCA 1961, ss 2–4 then apply[2].

1 Electricity Act 1989, Sch 4, para 7(3).
2 Electricity Act 1989, Sch 4, para 7(4). As to references to the Lands Tribunal, see **Division H**.

[2105]
A licence holder has a power of entry:

(*a*) for the purpose of felling or lopping trees which interfere with the line or create a source of damage[1]; and
(*b*) for survey purposes[2].

In the event of damage or disturbance to the land or moveables as a result of the exercise of these powers, a right to compensation arises[3]. Any question of disputed compensation shall be referred to and determined by the Upper Tribunal. Sections 2 and 4 of the Land Compensation Act 1965 apply.

1 Electricity Act 1989, Sch 4, para 9.
2 Electricity Act 1989, Sch 4, para 10.
3 Electricity Act 1989, Sch 4, para 11(2).

D Telecommunications

[2106]
A public telecommunications operator[1] has the power to acquire land compulsorily, including new rights over land[2]. The Acquisition of Land Act 1981 will apply. In addition, an operator may acquire rights to install and maintain apparatus under the Telecommunications Code[3] without acquiring land or rights by compulsory purchase. The operator must seek the consent of the occupier[4], but, if this cannot be achieved, he may apply to the county court for an order granting the rights required. If the court makes such an

order, it may direct that specified terms and conditions shall apply[5] and, in particular, may include terms, with respect to:

(*a*) the payment of consideration which appears to the court to be fair and reasonable; and
(*b*) for ensuring that those bound by the order are adequately compensated for any loss or damage sustained by them in consequence of the order[6].

If the owner confers or varies the right to carry out works (etc) under the Telecommunications Code, a right to compensation may arise in the event of depreciation being caused to any 'relevant interest'[7] in the land[8]. The depreciation must be caused by the fact that paragraph 21 of the Telecommunications Code (restriction on the right to require the removal of apparatus) will apply when the owner of the interest becomes the occupier of the land.

1 Ie a person authorised by a licence to run a public telecommunications system: Telecommunications Act 1984, s 9(3).
2 Telecommunications Act 1984, s 34. See para **[2101]**, note 1.
3 Telecommunications Act 1984, Sch 2.
4 Telecommunications Act 1984, Sch 2, para 2.
5 Telecommunications Act 1984, Sch 2, para 5(4).
6 Telecommunications Act 1984, Sch 2, para 7(1).
7 Defined in Telecommunications Act 1984, Sch 2, para 4(5) as meaning, in relation to land subject to a right conferred or varied in accordance with para 2 of the Code, any interest in respect of which the following two conditions are satisfied at the time the right is conferred or varied – (*a*) the owner of the interest is not the occupier of the land but may become the occupier by virtue of that interest; and (*b*) the owner of the interest becomes bound by the right or variation by virtue only of para 2(3) of the Code.
8 Telecommunications Act 1984, Sch 2, para 4(4).

[2107]–[2400]

Any dispute as to a person's entitlement to, or as to the amount of, compensation is to be determined by the Upper Tribunal. Sections 2 and 4 of the Lands Compensation Act 1961 applies with the necessary modifications[1]. The operator must be given notice of the claim and the claim must specify particulars of:

(*a*) the land in respect of which the claim is made;
(*b*) the claimant's interest in the land and, so far as known to the claimant, any other interests in the land;
(*c*) the right or variation in respect of which the claim is made; and
(*d*) the amount of compensation claimed.

The claim may be made at any time before the claimant becomes the occupier of the land or at any time within three years of the claimant becoming the occupier[2]. In addition to any compensation, the operator shall also pay to the claimant any reasonable valuation or legal expenses incurred by the claimant in the[3] preparation and prosecution of his claim.

1 Telecommunications Act 1984, Sch 2, para 4(6). As to references to the Upper Tribunal, see **Division H**.
2 Telecommunications Act 1984, Sch 2, para 4(7).
3 Telecommunications Act 1984, Sch 2, para 4(9).

Division H

Determination and recovery of compensation

Contents

References in bold are to paragraph numbers.

Determination and recovery of compensation

Determination and recovery of compensation

Contents

A Introduction

[1]

This Division explains the process by which compensation for compulsory purchase and certain other forms of compensation is determined by the Upper Tribunal (Lands Chamber) where the parties are unable to reach agreement[1] and the process by which an award of compensation may be enforced.

1 Despite the wording of the relevant statutory provisions, there is encouragement in policy and procedure to use alternative dispute resolution techniques, such as mediation, to resolve questions of compensation: ODPM Circular 06/04, para 26; Tribunal Procedure (Upper Tribunal) (Lands Chamber) Rules 2010, SI 2010/2600, rr 2 and 3; Lands Chamber Practice Directions 2010, para 2. The parties are advised to consider whether or not they should be using these options and are reminded of their obligation to consider such a course as part of the overriding duty.

[2]
Under the Land Clauses Consolidation Act 1845 (LCCA 1845)[1], different methods of resolution applied according to the amount of the claim: small claims were settled by two justices, larger claims by arbitration or, in certain circumstances, by a jury summonsed by the sheriff of the county. Under the Acquisition of Land (Assessment of Compensation) Act 1919 these were replaced by expert valuers acting as official arbitrators. These, in turn, were replaced by the Lands Tribunal, which was created[2] in 1950 to combine valuation and legal expertise in one body, with jurisdiction in relation to compensation for land compulsorily acquired, as well as for a range of other matters concerning or affecting the valuation of interests in land. In 2009, the Lands Tribunal ceased to exist and its jurisdiction was transferred to the Upper Tribunal (Lands Chamber)[3],which is referred to in this Division as 'the tribunal'. Although it operates under new procedural rules and practice directions which are described in the paragraphs which follow, in general the tribunal operates in much the same way as the Lands Tribunal used to operate.

1 For the history of the compensation legislation, see **Division E**.
2 Lands Tribunal Act 1949.
3 Following the approach in the Land Valuations and Housing Tribunals: The Future: Law Commission, Report No 281 and the Tribunal Procedure (Upper Tribunal) (Lands Chamber) Rules 2010, SI 2010/2600. It should be noted that by virtue of the Tribunal Procedure (Upper Tribunal) Rules 2008, SI 2008/2698, r 1(2), as amended, those rules do not apply to proceedings in the Lands Chamber.

[3]
Any question of disputed compensation following the acquisition of land or an interest in land authorised to be acquired compulsorily by or under any statute must now be referred to the Upper Tribunal for determination[1]. In addition, the tribunal has jurisdiction over a range of other compensation claims, arising under various enactments, where land has not been compulsorily acquired[2].

1 Land Compensation Act 1961 (LCA 1961), s 1 and the Compulsory Purchase Act 1965 (CPA 1965), s 6.
2 For example, the rights to compensation described in **Division F** and most of those described in **Division G**. Disputes in relation to some types of compensation described in **Division G** are to be referred to arbitration or other forms of determination; these are not described in this work. The tribunal has power to act as arbitrator on a reference by consent under the Lands Tribunal Act 1949, s 1(5); when it does so, the Tribunal Procedure (Upper Tribunal) (Lands Chamber) Rules 2010, SI 2010/2600 , Pt 5, r 30 applies a number of sections of the Arbitration Act 1996 to such proceedings.

B The Upper Tribunal (Lands Chamber) – 'the tribunal'

[4]
The tribunal is composed of a President[1] and members, who are either lawyers ('judges') or persons of experience in the valuation of land ('members') appointed after consultation with the President of the Royal Institution of Chartered Surveyors. The jurisdiction of the tribunal may be exercised by any one or more of its judges or members[2] who are selected by the President for a particular case or for a class or group of cases.

Additionally, if it appears to the President that any case calls for special knowledge he may appoint one or more assessors.

1 Within the Upper Tribunal there is a Senior President of Tribunal judges: Sir Robert Carnwath. The Chamber President Upper Tribunal (Lands Chamber) must either have held judicial office or have a seven-year general qualification within the meaning of the Courts and Legal Services Act 1990. The President is George Bartlett QC.

2 The current judges are: the Hon Mr Justice Morgan; His Honour Judge Reid QC, His Honour Judge Mole QC; His Honour Judge Huskinson; Her Honour Judge Alice Robinson; His Honour Judge Milwyn Jarman QC. The current members are Norman Rose FRICS, Paul Francis FRICS and Andrew Trott FRICS.

[5]

The Lands Tribunal was regarded as a 'court of law' which had judicial, rather than essentially administrative, characteristics[1] and presumably the same applies to the tribunal. It is designated as a tribunal under the Tribunals and Inquiries Act 1992 and supervised under the Tribunals, Courts and Enforcement Act 2007 by the Administrative Justice and Tribunals Council. Its procedure is governed by the Tribunal Procedure (Upper Tribunal) (Lands Chamber) Rules 2010[2] and its own Lands Chamber of the Upper Tribunal Practice Directions 2010[3]. Also available are an *Explanatory Leaflet of Guidance for Users* dated January 2011 and Procedural Flowcharts.

The rules apply the same overriding objective as in the High Court and county court under the Civil Procedure Rules[4]. That overriding objective is to apply the rules and practice directions so as to enable the tribunal to deal fairly and justly with cases:

(*a*) by dealing with the case in ways which are proportionate to the importance of the case, the complexity of the issues, the anticipated costs and the resources of the parties;
(*b*) by avoiding unnecessary formality and seeking flexibility in the proceedings;
(*c*) by ensuring, as far as is practicable, that the parties are able to participate fully in the proceedings;
(*d*) by using any special expertise of the tribunal effectively;
(*e*) by avoiding delay, so far as compatible with proper consideration of the issues[5].

The tribunal is not constrained by its rules and may rely upon the supplemental powers in respect of the attendance and examination of witnesses, the production and inspection of documents and all other matters incidental to its functions, provided by the Tribunals, Courts and Enforcement Act 2007, s 25(2)(*c*).

1 *Hillingdon London Borough Council v ARC Ltd* [1999] Ch 139, CA and in the former Practice Notes 1997, para 2: 'Practitioners are reminded that the Lands Tribunal is a court of law.' Although this reference to status was repeated in para 18.1 of the 2006 Practice Directions, it has not been included in subsequent Practice Directions.

2 SI 2010/2600. For proceedings started before the date on which the 2010 Rules came into force (29 November 2010), r 60 allows the tribunal to give any directions to ensure fair treatment and may apply the provisions of the Lands Tribunal Rules 1996, SI 1996/1022 or disapply the provisions of the Tribunal Procedure (Upper Tribunal) (Lands Chamber) Rules 2010, SI 2010/2600. Failure to comply with the rules does not render proceedings invalid unless the tribunal so directs: r 7.

3 Lands Chamber of the Upper Tribunal Practice Directions 29 November 2010 replace those previously issued.
4 Tribunal Procedure (Upper Tribunal) (Lands Chamber) Rules 2010, SI 2010/2600, r 2. Note, however, that the Civil Procedure Rules had no general application in the Lands Tribunal under the previous rules. This was highlighted in the decision of the Court of Appeal in *Purfleet Farms Ltd v Secretary of State for Transport, Local Government and the Regions* [2002] EWCA Civ 1430, [2002] RVR 368, which made it clear that the costs provisions of the Civil Procedure Rules and related case law have no application to decisions on costs in the Lands Tribunal. The approach in *Purfleet* was adopted in *Blakes Estate Ltd v Government of Montserrat* [2005] UKPC 46 at [25]. In *O'Donovan v Manchester (Ringway) Airport plc* [2009] UKUT 164 (LC), [2009] RVR 358 at para 10, the President said: 'The Civil Procedure Rules have no application in the Lands Tribunal (although they may have some persuasive force in terms of the way in which the tribunal exercises its powers). Certainly the CPR cannot under any principle of construction be used for the purposes of construing the Lands Tribunal Rules.'
5 Tribunal Procedure (Upper Tribunal) (Lands Chamber) Rules 2010, SI 2010/2600, r 2(2).

[6]

The Upper Tribunal (Lands Chamber) is located at 43-45 Bedford Square, London WC1B 3DN (tel: 020 7612 9710; fax: 020 7612 9723; e-mail: lands@tribunals.gsi.gov.uk; DX: 149065 Bloomsbury 9; Typetalk 18001 020 7612 9710; website: www.landstribunal.gov.uk), where the registrars (Donald Scannnell and Stella Rozanski) and administration are based, and where hearing rooms are available[1]. There is no statutory requirement for hearings to be located near to the land in question, but the tribunal will sit locally where necessary or, if so requested, will try to arrange suitable courtroom accommodation locally[2]. For this purpose, although it has no permanent courts or administration other than those in Bedford Square, arrangements will be made to use suitable premises, such as magistrates' or county courts. The choice of venue will be influenced by such considerations as the convenience of, and the costs to, the parties and the need to inspect the site and comparable property in the locality. Proceedings may be heard in part locally and in part in London, particularly if they are likely to last more than five days. All hearings of the tribunal are in public, except where it is acting as an arbitrator on a reference by consent or it is satisfied that, by reason of disclosure of matters which are either confidential or concern national security, it is just and reasonable for the hearing or any part of it to be held in private[3].

1 The tribunal has a website, www.justice.gov.uk/guidance/courts-and-tribunals/tribunals/lands/index, which provides links to the rules, practice directions, explanatory leaflet, flowcharts and forms, and a library of decisions, as well as other archived information.
2 Explanatory Leaflet, January 2011, para 11.1: Venues.
3 LCA 1961, s 2(2); The Tribunal Procedure (Upper Tribunal) (Lands Chamber) Rules 2010, SI 2010/2600, r 48. Where a hearing is held in private, it may be attended by the Senior President or any other judge or member, and with the consent of the parties, any other person: r 48(4), (5).

C Jurisdiction of the tribunal

[7]

The tribunal depends for the precise extent of its jurisdiction upon the powers conferred upon it by statute, by Orders in Council, by statutory instrument or, where the tribunal is acting as an arbitrator, the terms of the arbitration agreement. The tribunal has no inherent jurisdiction and must satisfy itself that the facts and issues for determination are sufficient to found jurisdiction before proceeding to hear those matters[1]. Any decision of the tribunal as to jurisdiction[2] may be questioned in subsequent proceedings.

1 For example: *Re London and Winchester Properties Ltd's Appeal* (1983) 45 P & CR 429, Lands Tribunal; *Simmonds v Kent County Council* [1990] 1 EGLR 227, Lands Tribunal; *Donovan v Welsh Water and Alfred McAlpine Homes Midlands Ltd* (1993) 67 P & CR 233, Lands Tribunal; *Williams v Blaenau Gwent Borough Council* (1994) 67 P & CR 393, Lands Tribunal; *Dodd and Dodd v Stansted Airport* (1998) 76 P & CR 456. In *Mean Fiddler Holdings Ltd v Islington London Borough Council (No 2)* [2003] 3 EGLR 61, [2003] RVR 375 the Lands Tribunal decided that it had jurisdiction to enforce its rules of procedure and to suppress an abuse of its process and disagreed with *Finsbury Business Centre Ltd v Mercury Communications* [1994] RVR 108, where the tribunal had decided that it could not strike out a reference.

2 The Upper Tribunal (Lands Chamber) may determine questions of jurisdiction under the powers conferred by the Tribunals, Courts and Enforcement Act 2007: see para **[9]**, note 2 below.

[8]

The jurisdiction now conferred upon the tribunal may for present purposes be summarised as follows:

(*a*) to determine questions of disputed compensation for land which has been compulsorily acquired[1];
(*b*) to determine questions of disputed compensation for injurious affection or loss where land has not been compulsorily acquired[2];
(*c*) to determine compensation where the owner of land being acquired compulsorily is absent or abroad[3] or where no effectual meeting of commoners has taken place[4];
(*d*) to determine questions referred to it by virtue of Orders in Council[5];
(*e*) to determine compensation arising by virtue of various enactments[6];
(*f*) to act as an arbitrator by consent of the parties[7];
(*g*) to determine objections to blight notices[8]; and
(*h*) to issue certificates of value pursuant to the LCA 1961, s 35[9].

Functions are allocated to the Upper Tribunal (Lands Chamber) by the First-Tier Tribunal and Upper Tribunal (Chambers) Order 2010[10].

1 LTA 1949, s 1(3)(*a*); LCA 1961, s 1; and CPA 1965, s 6.
2 Ie, under the LCCA 1845, s 10; LTA 1949, s 1(3)(*b*); under CPA 1965, ss 6, 7; or under the Land Compensation Act 1973, s 16. As to injurious affection where no land is taken, see **Division F, Chapter 2**.
3 LCCA 1845, s 58; CPA 1965, s 5(3), Sch 2.
4 LTA 1949, s 1(6); LCCA 1845, s 106; CPA 1965, s 21, Sch 4, para 6.
5 LTA 1949, s 4; eg the National Parks and Access to the Countryside Act 1949, s 107.
6 For example, the enactments explained in **Divisions F** and **G**.
7 LTA 1949, s 1(5). The tribunal may be given jurisdiction to act as an arbitrator even where the tribunal holds that it has no jurisdiction under the statute referred to in the notice of reference: *Simmonds v Kent County Council* [1990] 1 EGLR 227, Lands Tribunal.
8 See **B[1210]–[1269]**.
9 LCA 1961, s 35 and formerly covered by the Lands Tribunal Rules 1996, SI 1996/1022, r 40. This provides protection to trustees and others who are required to achieve the best price that can reasonably be obtained.
10 The First-Tier Tribunals and Upper Tribunal (Chambers) Order, SI 2010/2655, art 12 allocates to the Lands Chamber:

'(a) all functions relating to –
  (i) compensation and other remedies for measures taken which affect the ownership, value, enjoyment or use of land or water, or of rights over or property in land or water;
  (ii) appeals from decisions of leasehold valuation tribunals, residential property tribunals, the Valuation Tribunal for England or a valuation tribunal for Wales;
  (iii) the determination of questions of the value of land or an interest in land arising in tax proceedings;
  (iv) proceedings in respect of restrictive covenants, blight notices or the obstruction of light;.

(*b*) the Upper Tribunal's function as arbitrator under section 1(5) of the Lands Tribunal Act 1949;

(*c*) an application for the Upper Tribunal to grant the relief mentioned in section 15(1) of the Tribunal's, Courts and Enforcement Act 2007 (Upper Tribunal's 'judicial review' jurisdiction) which relates to a decision of a tribunal mentioned in sub-paragraph (*a*)(iii);

(*d*) any other functions transferred to the Upper Tribunal by the Transfer of Tribunal Functions (Lands Tribunal and Miscellaneous Amendments) Order 2009.'

[9]

The tribunal has jurisdiction to determine any question of law that arises on a reference. Although it does not have jurisdiction to make binding decisions as to title[1], it does have jurisdiction to make decisions on title which only have effect for the purpose of the decision before it and the legal consequences that flow from that decision, such as the existence of compensatable interests[2]. If a reference has proceeded upon a presumption as to title the acquiring authority will be able to resist the payment of compensation determined by the tribunal if the claimant is unable to make out title.

While the courts have no jurisdiction to determine questions of the amount of compensation[3], they will determine questions of law which arise in the context of a claim[4].

The tribunal is not bound to follow its own decisions[5], although, in practice, they are often cited and, in so far as they determine points of law, practice or valuation principle, the tribunal will take them into account[6]. The status of a decision of the Lands Tribunal as a precedent or guideline as to methods of valuation was considered in *Earl Cadogan v Sportelli*[7].

1 *Re Purkiss' Application* [1962] 1 WLR 902, subsequently reversed in respect of restrictive covenants only by the Law of Property Act 1969, s 84(3A).

2 *Union Railways (North) Ltd v Kent County Council* [2008] RVR 217 at 228, paras 77 and 78(*c*): 'If … the question is whether the claimant is entitled to claim compensation and whether, therefore, the tribunal has jurisdiction to determine the reference, the tribunal must determine that question.' In the Court of Appeal ([2009] EWCA Civ 363), Carnwath LJ observed that as an Upper Tribunal Lands Chamber: 'the Chamber will, in appropriate cases, be able to call on the expertise of High Court judges to assist in the determination of complex issues of title.'

3 *Harrison v Croydon London Borough Council* [1968] Ch 479.

4 *Argyle Motors (Birkenhead) Ltd v Birkenhead Corpn* (1971) 22 P & CR 829, Ch D, where it was held that a claimant could bring an action for a declaration as to his entitlement to compensation. The substantive issues in this case reached the House of Lords: [1975] AC 99. See also *Duttons Brewery Ltd v Leeds City Council* (1980) 42 P & CR 152; affd on other grounds (1982) 261 Estates Gazette 885; *Munton v Greater London Council* [1976] 1 WLR 649, CA. If proceedings are already before the tribunal, relief may be refused: *Grand Junction Waterworks Co v Hampton UDC* [1898] 2 Ch 331.

5 *West Midland Baptist (Trust) Association (Incorporated) v Birmingham City Corpn* [1968] 2 QB 188, [1968] 1 All ER 205, CA; affd on other grounds sub nom *Birmingham Corpn v West Midland Baptist (Trust) Association (Incorporated)* [1970] AC 874, [1969] 3 All ER 172, HL.

6 It is submitted that this states the practice of the tribunal accurately. However, in *W Clibbet Ltd v Avon County Council* [1976] RVR 131, Lands Tribunal, at 132, the tribunal commented that previous decisions of the tribunal are 'relevant only to arguments on law and procedure'; it is submitted that this is not correct and does not reflect the practice of the tribunal.

7 [2006] RVR 382, Lands Tribunal, at paras 113–124; [2007] RVR 314, CA, at paras 91–99. The Court of Appeal agreed that it was an important part of its role for the tribunal to promote consistent practice in land valuation matters and to issue guidance. The court declined, however, to consider the status of Lands Tribunal decisions on issues of law, valuation and fact respectively because the tribunal was about to be subsumed in an Upper Tribunal which would be a 'superior court of record' under the Tribunals, Courts and Enforcement Act 2007. Carnwath LJ stated (at para 99) that: 'It will be principally for the new tribunal to lay down guidelines as to the precedent effect of its decisions for different purposes.'

[9.1]

The manner in which the tribunal exercises its jurisdiction is regulated by the Tribunal Procedure (Upper Tribunal) (Lands Chamber) Rules 2010[1], by the Lands Chamber of the Upper Tribunal Practice Directions 2010 and by an Explanatory Leaflet dated January 2011. A failure to comply with the rules, a practice direction or a direction of the tribunal does not of itself render proceedings void[2] and the rules provide various means by which breaches of the rules may be remedied[3].

1 SI 2010/2600.

2 Tribunal Procedure (Upper Tribunal) (Lands Chamber) Rules 2010, SI 2010/2600, r 7(1).

3 Tribunal Procedure (Upper Tribunal) (Lands Chamber) Rules 2010, SI 2010/2600, r 7(2) by:

(*a*) waiving the requirement;

(*b*) requiring the failure to be remedied;

(*c*) exercising the equivalent High Court powers under s 25 of the Tribunals, Courts and Enforcement Act 2007 in respect of attendance and examination of witnesses; production and inspection of documents; and all other matters incidental to the tribunal's functions in a manner not limited by the rules of the tribunal; or

(*d*) exercising its power under, r 8 of the Tribunal Procedure (Upper Tribunal) (Lands Chamber) Rules 2010, SI 2010/2600 to strike out a party's case.

D Notice of claim

[10]–[20]

Where land has been compulsorily acquired, there is no statutory requirement for the claimant to serve a notice of claim[1]. However, failure to provide particulars of claim in time to enable the acquiring authority to make an unconditional offer of compensation may not only prejudice the progress of the claim but also result in an order that the claimant be liable for not only his own costs but also those of the acquiring authority[2]. In relation to claims for compensation where no land has been taken, a formal notice of claim is in many circumstances required[3].

1 The tribunal's jurisdiction is to determine questions of disputed compensation, see para **[8]**; this implies that the claimant has at least indicated the nature of his claim sufficiently for a dispute to have arisen.

2 LCA 1961, s 4. See further para **[82]** below. It is now a procedural requirement in relation to all claims for compensation for the notice of reference to include a statement of the amount claimed, an explanation of how that amount is calculated and a summary of the reasons for making that claim: The Tribunal Procedure (Upper Tribunal) (Lands Chamber) Rules 2010, SI 2010/2600, r 28(3)(*g*) and the Lands Chamber of the Upper Tribunal Practice Directions 2010, para 6.3(2)(*a*). Notice of Reference Form REF Claimant requires a copy of the 'Notice of Claim' to be enclosed.

3 See **Divisions F** and **G**.

E Commencement of proceedings

1 Notice of reference

[21]

Proceedings for the determination of a claim for compensation by the tribunal are initiated by either party sending to the registrar a 'notice of reference', together with sufficient copies for service upon every other person named in the reference[1] and the appropriate fee[2]. The parties to the proceedings are the person who lodged the notice of reference and any other person named in it[3]. Where land is in joint ownership, the notice of reference must be made by all the joint owners[4]. In relation to a claim for compensation for compulsory purchase, only one reference may be made[5].

1 Tribunal Procedure (Upper Tribunal) (Lands Chamber) Rules 2010, SI 2010/2600, r 28(1).

2 Upper Tribunal (Lands Chamber) Fees Order 2009, SI 2009/1114, as amended by SI 2010/2601. The order also provides for the reduction or omission of fees in exceptional circumstances, ie those involving undue financial hardship (art 7) and those where such fees would have been reduced or remitted if all circumstances had been known at the time of payment (art 8).

3 Tribunal Procedure (Upper Tribunal) (Lands Chamber) Rules 2010, SI 2010/2600, r 28(2).

4 *Williams v British Gas Corpn* (1980) 41 P&CR 106; *Earle and Earle v East Riding of Yorkshire Council* [1999] RVR 200, Lands Tribunal.

5 Because compensation for compulsory purchase is a single lump sum (as to which, see **Division E**): *Thameside Estates Ltd v Greater London Council* [1979] 1 EGLR 167, 249 Estates Gazette 346, Lands Tribunal and the authorities cited in paras **[448]–[449]**.

[22]

A specific form is no longer required[1], but the notice of reference must contain[2]:

(*a*) the name and address[3] of the person lodging the reference, together with the name, address and profession of any representative;
(*b*) the name and address of any other person with an interest in the land to which the reference relates;
(*c*) the address or description of the land;
(*d*) the nature of the interest in the land of the person lodging the reference;
(*e*) the statutory provision under which the reference is made;
(*f*) the signature of the person lodging the reference or his representative and the date on which the reference was signed;
(*g*) where the reference is made by a claimant, the amount claimed, an explanation of how that amount is calculated and a summary of the reasons for making the claim;
(*h*) the matter upon which a determination is sought and a summary of the reasons for seeking it; and
(*i*) whether the claimant wants the reference to be determined without a hearing.

1 There is a Form REF (Claimant) provided on the tribunal website. The form has been amended to accord with the requirements of the rules. Although it was agreed in *O'Donovan v Manchester (Ringway) Airport plc 2009* [2009] RVR 358 at para 7 that a predecessor form was not an obligatory form, the Explanatory Leaflet, January 2011 now states at para 4.2 that: 'To bring a case to the tribunal you must file **two copies** of a notice of reference using the **correct form**.' No source is given for the statement. It appears, however, that the decision in *O'Donovan* that it was the date of posting and not the date of receipt or filing that constitutes the bringing of proceedings on a reference should no longer be relied upon.

2 Tribunal Procedure (Upper Tribunal) (Lands Chamber) Rules 2010, SI 2010/2600, r 28(3).
3 A change of address should be notified to the tribunal: the Tribunal Procedure (Upper Tribunal) (Lands Chamber) Rules 2010, SI 2010/2600, r 13(5).Unless and until notified in writing of a change, the previous address may be assumed to be the correct address for delivery of documents.

[23]
Where the reference relates to compensation for compulsory purchase, the notice of reference should be accompanied by any notice to treat, notice of entry and notice of claim received or sent (including any amendments); in any other case, it should be accompanied by a copy of the order or other document which gives rise to the proceedings[1]. Where a solicitor commences or responds to proceedings on behalf of a party, he is noted on the record as acting for that party; the solicitor, while on the record, is responsible for all fees in respect of that party[2]. Where a party is represented by any person, written notice of the representative's name and address must be sent to the tribunal[3].

1 Tribunal Procedure (Upper Tribunal) (Lands Chamber) Rules 2010, SI 2010/2600, r 28(4).
2 Lands Chamber of the Upper Tribunal Practice Directions 2010, para 11.
3 Tribunal Procedure (Upper Tribunal) (Lands Chamber) Rules 2010, SI 2010/2600, r 11(2).

2 Time limits for references

The earliest date

[24]
A reference relating to compensation for compulsory purchase may not be made until one month has elapsed after the date of actual or deemed service of the notice to treat or of the making of a claim, if there is no service of a notice to treat[1].

1 The Tribunal Procedure (Upper Tribunal) (Lands Chamber) Rules 2010, SI 2010/2600, r 28(6). Notices of Reference in respect of claims under the provisions listed in, r 28(7) must be made *within one month*. These are claims arising under the Town and Country Planning Act 1971, s 153(1); or under the Town and Country Planning (Compensation and Certificates) Regulations 1974, SI 1974/1242, regs 7(1), 12(1) or 15(1).

The latest date

[24.1]
A reference to the tribunal to determine a question of compensation is an action to recover compensation for the purposes of the Limitation Act 1980, s 9, which may not be commenced more than six years after the cause of action arises[1]. In the case of compulsory purchase, it would appear that the cause of action would arise for the purposes of the Limitation Act when the compulsory purchase is implemented by the acquiring authority entering on the land following notice to treat and notice of entry[2]. Where the general vesting declaration procedure is used to implement a compulsory purchase, a six-year limitation period applies[3] from the time of vesting under s 10(1) or from when the person claiming compensation first knew or could reasonably be expected to have known of the vesting of the interest in land, although the Lands Tribunal has held that this may be waived[4]. There is also a six-year limitation upon

claims under the LCA 1973, Pt I. In a number of cases the strict application of the limitation period has been modified on the facts of the case[5]. The bringing of an action on a reference is commenced when a notice of reference is posted and not when it is received or filed[6]. Where a contractual agreement has the effect of extending time, the reference may come before the tribunal as an arbitration on a reference by consent rather than as a statutory reference. Where a notice to treat is served but no further steps have been taken, the notice lapses after three years and with it the ability to make a reference[7].

1 *Hillingdon London Borough Council v ARC Ltd* [1999] Ch 139, CA. This was later held not to apply in circumstances where the parties had entered into an agreement for the sale of the land which the authority was authorised to acquire compulsorily on the basis that the consideration would, if not agreed, be assessed in accordance with the compensation code. The Court of Appeal, reversing a decision of the Lands Tribunal, held that the agreement took effect as an arbitration agreement and the reference to the Lands Tribunal was therefore a reference by consent under the Lands Tribunal Act 1949, s 1(5), rather than one under s 1(3): *BP Oil UK Ltd v Kent County Council* [2003] EWCA Civ 798, [2003] RVR 276.
2 As to notice to treat and entry, see **Division D**.
3 Compulsory Purchase (Vesting Declarations) Act 1981 (CP(VD)A 1981), s 10(3), see **Division D**.
4 See **Division F, Chapter 2:** *Bateman v Lancashire County Council* [1999] RVR 125.
5 In *Hillingdon London Borough Council v ARC Ltd (No 2)* [2000] RVR 283 the Court of Appeal held on the facts of the case that the acquiring authority was not estopped from relying upon expiry of the limitation period to resist payment of compensation. See: *SITA v Surrey County Council* [2001] RVR 56, Lands Tribunal; *RWE Npower plc v Kent County Council* [2006] RVR 103; *Co-operative Wholesale Society Ltd v Chester le Street District Council* (1996) 73 P&CR 111, Lands Tribunal; *Dodd and Dodd v Stansted Airport Ltd* (1998) 76 P&CR 456, Lands Tribunal. See also *Williams v Blaenau Gwent County Borough Council (No 2)* [1999] 2 EGLR 195; *Lillis v North West Water Ltd* [1999] RVR 12; *Rotherwick's Executors v Oxfordshire County Council* [2000] 2 EGLR 84; *Bateman v Lancashire County Council* [1999] RVR 125; *Bhattacharjee v Blackburn with Darwen Borough Council* [2002] RVR 55; *BP Oil UK Ltd v Kent County Council* [2003] EWCA Civ 798, [2003] RVR 276; *Wiberg v Swansea City and County Council* [2002] RVR 143; *Llanelec Precision Engineering Ltd v Neath Port Talbot Borough Council* [2000] EGLR 158; *Oakglade Investments v Greater Manchester Passenger Transport Executive* [2009] VR 39, Lands Tribunal; and *Bridgestart Properties Ltd v London Underground Ltd* [2005] 1 P&CR 15, [2004] RVR 196, CA. This reliance on estoppel has survived the decision of the House of Lords in *R v East Sussex County Council, ex p Reprotech (Pebsham) Ltd* [2002] UKHL 8, [2003] 1 WLR 348 that: '… these concepts of private law should not be extended into "the public law of planning control, which binds everyone".' In *RWE Npower plc v Kent County Council* [2006] RVR 103 at para 18 the tribunal held that: 'Although a claim for compensation on compulsory acquisition arises under statute, it is, at least for these purposes, a claim in private law against the Acquiring Authority, and decisions as to conduct of the claim affect only the parties to it.'
6 *O'Donovan v Manchester (Ringway) Airport plc* [2009] RVR 358 but see para **[22]** note 1 above and Explanatory Leaflet, January 2011, para 4.2, which takes the date of filing as the date for subsequent time-limits.
7 Compulsory Purchase Act 1965, s 5(2A). See also deemed notices to treat pursuant to purchase notices.

3 Entry of reference

[25]

On receipt of a notice of reference, the tribunal gives the reference a number, which then becomes the title of the proceedings, and enters particulars of it on the register of references. The tribunal sends a copy of the notice and its number to every other party to the proceedings[1].

1 Tribunal Procedure (Upper Tribunal) (Lands Chamber) Rules 2010, SI 2010/2600, r 28(8) and Explanatory Leaflet, January 2011, para 4.2.

4 Withdrawal of reference

[26]
Once lodged and entered, a reference may be withdrawn by sending to the tribunal a written notice of consent signed by or on behalf of all parties to the proceedings[1]. Any party may give notice in writing to the tribunal at any stage before the hearing or orally at the hearing to have the reference dismissed[2]. A party that has withdrawn part or all of its case may apply to the tribunal, in writing within 1 month of the date of receipt of the notice to withdraw or of the oral hearing, to reinstate its case[3].

1 Tribunal Procedure (Upper Tribunal) (Lands Chamber) Rules 2010, SI 2010/2600, r 50 and r 20(3)(*b*).
2 Tribunal Procedure (Upper Tribunal) (Lands Chamber) Rules 2010, SI 2010/2600, r 20(1)(*a*).
3 Tribunal Procedure (Upper Tribunal) (Lands Chamber) Rules 2010, SI 2010/2600, r 20(4)–(5).

5 Statements of case

[27]
Where the notice of reference is made by a claimant, a statement of case must be contained in or provided with the notice of reference[1] and the reference and any accompanying documents will be forwarded by the tribunal to the other named parties[2]. Where the notice of reference is made by the acquiring authority, there is no such requirement in the rules. It appears to be the intention that the claimant should serve a statement of case before the acquiring authority responds[3].

1 Lands Chamber of the Upper Tribunal Practice Directions 2010, para 6.3(1)(*a*) but note Tribunal Procedure (Upper Tribunal) (Lands Chamber) Rules 2010, SI 2010/2600, r 29(3)(*a*), which appears to envisage that the practice direction will specify a later date for the statements of case as it is now a procedural requirement in relation to all claims for compensation for the notice of reference to include a statement of the amount claimed, an explanation of how that amount is calculated and a summary of the reasons for making that claim: The Tribunal Procedure (Upper Tribunal) (Lands Chamber) Rules 2010, SI 2010/2600, r 28(3)(*g*) and the Lands Chamber of the Upper Tribunal Practice Directions 2010, para 6.3(2)(*a*).
2 Tribunal Procedure (Upper Tribunal) (Lands Chamber) Rules 2010, SI 2010/2600, r 28(8).
3 The Practice Directions do not distinguish between a claimant's notice of reference and an acquiring authority's reference, while the rules do.

[27.1]
A person to whom a notice of reference (and any accompanying statement of case) has been sent by the tribunal must, within one month of the date on which the tribunal sent the notice, send or deliver to the tribunal and to the claimant a response to the notice of reference[1].

The response to the statement of case must be signed, dated and state whether the respondent intends to take part in the proceedings. If so, it must state the name, address and professional capacity of any representative; provide an address for service of documents; and summarise the respondent's contentions.

Upon receipt of the response the tribunal must direct that the respondent either:

(*a*) send or deliver to the tribunal and to the claimant, within a specified period, a statement of case; *or*
(*b*) that the notice of reference shall stand as the respondent's statement of case[2].

It should be noted that the Practice Direction differs from the rules in respect of the timing and need for a statement of case as well as a response[3]. Paragraph 6.3 of the Practice Direction requires that the statement of case must be contained in or be provided with the reference or response and that, if it is not, an application must be made at the time the response is provided or made for an extension of time for providing the statement of case. The Practice Direction para 6.3(4) also appears to preclude, r 29(3)(ii) (above) of the rules[3] from ever applying as it states that where no statement of case is provided with the response the tribunal will order that one be provided.

1 Tribunal Procedure (Upper Tribunal) (Lands Chamber) Rules 2010, SI 2010/2600, r 29(1).
2 Tribunal Procedure (Upper Tribunal) (Lands Chamber) Rules 2010, SI 2010/2600, r 29(3).
3 Lands Chamber of the Upper Tribunal Practice Directions 2010, para 6.3(1)(*b*) and (3).

6 Alternative dispute resolution

[27.2]
Before a case is allocated the parties should have considered resolving all or some of their differences by alternative dispute resolution or mediation. Even after cases have been allocated, the tribunal will allow a short stay of proceedings for the parties to pursue a mediated settlement outside the tribunal process[1]. If a stay is required, a short period of six weeks may be applied for under the Tribunal Procedure (Upper Tribunal) (Lands Chamber) Rules 2010[2], r 6 and will normally be granted unless a longer period can be justified[3]. The parties may apply for a second or longer stay in alternative dispute resolution proceedings[4].

Three different mediation schemes are offered[5] (although not exclusively):

(*a*) The National Mediation Helpline.
(*b*) The Centre for Effective Dispute Resolution.
(*c*) The Royal Institution of Chartered Surveyors.

The Practice Directions warn that a party's refusal to mediate may be drawn to the attention of the tribunal when its discretion as to costs being paid by another party or by its legal or other representatives is being considered[6].

In *Dunnett v Railtrack plc*[7] the Court of Appeal refused to make a costs order to a successful party because the court's indication that mediation might be attempted had subsequently been rejected by that party. The court indicated that mediation might be appropriate even where one of the parties did not intend to pay any more money than had already been offered.

1 Tribunal Procedure (Upper Tribunal) (Lands Chamber) Rules 2010, SI 2010/2600, r 3(1).
2 SI 2010/2600.
3 Lands Chamber of the Upper Tribunal Practice Directions 2010, para 2.1.
4 Lands Chamber of the Upper Tribunal Practice Directions 2010, para 2.2.
5 Explanatory Leaflet, January 2011 para 2.10 at p 15.
6 Lands Chamber of the Upper Tribunal Practice Directions 2010, para 2.2.
7 [2002] EWCA Civ 303, [2002] 2 All ER 850, a case relating to CPR 1.4.

7 Case allocation

[28]

After receipt of a reference and bearing in mind any preference for procedure that has been expressed, the tribunal will assign the reference to one of the four case management procedures[1]:

(*a*) Written procedure.
(*b*) Simplified procedure.
(*c*) Standard procedure.
(*d*) Special procedure.

1 Lands Chamber of the Upper Tribunal Practice Directions 2010, para 3.1.

8 Addition, substitution and removal of parties

[28.1]

The tribunal may direct that any party be added, removed or substituted as a party and may make appropriate consequential directions[1]. Any person may apply to be added or substituted as a party[2].

1 Tribunal Procedure (Upper Tribunal) (Lands Chamber) Rules 2010, SI 2010/2600, r 9(1) and (2).
2 Tribunal Procedure (Upper Tribunal) (Lands Chamber) Rules 2010, SI 2010/2600, r 9(3). If a person is entitled to be a party by virtue of satisfying the requirements of another enactment, the tribunal must give a direction adding that party: r 9(4).

F Service of documents

[29]

Parties to proceedings must notify the tribunal of an address for service of documents[1]. Documents required by the rules to be served are to be deemed to have been sent or delivered to that person if sent or delivered to the last address given for service[2]. Documents to be sent to the tribunal are to be sent to its office[3]. Where any person to whom a document is required to be sent cannot be found, after diligent inquiries, or has died without personal representatives or is out of the United Kingdom or, for any other reason, service cannot be effected, the tribunal may dispense with service upon that person or make an order for substituted service[4]. Documents may be sent by pre-paid post; document exchange, hand, fax or e-mail subject to any contrary request from the tribunal or other party[5]. Where a party intends to call expert evidence, he must comply with any request under the Tribunal Procedure (Upper Tribunal) (Lands Chamber) Rules 2010, r 18 for the production of documents[6].

1 Tribunal Procedure (Upper Tribunal) (Lands Chamber) Rules 2010, SI 2010/2600, r 28(3)(*a*)(i).
2 Tribunal Procedure (Upper Tribunal) (Lands Chamber) Rules 2010, SI 2010/2600, r 13(5).
3 Tribunal Procedure (Upper Tribunal) (Lands Chamber) Rules 2010, SI 2010/2600, r 13(1)(*a*).
4 Tribunal Procedure (Upper Tribunal) (Lands Chamber) Rules 2010, SI 2010/2600, r 14.
5 Tribunal Procedure (Upper Tribunal) (Lands Chamber) Rules 2010, SI 2010/2600, r 13(1)(*a*)–(*c*).
6 Tribunal Procedure (Upper Tribunal) (Lands Chamber) Rules 2010, SI 2010/2600, r 18(1)(*b*) and the section on expert evidence at paras **[65]–[66]** below.

G Determination of proceedings by striking out

[30]
If a direction states that failure to comply would lead to the proceedings being struck out and there is such a failure, the proceedings or part of them will be *automatically* struck out[1].

If any part of the proceedings are outside the jurisdiction of the tribunal, that part *must* either be struck out[2] or transferred to another court or tribunal with jurisdiction[3].

The tribunal may strike out all or part of the proceedings[4] if there has been:

(*a*) failure to comply with a direction indicating that such failure could lead to striking out of part or all of proceedings; or
(*b*) failure by a claimant to co-operate with the tribunal; or if there is a
(*c*) lack of any reasonable prospect of success on all or part of a claim.

No notice is required where there has been an automatic strike out for failure to comply with a requirement in a direction or for want of jurisdiction[5] but the claimant may apply in writing to the tribunal, within 14 days of notification, for reinstatement[6].

The tribunal may not strike out any part of proceedings on the grounds of lack of jurisdiction, or for failure to co-operate with the tribunal, or where the tribunal considers there to be no reasonable prospect of success without first giving the claimant an opportunity to make representations[7].

1 Tribunal Procedure (Upper Tribunal) (Lands Chamber) Rules 2010, SI 2010/2600, r 8(1).
2 Tribunal Procedure (Upper Tribunal) (Lands Chamber) Rules 2010, SI 2010/2600, r 8(2)(*a*).
3 Tribunal Procedure (Upper Tribunal) (Lands Chamber) Rules 2010, SI 2010/2600, r 8(2)(*b*), applying r 5(3)(*k*)(i).
4 Tribunal Procedure (Upper Tribunal) (Lands Chamber) Rules 2010, SI 2010/2600, r 8(3)(*a*)–(*c*).
5 Tribunal Procedure (Upper Tribunal) (Lands Chamber) Rules 2010, SI 2010/2600, r 8(1) and (3)(*a*), as applied by r 8(4).
6 Tribunal Procedure (Upper Tribunal) (Lands Chamber) Rules 2010, SI 2010/2600, r 8(5).
7 Tribunal Procedure (Upper Tribunal) (Lands Chamber) Rules 2010, SI 2010/2600, r 8(4), applied to r 8(2) and (3)(*b*)–(*c*).

H Determination of proceedings by consent order

[31]–[38]
A reference may be determined by consent where the parties to proceedings agree the terms of an order to be made by the tribunal. They must send particulars of those terms to the tribunal signed by all parties or their representatives and the tribunal may make an order, in accordance with those terms, in the absence of the parties[1].

1 Tribunal Procedure (Upper Tribunal) (Lands Chamber) Rules 2010, SI 2010/2600, r 50.

I Determination of proceedings by the written representations procedure

[39]
A reference may be determined without an oral hearing, where the parties consent and the tribunal agrees that it is a proper case[1]. The tribunal will give

directions for the filing of documents and written representations[2]. The tribunal will carry out a site visit if necessary[3]. The normal rules relating to costs of the proceedings do not apply[4]. At any time a registrar or the judge or member to whom the case has been allocated for case management may direct that it should be assigned to one of the other procedures[5].

1 Lands Chamber of the Upper Tribunal Practice Directions 2010, para 3.5(1); Explanatory Leaflet, January 2011, para 2.12.
2 Lands Chamber of the Upper Tribunal Practice Directions 2010, para 3.5(2).
3 Lands Chamber of the Upper Tribunal Practice Directions 2010, para 3.5(2).
4 Tribunals, Courts and Enforcement Act 2007, s 29(1)(*b*) and (3) provide that the costs of all proceedings in the Upper Tribunal shall be in the discretion of the Lands Chamber subject to Tribunal Procedure Rules. The Tribunal Procedure (Upper Tribunal) (Lands Chamber) Rules 2010, SI 2010/2600, r 10 gives the tribunal full discretion to award costs on an application. However, the Lands Chamber of the Upper Tribunal Practice Directions 2010, paras 3.5(3) and 12.8 restrict an award of costs in the written representation procedures to circumstances where there has been an unreasonable failure on the part of the claimant to accept an offer to settle; or where either party has otherwise behaved unreasonably; or where the circumstances are in some other respect exceptional. This reverses the general rule at para 12.3(1) of the rules that a claimant for compensation in respect of the acquisition of an interest in his land should recover his costs in the tribunal, subject to the period following any sealed offer being discretionary. There is no reason given for the reversal of the general rule in the Explanatory Leaflet, January 2011 at paras 2.4, 2.12 and 4.6.
5 Lands Chamber of the Upper Tribunal Practice Directions 2010, para 3.1(2).

J Determination of proceedings by means of simplified procedure

[40]

A reference may be determined by means of a simplified procedure, the purpose of which is to provide for the speedy and economical determination of cases in which no substantial issue of law or valuation practice, or substantial conflict of fact, is likely to arise[1]. The object is to save time and costs in simpler cases where legal representation is not required; where a chartered surveyor will be allowed to act as advocate and expert witness; where the procedure is informal and witnesses are not sworn-in[2].

The procedure is initiated by a request to the tribunal that the proceedings should be determined in this way[3]. There is provision for any other party to object, and for determining such objection as an interlocutory matter[4]. A statement of case must be provided with the notice of reference[5] and both will be forwarded to the other named parties by the tribunal[6]. Not later than one month before the hearing the parties must exchange copies of all documents to be relied upon[7]. Not later than 14 days before the hearing each party must file and exchange an expert's report if one is relied upon and a list of witnesses to be called[8]. The tribunal acts as if it were an arbitrator at an informal hearing adopting any procedure that it considers fair. Strict rules of evidence do not apply and the evidence is not taken on oath, unless the tribunal orders otherwise.

The normal rule as to costs is that there will be no order; in other words, each party will bear its own. However, exceptions are made for references to which the LCA 1961, s 4[9] applies, when costs will be ordered in accordance with that section. Where the tribunal considers it appropriate to have regard to the making of an offer of settlement; or in circumstances which the tribunal regards as exceptional; or where the tribunal considers that an award of wasted cost should be made, costs may be awarded, but may not exceed the amount that would be allowed if the proceedings had been heard in the County Court[10].

At any time a registrar or the judge or member to whom the case has been allocated for case management may direct that it should be assigned to one of the other procedures[11].

1 Lands Chamber of the Upper Tribunal Practice Directions 2010, para 3.3(1).
2 Explanatory Leaflet, January 2011, para 2.12.
3 Lands Chamber of the Upper Tribunal Practice Directions 2010, para 3.1(2) and Form REF (Claimant).
4 Tribunal Procedure (Upper Tribunal) (Lands Chamber) Rules 2010, SI 2010/2600, r 10(3)(*g*).
5 Lands Chamber of the Upper Tribunal Practice Directions 2010, paras 3.3(2) and 6.3. See also para **[27]** note 3 above.
6 Tribunal Procedure (Upper Tribunal) (Lands Chamber) Rules 2010, SI 2010/2600, r 28(8).
7 Lands Chamber of the Upper Tribunal Practice Directions 2010, para 3.3(3).
8 Lands Chamber of the Upper Tribunal Practice Directions 2010, para 3.3(3).
9 Lands Chamber of the Upper Tribunal Practice Directions 2010, para 3.3(4). This is different from the provision in respect of the written representation procedure and appears to expand the description of costs available as described in para 12.8. LCA 1961, s 4 provides for three situations: where a claimant has not delivered to an acquiring authority particulars of his claim in sufficient time to enable it to make an unconditional offer; where the acquiring authority has made an unconditional offer which exceeds the tribunal's award; or where the claimant had made an unconditional offer to accept a certain sum which is less than the tribunal's award: see further para **[81]**. See also **Division E**. See also para **[39]** note 4 above for the restriction on costs awards under this procedure.
10 Lands Chamber of the Upper Tribunal Practice Directions 2010, para 3.3(4). For exceptions see *Nicholls v Highways Agency* [2000] RVR 230 and *Cook and Pullen v Highways Agency* (3 May 2002, unreported), Lands Tribunal.
11 Lands Chamber of the Upper Tribunal Practice Directions 2010, para 3.1(2).

K Determination of proceedings by means of the special and standard procedures

[41]

A reference will be assigned to the special procedure if it requires case management by a judge or member in view of its complexity, the amount in issue or its wider importance. Such cases normally concern large or complex matters which require non-standard orders for directions[1].

An early case management hearing will be held for appropriate directions. Not less than seven days before that hearing the parties must file an agreed position statement summarising the subject-matter of the case and issues likely to be raised. The parties should also state the areas of expertise and the general scope of the evidence of each expert that they wish to rely upon[2].

The purpose of the early hearing is to ensure so far as practicable that all appropriate directions are given for the fair, expeditions and economical conduct of the proceedings. The parties should consider what orders are necessary and whether directions are required for the determination of a preliminary issue or for permission to call more than the permitted number of expert witnesses[3].

Where appropriate, at the early case management hearing, a main hearing date will be fixed and a timetable set by reference to that date.

At any time a registrar or the judge or member to whom the case has been allocated for case management may direct that it should be assigned to one of the other procedures[4].

1 Lands Chamber of the Upper Tribunal Practice Directions 2010, para 3.4; Explanatory Leaflet, January 2011, para 2.12.
2 Lands Chamber of the Upper Tribunal Practice Directions 2010, para 3.4(3).
3 Lands Chamber of the Upper Tribunal Practice Directions 2010, para 3.4(2).
4 Lands Chamber of the Upper Tribunal Practice Directions 2010, para 3.1(2).

[41.1]
The standard procedure[1] applies in all cases where the written representation, simplified and special procedures are not appropriate. Under this procedure case management will be in the hands of the registrars. A case management hearing will be held should it appear appropriate. It will consider any of the elements that might arise in connection with a special procedure case, should they arise in the context of the standard procedure case in question.

1 Lands Chamber of the Upper Tribunal Practice Directions 2010, para 3.2; Explanatory Leaflet, January 2011, para 2.12.

L Case management procedures

1 Stay of proceedings pending negotiation of ADR

[42]
If a stay is required, a short period of six weeks may be applied for under Rule 6 and will normally be granted for that short period unless a longer period can be justified[1]. The parties may apply for a second or longer stay once alternative dispute resolution proceedings are in progress[2].

1 Lands Chamber of the Upper Tribunal Practice Directions 2010, para 2.1.
2 Lands Chamber of the Upper Tribunal Practice Directions 2010, para 2.2.

2 Consolidation, hearing together or selection of a lead case

[43]
Where two or more references have been made which:

(*a*) are in respect of the same land or buildings;
(*b*) relate to different interests in the same land; or
(*c*) raise the same issues,

the tribunal may of its own motion or on the application of a party to the proceedings, order that the references be consolidated or heard together or treat one case as a lead case[1]. Such an order may relate to some only of the matters to which the references relate.

There is a difference between consolidation and hearing together. However, the Rules have never clearly differentiated between the two. Rule 23 of the

Lands Tribunal Rules 1949 referred to hearing together except where the tribunal consolidated some only of the matters (r 23(3)); r 36 of the 1975 Rules referred to consolidation where more than one notice had been given in respect of the same land (r 36(1)) and to hearing together where two or more notices had been given in respect of different land but raising the same issues (r 36(2)). The 1975 Rules were clearly drafted. 'Consolidation' applied to (*a*) and (*b*) above and 'hearing together' applies to similar issues in respect of different land as in (*c*) above. Rule 30 of the 1996 Rules[2] elided the two terms and removed from (*c*) the reference to 'relating to different land' and only left '[*which*] raise the same issues'. The 2010 Rules now further elide and widen the power. They merely say 'consolidate or hear together two or more sets of proceedings or parts of proceedings raising common issues, or treat a case as a lead case'.

1 Tribunal Procedure (Upper Tribunal) (Lands Chamber) Rules 2010, SI 2010/2600, r 5(3)(*b*).
2 Lands Tribunal Rules 1996, SI 1996/1022, r 30(2).

3 Application for permission to call more than one expert

[44]
Each side is permitted to call only one expert witness unless the tribunal orders otherwise[1], except where the proceedings relate to either mineral valuations or business disturbance for which not more than two experts are permitted unless the tribunal orders otherwise[2]. It is necessary to apply for permission to call more than the permitted number of expert witnesses. Such permission may be sought by means of an interlocutory application[3] made to the tribunal at any time[4]. Expert evidence is to be given in a written report unless the tribunal orders otherwise[5].

1 Tribunal Procedure (Upper Tribunal) (Lands Chamber) Rules 2010, SI 2010/2600, r 17(2).
2 Tribunal Procedure (Upper Tribunal) (Lands Chamber) Rules 2010, SI 2010/2600, r 17(3).
3 As to the procedure for case management applications, see para **[50]** below.
4 Tribunal Procedure (Upper Tribunal) (Lands Chamber) Rules 2010, SI 2010/2600, rr 5(2) and 16(1)(*c*)–(*d*).
5 Tribunal Procedure (Upper Tribunal) (Lands Chamber) Rules 2010, SI 2010/2600, r 17(4).

4 Discovery, further and better particulars etc

[45]
The tribunal may, on its own initiative or on the application of any party, order any party[1]:

(*a*) to provide any document, information, evidence or submissions to the tribunal or to a party[2];
(*b*) to answer any questions or produce any documents in that person's possession or control which relate to any issue in the proceedings[3].

1 Tribunal Procedure (Upper Tribunal) (Lands Chamber) Rules 2010, SI 2010/2600, r 6(1).
2 Tribunal Procedure (Upper Tribunal) (Lands Chamber) Rules 2010, SI 2010/2600, r 5(3)(*d*). The tribunal is not constrained by its rules and may rely upon supplemental powers in respect of the production and inspection of documents provided by the Tribunals, Courts and Enforcement Act 2007, s 25(2)(*b*).
3 Tribunal Procedure (Upper Tribunal) (Lands Chamber) Rules 2010, SI 2010/2600, r 18(1)(*b*).

[46]

No person may be compelled by an order to give any evidence or produce any document that the person could not be compelled to give or produce in an action in a court of law[1]. This reflects the approach previously taken[2]. In the tribunal, discovery of the actual letter of instruction of an expert, although not privileged, will be ordered only when there are reasonable grounds to consider that the summary is inaccurate or incomplete[3]. A letter expressed to be written 'without prejudice' does not of itself confer privilege on that document[4]. Such a letter and references to it in evidence will be inadmissible if its nature and purpose form part of negotiations for a settlement[5] and if it is not an assertion of rights[6] and if the recipient would not be prejudiced by its inadmissibility[7]. The President of the tribunal has said that, in the overwhelming majority of cases, the desirability of making an order for discovery could not be judged until after the, r 17 documents have been lodged[8].

The tribunal may issue a witness summons requiring any person to attend at the time and place specified in the summons[9]. The summons must give 14 days' notice to the person required to attend or such shorter period as the tribunal may direct[10]. The summons must state the consequences of failure to comply[11].

1 Tribunal Procedure (Upper Tribunal) (Lands Chamber) Rules 2010, SI 2010/2600, r 28(8).

2 The approach adopted by the tribunal under its former rules was to accept that the same considerations apply in the tribunal as in the High Court, and that discovery will be ordered where it is necessary for disposing of the proceedings fairly, whether or not the documents are confidential: *City of London Corpn v Watneys (London) Ltd* (1981) 258 Estates Gazette 561, Lands Tribunal. See also *City of London Corpn v Watneys (London) Ltd* [1983] RVR 5, in which the High Court refused to interfere with the tribunal's decision not to grant an order for discovery. Unlike in the High Court, the Lands Tribunal Rules 1996 did not provide expressly for protection from discovery on the grounds of privilege, nor were documents protected from discovery by reason of confidentiality alone, although it was a factor to be taken into account, together with relevance, in considering the necessity of discovery: *Science Research Council v Nassé* [1980] AC 1028, HL. For example, an order was made under former, r 39 for the production of a witness statement referred to but not exhibited in an expert's report. It was not accepted that the statement was merely setting out the expert's instructions: *Malcolm Electropainting Group v West Midlands Passenger Transport Executive* 4 February 2003, ACQ/59/2002. No order was sought or made in respect of such a letter. Instructions should be summarised in the expert report.

3 Lands Chamber of the Upper Tribunal Practice Directions 2010, para 8.2(2). Instructions will not be privileged against disclosure but the tribunal will not, in relation to those instructions, order disclosure of any specific document or permit any questioning in the tribunal, other than by the party who instructed the expert, unless it is satisfied that there are reasonable grounds to consider the statement of instructions given in the report to be inaccurate or incomplete.

4 *South Shropshire District Council v Amos* [1986] 1 WLR 1271; *Rush & Tompkins Ltd v Greater London Council* [1988] 3 WLR 939 at 942F; *Optical Express (Southern) Ltd v Birmingham City Council* [2005] RVR 230; *Secretary of State for Transport v Christos* [2003] EWCA Civ 1073, [2004] 1 P&CR 228.

5 *Malcolm Electropainting Group v West Midlands Passenger Transport Executive* 4 February 2003 ACQ/59/2002, paras 37–41 and the cases reviewed therein; also *Matthews and Matthews v Walsall Metropolitan Borough Council* [2003] RVR 163.

6 *Buckinghamshire County Council v Moran* [1989] 2 All ER 225.

7 In *Re Daintrey, ex p Holt* [1893] 2 QB 116 at 119–120; *Unilever plc v Proctor & Gamble Co* [2001] 1 All ER 783 at 795f; *Malcolm Electropainting Group v West Midlands Passenger Transport Executive* 4 February 2003, ACQ/59/2002, paras 42–43.

8 *Henry Foster Building Products Ltd v National Coal Board* (1966) 12 RRC 326, Lands Tribunal, although in that case, the tribunal did make an order before such documents were lodged.

9 Tribunal Procedure (Upper Tribunal) (Lands Chamber) Rules 2010, SI 2010/2600, r 18(1)(*a*).

10 Tribunal Procedure (Upper Tribunal) (Lands Chamber) Rules 2010, SI 2010/2600, r 18(2)(*a*).
11 Tribunal Procedure (Upper Tribunal) (Lands Chamber) Rules 2010, SI 2010/2600, r 18(6)(*b*).

5 Determination of preliminary issues

[47]

The tribunal may, on the application of any party to the proceedings or on its own initiative , order any issue to be determined at a preliminary hearing[1]. The issues which may be determined in this way are not restricted to preliminary points of law[2] but must be properly severable. However, not all issues should be considered separately from the case as a whole[3]. For example, in a case where compensation was claimed under, r 5[4] (equivalent reinstatement), the House of Lords commented that this should not have been heard as a preliminary issue because the tribunal had a discretion whether to award compensation on that basis and evidence was required for the exercise of that discretion[5]. There is a right of appeal against a decision of the tribunal on a preliminary issue[6]. There is no requirement that a legally qualified member be selected to hear and determine a preliminary issue that concerns a point of law[7].

> 'Costs in respect of the preliminary issues may be awarded on an interim basis notwithstanding that no hearing has taken place. If there is agreement over preliminary issues, it does not follow that one party has necessarily been a successful party on those issues or is entitled to an award of costs.'[8]

A preliminary issue is not a split hearing or split determination. No such procedures are referred to in the Rules or Practice Direction.

1 Tribunal Procedure (Upper Tribunal) (Lands Chamber) Rules 2010, SI 2010/2600, r 5(3)(*e*) and Lands Chamber of the Upper Tribunal Practice Directions 2010, para 7.
2 For example, a lay member ordered that the question of the reasonableness of relocation was suitable for a preliminary hearing since it would ascertain the basis of the claim: *Malcolm Electropainting Group v West Midlands Passenger Transport Executive* 4 February 2003, ACQ/59/2002, at para 11. Planning assumptions were also treated as preliminary matters in *Nomad Development Ltd v Gateshead Borough Council* [2005] RVR 187 and in *Waters v Welsh Development Agency* [2004] UKHL 19, [2004] RVR 153.
3 See the remarks of Lord Wilberforce and Lord Scarman in *Tilling v Whiteman* [1980] AC 1 at 17F–18A and 25B-C. It may be that the approach advocated by the House of Lords in *Waters* will lead to the treatment of planning assumptions not being separated from valuation, in future cases.
4 LCA 1961, s 5, r 5 as to which, see **Division E**.
5 *Harrison and Hetherington Ltd v Cumbria County Council* (1985) 50 P&CR 396, HL, at 397.
6 *Magdalen, Jesus and Keble Colleges, Oxford v Howard (Valuation Officer) and City of Oxford* (1960) 7 RRC 123, CA, at 126; *Jones v Stockport Metropolitan Borough Council* [1984] RVR 34, Lands Tribunal; [1984] RVR 35, CA. In contrast, there is no right of appeal against the refusal to grant an interlocutory direction: see para **[50]** below. As to the right of appeal, see paras **[85]–[85.1]** below.
7 *Myers v Milton Keynes Development Corpn* [1974] 1 WLR 696, CA, at 701B–C.
8 *Roadchef Motorways Ltd v Secretary of State for Transport* [2007] RVR 5, although it may be as appropriate to reserve such costs: *Esso Petroleum Company Limited v Secretary of State for Transport* [2008] RVR 351.

6 Case management powers

[48]

The Senior President of Tribunals may delegate any matter to the staff of a Tribunal[1]. Within 14 days after the date on which a delegated decision is sent to a party, that party may apply in writing to the tribunal for the decision to be considered afresh by a judge[2]. Case management under the standard procedure will be in the hands of a registrar; case management under the special procedure will be supervised by a judge or member[3].

The tribunal regulates its own procedures. It may give a direction in relation to the conduct or disposal of proceedings at any time and may amend, suspend or set aside its earlier directions.

The object is to ensure that all parties make all such admissions and agreements as ought reasonably to be made before the full hearing commences. The powers under, r 5 include reviewing and defining the issues, agreeing documentation, plans, photographs and any discovery necessary before the full hearing, fixing the venue, the likely duration and the date of the full hearing, and requiring the preparation of an agreed statement of facts and hearing bundle[4]. Appropriate directions may be made orally or in writing, in the presence or absence of any party[5].

1 Delegation of Functions to the Staff on or after 29 November 2010 Practice Statement by the Senior President of Tribunals, 29 November 2010 subject to the authorisation of the registrar by the Chamber President and the Tribunal Procedure (Upper Tribunal) (Lands Chamber) Rules 2010, SI 2010/2600, r 4(1).
2 Tribunal Procedure (Upper Tribunal) (Lands Chamber) Rules 2010, SI 2010/2600, r 4(3).
3 Lands Chamber of the Upper Tribunal Practice Directions 2010, paras 3.2(1) and 3.4(1).
4 Tribunal Procedure (Upper Tribunal) (Lands Chamber) Rules 2010, SI 2010/2600, r 5 contains a non-exclusive list of items.
5 Tribunal Procedure (Upper Tribunal) (Lands Chamber) Rules 2010, SI 2010/2600, r 46.

7 Extensions of time

[49]
The time for doing anything under the rules or for taking any steps in connection with proceedings may be extended by a direction. Such an extension may be made after the time limit has expired[1]. In general, justification for any such extension will be required, and the application will be consider having regard to the overriding objective set out in, r 2. The application must state that the other party has been sent a copy; must tell that party that any response must be made within 10 days of the date it has been served on that party; and must state the term of the extension sought and the reasons[2].

1 Tribunal Procedure (Upper Tribunal) (Lands Chamber) Rules 2010, SI 2010/2600, r 5(3)(*a*). As to the procedure for such an application, see case management applications at para **[50]** below.
2 Explanatory Leaflet, January 2011, para 9.1.

8 Procedure for case management applications

[50]–[60]
An application for directions, including an interlocutory application made during the course of proceedings, may be made in writing or orally during the course of a hearing[1]. A written application should be sent to the other parties and their representatives, as well as to the tribunal[2]. The application should state the title of the proceedings; the reasons for the application[3];

confirmation that the other parties have been sent a copy of the application and that they have been notified that they have ten days in which to object in writing to the tribunal; and a cheque for the appropriate fee[4] should be enclosed. Where the application is made with the consent of all parties, it must be accompanied by consents signed by all parties and no further copies of the application need be sent to those parties[5]. Any party who objects to the application must, with ten days of being sent a copy of the application, send to the tribunal and to the applicant written notice of objection[6]. The tribunal may determine the application with or without a hearing. If a party requests a hearing the tribunal must have regard to any view expressed when determining whether or not to hold a hearing and the form of such hearing[7]. The tribunal must send written notice of any direction to every party and to any other person affected by it, unless there is good reason not to[8]. If a party or any other person affected by the direction wishes to challenge a direction, they may do so by applying for another direction which amends, suspends or sets aside the first direction[9]. The tribunal has power to award costs, in relation to case management and interlocutory matters[10], although, in practice, they are often reserved until the determination of the reference[11]. It was held that there was no right of appeal against an interlocutory decision of the Lands Tribunal[12], presumably the same applies to a case management decision of the tribunal.

1 Tribunal Procedure (Upper Tribunal) (Lands Chamber) Rules 2010, SI 2010/2600, r 6(2); Explanatory Leaflet, January 2011, para 2.3 and 2.7.3.
2 Explanatory Leaflet, January 2011, para 2.7.2.
3 Tribunal Procedure (Upper Tribunal) (Lands Chamber) Rules 2010, SI 2010/2600, r 6(3).
4 Explanatory Leaflet, January 2011, para 2.7.3. The cheque (£100 in the Upper Tribunal (Lands Chamber) Fees (Amendment) Order 2010, SI 2010/2601) should be made out to 'Tribunal Service' and not to the Lands Chamber.
5 Tribunal Procedure (Upper Tribunal) (Lands Chamber) Rules 2010, SI 2010/2600, r 6(4), (5).
6 Tribunal Procedure (Upper Tribunal) (Lands Chamber) Rules 2010, SI 2010/2600, r 6(6).
7 Tribunal Procedure (Upper Tribunal) (Lands Chamber) Rules 2010, SI 2010/2600, r 46(2).
8 Tribunal Procedure (Upper Tribunal) (Lands Chamber) Rules 2010, SI 2010/2600, r 6(7).
9 Tribunal Procedure (Upper Tribunal) (Lands Chamber) Rules 2010, SI 2010/2600, r 6(8).
10 Tribunals, Courts and Enforcement Act 2007, s 29(1)(*b*); Tribunal Procedure (Upper Tribunal) (Lands Chamber) Rules 2010, SI 2010/2600, r 10(1).
11 *Esso Petroleum Company Limited v Secretary of State for Transport* [2008] RVR 351.
12 *R v Lands Tribunal, ex p City of London Corpn* [1982] 1 WLR 258, CA. As to the test whether an order is interlocutory or final, see *Salter Rex & Co v Gosh* [1971] 2 QB 597, CA; *White v Brunton* [1984] QB 570, [1984] 2 All ER 606, CA. Tribunal Procedure (Upper Tribunal) (Lands Chamber) Rules 2010, SI 2010/2600, r 56(1) refers to appeals against decisions and not against directions. The correct remedy is to apply for a different order amending, suspending or setting aside the first direction under, r 6(8).

M The hearing[1]

1 Rights of audience

[61]
Any party may appear in person or be represented by any other person, whether a legal representative or not[2]. The tribunal is, however, reluctant to allow individuals to represent companies whose shareholders may be unknown to the tribunal[3] or to allow a surveyor or valuer to represent a party

in hearings other than in simple cases or those following the simplified procedure[4]. If a party appoints a representative, that party, or the representative if a legal representative, must send or deliver to the tribunal and to each other party, a written notice of the representative's name and address[5]. Once notified, other parties must send a copy of any document to the representative and need not provide it to the person who has appointed the representative. This continues until a written notice revoking the representation is received[6]. If no representative has been notified, a party may still be accompanied by another person at the hearing and that person may, with the permission of the tribunal, act as representative or otherwise assist in presenting the party's case[7].

1 For information about how and when the hearing is listed see the Explanatory Leaflet, January 2011, s 11.
2 Tribunal Procedure (Upper Tribunal) (Lands Chamber) Rules 2010, SI 2010/2600, r 11(1). Formerly, permission was required for representation by a person who was not a lawyer. There is no longer such a requirement.
3 In *Koppel Investments Ltd v Thames Water Authority* [1984] RVR 176, the tribunal commented after giving leave to the principal shareholder to represent the company: 'by way of footnote this is a somewhat complicated matter with a long involved history of negotiations … I was not assisted at all by [his] not being legally represented and not putting forward expert evidence.' See also *Franks v Towse* [2001] EWCA Civ 9, [2002] RVR 15.
4 The former Lands Tribunal Interim Practice Directions and Guidance 2009, para 18.1 explained the reasoning:

> '… In simple cases, permission will usually be granted for a surveyor or valuer to represent a party in order to avoid the additional costs of separate representation. In those cases allocated to the simplified procedure under rule 28, such representation may well be the norm. In general, however, it is difficult and undesirable for the same person to act both as advocate and expert witness. Accordingly, permission will not be granted for a non-lawyer to represent a party in any case where the tribunal considers that the responsibilities of advocate and of expert witness are likely to conflict.'

The Explanatory Leaflet, January 2011 provides no such constraints at paras 2.8 and 11.3 but does advise at para 2.8 that: 'Except in small or simple cases the tribunal considers that experts should not act both as advocates and expert witnesses.'
5 Tribunal Procedure (Upper Tribunal) (Lands Chamber) Rules 2010, SI 2010/2600, r 11(2).
6 Tribunal Procedure (Upper Tribunal) (Lands Chamber) Rules 2010, SI 2010/2600, r 11(4).
7 Tribunal Procedure (Upper Tribunal) (Lands Chamber) Rules 2010, SI 2010/2600, r 11(5).

2 Failure to appear

[62]

If any party to a reference fails to attend or be represented at the hearing the tribunal may proceed, hear and determine the reference in the party's absence[1]. The tribunal must be satisfied that reasonable steps have been taken to notify the party of the hearing and that to proceed would be in the interests of justice. Where proceedings have been dismissed or determined in these circumstances, a party may apply in writing within one month after the date of the notice of decision for it to be set aside and re-made. The ground for such an application would be that the party or the party's representative was not present at the hearing and that it is in the interests of justice for the decision to be set aside[2].

1 Tribunal Procedure (Upper Tribunal) (Lands Chamber) Rules 2010, SI 2010/2600, r 49.
2 Tribunal Procedure (Upper Tribunal) (Lands Chamber) Rules 2010, SI 2010/2600, r 54(1) and (2)(*c*).

3 Procedure

[63]

The procedure at the hearing is as the tribunal may direct, but will generally follow High Court procedure[1]. The claimant usually begins by opening the case and calling the evidence for the claimant[2]. Reports or proofs of evidence may be read, summarised or taken as read. The tribunal may permit the introduction of additional evidence at the hearing if proper notice has been given to the opposing party.

1 Lands Chamber of the Upper Tribunal Practice Directions 2010, para 9.1: 'Except under the simplified procedure, the procedure adopted will generally accord with the practice in the High Court and County Courts. In particular, the claimant will begin and will have a right of reply, evidence will be taken on oath, and the rules of evidence will be applied. The tribunal will throughout seek to adopt a procedure that is proportionate, expeditious and fair in accordance with the overriding objective.' Explanatory Leaflet, January 2011, para 11.6: It is customary to address the tribunal as 'Sir'or 'Madam', notwithstanding that a legal member of the tribunal is described as a judge and may also sit in that role elsewhere: eg as High Court or county court judge. Cases under the simplified procedure will be heard informally.

2 The tribunal may direct a witness to be excluded from the hearing until that witness gives evidence: Tribunal Procedure (Upper Tribunal) (Lands Chamber) Rules 2010, SI 2010/2600, r 48(7).

4 Evidence: general

[64]

Evidence and submissions are subject to directions under, r 16(1) of the Tribunal Procedure (Upper Tribunal) (Lands Chamber) Rules 2010[1]. Evidence may be given orally on oath or affirmation or, if the parties consent or the tribunal so orders, by written submission or witness statement, although the tribunal may, at any stage, require the deponent to attend. The tribunal is not constrained by its Rules and may rely upon supplemental powers in respect of the attendance and examination of witnesses provided by the Tribunals, Courts and Enforcement Act 2007, s 25(2)(a). The tribunal has power to administer oaths and take affirmations for the purpose of witness statements or for the purpose of the giving of oral evidence[2]. Those giving evidence at a hearing, whether of fact or as expert witness, should provide a witness statement verified by a statement of truth[3]. Where a witness is called to give evidence, their witness statement will stand as their evidence in chief unless the tribunal directs otherwise[4]. The tribunal may allow amplification of the witness statement or evidence in relation to new matters that have arisen since the witness statement was provided[5]. The tribunal should not conduct experiments or take account of evidence obtained itself which have not been open to cross-examination[6], nor should it arrive at its determination on a basis different from that relied upon by either party without informing the parties[7]. The evidence should not make reference to negotiations or correspondence which have been undertaken on a 'without prejudice' basis[8]. No written or oral evidence should be given in the course of a site inspection[9], although further evidence has, on occasion, been admitted after closing submissions and after a site inspection[10]. Parties are expected to provide, prior to the hearing, bundles of relevant documents, properly paginated and excluding any irrelevant material[11].

1 SI 2010/2600.
2 Tribunal Procedure (Upper Tribunal) (Lands Chamber) Rules 2010, SI 2010/2600, r 16(3).
3 Tribunal Procedure (Upper Tribunal) (Lands Chamber) Rules 2010, SI 2010/2600, r 16(4).
4 Tribunal Procedure (Upper Tribunal) (Lands Chamber) Rules 2010, SI 2010/2600, r 16(5).
5 Tribunal Procedure (Upper Tribunal) (Lands Chamber) Rules 2010, SI 2010/2600, r 16(5)(*a*)–(*b*).
6 *Hickmott v Dorset County Council* (1978) 35 P & CR 195, CA.
7 *Aquilina and Carberryv Havering London Borough Council* (1992) 66 P & CR 39, CA; *Faraday v Carmarthenshire County Council* [2004] EWCA Civ 649, [2004] RVR 236, CA.
8 Tribunal Procedure (Upper Tribunal) (Lands Chamber) Rules 2010, SI 2010/2600, r 19. Lands Chamber of the Upper Tribunal Practice Directions 2010, para 10(2). Explanatory Leaflet, January 2011, para 2.9.
9 *Unilever plc v Proctor & Gamble Co* [2001] 1 All ER 783, CA, at 789f; *South Shropshire District Council v Amos* [1987] 1 All ER 340, CA, at 344c; *Buckingham County Council v Moran* [1989] 2 All ER 225, Court of Appeal; *Matthews and Matthews v Walsall Metropolitan Borough Council* [2003] RVR 163, Lands Tribunal.
10 *Vesta Launderettes Ltd v Smith (Valuation Officer)* [1979] RA 317, Lands Tribunal, where evidence was admitted to correct a factual error in earlier evidence, following *Wexler v Playle (Valuation Officer)* [1960] 1 QB 217, CA.
11 Tribunal Procedure (Upper Tribunal) (Lands Chamber) Rules 2010, SI 2010/2600, r 5(3)(*i*) – a party may be required as part of case management to produce a bundle for the hearing.

5 Expert evidence

[65]

An expert witness may in evidence express his opinions on values, even though substantial contribution to the formation of those opinions has been made by hearsay. Prior to the Civil Evidence Act 1995, he could not give hearsay evidence as to the facts of transactions which lay outside his personal knowledge[1]. The rule against the admissibility of hearsay evidence in civil proceedings was abolished by the Civil Evidence Act 1995[2], subject to the requirement that notice be given, where reasonable and practicable, and the right to call a witness for cross-examination[3]. The tribunal must consider the weight to be attributed to hearsay evidence, for which purpose the Act sets out various factors which may be relevant[4]. In assessing expert evidence on appeal, a court should not apply the burden of proof to the conflicting evidence of experts but should seek to determine the correct answer to the valuation question in dispute in the light of the evidence: *Stephens and Stephens v Cannon and Cannon*[5].

1 For a general explanation of the position and role of an expert valuer prior to the Civil Evidence Act 1995, see the judgment of Megarry J in *English Exporters (London) Ltd v Eldonwall Ltd* [1973] Ch 415, [1973] 1 All ER 726, including the following at 423C:

> 'Putting matters shortly, and leaving on one side the matters that I have mentioned, such as the Civil Evidence Act 1968 and anything made admissible by questions in cross-examination, in my judgment a valuer giving expert evidence in chief (or in re-examination): (*a*) may express the opinions that he has formed as to values even though substantial contributions to the formulation of those opinions have been made by matters of which he has no first-hand knowledge; (*b*) may give evidence as to the details of any transactions within his personal knowledge, in order to establish them as matters of fact; and (*c*) may express his opinion as to the significance of any transactions which are or will be proved by admissible evidence (whether or not given by him) in relation to the valuation with which he is concerned; but (*d*) may not give hearsay evidence stating the details of any transactions not within his personal knowledge in order to establish them as matters of fact. To those propositions I would add that for counsel to put in a list of comparables ought to amount to a warranty by him of his intention to tender admissible evidence of all that is shown on the list.'

Megarry J's point (*d*) is no longer applicable since the Civil Evidence Act 1995, but the remainder continues to be valid.

2 Civil Evidence Act 1995, s 1.

3 Civil Evidence Act 1995, ss 2, 3. Tribunal Procedure (Upper Tribunal) (Lands Chamber) Rules 2010, SI 2010/2600, r 16(2) provides that the tribunal may admit any evidence whether or not it would be admissible in a civil trial and may exclude admissible evidence that does not comply with a direction or practice direction or which it would be unfair to admit.

4 Civil Evidence Act 1995, s 4.

5 [2006] RVR 126.

[65.1]

The tribunal may give directions as to whether the parties are permitted to provide expert evidence; whether that evidence is to be by a jointly appointed single expert; the manner in which any evidence or submissions are to be provided including the time by which they are to be provided[1]. Permission is required where more than one expert is to be called by a party[2].

A party may apply for an order that expert evidence should be given by a single joint expert and should answer the following questions:

(*a*) Is it proportionate to have separate experts on a particular issue bearing in mind the amount in dispute; the importance to the parties and the complexity of the issue?
(*b*) Would it be quicker and more cost effective?
(*c*) Is expert evidence to be given on liability, causation or quantum?
(*d*) Is there likely to be a range of expert opinions?
(*e*) Has one party already instructed an expert?
(*f*)–(*g*) Would questions put to a single expert deal with matters sufficiently?
(*h*) Would a conference with the expert be required and make joint instruction impractical?
(*i*) Do claims of privilege make joint instruction inappropriate?[3]

An expert's report should be addressed to the tribunal and not to the instructing party[4].

An expert's report should:

(*a*) give details of the expert's qualification;
(*b*) record any literature or other material relied upon in making the report;
(*c*) say who carried out any inspection or investigations relied upon and whether or not they were carried out under the expert's supervision;
(*d*) give the qualification of the person carrying out such inspection or investigations;
(*e*) summarise the range of opinions considered and give reasons for the experts own opinion;
(*f*) include a summary of conclusions reached;
(*g*) set out the substance of all written or oral instructions received, summarising the facts material to, or upon which the opinion expressed is based which were given to the expert[5];
(*h*) contain a statement that the expert understands the duty to the tribunal and has complied with it[6];
(*i*) contain the words 'I believe that the facts stated in this report are true and that the opinions expressed are correct'[7];
(*j*) be signed[8].

An expert's report should include:

(*a*) every plan and valuation of the land or property to which the proceedings relate,

(*b*) either:

   (i) full particulars of any comparable properties or transactions to which the party intends to refer in support of his case and a statement of the purpose for which the comparison is made, or

   (ii) a statement that no comparable properties or transactions will be referred to;

(*c*) full particulars and computations in support of the valuation which it is proposed to put in evidence;

(*d*) if computer-based valuations are to be relied upon, record that a common model has been agreed or that directions have been sought at an early stage to agree such a model and that it can be made available for use by the tribunal[9];

(*e*) such other supporting information and documents as may be relied upon[10].

Before and after exchange of experts' reports the tribunal requires the experts to meet in order to identify the issues to be resolved, to reach agreement as to facts, to agree any relevant plans and photographs and to settle as many issues as may be possible. These matters should be recorded in the form of statements of agreed matters and of matters not agreed with a summary of reasons for the matters not agreed[11]. The failure of the experts to co-operate in seeking to reach agreement as to the facts and issues is likely to be considered incompatible with the duty to the tribunal and may be reflected in costs[12]. The contents of the discussions between experts are not to be referred to at the hearing unless the parties agree and, where the experts reach agreement on an issue during their discussions, the agreement will not bind the parties unless the parties expressly agree to be bound[13].

Questions to an expert should be put in writing and preferably only once[14]. They should be put within one month of receipt of the expert's report and should only seek to clarify matters referred to in the report. The questions should be sent both to the expert and to any legal representative. Answers will be treated as part of the original report. Answers should be supplied within three weeks. The tribunal may order unanswered questions to be answered and may order different or differently worded questions to be answered. If a question is not answered the tribunal may order that the instructing party is not to rely upon that expert or that it may not recover any fees from another party in respect of that expert[15].

It would appear that expert's reports must be sent to the other party and to the tribunal within two months of filing and serving statements of case[16].

1 Tribunal Procedure (Upper Tribunal) (Lands Chamber) Rules 2010, SI 2010/2600, r 16(1).
2 Tribunal Procedure (Upper Tribunal) (Lands Chamber) Rules 2010, SI 2010/2600, r 17(2).
3 Lands Chamber of the Upper Tribunal Practice Directions 2010, para 8.6.
4 Lands Chamber of the Upper Tribunal Practice Directions 2010, para 8.2(1).
5 Lands Chamber of the Upper Tribunal Practice Directions 2010, para 8.2(1).
6 Tribunal Procedure (Upper Tribunal) (Lands Chamber) Rules 2010, SI 2010/2600, r 17(5)(*a*) and (1).

7 Tribunal Procedure (Upper Tribunal) (Lands Chamber) Rules 2010, SI 2010/2600, r 17(5)(*b*).
8 Tribunal Procedure (Upper Tribunal) (Lands Chamber) Rules 2010, SI 2010/2600, r 17(5)(*d*).
9 Lands Chamber of the Upper Tribunal Practice Directions 2010, para 8.5. *Railtrack plc v Guinness Ltd* [2003] EWCA Civ 188, [2003] RVR 280 at [55].
10 Explanatory Leaflet, January 2011, paras 4.4 and 10.2.
11 Lands Chamber of the Upper Tribunal Practice Directions 2010, para 8.4; Explanatory Leaflet, January 2011, para 10.2.
12 Lands Chamber of the Upper Tribunal Practice Directions 2010, para 8.4(1).
13 Lands Chamber of the Upper Tribunal Practice Directions 2010, para 8.4(2).
14 Lands Chamber of the Upper Tribunal Practice Directions 2010, para 8.3(1).
15 Lands Chamber of the Upper Tribunal Practice Directions 2010, para 8.3(2). In *Cook and Pullen v Highways Agency* (3 May 2002, unreported), Lands Tribunal, the acquiring authority was given two opportunities to file expert evidence concerning value but failed to do so, the tribunal debarred it from producing such evidence and proceeded on the basis of the claimant's evidence alone.
16 Explanatory Leaflet, January 2011, para 4.4 states that 'in most cases the expert reports must be filed and exchanged two months after the parties have filed and served their statements of case' and at para 10.2 it states in this context that: 'The witness statements and other documents must usually be sent to the other party and to the tribunal within two months of exchange of statements of case.' The source for this period and the starting date is unclear. Since statements of case are not exchanged simultaneously and since the timing of the statements of case differs between the rules and the Practice Directions and between a claimant and an acquiring authority, it would appear that any period will run from the date of receipt of the last statement of case. The intention is that neither party may take their opponents by surprise at the hearing by withholding material until the last minute.

[66]

The duties and responsibilities of expert witnesses in civil cases were summarised by Cresswell J[1] as follows:

(1) Expert evidence presented to the court should be, and should be seen to be, the independent product of the expert, uninfluenced as to form or content by the exigencies of litigation[2].
(2) An expert witness should provide independent assistance to the court by way of objective unbiased opinion in relation to matters within his expertise. An expert witness (in the High Court) should never assume the role of an advocate.
(3) An expert witness should state the facts or assumptions upon which his opinion is based. He should not omit to consider material facts which could detract from his concluded opinion.
(4) An expert witness should make it clear when a particular question or issue falls outside his expertise.
(5) If an expert's opinion is not properly researched because he considers that insufficient data is available, then this must be stated with an indication that the opinion is no more than a provisional one. In cases where an expert witness, who has prepared a report, could not assert that the report contained the truth, the whole truth and nothing but the truth without some qualification, that qualification should be stated in the report.
(6) If, after exchange of reports, an expert witness changes his view on a material matter having read the other side's expert's report, or for any other reason such change of view should be communicated (through legal representatives) to the other side without delay and, when appropriate, to the court.

(7) Where expert evidence refers to photographs, plans, calculations, analyses, measurements, survey reports or other similar documents, these must be provided to the opposite party at the same time as the exchange of reports.

1 *National Justice Cia Naviera SA v Prudential Assurance Co Ltd, The Ikarian Reefer* [1993] 2 EGLR 183, referring to a number of other cases; approved and extended in *Stevens v Gullis* [2000] 1 All ER 527, CA, in which the expert's overriding duty to the court was emphasised.

2 See *Keen and Keen v Worcestershire County Council* LCA/44/2001, in which the tribunal did not attach any weight to the opinions of an expert who had a financial interest in the outcome of the case. The expert was funding the case with a view to the decision becoming a benchmark for other outstanding claims in the vicinity, on which he would earn fees.

6 Documentation for the hearing

[66.1]

The tribunal may direct on case management that a party produce a bundle for the hearing[1]. There is no other guidance in the Rules or Explanatory Leaflet, January 2011. In cases assigned to the special or standard procedures, unless the tribunal directs otherwise, it would seem advisable for the parties to lodge with the tribunal not less than 14 days prior to the hearing sufficient copies (for the numbers of judges or members sitting) of the following[2]:

(*a*) an agreed trial bundle, fully paginated and containing all documents to be relied upon;
(*b*) expert witness reports, including all appendices, photographs and plans referred to;
(*c*) witness statements;
(*d*) a statement of agreed facts and issues to be determined; and
(*e*) (not less than seven days before the hearing) the advocates' skeleton arguments[3].

Sufficient copies for the tribunal and the other party should be made of any additional documents that may require to be produced at the hearing, suitably annotated to facilitate cross reference to the evidence.

Plans and photographs should be appropriately annotated and indexed and, wherever possible, agreed. Plans should be in A4 or A3 format unless there is good reason to use some other size.

The Rules, Practice Directions and Explanatory Leaflet of January 2011 make no express mention of skeleton arguments. It was the practice of the Lands Tribunal to require skeleton arguments to be provided in all but the simplest cases and it is likely that the tribunal will continue that practice[4].

1 Tribunal Procedure (Upper Tribunal) (Lands Chamber) Rules 2010, SI 2010/2600, r 5(3)(*i*).

2 This list has been taken from the former Interim Practice Directions and Guidance 2009, para 15, with the addition of the Statements of Case required under Lands Tribunal Interim Practice Directions and Guidance 2009, para 9.

3 Taken from the former Lands Tribunal Interim Practice Directions and Guidance 2009, para 15.2, as there is no reference to times for skeleton arguments in the new Rules, Practice Direction or Explanatory Leaflet, January 2011.

4 It would appear that the tribunal would have power by virtue of the very wide and general words of the Tribunal Procedure (Upper Tribunal) (Lands Chamber) Rules 2010, SI 2010/2600, r 5(2) to direct that skeleton arguments be provided.

N Site inspections

[67]

> 'A view by the Tribunal is desirable where the weight to be given to expressions of opinion by the witnesses can only be resolved by inspection; it is not for the purpose of adding to the evidence given in court.'[1]

The tribunal is authorised to enter and inspect the land or property which is the subject of the proceedings and, so far as practicable, any comparable land or property to which the tribunal's attention has been drawn[2]. The parties must be given notice of an intention to inspect[3] and may be represented, although the number of representatives will be limited to one representative from each side unless the tribunal agrees to more[4]. No written or oral evidence should be given in the course of a site inspection[5] but parties may point out any features of the land or building that they wish to draw to the tribunal's attention[6]. The tribunal should not conduct experiments or take account of evidence obtained itself which have not been open to cross-examination[7].

1 Per H P Hobbs Esq, member of the Lands Tribunal, in *Dunne v Secretary of State for Air* (1959) 10 P & CR 157 at 161; the member declined to view because he had been given so little information about the property that he felt that by viewing he would be bound to add to the evidence given.
2 Tribunal Procedure (Upper Tribunal) (Lands Chamber) Rules 2010, SI 2010/2600, r 19.
3 Tribunal Procedure (Upper Tribunal) (Lands Chamber) Rules 2010, SI 2010/2600, r 19 (2)(*b*).
4 Lands Chamber of the Upper Tribunal Practice Directions 2010, para 10.2.
5 Lands Chamber of the Upper Tribunal Practice Directions 2010, para 10.2.
6 Explanatory Leaflet, January 2011, para 2.9.
7 *Hickmott v Dorset County Council* (1977) 35 P & CR 195, CA.

O The tribunal's decision

1 The decision

[68]

The tribunal may give its reasons orally at a hearing and is required to give a decision notice in writing and notification of any rights of and time limits for review or appeal as soon as reasonably practicable after making a decision[1]. This applies to both a preliminary issue and to a final decision. Written reasons may be given for any other decisions[2]. Written reasons may be dispensed with if the decision was made with the consent of the parties or the parties have agreed to dispense with written reasons[3]. In practice, decisions are usually reserved and sent to the parties with an invitation to make written submissions on costs[4]. The written decision may then be issued later incorporating the decision on costs. Following issue of the reasoned decision a brief formal order is issued stating the effect of the decision[5]. To be adequate, the reasoned decision must not only be intelligible, but also must deal with the substantial points which have been raised by the parties[6]. Where an amount awarded or a value determined is dependent upon a point of law, the tribunal is no longer required to state in its decision the alternative amount which it would have awarded or determined, if it had reached a different decision on the point of law.

1 Tribunal Procedure (Upper Tribunal) (Lands Chamber) Rules 2010, SI 2010/2600, r 51(2).
2 Tribunal Procedure (Upper Tribunal) (Lands Chamber) Rules 2010, SI 2010/2600, r 51(4).
3 Tribunal Procedure (Upper Tribunal) (Lands Chamber) Rules 2010, SI 2010/2600, r 51(3).
4 Explanatory Leaflet, January 2011, para 12.1.
5 Explanatory Leaflet, January 2011, para 12.3.
6 *Re Poyser and Mills' Arbitration* [1964] 2 QB 467, CA. For an example of inadequate reasons, see *Batchelor v Kent County Council* (1989) 59 P & CR 357. See also para **[88] below.**

2 Correction of errors

[69]
The tribunal has four powers of correction of a decision:

(*a*) errors and omissions before the final decision is delivered;
(*b*) correction of clerical mistakes and accidental slips or omissions after decision issued (r 53);
(*c*) review of a final decision (r 57); and
(*d*) setting aside a final decision which disposes of proceedings (r 54).

Errors or omissions before the final decision has been issued

[69.1]
Before it is issued the parties can in some circumstances ask for the hearing to be re-opened, for example where clarification is required or a material point has been overlooked[1].

1 *Shraff Tip Ltd v Highways Agency (No 2)* [1999] RVR 322, Lands Tribunal. This approach was approved by the Court of Appeal in *Railtrack plc v Guinness Ltd* [2003] EWCA Civ, RVR 280 at [55]. For a detailed examination of the principle involved and the test adapted by the Court of Appeal on a challenge to a refusal by the tribunal to re-open a hearing before issuing its final decision, see *Ridgeland Properties Ltd v Bristol City Council* [2011] EWCA Civ 649, [2011] NLJR 811.

Errors and omissions after the decision is perfected

[69.2]
The tribunal may, on its own initiative or on the application of a party, at any time correct a decision by removing any clerical mistake or error arising from an accidental slip or omission[1]. The tribunal may no longer clarify or remove any ambiguity in its decision except in the case of a reference by consent to which certain provisions of the Arbitration Act 1996 are applied[2].

1 Tribunal Procedure (Upper Tribunal) (Lands Chamber) Rules 2010, SI 2010/2600, r 53.
2 Tribunal Procedure (Upper Tribunal) (Lands Chamber) Rules 2010, SI 2010/2600, rr 3(2) and 30(*g*) applying the Arbitration Act 1996, s 57(3)(*a*) to references by consent. Formerly, the power to correct ambiguities was applied by the Lands Tribunal Rules 1996, SI 1996/1022, r 32(*c*) to all proceedings. For an example of an error which was corrected and others which were not, see *Craske v Norfolk County Council* (1991) 62 P&CR 434, Lands Tribunal.

Review of a decision

[69.3]
The tribunal may review a decision on receiving an application for permission to appeal if, but only if:

(*a*) the tribunal overlooked a legislative provision or binding authority when making the decision which could have had an effect on the decision; or
(*b*) since the tribunal's decision, a court has made a decision which is binding on the tribunal and which could have been material had it been decided earlier[1].

The tribunal must notify the parties in writing of the outcome of any review and of the rights of review or appeal[2]. If a party did not have the opportunity to make representations, the notice must state this and allow the party an opportunity to apply for such action as has been taken to be set aside and for further review[3].

1 Tribunal Procedure (Upper Tribunal) (Lands Chamber) Rules 2010, SI 2010/2600, rr 57(1) and 56(1).
2 Tribunal Procedure (Upper Tribunal) (Lands Chamber) Rules 2010, SI 2010/2600, r 57(2).
3 Tribunal Procedure (Upper Tribunal) (Lands Chamber) Rules 2010, SI 2010/2600, r 57(3).

Setting aside

[69.4]
If the tribunal considers it to be in the interests of justice it may set aside a decision or part of a decision which disposes of proceedings in the following cases:

(*a*) a document relating to the proceedings was not sent or delivered to or was not received at an appropriate time by a party or a party's representative; or
(*b*) a document was not sent or delivered to the tribunal at an appropriate time; or
(*c*) a party or a party's representative was not present at a hearing; or
(*d*) there has been some other procedural irregularity in the proceedings[1].

A written application to set aside part or all of a decision must be sent to the tribunal and to all parties, to be received within one month after the date on which the tribunal sent the decision to the parties[2].

1 Tribunal Procedure (Upper Tribunal) (Lands Chamber) Rules 2010, SI 2010/2600, r 54(2).
2 Tribunal Procedure (Upper Tribunal) (Lands Chamber) Rules 2010, SI 2010/2600, r 54(3).

P Fees and costs

1 General

[70]
A distinction is to be drawn between the costs of the reference and costs which properly form part of the claim for compensation (including pre-reference costs[1]); these paragraphs are concerned with the former, the latter being explained elsewhere[2]. The tribunal has a general discretionary power to order that the costs of any proceedings before it, be paid by any other party or their legal representative[3], but this is supplemented by the LCA 1961, s 4, which is explained below. The rules provide for the tribunal to settle the

amount summarily or to direct that they be subject to detailed assessment by a registrar[4]. The discretion to award costs must be exercised judicially[5].

A written application for costs must be sent to the tribunal and to the person against whom cost are sought[6]. The application may contain a schedule of costs in sufficient detail to allow for summary assessment[7]. The application may be made at any time[8] but not later than 14 days after the date on which the tribunal sends the decision finally disposing of all issues; or notice of withdrawal under Rule 20 ending the proceedings; or notice of withdrawal by consent. Before an order is made, the party against whom the order is sought must be given an opportunity to make representations[9].

In practice, the decision is issued in writing some time after the close of the hearing with an invitation to the parties to make submissions as to costs. An addendum on costs is then issued[10]. The tribunal has power to make an order for wasted costs[11]. The Litigants in Person (Costs and Expenses) Act 1975 applies to the tribunal[12].

1 Pre-reference costs are part of the compensation and are not dependent upon a claim having been made. They may include the reasonable costs of seeking a s 17 Land Compensation Act 1961 certificate from the local planning authority. They should be dealt with by the tribunal as part of the claim and not later as part of the costs of the reference before the tribunal: *Re Spirerose Ltd (in administration)* [2007] 49 EG 102 (CS), paras 147–151, upheld on appeal on a different point [2009] RVR 18; *Jumbuk Ltd v West Midlands Passenger Transport Executive* [2008] RVR 186, para 66.

2 See **E[2004]**.

3 Tribunals, Courts and Enforcement Act 2007, s 29. Tribunal Procedure (Upper Tribunal) (Lands Chamber) Rules 2010, SI 2010/2600, r 10 and Lands Chamber of the Upper Tribunal Practice Directions 2010, paras 12.2 and 12.1(1). Although the discretion is wide, it must be exercised judicially; the tribunal was held to have erred in law in ordering an acquiring authority to pay a claimant's costs when it awarded no compensation to the claimant: *Pepys v London Transport Executive* (1974) 29 P&CR 248, CA. See also *English Property Corpn v Royal Borough of Kingston upon Thames* (1988) 77 P&CR 1, CA. Costs are not normally awarded where the simplified procedure is followed but the tribunal may award costs where there has been an unreasonable failure to settle or if there has been unreasonable behaviour or if it regards the circumstances as exceptional: Lands Chamber of the Upper Tribunal Practice Directions 2010, para 12.8 and *Cook and Pullen v Highways Agency* (3 May 2002, unreported), Lands Tribunal; *Nicholls v Highway Agency* [2000] RVR 230.

4 A party dissatisfied by the registrar's assessment may apply to the registrar for a review and, if still dissatisfied, may apply to the Chamber President for a further review: Lands Chamber of the Upper Tribunal Practice Directions 2010, para 12.10(2).

5 *Gray v Lord Ashburton* [1917] AC 26, HL; *Bradshaw v Air Council* [1926] Ch 329; *Wootton v Central Land Board* [1957] 1 All ER 441, CA; *Church Cottage Investments v Hillingdon London Borough Council (No 2)* [1991] 2 EGLR 13, CA.

6 Tribunal Procedure (Upper Tribunal) (Lands Chamber) Rules 2010, SI 2010/2600, r 10(2)(*a*).

7 Tribunal Procedure (Upper Tribunal) (Lands Chamber) Rules 2010, SI 2010/2600, r 10(2)(*b*).

8 Tribunal Procedure (Upper Tribunal) (Lands Chamber) Rules 2010, SI 2010/2600, r 10(3).

9 Tribunal Procedure (Upper Tribunal) (Lands Chamber) Rules 2010, SI 2010/2600, r 10(3)(*a*)–(*c*).

10 Lands Chamber of the Upper Tribunal Practice Directions 2010, para 12.9.

11 Formerly, the President decided that the Lands Tribunal had no power to make an order for wasted costs: *Welford v Transport for London* [2008] RVT 178 at 182, para 30. However, such a power is now applied by the Tribunals, Courts and Enforcement Act 2007, s 29(4).

12 Tribunals, Courts and Enforcement Act 2007, Sch 8, para 6. The litigant in person may be awarded costs in respect of any work done and expenses and losses incurred in connection with the proceedings. Under the CPR such costs should not exceed two-thirds of those that would have been allowed to a legal representative and full disbursements. A litigant in person claiming attendance costs to conduct his case may not claim a witness attendance fee in addition. He should be allowed:

(i) costs and disbursements for the types of work that would have been done by a legal representative;
(ii) costs in respect of payments made for legal services relating to the conduct of the proceedings;
(iii) costs of expert assistance in assessing costs.

[71]–[80]
In exercising its discretion the tribunal will take into account all the circumstances, including:

(*a*) the conduct of the parties both before and during the proceedings;
(*b*) whether a party has acted reasonably in pursuing or contesting an issue;
(*c*) the manner in which the case has been conducted;
(*d*) whether or not the claim has been exaggerated;
(*e*) whether a party has succeeded on part of the case even if not on the whole case;
(*f*) any admissible offers to settle[1].

The general rule is that the successful party ought to receive their costs[2]. In a compulsory acquisition these costs are seen as part of the costs imposed on the claimant by the acquisition, subject to the particular rules under s 4 of the Land Compensation Act 1961.

1 Lands Chamber of the Upper Tribunal Practice Directions 2010, para 12.2.
2 Lands Chamber of the Upper Tribunal Practice Directions 2010, para12.3.

2 Land Compensation Act 1961, section 4

[81]
Where the acquiring authority has made an unconditional offer in writing and the tribunal's award does not exceed the offer, the tribunal must, unless there are special reasons not to do so, order that the claimant bear its own costs and pay those of the acquiring authority, in so far as they were incurred after the offer was made[1]. Similarly, where a claimant has failed to provide the acquiring authority with a notice in writing of the amount claimed supported by particulars[2] in time for them to make an offer, the tribunal is also required to order that the claimant pay the authority's costs, unless there are special reasons not to do so[3]. Where a claimant has provided to the acquiring authority a written notice of claim containing the required particulars and has made an unconditional offer in writing to accept a sum, then, if the tribunal's award is equal to or exceeds that sum[4], the tribunal is required, unless there are special reasons, to order the acquiring authority to bear its own costs and to pay those of the claimant, in so far as they were incurred after the offer was made[5].

1 LCA 1961, s 4(1)(*a*); Lands Chamber of the Upper Tribunal Practice Directions 2010, para 12.3(2). The amount of costs may be deducted from the amount of compensation awarded: s 4(5) or may be recovered as a civil debt: s 4(6). In *Hood Investment Co Ltd v Marlow UDC* (1963) 15 P & CR 229 it was held that a claimant can in appropriate circumstances be ordered to pay the acquiring authority's costs, even though no unconditional offer has been made; see also *Potter and Potter v Hillingdon London Borough Council* [2010] RVR 271, paras 95–99. An example of special reasons not to follow the normal rule is *Christodoulou v Islington London Borough Council* (1973) 230 Estates Gazette 233, Lands Tribunal, where the tribunal refused to

order that the claimant pay the acquiring authority's costs, even though the sealed offer had exceeded the amount awarded, because the authority had delayed delivering its offer until just before the hearing.

2 Ie the particulars identified in the LCA 1961, s 4(2).

3 LCA 1961, s 4(1)(*b*); Lands Chamber of the Upper Tribunal Practice Directions 2010, para 12.2(3). An example of the operation of the LCA 1961, s 4 is contained in *Colneway Ltd v Environment Agency* [2004] RVR 37.

4 Eviction costs incurred by the sheriff may be deducted and retained from compensation payable by the acquiring authority (LCA 1961, s 13) but they do not form part of the sum for assessment by the tribunal and would not count as a relevant part of a sealed offer for assessing whether the award exceeded the offer: *Prielipp v Secretary of State for the Environment, Transport and the Regions* [2002] RVR 169.

5 LCA 1961, s 4(3). For a case in which both parties had made sealed offers, both of which were exceeded by the award, but where the award of costs in favour of the claimant only ran from the date of the claimant's offer as provided by s 4(3) see *Toye v Kensington and Chelsea Royal London Borough Council* [1994] 1 EGLR 204. However, s 4(3) does not preclude a discretionary award of costs before that date if one is sought.

[81.1]

The LCA 1961, s 4 and relevant case law were reviewed and explained by the Court of Appeal in *Purfleet Farms Ltd v Secretary of State for Transport*[1]. The starting point for a decision on costs is the general rule that the costs of a reference to determine compensation fall on the acquiring authority without whose resort to the use of compulsory powers there would have been no need for the owner to be compensated[2]. In the absence of 'special reasons' to the contrary, a claimant will, therefore, be entitled to his costs so long as he is awarded more than the amount of any unconditional offer made by the acquiring authority (as to which see para **[81]** above). 'Special reason' means readily identifiable conduct leading to an obvious and substantial escalation in the costs over and above those costs which it was reasonable for the claimant to incur. Mere exaggeration of the claim alone might not be enough[3]. Costs may be the sole matter in a reference[4] and may be refused where the tribunal has no jurisdiction[5].

1 [2002] EWCA Civ 1430, [2003] 1 P&CR 20, [2003] 1 EGLR 9, [2002] RVR 368, followed in *Blakes Estate Ltd v Government of Montserrat* [2005] UKPC 46, [2005] All ER (D) 241 (Dec).

2 *Emslie & Simpson Ltd v Aberdeen District Council (No 2)* [1995] RVR 159; *Lesquende Ltd v Planning and Environmental Committee of the States of Jersey* [1998] 1 EGLR 137; *Munawar Hussain v Bradford Metropolitan District Council* ACQ/133/2000.

3 *Purfleet Farms Ltd v Secretary of State for Transport, Local Government and the Regions* [2002] EWCA Civ 1430, [2003] 1 P&CR 20. The decision of the Court of Appeal in this case also referred (at [40]) to the costs provisions of the Civil Procedure Rules 1998. The court held that the tribunal must have regard to whether the reasons for the exaggeration were defensible and whether the exaggeration had any effect on the time spent and costs incurred in the proceedings. Despite the similarities in procedure, a compensation reference before the Upper Tribunal (Lands Chamber) does not itself constitute 'ordinary litigation' and remains outside the purview of the CPR. The Lands Chamber of the Upper Tribunal Practice Directions 2010, para 12.2 now includes exaggeration as a justification for an award of costs to the other party

4 *Williams v Central Estate* [1972] RVR 466, Lands Tribunal; *Ford v Hartley Witney RDC* (1951) 2 P&CR 99, Lands Tribunal.

5 *Christian Salveson (Properties) Ltd v Central Electricity Generating Board* [1984] RVR 185, Lands Tribunal.

[81.2]

In *Colneway Ltd v Environment Agency*[1], the Lands Tribunal explained the operation of s 4 in some detail as follows. There are three circumstances in which it is mandatory for the tribunal to make a particular order for costs unless there are 'special reasons' not to do so:

(1) Where the acquiring authority has made an unconditional offer which is not exceeded by the amount of the award: here the claimant bears his own costs and pays the acquiring authority's costs after the date of the offer: s 4(1)(*a*).
(2) Where the claimant has failed to deliver a particularised claim to the acquiring authority in time to enable it to make a proper offer: here the claimant bears his own costs and pays the authority's costs after the time when the claim should have been delivered: s 4(1)(*b*).
(3) Where the claimant has made a particularised claim and has also made an unconditional offer to accept a sum as compensation and the award is equal to or exceeds that sum: here the acquiring authority bears its own costs and pays the claimants costs after the date of the offer: s 4(3).

1 [2004] RVR 37, Lands Tribunal, paras 65–72.

3 Sealed offers

[81.3]
Section 4 makes no express provision for the following circumstances:

(1) Where the acquiring authority has made an unconditional offer which is exceeded by the award, but the claimant has made a claim but no offer.
(2) Where the claimant has made a claim and has also made an offer which is for more than the sum awarded, but the acquiring authority has made no offer.
(3) Where the claimant has made a claim but has not made an offer, and the acquiring authority also has not made an offer.
(4) The period up to the time when the claim should have been delivered.

In *Colneway*[1] the tribunal went on to consider the approach which should be taken in these four circumstances where s 4 makes no provision. Applying the principle of equivalence and the judgments in *Emslie & Simpson Ltd v Aberdeen District Council (No 2)*[2] and *Purfleet Farms Ltd v Secretary of State for Transport*[3], the tribunal decided that in cases where the acquiring authority had made an offer it was appropriate to continue the tribunal's practice to award the claimant his costs up to the date of the offer even when the claimant had not himself made an offer[4].

1 *Colneway Ltd v Environment Agency* [2004] RVR 37, Lands Tribunal.
2 [1995] RVR 159 at 164.
3 [2002] EWCA Civ 1430, [2003] 1 P&CR 20, followed in *Blakes Estate Ltd v Government of Montserrat* [2005] UKPC 46, [2005] All ER (D) 241 (Dec).
4 *Colneway Ltd v Environment Agency* [2004] RVR 37, Lands Tribunal, paras 67–72.

[81.4]
Any party may offer to settle the claim or part of the claim with the other party[1]. The offer or making of any offer marked to the effect: 'without prejudice save as to costs' or as being a 'Calderbank' offer must not be referred to at the hearing. Such offers should identify which parts of the claim or issues are referred to and should state the period for acceptance[2]. If interest has been

claimed the rate and period should be stated if included in the offer. It should also state whether or not the offer includes costs and the amount or basis of those costs[3]. A copy of the offer should be sent to the tribunal within a sealed envelope enclosed with a covering letter[4]. Neither the judge nor member hearing the case will see the offer or be informed of its existence until the proceedings have ended. A party may request that the offer be viewed when costs are being considered. The promptness of response to an offer will affect the incidence of costs[5].

1 Lands Chamber of the Upper Tribunal Practice Directions 2010, para 12.7(1). If a sealed offer is accepted at or before the hearing, LCA 1961, s 4 does not apply because the tribunal has not made an award: *Stanford Marsh v Secretary of State for the Environment* [1997] 1 EGLR 178, Lands Tribunal. As to the effect of withdrawn sealed offers, see *Hepworth Building Projects v Coal Authority* [1999] 3 EGLR 99, [1999] 41 EG 157, CA.
2 Lands Chamber of the Upper Tribunal Practice Directions 2010, para 12.7(2).
3 Costs should be separately itemised. A sealed offer should not include costs within a single sum: *Balls v Metropolitan Board of Works* (1866) LR 1 QB 337. However, in *Eugene Shevlin v Trafford Park Development Corpn* [1998] 1 EGLR 115 the Lands Tribunal took the view that 'a sealed offer which omits any reference to the claimant's costs is weakened in effect and reduced in amount'. A similar approach was taken in *Tague v Lancaster City Council* [1999] 20 EG 156, [1999] 2 EGLR 103, Lands Tribunal. See also *Chapter Group plc v London Regional Transport* [2006] RVR 242 as to whether costs were included within a sealed offer and *Tollgate Hotels Ltd v Secretary of State for Transport* [2006] RVR 315 as to whether interest was included within a sealed offer. For a review of costs after sealed offers: see [2006] RVR 291. For the construction of 'Calderbank' letters see *Phyllis Trading Ltd v 86 Lordship Road Ltd* [2001] EWCA Civ 350, 82 P&CR 388.
4 Lands Chamber of the Upper Tribunal Practice Directions 2010, para 12.7(3).
5 *Stanford Marsh v Secretary of State for the Environment* [1997] 1 EGLR 178, Lands Tribunal: five days allowed for response to an offer. *L & B Holdings Ltd v Brent London Borough Council* [2010] UKUT 24, [2010] RVR 304: regard paid to High Court Rules which allowed 21 days and the delivery of an additional undertaking during that period.

4 Summary and detailed assessment

[82]

In proceedings determined by the simplified or written procedure, costs are restricted[1]. Where the tribunal directs that one party pay another party's costs, it may, in a simple case or hearing, make a summary assessment of costs by assessing the amount of costs payable as a fixed lump sum at the end of the hearing[2]. A party who proposes to apply for a summary assessment should prepare a summary of the costs and should serve it in advance on the other party[3]. The tribunal may simply award any sum agreed between the parties[4].

Alternatively, the tribunal may direct that there be a detailed assessment of the whole or of a specified part of the costs on the standard basis or, if specified in the costs order, on the indemnity basis. The claimant should prepare a bill of costs and the other party may file a document identifying points of dispute and challenging particular items or amounts claimed. The registrar will then carry out a detailed assessment[5].

Costs will normally be awarded on the standard basis. Any doubts as to whether costs were reasonably incurred or were reasonable and proportionate will be resolved in favour of the paying person. Exceptionally, the tribunal may award costs on the indemnity basis. The receiving party will then obtain all their costs except those that have been unreasonably incurred or which are unreasonable in amount. Any dispute as to reasonableness will be resolved in favour of the receiving party[6].

It may be directed that the costs be subject to an application to the Senior Courts Costs Office or to a county court where the application will be considered as if the CPR applied[7]. Any party dissatisfied with the decision on costs may, within one month, apply for permission to appeal[8].

1 Lands Chamber of the Upper Tribunal Practice Directions 2010, para 12.8 suggests costs will only be awarded where there has been unreasonable failure on the part of the claimant to accept an offer to settle, or if either party has behaved otherwise unreasonably, or the circumstances are in some other respect exceptional. However, see paras **[39]** and **[40]** above and Lands Chamber of the Upper Tribunal Practice Directions 2010, para 3.3(4) where it is suggested that the scope for costs differs between the two procedures.
2 Tribunal Procedure (Upper Tribunal) (Lands Chamber) Rules 2010, SI 2010/2600, r 10(5)(*a*).
3 Lands Chamber of the Upper Tribunal Practice Directions 2010, para 12.10(1).
4 Tribunal Procedure (Upper Tribunal) (Lands Chamber) Rules 2010, SI 2010/2600, r 10(5)(*b*).
5 Explanatory Leaflet, January 2011, para 14.1. The tribunal will charge 5p for every £1 of the total bill assessed.
6 Lands Chamber of the Upper Tribunal Practice Directions 2010, para 12.4.
7 Tribunal Procedure (Upper Tribunal) (Lands Chamber) Rules 2010, SI 2010/2600, r 10(5)(*c*); Lands Chamber of the Upper Tribunal Practice Directions 2010, para 12.10(2). The Civil Procedure Rules 1998 (CPR 1998), Pts 43–48 refer to the assessment of costs. The form of order will be for costs to be agreed or in default of agreement for there to be a detailed assessment in accordance with Pt 47. See CPR Practice Direction 44, r 4.1.
8 Tribunal Procedure (Upper Tribunal) (Lands Chamber) Rules 2010, SI 2010/2600, r 55(2)(*b*). It would also be possible to apply to set aside an order if any of the conditions in, r 54(2) applied.

Q Interest

[83]
A claimant is entitled to interest under a number of statutory provisions which do not require an order of the tribunal to be effective; these include the following:

(*a*) Under the CPA 1965, s 11, where the acquiring authority has entered and taken possession of the land, interest is payable at the prescribed rate until the compensation is paid[1].
(*b*) Under the CP(VD)A 1981, s 10, where an acquiring authority executes a general vesting declaration, interest is payable from the date of vesting until payment of compensation[2].
(*c*) Under the LCA 1973, s 52A, where an advance payment is made, interest is payable from the date of entry on the advance payment[3].
(*d*) Under the LCA 1973, s 63, where compensation is payable for injurious affection under the CPA 1965, s 10[4].
(*e*) Under the LCA 1973, 37(6) where a statutory disturbance payment is payable[5].
(*f*) Under the Planning and Compensation Act 1991, s 80, Sch 18, in relation to various rights to compensation where no land has been taken[6].

1 See **D[708]**.
2 See **D[350]**.
3 See **D[1081]**.
4 See **Division F, Chapter 2**.
5 See **Division E**.
6 See **Division G**.

[84]
In addition to the cases where no order for interest is necessary, the tribunal has a discretionary power in references by consent to award interest on a simple or compound basis, from such dates, at such rates and with such rests as it considers meets the justice of the case, on the whole or part of its award; or, where an amount has been paid prior to the award, up to the date of payment[1].

Although the Lands Tribunal had a discretionary power to award interest in other cases, the power of the tribunal to award interest appears to be limited to references by consent[2].

Compensation in respect of the compulsory acquisition of an interest in any land on which entry has been made before the payment of interest shall be at the statutory rate prescribed[3]. There is no reference to compound interest being payable[4]. The tribunal has no power to add interest to a subsequent award of the costs of an earlier quashed hearing[5].

1 Arbitration Act 1996, s 49, applied to references by consent: Tribunal Procedure (Upper Tribunal) (Lands Chamber) Rules 2010, SI 2010/2600, r 30(*f*).
2 The Arbitration Act is now specifically disapplied with respect to all references or generally (apart from references by consent) by the Tribunal Procedure (Upper Tribunal) (Lands Chamber) Rules 2010, SI 2010/2600, r 3(2). For a historical review of the application of these provisions, see *Aslam v South Bedfordshire District Council* [2001] RVR 65, CA.
3 Land Compensation Act 1961, s 32.
4 Circular of 12 March 1997, Annex, para 5.
5 *Barclays Bank plc v Kent County Council* [1998] 2 EGLR 14, CA.

R Appeals from and review of decisions by the tribunal

1 Right of appeal

[85]
A decision of the tribunal is final, but any person aggrieved by a decision, on the basis that it is erroneous in point of law, may appeal to the Court of Appeal[1]. Permission is required for such an appeal or for a cross-appeal and must first be sought from the tribunal.[2] A written application for permission to appeal must be received by the tribunal within one month of the latest of the dates upon which the tribunal sent:

(*a*) the written reasons for the decision;
(*b*) notification of a decision to award or refuse costs;
(*c*) notification of amended reasons for, or correction of, the decision following review; or
(*d*) notification that an application for the decision to be set aside has been unsuccessful[3].

If the application is received outside the one month allowed, the application must include a request for an extension of time and give the reason why the application is late[4]. Unless time is extended under, r 5(3)(*a*), the application must be refused[5]. The application must identify the decision to which it relates; identify the error(s) of law alleged; and state the result sought by the applicant[6].

On receiving an application for permission to appeal, the tribunal may review the decision if:

(*a*) a legislative provision or binding authority which could have had a material effect had been overlooked; or
(*b*) a court decision of material effect and binding on the tribunal has been made since the decision[7].

If the tribunal decides not to review the decision or reviews it and decides to take no action, the tribunal must consider whether to give permission to appeal[8]. A record of its decision must be sent to the parties as soon as practicable[8].

If permission to appeal is refused by the tribunal, a statement of reasons for refusal and notification of a right and time for making an application for permission to appeal to the Court of Appeal must be sent with the record of the decision[9]. A further application for permission may then be contained within an Appellant's notice of appeal to the Court of Appeal[10]. It must be submitted within 21 days of the date of the decision in respect of which the party wishes to appeal[11]. Upon further refusal by the Court of Appeal on paper a request for an oral hearing may be made[12]. Permission will only be granted by the Court of Appeal if it considers that there is a real prospect of success or some other compelling reason why the appeal should be heard.

The tribunal may give permission to appeal on limited grounds but if it does, it must notify the grounds which are refused and give notice of the right to appeal to the Court of Appeal in respect of those grounds. The tribunal has no express powers to impose other terms[13]. The Court of Appeal may give permission to appeal on such terms as to costs below and on the appeal as the Court considers appropriate[14].

1 Tribunals, Courts and Enforcement Act 2007, s 13; and see Explanatory Leaflet, January 2011, para 13.
2 *Girls' Day School Trust (1872) v Dadak* [2001] EWCA Civ 380, [2002] P&CR 49; Tribunals, Courts and Enforcement Act 2007, s 13(4); Tribunal Procedure (Upper Tribunal) (Lands Chamber) Rules 2010, SI 2010/2600, r 28(8); Explanatory Leaflet, January 2011 para 13. The tribunal may grant permission to appeal. In the case of an appeal against decision of a Leasehold Valuation Tribunal under the special provisions applicable it was held that s 3(4) of the 1949 Act does not preclude the operation of judicial review of decisions of the tribunal which fall outside the scope of that section: *R (Sinclair Investments (Kensington) Ltd) v Lands Tribunal* [2006] RVR 66.
3 Tribunal Procedure (Upper Tribunal) (Lands Chamber) Rules 2010, SI 2010/2600, r 55(2).
4 Tribunal Procedure (Upper Tribunal) (Lands Chamber) Rules 2010, SI 2010/2600, r 55(5)(*a*). Formerly, the application for permission would have been made straight to the Court of Appeal. In *Regalbourne v East Lindsey District Council* [1994] RA 1, when the application for permission was required to be made straight to the Court of Appeal, it was stated that an extension was unlikely to be granted easily and not without a full explanation of the reasons for delay.
5 Tribunal Procedure (Upper Tribunal) (Lands Chamber) Rules 2010, SI 2010/2600, r 55(5)(*b*).
6 Tribunal Procedure (Upper Tribunal) (Lands Chamber) Rules 2010, SI 2010/2600, r 55(6).
7 Tribunal Procedure (Upper Tribunal) (Lands Chamber) Rules 2010, SI 2010/2600, r 56(1).
8 Tribunal Procedure (Upper Tribunal) (Lands Chamber) Rules 2010, SI 2010/2600, r 56(2).
9 Tribunal Procedure (Upper Tribunal) (Lands Chamber) Rules 2010, SI 2010/2600, r 56(4).
10 There is authority cited under CPR 52 (at para 52.3.5 of the White Book) that: 'If the lower court purports to grant permission outside the time limit for appealing then (absent any extension of time) such "permission" is ineffective': *Lloyd Jones v T Mobile (UK) Ltd* [2003] EWCA Civ 1162, [2003] 49 EG 130. Similar considerations may apply to seeking permission

from the tribunal more than 21 days after the 'date of the decision' but within the one month allowed by the Tribunal Procedure (Upper Tribunal) (Lands Chamber) Rules 2010, SI 2010/2600, r 55(2) for permission applications to the tribunal. The Explanatory Leaflet, January 2011, para 13.1 states:

> 'If permission to appeal to the Court of Appeal is refused in whole or in part … you must file at least 3 copies of an Appellant's Notice and also ask permission to appeal … with the Court of Appeal within 21 days of the date that the tribunal's decision to refuse permission … was sent to the parties.'

However, CPR 52.4(2)(*b*) requires the Appellant's Notice to be filed: 'within … 21 days after the date of the decision of the lower court that the appellant wishes to appeal.' The decision to be appealed is the written reasons for the decision under the Tribunal Procedure (Upper Tribunal) (Lands Chamber) Rules 2010, SI 2010/2600, r 55(2)(*a*) and not the decision to refuse permission. (There is a renewed application for permission included with the Appellant's Notice). Consequently, the 21 days is likely to have expired either before a costs decision has been determined or before the end of the one month for making an application for permission to appeal to the tribunal or before the tribunal has determined the application for permission to appeal. The wording in the Explanatory Leaflet, January 2011 does not appear to be accurate and assumes that it is the refusal of permission to appeal which is the subject of the Appellant's Notice rather than the decision appealed against and does not consider whether that is the substantive decision or the costs decision. It may be that the tribunal considers that it can direct an extension of the 21-day period under CPR 53.4(2)(*a*). If so, the cautious advice is for applicants to request such an extension rather than relying upon the Explanatory Leaflet of January 2011.

11 Explanatory Leaflet, January 2011, para 13.1 – see note 10 above.

12 CPR 52.3(4). Under the Tribunal Procedure (Upper Tribunal) (Lands Chamber) Rules 2010, SI 2010/2600, r 46(1) the application for permission may be determined with or without a hearing. Unlike in the Court of Appeal, if it is determined without a hearing, there is no right to reconsideration at a hearing before the tribunal.

13 Tribunal Procedure (Upper Tribunal) (Lands Chamber) Rules 2010, SI 2010/2600, r 56(5); CPR 52.3(7)(*b*).

14 In *White v Herefordshire Council* [2007] EWCA Civ 1204, [2008] RVR 54 permission to appeal was granted by the Court of Appeal on an undertaking from the compensating authority that it would not seek to upset the award of costs in favour of the claimant in the tribunal, nor seek an award of costs if successful on the appeal.

[85.1]

Time limits explained:

(*a*) acts required to be done on or by a particular day means by 5 pm on that day;

(*b*) if time ends on a non-working day, the act is within time if done on the next working day;

(*c*) working day means Monday to Friday excluding Christmas Day, Good Friday or a bank holiday[1].

'One month' is not defined, but both the Interpretation Act 1978, Sch 1 and RSC 2.10 define 'month' as 'calendar month'.

1 Tribunal Procedure (Upper Tribunal) (Lands Chamber) Rules 2010, SI 2010/2600, r 12.

2 Review by the tribunal

[86]

The tribunal may itself review its own decision on receiving an application for permission to appeal[1]. If satisfied that it has overlooked a legislative provision or binding authority which could have had a material effect on the decision or if there has been a subsequent binding decision of a court of similar effect, the tribunal may notify the parties and take appropriate action in relation to the decision. All parties should be given an opportunity to make representations and may apply for the remedial action to be set aside and for a further review if they have not been given such an opportunity[2]. As a matter of practice, a party seeking a review should apply for permission to appeal to the Court of Appeal and also ask the tribunal to review its decision. If the tribunal decides not to review the decision or upon reviewing it decides not to vary it, it will then consider whether to give permission to appeal the whole or part of the decision[3].

1 Tribunal Procedure (Upper Tribunal) (Lands Chamber) Rules 2010, SI 2010/2600, r 57.
2 Tribunal Procedure (Upper Tribunal) (Lands Chamber) Rules 2010, SI 2010/2600, r 57(3).
3 Explanatory Leaflet, January 2011, para 13.2.

3 Powers of the Court of Appeal

[87]
The Court of Appeal has all the powers of the tribunal[1]. It also has the power to affirm, set aside or vary any order or judgment of the tribunal[2]. It can refer any claim or issue for determination by the tribunal[3] and can order a new trial or hearing[4]. It has power to make orders for payment of interest[5] and to make cost orders[6]. It may order that security for costs be provided[7].

1 Civil Procedure (Amendment) Rules 2000, SI 2000/221, Pt 52, r 10(1).
2 SI 2000/221, Pt 52, r 10(2)(*a*).
3 SI 2000/221, Pt 52, r 10(2)(*b*).
4 SI 2000/221, Pt 52, r 10(2)(*c*).
5 SI 2000/22,1 Pt 52, r 10(2)(*d*), notwithstanding that the tribunal may not have such power.
6 SI 2000/221, Pt 52, r 10(2)(*e*).
7 SI 2000/221, Pt 25, r 15.

4 Jurisdiction of the Court of Appeal

[88]
Since the right of appeal is on a point of law[1] only, the Court of Appeal has no jurisdiction to review the facts or valuation judgments[2]. The following citations from a number of different cases usefully summarise the scope of the court's jurisdiction:

> 'The evident intention of the Act and the [Lands Tribunal Rules] is to create and define a severely restricted right of appeal, which is to be only on a point of law [and only by way of case stated] … There is no provision for an appeal on questions of fact, nor for any review of the findings of fact on a consideration of the evidence.'[3]

> 'It might be open … to attack a conclusion of fact on the ground that there is no evidence to support it, and that may very well raise a question of law … If a party thinks that a conclusion to which an umpire may come adverse to himself is one that cannot be supported on any evidence that is before him, he may require the umpire to leave the question of law stated in that form; then no doubt it is the duty of the umpire to set out all the material evidence which justifies his conclusion.'[4]

'... it may be that the facts found are such that no person acting judicially and properly instructed as to the relevant law could have come to the determination under appeal. In those circumstances, the court must intervene. It has no option but to assume that there has been some misconception of the law and that this has been responsible for the determination. So there too there has been error in point of law ...'[5]

'The existence in the last resort of a power to find errors of law by inference is a salutary check upon arbitrariness on the part of an administrative tribunal; but courts must sternly resist the temptation to infer errors of law in an expert tribunal, such as the [Tribunal], when all that has happened is that the tribunal's decision is different from that which the court itself, lacking comparable expertise, would have reached on the same evidence.'[6]

1 For comments upon what constitutes a point of law, see Lord Denning MR in *Cardiff Corpn v Williams (Valuation Officer)* [1973] RA 46, CA, at 53. See also the comments of Carnwath LJ in *Railtrack plc v Guinness Ltd* [2003] EWCA Civ 188, [2003] RVR 280 at para 51. For the approach of the Court of Appeal on an appeal against a refusal to re-open a hearing, see *Ridgeland Properties Ltd v Bristol City Council* [2011] EWCA Civ 649, [2011] NWR 811.
2 The Court of Appeal will not reconsider the valuations, but it may remit the case back to the tribunal to determine the amount of compensation within stated legal criteria: *Myers v Milton Keynes Development Corpn* [1974] 2 All ER 1096, CA.
3 Per Pearson LJ in *Festiniog Rly Society Ltd v Central Electricity Generating Board* [1962] RVR 202, CA.
4 Per Devlin J in *Nello Simoni v A/S M/S Straum* (1950) 83 Ll L Rep 157 at 161.
5 Per Lord Radcliffe in *Edwards (Inspector of Taxes) v Bairstow* [1956] AC 14, HL, at 29.
6 Per Lord Diplock in *Baker Britt v Hampsher (Valuation Officer)* (1976) 19 RRC 62, HL, at 83.

[89]
A failure to provide adequate or intelligible reasons amounts to an error of law; to be adequate, its reasons must deal with the substantial points which have been raised by the parties[1]. The tribunal will not be held to have erred in law merely because it has not supported every step of its valuation; it is a specialist tribunal charged with problems of compensation and is entitled to come to its own conclusions on certain matters[2].

1 *Re Poyser and Mills' Arbitration* [1964] 2 QB 467, CA. For an example of inadequate reasons, see *Batchelor v Kent County Council* (1989) 59 P&CR 357.
2 Per Glidewell LJ in *Abbey Homesteads (Developments) Ltd v Northamptonshire County Council* [1992] 2 EGLR 18, CA.

5 Appeal to the Supreme Court

[90]
An appeal against a decision of the Court of Appeal may be brought to the Supreme Court, but only with the permission of the Court of Appeal or the Supreme Court[1].

1 Constitutional Reform Act 2005, s 40(2).

S Enforcement of the tribunal's award

[91]–[100]
An award payable in pursuance of a decision of the tribunal is recoverable as if it were payable under an order of a county court or High Court[1].

H [91] *Determination and recovery of compensation*

An award of compensation by the tribunal on a reference by consent can be enforced in the same manner as a judgment or order of the court, but permission of the court is required. When permission is given, judgment may be entered in the terms of the award[2]. Permission will be granted unless there is any real ground for doubting the validity of the award[3].

1 Tribunals, Courts and Enforcement Act 2007, s 27(1).
2 Arbitration Act 1996, applied by the Tribunal Procedure (Upper Tribunal) (Lands Chamber) Rules 2010, SI 2010/2600, r 30(i). The Act, which precedes the CPR 1998, still uses the term 'leave', but the CPR 1998 now uses the word 'permission' instead.
3 *Middlemiss and Gould (a firm) v Hartlepool Corpn* [1973] 1 All ER 172, CA, at 175.

Index

Please note that references are to paragraph numbers; the letters printed in bold indicate the relevant division.

All references to CPA 1965 refer to Compulsory Purchase Act 1965.

B